MUSLIM AND CHRISTIAN CONTACT
IN THE MIDDLE AGES

READINGS IN MEDIEVAL CIVILIZATIONS AND CULTURES: XVIII
series editor: Paul Edward Dutton

MUSLIM AND CHRISTIAN CONTACT IN THE MIDDLE AGES

A READER

edited by

JARBEL RODRIGUEZ

UNIVERSITY OF TORONTO PRESS

LIBRARY AND ARCHIVES CANADA CATALOGUING IN PUBLICATION

Muslim and Christian contact in the Middle Ages : a reader / edited by
    Jarbel Rodriguez. (Readings in medieval civilizations and cultures series ; XVIII)

Includes bibliographical references and index.
Issued in print and electronic formats.
ISBN 978-1-4426-0819-1 (bound).—ISBN 978-1-4426-0066-9 (pbk.).—
ISBN 978-1-4426-0424-7 (html).—ISBN 978-1-4426-8656-4 (pdf)

    1. Islam—Relations—Christianity—History—To 1500. 2. Christianity and other religions—Islam—History—To 1500. 3. Church history—Middle Ages, 600–1500. I. Rodriguez, Jarbel, 1971–, editor II. Series: Readings in medieval civilizations and cultures ; XVIII

BP172.M88 2014   261.2'70902   C2014-906017-3
                                             C2014-906018-1

We welcome comments and suggestions regarding any aspect of our publications—please feel free to contact us at news@utphighereducation.com or visit our Internet site at www.utppublishing.com.

North America   UK, Ireland, and continental Europe
5201 Dufferin Street   NBN International
North York, Ontario, Canada, M3H 5T8 Estover Road, Plymouth, PL6 7PY, UK
                                     ORDERS PHONE: 44 (0) 1752 202301
2250 Military Road   ORDERS FAX: 44 (0) 1752 202333
Tonawanda, New York, USA, 14150   ORDERS E-MAIL: enquiries@nbninternational.com

ORDERS PHONE: 1–800–565–9523
ORDERS FAX: 1–800–221–9985
ORDERS E-MAIL: utpbooks@utpress.utoronto.ca

Every effort has been made to contact copyright holders; in the event of an error or omission, please notify the publisher.

The University of Toronto Press acknowledges the financial support for its publishing activities of the Government of Canada through the Canada Book Fund.

Printed in the United States of America

CONTENTS

ACKNOWLEDGMENTS

No book like this is a singular effort, and this one is no different. I have had the support of numerous friends, colleagues, and institutions throughout the writing of this book. In my home department at San Francisco State, Barbara Loomis, Laura Lisy-Wagner, Fred Astren, Trevor Getz, and others provided ideas, suggestions, and, most importantly, support when I have needed it over the last few years. My students, particularly those in my graduate seminar on inter-faith Spain, likewise made suggestions and proved a valuable forum as I tried out some of the sources and ideas incorporated here. The participants in the NEH Summer Seminar in Barcelona in the summer of 2010 gave me new insights into how to approach the medieval Mediterranean world and into possible sources to pursue. I would particularly like to thank Abigail Balbale, Adam Gaiser, Camilo Gomez-Rivas, Jocelyn Hendrickson, and Yuen-Gen Liang, as well as the organizers, Brian Catlos and Sharon Kinoshita, and the participating faculty for their wonderful lectures. It was in discussions with them and others, typically on very pleasant Barcelona afternoons, that much of the final structure of this book began to take shape. Thanks are also due to the host of scholars who have worked on the history of Christian/Muslim relations and whose scholarship has educated, influenced, and guided me. Paul Dutton, the editor of this series, has been unfailingly kind and attentive to my questions, as has Natalie Fingerhut and the staff at the University of Toronto Press. Like Pietro Casola (see Doc. 72), I am sure they've had to tap at least two of their three sacks as I worked to finish this book. Finally, I would like to thank my family, especially my patient wife Claudia and sometimes not so patient son Tristan, who have put up with my absences and inattention as I was preoccupied with finding sources, translating, and writing.

INTRODUCTION

This book explores the history of Muslim–Christian relations in the Middle Ages through the writing and actions of contemporaries. To study the interactions between Christians and Muslims in the medieval period is to study a history of conflict and coexistence. It is a history of warfare, piracy, and raiding, typically along religious lines, but also a history of commerce, intellectual exchanges, and personal relationships that transcended religious differences. Although modern students might be most familiar with the conflict that existed between Christians and Muslims during the Middle Ages, the coexistence, pragmatism, and interdependence that crossed or ignored confessional boundaries are worth remembering and studying as well. This collection of sources aims to give students engaging and informative readings that highlight the many facets of this complex relationship.

The history of Muslim–Christian relations can be said to have its origins in the book of Genesis in the Hebrew Bible and predates, by centuries, the development of both Christianity and Islam. According to the story, the patriarch Abraham and his wife Sarah were trying to conceive a child. As she got older (into her seventies) and remained childless, Sarah convinced Abraham to take her Egyptian slave Hagar to be his wife and father her child, a son named Ishmael. Some 14 years later, at the age of 90, Sarah gave birth to her own son with Abraham, a child named Isaac. Soon thereafter, on Sarah's insistence, Abraham expelled Hagar and her son into the wilderness. When they were on the verge of death, an angel of God found them, led them to water, and proclaimed that Ishmael would be the father of a great nation. This event became the foundational story for Judaism, Christianity, and Islam, as Jews and Christians traced their origins back to Abraham through Isaac, while Muslim belief held that the Arabs were the descendants of Ishmael. Consequently, numerous traditions that we associate with each of the three Abrahamic faiths have their basis in the story of Isaac and Ishmael. Included among them are the widely held practice of circumcision among Muslims (Ishmael was circumcised), the medieval Christian practice of calling Muslims Hagarenes (to insinuate that they were the descendants of slaves) and Ishmaelites, and the Muslim belief that the Kaaba (the holiest site in Islam) was built by Abraham and Ishmael. Ultimately, moreover, the story reveals the close kinship that existed (and still exists) between Christians and Muslims in their religious traditions, bound as they are by a common ancestor in Abraham, as well as hinting at some of the reasons for their estrangement and continued conflict.

The history of Christian–Muslim relations is closely tied to that of the Roman Empire. Christ, the messiah or savior in the Christian tradition, was born in the Roman Empire, and it was the Romans who crucified him, thus bringing about his death and the beginnings of Christianity as a religion. In the centuries after Christ died, his followers—who believed that he was the Son of God, had been resurrected, and could offer them eternal life—spread throughout the Roman Empire. As monotheists in a largely polytheistic world, the Christians were not popular among their fellow Roman citizens and were often the targets of persecutions that led to many being martyred by Roman authorities. In 313, the emperor Constantine (r. 306–337) granted Christians religious freedom, and thereafter they began to gain power rapidly; by the end of the century Christianity had become the official religion of the Roman Empire, and traditional Roman religious practices had been banned.

This was a turbulent period for the Roman world, and not just because of the changes in religious practices brought on by Christianity. Invasions and internal problems sapped the Roman Empire of much of its strength and forced it to split into a western half with its capital in Rome and an eastern half centered on Constantinople. By 476 the western half had collapsed, overrun by Germanic invaders who then settled throughout much of the former imperial territory and began the long, arduous process of centralization and rebuilding.

As the western empire collapsed, the eastern half, called the Byzantine Empire by later historians, soldiered on, increasingly becoming more Greek than Latin and evolving quite differently from the nascent Germanic kingdoms in the west. Indeed, over the next few centuries, the most important characteristic that east and west continued to share was Christianity, and even here there were enough important theological and ritual differences to render the two faiths quite distinctive from one another. The existence of the eastern empire, moreover, proved precarious. The collapse of the western empire had shattered the political unity that had once bound much of Europe, northern Africa, and western Asia. The Mediterranean Sea, for all practicalities a Roman lake, as all its waters touched imperial shores, ceased to be so and fragmented into numerous political zones. In the aftermath of this calamity, new groups and faiths began to make claims on the Mediterranean and to challenge the Byzantines for supremacy.

By far the most successful of these new arrivals were the Arabs. Around 610, a young Arab by the name of Muhammad ibn Abd Allah began to experience visions that he believed were a message from God (the same God worshipped by Christians and Jews and called Allah by Muslims). These revelations were eventually recorded in the Quran, the sacred scriptures of Islam. Armed with these revelations, Muhammad began to preach and in time ascended to political power over the cities of Medina and Mecca. By the time of his death in 632, he had created a willing and active confederation of believers ready to spread his message, by force if necessary. This was followed by an extraordinary century of expansion that saw Islamic armies vanquish the Sasanian (Persian) Empire and come close to doing the same to the Byzantines. Similar expansion came along the North African coast as Muslim armies reached the Atlantic and by 711 had crossed into Spain. In 732 at the Battle of Tours, further expansion into Europe was halted by Charles Martel, leader of the Germanic tribe known as the Franks who had settled in what is now modern-day France and Germany. Despite some minor or short-term conquests, this is how the situation remained in the Mediterranean for the next three centuries.

In the eleventh century, Christian Europe began to reassert itself militarily, politically, and economically in the Mediterranean world. The eleventh century witnessed the beginnings of what some modern historians have called the Reconquest of Spain, as the Christian kingdoms that had lingered in the north took advantage of the collapse of Islamic political power in the Iberian Peninsula and began to push south and claim land that they believed rightfully belonged to them. At roughly the same time, a wave of Turkish invaders, recently converted to Islam, began to put renewed pressure on the Byzantines, prompting the latter to ask the West for help. The help came in the form of the Crusades. Yet this renewal of intense warfare between western (or Latin) Christians, Byzantines, and Muslims also led to other types of contact including commercial, intellectual, religious, and personal ones. The next 500 years were to be a period of intense confrontation and interaction, and they form the chronological core of this book.

This has not been an easy book to organize, simply because of its scope, both geographical and chronological. In order to focus the readings more effectively, I have given limited attention to some periods and regions so as to give a more complete picture of others. The first chapter serves as an introduction to the history of Muslim–Christian relations, covering the period between the rise of Islam and the eleventh century. As well as providing a rough history of events, I have also tried to include sources that introduce some of the salient themes developed in more detail in later chapters. Chapters Two and Three cover most of the political and military history of the period between the years 1000 and 1500, with Chapter Two covering the eastern Mediterranean and Chapter Three focusing on Spain and the western Mediterranean. The remaining seven chapters cover specific aspects of Muslim–Christian relations, including diplomacy, economic interactions, intellectual and religious exchanges, and personal relations.

Although I have done my best to keep sources on topic for any given chapter, undoubtedly there are overlaps, as some could easily fit in several chapters—the original authors were not writing with this book in mind and did not organize their materials in a way that would make the editor's job easier. Instructors and students might wish to arrange things somewhat differently to suit their own purposes. Where possible I have tried to provide multiple sources on the same event or topic to give readers other points of view and limit the bias inherent in most of the sources. And there is bias, prejudice, and intolerance found in many (if not most) of the sources in this book. Medieval writers were not particularly concerned with modern ideas of political correctness, and most of their works were written in a polemical tone that thought little of criticizing, ridiculing, and maligning those about whom they wrote, their sacred teachings, and their religious figures. Yet even these biases, misconceptions, and chauvinisms can be used by the careful student to learn more about his or her historical subjects, their beliefs, and aspirations.

CHAPTER ONE

ORIGINS AND BACKGROUND TO CHRISTIAN/ISLAMIC INTERACTIONS

Figure 1.1: Mosque of Cordoba.

Source: Albert F. Calvert, *Moorish Remains in Spain* (London: John Lane, 1906), 67.

1. THE PACT OF UMAR

Much of the interaction between Muslims, Christians, and Jews was regulated by the Quran, the Islamic sacred scriptures. The Quran calls Christians and Jews 'ahl al kitāb, or the "People of the Book," a reference to the sacred texts at the center of each faith. As "People of the Book," Christians and Jews were to be tolerated and enjoyed certain rights under Islamic law. They were given dhimmi *(protected) status, which entailed some privileges such as the right to freely practice their faith in private (not in public), but also entailed obligations to the Muslim polity and legal restrictions as well.* Dhimmis *were required to pay a special poll tax called the* jizya *in return for the protections granted to them. Failure to pay the* jizya *(or any other breach of the* dhimmi *contract) could result in revocation of the* dhimmi *status, and offenders could then be given a choice of conversion to Islam, enslavement, or death.* Dhimmis *were also barred from bearing arms or serving in the military and had a limited voice in Islamic legal courts. Beyond the guidelines offered in the Quran, numerous later documents helped to standardize and define the status of the* dhimmi *in Islam. Among the earliest and most important of these documents is the so-called Pact of Umar. The origins of the pact and its original usage are disputed by modern scholars. Some argue that the pact represents a specific treaty made between conquering Muslims and the native Christian population. On the other hand, there is strong evidence that there may have been multiple documents, all of which were called "the Pact of Umar," or that the "Pact" was simply a model treaty drawn up in early Islamic law schools. The document presented here is one of these law-school model "Pacts." This document drew on earlier versions of treaties between Muslims and the People of the Book, as well as possibly Byzantine legal codes, in order to create a model treaty. Whatever the case may be as to its origins, the "Pact" remains an important source, both for understanding the process by which communities of People of the Book were assimilated into the Muslim caliphate and for helping us to understand the rights, obligations, and limitations placed upon the* dhimmi.

Source: trans. A.S. Tritton, *The Caliphs and Their Non-Muslim Subjects: A Critical Study of the Covenant of Umar* (London: F. Cass, 1970), 12–16.

I, and all Muslims, promise you and your fellow Christians security as long as you and they keep the conditions we impose upon you. Which are: you shall be under Muslim laws and no other, and shall not refuse to do anything we demand of you. If any of you says of the Prophet, of God's book or his religion what is unfitting, he is debarred from the protection of God, the Commander of the Faithful, and all Muslims; the conditions on which security was given are annulled; and the Commander of the Faithful has put his property and life outside the pale of the law, like the property and lives of enemies. If one of you commits fornication with or marries a Muslim woman, or robs a Muslim on the highway, or turns a

Muslim from his religion, or helps their enemies as a soldier or guide to Muslim weaknesses, or shelters their spies, he has broken his agreement, and his life and property are without the law. He who does lesser harm than this to the goods or honor of a Muslim shall be punished. We shall scrutinize your dealings with Muslims, and if you have done anything unlawful for a Muslim we shall undo it and punish you; e.g. if you have sold to a Muslim any forbidden thing, as wine, pigs, blood, or an [unclean] carcass, we shall annul the sale, take the price from you (if you have received it) or withhold it from you (if it has not been paid); we shall pour out the wine or blood and burn the carcass. If he [the Muslim] wishes it to be destroyed we shall do nothing to him, but we shall punish you. You shall not give him any forbidden thing to eat or drink, and shall not give him a wife in the presence of your witnesses nor in an illegal marriage. We shall not scrutinize nor enquire into a contract between you and any other unbeliever. If either party wishes to annul the contract, and brings a request to us, if we think that it should be annulled we shall annul it, if it is legal we shall allow it. But if the object has been taken and lost we shall not restore it, for a sale between unbelievers has been finished. If you or any other unbeliever asks for judgment we shall give it according to Muslim law; if we are not approached we shall not interfere between you. If you kill accidentally a Muslim or an ally, Christian or not, then the relatives [of the homicide] shall pay blood money, as among Muslims. For you, relatives are on the father's side. If a homicide has no relatives then his estate must pay. A murderer shall be killed unless the heirs wish to take blood money, which shall be paid at once. A thief, if his victim complains, shall have his hand cut off, if this is the punishment, and shall pay a fine. The slanderer shall be punished if the punishment is fixed; if not, he shall be punished according to Muslim law. You shall not display in any Muslim town the cross nor parade your idolatry, nor build a church nor place of assembly for your prayers, nor beat the *nākūs* [small drums], nor use your idolatrous language about Jesus, the son of Mary, to any Muslim. You shall wear the *zunnār* [belt or girdle worn by Christians so that they could be distinguished from Muslims] above all your clothes, cloaks and others, so that it is not hidden; you shall use peculiar saddles and manner of riding, and make your *kalansuwas* [tall caps] different from those of the Muslims by a mark you put on them. You shall not take the crest of the road nor the chief seats in assemblies, when Muslims are present. Every free adult male of sound mind shall pay [the] poll-tax, one dinar of full weight, at new year. He shall not leave his town till he has paid and shall not appoint a substitute to pay it, one who pays no *jizya* till the beginning of the year. A poor man is liable for his *jizya* until it is paid; poverty does not cancel any of your obligations nor abrogate the protection given you. If you have anything we shall take it. The *jizya* is the only burden on your property as long as you stay in your town or travel in Muslim land, except as merchants. You may not enter Mecca under any conditions. If you travel with merchandise you must pay one-tenth to the Muslims, you may go where you like in Muslim land, except Mecca, and may stay in any Muslim land you like except the Hedjaz, where you may stay three days only till you depart.

These terms are binding on him who has hair under his clothes, is adult, or has completed fifteen years before this date, if he agrees to them; if not, there is no treaty with him. Your little boys, immature lads, lunatics, and slaves do not pay *jizya*. If a lunatic becomes sane, a boy grows up, a slave is set free and follows your religion, he pays *jizya*. The terms are binding on you and those who accept them; we have no treaty with those who refuse them. We will protect you and your lawful (according to our law) property against any one, Muslim or not, who tries to wrong you, as we protect ourselves and our own property; our decisions about it will be the same as those about our own property, and ourselves. Our protection does not extend to forbidden things, like blood, carcasses, wine and pigs, but we will not interfere with them; only you must not obtrude them on Muslim towns. If a Muslim or other buys them we will not force him to pay, for they are forbidden and have no price; but we will not let him annoy you about them, and if he does it again we will punish him, but will not force him to pay. You must fulfill all the conditions we have imposed on you. You must not attack a Muslim nor help their enemies by word or deed.

The treaty of God and His promise and the most complete fulfillment of promise He has imposed on any of His creatures; you have the treaty of God and His promise and the protection of N.N. [most likely a placeholder for a name] the Commander of the Faithful, and of the Muslims to fulfill their obligations towards you. Your sons, when they grow up, have the same obligations as you. If you alter or change them then the protection of God, of N.N. the Commander of the Faithful, and of the Muslims is taken from you. He, who is at a distance, yet receives this document and approves it, these are the terms that are binding on him and on us, if he approves them; if he does not approve, we have no treaty with him.

2. THE CONQUEST OF ALEXANDRIA

One of the primary reasons why the Quran and Muslim legal scholars and political leaders were so concerned with the status of dhimmis is due to Islam's rapid early expansion. In the century after Muhammad's death, Muslim armies quickly toppled the once mighty Persian Empire, conquered large portions of the Byzantine world, notably in the Middle East and northern Africa, and took over most of the Iberian Peninsula. This led to large numbers of dhimmis coming under Muslim domination. The source below details the conquest of the Byzantine city of Alexandria in Egypt in 641 during the reign of the emperor Heraclius. It highlights the considerable power of the Muslim armies, as well as the aftermath of conquest and the interaction between the invading Islamic forces and the native Byzantine Christian population.

Source: trans. Basil Evetts, *Sawirus ibn al-Muqaffa: History of the Patriarchs of the Coptic Church of Alexandria*, from *Patrologia Orientalis* I (Paris: Firmin-Didot, 1907), 492–97.

And in those days Heraclius saw a dream in which it was said to him: "Truly there shall come against you a circumcised nation, and they shall vanquish you and take possession of the land." So Heraclius thought that they would be the Jews, and accordingly gave orders that all the Jews and Samaritans should be baptized in all the provinces which were under his dominion. But after a few days there appeared a man of the Arabs, from the southern districts, that is to say, from Mecca or its neighborhood, whose name was Muhammad; and he brought back the worshippers of idols to the knowledge of the One God, and bade them declare that Muhammad was his apostle; and his nation were circumcised in the Hesh, not by the law, and prayed towards the South, turning towards a place which they called the Kaabah. And he took possession of Damascus and Syria, and crossed the Jordan, and dammed it up. And the Lord abandoned the army of the Romans before him, as a punishment for their corrupt faith, and because of the anathemas uttered against them, on account of the council of Chalcedon, by the ancient fathers.

When Heraclius saw this, he assembled all his troops from Egypt as far as the frontiers of Aswan. And he continued for three years to pay to the Muslims the taxes which he had demanded for the purpose of applying them to himself and all his troops; and they used to call the tax the *bakt*, that is to say that it was a sum levied at so much a head. And this went on until Heraclius had paid to the Muslims the greater part of his money; and many people died through the troubles which they had endured.

So when ten years were over of the rule of Heraclius together with the Colchian, who sought for the patriarch Benjamin, while he was fleeing from him from place to place, hiding himself in the fortified churches, the prince of the Muslims sent an army to Egypt, under one of his trusty companions, named Amr ibn Al-Asi, in the year 357 of Diocletian [641 CE], the slayer of the martyrs. And this army of Islam came down into Egypt in great force, on the twelfth day of Baunah, which is the sixth of June, according to the months of the Romans.

Now the commander Amr had destroyed the fort, and burnt the boats with fire, and defeated the Romans, and taken possession of part of the country. For he had first arrived by the desert; and the horsemen took the road through the mountains, until they arrived at a fortress built of stone, between Upper Egypt and the Delta, called Babylon [Cairo]. So they pitched their tents there, until they were prepared to fight the Romans, and make war against them; and afterwards they named that place, I mean the fortress, in their language, Bablun Al-Fustat; and that is its name to the present day.

After fighting three battles with the Romans, the Muslims conquered them. So when the chief men of the city saw these things, they went to Amr, and received a certificate of security for the city, that it might not be plundered. This kind of treaty which Muhammad, the chief of the Arabs, taught them, they called the Law; and he says with regard to it: "As for the province of Egypt and any city that agrees with its inhabitants to pay the land-tax to you and to submit to your authority, make a treaty with them, and do them no injury. But plunder and take as prisoners those that will not consent to this and resist you." For this reason the Muslims kept their hands off the province and its inhabitants, but destroyed the nation of the Romans, and their general who was named Marianus. And those of the Romans who escaped fled to Alexandria, and shut its gates upon the Arabs, and fortified themselves within the city.

And in the year 360 of Diocletian, in the month of December, three years after Amr had taken possession of Memphis, the Muslims captured the city of Alexandria, and destroyed its walls, and burnt many churches with fire. And they burnt the church of Saint Mark, which was built by the sea, where his body was laid; and this was the place to which the father and patriarch, Peter the Martyr, went before his martyrdom, and blessed Saint Mark, and committed to him his reasonable flock, as he had received it. So they burnt this place and the monasteries around it....

When Amr took full possession of the city of Alexandria, and settled its affairs, that infidel, the governor of Alexandria, feared, he being both prefect and patriarch of the city under the Romans, that Amr would kill him; therefore he sucked a poisoned ring, and died on the spot. But Sanutius, the believing dux [ruler], made known to Amr the circumstances of that militant father, the patriarch Benjamin, and how he was a fugitive from the Romans, through fear of them. Then Amr, son of Al-Asi, wrote to the provinces of Egypt a letter, in which he said: "There is protection and security for the place where Benjamin, the patriarch of the Coptic Christians is, and peace from God; therefore let him come forth secure and tranquil, and administer the affairs of his Church, and the government of his nation." Therefore when the holy Benjamin heard this, he returned to Alexandria with great joy, clothed with the crown of patience and sore conflict which had befallen the orthodox people through their persecution by the heretics, after having been absent during thirteen years, ten of which were years of Heraclius, the misbelieving Roman, with the three years before the Muslims conquered Alexandria. When Benjamin appeared, the people and the whole city rejoiced, and made his arrival known to Sanutius, the dux who believed in Christ, who had settled with the commander Amr that the patriarch should return, and had received a safe-conduct from Amr for him. Thereupon

Sanutius went to the commander and announced that the patriarch had arrived, and Amr gave orders that Benjamin should be brought before him with honor and veneration and love. And Amr, when he saw the patriarch, received him with respect, and said to his companions and private friends: "Truly in all the lands of which we have taken possession hitherto I have never seen a man of God like this man." For the Father Benjamin was beautiful of countenance, excellent in speech, discoursing with calmness and dignity.

Then Amr turned to him, and said to him: "Resume the government of all your churches and of your people, and administer their affairs. And if you will pray for me, that I may go to the West and to Pentapolis, and take possession of them, as I have of Egypt, and return to you in safety and speedily, I will do for you all that you shall ask of me." Then the holy Benjamin prayed for Amr, and pronounced an eloquent discourse, which made Amr and those present with him marvel, and which contained words of exhortation and much profit for those that heard him; and he revealed certain matters to Amr, and departed from his presence honored and revered. And all that the blessed father said to the commander Amr, son of Al-Asi, he found true, and not a letter of it was unfulfilled.

3. THE COMING OF ISLAM AND THE DESTRUCTION OF THE (ROMAN) WORLD

The conquest of Alexandria was only one episode in a broader campaign by the Muslims to take over large parts of the once mighty Roman Empire. As Muslim armies continued to have successes against their eastern Roman counterparts, numerous writers began to voice their alarm and even panic as to what these Muslim conquests represented. A few of these interpreted the Muslim conquests as nothing less than the end of the Roman Empire, prophesied by numerous books of the Bible in both the Old and New Testaments. Among the most anguished sources is the Apocalypse of Pseudo-Methodius, *partially reproduced below. The* Apocalypse *claims to be the vision of Methodius, bishop of Olympas who had died around 311, but was in fact written sometime around 692. Consequently, while clad in the guise and authority of a prophetic vision, the* Apocalypse *allowed its author to portray the Arab expansion in the most horrific terms possible and not always supported by historical reality, while also comforting its readers with the knowledge that the Arabs too would be overthrown in their own time. Yet, even though it takes numerous liberties with the truth, the* Apocalypse *does give the modern reader a sense of the dread and fear felt by many eastern Romans in the face of the unstoppable Muslim expansion.*

Source: trans. Walter Emil Kaegi, "Initial Byzantine Reactions to the Arab Conquest," *Church History* 38.2 (1969): 144–46.

The land of Persia will be delivered over to ruin and destruction and her inhabitants to captivity and the sword. Cappadocia and her inhabitants will be swallowed down in similar ruin, captivity, and slaughter. Sicily will become desolate and her inhabitants will meet slaughter and captivity. Hellas and [its] inhabitants will meet destruction, captivity and the sword. Romania [Asia Minor] will undergo destruction and her people will be turned to flight. The islands of the sea will become desolate and their inhabitants will perish through the sword and captivity. Egypt, the East and Syria will be loaded with an immeasurable yoke of affliction. They mercilessly will be pressed into service and their souls will be lured by an irresistible amount of gold. The inhabitants of Egypt and Syria will experience distress and affliction seven times worse than captivity. The land of the Gospel will be smitten from the four winds beneath the heavens and will be as dust in a mass which is gathered by the wind. There will be plague and famine upon them. The hearts of the destroyers will be uplifted and raised in contempt and they will babble excessively until their appointed time. They will gain mastery over the entrance and exit from the north and east to the west and the sea. All men will be beneath their yoke and birds and all waters of the sea will be subject to them, and the deserts, where their inhabitants hunt, will be theirs. They will register claim for themselves of the mountains as well as the deserts, fish of the sea, wood of the hills, soil of the land, rocks and the land's productivity will be their revenues. They will possess the labors and sweat of the farmers, the property of the rich, the offerings to the saints, whether gold, silver, precious stones, copper or iron, the holy and glorious vestments, every food and all honorable things. Their hearts will be exceedingly exalted until they demand the corpses themselves equally of widows, orphans, and saints. They will have no mercy on laborers, the poor, they will dishonor the aged and will afflict and have no mercy on the weak and infirm, but will mock and laugh at those who are distinguished in wisdom and in political and civic affairs. Everyone will be shamed into silence and will be afraid since they will not have the strength to reply or to say anything plainly. All of the inhabitants of the earth will be astonished and their wisdom and education, of evil origin, will be powerless to retort to or to alter their [the Arabs'] proclamations. Their course will be from sea to sea, from east to west, and from the north to the desert of Yathrib. Their way will be named the way of difficulty and presbyters and presbyteresses, poor and rich, laborers and the thirsty and prisoners, will travel it and will bless the dead.... For apostasy is education and it will educate all of the earth's inhabitants. Since God called Ishmael, their father, a wild ass, accordingly, wild asses and scorpions of the desert and every kind of wild and tame beast will be captured, all of the wood of the hillside will be extirpated, the beauty of the mountains will vanish, cities will become desolate, lands will become impassable because of the reduction of the human population and the earth will be polluted by blood and they

8

[the Arabs] will gain hold of its fruit. For the tyrannically conquering barbarians are not men, but sons of the desert who will come to desolation, are ruined, and will welcome hate. And in the beginning, at the time of their exodus, pregnant women will be won by their [the Arabs'] swords and will become food for the wild beasts. They will slaughter the priests at home, defiling the holy places, and they will lie with their wives in the revered and holy places where the mystical and bloodless sacrifice is performed. Their wives, sons, and daughters will put on the holy vestments, they will place these on their horses, they will spread them on their beds, and they will tie their cattle in the coffins of the saints. They will be corrupted murderers, like a fire testing the race of the Christians....

... Then suddenly the emperor of the Greeks or Romans will rise up against them with great wrath and will be awakened like a man from his sleep who had been drinking wine, whom men had thought to be a corpse and of no use. This man will come out against them from the sea of the Ethiopians and will thrust his sword and desolation as far as Yathrib, that is, into their fatherland, and will make captive their wives and children. The sons of the emperor will descend upon the inhabitants of the land of the Gospel and will eradicate them from the earth. Fear will fall upon them from all directions. Their wives and children, those nursing babes, all of their encampments and the property of their fathers in their lands will be delivered into the hands of the emperor of the Romans, that is, to the sword, captivity, death, and destruction. The yoke of the emperor of the Romans will be seven times worse upon them than their own yoke had been. Great distress will seize them—dirt, thirst, affliction—they and their wives will be the slaves of their [former] slaves. Their slavery will be a hundred times more bitter and painful. The earth, which they had desolated, will be at peace and each man will return to his own property and to that of his fathers. Armenia, Cilicia, Isauria, Africa, Hellas, Sicily, and everyone who was abandoned will return to his property and to that of his fathers. Men will multiply on the desolate earth like the locusts of Egypt. Arabia will be devastated by fire, Egypt will be burned, and the coast will be at peace. The entire wrath of the emperor of the Romans will be upon those who deny our Lord Jesus Christ. The earth will be at peace and there will be a general calm on earth such as never has existed and will not again exist, as it is the end. There will be merriment on earth and men will dwell in peace and rebuild cities, will free priests from their pains, and men will cease to have afflictions in that time.

4. AL-JĀHIZ'S WARNINGS ABOUT THE CHRISTIANS

The persistent conflict between Christians and Muslims on the battlefields was at times echoed in polemical literature. The Apocalypse of Pseudo-Methodius *(see Doc. 3) is a good example of this on the Christian side, and something to which Muslim writers replied in kind with their own literary attacks. The source below, which includes only about one-third of the original work, is one of these polemical tracts written by the Muslim philosopher Abū 'Uthmān 'Amr ibn Bahr al-Jāhiz (ca. 776–868). Al-Jāhiz was the author of over 200 works ranging from the theological, such as the source below, to more comical and lewd pieces.* He wrote Contra Christianorum [sic] *to give Muslims suitable arguments to use against Christians in Iraq, who were considered to have influence and power beyond their limited number. The source is fascinating in that while attacking many Christian beliefs and practices, it also provides extensive details on the daily interactions between Christians and Muslims living in the Abbasid Caliphate. What emerges is a snapshot of a society that seems to have practiced a healthy amount of toleration but that was under pressure from some of its more orthodox members to minimize these friendly relations.*

Source: trans. Jim Colville, *Contra Christianorum* in *Sobriety and Mirth: A Selection of the Shorter Writings of al-Jāhiz* (London: Kegan Paul, 2002), 73–80.

I shall begin by considering why the Muslim masses are more favorably disposed towards Christians than they are towards Zoroastrians and why they believe them to be more trustworthy, more sociable, less pernicious, lesser infidels and, generally, less of a torment than Jews. The reasons for this are many and quite unmistakable. They will be recognized by the thoughtful but remain a mystery to the ignorant.

The first point to note is that Jews and Muslims were neighbors in Medina (and elsewhere) and the hostility between neighbors is akin to the implacable hostility and jealousy that exist between members of the same family. A man only falls out with someone he knows and directs his resentment at someone he sees. It is men of his acquaintance whose faults he notes. Love and hate are functions of distance and proximity, respectively. For this reason, feuds between neighbors and members of the same family last longer and are more acrimonious than those involving other peoples and tribes.

When the Muslim émigrés from Mecca joined forces with the Medinese stalwarts, the Jews of Medina came to resent their neighbors, the twin blessing of their faith and new alliance. They sowed suspicion among the common people and sought to turn the heads of the simple. They gave succor to the Muslims' enemies and malcontents. Then they went beyond mere slander and the spreading of doubt to open hostility. They conspired against the Muslims, mobilizing men and materiel for war and driving them from their homes. The situation worsened and the hatred became ingrained.

However, because their lands were distant from both Mecca and Medina, Christians never resorted to intrigue, vilification and open hostility against Muslims. This is the principal reason why Muslim opinion became set against Jews but remains tolerant of Christians. The emigration of Muslims to Abyssinia and the support they received from the authorities there further endeared Christians to the Muslim masses.

As a general rule, people tend to be inimical towards the enemies of their friends and, as dislike of Christians diminished, so dislike of Jews increased. It is normal to like someone who does you a good turn or whose actions result in some benefit to you, regardless of whether or not it was intentional and whether or not it was so willed by God.

One of the most compelling reasons of all concerns the interpretation of certain Quranic verses which have been misunderstood by the Muslim masses and over which even the elite have disputed. Christians have picked up on them and used them to bend the ears of the rabble. These are the verses in which God says, You shall find that pagans and Jews are the most hostile towards believers, while those who say "We are Christians" are the most sympathetic, for among them there are priests and monks who are not arrogant. When they hear what has been revealed to the Messenger, you can see their eyes fill with tears, for they recognize the truth. "Lord," they cry, "we believe, so inscribe our names among those who bear witness. How can we fail to believe in God and the truth revealed to us, when we have longed for our Lord to admit us to the company of the righteous?" And God has rewarded them for their prayers with gardens through which rivers flow, wherein they shall dwell forever. Such is the reward of the righteous.

However, these same verses provide powerful evidence that God was not referring to such Christians as the ones you speak of and their Melchite and Jacobite coreligionists but, rather, to the likes of Bahlra and the monks whom Salman served. Just because they all claim to be Christian does not mean we have to treat them all alike.

At the coming of Islam, there were two Arab kings, one from the tribe of Ghassan and the other from Lakhm, and both of them were Christian. The Arab tribes owed allegiance and paid tribute to both—a respect that had its roots in reverence for the Christian religion. Although the people of the Tehom maintained their independence and paid no tribute, submitting to neither the spiritual nor temporal authority, they nevertheless held the same values as the rest of the Arabs. If the Christianity of Nu'man and the Ghassanid kings was not already well-known to the Arab genealogists, I would illustrate it here with celebrated verses and authenticate historical narratives.

The kingdoms of Lakhm and Ghassan traded with Syria and their merchants ventured as far afield as the courts of the Byzantine emperors. They organized summer and winter caravans, trading with Abyssinia, Syria, and Medina. They summered in Ta'if and, occasionally, in Yemen to reaffirm respect for its ruler. That they were wealthy men is attested in the Quran and known by scholars to be true.

When the Muslims emigrated to Abyssinia and came as a delegation to the Porte of the Negus, they were cordially received and treated with respect. The kings of Persia never accorded Muslims such recognition and hospitality. The *negus* of Abyssinia and emperor of Byzantium were both Christian, making a further point in Christianity's favor. It is a fact that subsequent generations tend to adopt the values of their predecessors.

Another point to note is that Christianity, unlike Judaism and Zoroastrianism, had spread among the Bedouin, eventually becoming the dominant religion among the tribes, with the exception of Mudhar. The only Mudhar clan to adopt Christianity was one that settled at Hira, becoming known as "Votaries" but, with their relatively small numbers, they were soon submerged among other tribes. For the most part, Mudhar adhered to Arab paganism and, subsequently, to Islam.

Christianity prevailed among the Arab kings and the tribes of Lakhm, Ghassan, Harith ibn Ka'b at Najran, Qudha'a, and Tayy, to name but a few. It later spread among Rabl'a, Tighlab, Abd Qays, obscure elements of Bakr, and, in particular, among the Dhu'ljaddayn. However, by the time of the coming of Islam, there were no predominantly Jewish tribes outside the Yemen, except for insignificant elements of Iyyad and Rabl'a. Most Jews lived in Medina, Himyar, Tayma, and Wadi'l Qura, and, as descendants of Aaron, were not of true Arab origin.

Many Arabs are favorably disposed towards Christians because of the influence they wield and by virtue of kinship. Our masses appreciate the fact that the emperor of Byzantium is Christian and that many Arabs are themselves Christian. They can see that Byzantine women bear the children of highly-placed Muslims and that Christians are scholastics, physicians, and astrologers. Consequently, the popular belief has formed that Christians, unlike Jews, are philosophers and sages.

The reason why Christians and Jews are different in this respect is that the latter treat metaphysical speculation as unbelief and scholastic theology as a heresy that acts as a magnet for doubt. The Jewish position is that there is no worthwhile knowledge except that contained in the Pentateuch and Books of the Prophets. Faith in medicine and belief in astrology lead directly to materialism and atheism, so they say, and conflict with their tradition. They even dismiss the elements of those disciplines which are generally recognized and deny freedom of speech to those who would practice them.

If the masses only realized that Christians and Byzantines possess no wisdom, enlightenment, or any sort of cultural depth beyond a certain competence in crafts like turnery [woodturning], carpentry, drawing, and embroidery, they would remove them from the ranks of the cultured and erase them from the register of philosophers and sages.

The Organon, On Generation and Corruption, The Metaphysics, etc. were written by Aristotle, who was neither Byzantine nor Christian. *The Almagest* was written by Ptolemy who, likewise, was neither Byzantine nor Christian. Euclid, too, was neither Byzantine nor Christian. Galen, the author of the standard treatise on medicine, was neither Byzantine nor Christian. The same is true of Democritus, Hippocrates, Plato, et al. They belonged to a long-gone society but the imprint of their intellects has endured. They were Greeks whose religion and culture were not those of Christianity. They were scholars, while the Christians in our society are mere tradesmen, who have assumed the rights to their writings by virtue of geographical proximity, ascribing some of their works to themselves and adapting others to the tenets of their creed. Unable to plagiarize the better-known works, they claim that the ancient Greeks were a Byzantine tribe and boast of their mythology to the Jews, flaunt it in front of the Arabs, and broadcast it to the Hindus. They even go so far as to claim that our doctors imitate theirs and our philosophy is a mere parody. So be it!

Christianity resembles atheism and has much in common with the doctrines of materialism. That this is a principal cause of doubt and confusion is borne out by the fact that no more heretical, perplexed, and unstable religious community exists than Christendom.

Such is the case of all who would speculate on esoteric matters with feeble intellect. Do you not agree that most of the professing Muslims executed for atheism were children of Christian parents? Count the number of skeptics around nowadays and you will find almost all of them in the same boat.

What impresses the rabble so much about Christians is that they are the secretaries to sultans, valets to princes, physicians to the court, as well as perfumiers and bankers. Jews, on the other hand, are the tanners, dyers, barbers, butchers, and tinkers. Consequently, the masses suppose that the Jewish faith compares with other faiths as their trades compare with other trades and that their unbelief is of the lowest sort, since their trades are society's most menial.

Despite their hideous looks, Christians are less of an eyesore than Jews because the latter take wives only from within their own community and do not let their womenfolk marry outside it. The absence of intermarriage means that the vigorous blood of other races does not mix with theirs. They beget no intellect, vitality, or grace. The same phenomenon can be observed at work among horses, donkeys, camels, and pigeons.

I have no quarrel with the popular perception that Christians possess considerable wealth and influence, that their clothes are cleaner than Jewish clothes, and that their professions are of the higher sort. Where I disagree is over the difference between the relative intolerance of the two forms of unbelief, the extent of their intrigue against the good people of Islam, and the inherited deficiencies and ethnic taints of their adherents.

As regards influence, power, and position in society, we all know that Christians ride pedigree horses, hold riding tournaments, and play polo. They comb their forelocks fashionably and dress sharply in double-breasted tunics tailored from blended fabrics. They even employ bodyguards. They call themselves good Muslim names like Hassan, Hussayn, Abbas, Fadhl, and Ali. About the only names left which they have not appropriated are Muhammad and Abu'l Qasim. Consequently, Muslims fall over themselves beating a path to their door. Many Christians have stopped wearing the obligatory waistband or have taken to wearing it under their tunics. Many of their grandees are too proud to pay the poll-tax, although it is well within their means. They exchange insults and blows with Muslims. And what is to stop them behaving so—and even worse—when most of our judges believe that the blood of a primate, archbishop, and bishop is equal to that of aja'far, an Ali, an Ayyas, and a Hamza and think it is enough to let off with a reprimand a Christian who has accused the Prophet's mother of easy virtue and then justified himself by saying that the Prophet's mother was not a Muslim?! God Almighty, what a staggering thing to say and what a patently feeble excuse! The Prophet ruled, "No one is our equal in court. If they insult you, beat them and if they beat you, kill them."

To top it all, the same Christian who accused the Prophet's mother of indecency receives nothing more than a reprimand from his own community, who claim that slander of the Prophet does not constitute a breach of the covenant or violation of their oath of allegiance. However, the Prophet ordered them to pay us the levy and ordered us to take it with the upper hand. We, in turn, are obliged to give them protection and do them no harm. God condemned them to humility and obedience. Even a dunce ought to realize that the first four caliphs and their successors did not make a promise not to slander the Prophet or his mother a condition of receiving the poll-tax and of guaranteeing protection. It was so self-evident that it did not require to be written in stone, stated as an explicit condition, and noted in the public record. If it had, it would have been taken as a sign of weakness and opened the door to other demands. It would have been assumed that the Muslim position was so insecure that that sort of thing was needed.

Conditions are stipulated in writing and the details of an agreement made explicit only if there is a likelihood that confusion or misunderstanding will arise, a judge will make an oversight, a witness will forget or a lawsuit will be brought. However, when something is so patently obvious as to exclude any confusion, what is the point of stipulating it as a condition and taking the trouble to write it down?

Conditions that legitimately required to be stated in the terms of the Muslim/non-Muslim covenant—humility, obedience, payment of the poll-tax, the allegiance of the churches, impartiality in disputes between Muslims, etc.—were made explicit. However, since saying to someone who is lower than low and smaller than small, who seeks and desires that his tribute be taken, who is blessed by the receipt of his poll-tax and the sparing of his blood: "You shall be required not to insult the community of the Messenger of the Lord of the Universe, the seal of the prophets, and the master of men past and future," would not be required by ordinary men, why should it be of the majestic and glorious, the leaders of men, the lights in the darkness, and the beacons of guidance—particularly given Arab pride, the prestige of the sultan, the authority of the state, the glory of Islam, the epiphany of proof, and the promise of salvation and triumph?

In actual fact, the Muslim community has not been blighted half as much by Jews, Zoroastrians, and Mandaeans as it has been by Christians. They pick up on any contradictory aspects of our traditions, weak chains of transmission, and ambiguous verses in the Quran. Then they corner our weak-minded brethren—who know little about heretical sophistry and damned atheism—and start putting questions to them. At the same time, they come over all innocent with our scholars and intellectuals. They prompt doubt among rational men and perplex the simple folk. It is a regrettable fact that every Muslim thinks of himself as a scholastic and just as qualified to dispute with heretics as anybody else.

Were it not for Christian theologians, doctors, and astrologers, our simpletons, popinjays, and under-age dandies would never have heard about Manichaeism, obscure sects of Zoroastrianism, and all sorts of other -isms. They would know only the Quran and the Sunna of the Prophet. The scriptures of those other creeds would have remained within the confines of their own communities. Every single look of despair that I have ever seen on the faces of our simple folk and juveniles can be traced to Christian influence.

When you hear what they have to say about forgiveness, the mendicant life, chastity and the renunciation of issue, their aversion to meat and appetite for fruit and vegetables (particularly berries), and their reverence for ecclesiarchs, you quickly come to see the link between Christianity and atheism, with which they clearly sympathize.

It is simply astonishing that no primate, bishop, archbishop, Jacobite hermit, Nestorian (or any other) monk or nun anywhere engages in procreative activity, in spite of the legion of monks and nuns around, the army of priests who follow their lead, the hordes of campaign veterans in their ranks and their share of normal male and female sterility. Christians who do take a wife cannot divorce and remarry or take a second wife or concubine. Even so, they have filled the furthest corners of the world and colonized the horizons. They have overwhelmed other faiths with their rabble of brats and by sheer weight of numbers, thereby adding to our torment and distress. Their numbers keep increasing because, while they make many converts from other religions, few of them ever convert. This is the case with any religion that is successor to another.

Proof of the moral corruption and lack of compassion of Christians is that they, uniquely, practice that grimmest of all human customs: castration. They even perform it on innocent children. The only countries I know of where human castration is practiced are [Christian] Byzantium and Abyssinia; it is rare—almost unknown, in fact—anywhere else. Moreover, it is an indigenous custom there, not the product of external influence. They even castrate their own sons and put them up for sale. A Mandaean may castrate himself but does not have the right to castrate his son. If this wish to castrate their sons for the purposes of chastity were to be realized, their lineage would vanish, their religion disappear and a blight descend upon their people.

He may be better dressed, practice a higher profession, and be less hideous to look at than the Jew but the Christian is, at heart, a foul and dirty creature. Why? Because he is uncircumcised, does not wash after intercourse, and eats pig meat. His wife does not wash after intercourse, either, or even after menstruation and childbirth, which leaves her absolutely filthy. Furthermore she, too, is uncircumcised.

Despite their wicked natures and subservience to lust, Christianity contains no admonitions such as the everlasting fire of hell and the various forms of legal punishment provided for in this life by Islam. So how can a Christian avoid being corrupted and follow the path of salvation? How can he make the world a better place? Is he not more likely to corrupt it?

Even if you made a supreme mental effort to grasp their teaching on the Messiah and, in particular, the doctrine of the nature of the divinity, you would fail to understand the essential point of Christianity. How could you? If you corner a Nestorian and ask him about the doctrine of the Messiah, he will tell you one thing. If you then corner his brother (also a Nestorian) and ask him the same thing, he will tell you something else. The same goes for Jacobites and Melchites. In consequence, we cannot grasp the truth of Christianity as we can of all other religions.

They claim that religion is not tractable to reason, supported by disputation, or assayed in the crucible of open debate, but is a matter of accepting what scripture says and conforming to tradition. Whoever adheres to such a religion has little choice but to come up with such an excuse!

Christians maintain that the profession of a different faith, such as Zoroastrianism, Mandaeanism, and Manicaenism, is tolerable as long as such a falsehood has not been consciously adopted and the truth is not opposed. They denounce Jews for intransigence but absolve them from charges of transgression and sophistry.

5. A MUSLIM AMBASSADOR IN CONSTANTINOPLE

By the middle of the eighth century, the military situation between the Muslim caliphate and the Byzantine Empire was beginning to reach equilibrium with the ending of Islamic expansion in western Asia. And while conflict between the two states continued, sometimes for high stakes but more often at a low level, we begin to see numerous mercantile, intellectual, and diplomatic exchanges. Among the latter was the embassy undertaken by Abu Ishak ibn Shahrām, a functionary in the court of 'Adud al-Dawla (r. 949–983), the ruling emir in much of what is modern-day Iraq and Iran. By the time this diplomatic exchange took place in 981–982, the Abbasid dynasty had lost its nearly absolute control over the Muslim world, ceding significant parts of the Middle East and central Asia to local rulers (emirs), and Spain to a descendant of the Umayyads. As a result, warfare between the different Muslim polities was relatively common, and it was not unusual for some of these rulers to ally with the Byzantines. On the Byzantine side, there was similar conflict, with pretenders to the throne sometimes challenging the emperor and allying themselves with anyone who could help—often regional Muslim powers. Such was the case in 976, when Bardas Sclerus, a Byzantine general (domesticus) rose up in rebellion against the emperor Basil II (r. 976–1025). In 979, the rebellion was put down and Sclerus fled to Baghdad and the safety of his Muslim allies. In the aftermath of the rebellion, a series of embassies were exchanged between Constantinople and Baghdad as Basil tried to convince the Muslims to turn Sclerus over to him. The embassy of ibn Shahrām, which intended to discuss the possible return of Sclerus to Constantinople in exchange for a border fortress and tax levies, is recorded in the following source taken from the notes of ibn Shahrām.

Source: trans. H.F. Amedroz, "An Embassy from Baghdad to the Emperor Basil II," *Journal of the Royal Asiatic Society* (1914): 919–31; rev. Jarbel Rodriguez.

An Account of the Negotiations between 'Adud al-Dawla and the Byzantine Ruler by Exchange of Verbal Communications

The occasion for these communications was the fact already stated, that Bardas had entered Islamic territory; this alarmed the Byzantine sovereign and he dispatched an envoy thereon to 'Adud al-Dawla. The reply was sent by Abu-Bakr Muhammad b. al-Tayyib al-Ash'ari, known as Ibn al-Bākilāni, and he came back with an envoy known as Ibn Kūnis, who, on his return, went accompanied by Abu Ishak b. Shahrām with a claim against the Byzantine sovereign for a number of strongholds. He now arrived accompanied by Nicephorus the Kanikleios [senior chancery official], who was the bearer of a handsome gift.

Summary of the Whole Transaction Extant in the Words of Ibn Shahrām, Pointing to His Sagacity, His Caution, and His Firmness

It runs thus: On reaching Kharshana I learnt that the *domesticus* [Bardas Phocas] had left Constantinople and had begun his preparations, and that with him was an envoy from Aleppo known as Ibn Māmak, and Kulaib, brother-in-law to Abu

Sālih al-Sadīd. Kulaib was one of Bardas's partisans and was among the rebels who had been amnestied and settled on Byzantine territory after being levied a fine. The Byzantines thought of fining him after the examples of others, and to forfeit the estates which had been granted him when he contrived the surrender to them of the fortress of Barzūya [ca. 974], but he found the means of gaining over the chamberlain and the *domesticus*, and managed to procure for the Byzantine ruler undertakings as regards Aleppo and elsewhere which sufficed to ward off imminent danger, together with an offer to secure immediate payment of what was attributable to the land-tax on Aleppo and Emesa, since it was his relative [who had promised] and he would not oppose him. On this ground he was let off. With the envoy from Aleppo nothing was settled, but a claim was made for arrears of land tax for past years.

On the *domesticus* arriving at a place which was off the post route, Ibn Kūnis and I proceeded to join him. He proved to be young and self-satisfied, and averse to completing the truce on various grounds: one being that he could dispense with its necessity for the moment and that it would prejudice his repute; another that the Byzantine ruler was eager for it, "and we are in fear of mischief from him"; and thirdly his own personal hopes and wishes. But at the same time he showed us courtesy and did accept the proposed peace with an expression of thanks.

He then inquired the object of my coming, and I fully informed him. Ibn Kūnis drew his attention to the stipulated terms, on which he said: were the chiefs to succeed in getting us to cede to them amicably the districts and fortresses they ask, each one of them would set about scheming to avoid the necessity of keeping a force of men and of making money payments. I replied that where policy was backed by force and ability it was a proof of nobility of character, and should be met by compliance. "But what about Aleppo?" he asked: "it is no part of your ['Adud al-Dawla's] territory, and its ruler has no regard for you; his envoy here and Kulaib are tendering us its land-tax and asking for our protection. And as for the fortresses, they were taken in the time of my uncle Nicephorus [Byzantine emperor, r. 963–969] and of other sovereigns, and we are not at liberty to relinquish them, so if you can make any other proposal, do so, otherwise spare yourself the long journey." I replied: "If you have your sovereign's order for my departure I will go, but if you say this from yourself only, then the sovereign ought to hear my own words and I his reply, so as to return with authentic information." And he permitted my going on.

So I proceeded to Constantinople and made my entry after I had been met and most courteously escorted by court officials. I was honorably lodged in the palace of Kanikleios Nicephorus (the envoy who had come [with] me) who stood in favor with the sovereign. Next, I was summoned to the presence of the chamberlain [the eunuch Basil], who said: "We are acquainted with the correspondence which bears on your message, but state your views." Thereupon I produced the actual agreement, which he inspected and then said: "Was not the question of relinquishing the land-tax on Abu Taghlib's territory, both past and future, settled with al-Bākilāni in accordance with your wishes, and did he not assent to our terms as to restoring the fortresses we had taken, and as to the arrest of Bardas? Your master accepted this agreement and complied with our wishes, for you have his ratification of the truce under his own hand." I said that al-Bākilāni had not come to any agreement at all; he replied that he had not left until he had settled the terms of the agreement of which the ratification under the hand of his sovereign was to be forwarded, and that he had previously produced his letter approving the whole of the stipulations. Accordingly, I was driven to find some device in order to meet this argument.

The Excellent Idea That Occurred to Ibn Shahrām for Rebutting His Adversary's Case

I said this: "Ibn al-Bākilāni came to no agreement with you; it was Ibn Kūnis who made this compact and took a copy of it in the Greek language." At this the chamberlain broke out and asked Ibn Kūnis "Who has authorized this?" to which he answered that neither he nor al-Bākilāni had settled anything and I withdrew.

A few days later the chamberlain summoned me and resumed reading the agreement. He paused at a point where it spoke of "what might be settled with Ibn Shahrām on the basis of what was contained in the third copy," and said that this was one copy but where were the other two? On referring to this passage I saw the blunder that had been committed in letting this stand, and said: "The meaning of the passage is that the agreement was to be in triplicate, one part to remain with the Byzantine ruler, one to be in Aleppo, and the third in the capital [Baghdad]." This Ibn Kūnis traversed, saying that his instructions had been to note down the exact sense of the agreement, and the chamberlain said that this copy was the ruling one; that the second copy referred to giving up the fortresses, while the third omitted all mention of Aleppo; that the agreement had been signed on the terms agreed upon with Ibn al-Bākilāni, and the sole object in sending this copy was to procure the sovereign's hand and seal thereto. To which I said: "This cannot be so; my instructions are merely what I have stated as regards Aleppo and the fortresses, in accordance with the agreement which you have seen." He replied: "Were Bardas [Sclerus] here in force and you had made us all prisoners you could not ask for more than you are asking; and Bardas is, in fact, a prisoner."

Ibn Shahrām's Well-Directed Rejoinder

I replied: "Your supposed case of Bardas being here in force is of no weight for you are well aware that when Abu Taghlib, who is not on part with the lowest of 'Adud al-Dawla's followers, assisted Bardas he foiled the Byzantine sovereigns for seven years; how would it be, then, were 'Adud al-Dawla to assist him with his army? Bardas, although a prisoner in our hands, is not exposed as your captives are to mutilation; his presence in the capital is the best thing for us, for we have not made a captive of him. It may be that he will fret at our putting him off, will despair of us, become estranged, and go away, but at present he is acting with us and is reassured by the pomp and security he witnesses at the capital. We hold, in truth, all the strings."

My words impressed and nonplussed him greatly, for he knew them to be true, and he said: "What you ask cannot be granted; we will ratify, if you will, what was agreed on with al-Bākilāni—else depart." I replied: "If you wish me to depart without having had a hearing from the sovereign I will do so." To this he said that he spoke for the sovereign, but that he would ask an audience for me.

And in a few days' time I was summoned and attended. The Byzantine sovereign [Basil] caused what had passed to be repeated to him in my presence, and said: "You have come on a reprehensible errand; your envoy came and procured our consent to certain terms, which included the restoring of fortresses taken during the revolt; you are now asking to have ceded other fortresses which were taken by my predecessors. Either consent to what was originally stipulated or go in peace." I replied: "But al-Bākilāni agreed on nothing, for, as for the document he brought, you deprived us under its terms of half our territory; how can we admit such a thing against ourselves? Of these fortresses in Diyār Bakr none are held by you; now Diyār Bakr belongs to us; all you can do is dispute it, and you do not know what will be the issue of the struggle." Here the chamberlain interposed, saying: "This envoy is skilled in controversy and makes up a fine story; death is better for us than submission to these terms. Let him return to his master." The sovereign then rose and I withdrew.

When I had spent two months in Constantinople I was summoned by the chamberlain. He had with him the marshal, father of the *domesticus*, who had been blinded, and a number of patricians besides, and we discussed the question of the fortresses. They offered to cede the land-tax of Husn Kaifā [held by Abu Taghlib's mother, who received the tax] to which I replied: "And I, in turn, will cede you the land-tax of Samand." And on their asking what I meant I said: "It is only the extreme limits that are specified in the agreement so as to make it clear that all within the limits is comprised in the peace; Husn Kaifā is five days' journey short of Amid; how come you to name it?"

The dispute as to Aleppo went on until the marshal said: "If the ruler of Aleppo pays over the land-tax to us we shall know that your statements were not justified and that he prefers us to you." I answered: "And what assurance have we that you have induced his secretary and brother-in-law Kulaib to make you some payment to be adduced as proof? For, short of fraud, I know the thing to be out of the question." And thereupon I went away.

Next I was summoned by the sovereign. By this time that Aleppo land-tax had arrived, and I found their earlier tone altered in vehemence and decision, for they said: "Here is the Aleppo land-tax come in, and its ruler has asked us to come to an agreement with him as regards the towns of Harrān and Sarūj, and to aid him in attacking you and other powers." And I said: "Your receipt of the land-tax I know to be a trick, for 'Adud al-Dawla did not imagine that you would regard it as lawful to act as you have acted, or he would have sent an army to stop yours. As for your story about Aleppo's ruler, I am better informed as to his views, and all you have been told about him is untrue; the overlordship of Aleppo is held by 'Adud al-Dawla." They asked me whether I had anything to add, and on my replying "No," said that I might take leave of the sovereign and depart with my escort. I said I would forthwith do this, and I turned towards the sovereign to take my leave of him.

Ibn Shahrām's Sound Resolve in This Predicament

I considered the position, perceiving that the chamberlain, the marshal, and the rest of them were averse to the proposed peace, (the military men being apprehensive that their swords would not be required, and that their stipends would be reduced, as was the way at Byzantium when peace was made), and the only way left to me was to gain over and conciliate the sovereign, so I said to him: "Will your majesty consider 'Adud al-Dawla's conduct towards you in not assisting your enemy and in not attacking your territory during the time you were occupied with those in revolt against you; for you know that if you do not satisfy him by himself, he being the monarch of Islam, well and good, but, failing this, you will have to satisfy thousands of your partisans, and their consent is uncertain. And if you fail to procure it you may have to satisfy 'Adud al-Dawla later on. You know, too, that all those around him are averse to the proposed peace; he alone is in its favor and he is able to give effect to his pleasure, for no one ventures to dispute it. You I perceive to be in favor of peace, but it may be that your wish is not furthered by those around you." He was moved by my speech, and his expression showed his concern at my being aware of the opposition of his advisers, and he rose and departed.

Now, the person most intimately placed towards the sovereign and the one who imposed the purple signature on his behalf, and was privy to all his official acts was Nicephorus, the kanikleios, who had accompanied me as envoy, and I asked him to withdraw with me, and he did so.

The Arrangement Come to by Ibn Shahrām with the Sovereign's Confidential Adviser, whereby He Effected His Purpose

When we were alone together I spoke thus: "I wish you to convey a communication from me to the sovereign. My stay here has been protracted, so inform me of his final resolve. If he meets my wishes, well and good; if not, there is no occasion for me to remain any longer." And I made the kanikleios a complimentary present from what I had brought with me, with fair promises on behalf of 'Adud al-Dawla. My communication was this: "Your majesty's first care should be to guard your person, next your sovereignty, and next your partisans. You should not trust one whose interest it is to do you prejudice, for it is Abu Taghlib's aid that has brought about what has taken place in your dominions; what then will happen if 'Adud al-Dawla joins forces against your majesty? The conclusion of peace between yourself and the first of men and ruler of Islam is not, I see, to the taste of your advisers. Now a man fails to realize only that of which he has had no experience, and you have had seven years' experience of revolt against yourself and your rule. Moreover, the continuance of the state does not imply your continued existence, for the Byzantines are indifferent as to who is the emperor over them [there is a corruption in the text here.] This is on the assumption that 'Adud al-Dawla does not move in person. I gave you good advice, knowing as I do my master's leaning and regards towards you; consider therefore my words and act as you may deem best." Nicephorus on his return said: "The answer is that things are as you say, but it is not in my power to resist the general body, who already regard me as their deceiver and undoer. Nevertheless I shall carry the matter through and act so far as I am able."

By a fortunate coincidence the chamberlain now fell seriously ill and was unable to go out. My correspondence with the sovereign went on, and he gave me audience on successive days and conversed with me in person, the kanikleios assisting me owing to his hatred and jealousy of the chamberlain, until the peace was agreed to in accordance with all the stipulations in the agreement, any attempts to have Aleppo excluded not being assented to. On my pressing this point vigorously and saying, "Without Aleppo this cannot go through," he said, "Give up insisting, for we will not cede more than we have ceded, nor will we evacuate territory whose revenue we receive, except under duress. But I will send a letter by you to my friend your sovereign, for I know his noble nature, and that once he knows the truth he will not deviate from it." He then told those near to leave, and said to me secretly from all: "Tell your sovereign that I truly desire his goodwill, but that I must have proof of it. If you wish us to transfer to you the Aleppo land-tax, or that I should leave you to collect it on the terms of Ibn Hamdān being ousted from Aleppo, perform what you promised by the mouth of Ibn Kūnis [the surrender of Bardas Sclerus]. And I said: "I have not

22

heard of this and was not present thereat, but I think the performance unlikely." This he resented, and said: "Give up this delaying, for there remains nothing more for you to argue with me." He then ordered the replies to be drawn up, and I wrote mine and attended to take my leave.

A Fortunate Occurrence for Ibn Shahrām

Afraid lest fate should, as happens in such cases, bring about the death of the man whose surrender they required, and in order that the peace should include all our territory to be beyond the Euphrates and the territory of Bād to the exclusion of Aleppo, I said: "You know that I am a servant under orders and not a sovereign, and that I must not go beyond the instructions which I have faithfully reported to you. And as for the stipulations about Aleppo I have sworn to you that I heard nothing on this topic at Baghdad. But is your majesty prepared to consider a plan which has occurred to me as being the right one for him to adopt?" "What is that?" he asked, and I said: "To draw up a treaty of peace between us to include all our territory from Emesa to Bād's district without any mention of the question of the surrender you ask—so much and no more. This you will swear to on your religion, sign it with your hand, and seal it with your seal in my presence. Your envoy will convey it to the capital with me, where either it will be ratified or your envoy will bring it back." I was asked, "And you will give a similar written undertaking?" "Yes," I said, "on your handing in the terms you require." "But you," he replied "will mention in your document the man's surrender?" I replied: "I cannot mention what is outside my authority." "Then," said he, "I will have two agreements prepared, one of them for what lies beyond the Euphrates and Bād's territory, the other dealing with Emesa and Aleppo as stipulated; then if your sovereign chooses the one which extends beyond the Euphrates on the terms of his removing Bardas he can take it, or if he prefer the other he can give effect to his preference." I suggested the agreement being drawn up without any mention of this question, to which he said: "You then put it into writing, for I will not give anything written without receiving the same." "Then let your interpreter," I said, "make a copy of my words and should 'Adud al-Dawla ratify them they can be copied out in his presence and be signed by him," and this he agreed to. On this footing the terms were put into writing and a peace was made for ten years. When this was finished I said: "Do not put your envoy on the footing of a mere courier, but inform him of what you wish to do in pursuance of this agreement we have come to, and in accordance with what he himself knows, and ratify whatever he may ratify." To this he agreed, and it was so specified in the document.

The chamberlain, on coming out after his recovery, was highly incensed at several matters, one being the intimacy of the kanikleios with his master, another the conclusion of the business in his absence, and a third the question of Aleppo and Emesa and the promises made to him by Kulaib.

Words by Which the Byzantine Sovereign Conciliated the Chamberlain's Feelings

According to the report of some of the courtiers he spoke thus: "There is no one about me, as you know, chamberlain, who has your affection for me or holds your place in my esteem, for you are nearest me in lineage and in affinity; the rest, as the envoy said, are indifferent as to whether it be I or someone else who is emperor. You must safeguard both our lives and not heed what the marshal [Leo Phocas] may say, nor trust to him or to his advice. For you know Ibrāhīm's story about him and his son [Bardas Sclerus], how they harbored treachery to our rule and intended deceit towards us." I asked my informant who Ibrāhīm was, and he said, "An envoy from the *domesticus* to yourselves; he it was who disclosed faithfully to the sovereign that the *domesticus* [Bardas Sclerus] had sent him to you [the Muslims] to ask you to assist him in rebelling."

The chamberlain accepted the sovereign's statement, and on his sending for me I noticed in him a tone and familiarity with me quite other than before, while at the same time his looks gave evidence of his disapproval of the terms agreed on. The kanikleios was named envoy with me after he had declined the office, but the sovereign finding no one else of his capacity put pressure on him, and the chamberlain aided him saying: "You and I are the two most important personages at court, and one of us must go." And so zealous was he in the matter that I attributed it to a desire that he should be at a distance, and to jealousy at the intimate footing he saw he was on with the sovereign.

This, concisely, is the sense of the words used by Ibn Shahrām. At this moment 'Aḍud al-Dawla was in ill-health, and access to him was forbidden, and he ordered a statement of what had happened to be laid before him. This illness was that which proved fatal to 'Aḍud al-Dawla, and after his death the Byzantine envoy had an audience with Samsān al-Dawla ['Aḍud's second son and successor] and was handed presents from him and settled the business he had come on. Two agreements were drawn up, the one being the agreement come to with Ibn Shahrām on the footing of its being a complete and permanent one, the other the earlier agreement made with Nicephorus.

The Agreement Come to as Regards Bardas, His Brother, and His Son

The result of deliberations was that Nicephorous was to remain at Baghdad, and was to send an envoy of his own with coming from the capital [Baghdad] to take the sovereign's signature and seal for Bardas's brother and son, with a safe-conduct and a guarantee assuring them his favor and restoration to their former offices and to a settled position. And that on this being sent they were then to be conducted to the Byzantine sovereign by Nicephorus, while Bardas himself was to remain in Muslim territory, and was to be prevented from approaching Byzantine territory with a view to mischief. And that, when the fair treatment of the other two in accordance with the undertaking had become apparent, then Bardas too should be sent after them in the course of the third year following on the above undertaking, on terms no less satisfactory than in the case of his brother and son. And that the sum paid as tribute for Emesa and Aleppo by Ibn Hamdān to the Byzantine sovereign should, as from the sending of Bardas to Byzantium, be paid into the treasury of Samsān al-Dawla, and that if Ibn Hamdān delayed making the payment, the Byzantine sovereign was to compel him and thus spare Samsān al-Dawla the necessity of sending a force against him. And that an equivalent should be assigned as against Bād's territory for the complimentary presents he used to make to the Byzantine sovereign, on the understanding that the latter was not to assist Bād nor to protect him if he took refuge with the Byzantines. Both agreements were sent off together and both were ratified.

6. THE CONQUEST OF THE IBERIAN PENINSULA

The success of Muslim armies in western and central Asia against the Persians and Byzantines was matched by a host of victories in northern Africa and the western Mediterranean. The conquest of northern Africa brought Muslim armies within striking distance of western Europe, and most notably the Iberian Peninsula. Early in the spring of 711, a Muslim force under the command of Tariq ibn Ziyad crossed the Strait of Gibraltar with a modest army. In July of that year, with his army now reinforced, Tariq met Roderick (Rodrigo), king of the Visigoths who controlled Spain, killing him and routing his army. It was a momentous event, as the Muslim conquest of Spain initiated a long period of conflict and contact between the scattered Christian survivors, who retreated to the mountains in the north and there struggled to survive, and the Islamic-dominated south where a well-governed, highly educated, and cosmopolitan society emerged. The source that best records the events of the conquest is the Christian Chronicle of 754, *written some years after the events described here. The* Chronicle *captures the immediate horrors of the conquest for the Christians as well as the political instability that followed. There are also numerous Muslim sources that depict the conquest, but they all postdate the events by at least a century. Of these, one of the most readable is the* Kitab ar-Rawd al M'itar (The Book of the Fragrant Garden), *a compilation of geographical and historical vignettes assembled by Muhammad bin Abd al-Munim al-Himyari in the late fifteenth century from numerous earlier sources. While lacking the more immediate knowledge of the* Chronicle of 754, *the* Kitab *makes up for it with its readability and the inclusion of many of the stories and legends that are now associated with the Muslim arrival in Iberia.*

Sources: trans. Kenneth B. Wolf, *The Chronicle of 754*, in *Conquerors and Chroniclers of Early Medieval Spain* (Liverpool: Liverpool University Press, 1990), 130–35; and trans. Jarbel Rodriguez from Maria Pilar Maestro González, *Al Himyari, Kitab ar-Rawd al-Mi'tar* (Valencia: Graficas Bautista, 1963), 24–32.

Chronicle of 754

In Justinian's time [Byzantine emperor Justinian II, r. 705–711] in the aforesaid year, the first year of his rule and the eighty-ninth of the Arabs, Walid held the kingship among the Arabs [Umayyad caliph, r. 705–715]. In Spain, Witiza continued to rule for his fifteenth year.

In Justinian's time, in the era 747 [709], in his fourth year as emperor and the ninety-first of the Arabs, Walid received the scepter of the kingdom of the Saracens, as his father had arranged, and fought various peoples for four years. He was victorious and, endowed with great honors, exercised his rule for nine years. He was a man of great prudence in deploying his armies to the extent that, though lacking in divine favor, he crushed the forces of almost all neighboring peoples, made Romania especially weak with constant raiding, nearly brought the islands to their destruction, raided and subdued the territory of India, brought cities to utter destitution, besieged fortresses, and, from the twisted paths of Libya, subjugated all of Mauretania. In the western regions, Walid, through a general of his army by the name of Musa, attacked and conquered the kingdom of the Goths—which had been established with ancient solidity almost 350 years ago from its foundation in the era 400 [362] and which had been extended peacefully throughout Spain from the time of Leovigild for almost 140 years up to the era 750 [712]—and having seized the kingdom, he made it pay tribute.

In Justinian's time, in the era 749 [711], in his fourth year [*sic*] as emperor and the ninety-second of the Arabs, with Walid retaining the scepter of the kingdom for the fifth year, Roderick rebelliously seized the kingdom at the instigation of the senate. He ruled for only one year. Mustering his forces, he directed armies against the Arabs and the Moors sent by Musa, that is against Tariq ibn Ziyad and the others, who had long been raiding the province consigned to them and simultaneously devastating many cities. In the fifth year of Justinian's rule, the ninety-third of the Arabs, and the sixth of Walid, in the era 750 [712], Roderick headed for the Transductine mountains to fight them and in that battle the entire army of the Goths, which had come with him fraudulently and in rivalry out of ambition for the kingship, fled and he was killed. Thus Roderick wretchedly lost not only his rule but his homeland, his rivals also being killed, as Walid was completing his sixth year of rule.

In Justinian's time, in the era 749 [711], in his fourth year as emperor, the ninety-second of the Arabs, and the fifth of Walid, while Spain was being devastated by the aforesaid forces and was greatly afflicted not only by the enemy but also by domestic fury, Musa himself, approaching this wretched land across the straits of Cadiz and pressing on to the pillars of Hercules—which reveal the entrance to the port like an index to a book or like keys in his hand revealing and unlocking the passage to Spain—entered the long plundered and godlessly invaded Spain to destroy it. After forcing his way to Toledo, the royal city, he imposed on the adjacent regions an evil and fraudulent peace. He decapitated on a scaffold those noble lords who had remained, arresting them in their flight from Toledo with the help of Oppa, King Egica's son. With Oppa's support, he killed them all with the sword. Thus he devastated not only Hispania Ulterior, but Hispania Citerior up to and beyond the ancient and once flourishing city of Zaragoza, now, by the judgment of God, openly exposed to the sword, famine, and captivity. He ruined beautiful cities, burning them with fire, condemned lords and powerful men to the cross and butchered youths and infants with the sword. While he terrorized everyone in this way, some of the cities that remained sued for peace under duress and, after persuading and mocking them with a certain craftiness, the Saracens granted their requests without delay. When the citizens subsequently rejected what they had accepted out of fear and terror, they tried to flee to the mountains where they risked hunger and various forms of death. The Saracens set up their savage kingdom in Spain, specifically in Cordoba, formerly a patrician see and always the most opulent in comparison to the rest of the cities, giving its first fruits to the kingdom of the Visigoths.

In the era 750 [712], in Justinian's sixth year [*sic*] as emperor and the ninety-fourth of the Arabs, Musa, after fifteen months had elapsed, was summoned by order of the princes and, leaving his son Abd al-Aziz in his place, he returned to his homeland and presented himself to the king Walid in the last year of his reign. Musa brought with him from Spain some noblemen who had escaped the sword; gold and silver, assayed with zeal by the bankers; a large quantity of valuable ornaments, precious stones, and pearls; ointments to kindle women's desire; and many other things from the length and breadth of Spain that would be tedious to record. When he arrived, by God's will he found Walid angry. Musa was ignominiously removed from the prince's presence and paraded with a rope around his neck.

At the same time, in the era 753 [715], in Justinian's ninth year [*sic*] as emperor and the ninety-seventh of the Arabs, Abd al-Aziz pacified all of Spain for three years under the yoke of tribute. After he had taken all the riches and positions of honor in Seville, as well as the queen of Spain, whom he joined in marriage, and the daughters of kings and princes, whom he treated as concubines and then rashly repudiated, he was eventually killed on the advice of Ayub by a revolt of his own men while he was in prayer. After Ayub had held Spain for a full month, Al-Hurr succeeded to the throne of Hesperia by order of the prince, who was informed about the death of Abd al-Aziz in this way: that on the advice of Queen Egilona, wife of the late king Roderick, whom he had joined to himself, he tried to throw off the Arab yoke from his neck and retain the conquered kingdom of Iberia for himself.

Kitab ar-Rawd al-M'itar

During this time, Toledo was the capital of the kingdom in al-Andalus. In the city, there was a locked house that it was forbidden to open; only those whom the Goths [Visigoths] trusted were allowed to guard it permanently. This was a very honorable position and it was passed from generation to generation. Each time a new king ascended to the throne, he would add a new lock to those that already protected the house. When Roderick took power, he decided to open the door to this house and find out for himself what was kept inside. This terrified the Gothic nobles who pleaded with Roderick to abandon his curiosity.

Roderick refused, convinced that the building housed a treasure. He broke the locks and entered the house. He found it empty save for a locked chest. After ordering that the chest be opened, he likewise found it empty, save for a piece of cloth on which was drawn Arabs on horseback. They wore their turbans, had sword blades hanging from their waists, and bows on their backs, and in their hands they carried lances held upright with flags flying. In the upper section of the piece of cloth was something written in a language that was not Arabic. The inscription was read and it said as follows: "When the locks that bar this house have been broken, when this chest has been opened and these images brought to the light of day, that will be the sign that the people represented in these images will be on the verge of taking over al-Andalus and holding dominion there." Roderick lowered his eyes, overcome with an anxiety that was shared by the other Goths. He gave the order to replace the locks and to keep the guards at their station.

According to the customs of the Christians of al-Andalus, the nobles of the country would send their children to the [royal] court to receive a princely education and to benefit from its favors. When they reached a suitable age, the king would marry them with each other, thereby showing his benevolence with their fathers. He would even pay for the dowry of the grooms and the bride's bedroom linens.

Following this custom, Julian, the Governor of Ceuta [in northern Africa], sent one of his daughters to Roderick's court. She was exceedingly beautiful and her father loved her very much. Roderick put his eyes on her, was attracted to her, and ravished her. She was able to send a message to her father in secret using an agreed upon phrase. When he found out about the insult, Julian full of irritation exclaimed: "By the religion of the messiah, I swear that I will put an end to that man's power!" And it was this anger, caused by the dishonor to his daughter, which brought about, along with the will of Allah, the conquest of al-Andalus by the Muslims. Julian took ship immediately at Ceuta and crossed the Straits of Gibraltar during the time that it was most difficult to cross, that is during the month of January. Continuing on his path, he arrived in Toledo, Roderick's capital. Roderick disapproved of his trip during the winter and asked him his motive. Julian responded that his wife was suffering too much the separation from their daughter, who now resided in his [Roderick's] court and that she wanted to see her again before she died. She had begged that he take their daughter to her and he wanted to give his wife that satisfaction. Thus, he asked the king to allow his daughter to return with him to Ceuta. The king granted Julian's request and he allowed the young woman to depart, but not without extracting her promise to keep their relations a secret. He favored her and her father with gifts and they then returned home.

It is told that when Julian first entered Roderick's house to ask his permission, the king told him, "When you see us again, bring us some pedigreed falcons for our hunts." Julian replied, "My king, I swear to you by the messiah, that I will bring falcons, the likes of which you have never received." He, thus, made an allusion to the plan that he had begun to conceive in his mind, bringing Arab warriors to war with al-Andalus. The king did not understand this allusion. For his part, Julian, upon returning to Ceuta, put aside all his other concerns, and made plans to meet with Musa ibn Nusayr [Muslim governor of northern Africa], whom he found in Ifriqiya [mostly modern-day Tunisia]. He persuaded him to undertake the conquest of al-Andalus. He wrote to him about the beauty of the country, its advantages and superiority and he showed him how the weakness of its inhabitants would facilitate the conquest. Musa, while expressing his best sentiments to the Muslims, made a treaty of friendship with Julian and he urged him to open hostilities against his coreligionists in al-Andalus. Julian agreed and he landed on the coast of Algeciras [on the southern coast of Iberia]. He inflicted numerous casualties and took captives and booty and remained several days in the region, which he ruined with his incursions. The news of his landing spread among the Muslims, who, after that, no longer doubted his loyalty. These events occurred around the end of the year 90 AH [709 CE].

Musa ibn Nusayr wrote to al-Walid to inform him of the proposition Julian had made and to ask for authorization to begin the conquest of al-Andalus. Al-Walid responded: "Send cavalry detachments to explore that country so that you are well informed of the current situation, but be wary of exposing the Muslims to the dangers of violent storms at sea!" To this, Musa responded: "This is not really a sea, but a strait, where one can see one coast from the other." "Even so," answered al-Walid, "it does not make it any less important that you scout the country with the cavalry units." Musa then sent one of his freed Berbers, Tarif ibn Malik, who bore the honorific Abu Z'ura, at the head of a 400-man detachment. He crossed the Straits and landed on the isle that since then bears his name [Tarifa]. Then he made an incursion into Algeciras and its surroundings and took captive people of such beauty that neither Musa nor his companions had ever seen their equal. Likewise, he took a considerable booty of coins and precious objects. This occurred in the month of Ramadān of the year 91 AH [July 710 CE].

With these results, the Muslims hastened their efforts to penetrate al-Andalus. Musa then called upon one of his freedmen who commanded his vanguard and was called Tariq ibn Ziyad. It is said that he was a Persian or one of the Berbers of Nafsa. Musa gave him command of the upcoming expedition and ordered him to depart leading 7,000 Berbers and freedmen. The contingent only had a small number of Arabs. [Count] Julian equipped the necessary ships for the crossing and Tariq disembarked at the foot of Gabal Tariq [Tariq's Rock or Gibraltar] on a Saturday in the month of Sha'bān of the year 92 [May–June 711] at the head of an army of 12,000 men that had only a small number of Arabs.

By chance, Tariq came across an old woman from Algeciras. "I had a husband," she told him, "who was gifted in the art of divination; he foretold the coming of a chieftain to this country. According to the vision that he saw, this chieftain would have a big head like yours and a patch of hair on his left shoulder. If you have this patch of hair, are you then the chieftain in question?" After hearing her words, Tariq opened his clothing and, in fact, did have the hairy patch on his shoulder, just as the old woman had described it. Tariq and his men believed this coincidence to be a good omen.

Another story is also told about Tariq that while he slept on board the ship that transported him [to Spain], he saw in a dream the Prophet and the four caliphs [who ruled immediately after Muhammad] advancing on the water and reaching the shore with him. The Prophet then announced the upcoming victory and ordered him to treat the Muslims with kindness and to remain loyal to the pact. According to another story, when Tariq boarded his ship, he fell into a deep sleep and saw the Prophet surrounded by the Muhajirun [Muhammad's closest followers] and the Ansar [citizens of Medina]. They all carried their swords at their belts and their bows on their backs. The Prophet told him: "Oh Tariq, go and carry out your mission." And Tariq saw him go into al-Andalus surrounded by his companions. Tariq then told his soldiers and no longer doubted his victory.

He landed thus in Gibraltar and launched several raids on the surrounding plains. Roderick, who was at that time on an expedition, was not on hand [to meet him]. When the news of the Muslim landings reached him, he judged that the situation was critical and understood the motives that had caused Julian to make an alliance with the Muslims. He returned with all haste at the head of his army and for several days he remained in Cordoba, where more troops joined him. During his advance, he gave command of his right wing to Sisebut, the son of king Witiza and the left wing to his brother [Oppa]. These were the two princes from whom Roderick had stripped the royal throne.

The two brothers sent a message to Tariq asking for his protection and letting him know that if he granted it they would turn coat along with their retainers in the midst of the battle. In exchange, they asked that Witiza's personal lands be turned over to them if the Muslims were victorious. Tariq accepted their offer and made a pact with them on these terms. When the two armies clashed, the two princes sided with Tariq and it was this that brought victory to the Muslims. King Roderick commanded an army of 600,000 horsemen [more likely, around 40,000].

7. THE BATTLE OF TOURS

After consolidating their gains in Spain, Muslim armies began to venture north of the Pyrenees as they made incursions into modern-day France. By 720/721, they were frequently raiding in Aquitaine, and in 732 (or 733) they defeated Eudo, the local duke, in battle. With his duchy on the verge of collapse, Eudo was forced to call on Charles Martel, a chieftain of the Franks (r. 718–741) who controlled much of central and northern France. Eudo had a deep mistrust of Charles and his opportunistic ways, but he had little choice. In October of 732 (or 733) Charles was able to defeat a Muslim army near Tours. In time, the Battle of Tours would acquire almost mythic qualities as Romantic-era European writers credited Charles with saving Christendom from Islam. The reality, however, is less sensational. While Charles and the Franks certainly enjoyed a significant victory, there is little evidence to suggest that the Muslim army he defeated was any more than a raiding force and not one bent on conquest. The battle did coincide with a decline in Muslim raiding activity in southern France and gave Charles the influ-ence and political capital to begin taking full control of the Frankish kingdom, a process that would reach its culmination under his grandson Charlemagne (r. 768–814). The three brief sources below offer different points of view on the battle and the participants. Note, in particular, the penchant of medieval chroniclers to inflate the number of enemy soldiers and casualties, as the Muslim army had nowhere near the 300,000 fatalities that the Chronicle of Saint Denis claims Charles inflicted upon them.

Source: trans. William Stern Davis, *Readings in Ancient History from the Sources—II. Rome and the West* (Boston: Allyn and Bacon, 1913), 362–64.

From an Arab Chronicler

The following opinion was expressed about the Franks by the emir who con-quered Spain, and who—had he not been recalled—might have commanded at Tours. It shows what the Arab leaders thought of the men of the North up to the moment of their great disillusionment by "The Hammer" [Charles Martel].

[Musa being returned to Damascus, the Kalif Abd-el-Melek asked of him about his conquests,] saying: "Now tell me about these Franks,—what is their nature?" "They," replied Musa, "are a folk right numerous, and full of might: brave and impetuous in the attack, but cowardly and craven in event of defeat."

"And how has passed the war between them and thyself? Favorably or the reverse?"

"The reverse? No, by Allah and the prophet!" spoke Musa. "Never has a company from my army been beaten. And never have the Muslims hesi-tated to follow me when I have led them; though they were two score to fourscore."

Isidore of Beja's *Chronicle*

Then Abdrahman [the Muslim emir], seeing the land filled with the multitude of his army, crossed the Pyrenees, and traversed the defiles [in the mountains] and the plains, so that he penetrated ravaging and slaying clear into the lands of the Franks. He gave battle to Duke Eudo [of Aquitaine] beyond the Garonne and the Dordogne, and put him to flight—so utterly [was he beaten] that God alone knew the number of the slain and wounded. Whereupon Abdrahman set out in pursuit of Eudo; he destroyed palaces, burned churches, and imagined he could pillage the basilica of Saint Martin of Tours. It is then that he found himself face to face with the lord of Austrasia, Charles, a mighty warrior from his youth, and trained in all the occasions of arms.

For almost seven days the two armies watched one another, waiting anx-iously the moment for joining the struggle. Finally they made ready for combat. And in the shock of the battle the men of the North seemed like unto a sea that cannot be moved. Firmly they stood, one close to another, forming as it were a bulwark of ice; and with great blows of their swords they hewed down the Arabs. Drawn up in a band around their chief, the people of the Austrasians carried all before them. Their tireless hands drove their swords down to the breasts [of the foe].

At last night sundered the combatants. The Franks with misgivings, low-ered their blades, and beholding the numberless tents of the Arabs, prepared themselves for another battle the next day. Very early, when they issued from their retreat, the men of Europe saw the Arab tents ranged still in order, in the same place where they had set up their camp. Unaware that they were utterly empty, and fearful that the phalanxes of the Saracens were drawn up for combat, they sent out spies to ascertain the facts. These spies discovered that all the squadrons of the "Ishmaelites" had vanished. In fact, during the night they had fled with the greatest silence, seeking with all speed their home land. The Europeans, uncertain and fearful, lest they were merely hidden in order to come back [to fall upon them] by ambushes, sent scouting parties everywhere, but to their great amazement found nothing. Then without troubling to pursue the fugitives, they contented themselves with sharing the spoils and returned right gladly to their own country.

Chronicle of Saint Denis

[The Muslims planned to go to Tours] to destroy the church of Saint Martin, the city, and the whole country. Then came against them the glorious prince Charles at the head of his whole force. He drew up his host, and he fought as fiercely as the hungry wolf falls upon the stag. By the grace of Our Lord, he wrought a great slaughter upon the enemies of Christian faith, so that—as history bears witness—he slew in that battle 300,000 men, likewise their "king" by name Abdrahman. Then was he [Charles] first called "Martel," for as a hammer of iron, of steel, and of every other metal, even so he dashed and smote in the battle all his enemies. And what was the greatest marvel of all, he only lost in that battle 1500 men. The tents and harness [of the enemy] were taken, and whatever else they possessed became a prey to him and his followers.

Eudo, duke of Aquitaine, being now reconciled with Prince Charles Martel, later slew as many of the Saracens as he could find who had escaped from the battle.

8. CHRISTIANS AND MUSLIMS IN THE AGE OF CHARLEMAGNE

A few years after the Battle of Tours, the Muslim world was rocked by a dynastic struggle in which the ruling Umayyad family was overthrown by the Abbasids. By 750, the conflict was mostly over, with the Abbasids assuming control of the Islamic caliphate and most of the Umayyads dead. One of the very few Umayyads to survive this insurrection was Abd al-Rahman I, a young royal prince who made his way to Spain and in 755 founded an Umayyad polity there, separate from the traditional caliphate now ruled by the Abbasids from Baghdad. Thus there were now two distinct Muslim political entities, each of which had its own set of relations with the Christian world. This becomes evident when we look at the relations maintained by Charlemagne, the Carolingian emperor and ruler of much of western Europe, and his sons, with the Abbasids in Baghdad on the one hand and with the Umayyads in Spain on the other. The first source below is a well-known passage from The Life of Charlemagne *written by a monk of St-Gall in 883–884 and detailing the diplomatic relationships between Charlemagne and the Abbasid caliph Harun al-Rashid (r. 786–809). Unfortunately, there are no Muslim sources that speak about this embassy. The second source is a series of entries from the* Royal Frankish Annals, *detailing events between the years 778 and 827. These entries, although simple and unadorned, do provide a sense of the complexity of the relationship that the Carolingians and their Spanish allies in northern Spain had with the Spanish Muslims. One noteworthy event that they mention is Charlemagne's incursion into Spain in 778 and the subsequent destruction of the rear guard by the Basques. This event would form the basis of the twelfth-century poem* The Song of Roland, *but in the poem, written during the crusades, the Basques are replaced by Muslims.*

Sources: trans. A.J. Grant, "The Life of Charlemagne by the Monk of St. Gall" in *Early Lives of Charlemagne by Einhard and the Monk of St. Gall* (London: Chatto and Windus, 1926), 116–25; trans. Bernhard Walter Scholz with Barbara Rogers, "Royal Frankish Annals" in *Carolingian Chronicles* (Ann Arbor: University of Michigan Press, 1970), 56, 77–78, 86–87, 91, 96, 101–2, 120–22.

The Life of Charlemagne by the Monk of St-Gall

About the same time also envoys of the Persians [Muslims] were sent to him. They knew not where Frankland lay; but because of the fame of Rome, over which they knew that Charles had rule, they thought it a great thing when they were able to reach the coast of Italy. They explained the reason of their journey to the bishops of Campania and Tuscany, of Emilia and Liguria, of Burgundy and Gaul and to the abbots and counts of those regions; but by all they were either deceitfully handled or else actually driven off; so that a whole year had gone round before, weary and footsore with their long journey, they reached Aix at last and saw Charles, the most renowned of kings by reason of his virtues. They arrived in the last week of Lent, and, on their arrival being made known to the emperor, he postponed their presentation until Easter Eve. Then when that incomparable monarch was dressed with incomparable magnificence for the chief of festivals, he ordered the introduction of the envoys of that race that had once held the whole world in awe. But they were so terrified at the sight of the most magnificent Charles that one might think they had never seen a king or emperor before. He received them however most kindly, and granted them this privilege—that they might go wherever they had a mind to, even as one of his own children, and examine everything and ask what questions and make what inquiries they chose. They jumped with joy at this favor, and valued the privilege of clinging close to Charles, of gazing upon him, of admiring him, more than all the wealth of the east.

They went up into the ambulatory that runs round the nave of the cathedral and looked down upon the clergy and the nobles; then they returned to the emperor, and, by reason of the greatness of their joy, they could not refrain from laughing aloud; and they clapped their hands and said: "We have seen only men of clay before: here are men of gold." Then they went to the nobles, one by one, and gazed with wonder upon arms and clothes that were strange to them; and then came back to the emperor, whom they regarded with wonder still greater. They passed that night and the next Sunday continuously in church and, upon the most holy day itself, they were invited by the most munificent Charles to a splendid banquet, along with the nobles of Frankland and Europe. There they were so struck with amazement at the strangeness of everything that they had hardly eaten anything at the end of the banquet.... Then Charles, who would never endure idleness and sloth, went out to the woods to hunt the bison and the aurochs [large wild cattle now extinct] and made preparations to take the Persian envoys with him. But when they saw the immense animals they were stricken with a mighty fear and turned and fled. But the undaunted hero Charles, riding on a high-mettled charger, drew near to one of these animals and drawing his sword tried to cut through its neck. But he missed his aim, and the monstrous beast ripped the boot and leg-thongs of the emperor; and, slightly wounding his calf with the tip of its horn, made him limp slightly: after that, furious at the failure of its stroke, it fled to the shelter of a valley, which was thickly covered with stones and trees. Nearly all his servants wanted to take off their own hose to give to Charles, but he forbade it saying: "I mean to go in this fashion to Hildegard." Then Isambard, the son of Warin (the same Warin that persecuted your patron Saint Othmar), ran after the beast and not daring to approach him more closely, threw his lance and pierced him to the heart between the shoulder and the wind-pipe, and brought the beast yet warm to the emperor. He seemed to pay no attention to the incident; but gave the carcass to his companions and went home. But then he called the queen and showed her how his leg-coverings were torn, and said: "What does the man deserve who freed me from the enemy that did this to me?" She answered: "He deserves the highest boon." Then the emperor told the whole story and produced the enormous horns of the beast in witness of his truth so that the empress sighed and wept and beat her breast. But when she heard that it was Isambard, who had saved him from this terrible enemy, Isambard, who was in ill favor with the emperor and who had been deprived of all his offices—she threw herself at his feet and induced him to restore all that had been taken from him and a largess was given to him besides.

These same Persian envoys brought the emperor an elephant, monkeys, balsam, nard, unguents of various kinds, spices, scents, and many kinds of drugs:

in such profusion that it seemed as if the east had been left bare that the west might be filled. They came by-and-by to stand on very familiar terms with the emperor; and one day, when they were in a specially merry mood and a little heated with strong beer, they spoke in jest as follows: "Sir emperor, your power is indeed great; but much less than the report of it which is spread through all the kingdoms of the east." When he heard this he concealed his deep displeasure and asked jestingly of them: "Why do you say that, my children? How did that idea get into your heads?" Then they went back to the beginning and told him everything that had happened to them in the lands beyond the sea; and they said: "We Persians and the Medes, Armenians, Indians, Parthians, Elamites, and all the inhabitants of the east fear you much more than our own ruler Harun. And the Macedonians and all the Greeks [the Byzantines with whom Charlemagne was often at odds] they are beginning to fear your overwhelming greatness more than the waves of the Ionian Sea. And the inhabitants of all the islands through which we passed were as ready to obey you, and as much devoted to your service, as if they had been reared in your palace and loaded with your favors. But the nobles of your own kingdom, it seems to us, care very little about you except in your presence, for when we came as strangers to them, and begged them to show us some kindness for the love of you, to whom we desired to make our way, they gave no heed to us and sent us away empty-handed." Then the emperor deposed all counts and abbots, through whose territories those envoys had come, from all the offices that they held, and fined the bishops a huge sum of money. Then he ordered the envoys to be taken back to their own country with all care and honor.

There came to him also envoys from the king of the Africans, bringing a Marmorian lion and a Numidian bear, with Spanish iron and Tyrian purple, and other noteworthy products of those regions. The most munificent Charles knew that the king and all the inhabitants of Africa were oppressed by constant poverty; and so, not only on this occasion but all through his life, he made them presents of the wealth of Europe, corn and wine and oil, and gave them liberal support; and thus he kept them constantly loyal and obedient to himself, and received from them a considerable tribute.

Soon after the unwearied emperor sent to the emperor of the Persians horses and mules from Spain; Frisian robes, white, grey, red and blue, which in Persia, he was told, were rarely seen and highly prized. Dogs too he sent him of remarkable swiftness and fierceness, such as the king of Persia had desired, for the hunting and catching of lions and tigers. The king of Persia cast a careless eye over the other presents, but asked the envoys what wild beasts or animals these dogs were accustomed to fight with. He was told that they would pull down quickly anything they were set on to. "Well," he said, "experience will test that." Next day the shepherds were heard crying loudly as they fled from a lion. When the noise came to the palace of the king, he said to the envoys: "Now, my friends of Frankland, mount your horses and follow me." Then they eagerly followed after the king as though they had never known toil or weariness. When they came in sight of the lion, though he was yet at a distance, the satrap of the satraps said to them: "Now set your dogs on to the lion." They obeyed and eagerly galloped forward; the German dogs caught the Persian lion, and the envoys slew him with swords of northern metal, which had already been tempered in the blood of the Saxons.

At this sight Harun, the bravest inheritor of that name, understood the superior might of Charles from very small indications, and thus broke out in his praise: "Now I know that what I heard of my brother Charles is true. How that by the frequent practice of hunting, and by the unwearied training of his body and mind, he has acquired the habit of subduing all that is beneath the heavens. How can I make worthy recompense for the honors which he has bestowed upon me? If I give him the land which was promised to Abraham and shown to Joshua, it is so far away that he could not defend it from the barbarians: or if, like the high-souled king that he is, he tried to defend it I fear that the provinces which lie upon the frontiers of the Frankish kingdom would revolt from his empire. But in this way I will try to show my gratitude for his generosity. I will give that land into his power; and I will rule over it as his representative. Whenever he likes or whenever there is a good opportunity he shall send me envoys; and he will find me a faithful manager of the revenue of that province."

Thus was brought to pass what the poet spoke of as an impossibility: "The Parthian's eyes the Arar's stream shall greet and Tigris' waves shall wash the German's feet," for through the energy of the most vigorous Charles it was found not merely possible but quite easy for his envoys to go and return and the messengers of Harun, whether young or old, passed easily from Parthia into Germany and returned from Germany to Parthia. (And the poet's words are true, whatever interpretation the grammarians put on "the river Arar," whether they think it an affluent of the Rhone or the Rhine; for they have fallen into confusion on this point through their ignorance of the locality). I could call on Germany to bear witness to my words; for in the time of your glorious father Louis [the Pious, r. 814–840] the land was compelled to pay a penny for every acre of land held under the law towards the redemption of Christian captives in the Holy Land; and they made their wretched appeal in the name of the dominion anciently held over that land by your great-grandfather Charles and your grandfather Louis.

The Royal Frankish Annals

778: The Lord King Charles marched to Spain by two different routes. One was by Pamplona, which the great king himself took as far as Zaragoza. To Zaragoza came his men from Burgundy, Austrasia, Bavaria, as well as Provence and Septimania, and a part of the Lombards. Arriving from two sides the armies united at Zaragoza. The king received hostages from ibn al-Arabi and Abu Taher and many Saracens, destroyed Pamplona, and subjugated the Spanish Basques and the people of Navarre. Then he returned to Francia. On the heights of the Pyrenees the Basques prepared an ambush, attacked the rearguard, and threw the whole army into confusion. Although the Franks were obviously their betters in arms and valor, they nevertheless suffered a defeat due to the unfavorable terrain and the unequal method of fighting. In this engagement a great many officers of the palace, whom the king had given positions of command, were killed; the baggage was plundered, and the enemy was able to vanish in all directions because he knew the lay of the land. To have suffered this wound shadowed the king's view of his success in Spain.

798: In this year the star called Mars could not be seen anywhere in the entire sky from July of the preceding year to July of this year. The Balearic Islands were plundered by Moors and Saracens. During the winter King Alfonso of Galicia and Asturias, after plundering Lisbon, the remotest city of Spain, as tokens of his victory, sent coats of mail, mules, and captive Moors to the lord king by his envoys Froia and Basiliscus. In this palace the lord king celebrated Christmas and Easter.

799: In the same year the tribe of the Avars broke the faith which it had promised, and Eric, duke of Friuli, after many successes, fell a victim to an ambush of its inhabitants near the city of Tarsatika in Liburnia. Count Gerold, commander of Bavaria, perished in a battle against the Avars. The Balearic Islands, which had been plundered the year before by Moors and Saracens and had sought and received aid from us, submitted to us and with God's help and ours were defended against the raids of the pirates. Military insignia of the Moors were carried away in battle and presented to the lord king.

806: In the same year a fleet was dispatched by Pepin from Italy to Corsica against the Moors who had pillaged the island. Without awaiting its arrival the Moors made away. But one of our men, Hadumar, count of the city of Genoa, was killed when he carelessly got into a fight with them. In Spain, the people of Navarre and Pamplona, who had defected to the Saracens during the last years, were again placed under our authority.

807: In the same year he sent his marshal Burchard with a fleet to Corsica to defend the island against the Moors, who in past years used to come there and pillage. The Moors embarked, as usual, from Spain and went ashore first in Sardinia, where they waged a battle with the Sardinians and lost many men—three thousand are said to have died there. Then they came by a direct route to Corsica. Here they again engaged in battle with the fleet under Burchard's command, in a harbor of this island. They were defeated and put to flight with thirteen ships lost and most of their men killed. The Moors in this year were plagued by so much misfortune everywhere that they themselves admitted that this had happened because the year before they had unjustly carried away sixty monks from Pantelleria and sold them in Spain. But some of these monks returned home again through the largesse of the emperor.

809: Count Aureolus died. He had been stationed on the border of Spain and Gaul, on the other side of the Pyrenees over against Huesca and Zaragoza. Amorez, the governor of Zaragoza and Huesca, assumed the count's position, placed garrisons in his castles, and sent an embassy to the emperor, promising that he was willing to submit to him with everything he had.

813: Count Irmingar of Ampurias prepared an ambush near Majorca against the Moors who were returning with much booty from Corsica to Spain. Irmingar captured eight Moorish ships, on which he found more than five hundred Corsican prisoners. The Moors wanted revenge and ravaged Civitavecchia in Tuscany and Nice in the province of Narbonne. They also attacked Sardinia, but were repelled and defeated in battle by the Sardinians and turned back after losing many of their men.

817: Envoys of Abd al-Rahman, son of Abul Aas, king of the Saracens, were dispatched from Zaragoza and came to ask for peace. They were received by the emperor [Louis the Pious] at Compiègne and then told to travel ahead of him to Aachen. When the emperor arrived in Aachen, he received an envoy of Emperor Leo by the name of Nicephorus who had been sent from Constantinople because of the Dalmatian question. Since Cadolah, who was in charge of that frontier, was not present but was believed to be arriving shortly, Nicephorus was ordered to wait for him. After Cadolah's arrival, negotiations took place between him and the emperor's envoy about the complaints which Nicephorus submitted. Since this matter concerned a great number of Romans as well as Slavs and apparently could not be settled if all parties were not present, a decision was postponed until then. For this purpose Albgar, nephew of Unroch, was sent to Dalmatia with Cadolah and the imperial envoy. The envoys of Abd al-Rahman were also sent back. They had been kept waiting for three months and were beginning to think they would never get home.

826: A general assembly was planned for the middle of October and all other business settled as usual. The emperor then traveled with his retinue across the Rhine to the royal villa of Salz. There envoys of the people of Naples came to him, and when they had received an answer they returned home again. At Salz Aizo's flight and treachery were brought to his attention: how he artfully entered Vich [in northern Spain], was received by the people of Roda, whom he cunningly deceived and whose city he destroyed, fortified the stronger castles of this country, sent his brother to Abd al-Rahman, king of the Saracens, and requested and accepted this king's aid against us. Although the news of this matter infuriated the emperor, he believed that nothing should be done on the spur of the moment and decided to wait for the arrival of his counselors. When the fall hunting was over, about October 1, he traveled down the Main to Frankfurt.

827: The emperor sent the priest and abbot Helisachar and with him Counts Hildebrand and Donatus to stamp out the revolt in the Spanish March. Before their arrival Aizo, trusting in the assistance of the Saracens, had inflicted much damage on the guards of this border. By constant invasions he had worn them out so thoroughly that some of them deserted the castles, which they were to defend and retreated. Willemund, son of Bera, defected to him as did some others equally anxious for change, which is just what might be expected of this fickle people. They joined the Saracens and Moors and molested Cerdana and Valles with daily robbing and burning. Abbot Helisachar, dispatched with others by the emperor to calm down the Goths and Spaniards living in this territory, made many prudent arrangements due to his personal concern over the problem and to the counsel of his companions. Bernard, count of Barcelona, stubbornly resisted the ambushes of Aizo and the cunning and treacherous machinations of those who had defected to him and frustrated their daring attempts. An army sent to Aizo's aid by Abd ar-Rahman, king of the Saracens, was reported to have arrived at Zaragoza. Abumarvan, a relative of the king, had been made its commander, and he promised, on the insurance of Aizo, that victory was not in doubt. Against Abumarvan the emperor sent his son Pepin, king of Aquitaine, with innumerable Frankish troops and ordered him to defend the borders of his kingdom. This would have been done if the army had not arrived in the march too late, due to the negligence of the leaders he had put in command. This delay was so disastrous that Abumarvan laid waste the fields and burned the villages around Barcelona and Gerona, pillaged everything found outside the cities, and retreated to Zaragoza with his army intact before our men ever caught sight of him. People were sure they saw battle lines and shifting lights in the sky at night and that these marvels foreboded the Frankish defeat.

9. CONVERTING CHURCHES INTO MOSQUES IN SPAIN

The Muslim society that emerged in Spain, also known as the caliphate of Cordoba, achieved a high level of religious tolerance and integration of the Jewish and Christian communities that had existed in the peninsula before the arrival of Islam. This was encouraged partly by the Quran's command to allow dhimmis to worship in peace as long as they respected the Islamic faith and the Prophet Muhammad, and also by practical considerations, as the Christian community in Iberia in the eighth century was substantially larger than the Muslim one, and all matters of faith had to be handled with some delicacy. This did not mean that there were no conflicts, however. A story that may be colored by artistic license describes one of these conflicts, peacefully resolved. At some point after the conquest of the city of Cordoba, the new Muslim rulers asked the local Christian community (commonly called the Mozarabs, as over time they incorporated many Muslim and Arab traditions into their daily lives while maintaining their Christian faith) to turn over half of the church of Saint Vincent to serve as a mosque. During the reign of Abd al-Rahman I (r. 754–788), this process was finished as the Christians gave up their half of the church in exchange for permission to build a church outside the city walls and a cash payment. Abd al-Rahman then proceeded to demolish the entire structure that had once been Saint Vincent and build the grand mosque of Cordoba on its grounds. The source below, by the Muslim historian al-Razi, describes the events that transpired, culminating in the building of the Cordoban mosque that still stands there today.

Source: trans. Jarbel Rodriguez from Francisco Javier Simonet, *Historia de los Mozarabes de España* (Madrid: Establecimiento tipográfico de la viuda é hijos de M. Tello, 1897, 1903, repr. 2005), 806–7.

When the Muslims conquered al-Andalus, they imitated what Abū 'Ubaidah ibn al-Jarrāh and Khālid ibn al-Walīd [Muhammad's companions] had done in Syria, taking from the Rum [Christians] half their churches as they did in Damascus and other conquered cities. Thus, the Muslims took from the Mozarabs of Cordoba half of the main church, which was inside the city under the wall, and was known as Saint Vincent. In this half, they built a mosque for congregation. The other part [of the church] remained under the control of the Christians, while all remaining churches in Cordoba were destroyed. The Muslims were satisfied with their half until their numbers started to multiply and the population of Cordoba began to grow. When the emirs and their armies began to settle in Cordoba, with the mosque being so narrow, they placed hanging galleries from the roofs, right over where people sat. But it became exhausting to enter the great mosque with the roofs being so close, the doors so narrow, and the dome so low, to the point that the majority of the congregants could not easily rise due to the proximity between the ceiling and the floor. The mosque, however, continued this way until the arrival of the emir Abd al-Rahman [I] and his takeover of [al-Andalus]. As he began to live and hold court in Cordoba, the population grew. Abd al-Rahman began to look after the affairs of the mosque and began efforts to widen it. He called the leaders of the Christians and demanded that they sell [to him] the half of the church that they still held next to the mosque, promising to indemnify them according to the guidelines stipulated in their surrender treaty. The Christians, at first, refused to sell the half that they held, but after much effort they agreed to cede it to the Muslims in exchange for permission to rebuild the churches that had been destroyed outside the city. This is how the affair finished in the year 168 AH [784 CE], with Abd al-Rahman then proceeding to construct the congregation mosque. A certain writer says that Abd al-Rahman spent 80,000 dinars on the construction of the mosque in addition to the 100,000 dinars he spent buying the [half of the] church [from the Christians], and God knows this better than anyone.

10. SUPPORT FOR THE *DHIMMIS*

The second-class status of the Christians in Spain at times led to their reaching out to foreign Christian powers to ask for help. One such case occurred in 830 when they were in contact with Louis the Pious, the Carolingian emperor. Louis's response included an offer of alliance as well as possible integration into his kingdom.

Source: Paul Edward Dutton, *Charlemagne's Courtier: The Complete Einhard* (Toronto: University of Toronto Press, 1998), 148–49.

In the name of the Lord God and our Savior, Jesus Christ, N. [that is, Louis the Pious], emperor and augustus by the design of divine providence, [sends his] greetings in the Lord to all the leading men and to the entire population of Merida.

We have heard of your troubles and of the various difficulties you are enduring because of the savagery of King Abd al-Rahman [II, r. 822–852], who has oppressed you constantly and violently with his greedy desire for your possessions, which he has attempted to steal from you. We know that his father Abul Aas [al-Hakam, emir of Cordoba until 822] did the same, forcing you through the imposition of unfair charges to pay taxes to him though you were not indebted to him. In this way [Abul Aas] made enemies out of his friends and rebellious and disobedient [subjects] out of obedient ones, for he was attempting to take away your freedom and to oppress and humble you with unfair taxes and tribute. But we have heard that you always courageously fought back as courageous men against the damage done to you by evil kings and that you have bravely resisted their cruelty and greed. We have [also] learned from the accounts of many people that you are doing this [even] now.

Therefore, it pleased us to send this letter to you to console you and urge you to persevere in that very defense of your freedom, which you have [already] begun, against an extremely cruel king, and to refuse to submit to his fury and raging madness, as you have so far done. And since that very king is our absolute enemy and opponent as much as he is yours, we should resist his raging madness with shared resolve.

For we want, with the almighty God's help, to send our army next summer to our [Spanish] march [frontier], where it might see up camp and remain ready and waiting for you to send word that it should advance [into Spain]. If it seems appropriate to you, we shall, in order to assist you, [first] send this army against our common enemies living in our march, so that if Abd al-Rahman or his army wants to proceed against you, they will be stopped by our army and no one [from the march] will be able to proceed against you in order to help [Abd al-Rahman] and his army.

For we reassure you that if you wish to abandon him and to come over to us, we shall grant you your ancient rights to the fullest extent without any reduction and we shall permit you to be free of tax or tribute and shall command you to follow no other law than the one under which you wish to live. Nor do we desire to treat and regard you except honorably as friends and allies in the defense of our kingdom.

We hope that you always prosper in the Lord.

11. THE MARTYRS OF CORDOBA

The negotiations that Abd al-Rahman I undertook with the Christians in order to gain full control of the church of Saint Vincent speaks to the bargaining power of the Mozarab community in Cordoba and the Muslim willingness to observe the rights and religious practices to which they were entitled to as dhimmis. *Many local Christians were also integral members of the Muslim government structure, serving as tax collectors and translators, and even trusted as bodyguards to the emirs. Moreover, although al-Razi notes above (see Doc. 9) that all of the churches in Cordoba except Saint Vincent were demolished by the Muslim conquerors, it seems certain that the emirs who ruled after the conquest allowed many of them to be rebuilt. Yet as* dhimmis *the Christians were still second-class citizens with limited rights and certain obligations, such as paying the* jizya, *that were not imposed on Muslims. The majority of Mozarabs seem to have accepted this as the cost of living as a religious minority and partaking of the rich, vibrant, and intellectually advanced Muslim civilization that by the ninth and tenth centuries dominated most of the Mediterranean both militarily and culturally. However, while the Christians were relatively tranquil over the first half of the ninth century, there had been some outbursts of insurrection among the local Muslims in Cordoba and other parts of Spain, putting the authorities on edge and creating a climate of political uncertainty for the caliph, Abd al-Rahman II (r. 822–852). Consequently, in 851, when a small group of Christian monks began to denounce Islam and blaspheme the Prophet Muhammad, the authorities were quick to react. The monks were arrested and then decapitated for violating the prohibitions against insulting Islam or its prophet. Over the course of the next eight years, a total of 48 Christians, mostly monks and clerics but also some lay people, were executed in Cordoba for blasphemy as they actively engaged in a campaign of antagonism seeking martyrdom; this left the authorities with little alternative but capital punishment. This period of heightened martyrdom, which likely continued at a lesser pace into the tenth century, was recorded by two sources. The first of these was the* Martyrology of Eulogius, *who was himself among the last to die in 859. The second source, included here,* The Life of Eulogius (Vita Eulogii) *was the work of Paulus Alvarus, a layman. Alvarus's source, while having the merit of being contemporary, was also written as an apologetic work that tried to explain the reasons for the martyrs' acts.*

Source: trans. Carleton M. Sage, *Paul Albar of Cordoba: Studies on His Life and Writings* (Washington, DC: The Catholic University of America Press, 1943), 201–10.

12. At the time when the savage rule of the Arabs miserably laid waste all the land of Spain with deceit and imposture, when Muhammad with unbelievable rage and unbridled fury determined to root out the race of Christians, many terrified by fear of the cruel king and hoping to allay his madness, by a cruel use of evil will endeavored to assail Christ's flock with various and ingenious temptations. Many by denying Christ threw themselves into the abyss; others were shaken by severe trials. But others were established and confirmed in flourishing virtue. In his times, as we have said, the martyrdom [or, testimony] of the faithful shone gloriously, and the error of the gainsayers was as shifting as waves [cf. James 1:6]. For some who were holding the Christian faith only in secret by God's grace brought out into the open what they had concealed, and without being searched out they sprang forward to martyrdom and snatched their crown from the executioners. Among these was blessed Christopher, of an Arab family, the story of whose passion we plan to write in another place. Among them also were blessed Aurelius and holy Felix, who having practiced Christianity in secret, came forward with their wives to the glory of martyrdom. Another of them was the blessed virgin Flora, who indeed flowered with virtues, and despising the transitory pomp of the world won an eternal crown. Our holy doctor Eulogius described the combat of each of these and wrote their lives and acts in a brilliant style.

    13. At this time there was a certain girl named Leocritia, of noble family, but nobler in soul, begotten of the filth of the Muslims and born from the womb

of wolves, baptized some time earlier by a Christian nun, Litiosa, who was of her kindred. Secretly she blossomed in the Christian faith she had adopted, and knowledge of her spread abroad as a sweet odor. For as in her childhood she visited the nun as relatives do, and Litiosa daily instructed her as well as she could; at length by divine grace Leocritia received Christian faith and preserved it in her breast with the fire of love. When she came to years of wisdom and attained the lights of knowledge, that faith which she had secretly learned in her earliest childhood, increased by spiritual food day by day, she nourished to still greater growth, at first in secret, then publicly and openly. Her parents gave her earnest warnings, but as this had no effect, they tried to assail her with whipping and beating in order to coerce her by punishment, since she was not to be moved by gentler means. But that flame which Christ sent into the hearts of the faithful cannot yield to any threats. When in this conflict she was beaten day and night, and saw herself attacked with severe punishments and tied with heavy bonds, and fearing that if she did not profess her faith publicly she would be burned in hell for her infidelity, she made her case known through messengers to blessed Eulogius, who was already much esteemed in many such cases, and to his sister, Anulo, a virgin dedicated to God. She explained that she wished to go to safer places among the faithful where she might without fear make her faith known. Thereupon blessed Eulogius recognized his accustomed office, and as he was a zealous partisan of the martyrs, he directed her through the same messengers to leave home secretly. She quickly planned a stratagem, and pretending to yield to her parents, and attacking our faith in words, according to plan she donned all her best ornaments and appeared in the manner of those who are out to please and marry in the world; she set out to change their minds by attiring herself in a way she hated. When she saw that everything was now safe for her, pretending to go to the wedding of some of her kindred which was then being celebrated, beautifully dressed as befitted the occasion, she hurried off to the protection of blessed Eulogius and his sister Anulo. At once they received her with joy, and turned her over to trusted friends to be kept in hiding. Her father and mother awaited her, and when they did not see their daughter, wailing that they had been deceived and torturing themselves into an unheard of rage and grief never before seen, they upset everything, confused everything, running about among friends and strangers, using force and the authority of the judge, they loaded into prisons and chains all whom they suspected; they afflicted with stripes and imprisonment men, women, confessors, priests, nuns, and whom they could, hoping that by these and other measures they might in some way get their daughter back. But the saint unmoved changed her from place to place, taking every precaution that the sheep should not fall into the hands of wolves. Meanwhile she austerely wore down her body, being constant in fasting and vigils, wearing haircloth and sleeping on the ground. The blessed man Eulogius, whose name is to be spoken with reverence, applying himself to nocturnal vigils, and praying prostrate on the ground in the basilica of San Zoylo, spent nights without sleep, beseeching the Lord for help and strength for the maiden, and consecrating her to the Lord by these exercises.

14. Meanwhile the serene maiden wished to see Eulogius's sister, whom she loved with warm affection, and came by night to their dwelling, moved by a revelation of the Lord and led by her desire of consolation, to spend just one day with them and then return to her usual hiding place. She told them that twice while praying her mouth had been filled with honey, that she had not dared to spit it out but had swallowed it, wondering at the nature of the thick substance. The saint interpreted this to her as a presage that she would enjoy the sweetness of the heavenly kingdom.

15. The next day when the maiden prepared to go back, it happened that her attendant did not come at the accustomed hour but only when dawn was breaking. She could not set out, for she used to travel at night to avoid being caught. So it was arranged that the virgin of God should stay where she was that day until the sun should put a term to its light for the earth and the shades of night should grant again the desired quietude. It was indeed by human counsel, but really by God's decree that she was held back, in order that he might give her her crown, and bestow the diadem of glory on the blessed Eulogius. For on that day, I know not at whose suggestion nor by whose plotting and betrayal, the hiding-place was made known to the judge, and suddenly their whole dwelling was surrounded by soldiers sent for the purpose. It happened that the elect and predestined martyr was there in person. Bringing Leocritia into Eulogius's presence they arrested both together, and beating them and treating them with disrespect, they brought them to the unjust and infamous judge. The judge at once thought to kill them by scourging, and roused to vehement fury, with truculent face and impatient mind he questioned Eulogius in furious words, and inquired with threatening why he had detained the girl at his house. Eulogius answered him patiently and with good grace, as he commonly spoke, and splendidly made clear the truth of the matter as follows: "Sir, the office of preaching is laid upon us, and it is a part of our faith that we should hold out the light of faith to those seeking it of us, and that we should deny it to no one who is hastening to the highways of life which are holy. This is the duty of priests, true religion demands it, and this also Christ our Lord taught us: that whoever is athirst and wishes to draw from the rivers of faith will find double the drink that he sought. And as this girl asked us for the rule of our holy faith, our purpose necessarily applied itself to her the more gladly as her desire was the more ardent. It was not proper to turn away a person asking this, especially not proper for one who for this purpose was endowed with the office of Christ. Hence as I was able I have enlightened and taught her, and I have shown her

that the faith of Christ is the road of the kingdom of heaven. In the same way I should be glad to do it for you, if you should care to ask me." Then the judge with stormy visage commanded rods to be brought in, threatening to put him to death by scourging. The saint said to him: "What do you intend to do with those rods?" He replied: "I mean to put you to death with them." Eulogius said: "Sharpen and prepare the sword with which you may send my soul, released from the bondage of the body, back to Him who gave it. Do not imagine that you will cut my body apart with scourges." And straightway reproaching with clear invective and much eloquence the falseness of their prophet and law, and redoubling what he had said, he was hurried off to the palace and brought before the king's councilors. One of them who was very well known to him addressed him sympathetically: "Even though fools and idiots are borne to this miserable ruin of death, you who are girt with the beauty of wisdom, and famous for your excellent life, what madness drove you to commit yourself to this fatal ruin, forgetting the natural love of life? Please listen to me, and do not rush into this headlong destruction, I beg you. Say only a word in this hour of your need, and afterward practice your faith where you will. We promise not to search for you anywhere." The blessed martyr Eulogius answered him smiling: "If only you could know what things are laid up for those of our faith! Or if I could place in your breast what I possess in my own; then you would not try to hold me back from my purpose, but even more gladly would you yourself think of giving up your worldly position." And he began to offer them the teaching of the everlasting Gospel, and with bold freedom to pour forth the preaching of the Kingdom. But not wishing to hear him, those present ordered him to be put to the sword. While he was being led away, one of the king's eunuchs slapped him. Turning the other cheek, Eulogius said: "Please strike this too, and make it equal to the other." When this had been struck, he patiently and meekly turned the first again. But the soldiers hurried him out to the place of execution, and there kneeling in prayer and raising his hands to heaven, making the sign of the cross and saying a few words of prayer silently, he stretched out his neck for the blade, and, despising the world, by a swift blow he found life. He was martyred in mid-afternoon of Saturday, the eleventh of March [859]. O blessed and wonderful man of our age, who in many martyrs sent the fruit of his work ahead of him, and in the virgin Leocritia left another to follow! Raising in his hands the standard of victory, and dedicating to the Lord the sheaf of his labor for himself, offering a pure oblation and peaceful sacrifices, and what things he had taught others, now in himself he presented to Christ the Lord of all things. As soon as his body was thrown from the upper level onto the river-bank, a dove of snowy whiteness, gliding through the air, in the sight of all flew down and sat on the martyr's body. They all tried to drive it away by throwing stones from all sides, but being nevertheless unable to move it as it sat there, they sought to put it to flight directly with their hands. But the dove, fluttering rather than flying around the body, came to rest on a tower overlooking the corpse, with its beak pointed towards the blessed man's body. And I must not be silent about the miracle that Christ worked for the glory of his name over the body of the martyr. A native of Ecija, while performing with others his monthly service in the palace and taking his turn with the watch, at night desiring a drink of water arose and went to the projecting water outlet which comes to that place. There he saw above Eulogius's body, which lay lower down, priests glistening white as snow, holding dazzling lamps, and earnestly reciting psalms. Frightened by this vision he went back to his station, fleeing rather than returning. After telling a companion all about it, he decided to go with him again to the place; but this second time he was unable to see it. On the next day the effort of the Christians obtained the blessed man's head, and on the third day they gathered the rest of the body, and buried it in the church of the blessed martyr San Zoylo.

16. As for the blessed virgin Leocritia, though they tried to seduce her with many delights and move her with many promises, she was by God's grace strengthened in the firmness of faith, and on the fourth day after Eulogius's martyrdom was herself beheaded and thrown in the Guadalquivir. But she could not be submerged nor hidden in the water, for moving with body erect she presented an astonishing sight to all. So she was taken out by the Christians and buried in the basilica of the martyr Saint Genesius, which is in the place called Terzos. Such was the end of the blessed doctor Eulogius, this his admirable departure, such his crossing over after many labors.

CHAPTER TWO

WARFARE IN THE EASTERN
MEDITERRANEAN AND THE HOLY LAND

Figure 2.1: Façade of the Holy Sepulcher.

Source: Paul LaCroix, *Military and Religious Life in the Middle Ages and the Period of the Renaissance* (London: Bickers and Son, n.d.), 106.

12. THE COMING OF THE SELJUK TURKS

The frontiers between the Byzantines and the neighboring Muslim polities were dramatically altered in the early eleventh century with the arrival of the nomadic Turks in western Asia. Originating in central Asia, the Turks had converted to Islam in the mid-tenth century and begun to migrate westward; there they found a fractured and, in their view, deeply corrupted Muslim world that had to be cleansed and expanded. The dominant clan among the Turks were the Seljuks, who by the late 1030s had settled in Khorasan (modern-day Iran). In 1055, the chief of the Seljuks was proclaimed sultan in Baghdad, and soon thereafter they began to send raiding expeditions against the Byzantines in Asia Minor. In 1071, as the Byzantine emperor Romanus Diogenes (r. 1068–71) sought to stop their advances, he was met in battle by the Turks under the command of Alp Arslan (r. 1063–72). In the resulting battle at Manzikert (1071), the Turks crushed the Byzantines, captured the emperor, and in the ensuing turmoil weakened Byzantine power in eastern Asia Minor and Armenia. Matthew of Edessa, an Armenian historian writing in the early twelfth century, is one of the best sources that we have to help us understand the arrival of the Turks and their movement into Armenia and the Byzantine Empire. The selection below, taken from his Chronicle, *details the arrival of the Turks in Armenia in the early eleventh century and the annexation of Armenian territory by the Byzantines, ostensibly so that they could protect it from the Turkish threat.*

Source: trans. Ara Edmond Dostourian, *Armenia and the Crusades—Tenth to Twelfth Centuries: The Chronicle of Matthew of Edessa* (Lanham, MD: University Press of America, 1993), 44–46.

The Arrival of the Turks

When the year 467 of the Armenian era [1018–19] began, the divine-rebuking wrath of God was awakened against all the Christian peoples and against those worshiping the holy cross, for a fatal dragon with deadly fire rose up and struck those faithful to the Holy Trinity. In this period the very foundations of the apostles and prophets were shaken, because winged serpents came forth and were intent on spreading like fire over all the lands of the Christian faithful. This was the first appearance of the bloodthirsty beasts. During these times the savage nation of infidels called Turks gathered together their forces. Then they came and entered Armenia in the province of Vaspurakan and mercilessly slaughtered the Christian faithful with the edge of the sword.

The news of this event reached King Senek'erim. Thereupon, his eldest son David, gathering together forces of the noblemen, advanced against the Turkish camp, and the two armies clashed violently in a horrible battle. Until that time the Armenians had never seen Turkish cavalry forces. When they encountered these Turks, armed with bows and having flowing hair like women, they found them strange-looking. The Armenian troops were not accustomed to resisting arrows. Nevertheless, they bravely attacked the infidels, fully unsheathing their swords from the scabbard; thus the courageous Armenian army bravely rushed into battle and killed many of the infidels. However, the infidels, shooting arrows, hit and wounded many of the Armenian troops. Seeing all this, Shapuh [an Armenian general] said to David: "Turn back, O king, from before the enemy, for the greater part of our troops have been wounded by arrows. Let us withdraw and defend ourselves against these weapons we see in the hands of the infidels by preparing other types of garments which will resist their arrows." But David, being conscious of his high rank, became arrogant with great pride and did not heed Shapuh's advice to withdraw from the battle. Then Shapuh, irritated by this, ran after David and, striking his back with his fist, vehemently forced him to turn back. For Shapuh was a brave and mighty warrior, besides which he had raised and educated David and, because of all this, did not fear him. In this manner Shapuh forced David to withdraw together with his troops. The Armenian forces went back to the city of Ostan and related everything to King Senek'erim, telling him about the appearance of the infidels. When Senek'erim heard this, he became greatly distressed. He neither ate nor drank, but rather became pensive, grief-stricken, and passed the whole night sleepless. Sitting down, he examined the chronicles and utterances of the divinely-inspired prophets, the holy vardapets [theological scholars], and found written in these books the time specified for the coming of the forces and soldiers of the Turks. He also learned of the impending destruction and end of the whole world. In these books he found written the following: "At that time they will flee from the east to the west, from the north to the south, and they will not find rest upon the earth, for the plains and the mountains will be covered with blood;" and this is what Isaiah said: "The hoofs of their stallions are unfaltering."

After this Senek'erim resolved to hand over the land of his ancestors to the Greek emperor Basil and in its stead to obtain Sebastia; so he immediately wrote to the emperor. When the emperor Basil heard this, he rejoiced greatly and gave the Armenian king Sebastia. In turn Senek'erim handed over the land of Vaspurakan to the emperor, including seventy-two regional fortresses and four thousand four hundred villages and the monasteries; he did not give up, but kept, one hundred and fifteen monasteries where prayers were said for him. He gave all of this in writing to Basil. Then the emperor asked the Armenian king to send him David in royal splendor; so Senek'erim sent his son and with him the sons of the noblemen; the bishop, his lordship Eghishē; three hundred pack-mules, laden with treasure and various articles; and also one thousand Arabian horses. With such a splendid train David entered Constantinople. The city was stirred up and everyone came to meet him. The streets and palaces were decorated and the populace strewed money on him [as he went forth]. The emperor Basil rejoiced greatly when he saw David and, taking him to Saint Sophia, made him his adopted child, and the populace honored him as the emperor's son. After this Basil gave David many gifts and sent him back to his father, and he gave Senek'erim Sebastia with its innumerable surrounding districts. Senek'erim, going forth with his whole household and people, came to Sebastia; and thus Armenia was abandoned by its kings and princes.

13. CALLING THE CRUSADES

The disaster at the hands of the Seljuks at Manzikert ultimately led to the collapse of the Byzantine frontier in Anatolia and the methodical advance of Turkish forces toward the Byzantine capital of Constantinople. As the situation deteriorated, reports from pilgrims began to filter to the West, prompting Pope Gregory VII (r. 1073–85) to issue an encyclical in 1074 urging Christians to go to the East and help the Byzantines fight the Turks. This is our first source below. This papal command seems to have yielded very limited results, but that was not the case the next time the pope urged Latin Christians to march eastward. In the spring of 1095, in an effort to dislodge the Turks from their recent conquests, the Byzantine emperor Alexios I (r. 1081–1118) made an appeal to the pope, by now Urban II (r. 1088–99), asking for mercenaries to help the Byzantines in their wars. The appeal to the West came at a time when relations between Latin (Western) and Orthodox (Byzantine) Christians were still strained as a result of the Great Schism (1054). Nevertheless, Urban reacted quickly and vigorously to Alexios's call for help, in the process setting in motion the events that would lead to the First Crusade. In November of 1095 at a church council in the French town of Clermont, Urban preached his call to arms to an assembled audience of the leading clergy and nobility of France and neighboring regions. No exact transcript exists of Urban's speech. The two accounts provided here by Fulcher of Chartres and Robert the Monk were written at the conclusion of the First Crusade (1096–99), although it is likely that Fulcher and Robert were present at Clermont.

Source: trans. O.J. Thatcher and E.H. McNeal, *A Source Book for Medieval History: Selected Documents Illustrating the History of Europe in the Middle Ages* (New York: Charles Scribner and Sons, 1905), 512–21; rev. Jarbel Rodriguez.

Appeal by Gregory VII, 1074

Gregory, bishop, servant of the servants of God, to all who are willing to defend the Christian faith, greeting and apostolic benediction.

We hereby inform you that the bearer of this letter, on his recent return from across the sea [from Palestine], came to Rome to visit us. He repeated what we

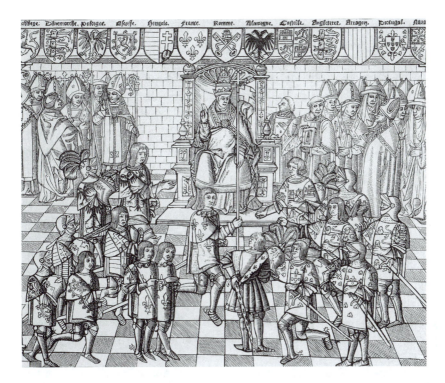

Figure 2.2: Urban II at Clermont.

Source: Paul LaCroix, *Military and Religious Life in the Middle Ages and the Period of the Renaissance* (London: Bickers and Son, n.d.), facing 262.

had heard from many others, that a pagan race had overcome the Christians and with horrible cruelty had devastated everything almost to the walls of Constantinople, and were now governing the conquered lands with tyrannical violence, and that they had slain many thousands of Christians as if they were but sheep. If we love God and wish to be recognized as Christians, we should be filled with grief at the misfortune of this great empire [the Greek] and the murder of so many Christians. But simply to grieve is not our whole duty. The example of our Redeemer and the bond of fraternal love demand that we should lay down our lives to liberate them. "Because he laid down his life for us: and we ought to lay down our lives for the brethren" [1 John 3:16]. Know, therefore, that we are trusting in the mercy of God and in the power of his might and that we are striving in all possible ways and making preparations to render aid to the Christian empire [the Greek] as quickly as possible. Therefore we beseech you by the faith in which you are united through Christ in the adoption of the sons

53

of God, and by the authority of Saint Peter, prince of apostles, we admonish you that you be moved to proper compassion by the wounds and blood of your brethren and the danger of the aforesaid empire and that, for the sake of Christ, you undertake the difficult task of bearing aid to your brethren [the Greeks]. Send messengers to us at once to inform us of what God may inspire you to do in this matter.

Urban's Speech—Version of Fulcher of Chartres

"Most beloved brethren: Urged by necessity, I, Urban, by the permission of God chief bishop and prelate over the whole world, have come into these parts as an ambassador with a divine admonition to you, the servants of God. I hoped to find you as faithful and as zealous in the service of God as I had supposed you to be. But if there is in you any deformity or crookedness contrary to God's law, with divine help I will do my best to remove it. For God has put you as stewards over his family to minister to it. Happy indeed will you be if he finds you faithful in your stewardship. You are called shepherds; see that you do not act as hirelings. But be true shepherds, with your crooks always in your hands. Do not go to sleep, but guard on all sides the flock committed to you. For if through your carelessness or negligence a wolf carries away one of your sheep, you will surely lose the reward laid up for you with God. And after you have been bitterly scourged with remorse for your faults, you will be fiercely overwhelmed in hell, the abode of death. For according to the gospel you are the salt of the earth [Matt. 5:13]. But if you fall short in your duty, how, it may be asked, can it be salted? O how great the need of salting! It is indeed necessary for you to correct with the salt of wisdom this foolish people which is so devoted to the pleasures of this world, lest the Lord, when he may wish to speak to them, find them putrefied by their sins, unsalted and stinking. For if he shall find worms, that is, sins, in them, because you have been negligent in your duty, he will command them as worthless to be thrown into the abyss of unclean things. And because you cannot restore to him his great loss, he will sorely condemn you and drive you from his loving presence. But the man who applies this salt should be prudent, provident, modest, learned, peaceable, watchful, pious, just, equitable, and pure. For how can the ignorant teach others? How can the licentious make others modest? And how can the impure make others pure? If anyone hates peace, how can he make others peaceable? Or if anyone has soiled his hands with baseness, how can he cleanse the impurities of another? We read also that if the blind lead the blind, both will fall into the ditch [Matt. 15:14]. But first correct yourselves, in order that, free from blame, you may be able to correct those who are subject to you. If you wish to be the friends of God, gladly do the things which you know will please him. You must especially let all matters that pertain to the church be controlled by the law of the church. And be careful that simony does not take root among you, lest both those who buy and those who sell [church offices] be beaten with the scourges of the Lord through narrow streets and driven into the place of destruction and confusion. Keep the church and the clergy in all its grades entirely free from the secular power. See that the tithes that belong to God are faithfully paid from all the produce of the land; let them not be sold or withheld. If anyone seizes a bishop let him be treated as an outlaw. If anyone seizes or robs monks, or clergymen, or nuns, or their servants, or pilgrims, or merchants, let him be anathema [that is, cursed]. Let robbers and incendiaries and all their accomplices be expelled from the church and anathematized. If a man who does not give a part of his goods as alms is punished with the damnation of hell, how should he be punished who robs another of his goods? For thus it happened to the rich man in the Gospel [Luke 16:19]; for he was not punished because he had stolen the goods of another, but because he had not used well the things which were his.

"You have seen for a long time the great disorder in the world caused by these crimes. It is so bad in some of your provinces, I am told, and you are so weak in the administration of justice, that one can hardly go along the road by day or night without being attacked by robbers; and whether at home or abroad, one is in danger of being despoiled either by force or fraud. Therefore it is necessary to reenact the truce, as it is commonly called, which was proclaimed a long time ago by our holy fathers. I exhort and demand that you, each, try hard to share the truce kept in your diocese. And if anyone shall be led by his cupidity or arrogance to break this truce, by the authority of God and with the sanction of this council he shall be anathematized."

After these and various other matters had been attended to, all who were present, clergy and people, gave thanks to God and agreed to the pope's proposition. They all faithfully promised to keep the decrees. Then the pope said that in another part of the world Christianity was suffering from a state of affairs that was worse than the one just mentioned. He continued:

"Although, O sons of God, you have promised more firmly than ever to keep the peace among yourselves and to preserve the rights of the church, there, remains still an important work for you to do. Freshly quickened by the divine correction, you must apply the strength of your righteousness to another matter which concerns you as well as God. For your brethren who live in the east are in urgent need of your help, and you must hasten to give them the aid which has often been promised them. For, as the most of you have heard, the Turks and Arabs have attacked them and have conquered the territory of Romania [the Byzantine Empire] as far west as the shore of the Mediterranean and the Hellespont, which is called the Arm of Saint George. They have occupied more and more of the lands of those Christians, and have overcome them in seven battles. They have killed and captured many, and have destroyed the churches and devastated the empire. If you permit them to continue thus for awhile with impunity, the faithful of God will be much more widely attacked by them. On this account I, or rather the Lord, beseech you as Christ's heralds to publish this everywhere and to persuade all people of whatever rank, foot-soldiers and knights, poor and rich, to carry aid promptly to those Christians and to destroy that vile race from the lands of our friends. I say this to those who are present, it is meant also for those who are absent. Moreover, Christ commands it.

"All who die by the way, whether by land or by sea, or in battle against the pagans, shall have immediate remission of sins. This I grant them through the power of God with which I am invested. O what a disgrace if such a despised and base race, which worships demons, should conquer a people which has the faith of omnipotent God and is made glorious with the name of Christ! With what reproaches will the Lord overwhelm us if you do not aid those who, with us, profess the Christian religion! Let those who have been accustomed unjustly to wage private warfare against the faithful now go against the infidels and end with victory this war which should have been begun long ago. Let those who, for a long time, have been robbers, now become knights. Let those who have been fighting against their brothers and relatives now fight in a proper way against the barbarians. Let those who have been serving as mercenaries for small pay now obtain the eternal reward. Let those who have been wearing themselves out in both body and soul now work for a double honor. Behold I on this side will be the sorrowful and poor, on that the rich; on this side, the enemies of the Lord, on that his friends. Let those who go not put off the journey, but rent their lands and collect money for their expenses; and as soon as winter is over and spring comes, let them eagerly set out on the way with God as their guide."

Urban's Speech—The Version of Robert the Monk

In 1095 a great council was held in Auvergne, in the city of Clermont. Pope Urban II, accompanied by cardinals and bishops, presided over it. It was made famous by the presence of many bishops and princes from France and Germany. After the council had attended to ecclesiastical matters, the pope went out into a public square, because no house was able to hold the people, and addressed them in a very persuasive speech, as follows: "O race of the Franks, O people who live beyond the mountains, O people loved and chosen of God, as is clear from your many deeds, distinguished over all other nations by the situation of your land, your catholic faith, and your regard for the holy church, we have a special message and exhortation for you. For we wish you to know what a grave matter has brought us to your country. The sad news has come from Jerusalem and Constantinople that the people of Persia, an accursed and foreign race, enemies of God, 'a generation that set not their heart aright, and whose spirit was not steadfast with God' [Ps. 78:8], have invaded the lands of those Christians and devastated them with the sword, rapine, and fire. Some of the Christians they have carried away as slaves, others they have put to death. The churches they have either destroyed or turned into mosques. They desecrate and overthrow the altars. They circumcise the Christians and pour the blood from the circumcision on the altars or in the baptismal fonts. Some they kill in a horrible way by cutting open the abdomen, taking out a part of the entrails and tying them to a stake; they then beat them and compel them to walk until all their entrails are drawn out and they fall to the ground. Some they use as targets for their arrows. They compel some to stretch out their necks and then they try to see whether they can cut off their heads with one stroke of the sword. It is better to say nothing of their horrible treatment of women. They have taken from the Greek empire a tract of land so large that it takes more than two months to walk through it. Whose duty is it to avenge this and recover that land, if not yours? For to you more than to other nations the Lord has given the military spirit, courage, agile bodies, and the bravery to strike down those who resist you. Let your minds be stirred to bravery by the deeds of your forefathers, and by the efficiency and greatness of Charlemagne, and of his son Louis the Pious, and of the other kings who have destroyed Turkish kingdoms, and established Christianity in their lands. You should be moved especially by the holy grave of our Lord and Savior, which is now held by unclean peoples, and by the holy places which are treated with dishonor and irreverently befouled with their uncleanness.

"O bravest of knights, descendants of unconquered ancestors, do not be weaker than they, but remember their courage. If you are kept back by your love for your children, relatives, and wives, remember what the Lord says in the Gospel: 'He that loves father or mother more than me is not worthy of me' [Matt. 10:37]; 'and everyone that hath forsaken houses, or brothers, or sisters, or father, or mother, or wife, or children, or lands for my name's sake, shall receive a hundredfold and shall inherit everlasting life' [Matt. 19:29]. Let no possessions keep you back, no solicitude for your property. Your land is shut in on all sides by the sea and mountains, and is too thickly populated. There is not much wealth here, and the soil scarcely yields enough to support you. On this account you kill and devour each other, and carry on war and mutually destroy each other. Let your hatred and quarrels cease, your civil wars come to an end, and all your dissensions stop. Set out on the road to the Holy Sepulcher, take the land from that wicked people, and make it your own. That land which, as the Scripture says, is flowing with milk and honey, God gave to the children of Israel. Jerusalem is the best of all lands, more fruitful than all others, as it were a second Paradise of delights. This land our Savior made illustrious by his birth, beautiful with his life, and sacred with his suffering; he redeemed it with his death and glorified it with his tomb. This royal city is now held captive by her enemies, and made pagan by those who know not God. She asks and longs to be liberated and does not cease to beg you to come to her aid. She asks aid especially from you because, as I have said, God has given more of the military spirit to you than to other nations. Set out on this journey and you will obtain the remission of your sins and be sure of the incorruptible glory of the kingdom of heaven."

When Pope Urban had said this and much more of the same sort, all who were present were moved to cry out with one accord, "It is the will of God, it is the will of God." When the pope heard this he raised his eyes to heaven and gave thanks to God, and, commanding silence with a gesture of his hand, he said: "My dear brethren, today there is fulfilled in you that which the Lord says in the Gospel, 'Where two or three are gathered together in my name, there am I in the midst' [Matt. 18:20]. For unless the Lord God had been in your minds you would not all have said the same thing. For although you spoke with many voices, nevertheless it was one and the same thing that made you speak. So I say unto you, God, who put those words into your hearts, has caused you to utter them. Therefore let these words be your battle cry, because God caused you to speak them. Whenever you meet the enemy in battle, you shall all cry out, 'It is the will of God, it is the will of God.' And we do not command the old or weak to go, or those who cannot bear arms. No women shall go without their husbands, or brothers, or proper companions, for such would be a hindrance rather than a help, a burden rather than an advantage. Let the rich aid the poor and equip them for fighting and take them with them. Clergymen shall not go without the consent of their bishop, for otherwise the journey would be of no value to them. Nor will this pilgrimage be of any benefit to a layman if he goes without the blessing of his priest. Whoever therefore shall determine to make this journey and shall make a vow to God and shall offer himself as a living sacrifice, holy, acceptable to God [Rom. 12:1], shall wear a cross on his brow or on his breast And when he returns after having fulfilled his vow he shall wear the cross on his back. In this way he will obey the command of the Lord, 'Whosoever doth not bear his cross and come after me is not worthy of me'" [Luke 14:27]. When these things had been done, while all prostrated themselves on the earth and beat their breasts, one of the cardinals, named Gregory, made confession for them, and they were given absolution for all their sins. After the absolution, they received the benediction and the permission to go home.

14. THE FIRST CRUSADE

Urban II's call for a Holy War spread like wildfire, succeeding beyond even his wild-est expectations. Within months, armies raised by some of the most prominent western European nobles began their long march to the east. But they were not the only ones who sought to gain the spiritual benefits that Urban had promised at Clermont. A multitude of non-combatants, numbering in the tens of thousands and including women, children, the frail, and the old began their march eastward before the nobles and their soldiers could get under way. Many of these coalesced around a French preacher who went by the name of Peter the Hermit (d. 1115). The first selection below from the anonymous Gesta Francorum *captures their peregrination to Constantinople and their encounters with Turkish armies, which ended in disaster for Peter and his followers. The professional knightly armies raised by high-ranking nobles including Raymond of Provence, Geoffrey of Lorraine, Bohemond of Taranto, and Robert of Normandy, among others, acquitted themselves much better in their clashes with the Turks. But in spite of their military prowess, the march to the east proved to be an incredibly difficult one that saw the crusader ranks diminished by military clashes, disease, famine conditions, and desertions. Still, overcoming these obstacles (which was helped significantly by Muslim political and military division) and reinforced by late arrivals, the armies reached Jerusalem on 7 June 1099, nearly three years after they had departed from western Europe. After a siege lasting over a month, the crusaders were able to capture Jerusalem on 15 July, putting the bulk of the population, Christians, Muslims, and Jews alike, to the sword. The last three selections below are all accounts of the fall of Jerusalem; the first two from the anonymous* Gesta Francorum *and the* Historia Francorum *of Raymond d'Aguiliers are both from the Christian perspective, while the last source by Ibn al-Athīr (1160–1233) captures the Muslim reaction.*

Sources: trans. O.J. Thatcher and E.H. McNeal, *A Source Book for Medieval History: Selected Documents Illustrating the History of Europe in the Middle Ages* (New York: Charles Scribner and Sons, 1905), 523–26, for the first selection from the *Gesta Francorum*; trans. A.C. Krey, *The First Crusade: The Accounts of Eye-witnesses and Participants* (Princeton, NJ: Princeton University Press, 1921), 256–62 for the second selection from the *Gesta Francorum* and the *Historia Francorum*; trans. E.J. Costello and Francesco Gabrieli, *Arab Historians of the Crusades*, ed. Francesco Gabrieli (Berkeley: University of California Press, 1969), 10–11.

Peter the Hermit and His Followers from the *Gesta Francorum*

One of the divisions of the Franks passed through Hungary. The leaders of these were Peter the Hermit, Godfrey, his brother Baldwin, and Baldwin, count of Mt. Henno. These most powerful knights and many others, whose names I do not know, went by the road that Charlemagne, the famous king of France, had caused to be made to Constantinople. But Peter, with a large number of Germans, preceded all the others to Constantinople, which he reached August 1 [1096]. There he found some Lombards, [other] Italians, and many others assembled. The emperor had given them a market and had told them not to cross the strait until the great body of crusaders should come, because they were not numerous enough to meet the Turks in battle. But these crusaders were conducting themselves badly. They were destroying and burning palaces [in the suburbs of Constantinople], and they stole the lead with which the churches were covered, and sold it to the Greeks. At this the emperor became angry and ordered them to cross the strait. But after they crossed they continued to do all the damage possible, burning and plundering houses and churches. At length they came to Nicomedia where, because of the haughtiness of the French, the Lombards, Italians, and Germans separated from them and chose a leader named Raynald. They then marched four days into the interior. Beyond Nicaea they found a castle, named Xerigordon, which had no garrison. They took it and found in it a good deal of grain, wine, and meat, and an abundance of all kinds of provisions. The Turks, hearing that the Christians were in this castle, came to besiege it. Before the gate of the castle was a well and at the foot of the castle a spring of water. Near this spring Raynald laid an ambush to catch the Turks. But they came on St. Michael's day [29 September], and discovered the ambuscade and fell upon Raynald and those who were with him, and killed many of them. Those who escaped fled into the castle. The Turks laid close siege to the castle and cut off its supply of water. And the crusaders suffered so from thirst that they bled the horses and donkeys and drank their blood. And some let down girdles and pieces of rags into the cistern and squeezed the water out of them into their mouths. Some even drank urine, and others, to relieve their thirst, dug holes in the ground and, lying on their backs, covered their breasts with the moist earth. The bishops and priests comforted them and urged them not to give up, saying, "Be strong in the faith of Christ, and fear not those who persecute you, as the Lord said, 'Fear not them which kill the body, but are not able to kill the soul'" [Matt. 10:28]. This continued for eight days. Finally, the leader of the Germans agreed with the Turks to betray his companions to them. So, pretending to go out to fight, he fled to the Turks and many went with him. But those who would not deny their Lord were killed. The Turks took some prisoners and divided them like sheep among themselves. Some of these they put up as targets and shot arrows at them. Others they sold or gave away as if they were animals. Some took their prisoners home with them as slaves. In this way some of the Christians were taken to Khorasan, some to Antioch, some to Aleppo, and still others to other places. These were the first to suffer a glorious martyrdom for the name of the Lord Jesus.

Now the Turks, learning that Peter the Hermit and Walter the Penniless were at Civitot, which is above Nicaea, came thither with great rejoicing to kill them and those who were with them. Walter was leading his men out toward Xerigordon when the Turks met them and killed them. But Peter the Hermit had a short time before gone back to Constantinople because he could not control his people, who refused to obey him. The Turks then attacked those who were encamped near Civitot, some of whom they found asleep, others lying down, and others naked, and killed them. Among them they found a priest saying mass and killed him at the altar. Those who were able to escape fled into Civitot. Some sprang into the sea, and others hid in the woods and mountains. The Turks followed those who went into the castle, and gathered wood to burn them with the castle. But the Christians in the castle threw fire into the piles of wood, and the fire, turned against the Turks, burned some of them. But God delivered ours from the fire. But at length the Turks took them alive, divided them among themselves, as they had done before, and scattered them through all those regions. Some were sent to Khorasan and others into Persia. All this was done in the month of October [1096].

The Conquest of Jerusalem from
the *Gesta Francorum*

At length, our leaders decided to beleaguer the city with siege machines, so that we might enter and worship the Savior at the Holy Sepulcher. They constructed wooden towers and many other siege machines. Duke Godfrey [of Bouillon] made a wooden tower and other siege devices, and Count Raymond [of Provence] did the same, although it was necessary to bring wood from a considerable distance. However, when the Saracens saw our men engaged in this work, they greatly strengthened the fortifications of the city and increased the height of the turrets at night. On a certain Sabbath night, the leaders, after having decided which parts of the wall were weakest, dragged the tower and the machines to the eastern side of the city. Moreover, we set up the tower at earliest dawn and equipped and covered it on the first, second, and third days of the week. The Count of St-Gilles erected his tower on the plain to the south of the city.

While all this was going on, our water supply was so limited that no one could buy enough water for one denarius to satisfy or quench his thirst. Both day and night, on the fourth and fifth days of the week, we made a determined attack on the city from all sides. However, before we made this assault on the city, the bishops and priests persuaded all, by exhorting and preaching, to honor the Lord by marching around Jerusalem in a great procession, and to prepare for battle by prayer, fasting, and almsgiving. Early on the sixth day of the week we again attacked the city on all sides, but as the assault was unsuccessful, we were all astounded and fearful. However, when the hour approached on which our Lord Jesus Christ deigned to suffer on the Cross for us, our knights began to fight bravely in one of the towers—namely, the party with Duke Godfrey and his brother, Count Eustace. One of our knights, named Lethold, clambered up the wall of the city, and no sooner had he ascended than the defenders fled from the walls and through the city. Our men followed, killing and slaying even to the Temple of Solomon, where the slaughter was so great that our men waded in blood up to their ankles.

Count Raymond brought his army and his tower up near the wall from the south, but between the tower and the wall there was a very deep ditch. Then our men took counsel how they might fill it, and had it proclaimed by heralds that anyone who carried three stones to the ditch would receive one denarius. The work of tilling it required three days and three nights, and when at length the ditch was filled, they moved the tower up to the wall, but the men defending this portion of the wall fought desperately with stones and tire. When the count heard that the Franks were already in the city, he said to his men, "Why do you loiter? Lo, the Franks are even now within the city." The emir who commanded the Tower of St-David surrendered to the count and opened that gate at which the pilgrims had always been accustomed to pay tribute. But this time the pilgrims entered the city, pursuing and killing the Saracens up to the Temple of Solomon, where the enemy gathered in force. The battle raged throughout the day, so that the Temple was covered with their blood. When the pagans had been overcome, our men seized great numbers, both men and women, either killing them or keeping them captive, as they wished. On the roof of the Temple a great number of pagans of both sexes had assembled, and these were taken under the protection of Tancred and Gaston of Beert. Afterward, the army scattered throughout the city and took possession of the gold and silver, the horses and mules, and the houses filled with goods of all kinds.

Later, all of our people went to the Sepulcher of our Lord, rejoicing and weeping for joy, and they rendered up the offering that they owed. In the morning, some of our men cautiously ascended to the roof of the Temple and attacked the Saracens, both men and women, beheading them with naked swords; the remainder sought death by jumping down into the temple. When Tancred heard of this, he was filled with anger.

The Conquest of Jerusalem from
the *Historia Francorum*

The duke [Godfrey of Bouillon] and the counts [Robert] of Normandy and [Robert of] Flanders placed Gaston of Beert in charge of the workmen who constructed machines. They built mantlets and towers with which to attack the wall. The direction of this work was assigned to Gaston by the princes because he was a most noble lord, respected by all for his skill and reputation. He very cleverly hastened matters by dividing the work. The princes busied themselves with obtaining and bringing the material, while Gaston supervised the work of construction. Likewise, Count Raymond [of Provence] made William Ricau superintendent of the work on Mount Zion and placed the bishop of Albara in charge of the Saracens and others who brought in the timber. The count's men had taken many Saracen castles and villages and forced the Saracens to work, as though they were their serfs. Thus for the construction of machines at Jerusalem fifty or sixty men carried on their shoulders a great beam that could not have been dragged by four pair of oxen. What more shall I say? All worked with a singleness of purpose, no one was slothful, and no hands were idle. All worked without wages, except the artisans, who were paid from a collection taken from the people. However, Count Raymond paid his workmen from his own treasury. Surely the hand of the Lord was with us and aided those who were working!

When our efforts were ended and the machines completed, the princes held a council and announced: "Let all prepare themselves for a battle on Thursday; in the meantime, let us pray, fast, and give alms. Hand over your animals and your boys to the artisans and carpenters, that they may bring in beams, poles, stakes, and branches to make mantlets. Two knights should make one mantlet and one scaling ladder. Do not hesitate to work for the Lord, for your labors will soon be ended." This was willingly done by all. Then it was decided what part of the city each leader should attack and where his machines should be located.

Meanwhile, the Saracens in the city, noting the great number of machines that we had constructed, strengthened the weaker parts of the wall, so that it seemed that they could be taken only by the most desperate efforts. Because the Saracens had made so many and such strong fortifications to oppose our machines, the duke, the count of Flanders, and the count of Normandy spent the night before the day set for the attack moving their machines, mantlets, and platforms to that side of the city which is between the church of Saint Stephen and the valley of Josaphat. You who read this must not think that this was a light undertaking, for the machines were carried in parts almost a mile to the place where they were to be set up. When morning came and the Saracens saw that all the machinery and tents had been moved during the night, they were amazed. Not only the Saracens were astonished, but our people as well, for they recognized that the hand of the Lord was with us. The change was made because the new point chosen for attack was more level, and thus suitable for moving the machines up to the walls, which cannot be done unless the ground is level; and also because that part of the city seemed to be weaker, having remained unfortified, as it was some distance from our camp. This part of the city is on the north.

Count Raymond and his men worked equally hard on Mount Zion, but they had much assistance from William Embriaco and the Genoese sailors, who, although they had lost their ships at Joppa, as we have already related, had been able, nevertheless, to save ropes, mallets, spikes, axes, and hatchets, which were very necessary to us. But why delay the story? The appointed day arrived and the attack began. However, I want to say this first, that, according to our estimate and that of many others, there were sixty thousand fighting men within the city, not counting the women and those unable to bear arms, and there were not many of these. At the most we did not have more than twelve thousand able to bear arms, for there were many poor people and many sick. There were twelve or thirteen hundred knights in our army, as I reckon it, not more. I say this that you may realize that nothing, whether great or small, which is undertaken in the name of the Lord can fail, as the following pages show.

Our men began to undermine the towers and walls. From every side stones were hurled from the *tormenti* and the *petrariae* [siege engines], and so many arrows that they fell like hail. The servants of God bore this patiently, sustained by the premises of their faith, whether they should be killed or should presently prevail over their enemies. The battle showed no indication of victory, but when the machines were drawn nearer to the walls, they hurled not only stones and arrows, but also burning wood and straw. The wood was dipped in pitch, wax, and sulfur; then straw and tow were fastened on by an iron band, and, when lighted, these firebrands were shot from the machines. [They were] all bound together by an iron band. I say, so that wherever they fell, the whole mass held together and continued to burn. Such missiles, burning as they shot upward, could not be resisted by swords or by high walls; it was not even possible for the defenders to find safety down behind the walls. Thus the fight continued from the rising to the setting sun in such splendid fashion that it is difficult to believe anything more glorious was ever done. Then we called on Almighty God, our Leader and Guide, confident in his mercy. Night brought fear to both sides. The Saracens feared that we would take the city during the night or on the next day, for the outer works were broken through and the ditch was filled, so that it was possible to make an entrance through the wall very quickly. On our part, we feared only that the Saracens would set fire to the machines that were moved close to the walls, and thus improve their situation. So on both sides it was a night of watchfulness, labor, and sleepless caution: on one side, most certain hope, on the other doubtful fear. We gladly labored to capture the city for the glory of God, they less willingly strove to resist our efforts for the sake of the laws of Muhammad. It is hard to believe how great were the efforts made on both sides during the night.

When the morning came, our men eagerly rushed to the walls and dragged the machines forward, but the Saracens had constructed so many machines that for each one of ours they now had nine or ten. Thus they greatly interfered with our efforts. This was the ninth day, on which the priest had said that we would capture the city. But why do I delay so long? Our machines were now shaken apart by the blows of many stones, and our men lagged because they were very weary. However, there remained the mercy of the Lord which is never overcome nor conquered, but is always a source of support in times of adversity. One incident must not be omitted. Two women tried to bewitch one of the hurling machines, but a stone struck and crushed them, as well as three slaves, so that their lives were extinguished and the evil incantations averted.

By noon our men were greatly discouraged. They were weary and at the end of their resources. There were still many of the enemy opposing each one of our men; the walls were very high and strong, and the great resources and skill that the enemy exhibited in repairing their defenses seemed too great for us to overcome. But, while we hesitated, irresolute, and the enemy exulted in our discomfiture, the healing mercy of God inspired us and turned our sorrow into joy, for the Lord did not forsake us. While a council was being held to decide whether or not our machines should be withdrawn, for some were burned and the rest badly shaken to pieces, a knight on the Mount of Olives began to wave his shield to those who were with the count and others, signaling them to advance. Who this knight was we have been unable to find out. At this signal our men began to take heart, and some began to batter down the wall, while others began to ascend by means of scaling ladders and ropes. Our archers shot burning firebrands, and in this way checked the attack that the Saracens were making upon the wooden towers of the duke and the two counts. These firebrands, moreover, were wrapped in cotton. This shower of fire drove the defenders from the walls. Then the count quickly released the long drawbridge which had protected the side of the wooden tower next to the wall, and it swung down from the top, being fastened to the middle of the tower, making a bridge over which the men began to enter Jerusalem bravely and fearlessly. Among those who entered first were Tancred and the duke of Lorraine [Godfrey of Bouillon], and the amount of blood that they shed on that day is incredible. All ascended after them, and the Saracens now began to suffer.

Strange to relate, however, at this very time when the city was practically captured by the Franks, the Saracens were still fighting on the other side, where the count was attacking the wall as though the city should never be captured. But now that our men had possession of the walls and towers, wonderful sights were to be seen. Some of our men (and this was more merciful) cut off the heads of their enemies: others shot them with arrows, so that they fell from the towers; others tortured them longer by casting them into the flames. Piles of heads, hands, and feet were to be seen in the streets of the city. It was necessary to pick one's way over the bodies of men and horses. But these were small matters compared to what happened at the Temple of Solomon, a place where religious services are ordinarily chanted. What happened there? If I tell the truth, it will exceed your powers of belief. So let it suffice to say this much, at least, that in the Temple and porch of Solomon, men rode in blood up to their knees and bridle reins. Indeed, it was a just and splendid judgment of God that this place should be filled with the blood of the unbelievers, since it had suffered so long from their blasphemies. The city was filled with corpses and blood. Some of the enemy took refuge in the Tower of David, and, petitioning Count Raymond for protection, surrendered the Tower into his hands.

Now that the city was taken, it was well worth all our previous labors and hardships to see the devotion of the pilgrims at the Holy Sepulcher. How they rejoiced and exulted and sang a new song to the Lord! For their hearts offered prayers of praise to God, victorious and triumphant, which cannot be told in words. A new day, new joy, new and perpetual gladness, the consummation of our labor and devotion, drew forth from all new words and new songs. This day, I say, will be famous in all future ages, for it turned our labors and sorrows into joy and exultation; this day, I say, marks the justification of all Christianity, the humiliation of paganism, and the renewal of our faith. "This is the day which the Lord hath made, let us rejoice and be glad in it," for on this day the Lord revealed himself to his people and blessed them.

On this day, the Ides of July [15 July], Lord Adhemar, bishop of Puy [who had died in Antioch in the summer of 1098], was seen in the city by many people. Many also testified that he was the first to scale the wall, and that he summoned the knights and people to follow him. On this day, moreover, the apostles were cast forth from Jerusalem and scattered over the whole world. On this same day, the children of the apostles regained the city and fatherland for God and the fathers. This day, the Ides of July, shall be celebrated to the praise and glory of the name of God, who, answering the prayers of his Church, gave in trust and benediction to his children the city and fatherland which he had promised to the fathers. On this day we chanted the Office of the Resurrection, since on that day he, who by his virtue arose from the dead, revived us through his grace. So much is to be said of this.

The Conquest of Jerusalem from Ibn al-Athir

Taj ad-Daula Tutūsh was the lord of Jerusalem but had given it as a fief to the emir Suqmān ibn Artūq the Turcoman. When the Franks defeated the Turks at Antioch the massacre demoralized them, and the Egyptians, who saw that the Turkish armies were being weakened by desertion, besieged Jerusalem under the command of al-Afdal ibn Badr al-Jamali. Inside the city were Artūq's sons, Suqmān and Ilghazi, their cousin Sunij and their nephew Yaquti. The Egyptians brought more than forty siege engines to attack Jerusalem and broke down the walls at several points. The inhabitants put up a defense, and the siege and fighting went on for more than six weeks. In the end the Egyptians forced the city to capitulate, in Sha'bān 489 [August 1096]. Suqmān, Ilghazi, and their friends were well treated by al-Afdal, who gave them large gifts of money and let them go free. They made for Damascus and then crossed the Euphrates. Suqmān settled in Edessa and Ilghazi went on into Iraq. The Egyptian governor of Jerusalem was a certain Iftikhār ad-Daula, who was still there at the time of which we are speaking.

After their vain attempt to take Acre by siege, the Franks moved on to Jerusalem and besieged it for more than six weeks. They built two towers, one of which, near Sion, the Muslims burnt down, killing everyone inside it. It had scarcely ceased to burn before a messenger arrived to ask for help and to bring the news that the other side of the city had fallen. In fact Jerusalem was taken from the north on the morning of Friday 22 Sha'bān 492 [15 July 1099]. The population was put to the sword by the Franks, who pillaged the area for a week. A band of Muslims barricaded themselves into the Oratory [or Tower] of David and fought on for several days. They were granted their lives in return for surrendering. The Franks honored their word, and the group left by night for Ascalon. In the Masjid al-Aqsa [the al-Aqsa Mosque] the Franks slaughtered more than 70,000 people, among them a large number of imams and Muslim scholars, devout and ascetic men who had left their homelands to live lives of pious seclusion in the Holy Place. The Franks stripped the Dome of the Rock of more than forty silver candelabra, each of them weighing 3,600 drams, and a great silver lamp weighing forty-four Syrian pounds, as well as a hundred and fifty smaller silver candelabra and more than twenty gold ones, and a great deal more booty. Refugees from Syria reached Baghdad in Ramadan, among them the qadi Abu Sa'd al-Hárawi. They told the caliph's ministers a story that wrung their hearts and brought tears to their eyes. On Friday they went to the Cathedral Mosque and begged for help, weeping so that their hearers wept with them as they described the sufferings of the Muslims in that Holy City: the men killed, the women and children taken prisoner, the homes pillaged. Because of the terrible hardships they had suffered, they were allowed to break the fast.

15. THE MUSLIM REACTION

The conquest of Jerusalem and the subsequent establishment of numerous Christian polities in the Holy Land were a catastrophe for the Islamic world. And in some cases, the popular reaction was much more noteworthy than the official one, as popular preachers, rallying around the notion of jihad, called on all Muslim believers to march against Jerusalem and expel the invaders. The first selection below, from the writings of Ibn al-Qalanisi (1073–1160), offers a first-hand account of one such popular reaction and the conflict that it created with established institutions. Yet these calls for holy war galvanized the Muslim world and played a critical role in the numerous counter-offensives that were launched against the Christian principalities. The most successful of these early attacks were carried out under the leadership of 'Imad ad-Din Zengi (r. 1127–46), the governor of Mosul. Zengi was an adept manipulator of the concept of jihad, parlaying it into impressive victories against his enemies, most notably the conquest of the County of Edessa in 1146. This would be the first crusader state to be retaken by Islamic forces. The second source below, from the Mesopotamian historian Ibn al-Athir (1160–1233), describes the conquest of Edessa and highlights Zengi's willingness to wage war against both Christians and Muslims who stood in his path.

Source: trans. E.J. Costello and Francesco Gabrieli, *Arab Historians of the Crusades*, ed. Francesco Gabrieli (Berkeley: University of California Press, 1969), 28–29, 50–53.

Call for Holy War, 1110

In Jumādā II 504 [November–December 1110] the sultan Ghiyāth ad-Dunya wa d-Din Muhammad ibn Malikshāh traveled from Hamadhān to Baghdad. Messengers and messages reached him there from Syria reporting on the situation there, the movements of the Franks after their retreat from the Euphrates, and events in Sidon, Ātharib, and the province of Aleppo. On the first Friday of sha'bān a Hashimite Sharif from Aleppo appeared in the Sultan's mosque at Baghdad, with a group of sufis, merchants and lawyers, and began to beseech aid for Syria. They made the preacher come down from the pulpit and then smashed it to pieces. They wept and groaned for the disaster that had befallen Islam with the arrival of the Franks, for the men who had died and the women and children who had been sold into slavery. They made such a commotion that the people could not offer the obligatory prayers. To calm them, the servers and imams promised, on the caliph's behalf, that troops would be sent to support Islam against the infidel. On the following Friday the men came back and repeated their noisy laments and cries for help, in the caliph's mosque. Not long after this the sultan's sister, who was the wife of the caliph, arrived in Baghdad from Isfahan, bringing a train of endless and indescribable splendor: jewels, rich furnishings, horses and trappings, clothes and equipage, slaves and pages, handmaids, and servants. The sharif's cries for help disturbed the gaiety and joyousness of the occasion. The caliph, the prince of the Faithful al-Mustazhir bi-llah, was extremely annoyed and wanted to arrest the offenders and punish them severely. But the Sultan intervened, pardoned the offenders and ordered the emirs and army commanders to return to their posts and prepare to march in the Holy War against the infidel enemies of God.

The Conquest of Edessa, 1144

On 6 Jumādā II of that year [1144] the atabeg 'Imad ad-Din Zengi ibn Aq Sunqūr seized from the Franks the city of Edessa and other forts in the Jazira. The Franks had penetrated far into this area, as far as Amid and Nusaibīn, Ras al-'Ain and ar-Raqqa. Their influence extended from near Mardin to the Euphrates, and covered Edessa, Sarūj, al-Bira, Sinn ibn 'Utaīr, Jamlin, al-Mu'azzar, Quradi, and other cities as well. All these and other regions west of the Euphrates belonged to Joscelin, the most famous of the Franks and the leader of their army by virtue of his valor and command of strategy. Zengi knew that if he made a direct attack on Edessa the Franks would concentrate there to defend it, and it was too well fortified to be an easy conquest. He moved to Diyār Bakr, to give the Franks the impression that his interests lay elsewhere and that he was in no position to attack their kingdom. When the Franks felt sure that he could not extract himself from the war he was fighting with the Artuqids and other princes at Diyār Bakr, and so felt safe from him, Joscelin left Edessa and crossed the Euphrates to move westwards. As soon as Zengi's spies informed him of this, he issued orders to his army to set out the next day for Edessa. His emirs were summoned to his presence, and he ordered food to be served. "No one," he said, "shall eat with me at this table unless he is prepared to hurl his lance with me tomorrow at the gates of Edessa." The only ones who dared to come forward were a solitary emir and a youth of humble birth whose bravery and prowess were known to all, for he had no equal in battle. The emir said to him, "What are you doing here?" but the atabeg [that is, Zengi] intervened: "Leave him, for his, I can see, is not a face that will be lagging behind me in battle."

The army set out and reached the walls of Edessa. Zengi was the first to charge the Franks, but the young man was at his side. A Frankish knight lunged at Zengi from the side, but the emir faced him and transfixed him with his lance, and Zengi was saved.

They besieged the city and attacked it for three weeks. Zengi made several assaults on it, and used sappers to mine the walls. He was straining every nerve in the struggle, for fear that the Franks should marshal their forces and march on him to relieve the fortress. Then the sappers undermined the wall and it collapsed, and Zengi took the city and besieged the citadel. The citizens and their goods were seized, the young taken captive, the men killed. But when Zengi inspected the city he liked it and realized that it would not be sound policy to reduce such a place to ruins. He therefore gave the order that his men should return every man, woman, and child to his home together with the goods and chattels looted from them. This was done in all but a very few cases, in which the captor had already left the camp. The city was restored to its former state, and Zengi installed a garrison to defend it. Then he received the surrender of Sarūj and other cities west of the Euphrates. The only exception was al-Bira, a strongly defended fort on the bank of the Euphrates. So he marched on it and besieged it, but it was well stocked and well guarded, and so after some time, as by God's will we shall describe, he lifted the siege.

It is said that a great authority on genealogies and biographies tells the following story: the king of Sicily sent a naval expedition that ravaged Tripoli in northern Africa. Now there was in Sicily a learned, God-fearing Muslim whom the king held in great respect, relying on his advice rather than that of his own priests and monks; so much so that the people used to say that the king was really a Muslim. One day, as the king was standing at a window overlooking the sea, he saw a small boat come into the harbor. The crew told him that his army had invaded Muslim territory, laid it waste and returned victorious. The Muslim sage was dozing at the king's side. The king said to him: "Did you hear what they said?" "No." "They told me that we have defeated the Muslims in Tripoli. What use is Muhammad now to his land and his people?" "He was not there," replied the old man, "he was at Edessa, which the Muslims have just taken." The Franks who were present laughed, but the king said, "'Do not laugh, for by God this man is incapable of speaking anything but the truth." And a few days later news came from the Franks in Syria that Edessa had been taken. Certain honest and godly men have told me that a holy man saw the dead Zengi in a dream and asked him, "How has God treated you?" and Zengi replied, "God has pardoned me, because I conquered Edessa."

16. RICHARD THE LIONHEART AND SALADIN

The conquest of Edessa was one of the many calamities that would befall the crusader states over the course of the twelfth century as the weight of Muslim arms began to whittle away at the Christian conquests. On 4 July 1187, the bulk of the crusader armies were wiped out at the Battle of Hattin, which left Jerusalem virtually defenseless. Over the next three months, Saladin (r. 1171–93), sultan of Egypt and Syria and the victor at Hattin, overwhelmed numerous crusader cities and fortifications, lightly defended as they now were. He crowned his conquests with the capitulation of Jerusalem itself on 2 October after a brief siege. The loss of Jerusalem was met with disbelief and dismay in the Latin West, which once again reacted to a major territorial loss by calling for another crusade. This Third Crusade was a gigantic enterprise led by three of the most powerful rulers of western Europe: Frederick Barbarossa, Holy Roman emperor and king of Germany (r. 1156–90); Philip Augustus, king of France (r. 1180–1223); and Richard the Lionheart, king of England (r. 1189–99). The crusade, which began with so much promise, quickly ran into trouble when Frederick Barbarossa drowned on the way to Jerusalem, throwing his army into panic, with the bulk of his forces either returning to Germany or being killed. The French and English contingents did not fare much better, as they fell to squabbling that led to Philip's returning to France just a few months after his arrival in the East—he departed on 31 July 1191. This left Richard to face off against Saladin. The interactions between the two men would later become the source of legend and chivalric romance. In the two sources below, the first

Muslim, the second Christian, we get a more accurate sense of their true relationship as they tried to reach a truce.

Sources: trans. E.J. Costello and Francesco Gabrieli, *Arab Historians of the Crusades*, ed. Francesco Gabrieli (Berkeley: University of California Press, 1969), 225–34; and H.G. Bohn, *The Chronicles of the Crusades* (London: Henry G. Bohn, 1848), 329–33.

Baha ad-Din on the Peace Negotiations

On 26 Ramadān [587; 17 October 1191] al-Malik al-ʿAdil [Saladin's brother] was on duty with the outposts when the king of England asked him to send over a messenger. He sent his secretary and favorite Ibn an-Nahhal, a fine young man. He met Richard at Yazūr, where the king had gone with a large detachment of infantry, which was now scattered over the plain. Richard had long private talks with him to discuss the peace, and Richard said, "I shall not break my word to my brother and my friend," meaning al-ʿAdil, and the secretary reported his words to al-Malik al-ʿAdil. He also sent a letter to the sultan, through an-Nahhāl, which said in effect, "I am to salute you, and tell you that the Muslims and Franks are bleeding to death, the country is utterly ruined and goods and lives have been sacrificed on both sides. The time has come to stop this. The points at issue are Jerusalem, the Cross [a piece of the True Cross captured by Saladin at Hattin], and the land. Jerusalem is for us an object of worship that we could not give up even if there were only one of us left. The land from here to beyond the Jordan must be consigned to us. The Cross, which is for you simply a piece of wood with no value, is for us of enormous importance. If the sultan will deign to return it to us, we shall be able to make peace and to rest from this endless labor."

When the sultan read this message he called his councilors of state and consulted them about his reply. Then he wrote, "Jerusalem is ours as much as yours; indeed it is even more sacred to us than it is to you, for it is the place from which our Prophet accomplished his nocturnal journey and the place where our community will gather [on the Day of Judgment]. Do not imagine that we can renounce it or vacillate on this point. The land was also originally ours, whereas you have only just arrived and have taken it over only because of the weakness of the Muslims living there at the time. God will not allow you to rebuild a single stone as long as the war lasts. As for the Cross, its possession is a good card in our hand and it cannot be surrendered except in exchange for something of outstanding benefit to all Islam." This reply was sent to Richard by the hand of his own messenger.

On 22 Ramadān [20 October] al-Malik al-ʿAdil sent for me, together with ʿAlām ad-Din Sulaimān ibn Jandar, Sabiq ad-Din of Shaizar, ʿIzz ad-Din ibn al-Muqaddam, and Husām ad-Din Bishara, and showed us the proposals that had been sent to the king of England by his messenger. He said that his plan was that he himself should marry the king's sister [Joanna of Sicily], whom Richard had brought with him from Sicily where she had been the wife of the late king. Her brother had taken her along with him when he had left Sicily. She would live in Jerusalem, and her brother was to give her the whole of Palestine that was in his hands: Acre, Jaffa, Ascalon, and the rest, while the sultan was to give al-'Adil all the parts of Palestine belonging to him and make him their king, in addition to the lands and fees he already held. Saladin was also to hand over the True Cross to the Franks. Villages and forts belonging to the Templars were to remain in their hands, Muslim and Frankish prisoners were to be freed, and the king of England was to return home by sea. In this way the problem was to be resolved.

Such were the proposals brought by al-'Adil's messenger to the king of England. Al-'Adil thought them feasible, and so he sent for us, and sent us with a message to that effect to the sultan, charging me to speak and the others to listen. We were to present the project to the sultan, and if he approved and thought it to the advantage of Islam we were to bear witness that he had authorized and approved the treaty, and if he disapproved we were to bear witness that negotiations had reached this point, and that the sultan had decided not to confirm them. When we came before the sultan I expounded the matter to him and read him the message, in the presence of the men I have already named. Saladin immediately approved the terms, knowing quite well that the king of England would never agree to them and they were only a trick and a practical joke on his part. Three times I repeated to him the formula of consent and Saladin replied "Yes," calling on those present to bear witness. Now that we were sure of his views we returned to al-'Adil and told him what had happened, and the others told him that I had repeated to Saladin the declaration that took effect from the oath taken by him, and that Saladin had insisted on authorizing it. In this way he firmly accepted the proposed terms.

On 13 Shawwāl [3 November], the arrival was announced of the prince of Sidon as ambassador from the marquis of Tyre [Conrad of Montserrat, a claimant to the crown of Jerusalem]. Conversations had already been held between us on several occasions, the essence of which was that the marquis and his men were tired of the Franks and of supporting them, and wanted to make common cause with us against them. This arose from a quarrel that had been blowing up between the marquis and the Frankish kings as a result of his marriage to the wife of King Guy's brother, a scandalous affair according to certain tenets of their faith. This led to a division of opinions, and the marquis, fearing for his life, took his wife and fled by night to Tyre. There he had begun to incline to the sultan, and made certain gestures of reconciliation toward him. The split between the marquis and the Franks was of advantage to the Muslims, for he was the strongest and most experienced of their generals, as well as a good governor. When the news of their ambassador's arrival reached the sultan he gave orders that he was to be treated with honor and respect. He had a tent erected for him, surrounded with an enclosure of cloth and containing as many cushions and carpets as are suitable when princes and kings meet. Saladin ordered that he should be shown to his quarters near the stores to rest, and then held a secret conference with him.

On 19 Shawwāl [9 November] the sultan gave an audience and summoned the prince of Sidon to hear his message and statement. He appeared with a whole group of companions—I was present at the audience—and Saladin treated him with great honor. He entered into conversation with him and had a sumptuous banquet served for them. After the meal he led them aside; their proposal was for the sultan to make peace with the marquis with whom various great Frankish lords had made common cause, among them the prince of Sidon himself and other distinguished persons. We have already stated his position. A condition of accepting his offer was that he should break openly with the Franks of Outremer, because of his great fear of them and because of the matter of his wife. The sultan appeared to be disposed to accept his proposal on certain conditions, by which he hoped to create discord among the Franks and to set them at loggerheads. Now, after listening to him, the sultan promised to give him a reply later, and the ambassador retired for the day to the tent erected for him.

That night an ambassador came from the king of England: the son of Humphrey, one of the great Frankish leaders and kings (in his train was an old man who was said to be a hundred years old). The sultan sent for him and listened to what he had to say. His message was, "The king says, 'your friendship and affection are dear to me. I told you that I would give these regions of Palestine to your brother, and I want you to be the judge between us in the division of the land. But we absolutely must have a foothold in Jerusalem. I want you to make a division that will not bring down on you the wrath of the Muslims, or on me the wrath of the Franks.'"

The sultan replied immediately with fine promises and allowed the messenger to return at once. He was impressed by the message. He sent someone after the ambassador to check on the matter of prisoners, which was treated separately from the terms of the peace. "If there is peace," he said, "it will be a general peace, and if there is no peace the matter of prisoners will be of no account." The sultan's real object was to undermine the foundations of peace on those terms. When the audience was at an end and the Franks had gone, he turned to me and said, "When we have made peace with them, there will be nothing to prevent their attacking us treacherously. If I should die the Muslims would no longer be able to muster an army like this and the Franks would have the upper hand. It is better to carry on the Holy War until we have expelled them from Palestine, or death overtakes us." This was his opinion, and he only moved toward peace in response to external pressures.

On 21 shawwāl [11 November] the sultan summoned his emirs and councilors and explained to them the terms of the agreement sought by the marquis, which for his part he was inclined to accept. The terms were that they should hand Sidon over to him in return for his military support against the Franks in open warfare. On the other hand, he was impressed by the terms proposed by king [Richard]—that either he should have certain points on the coast and we the mountain region, or we should divide the total number of settlements in half. In both cases the Franks stipulated that their priests should have the churches and oratories of Jerusalem, and the king of England left us to decide between the alternatives. Saladin explained the situation to the emirs and asked them to reveal their hearts to him and tell him which plan, the king's or the marquis's, seemed preferable to them, and if the former, which of the two divisions mentioned above, proposed by the king of England. The councilors held that peace must be made with the king, since it was improbable that Franks and Muslims would live amiably side by side, and they had no security against treacherous attacks.

So the treaty [with the marquis] came to nothing and the peace negotiations continued, ambassadors coming and going to settle the terms. A basic condition was that the king should give his sister in marriage to al-'Adil who would, as her husband, acquire the whole of Palestine, Muslim and Frankish, the Frankish regions from the princess's brother and the Muslim from al-'Adil's brother, the sultan. But the king's final message on this matter said, "The Christian people disapprove of my giving my sister in marriage without consulting the pope, the head and leader of Christianity. I have therefore sent a messenger who will be back in three months. If he authorizes this wedding, so much the better. If not, I will give you the hand of one of my nieces, for whom I shall not need papal consent." While all this was going on the hostilities continued and took their inevitable course.

The prince of Sidon sometimes went riding with al-'Adil, and they would go and inspect the Frankish positions. Every time the Franks saw him they would reiterate their offers of peace, for fear of an alliance between the Muslims and the marquis, and their strength of mind weakened. This continued until 25 shawwāl.

Yusuf, one of the prince of Sidon's pages, came from the marquis to seek peace from the Muslims. One of the conditions imposed by the sultan was that the marquis should undertake to fight his compatriots and to detach himself from them. The Frankish territories that he himself took after the peace were to be his, those taken by us alone were to be ours, and of those taken by both together, he should have the city and we the Muslim prisoners and whatever else the place contained. He was to release all the Muslim prisoners in his domains, and if the king of England should make him governor of the city by some agreement between them, peace between him and us should be based on the conditions laid down between us and the king of England, except for Ascalon and the region beyond, which should not be subject to the treaty. The coastal region was to be his and the region held by us, ours, and the area between was to be divided between us. The messenger left to carry these terms to the marquis [Conrad was assassinated before the conclusion of the truce].

[In Sha'ban 588 (late August 1192)] al-'Adil came to Jaffa and was lodged in a tent outside the city while the king was informed of his arrival. He was then sent for with the rest of the delegation, and presented the text of the treaty. The king, who was ill, said, "I have not the strength to read it now. But I agree to the peace, and here is my hand on it." The Muslim delegates conferred with Count Henry [of Champagne] and Ibn Barzah [Balian of Ibelin] and submitted the document to them. They accepted the division of Lydda and Ramla, and everything else in the text. They agreed to take the oath on Wednesday morning, as they had already eaten that day and it is not their custom to take an oath after they have broken their fast. Al-'Adil sent the news to the sultan.

On Wednesday 22 Sha'bān [2 September] the whole Muslim delegation was conducted into the king's presence. They took his hand and meant to take the oath with him, but he excused himself, saying that kings do not take oaths, and the sultan was content with this declaration. So they took the oath at the hands of Count Henry, and his nephew, whom he [Richard] had made ruler of Palestine, and of Balian ibn Barzan, lord of Tiberias, with the agreement of the Templars, the Hospitallers, and other Frankish leaders. In the course of that day they returned to the sultan's tent and joined him for the evening prayer, accompanied from the Frankish side by Humphrey's son, Ibn Barzan, and a group of their generals. They were received with great honor and a tent worthy of them was erected. Al-'Adil presented his report to the sultan. Next day, 23 sha'bān, the king's ambassador presented himself to the sultan, took his noble hand and undertook to keep the peace on the terms laid down. They proposed that oaths to this effect should be sworn by al-Malik al-'Adil, al-Malik al-Afdal, al-Malik az-Zahir, 'Ali ibn Ahmad al-Mash-tūb, Badr ad-Din Yildirīm, al-Malik al-Mansūr, and all the rulers whose territories bordered on those of the Franks, such as Ibn al-Muqaddam of Shaizar. The sultan for his part promised that he would send a messenger with them to all their neighbors to extract the oath from them. The king's ambassador also took the oath on behalf of the prince of Antioch and Tripoli, on condition that the Muslims did the same on behalf of the other Muslims. If not, the treaty was annulled. Then the sultan ordered a proclamation to be issued to all military camps and markets stating that a general peace extended over the whole territory and that unrestricted coming and going was permitted between their land and ours. He also proclaimed that the route of the pilgrimage through Syria was open and expressed his intention of going on the pilgrimage himself, an idea that occurred to him when I was with him. He also sent a hundred sappers under the command of a great emir to break down the walls of Ascalon and to enable the Franks to evacuate it. A Frankish delegation was to accompany them until the walls were down, for fear that we should leave them standing.

It was a memorable day, one on which the two sides expressed unimaginable joy and happiness. But it is well known that the peace did not entirely please the sultan. In conversation with me he said, "I am afraid of making peace. I do not know what might happen to me, and the enemy would gain strength from my death because these lands are still in their hands. They would take the opportunity of attacking us and recovering the rest. You see how each of them is perched on his own hilltop," meaning their forts; and he concluded, "As soon as I am gone, the Muslims will be destroyed."

These were his words, and it happened just as he said. Yet he felt that the peace was a good thing in that the army was tired and openly hostile [to a continuation of the war]. It was indeed a good thing, as God in his prescience knew, for Saladin died soon afterward, and if he had died during a campaign Islam would have been in danger. Peace was therefore an act of divine providence and a fortunate occurrence for Islam.

Geoffrey de Vinsauf on the Peace Negotiations

27. How the king wished to return to Acre to be cured, but, on the people opposing it, he asked of Saladin a truce for three years, which was granted—In the meantime the king began to be anxious about his health, and after long reflection he sent for his relation Count Henry [of Champagne], with the Templars and Hospitallers, to whom he explained the enfeebled state of his body, and protested that in consequence of the vitiated atmosphere, and the bad state of the fortifications, he must immediately leave the place. He then appointed some of them to go and take charge of Ascalon, and to others to guard Joppa, while he went himself to Acre to be cured, as was now absolutely necessary for him. To this proposition they all with one heart and one voice made objection, saying, that they could not possibly guard Joppa or any other fortress after he was gone and persisting in this refusal, they kept aloof, and no longer acted in concert with the king. Richard was vexed and embarrassed by this conduct, and it gave him the most bitter pain that none of them sympathized with his intentions or wishes. He then began to waver as to what he should do, but in all his deliberations he came only to the same conclusion, that there was none of them to sympathize with his misfortunes. Seeing, then, that all left him, and that none took the slightest interest in the common cause, he ordered a proclamation to be made that whoever wished to receive the king's pay should come together to give him their help. At once two thousand footmen and fifty knights came forward. But the king's health now began to get so bad, that he despaired of getting any better. Thus, in his anxiety both for the others and for himself, he thought it best, of all the plans which suggested themselves, to ask a truce, rather than to leave the land a prey to devastation, as many others had done, by sailing home in numbers to their own country. Thus the king, perplexed and hesitating what he had best do, requested Saphadin, the brother of Saladin, to mediate between them, and obtain the most honorable terms of truce in his power. Now Saphadin was a man of extraordinary liberality, who on many occasions paid great honor to the king for his singular virtues; and he now with great zeal procured for Richard a truce on the following conditions; namely, that Ascalon, which had always been a cause of annoyance to Saladin's government, should be destroyed, and not rebuilt for the space of at least three years, beginning at the following festival of Easter; but at the end of that time, whoever could get possession of it might fortify it; that the Christians should be allowed to inhabit Joppa without let or molestation, together with all the adjoining country, both on the seacoast and in the mountains; that peace should strictly be observed between the Christians and Saracens, each having free leave to come and go wherever they pleased; that pilgrims should have free access to the Holy Sepulcher, without any payment or monetary exaction whatever, and with leave to carry merchandise for sale through the whole land, and to practice commercial pursuits without opposition. This treaty was presented in writing to King Richard, who gave it his approval, for in his weak condition, and having so few troops about him, and that too within two miles of the enemy, he did not think it in his power to secure more favorable terms. Whoever entertains a different opinion concerning this treaty, I would have him know that he will expose himself to the charge of perversely deviating from the truth.

28. How the king and Saladin corresponded amiably with one another by means of messengers—When therefore the king, in his present emergency, had settled matters in the way described, he, in his magnanimity, which always aimed at something lowly and difficult, sent ambassadors to Saladin, announcing to him, in the presence of numerous of his chiefs, that he had only asked for a truce of three years for the purpose of revisiting his country, and collecting more men and money, and then to return and rescue all the land of Jerusalem from his domination, if indeed Saladin should have the courage to face him in the field. To this Saladin replied, calling his own Holy Law and God Almighty to witness, that he entertained such an exalted opinion of King Richard's honor, magnanimity, and general excellence, that he would rather lose his dominions to him than to any other king he had ever seen, always supposing that he was obliged to lose his dominions at all. Alas! How blind are men, while they lay plans for many years to come, they know not what tomorrow may bring forth. The king's mind was looking forward into the future, and he hoped to recover the sepulcher of our Lord; but he did not....

30. How the French, by the king's agency, for their malice, were forbidden to visit the Holy Sepulcher, while the others had permission—In the meantime the French, who had been long enjoying a holiday at Acre, were getting ready to return home; but though they had venomously opposed the truce, they now, before leaving the country, wished to complete their pilgrimage by visiting our Lord's sepulcher. The king, remembering their refusal to assist him at Joppa, as we have related, and also on many other occasions, sent messengers to request that neither Saladin nor Saphadin, his brother, would allow anyone to visit the Holy Sepulcher who did not bring a passport from either himself or Count Henry. The French were much vexed at this, and foiled of their object, soon afterwards returned to their own country, carrying back nothing with them but the reproach of ingratitude. The king, hearing that the greater part of the French who did their utmost to defame him were gone home, and that the mouths of his slanderers were stopped, caused it to be announced by proclamation, that whoever wished might visit our Lord's tomb, and bring back their offerings to help in repairing the walls of Joppa.

31. Of the first company who made the pilgrimage to Jerusalem, led by Andrew de Chavegui, and of the alarm occasioned by their indiscretion on the way—The people were now arrayed to visit Jerusalem in three companies, each of which was placed under a separate leader. The first was led by Andrew de Chavegui; the second by Ralph Teissun; and the third by Hubert, bishop of Salisbury. The first company then advanced under Andrew bearing letters from the king. But, for their sins, they fell into a snare on the journey; for when they reached the Plain of Ramula, they by common consent dispatched messengers to inform Saladin that they were coming with letters from King Richard, and that they wished to have a safe-conduct, coming and going. The messengers were noble men, and energetic in character, but on this occasion they rightfully incurred the charge of neglecting their duty. Their names were William des Roches, Girard de Tourneval, and Peter de Pratelles. When they came to "the Tower of the Soldier" they halted there to procure the authority of Saphadin for proceeding further; but there they fell asleep, and slept till sunset, and found on awaking that all the pilgrims, on whose behalf they came, had passed by and were gone on before them. The whole number crossed the plains and were approaching the hills, when Andrew de Chavegui and the rest, looking behind them, saw their own messengers coming after them as fast as they were able. Seeing this, they halted in much alarm, considering that they were in great danger of being put to death, for the army of the Turks had not yet departed, and their messengers, who ought to have brought back for them a safe-conduct from the Saracens, were now behind them. When therefore these came up, the others blamed them for their neglect, and told them once more to make haste on before, and do as they had been instructed. The messengers went on with all speed to Jerusalem, and found about 2,000 Turks, or more, encamped without the city. They inquired for Saphadin, and when they had found him, they explained what had happened, and he, rebuking them smartly, said it was evident that they did not value their lives, as they had come into the middle of a hostile army without passport or safeguard of any kind. It was now sunset, and the other pilgrims came up, not knowing what they ought to do, and having no arms to defend themselves. The Turks grinned and frowned on them as they passed, and it was manifest by their looks what enmity they harbored in their hearts, for the face is the window of the mind; and our men at that moment were so confounded that they wished themselves back again at Tyre, or even Acre, which they had just left. Thus they passed the night, near a certain mountain, in a state of great alarm.

32. How the Turks wished to take vengeance on our pilgrims, but Saladin and his chiefs would not allow it—The next day certain of the Turks appeared before Saladin, and earnestly entreated of him that they might be allowed to take vengeance on the Christians who were now in their power, for the death of their friends, fathers, brothers, sons, and relations who had been slain, first at Acre, and afterwards at other places, now, as they said, that they had so good an opportunity. Saladin sent for the Turkish chiefs to consult about this request, and Mestoc, Saphadin, Bedridin, and Dorderin were speedily in attendance. When the subject was placed before them, it was their unanimous opinion that the Christians should have leave to come and go, without injury or hindrance. "For," said they to Saladin, "it would be a deep stain upon our honor, if the treaty which has been made between you and the king of England should, by our interference, be broken, and the faith of the Turks for ever afterwards be called in question." In consequence of these observations, Saladin gave orders immediately that the Christians should be taken care of, and escorted to the city and back again without molestation. To discharge this commission, Spahadin was at his own request deputed; and under his protection the pilgrims had free access to the Holy Sepulcher, and were treated with the greatest liberality, after which they returned joyfully to Acre.

17. THE SEVENTH CRUSADE

The failure of numerous crusades in the early decades of the thirteenth century to reach Jerusalem did not deter subsequent crusading. In 1228, for example, Fredrick II, Holy Roman emperor, was able to negotiate the return of Jerusalem to Christian hands as part of a ten-year truce. The expiration of the truce and repeated infighting among the Christian nobility in the Holy Land led to the conquest of the city by the Khorezmians. Two months later, the Khorezmians and their Egyptian allies destroyed a large Christian army with a sizeable contingent of Muslim allies from Syria at the Battle of Harbiyah (La Forbie). The loss of Jerusalem once again prompted a call for crusade in Europe, and this time it was answered by Louis IX, the king of France (r. 1226–70). Louis's crusade (the Seventh) would begin well enough for the Christians with the conquest of Damietta in Egypt, but subsequent advances into the Egyptian interior, as well as an outbreak of dysentery, cost the Christians dearly; on 6 April, Louis and the bulk of his army were captured as they retreated to Damietta. While the Christians were in captivity, the sultan of Egypt, Turanshah (r. 1249–50), was overthrown by his own slave soldiers, known as Mamluks. The Mamluks now made themselves the rulers of Egypt and negotiated with Louis for his release and that of his men. On 6 May, after paying the massive sum of £400,000 and returning Damietta, Louis and his men were freed. Upon his release, Louis set sail for the Frankish principalities in the Holy Land, where he stayed for a further four years, stabilizing their military and political situation, before returning to France in 1254. The first source is by the Egyptian historian al-Makrisi and describes most of the important events discussed here, including the arrival and defeat of Louis and his crusaders and the emergence of the Mamluks. The second source, by Jean de Joinville, is one of the most famous sources of the crusades. Joinville, a French crusader and close friend of Louis IX, was an active participant in the events he described. His chronicle offers a more personal and intimate retelling of the events than al-Makrisi, who wrote over a century after the events occurred.

Sources: trans. Colonel Johnes, in *Chronicles of the Crusades: Being Contemporary Narratives of the Crusade of Richard Coeur de Lion by Richard of Devizes and Geoffrey de Vinsauf; and of the Crusade of Saint Louis by Lord John de Joinville* (London: Henry G. Bohn, 1848), 542–54 (for al-Makrisi); 415–19, 421–27, 431–41 (for Joinville); rev. Jarbel Rodriguez.

Al-Makrisi

On Friday, the 21st of the moon Safar, and in the year of the Hegira 647 [4 June 1249], the French fleet arrived off the coast, at two o'clock of the day, filled with an innumerable body of troops under the command of Louis [IX], son to Louis, king of France. The Franks, who were masters of Syria, had joined the French. The whole fleet anchored on the strand opposite to the camp of Fakhr ad-Din.

The king of France, before he commenced any hostilities, sent by a herald a letter to the sultan Najm al-Din, conceived in the following words: "You are not ignorant that I am the prince of those who follow the religion of Jesus Christ, as you are of those who obey the laws of Muhammad. Your power inspires me with no fear. How should it? I who make the Muslims in Spain tremble! I lead them as a shepherd does a flock of sheep. I have made the bravest among them perish, and loaded their women and children with chains. They endeavor by presents to appease me, and turn my arms to another quarter. The soldiers who march under my standards cover the plains, and my cavalry is not less redoubtable. You have but one method to avoid the tempest that threatens you. Receive priests, who will teach you the Christian religion; embrace it, and adore the Cross. Otherwise I will pursue you everywhere, and God shall decide whether you or I be master of Egypt."

Najm ad-Din, on reading this letter, could not restrain his tears. He caused the following answer to be written by the qadi Behaedin, his secretary: "In the name of the Omnipotent and All-merciful God, salvation to our prophet Muhammad and his friends! I have received your letter; it is filled with menaces, and you make a boast of the great number of your soldiers. Are you ignorant that we know the use of arms, and that we inherit the valor of our ancestors? No one has ever attacked us without feeling our superiority. Recollect the conquests we have made from the Christians; we have driven them from the lands they possessed; their strongest towns have fallen under our blows. Recall to your mind that passage of the Quran, which says, 'Those who make war unjustly shall Perish,' and also another passage, 'How often have the most numerous armies been destroyed by a handful of soldiers!' God protects the just, and we have no doubt of his protection, nor that he will confound your arrogant designs."

The French disembarked on the Saturday, on the same shore where Fakhr ad-Din had made his encampment, and pitched a red tent for their king. The Muslims made some movements to prevent their landing; and the emirs Najm al-Din [not the sultan] and Sarim ad-Din were slain in these skirmishes.

At the beginning of the night, the emir Fakhr ad-Din decamped with his whole army, and crossed the bridge which leads to the eastern shore of the Nile, whereon Damietta is situated. He took the road to Achmoum-Tanah, and by this march, the French were left masters of the western bank of that river.

It is impossible to paint the despair of the inhabitants of Damietta when they saw the emir Fakhr ad-Din march away from their town, and abandon them to the fury of the Christians. They were afraid to wait for the enemy, and quitted their town precipitously during the night. This conduct of the Muslim general was so much the less excusable as the garrison was composed of the bravest of the tribe of Beni-Kénané, and as Damietta was in a better state of resistance than when it was besieged by the Franks during the reign of the sultan al-Malik al-Kamel [sultan of Egypt during the Fifth Crusade when Damietta was also attacked]; for, although plague and famine afflicted the town, the Franks could not conquer it until after sixteen months' siege.

On the Monday morning [6 June 1249], the French came before the town; but, astonished to see no one, they were afraid of a surprise. They were soon informed of the flight of its inhabitants, and, without striking a blow, took possession of this important place, and all the ammunition and provision they found there.

When the news of the capture of Damietta reached Cairo, the consternation was general. They considered how greatly this success would augment the courage and hopes of the French; for they had seen an army of Muslims timorously fly before them, and were in possession of an innumerable quantity of arms of all sorts, with plenty of ammunition and provision. The disorder of the sultan, which daily grew worse, and hindered him from acting in this critical state of affairs, overwhelmed the Egyptians with despair. No one any longer doubted but that the kingdom would be conquered by the Christians.

The sultan, indignant at the cowardice of the garrison, ordered fifty of the principal officers to be strangled. In vain did they allege in their defense the retreat of the emir Fakhr ad-Din. The sultan told them they deserved death, for having quitted Damietta without his orders. One of these officers, condemned to death with his son, requested to be executed first; but the sultan refused him this favor, and the father had the misery to see his son expire before his eyes.

After this execution, the sultan, turning to the emir Fakhr ad-Din, asked with an enraged tone, "What resistance have you made? What battles have you fought? You could not withstand the Franks one hour. You should have shown more courage and firmness." The officers of the army, fearing for Fakhr ad-Din the rage of the sultan, made the emir understand by their gestures that they were ready to massacre their sovereign. Fakhr ad-Din refused his assent, and told them afterward that the sultan could not live more than a few days; and that, if the prince wished to trouble them, they were able at any time to get rid of him.

Najm ad-Din, notwithstanding his melancholy state, gave orders for his departure for Mansourah. He entered his boat of war, and arrived there on Wednesday the 25th of the moon Safar [9 June 1249]. He put the town in a posture of defense by employing his whole army on this service. The boats ordered by the prince before his departure arrived laden with soldiers, and all sorts of ammunition. Everyone able to bear arms ranged himself under his standards, and he was joined by the Arabs in great numbers. While the sultan was making his preparations, the French were adding new fortifications to Damietta, and filling it with a considerable garrison.

On Monday, the last day of the moon Rebiulewel [Rabī I; 12 July 1249], thirty-six Christian prisoners were conducted to Cairo; they had belonged to the guard of the camp against the inroads of the Arabs, among whom were two knights. The 5th of the same moon, thirty-seven were sent thither; on the 7th, twenty-two; and on the 16th, forty-five other prisoners, and among these last were three knights.

Different Christian princes, who held lands on the coast of Syria, had accompanied the French. As a result, their own castles and towns were weakened. The inhabitants of Damascus seized this opportunity to besiege Sidon, which, after some resistance, was forced to surrender. The news of this, when carried to Cairo, caused an excess of joy, and seemed to compensate for the loss of Damietta. Prisoners were made almost daily from the French, fifty of whom were sent to Cairo on the 18th of the moon Diemazilewel [Jumādā I; 29 August 1249].

The sultan continued daily to grow worse in health and the physicians despaired of his recovery, for he was attacked at the same time by a fistula and an ulcer in his lungs. At length he expired, on the night of the 15th of the moon Sha'bān [22 November 1249], after having appointed as his successor his son Turanshah. Najm al-Din was forty-four years old when he died, and had reigned ten years. It was he who instituted that militia of slaves, or of Mamluks, thus called from being quartered in the castle which this prince had built in the island of Roudah, opposite to old Cairo. This militia, in the course of time, seized the throne of Egypt.

As soon as the sultan had expired, the sultana Shajar al-Durr, his spouse, sent for the general Fakhr ad-Din and the eunuch Jamal ad-Din, to inform them of the death of the sultan, and to request their assistance in supporting the weight of government at such a critical period. All three resolved to keep the sultan's death a secret, and to act in his name as if he were alive. His death was not to be made public until after the arrival of Turanshah, to whom were sent messengers after messengers.

Notwithstanding these precautions, the French were informed of his death. Their army instantly quitted the plains of Damietta, and encamped at Fariskour. Boats laden with provision and stores came up the Nile, and kept the army abundantly supplied.

The emir Fakhr ad-Din sent a letter to Cairo, to inform the inhabitants of the approach of the French, and to exhort them to sacrifice their lives and fortunes in the defense of the country. This letter was read in the pulpit of the great mosque, and the people answered only with sighs and groans. Everything was in trouble and confusion and the death of the sultan, which was suspected, added to the consternation. The most cowardly thought of quitting a town which they believed unable to withstand the French but the more courageous, on the contrary, marched to Mansourah, to join the Muslim army.

On Tuesday, the 1st day of the moon Ramadān [7 December 1249], there were some trifling skirmishes between different corps of troops of each army. This, however, did not prevent the French army from encamping at Charmesah: the Monday following, being the 7th of the same moon, the army advanced to Bermoun.

On Sunday, the 13th day of the same moon, the Christian army appeared before the town of Mansourah; the branch of the Achmoum was between it and the Egyptian camp. Nasir Dawud, prince of Kerak, was on the western bank of the Nile with some troops. The French laid out their camp, surrounding it with a deep ditch surmounted by a palisade, and erected machines to cast stones at the Egyptian army. Their fleet arrived at the same time, so that there were engagements on water and on land.

On Wednesday, the 15th day of the same moon, six deserters passed over to the camp of the Muslims, and informed them that the French army was in want of provision.

On [6 January 1250] a great lord, and relation to the king of France, was made prisoner. Not a day passed without skirmishes on both sides, and with alternate success. The Muslims were particularly anxious to make prisoners, to gain information as to the state of the enemy's army, and used all sorts of stratagems for this purpose. A soldier from Cairo bethought himself of putting his head inside of a watermelon, with the interior scooped out, and of thus swimming toward the French camp. A Christian soldier, not suspecting a trick, leaped into the Nile to seize the melon, but the Egyptian was a stout swimmer, and catching hold of him, dragged him to his general.

On Wednesday, the 7th day of the moon Shawwāl [12 January 1250], the Muslims captured a large boat, in which were a hundred soldiers, commanded by an officer of distinction. On Thursday, the 15th of the same moon, the French marched out of their camp, and their cavalry began to move. The troops were ordered to file off, when a slight skirmish took place, and the French left on the field forty knights with their horses.

On the Friday, seventy prisoners were conducted to Cairo, among whom were three lords of rank. On the 22nd of the same moon, a large boat belonging to the French took fire. This was considered as a fortunate omen for the Muslims.

Some traitors having shown the ford over the canal of Achmoum to the French, fourteen hundred knights crossed it, and fell unexpectedly on the camp of the Muslims, on a Tuesday, the 5th day of the moon Zilkalde [Dhū al Qa'da; 8 February 1250], having at their head the brother of the king of France. The emir Fakhr ad-Din was at the time in the bath: he instantly quitted it with precipitation, and mounted a horse without saddle or bridle, followed only by some slaves. The enemy attacked him on all sides, but his slaves, like cowards, abandoned him when in the midst of the French: it was in vain he attempted to defend himself; he fell pierced with wounds. The French, after the death of Fakhr ad-Din, retreated to Djédilé, but their whole cavalry advanced to Mansourah, and, having forced one of the gates, entered the town with the Muslims fleeing to the right and left. The king of France had already penetrated as far as the sultan's palace, and victory seemed assured, when the Mamluk slaves, led by Baibars, advanced, and snatched it from his hands. Their charge was so furious that the French were obliged to retreat. The French infantry, during this time, had advanced to cross the bridge. Had they been able to join their cavalry, the defeat of the Egyptian army, and the loss of the town of Mansourah, would have been inevitable.

Night separated the combatants, when the French retreated in disorder to Djédilé, after leaving fifteen hundred of their men on the field. They surrounded their camp with a ditch and wall, but their army was divided into two corps. The smaller company was encamped on the branch of the Achmoum, and the larger on the great branch of the Nile that runs to Damietta.

A pigeon had been let loose to fly to Cairo the instant the French had surprised the camp of Fakhr ad-Din with a note under its wing to inform the inhabitants of this misfortune. This melancholy event had created a general consternation in the town, which the runaways had augmented, and the gates of Cairo were kept open all the night to receive them. A second pigeon bearing the news of the victory over the French had restored tranquility to the capital. Joy succeeded sorrow; and each congratulated the other on this happy turn of affairs, and public rejoicings were made.

When Turanshah heard of the death of his father, Najm ad-Din, he set out from Huns-Keifa. It was the 15th of the moon Ramadān [22 December 1249] when he departed, attended by only fifty horsemen, and he arrived at Damascus toward the end of that moon. After receiving the homage of all the governors of the towns in Syria, he set out on a Wednesday, the 27th day of the moon Shawwāl [2 February 1250], and took the road to Egypt. The news of his arrival raised the courage of the Muslims. The death of Najm ad-Din had not yet been publicly announced. The service of the sultan was performed as usual. His officers prepared his table as if he had been alive, and every order was given in his name. The sultana governed the kingdom, and found, in her own mind, resources for all. The moment she heard of Turanshah's arrival, she waited on him, and laid aside the sovereign command, to invest him with it. This prince was anxious to appear at the head of his troops, and set out for Mansourah, where he arrived on the 5th of the moon Zilkadé [Dhū al-Qa'da; 8 February 1250].

Boats sent from Damietta brought all sorts of provision to the French camp, and kept it abundantly supplied. The Nile was now at its greatest height. Turanshah caused many boats to be built, which were then disassembled, placed on the backs of camels, and carried to the canal of Méhalé. There they were put together again, launched on the canal, and filled with troops for an ambush.

As soon as the French fleet of boats appeared at the mouth of the canal of Méhalé, the Muslims left their hiding-place and attacked them. While the two fleets were engaged, other boats left Mansourah filled with soldiers, and fell on the rear of the French. They sought in vain to escape by flight; a thousand Christians were killed or made prisoners.

In this defeat, fifty-two of their boats laden with provision were taken, and their communication with Damietta by the navigation of the Nile was cut off, so that within a short time the whole army suffered the most terrible famine. The Muslims surrounded them on all sides, and they could neither advance nor retreat.

On the 1st of the moon Zilhijé [Dhū al-Hijja; 7 March 1250], the French surprised seven boats, but the troops on board had the good fortune to escape. In spite of the superiority of the Egyptians on the Nile, the French attempted to bring up another convoy from Damietta, but they lost it; thirty-two of their boats were taken and carried to Mansourah, on the 9th of the same moon. This new loss filled the measure of their woes, and caused them to propose a truce and send ambassadors to treat of it with the sultan. The emir Zeineddin and the qadi [judge] Bedreddin were ordered to meet and confer with them, when the French offered to surrender Damietta, on condition that Jerusalem, and some other places in Syria, should be given in exchange for it. This proposal was rejected, and the conferences broken up.

On Friday, the 27th of the moon Zilhijé [Dhū al-Hijja; 1 April 1250], the French set fire to all their machines of war and timber for building, and rendered almost all their boats unfit for use. During the night of Tuesday, the 3rd day of the moon Mahasem [Muharram; 5 April 1250], in the year of the Hegira 648, the whole of the French army decamped, and took the road to Damietta. Some boats which they had reserved fell down the Nile at the same time. The Muslims having perceived the retreat of the French, pursued and attacked them at daybreak on Wednesday.

The main combat took place at Fariskur. The French were defeated and put to flight. Ten thousand of their men fell on the field of battle; some say thirty thousand. Upwards of one hundred thousand horsemen, infantry, trades-people, and others, were made slaves. The booty was immense in horses, mules, tents, and other riches. There were but one hundred slain on the side of the Muslims. The Mamluk slaves, under the command of Baibars performed great acts of valor in this battle. The king of France had retired, with a few of his lords, to a small hillock, and surrendered himself, under promise of his life being spared, to the eunuch Djemaddelin Mahsun-Elsalihi. He was bound with a chain, and in this state conducted to Mansourah, where he was confined in the house of Ibrahim-ben Lokman, secretary to the sultan, and under the guard of the eunuch Sahil. The king's brother [either Charles of Anjou or Alfonse of Poitiers] was made prisoner at the same time, and carried to the same house. The sultan provided for their subsistence.

The number of slaves was so great, it was embarrassing, and the sultan gave orders to Seifeddin Jousef-ben-tardi to put them to death. Every night this cruel minister had from three to four hundred of the prisoners brought from their places of confinement, and, after he had caused them to be beheaded, had their bodies thrown into the Nile. In this manner perished one hundred thousand of the French.

The sultan departed from Mansourah, and went to Fariskur, where he had pitched a most magnificent tent. He had also built a tower of wood over the Nile and, being freed from a disagreeable war, he there gave himself up to all sorts of debauchery.

The victory he had just gained was so brilliant that he was eager to make all who were subjected to him acquainted with it. He wrote with his own hand a letter in the following terms, to the emir Djemal Edden-ben-Jagmour, governor of Damascus:

Thanks be given to the All-powerful, who has changed our grief to joy. It is to him alone we owe the victory. The favors he has condescended to shower upon us are innumerable, but this last is most precious. You will announce to the people of Damascus, or rather to all Muslims, that God has enabled us to gain a complete victory over the Christians, who were conspiring our ruin.

On Monday, the first day of this year, we opened our treasury, and distributed riches and arms to our faithful soldiers. We had called to our succor the Arabian tribes, and a numberless multitude of soldiers ranged themselves under our standards. On the nights between Tuesday and Wednesday, our enemies abandoned their camp with all their baggage, and marched towards Damietta. In spite of the obscurity of the night, we pursued them, and thirty thousand of them were left dead on the field, not including those who threw themselves into the Nile. We have beside slain our very numerous prisoners, and thrown their bodies into the same river. Their king had retreated to Meniat. He has implored our clemency, and we have granted him his life, and paid him all the honors due to his rank. We have regained Damietta.

The sultan, with this letter, sent the king's cap, which had fallen in the combat. It was of scarlet, lined with a fine fur. The governor of Damascus put the king's cap on his own head when he read to the public the sultan's letter. A poet made these verses on the occasion: "The cap of the French was whiter than paper. Our sabers have dyed it with the blood of the enemy, and have changed its color."

The gloomy and retired life the sultan led had irritated the minds of his people. He had no confidence but in a certain number of favorites, whom he had brought with him from Huns-Keifa, and whom he had invested with the principal offices of the state, in the room of the ancient ministers of his father. Above all, he showed a decided hatred to the Mamluks, although they had contributed so greatly to the last victory. His debaucheries exhausted his revenue, and, to supply the deficiencies, he forced the sultana Shajar al-Durr to render him an account of the riches of his father. The sultana, in alarm, implored the protection of the Mamluks, representing to them the services she had done the state in very difficult times, and the ingratitude of Turanshah, who was indebted to her for the crown he wore. These slaves, already irritated against Turanshah, did not hesitate to take the side of the sultana, and resolved to assassinate the prince. To execute this design, they fixed on the moment when he was at table; Baibars gave him the first blow with his saber, and, though he parried it with his hand, he lost his fingers. He then fled to the tower which he had built on the banks of the Nile, and which was but a short distance from his tent. The conspirators followed him, and, finding he had closed the door, set fire to it. The whole army saw what was occurring; but, as he was a prince universally detested, no one came forward in his defense.

It was in vain that he cried from the top of the tower, that he would abdicate his throne, and return to Huns-Keifa; the assassins were inflexible. The flames at length gaining on the tower, he attempted to leap into the Nile, but his dress caught as he was falling, and he remained some time suspended in the air. In this state, he received many wounds from sabers, and then fell into the river, where he was drowned. Thus, iron, fire, and water contributed to put an end to his life. His body continued three days on the bank of the Nile, without any one daring to bury it. At length, the ambassador from the caliph of Baghdad obtained permission and had it buried.

This cruel prince when he ascended the throne, had his brother, Adil Shah, strangled. Four Mamluk slaves had been ordered to execute this, but the fratricide did not long remain unpunished, and these same four slaves were the most bitter in putting him to death. With this prince was extinguished the dynasty of the Ayyubids, that had governed Egypt eighty years, under eight different kings.

After the massacre of Turanshah, the sultana Shajar al-Durr was declared sovereign of Egypt. She was the first slave who had reigned over this country. This princess was a Turk, but others said an Armenian. The sultan Najm al-Din had bought her, and loved her so desperately that he carried her with him to his wars, and never left her. She had a son by the sultan, called Khalil, but he died very young. The emir Aseddin-Aibegh, of the Turcoman nation, was appointed general of the army, and the name of the sultana was imprinted on the coin.

The emir Abū 'Alī was nominated to treat with the king of France for his ransom, and for the surrender of Damietta. After many conferences and disputes, it was agreed that the French should evacuate Damietta, and that the king, and all prisoners in Egypt, should be set at liberty, on condition of paying down one half of such ransom as should be agreed on. The king of France sent orders to the governor of Damietta to surrender that town, but he refused to obey, and new orders were necessary. At last, it was given up to the Muslims, after having remained eleven months in the hands of the enemy. The king paid four hundred thousand pieces of gold, as well for his own ransom as for that of the queen, his brother, and the other lords that had accompanied him.

All the Franks that had been made prisoners during the reigns of the sultans al-Kamil, Najm al-Din and Turanshah, obtained their liberty. They numbered twelve thousand one hundred men and ten women. The king, with all the French, crossed to the westward branch of the Nile, and embarked on a Saturday for Acre.

Jean de Joinville

All of us now galloped straight to Mansourah, and were in the midst of the Turkish army, when we were instantly separated from each other by the greater power of the Saracens and Turks. Shortly after, a sergeant at mace of the constable, with whom I was, came to him, and said the king was surrounded by the Turks, and his person in imminent danger. You may suppose our astonishment and fears, for there were between us and where the king was full one thousand or twelve hundred Turks, and we were only six persons in all. I said to the constable, that since it was impossible for us to make our way through such a crowd of Turks, it would be much better to wheel round and get on the other side of them. This we instantly did. There was a deep ditch on the road we took between the Saracens and us, and, had they noticed us, they must have slain us all, but they were solely occupied with the king, and the larger bodies. Perhaps also they might have taken us for some of their friends. As we thus gained the river, following its course downward between it and the road, we observed that the king had ascended it, and that the Turks were sending fresh troops after him. Both armies now met on the banks, and the event was miserably unfortunate, for the weaker part of our army thought to cross over to the division of the duke of Burgundy, but that was impossible from their horses being worn down, and the extreme heat of the weather. As we descended the river, we saw it covered with lances, pikes, shields, men, and horses unable to save themselves from death.

When we perceived the miserable state of our army, I advised the constable to remain on this side of the river, to guard a small bridge that was hard by, "for if we leave it," I added, "the enemy may come and attack the king on this side, and if our men be assaulted in two places, they must be discomfited."

There then we halted, and you may believe me when I say, that the good king performed that day the most gallant deeds that ever I saw in any battle. It was said, that had it not been for his personal exertions, the whole army would have been destroyed. But I believe that the great courage he naturally possessed was that day doubled by the power of God, for he forced himself wherever he saw his men in any distress, and gave such blows with battle-ax and sword, it was wonderful to behold.

The lord de Courtenay and Sir John of Salenay one day told me, that at this engagement six Turks caught hold of the bridle of the king's horse, and were leading him away, but this virtuous prince exerted himself with such bravery in fighting the six Turks, that he alone freed himself from them, and that many, seeing how valiantly he defended himself, and the great courage he displayed, took greater courage themselves, and abandoning the passage they were guarding, hastened to support the king.

After some little time, the count Peter of Brittany came to us who were guarding the small bridge from Mansourah, having had a most furious skirmish. He was so badly wounded in the face that the blood came out of his month, as if it had been full of water, and he vomited it forth. The count was mounted on a short, thick, but strong horse, and his reins and the pommel of his saddle were cut and destroyed, so that he was forced to hold himself by his two hands round the horse's neck for fear the Turks, who were close behind him, should make him fall off. He did not, however, seem much afraid of them, for he frequently turned round, and gave them many abusive words, by way of mockery.

Towards the end of this battle, Sir John of Soissons and Sir Peter of Noville, surnamed Cayer, came to us. They had suffered much from the blows they had received by remaining behind in the last battle. The Turks, seeing them, began to move to meet them, but observing us who were guarding the bridge, with our faces towards them, suffered them to pass, suspecting that we should have gone to their succor, as we certainly should have done. I addressed the count of Soissons, who was my first cousin: "Sir, I beg that you will remain here to guard this bridge. You will act right in so doing. For, if you leave it, the Turks whom you see before you will advance to attack us and the king may thus have his enemies in front and rear at the same moment." He asked, if he should stay, would I remain with him? To which I most cheerfully assented.

The constable, hearing our conversation and agreement, told me to defend this bridge, and not on any account to quit it, and that he would go and seek help. I was sitting quietly there on my horse, having my cousin Sir John of Soissons on my right and Sir Peter of Noville on my left hand, when a Turk, galloping from where the king was, struck Sir Peter of Noville so heavy a blow with his battle-ax on the back as felled him on the neck of his horse, and then crossed the bridge full speed to his own people, imagining that we would abandon our post and follow him, and thus they might gain the bridge. When they perceived that we would on no account quit our post, they crossed the rivulet, and placed themselves between it and the river. We turned toward them in such a way that we were ready to charge them, if they had further advanced.

In our front were two of the king's heralds. The name of one was Guillaume of Bron, and that of the other John of Gaymaches. Against them the Turks, led a rabble of peasants of the country, who pelted them with clods of earth and large stones. At last, they brought a villainous Turk, who thrice flung Greek fires at them; and by one of them was the tabard of Guillaume of Bron set on fire; but he soon threw it off, and good need had he, for if it had set fire to his clothes, he must have been burnt. We were also covered with these showers of stones and arrows which the Turks discharged at the two heralds.

I luckily found near me a gambeson [a garment made of padded cloth used as armor] of coarse cloth which had belonged to a Saracen, and turning the slit part inward, I made a sort of shield, which was of much service to me, for I was only wounded by their shots in five places, whereas my horse was hurt in fifteen. Soon after, as God willed it, one of my vassals of Joinville brought me a banner with my arms, and a long knife for war, which I needed, and then, when these Turkish villains, who were on foot, pressed on the heralds, we made a charge against them, and put them instantly to flight.

Thus when the good count of Soissons and myself were returned to our post on the bridge, after chasing away these peasants, he rallied me, saying, "Seneschal [Joinville was the seneschal of Champagne], let us allow this rabble to bawl and bray; and, by the 'Cresse Dieu,'" his usual oath, "you and I will talk over this day's adventures in the chambers of our ladies."

It happened that towards evening, about sunset, the constable, Sir Hymbert of Beaujeu, brought us the king's crossbows that were on foot. and they drew up in one front, while we, horsemen, dismounted under shelter of the cross-bows. The Saracens, observing this, immediately took to flight, and left us in peace. The constable told me that we had behaved well in thus guarding the bridge; and bade me go boldly to the king, and not leave him until he should be dismounted in his pavilion. I went to the king, and at the same moment Sir John of Valeri joined, and requested of him, in the name of the lord of Châtillon, that the said lord might command the rear guard, which the king very willingly granted. The king then took the road to return to his pavilion, and raised the helmet from his head. In turn, I gave him my iron skull-cap, which was much lighter, so that he might have more air.

Thus as we were riding together, Father Henry, prior of the hospital of Ronnay, who had crossed the river, came to him and kissed his hand, fully armed, and asked if he had heard any news of his brother, the count [Robert] of Artois. "Yes," replied the king, "I have heard all." That is to say, that he knew well he was now in paradise. The prior, thinking to comfort him for the death of his brother, continued, "Sire, no king of France has ever reaped such honor as you

have done, for with great intrepidity have you and your army crossed a dangerous river to combat your enemies, and have been so very successful, that you
have put them to flight and gained the field, together with their warlike engines,
with which they had wonderfully annoyed you, and concluded the affair by
taking possession this day of their camp and quarters."

The good king replied, that God should be adored for all the good he had
granted him; and then heavy tears began to fall down his cheeks, which many
great persons noticing, were oppressed with anguish and compassion, on seeing him
thus weep, praising the name of God, who had enabled him to gain the victory.

When we arrived at our quarters, we found great numbers of Saracens on
foot holding the cords of a tent which some of our servants were erecting, and
pulling against them with all their might. The master of the Temple, who had
the command of the vanguard, and myself, charged this rabble, and made them
run away. The tent remained, therefore, with us; not, however, that there was
any great fight, for which reason many boasters were put to shame. I could readily mention their names, but I abstain from doing so because they are deceased,
and we ought not to speak ill of the dead. Of Sir Guyon of Malvoisin I am
willing to speak, for the constable and I met him on the road, returning from
Mansourah, bearing himself gallantly, although hard pressed by the Turks, who
closely pursued him, for after they had scattered the count of Brittany and his
battalion, as I have before said, they followed the lord Guyon and his company.
He had not suffered much in this engagement, for he and his people had behaved
most courageously. This is not to be wondered at, as I have heard from those
who knew him and his family, that almost all his knights were of his kindred
and lineage, and his men-at-arms his liege vassals. This gave them the greater
confidence in their chief....

... In the evening of this severe engagement that I spoke of, and when we
had taken up our quarters in those from whence we had driven the Saracens,
my people brought me from the main army, a tent, which the master of the
Templars, who had the command of the van, had given me. I had it pitched
on the right of those machines we had won from the enemy, as each of us was
eager for repose. Indeed, we had need of it, from the wounds and fatigues we
had suffered in the late battle.

Before daybreak, however, we were alarmed by the cries of "To arms, to
arms!" and I made my chamberlain rise, who lay by my side, to go and see what
was the matter. He was not long in returning, much frightened, and crying out,
"My lord, get up instantly, for the Saracens have entered the camp, on both horse
and foot, and have already defeated the guard which the king had appointed for
our security and to defend the engines we had won from them."

These engines were in front of the king's pavilions, and of us who were
near to him. I immediately rose, threw a cuirass on my back, and put my iron

skull-cap on my head and having roused our people, wounded as we were, we drove the Saracens from the engines which they were so anxious to recover.

The king, seeing that scarcely any of us had armor on, sent Sir Walter of Châtillon, who posted himself between us and the Turks, to better guard the engines. After Sir Walter had several times repulsed the enemy, who made frequent attempts during the night to carry off these engines, the Saracens, finding they could not succeed, retreated to a large body of their horse, that were drawn up opposite to our lines, to prevent us from surprising their camp, which was in their rear.

Six of the principal Turks dismounted, armed from head to foot, and made themselves a rampart of large stones, as a shelter from our cross-bows, and from thence shot volleys of arrows, which often wounded many of our men. When I and my men-at-arms, who had the guard of that quarter, saw their stone rampart, we took counsel together, and resolved that, during the ensuing night, we would destroy this rampart, and bring away the stones.

Now I had a priest called John of Waysy, who, having overheard our counsel and resolution, did not wait so long, but set out alone towards the Saracens, with his cuirass on, his cap of iron, and his sword under his arm. When he was near the enemy, who neither thought of nor suspected anyone coming against them thus alone, he rushed furiously on, sword in hand, and gave such blows to these six captains, that they could not defend themselves, and took to flight, to the great astonishment of the other Turks and Saracens.

When the Turks saw their leaders fly, they stuck spurs into their horses, and charged the priest, who was returning to our army, whence had sallied fifty of our men to oppose them, as they were pursuing him on horseback. The Turks would not meet them, but wheeled off two or three times. It happened, however, that during these maneuvers, one of our men threw his dagger at a Turk, and hit him between the ribs. He carried off the dagger, but it caused his death. The other Turks, seeing this, were more shy than before, and never dared to approach while our men were carrying away the stones of the rampart. My priest was well-known ever after by the whole army, who said when they saw him, "That is the priest who, single-handed, defeated the Saracens."

These things happened during the first day of Lent, and this same day the Saracens elected another chief, in the place of their late chief Scecedin [Latinized name for Fakhr ad-Din], of whom mention has been made, and who died in the battle of Shrove-Tuesday, probably at the same time, that the good count [Robert] of Artois, brother to the king St. Louis, was slain. This new chief found among the other dead the body of the count of Artois, who had shown great intrepidity in this battle, magnificently dressed, becoming a prince. And this chief took the count's coat of armor, and, to give courage to the Turks and Saracens, had it hoisted before them, telling them it was the coat of armor of the king their enemy, who had been slain in battle, adding, "My lords, this should make you exert yourselves the more, for body without head is nothing, nor is an army without prince or chief to be feared. I advise, and you ought to have confidence in me, that we increase the force of our attacks on them, and on Friday next we must conquer and gain the battle, since they have now lost their commander." All who heard him cheerfully agreed to follow his advice.

You must know that the king had many spies in the Saracen army, who, having overheard their plans, knew their intentions, and how they meant to act. Some of them informed the king of the intended attack of the enemy, and that they believed him dead and the army without a leader.

Upon this, the king summoned all his captains, and commanded them to have their men-at-arms completely armed, and ready drawn up before their tents at midnight, and then to advance as far as the lines which had been made to prevent the Saracens entering the camp on horseback, although they were so constructed that they might pass them on foot. This was punctually executed according to the king's orders.

You may suppose that the Saracen chief lost no time in putting into execution the plan he had proposed and adopted.

On the Friday morning, by sunrise, 4,000 knights, well armed and mounted, were drawn up in battalions, alongside our army, which lay on the banks of the river toward Babylon [Cairo], and extending as far as a town called Ressil. When the pagan chief had thus drawn up his 4,000 knights in front of our army, he then brought another large body of Saracens on foot, and in such numbers that they surrounded all the other side of it. After doing this, he drew up at a short distance other companies in conjunction with the power of the sultan of Egypt, to succor and aid each of the two former, as necessity might dictate.

The chief of the Saracens, having now completed the arrangement of his army, advanced on horseback alone, to view and make his observations on the manner in which the king's army was formed. And where he saw ours was the strongest or weakest, he strengthened or diminished his own. After this he ordered 3,000 Bedouins, whose nature and character I have described, to march in front of the troops under the command of the duke of Burgundy, which were posted between the two branches of the Nile, thinking that part of the king's army might be under the duke, and his own so much the weaker, and that these Bedouins would effectively prevent the duke from affording any support to the king.

All these operations of the infidel chief took him up until about mid-day. This done, he ordered the nacaires [Arab timpani or kettledrums] and drums to be loudly sounded, according to the mode of the Turks, which is certainly very surprising to those who have not been accustomed to hear them, and then both horse and foot began to be in motion on all sides. I will speak first of the battalion under [Charles] the count of Anjou [youngest brother of Louis IX], which received the first attack, being posted the nearest to Cairo. The enemy advanced in a checkered manner, as in a game of chess, for their infantry ran towards our men, and burnt them with Greek fires, which they cast from instruments made for that purpose. On the other hand, the Turkish cavalry charged them with such rapidity and success, that the battalion of the count of Anjou was defeated. He himself was on foot among his knights, very uncomfortably situated.

When news was brought to the king of the danger his brother was in, nothing could check his ardor, nor would he wait for any one, but, sticking spurs to his horse, galloped into the midst of the battle, lance in hand, to where his brother was, and gave most deadly blows to the Turks, hastening always to where he saw the greatest crowd. He suffered many hard blows, and the Saracens covered all his horse's tail and rump with Greek fires. You may be assured that at such a time he had God in his heart and mind, and in good truth our Lord in this distress befriended him, and so far assisted him, that the king rescued his brother, the count of Anjou, and drove the Turks before him without the lines.

Next to the battalion of the count of Anjou was that commanded by Sir Guy of Guivelins, and his brother Baldwin, which joined the battalion of that bold and gallant man Sir Walter of Châtillon. He had with him numbers of chivalrous knights, and these two battalions behaved so vigorously against the Turks, that they were neither broken nor conquered.

The next battalion, however, fared but badly, under the command of Friar William of Sonnac, master of the Temple, who had with him the remnant of the men-at-arms that had survived the battle of Shrove Tuesday, which had been so severely murderous. The master of the Temple, having but few men, made of the engines that had been taken from the enemy, a sort of rampart in his front. This, nevertheless, availed him nothing, for although the Templars had added to them many planks of fir-wood, the Saracens burnt them with their Greek fire, and seeing there were but few to oppose them, they waited not until they were destroyed, but vigorously attacking the Templars, defeated them in a very short time. It is certain, that in the rear of the Templars there was about an acre of ground so covered with bolts, darts, arrows, and other weapons, that you could not see the earth beneath them, such showers of these had been discharged against the Templars by the Saracens. The commander of this battalion had lost an eye in the preceding battle of Shrove Tuesday, and in this battle he lost the other, and was slain. God have mercy on his soul!

Sir Guy of Malvoisin, a bold and valiant captain of another battalion, was severely wounded in the body, and the Saracens perceiving his gallant conduct and address, shot Greek fire at him incessantly, so that at one time when he was hit by it, his people had much difficulty to extinguish it. But notwithstanding this, he stood bold and firm, unconquered by the pagans.

From the battalion of Sir Guy of Malvoisin, the lines which enclosed our army descended to where I was, within a stone's cast of the river, and passed by the division of the lord William, count of Flanders, which extended to that branch of the river which entered the sea. Our battalion was posted opposite, and on that bank of the river where Sir Guy of Malvoisin was. The Saracens, observing the appearance of the division of the count of Flanders fronting them, dared not make any attack on us, for which I thanked God, as neither my knights nor myself could put on any armor, on account of the wounds we had received in the engagement of the Tuesday, which rendered it impossible to wear any defensive clothing.

The lord William of Flanders and his battalion did wonders. They gallantly and fiercely attacked the Turks on horseback and on foot, and performed great deeds of arms. Seeing their prowess, I ordered my crossbows to shoot strongly at the Turks who were on horseback during this engagement, and the moment they felt themselves or horses wounded by the arrows, they instantly took flight, and abandoned their infantry. The count of Flanders and his division, observing the Turks fly, passed the lines, and charged the pagans who were on foot, killing great numbers, and bringing off many targets. Among others, Sir Walter de la Horgne, who bore the banner of the count of Aspremont, displayed much courage.

Adjoining this battalion was that of my lord [Alphonse], the count de Poitiers, brother to the king. It was composed solely of infantry, and the only person on horseback was the count, which was unfortunate for him, for the Turks defeated this battalion, and made the count prisoner. They would surely have carried him away, had not the butchers, and all the other traffickers, men and women, who supplied the army with provision, hearing that the Turks were carrying off the count of Poitiers, set up a great shout, and rushed on the Saracens with such fury that they rescued the count of Poitiers, and drove the Turks beyond the lines.

The next battalion to that of the count de Poitiers was the weakest of the whole army, and commanded by Sir Josserant of Brancion, whom my lord of Poitiers had brought with him to Egypt. This division was also formed of dismounted knights, Sir Josserant and his son Sir Henry being the only persons on horseback. The Turks broke this battalion several times, and each time Sir Josserant and his son fell on the rear of the Turks, and cut them down with their swords. They pressed the enemy so much that they frequently turned on them again, leaving the main body of his men. In the end this would have been fatal, for the Turks must have slain the whole, if Sir Henry of One, a wise and valiant knight of the division under the duke of Burgundy, well knowing the weakness of the lord of Brancion's battalion, had not ordered the king's crossbows to shoot at them every time he saw the Turks make their charge on it. His tactic was so effective that the lord of Brancion escaped from this danger, but lost twelve of the twenty knights whom it was said he had, without counting other men-at-arms. He himself, was the victim of the wounds he received in the service of God, who, we are bound to believe, has well rewarded him for it....

... To return to our subject, the sultan, lately deceased, had left a son, who was twenty-five years old, well informed, prudent, and already full of malice. The last sultan, fearing he might dethrone him, kept him at a distance from his person, and had given him a kingdom in the East; but the moment his father was dead, the emirs of Cairo sent for him, and made him their sultan. On taking possession of his throne, he deprived the constable, marshals, and seneschals of his father of their golden wands, and the offices which they held, and gave them to those whom he had brought with him from the East.

This caused great discontent among those who had been removed, as also among those of the council of his late father, who suspected strongly that he would act against them, after seizing their wealth, in the same manner as the sultan had done against those who had taken the counts of Montfort and of Bar, as already related. They therefore unanimously agreed to put him to death, and found allies from those called La Hauleca, who were the sultan's guard.

After the two battles I have mentioned, which were marvelously sharp and severe, the one on Shrove Tuesday, and the other the first Friday in Lent, another great misfortune befell our army. At the end of eight or ten days, the bodies of those who had been slain in these two engagements, and thrown into the Nile, rose to the top of the water. It was said, this always happens when the gall is burst and rotten. These bodies floated down the river until they came to the small bridge that communicated with each part of our army; and the arch was so low it almost touched the water, and prevented the bodies passing underneath. The river was covered with them from bank to bank, so that the water could not be seen a good stone's throw from the bridge upward.

The king hired one hundred laborers, who spent eight full days separating the bodies of the Christians from the Saracens, which were easily distinguishable. The Saracen bodies they thrust under the bridge by main force, and floated them down to the sea; but the Christians were buried in deep graves, one over the other. God knows how great was the stench, and what misery it was to see the bodies of such noble and worthy persons lying so exposed. I witnessed the chamberlain of the late count of Artois seeking the body of his master, and many more hunting after the bodies of their friends, but I never heard that any who were thus seeking their friends amidst such an infectious smell ever recovered their health. You must know, that we ate no fish the whole Lent but eelpouts, which is a gluttonous fish that feeds on dead bodies. From this cause, and from the bad air of the country, where it scarcely ever rains a drop, the whole army was infected by a shocking disorder, which dried up the flesh on our legs to the bone, and our skins became darkened as black as the ground, or like an old boot that has long lain behind a coffer. In addition to this miserable disorder, those affected by it had another sore complaint in the mouth, from eating such fish, that rotted the gums, and caused a most stinking breath. Very few escaped death that were thus attacked, and the surest symptom of its being fatal was bleeding at the nose, for when that took place none ever recovered.

The better to cure us, the Turks, who knew our situation, fifteen days afterward attempted to starve us, as I shall now tell you. These villainous Turks had drawn their galleys overland, and launched them again below our army, so that those who had gone to Damietta for provision never returned, to the great astonishment of us all. We could not imagine the reason for this, until one of the galleys of the count of Flanders, having forced a passage, informed us how the sultan had launched his vessels, by drawing them overland, below us, so that the Turks watched all the galleys going toward Damietta, and had already captured fourscore of ours and killed their crews.

By this means all provision was exceedingly dear in the army; and when Easter arrived, a beef was sold for eighty livres, a sheep for thirty livres, a hog for thirty livres, a muid [a liquid unit used for measuring wine] of wine for ten livres, an egg for sixpence, and everything else in proportion.

When the king and his barons saw this, and that there was not any remedy for it, the barons advised the king to march the army from near Cairo, and join that of the duke of Burgundy, which was on the other bank of the river that flowed to Damietta. For the security of his retreat, the king had erected a barbican in front of the small bridge I have so often mentioned; and it was constructed in such a way that it might be entered on either side on horseback. As soon as this barbican was finished, the whole host armed, for the Turks made a vigorous attack, when they observed our intentions to join the duke of Burgundy's army on the opposite side of the river.

During the time we were entering the barbican, the enemy fell on the rear of our army, and took prisoner Sir Errart of Valeri, but he was soon rescued by his brother, Sir John of Valeri. The king, however, and his division never moved until the baggage and arms had crossed the river and then we all passed after the king, except Sir Walter of Châtillon, who commanded the rear-guard in the barbican.

When the whole army had passed, the rear-guard was much distressed by the Turkish cavalry; for from their horses they could shoot point blank, as the barbican was low. The Turks on foot threw large stones and clods of earth in their faces, without our men being able to defend themselves. They would surely have been destroyed, if the count of Anjou, brother to the king, and afterwards king of Sicily, had not boldly gone to their rescue, and brought them off in safety.

The day preceding Shrovetide I saw a thing which I must relate. On the vigil of that day died a very valiant and prudent knight, Sir Hugh of Landricourt, a knight under my banner. During his burial, six of my knights talked so loud they disturbed the priest as he was saying mass. On this I arose, and bade them be silent, for it was unbecoming for gentlemen thus to talk while the mass was celebrating. But they burst into laughter, and told me they were talking of marrying the widow of Sir Hugh, now in his bier. I rebuked them sharply, and said such conversation was indecent and improper, for that they had too soon forgotten their companion.

Now it happened on the morrow, when the first grand battle took place, although we may laugh at their follies, God took such vengeance on them, that of all the six not one escaped death, and remained unburied. The wives of all six re-married. This makes it credible, that God leaves no such conduct unpunished. With regard to myself, I fared little better, for I was grievously wounded in the battle of Shrove Tuesday. I had, besides, the disorder in my legs and mouth described earlier, and such a rheum [watery mucus discharge] in my head that it ran through my mouth and nostrils. In addition, I had a double fever, called a quartan, from which God defend us! With these illnesses, I was confined to my bed for half of Lent.

My poor priest was likewise as ill as myself, and one day when he was singing mass before me as I lay in my bed, at the moment of the elevation of the host, I saw him so exceedingly weak that he was near fainting. When I perceived he was on the point of falling to the ground, I flung myself out of bed, sick as I was, and taking my coat, embraced him, and bade him be at his ease, and take courage from Him whom he held in his hands. He recovered a little, but I never left him until he had finished the mass, which he completed. This was to be his last mass, for he never after celebrated another, but died. God receive his soul!

To return to our history. It is true there were some parleys between the councils of the king and of the sultan, regarding a peace, and a day was appointed for the further discussion of it. The basis of the treaty was agreed on—namely, that the king should restore to the sultan Damietta, and the sultan should surrender to the king the realm of Jerusalem. The sultan was also to take proper care of the sick in Damietta, and to give up the salted provision that was there, for neither Turk nor Saracen eat of it, and likewise return to us the engines of war; but the king was to send for all these things from Damietta.

The end of this was, that the sultan demanded what security the king would give him for the surrender of Damietta, and it was proposed that he should detain as prisoner one of the king's brothers, either the count of Poitiers or the count of Anjou, until it were affected. But the Turks refused to accept of any other hostage than the person of the king.

To this the gallant knight Sir Geoffrey of Sergines, replied that the Turks should never have the king's person and that he would rather the French should all be slain than it should be said they had given their king in pawn; and thus matters remained.

The disease I spoke of very soon increased so much in the army that the barbers [surgeons] were forced to cut away very large pieces of flesh from the gums, to enable their patients to eat. It was pitiful to hear the cries and groans of those on whom this operation was performed. They seemed like to the cries of women in labor, and I cannot express the great concern all felt who heard them.

The good king Louis, witnessing the miserable condition of great part of his army, raised his hands and eyes to heaven, blessing our Lord for all He had given him, and seeing that he could no longer remain where he was, without perishing himself as well as his army, gave orders to march on the Tuesday evening after the octave of Easter, and return to Damietta. He issued his commands to the masters of the galleys to have them ready to receive on board the sick, and convey them to Damietta. He likewise gave his orders to Josselin of Corvant and to other engineers, to cut the cords which held the bridges between the Saracens and us. But they neglected the orders which was the cause of much evil befalling us.

Perceiving that everyone was preparing to go to Damietta, I withdrew to my vessel, with two of my knights, all that I had remaining of those that had accompanied me, and the rest of my household. Towards evening, when it began to grow dark, I ordered my captain to raise the anchor, that we might float down the stream, but he replied, that he dared not obey me, since between us and Damietta were the large galleys of the sultan, which would certainly capture us.

The king's seamen had made great fires on board their galleys, to comfort the unfortunate sick and many others in the same state were waiting on the banks of the river for vessels to take them on board. As I was advising my sailors to make some little way, I saw by the light of the fires, the Saracens enter our camp, and murder the sick that were waiting on the banks of the Nile. As my men were raising the anchor, and we began to move down river, the sailors who were to take the sick on board advanced with their boats, but seeing the Saracens in the act of killing them, they retreated to their large galleys, cut their cables, and crashed into my small ship.

I expected every moment they would have sunk me, but we escaped this imminent danger, and made some way down the river. The king had the same illness as the rest of his army, dysentery, which, had he pleased, he might have prevented, by living on board his larger vessels, but he said that he would rather die than leave his people. The king, observing us make off, began to shout and cry for us to remain, and likewise ordered some heavy bolts to be shot at us, to stop our course until we had his orders to sail.

I will now break the course of my narration, and say in what manner the king was made prisoner, as he told me himself. I heard him say that he had left his own battalion and men-at-arms, and with Sir Geoffrey of Sergines, had joined the battalion of Sir Walter of Châtillon, who commanded the rear division. The king was mounted on a small courser, with only a covering of silk and of all his men-at-arms, there was only with him the good knight Sir Geoffrey of Sergines, who attended him as far as the town of Casel, where the king was made prisoner. But before the Turks could take him, I heard say, that Sir Geoffrey of Sergines defended him in like manner as a faithful servant does the cup of his master from flies; for every time the Saracens approached him, Sir Geoffrey guarded him with vigorous strokes of the blade and point of his sword, and it seemed as if his courage and strength were doubled.

By dint of gallantry, he drove them away from the king, and thus conducted him to Casel, where, having dismounted at a house, he laid the king in the lap of a woman who had come from Paris, thinking that every moment must be his last, for he had no hopes that he could ever pass that day without dying.

Shortly after arrived Sir Philip of Montfort, who told the king that he had just seen the emir of the sultan, with whom he had formerly treated for a truce, and that if it were his good pleasure, he would return to him again, and renew it. The king entreated him so to do, and declared he would abide by whatever terms they should agree on.

Sir Philip of Montfort returned to the Saracens, who had taken their turbans from their heads, and gave a ring, which he took off his finger, to the emir, as a pledge of keeping the truce, and that they would accept the terms as offered, and of which I have spoken.

Just at this moment a villainous traitor of an apostate sergeant, named Marcel, set up a loud shout to our people, and said, "Sir knights, surrender yourselves; the king orders you by me to do so, and not to cause yourselves to be slain." At these words, all were thunderstruck and thinking the king had indeed sent such orders, they each gave up their arms and staves to the Saracens.

The emir, seeing the Saracens leading the king's knights as their prisoners, said to Sir Philip of Montfort that he would not agree to any truce since the army had been captured. Sir Philip was greatly astonished at what he saw, for he was aware that although he was sent as ambassador to settle a truce, he should likewise be made prisoner, and knew not what to do. In pagan countries, they have a very bad custom, that when any ambassadors are dispatched from one king or sultan to another, to demand or conclude a peace, and one of these princes dies, and the treaty is not concluded before that event takes place, the ambassador is made prisoner, wherever he may he, and whether sent by sultan or king.

You must know that we, who had embarked on board our vessels, thinking to escape to Damietta, were not more fortunate than those who had remained on land; for we were also taken, as you shall hear. It is true, that during the time we were on the river, a dreadful tempest of wind arose, blowing towards Damietta, and with such force that, unable to go up river, we were driven towards the Saracens. The king, indeed, had left a body of knights, with orders to guard the invalids on the banks of the river; but it would not have been of any use to have headed in their direction, as they had all fled. Toward the break of day, we arrived at the pass where the sultan's galleys lay to prevent any provisions being sent from Damietta to the army. When they saw us, they made a great noise, and shot at us and at our horsemen who were on the banks, with large bolts armed with Greek fire, so that it seemed as if the stars were falling from the heavens.

When our mariners had gained the current, and we attempting to push forward, we saw the horsemen whom the king had left to guard the sick flying towards Damietta. The wind became more violent than ever, and drove us against the bank of the river. On the opposite shore were immense numbers of our vessels that the Saracens had taken and which we feared to approach, for we plainly saw them murdering their crews, and throwing the dead bodies into the water, and carrying away the trunks and arms they had thus gained.

Because we would not go near the Saracens who menaced us, they shot plenty of bolts at us, upon which, I put on my armor, to prevent them from hurting me. At the stern of my vessel were some of my people, who cried out to me, "My lord, my lord, because the Saracens threaten us, our steersman is determined to run us on shore, where we shall be all murdered." I instantly rose up, for I was then very ill, and, advancing with my drawn sword, declared I would kill the first person who should attempt to run us on the Saracen shore. The sailors replied that it was impossible to proceed and that I must determine which I would prefer, to be landed on the shore or to be stranded on the mud of the banks in the river. I preferred, very fortunately, as you shall hear, being run on a mud bank in the river to being carried toward shore, where I saw our men murdered, and they followed my orders.

It was not long before we saw four of the sultan's large galleys making toward us, having a full thousand men on board. I called upon my knights to advise me how to act, whether to surrender to the galleys of the sultan or to those who were on the shore. We were unanimous, that it would be more advisable to surrender to the galleys that were coming, for then we might have a chance of being kept together, whereas, if we gave ourselves up to those on the shore, we should certainly be separated, and perhaps sold to the Bedouins, of whom I have before spoken. To this opinion, however, one of my clerks would not agree, but said it would be much better for us to be slain, as then we should go to paradise, but we would not listen to him, for the fear of death had greater influence over us.

Seeing that we must surrender, I took a small case that contained my jewels and relics, and cast it into the river. One of my sailors told me, that if I would not let him tell the Saracens I was cousin to the king, we would all be put to death. In reply, I bade him say what he pleased. The first of these galleys now came next to us, and cast anchor close to our bow. Then, as I firmly believe, God sent to my aid a Saracen who was a subject of the emperor. Having on a pair of trousers of coarse cloth, and swimming straight to my vessel, he embraced my knees, and said, "My lord, if you do not believe what I shall say, you are a lost man. To save yourself, you must leap into the river, which will be unobserved by the crew, who are solely occupied with the capture of your bark." He had a cord thrown to me from their galley to my vessel, and I leaped into the water followed by the Saracen, who indeed saved me, and conducted me to the galley, for I was so weak I staggered, and should have otherwise sunk to the bottom of the river.

I was drawn into the galley, in which there were fourteen score men, besides those who had boarded my vessel, and this poor Saracen held me fast in his arms. Shortly after I was landed they rushed upon me to cut my throat. Indeed, I expected nothing else, for he that should do it would imagine he had acquired honor.

This Saracen who had saved me from drowning would not let go of me, but cried out to them, "The king's cousin! The king's cousin!"

I felt the knife at my throat, and had already cast myself on my knees to the ground; but God delivered me from this peril by the aid of the poor Saracen, who led me to the [ship's] castle where the Saracen chiefs were assembled.

When I was in their presence, they took off my coat of mail and from pity, seeing me so very ill, they flung over me one of my own scarlet coverlids, lined with miniver, which my lady-mother had given me. Another brought me a white leather girdle, with which I girthed my coverlid around me. One of the Saracen knights gave me a small cap, which I put on my head, but I soon began to tremble, so that my teeth chattered, partly from the fright I had and partly from illness.

On my complaining of thirst, they brought me some water in a pot, but I had no sooner put it to my mouth, and began drinking, than it ran back through my nostrils. God knows what a pitiful state I was in, looking more dead than alive, having an abscess in my throat. When my attendants saw the water run thus through my nostrils, they began to weep and to be very sorrowful. The Saracen who had saved me asked my people why they wept. They gave him to understand that I was nearly dead from an abscess in the throat which was choking me. The good Saracen, having always great compassion for me, went to tell this to one of the Saracen knights, who bade him to be comforted, for that he would give me something to drink that should cure me in two days. This he did and I was soon well, through God's grace, and the beverage which the Saracen knight gave me.

Soon after my recovery, the emir of the sultan's galleys sent for me, and demanded if I were cousin to the king as it was said. I told him I was not and related why it had been reported, and that one of my mariners had advised it out of fear of the Saracens in the galleys, believing that otherwise they would put us to death. The emir replied that I had been very well advised, for we should have been all murdered without fail, and thrown into the river. The emir again asked me if I had any acquaintance with the emperor Frederick II of Germany, then living, and if I were of his lineage. I answered truly that I had heard my mother say I was his second cousin. The emir replied that he would love me the better for it.

Thus, as we were eating and drinking, he sent for an inhabitant of Paris to come to me, who, on his entrance, seeing what we were doing, exclaimed, "Ah, sir, what are you doing?" "What am I doing?" I replied. He then informed me that I was eating meat on a Friday. I immediately threw my wooden plate behind me and the emir, noticing it, asked of my friendly Saracen, who was always with me, why I had stopped eating. He told him because it was a Friday, which I had forgotten. The emir said that God could never be displeased, because I had done it unknowingly. You must know, that the legate who had accompanied

Figure 2.3: Crac des Chevaliers.

Source: Claude Sauvageot, Crac des Chevaliers, reconstruction (engraving).

the king frequently reproached me for fasting when thus ill, and when there was not any statesman but myself left with the king, and that I should hurt myself by fasting. But notwithstanding this, and that I was a prisoner, I never failed to fast every Friday on bread and water.

18. THE CONQUEST OF ACRE AND THE END OF THE CRUSADER STATES

The emergence of the Mamluks as rulers of Egypt, and subsequently Syria, coupled with the failure of Louis IX's crusade, made the crusader position in the Holy Land precarious. Led by the sultan Baybars (r. 1260–77), the Mamluks methodically kept the pressure on the crusaders, taking numerous cities and strongholds. The crusaders were further hindered by their own internal political quarrels, which weakened them even more. Surrounded by a powerful and disciplined Mamluk Empire on all sides, the crusaders had few options beyond negotiating, and this at a disadvantage, with the Mamluks and asking their coreligionists in Europe for help. In an effort to rally the Christians and stave off their imminent downfall, Louis IX once again took the cross in 1267, but his second crusade, which finally departed France in 1270, never made it to the East, being instead diverted to Tunis. There Louis died, and with him went the last major crusade to the Holy Land. With little additional help coming from Europe, the Mamluks continued their advance, and by 1291 only the city of Acre (in modern-day Lebanon) and a few scattered fortresses were left under Christian control. On 5 April 1291, a massive Mamluk army arrived in Acre and began besieging the city, which fell on 28 May after a spirited defense. The conquest of Acre had a profound impact on both Latin Christendom and the Islamic world, and the telling of its fall was taken up by many writers. Among Christian writers, one of the most famous accounts was that put forth by the German traveler Ludolph von Suchem, who visited the Holy Land between 1336 and 1341, half a century after the events detailed here. In his account, he holds responsible the many defenders of Acre who were not able to overcome their political differences and make a common cause against the Muslims, but his writings are also filled with a certain nostalgia about what was lost when Acre fell. Unlike von Suchem, the Muslim nobleman Abu'l-Fidā was a witness to, and participant in, the Mamluk attack on Acre. Abu'l-Fidā was a poet and a scholar and a member of the ruling family of Hamāh, which gave him access to the inner circles of the Mamluk sultanate as well as information and intelligence. The excerpt here is from his al-Mukhtasar fī akhbār al-bashar *["A Short History of Mankind"], written around 1318.*

Sources: trans. Aubrey Stewart, Ludolph von Suchem, *Description of the Holy Land and of the Way Thither* (London: Palestinian Pilgrims' Text Society, 1895), 54–61, rev. Jarbel Rodriguez; trans. P.M. Holt, *The Memoirs of a Syrian Prince: Abu'l-Fidā, Sultan of Hamāh (672–732/1273–1331)* (Weisbaden: Franz Steiner Verlag GMBH, 1983), 16–17.

Ludolph von Suchem—The Loss of the City of Acre

After having told of the glories and beauties of Acre, I will now shortly tell you of its fall and ruin, and the cause of its loss, even as I heard the tale told by right truthful men, who well remembered it. While, then, the grand doings of which I have spoken were going on in Acre, at the instigation of the devil there arose a violent and hateful quarrel in Lombardy between the Guelfs and the Ghibellines, which brought all evil upon the Christians. Those Lombards who dwelt in Acre took sides in this same quarrel, especially the Pisans and Genoese, both of whom had an exceeding strong party in Acre. These men made treaties and truces with the Saracens, to the end that they might the better fight against one another within the city. When Pope Urban [IV] heard of this, he grieved for Christendom and for the Holy Land, and sent twelve thousand mercenary troops across the sea to help the Holy Land and Christendom. When these men came across the sea to Acre they did no good, but abode by day and by night in taverns and places of ill-repute, took and plundered merchants and pilgrims in the public streets, broke the treaty, and did much evil. Melot Saph-eraph, sultan of Babylon [Egypt], an exceedingly wise man, most potent in arms and bold in action, when he heard of this, and knew of the hateful quarrels of the people of Acre, called together his counselors and held a parliament in Babylon, wherein he complained that the truces had frequently been broken and violated, to the prejudice of himself and his people. After a debate had been held upon this matter, he gathered together a mighty host, and reached the city of Acre without any resistance, because of their quarrels with one another, cutting down and wasting all the vineyards and fruit-trees and all the gardens and orchards, which are most lovely thereabout. When the master of the Templars, a very wise and brave knight, saw this, he feared that the fall of the city was at hand, because of the quarrels of the citizens. He took counsel with his brethren about how peace could be restored, and then went out to meet the sultan, who was his own very special friend, to ask him whether they could by any means repair the broken truce. He obtained these terms from the sultan, to wit, that because of his love for the sultan and the honor in which the sultan held him, the broken truce might be restored by every man in Acre paying one Venetian penny. So the Master of the Templars was glad, and, departing from the Sultan, called together all the people and preached a ser-mon to them in the Church of St. Cross, setting forth how, by his prayers, he had prevailed upon the sultan to grant that the broken treaty might be restored by a payment of one Venetian penny by each man, so that everything might be settled and quieted. He advised them by all means to do so, declaring that the quarrels of the citizens might bring a worse evil upon the city than this—as indeed they did. But when the people heard this, they cried out with one voice that he was the betrayer of the city, and was guilty of death. The master, when he heard this, left the church, hardly escaped alive from the hands of the people, and took back their answer to the sultan. When the sultan heard this, knowing that, owing to the quarrels of the people, none of them would make any resistance, he pitched his tents, set up sixty machines, dug many mines beneath the city walls, and for forty days and nights, without any respite, assailed the city with fire, stones, and arrows, so that [the air] seemed to be stiff with arrows. I have heard a very honorable knight say that a lance which he was about to hurl from a tower among the Saracens was all notched with arrows before it left his hand. There were at that time in the sultan's army six hundred thousand armed men, divided into three companies; so one hundred thousand continually besieged the city, and when they were weary another hundred thousand took their place before the same, two hundred thousand stood before the gates of the city ready for battle, and the duty of the remaining two hundred thousand was to supply them with everything that they needed [these numbers are exaggerated]. The gates were never closed, nor was there an hour of the day without some hard fight being fought against the Saracens by the Templars or other brethren dwelling therein. But the numbers of the Saracens grew so fast that after one hundred thousand of them had been slain two hundred thousand came back. Yet, even against all this host, they would not have lost the city had they but helped one another faithfully; but when they were fighting outside the city, one party would run away and leave the other to be slain, while within the city one party would not defend the castle or palace belonging to the other, but purposely let the other party's castles, palaces, and strong places be stormed and taken by the enemy, and each one knew and believed his own castle and place to be so strong that he cared not for any other's castle or strong place. During this confusion the masters and brethren of the [Military] Orders alone defended themselves, and fought unceasingly against the Saracens, until they were nearly all slain. Indeed, the master and brethren of the house of the Teutonic Order, together with their followers and friends, all fell dead at one and the same time. As this went on with many battles and many thousands slain on either side, at last the fulfillment of their sins and the time of the fall of the city drew near. On the fortieth day of its siege, in the year of our Lord one thousand two hundred and ninety-two, on the twelfth day of the month of May, the most noble and glorious city of Acre, the flower, chief and pride of all the cities of the East, was taken. The people of the other cities, to wit, Jaffa, Tyre, Sidon, and Ascalon, when they heard this, left all their property behind and fled to Cyprus. When first the Saracens took Acre they got in through a breach in the wall near the king of Jerusalem's castle, and when they were among the people of the city within, one party still would not help the other, but each defended his own castle and palace, and the Saracens had a much longer siege, and fought at much less advantage when they were within the city than when they were without, for it was wondrously fortified. Indeed, we read in the stories of the loss of Acre that because of the sins of the people thereof the four elements fought on the side of the Saracens. First the air became so thick, dark, and cloudy that while one castle, palace, or strong place was being stormed or burned, men could hardly see in the other castles and palaces, until their castles and palaces were attacked, and then for the first time they would have willingly defended themselves, could they have come together. Fire fought against the city, for it consumed it. Earth fought against the city, for it drank up its blood. Water also fought against the city, for it being the month of May, wherein the sea is supposed to be very calm, when the people of Acre plainly saw that because of their sins and the darkening of the air they could not see their enemies, they fled to the sea, desiring to sail to Cyprus, and whereas at first there was no wind at all at sea, of a sudden so great a storm arose that no other ship, either great or small, could come near the shore, and many who tried to swim off to the ships were drowned. Nevertheless, more than one hundred thousand men escaped to Cyprus. I have heard from a most honorable lord, and from other truthful men who were present, that more than five hundred most noble ladies and maidens, the daughters of kings and princes, came down to the seashore, when the city was about to fall, carrying with them all their jewels and ornaments of gold and precious stones, of priceless value, in their bosoms, and cried aloud, asking whether there were any sailor there who would take all their jewels, and take whichever of them he chose to wife, if only he would take them, even naked, to some safe land or island. A sailor received them all into his ship, took them across to Cyprus, with all their goods, for nothing, and went his way. But who he was, from where he came, or where he went, no man knows to this day. Very many other noble ladies and damsels were drowned or slain. It would take long to tell what great grief and anguish was there. While the Saracens were within the city, but before they had taken it, fighting from castle to castle, from one palace and strong place to another, so many men perished on either side that they walked over their corpses as it were over a bridge. When all the inner city was lost, all who still remained alive fled into the very strong castle of the Templars, which was immediately invested on all sides by the Saracens; yet the Christians bravely defended it for two months, and before it almost all the nobles and chiefs of the sultan's army fell dead. For when the city inside the walls was burned, yet the towers of the city, and the Templars' castle, which was in the city, remained, and with these the people of the city kept the Saracens within the city from getting out, as before they had hindered their coming in, until of all the Saracens who had entered the city not one remained alive, but all fell by fire or by the sword. When the Saracen nobles saw the others lying dead, and themselves unable to escape from the city, they fled for refuge into the mines which they had dug under the great tower, that they might make their way through the wall and so get out. But the Templars and others who were in the castle, seeing that they could not hurt the Saracens with stones and the like, because of the mines wherein they were, undermined the great tower of the castle, and flung it down upon the mines and the Saracens therein, and all perished alike. When the other Saracens out-side the city saw that they had thus, as it were, failed utterly, they treacherously made a truce with the Templars and Christians on the condition that they should yield up the castle, taking all their goods with them, and should destroy it, but should rebuild the city on certain terms, and dwell therein in peace as heretofore. The Templars and Christians, believing this, gave up the castle and marched out of it, and came down from the city towers. When the Saracens had by this means got possession both of the castle and of the city towers, they slew all the Christians alike, and led away the captives to Babylon [Cairo]. Thus, Acre has remained empty and deserted even to this day. In Acre and the other places nearby a hundred and six thousand men were slain or taken, and more than two hundred thousand escaped from there. Of the Saracens, more than three hundred thousand were slain, as is well known even to this day. The Saracens spent forty days besieging the city, fifty days within the city before it was taken, and two months over the siege of the Templars' castle. When the glorious city of Acre thus fell, all the eastern people sung of its fall in hymns of lamentation, such as they are wont to sing over the tombs of their dead, bewailing the beauty, the grandeur, and the glory of Acre even to this day. Since that day all Christian women, whether gentle or simple, who dwell along the eastern shore [of the Mediterranean] dress in black garments of mourning and woe for the lost grandeur of Acre, even to this day.

After this the Saracens worked for many years endeavoring to utterly subvert and destroy down to their foundations all the walls, towers, castles, and palaces, lest the Christians should rebuild them; yet in hardly any place have they been able to beat them down to the height of a man, but all the churches, walls, and towers, and very many castles and palaces, remain almost entire, and, if it pleased God, could with great care be restored throughout to their former state. At this day about sixty Saracen mercenaries dwell in Acre as a garrison for the city and port, and make a living out of silk and birds, for there are so many partridges and pigeons to be found in Acre, that all the birds to be seen in this country are not to be compared to them. These mercenaries have an especial delight in Germans, whom they straightway recognize by their appearance and walk, and drink wine deeply with them, even though it is forbidden by their law. Thus, have I told how the glorious city of Acre was lost by quarrels, and from that time forth all the glory of the Holy Land, of its kings, princes, and other lords, has been carried over into Cyprus, as you have already heard.

Abu'l-Fidā

The Conquest of Acre

In Jumādā II of this year [June 1291] Acre was conquered. The reason for that was that the sultan al-Malik al-Ashraf marched on Acre with the Egyptian forces. He sent to order the Syrian forces to come and to bring the mangonels [a large catapult] with them. So al-Malik al-Muzaffar, the lord of Hamāh, and his uncle al-Malik al-Afdal, with all the Hamāh contingent went to Hisn al-Akrād [the castle of Crac des Chevaliers]. There we took delivery of a great mangonel called "al-Mansūrī," which made a hundred cart-loads. They were distributed among the Hamāh contingent, and one cart was put in my charge, for at that time I was an emir of Ten. Our journey with the carts was late in the winter-season, and we had rain and snowstorms between Hisn al-Akrād and Damascus. We suffered great hardship thereby because of the drawing of the carts, the oxen being weak and dying from the cold. Because of the carts we took a month from Hisn al-Akrād to Acre—usually about an eight days' journey for horses. The sultan al-Malik al-Ashraf similarly commanded mangonels to be brought there from all the fortresses, so there were collected against Acre great and small mangonels such as never were collected against any other place.

The descent of the Muslim armies on it was in the early part of Jumādā I of this year [May 1291], and severe fighting developed. The Franks did not close most of their gates but left them open and fought in them. The contingent from Hamāh was stationed at the head of the right wing, as was their custom, so we were beside the sea, with the sea on our right as we faced Acre. Ships with timber vaulting covered with ox-hides came to us firing arrows and quarrels. There was fighting in front of us from the direction of the city, and on our right from the sea. They brought up a ship carrying a mangonel which fired on us and our tents from the direction of the sea. This caused us distress until one night there was a violent storm of wind, so that the vessel was tossed on the waves and the mangonel it was carrying broke. It was smashed to pieces and never set up again. During the siege, the Franks came out by night, surprised the troops and put the sentries to flight. They got through to the tents and became entangled in the ropes. One of their knights fell into an emir's latrine and was killed there. The troops rallied against them and the Franks fell back routed to the town. The troops of Hamāh killed a number of them, and when morning came al-Malik al-Muzaffar, the lord of Hamāh, hung a number of heads of Franks on the necks of the horses which the troops had taken from them, and brought them to the sultan al-Malik al-Ashraf.

The troops tightened their grip on Acre until God Most High granted them its conquest by the sword on Friday, 17 Jumādā II [17 June]. When the Muslims stormed it, some of its inhabitants took flight in ships. Inside the town were a number of towers holding out like citadels. A great mass of Franks entered them and fortified themselves. The Muslims slew, and took an uncountable amount of booty from Acre. Then the sultan demanded the surrender of all who were holding out in the towers, and not one held back. The sultan gave the command and they were beheaded around Acre to the last man. Then at his command the city of Acre was demolished and razed to the ground.

By a strange coincidence the Franks had captured Acre, taking it from Salāh al-Dīn Saladin at noon on Friday, 17 Jumādā II 587 [12 July 1191], took the Muslims in it, and then killed them. God Almighty in his prescience decreed that it should be conquered in this year on Friday, 17 Jumādā II, at the hand of the sultan al-Malik al-Ashraf Salāh al-Dīn. So its conquest was like the day when the Franks took possession of it, and likewise the honorifics of the two sultans.

The Conquest of a Number of Fortresses and Cities

When Acre was conquered, God Most High cast alarm into the hearts of the Franks in the coastlands of Syria. They forthwith evacuated Sidon and Beirut, and al-Shuja'i received their surrender in late Rajab [July 1291]. The inhabitants of the city of Tyre likewise fled, and the sultan sent to receive its surrender. Then 'Athlīth surrendered at the beginning of Sha'bān [30 July]. Then Antartus [Tartus] surrendered on 5 Sha'bān [3 August]. All that was in the year 690, and the sultan enjoyed a felicity that had fallen to no other—the conquest of these great and well-fortified settlements without fighting or trouble. He commanded and they were utterly destroyed. By these conquests all the coastlands were brought back to Islam—an event too great to be hoped or wished. Syria and the coastlands were purged of the Franks after they had been on the brink of taking Egypt and getting possession of Damascus and other places in Syria—may God be praised and blessed. When these great conquests were completed, the sultan al-Malik al-Ashraf moved on and entered Damascus, where he stayed for a time. Then he returned to Egypt, entering it in this year.

19. THE OTTOMAN TURKS AND THE BATTLE OF NICOPOLIS

The fall of Acre eliminated the last Latin Christian foothold in the Holy Land, but it did not end the crusading spirit in Europe. Numerous crusades against the Mamluks were planned in the decades that followed the fall of Acre, only to fall apart before they could come to fruition. By the 1370s, however, the attention of the papacy and those among the aristocracy who favored crusading shifted from the Holy Land and northern Africa to the much more immediate threat posed by the Ottoman Turks. The Ottoman Turks had emerged as a regional power after the destruction of the Seljuks in the mid-thirteenth century. Over the next century, they carved out for themselves a formidable empire, largely at the expense of the Byzantines. By 1338, with their conquest of Nicea, Izmit, and Üsküdar, they were on the doorstep of Constantinople and its formidable defenses. Bypassing the Byzantine capital, they established a foothold in the Balkans, conquering most of Serbia and Bulgaria by 1393 under the leadership of the sultan Bayezid I (r. 1389–1402). This rapid expansion into Europe alarmed the papacy into action. Mounting a crusade at the time was made difficult by the ongoing events of the Hundred Years' War, which pitted France and its allies against England and its allies, and the Papal Schism, which had left Latin Christendom with two popes, one ruling from Rome and the other from Avignon. In 1394, King Sigismund of Hungary (r. 1387–1437) made an urgent plea to European courts for soldiers to come to his aid and drive the Turks out. Shortly thereafter, the Byzantine emperor added his calls for help, as Bayezid had begun a siege of Constantinople in 1395. The desperate appeals were enough to galvanize the countries of Europe and the divided papacy into action. By September 1396, some 15,000 crusaders—including Hungarians, French, English, Germans, Italians, and members of the Knights Hospitallers—had crossed the Danube and laid siege to the Turkish fortress-city of Nicopolis (in modern-day Bulgaria). Bayezid quickly abandoned the siege of Constantinople and rushed to meet the crusaders, arriving on 24 September. The next day, the two armies battled, resulting in a tremendous victory for the Turks and the destruction of the crusader army, including the capture of most of its leaders. The French chronicler Froissart (c. 1337–1410) included the events of the Nicopolis crusade in his Chronicles, based on information he received second hand. Froissart is very assertive in blaming the French crusaders for the debacle, claiming that their pride destroyed any chance the Christians had for success. His writings also give us an insight into the views of the Turks from someone who was far removed from the danger they posed to Christian Europe.

Source: trans. John Bourchier, Froissart, *The Chronicles of Froissart*, ed. G.C. Macaulay (London: Macmillan and Co., 1895), 442–48; rev. Jarbel Rodriguez.

213. How the siege before Nicopolis in Turkey was raised by Amurath-Baquin [Bayezid I] and how the Frenchmen were defeated and how the Hungarians fled—You have heard here before how the king of Hungary and the lords of France passed the river of Danube and entered into Turkey, and all the summer after the month of July they had done many enterprises and had brought many towns to their subjection, for there was none that resisted them, and had besieged the town of Nicopolis, and had brought it to close to surrendering, for they could bear no news of Amurath-Baquin. Then the king of Hungary said to the lords of France and to others, "Sirs, thanked be God, we have had a fair season and have destroyed part of Turkey. I reckon this town of Nicopolis ours when we attack. It is so sorely pressed that it cannot long hold. All things

considered, I counsel (that once we win this town) we go no further this season. We shall withdraw over the Danube into the realm of Hungary, where I have many cities, towns and castles readily furnished to receive you, seeing that you come so far to aid me to make war against the Turks, whom I have found hard and cruel enemies. And this winter we shall make new provision against the next summer, and send word to the French king of our situation, so that this next summer he may refresh us with new men, and I believe, when he knows what we have done and how everything stands, he will have a great desire to come here in his own person; for he is young and courageous and loves deeds of arms. And whether he comes or not, by the grace of God this next summer we shall win the realm of Armenia, and pass the Arm of Saint George [the Bosporus] and so into Syria, and win the ports of Jaffa and Beirut and conquer Jerusalem and all the Holy Land. And if the sultan comes forward, we shall fight with him, for he shall not depart without battle."

These or like words said the king of Hungary to the lords of France, and reckoned Nicopolis as already captured. However, fortune fell otherwise. All that season the king Bayezid, called Amurath-Baquin, had raised an army of Saracens, some from as far away as Persia. Many great men of the Saracens came to aid Amurath-Baquin to destroy Christendom. Two hundred thousand men passed the Arm of Saint George. To say the truth, the Christian men were not sure how many there were. This king Bayezid and his men approached near Nicopolis by covert ways. They knew their warcraft as much as might be expected, and this king was a valiant man, which showed well by reason of his strategy. He ordered his companies thus. His entire host was in a manner as wings, his men covered well over a mile of ground, and before this host, in the vanguard, a band of eight thousand Turks. The two wings of the army were open in the front and narrow behind, and Amurath-Baquin was in the heart of the army. Thus, they rode all in cover. These eight thousand Turks were ordered to make a demonstration, and that as soon as they should see the Christian men approach, they should slowly retire toward the center of the army, and then the two wings, which were open before were to close together and join into one company and then to fight with their enemies, once the Christians had entered between them. This was the order of their battle

Thus in the year of our Lord God a thousand three hundred fourscore and sixteen [1396], the Monday before the feast of Saint Michael, about ten of the clock, as the king of Hungary sat at dinner at the siege of Nicopolis, news arrived that the Turks were coming, and the scouts that came in showed how they had seen the Turks. But their reports were incorrect, for they had not ridden so far forward to see the two wings or the army behind. They had seen nothing more than the outriders and the vanguard, for as soon as they had seen these, they returned. The same day the greatest part of the host was at dinner. Then tidings were brought to the count of Nevers and to all the others by their scouts, who said, "Sirs, arm yourselves quickly so that you are not surprised, for the Turks are coming against you." These tidings greatly rejoiced the Christian men, such as they desired to do deeds of arms. Then every man rose from their dinners, pushed off from the tables, and demanded their harness and horses, and they were quite hot from drinking wine. Then every man drew into the field, banners and standards displayed, every man to his own banner, then the banner of our Lady was displayed, next to the valiant knight Sir John of Vienne, admiral of France. And the Frenchmen were the first that drew into the field freshly dressed, with little regard for the Turks. But they knew not that they were so many, or that Amurath-Baquin was there himself.

As these lords of France were in the field, the king of Hungary's marshal came to them in great haste. He was a valiant knight called Henry of Enstein-Schalle, upon a good horse, with a pennon of his arms, of silver a cross anchored in sable, called in heraldry the iron of a mill-stone. When he came before the banner of our Lady, he stood still and to the gathered host of the barons of France he said openly, "Sirs, I am sent here to you from the king of Hungary, and he desires that I ask that you not attack the enemy until such time as you have word again from him. For we do not know with certainty the number of the Turks. Within two hours, you shall hear more news, for we have sent other outriders forth to spy our enemies more substantially than the first did. And sirs, you may be sure the Turks shall not harm us, if you wait until all our strength is together. Sirs, this is the command that the king and his council have ordered. I must return again to the king." When he had departed, the French lords assembled to agree what was best for them to do. Then the Lord Coucy was asked what he thought best to be done. He answered and said, "I would counsel to obey the king of Hungary's command, for that order seems to be good." And as it was told to me, Sir Philip of Artois, count of Eu and constable of France, was not happy that he had not been asked first for advice. Then he, out of pride and spite, held the contrary opinion and said, "Yea, sir, yea, [if we wait] the king of Hungary would have the flower and chief honor of this battle. We have the vanguard, he has granted it to us, and now he would take it from us again. Obey him if you choose, for I will not." And then he said to the knight that carried his banner, "In the name of God and Saint George, ye shall see me this day a good knight."

When the Lord Coucy heard the constable speak these words, he took it to be done out of arrogance. Then he looked on Sir John of Vienne, who bore the standard of our Lady, and demanded of him what he thought best to be done. "Sir," said he, "whereas wise reason cannot be heard, then pride must reign, and if the Count of Eu attacks, then we must follow. However, we would be stronger if our host were together." Thus, as they deliberated in the field, the Turks approached, and the two wings, each of sixty thousand men, began to approach and to close, and caught the Christians between them, so that if they had wanted to retreat, they could not, for they were surrounded by the Saracens, the wings were so thick. Then many knights that were well experienced in combat saw well that the battle would go against them. However, they advanced and followed the banner of our Lady, borne by the valiant knight Sir John of Vienne. Every knight of France was in his coat of armor, so that every man seemed to be a king, they were so handsomely attired. And as it was told to me, when they first began to fight with the Turks, they were no more than seven hundred men. Lo, behold the great folly and outrage, for if they had waited for the king of Hungary, who had sixty thousand men, it is likely they would have done great deeds. But because of their pride, all was lost, and they received such damage that not since the battle of Roncesvalles, in which the twelve peers of France were slain, had Christendom received such a blow. However, they still managed to slay a great number of Turks. For the Frenchmen vanquished the first division of the Turks and had them in retreat until they came into a valley, where Amurath-Baquin was with his whole host. Then the Frenchmen would have returned to their own side, but they could not, for they were closed in on all sides. There was a terrible battle and the Frenchmen long endured. Then news came to the king of Hungary how the Frenchmen, Englishmen, and Germans were fighting with the Turks, and had broken his command and the counsel given them by his marshal. And he was very displeased, and not without good cause. Then he saw well how he was likely to lose that battle and he said to the grand master of Rhodes [grand master of the military order of John, also known as the Knights Hospitallers], who was next to him, "Sir, we shall this day lose the battle because of the pride of the Frenchmen, for if they would have obeyed me, we would had been strong enough to have fought with our enemies." And then the king of Hungary looked behind him and saw how his own men fled and were defeated. Then he saw clearly that there was no recovery, and those that were about him cried and said, "Save yourself, for if you are slain, all of Hungary is lost. You shall lose the field this day because of the pride of the Frenchmen. Their courage turned to foolish hardiness. They shall all be slain or captured and none is likely to escape. Therefore, sir, if you believe us, save yourself and escape this danger."

The king of Hungary was very displeased when he saw how he had lost the battle because of the disobedience of the Frenchmen, and saw no remedy but to flee or else be taken or slain. Great murder there was, for in fleeing they were chased and so killed. The soldiers of Hungary fled without order, and the Turks chased them. However, God aided the king of Hungary and the grand master of the Hospitallers, for they came to the Danube and found there a little barge belonging to the Hospitallers. They entered into it with only seven persons and pushed off from the shore, or else they would have been slain or captured. For the Turks came to the river side and there killed many Christians who had followed the king to save themselves.

Now let us speak of the Frenchmen and Germans who fought valiantly. When the Lord of Montcavrel, a right valiant knight of Artois, saw that they were about to be defeated, he had by him his son, a young man. Then he said to his squire, "Take here my son and lead him away and save him, and I will abide the fate of my fellow knights." When the child heard his father say so, he refused to depart, but the father insisted and, by force, the squire led him away out of peril and came to the river of Danube. But there the child was so concerned for his father, that he took small regard for himself, and he fell into the river between two barges and there was drowned without remedy. Also Sir William of Tremoville fought in that battle valiantly and there was slain, and his son with him; and Sir John of Vienne, bearing the banner of our Lady, was slain, with the banner in his hands. Thus, all the lords and knights of France that were there were destroyed in the manner that you have heard. Sir John of Burgundy, count of Nevers, was so richly dressed, as was Sir Guy de la Riviere and many other lords and knights of Burgundy, that they were taken prisoners. And there were two squires of Picardy right valiant men, called William Beu and William of Montquel, these two by courage two times passed through the field and returned again and did marvels, but finally they were slain. To say the truth, the Frenchmen and other foreigners that were there acquitted themselves valiantly, but the Frenchmen's pride lost all. There was a knight of Picardy called Sir Jacques of Helly, who had dwelt before in Turkey and had served Amurath-Baquin, and could somewhat speak the language of Turkey. When he saw the battle lost, he gave himself up, and the Saracens, who are covetous of gold and silver, took and saved him. Also a squire of Tour called Jacques du Fay, had before served the king of Tartary called Tamerlane, as soon as this Jacques knew that the Frenchmen came to make war in Turkey, he took leave of the king of Tartary and departed, and was on the said field and taken prisoner by the king of Tartary's men, who were there to help Amurath-Baquin, for king Tamerlane of Tartary had sent to him a great number of soldiers.

The Frenchmen were so richly attired, that they seemed like kings, whereby they were captured and their lives saved, for Saracens and Turks are covetous. They believed that they would receive great ransoms for those who were taken, and considered them greater lords than they were. Sir John of Burgundy count of Nevers was taken prisoner, likewise were the counts of Eu and de la Marche, the Lord Coucy, Sir Henry of Bar, Sir Guy de la Tremoville, Boucicault and many others. And Sir Philip of Bar, Sir John of Vienne, William of Tremoville and his son, slain, as well as many others. The fighting in this battle lasted three hours, and the king of Hungary lost all his baggage and all his plate and jewels, and was glad to save himself, with only seven persons with him in a little barge of the Hospitallers, otherwise he would have been taken or slain without recovery. There were more men slain in the chase than in the battle, and many drowned. Happy was he that might escape by any manner of means.

When this defeat was done and past, the Turks that had been sent out by the sultan were withdrawn into their lodgings, which were now the tents and pavilions that they had conquered. These they found well replenished with wine and garnished meat, and there they celebrated and reveled like people who had attained victory on their enemies. Then Amurath-Baquin with a great number of minstrels, according to their custom, came to the king of Hungary's chief tent, which was richly hung and decorated, and there he took great pleasure and glorified in his heart of the winning of that battle and thanked their God according to their law. Then he took off his weapons, and to refresh himself he sat down on a silk tapestry and caused all his great lords to come to him to chat and to talk with them. He rejoiced and said how he would shortly with great strength pass into the realm of Hungary and conquer the country and, after, other Christian countries, and bring them under his rule, for he said he was content that every man should live after their own laws, desiring nothing but the lordship. But he said he would reign like Alexander of Macedon, who was king of all the world for twelve years, and from whose lineage he said he was descended. All that heard him agreed to his saying. Then he gave three orders: the first was that whoever had any Christian prisoner, was to bring him forth by the next day into the presence of the sultan; the second was that all the dead bodies should be visited and searched, and such as were likely to be noblemen to be laid apart by themselves in their garments until he was able to see them himself; the third was to enquire correctly if the king of Hungary was dead or alive. All was done as he commanded.

After Amurath-Baquin had refreshed himself, to pass the time, he went to the battlefield to see the dead bodies, and it was shown to him that many of his men had been slain and that the battle had cost him greatly. He was greatly astonished at this and could not believe it. Then he mounted on his horse and a great number [of his men] went with him. He had with him two of his brothers called Ali-Bayezid and Sour-Bayezid, as some people said, but he would not acknowledge them, for he said he had no brothers. When he came to the place where the battle was fought, he found that there were many dead and slain. He saw that for each Christian dead, thirty Turks were slain and he was marvelously displeased, and openly said, "This has been a cruel battle and well fought by the Christians, but I shall make those that are alive pay for it dearly." Then the king went to his lodging and so passed that night with great anger in his heart, and in the morning, many people came to his tent to know what they should do with the Christian prisoners; the rumor was that they would all be put to death without mercy. Amurath-Baquin, for all his displeasure, ordered that such Christian men as were in the battle in great finery, and likely to be great men, should be all set together in one part, for he was told that they might well pay great ransoms. Also, there were many Saracens and pagans from Persia, of Tartary, of Arabia, and Syrians who had taken many prisoners, and believed that they had rights over them, as they had indeed. They hid them out of the way, so that they were not seen. Among others Sir Jacques of Helly was brought before Amurath-Baquin as he that held him dared to hide him no longer. Sir Jacques de Helly was known to some of the king's servants, who took him from those that had him, which was lucky for him, as you shall soon see, for many Christian were afterward cruelly slain and put to death.

King Bayezid had ordered his men to enquire which were the greatest of the Christian prisoners, and that they should be set aside with the intent of sparing their lives. So they were found and set apart, first the lord John of Burgundy, count of Nevers, who was chief above all others, and then Sir Philip of Artois, count of Eu, the count of Marche, the lord Coucy, Sir Henry of Bar, Sir Guy of Tremoville, and eight others, and Amurath-Baquin went to see and to speak with them, and beheld them for a long time, and he asked these lords by their faith and law to say the truth, if they were the same persons that they claimed to be, and they said, "Yes." And yet to be more certain, he sent to them the French knight Sir Jacques of Helly to identify them, for he had served Amurath-Baquin before, and therefore his life was spared. He was asked if he knew the French knights who were prisoners. He answered and said, "I think if I see them, I shall recognize them." Then he was commanded to go and view them and to say plainly their names. He did as he was commanded, and when he came to them, he told them his mission and how he had been sent to identify them properly. Then they said, "Ah, Sir Jacques, you know us all, and you see how fortune is against us and how we are in danger of this king. Therefore to save our lives make us rather greater than we in fact are, and show the king that we are men able to pay great ransoms." "Sirs," he said, "so shall I do, for I am bound to you." Then this knight returned to Amurath-Baquin and to his council, and said how those knights with whom he had spoken were of the greatest men in all France and were of the king's lineage, and able to pay great ransoms. Then Amurath-Baquin said how their lives should be saved, and all other prisoners to be slain and hewn to pieces as an example to the others. Then the king showed himself before all the people that were there assembled, and they all bowed to him. They made a lane for him to pass through, every man with his sword naked in his hand, and so he came to where the said lords of France stood together. Then he ordered that they witness the execution of the other prisoners, to which the Saracens all agreed.

Then the prisoners were all brought before Amurath-Baquin, naked in their shirts, and he beheld them a little and then turned from them and made a signal that they should all be slain, and so they were brought through the assembled Saracens, that had ready naked swords in their hands, and were slain and hewn all to pieces without mercy. This cruel justice did Amurath-Baquin that day carry out, by which more than three hundred knights of many nations were tormented and slain for the love of God, on whose souls Jesus have mercy. Among them was slain Sir Henry d'Antoine of Hainault. And so it was that Lord John Boucicault, marshal of France, was one of those brought naked before the king, and would have been slain with the others, had the count of Nevers not seen him. As soon as he saw him, he went straight to the king and kneeled down and begged him to spare Boucicault from death, saying how he was a great man in France and able to pay a great ransom. Amurath-Baquin agreed to the request of the count of Nevers, and so Sir Boucicault was set among them and spared. Thus, cruel justice was done that day upon the Christians, and so that his victory would be known in France, Amurath-Baquin ordered three of the French knights to come before him, of which Sir Jacques of Helly was one. Then the king demanded that the count of Nevers select which of the three knights he would choose to send to France to the king and to the duke of Burgundy, the count's father. Then the count of Nevers said, "Sir, if it pleases you, I would that this knight, Sir Jacques of Helly, should go to France from you and from us." So Sir Jacques waited with Amurath-Baquin, and the other two knights delivered to death and so slain, which was a pity.

Then Amurath-Baquin was well appeased of his anger and understood how the king of Hungary had escaped alive. He then decided to return into Turkey to a city called Bursa, and so he did, and all the prisoners were brought there. And then his army departed, especially those that came from far-off countries like Tartary, Persia, Media, Syria, Alexandria, and Lithuania. Then Sir Jacques Helly returned to France, and he was commanded to return through Lombardy and to praise Amurath-Baquin to the duke of Milan. He was also commanded to bring news of the victory that Amurath-Baquin had against the Christians through every place that he passed. The count of Nevers wrote to the French king for himself and all his company, and to his father the duke of Burgundy and to the duchess his mother. When this knight [Jacques Helly] had his orders and his credentials, he departed and made his way towards France. Before he departed, he was sworn and made to promise that as soon as he had delivered his message in France, he would return immediately [to Turkey]. This oath and promise he kept like a true knight.

20. THE CONQUEST OF CONSTANTINOPLE

Bayezid followed up his victory at Nicopolis by returning to the siege of Constantinople, but his plans for its conquest were derailed when Tamerlane, the great central Asian conqueror, began to war against the Ottomans. This culminated in Bayezid's capture and subsequent death in 1402. Tamerlane's incursions gave the Byzantines a reprieve, but only temporarily as subsequent sultans kept up the pressure and unsuccessfully attacked the city in 1422. In 1451, Mehmed II (r. 1451–81), Bayezid's great-grandson, ascended to the Ottoman throne and began preparations for the conquest of the city. The preparations alarmed Constantine XI (r. 1449–53), the Byzantine emperor, who called on the Latin West for help. But help from the West was not forthcoming. The distrust that had developed between the Latins and the Greeks—dating back to the split between the Catholic and Orthodox churches in 1054 and the Fourth Crusade, in which western Crusaders captured Constantinople and set up a Latin kingdom there for over five decades—limited any possible Latin aid. What help did come, mostly from the Italians, was inadequate or arrived too late to have much influence on the upcoming battle. Therefore, when the siege began in January 1453 with the arrival of the Ottoman forces outside the ancient walls of Constantinople, the defenders awaited with some 8,000 soldiers to oppose them. The besieging army may have numbered close to 100,000 men, including a corps of elite Janissaries, and an artillery train with fearsome firepower. The final attack began on 29 May, and after hours of fighting the Ottomans were able to breach the legendary defenses and capture the city, bringing an end to the Byzantine Empire. Among those present when the city fell was the Venetian doctor Nicolò Barbaro, who kept a diary recording the events that transpired during the siege.

Source: trans. J.R. Jones, Nicolò Barbaro, *Diary of the Siege of Constantinople, 1453* (New York: Exposition Press, 1969), 62–66.

On the twenty-ninth of May, 1453, three hours before daybreak, Mahomet Bey [Mehmed II], son of Murat the Turk, came himself to the walls of Constantinople to begin the general assault which gained him the city. The sultan divided his troops into three groups of fifty thousand men each: one group was of Christians who were kept in his camp against his will, the second group was of men of a low condition, peasants and the like, and the third group was of janissaries in their white turbans, these being all soldiers of the sultan and paid every day, all well-armed men strong in battle, and behind these janissaries were all the officers, and behind these the Turkish sultan. The first group, which was the Christians, had the task of carrying the ladders to the walls, and they tried to raise the ladders up, and at once we threw them to the ground with the men who were raising them, and they were all killed at once, and we threw big stones down on them from the battlements, so that few escaped alive; in fact, anyone who approached beneath the walls was killed. When those who were raising up the ladders saw so many dead, they tried to retreat towards their camp, so as not to be killed by the stones, and when the rest of the Turks who were behind saw that they were running away, at once they cut them to pieces with their scimitars and made them turn back towards the walls, so that they had the choice of dying on one side or the other; and when this first group was killed and cut to pieces, the second group began to attack vigorously. The first group was sent forward for two reasons, firstly because they preferred that Christians should die rather than Turks, and secondly to wear us out in the city; and as I have said, when the first group was dead or wounded, the second group came on like lions unchained against the walls on the side of San Romano, and when we saw this fearful thing, at once the tocsin [an alarm bell] was sounded through the whole city and at every post on the walls, and every man ran crying out to help; and the Eternal God showed us his mercy against these Turkish dogs, so that every man ran to ward off the attack of the pagans, and they began to fall back outside the barbicans. But this second group was made up of brave men, who came to the walls and wearied those in the city greatly by their attack. They also made a great attempt to raise ladders up to the walls, but the men on the walls bravely threw them down to the ground again, and many Turks were killed. Also, our crossbows and cannon kept on firing into their camp at this time and killed an incredible number of Turks.

When the second group had come forward and attempted unsuccessfully to get into the city, there then approached the third group, their paid soldiers the janissaries, and their officers and their other principal commanders, all very brave men, and the Turkish sultan behind them all. This third group attacked the walls of the poor city, not like Turks but like lions, with such shouting and sounding of castanets that it seemed a thing not of this world, and the shouting was heard as far away as Anatolia, twelve miles away from their camp. This third group of Turks, all fine fighters, found those on the walls very weary after having fought with the first and second groups, while the pagans were eager and fresh for the battle; and with the loud cries which they uttered on the field, they spread fear through the city and took away our courage with their shouting and noise. The wretched people in the city felt themselves to have been taken already, and decided to sound the tocsin through the whole city, and sounded it at all the posts on the walls, all crying at the top of their voices, "Mercy! Mercy! God send help from Heaven to this empire of Constantine, so that a pagan people may not rule over the empire!" All through the city all the women were on their knees, and all the men too, praying most earnestly and devoutly to our omnipotent God and his Mother, Madonna Saint Mary, with all the sainted men and women of the celestial hierarchy, to grant us victory over this pagan race, these wicked Turks, enemies of the Christian faith. While these supplications were being made, the Turks were attacking fiercely on the landward side by San Romano, by the headquarters of the most serene emperor and all his nobles, and his principal knights and his bravest men, who all stayed by him fighting bravely. The Turks were attacking, as I have said, like men determined to enter the city, by San Romano on the landward side, firing their cannon again and again, with so many other guns and arrows without number and shouting from these pagans, that the very air seemed to be split apart; and they kept on firing their great cannon which fired a ball weighing twelve hundred pounds, and their arrows, all along the length of the walls on the side where their camp was, a distance of six miles, so that inside the barbicans at least eighty camel-loads of them were picked up, and as many as twenty camel-loads of those which were in the ditch. This fierce battle lasted until daybreak.

Our men of Venice did marvels of defense in the part where the bastion was, where the Turks were concentrating their attack, but it was useless, since our eternal God had already made up his mind that the city should fall into the hands of the Turks; and since God had so determined, nothing further could be done, except that all we Christians who found ourselves at this time in the wretched city should place ourselves in the hands of our merciful Lord Jesus Christ and of his Mother, Madonna Saint Mary, for them to have mercy on the souls of those who had to die in the battle on this day. One hour before daybreak the sultan had his great cannon fired, and the shot landed in the repairs which we had made and knocked them down to the ground. Nothing could be seen for the smoke made by the cannon, and the Turks came on under cover of the smoke, and about three hundred of them got inside the barbicans. The Greeks and Venetians fought hard and drove them out of the barbicans, and a great number died, including almost all of those who were able to get inside. After the Greeks had fought this fight, they thought that they had indeed won the victory against the pagans, and we Christians were greatly relieved. But after being driven back from the barbicans the Turks again fired their great cannon, and the pagans like hounds came on behind the smoke of the cannon, raging and pressing on each other like wild beasts, so that in the space of a quarter of an hour there were more than thirty thousand Turks inside the barbicans, with such cries that it seemed a very inferno, and the shouting was heard as far away as Anatolia. When the Turks got inside the barbicans, they quickly captured the first row of them, but before they managed this, a great number of them died at the hands of those who were above them on the walls, who killed them with stones at their pleasure. After having captured the first row, the Turks together with the *axapi* [irregular infantry] made themselves strong there, and then there came inside the barbicans a good seventy thousand Turks with such force that it seemed a very inferno, and soon the barbicans from one end to the other, a full six miles, were full of Turks. As I have said before, those on the walls killed great numbers of Turks with stones, casting them down from above without stopping, and so many were killed that forty carts could not have carried away the dead Turks who had died before getting into the city. We Christians now were very frightened, and the emperor had the tocsin sounded through the whole city, and at the posts on the walls, with every man crying, "Mercy, eternal God!" Men cried out, and women too, and the nuns and the young women most loudly of all, and there was such lamentation that even the most cruel Jew would have felt pity. Seeing this, Zuan Zustignan [Giovanni Giustianni Longo], that Genoese of Genoa, decided to abandon his post [after being wounded], and fled to his ship, which was lying at the boom. The emperor had made this Zuan Zustignan captain of his forces, and as he fled, he went through the city crying, "The Turks have got into the city!" But he lied in his teeth, because the Turks were not yet inside. When the people heard their captain's words, that the Turks had got into the city, they all began to take flight, and all abandoned their posts at once and went rushing towards the harbor in the hope of escaping in the ships and the galleys. At this moment of confusion, which happened at sunrise, our omnipotent God came to his most bitter decision and decided to fulfill all the prophecies, as I have said, and at sunrise the Turks entered the city near San Romano, where the walls had been razed to the ground by their cannon. But before they entered, there was such a fierce struggle between the Turks and the Christians in the city who opposed them, and so many of them died, that a good twenty carts could have been filled with the corpses of the first Turks. Then the second wave followed the first and went rushing about the city, and anyone they found they put to the scimitar, women and men, old and young, of any condition. This butchery lasted from sunrise, when the Turks entered the city, until midday, and anyone whom they found was put to the scimitar in their rage. Those of our merchants who escaped hid themselves in underground places, and when the first mad slaughter was over, they were found by the Turks and were all taken and sold as slaves.

The Turks made eagerly for the piazza, five miles from the point where they made their entrance at San Romano, and when they reached it, at once some of them climbed up a tower where the flags of Saint Mark and the most serene emperor were flying, and they cut down the flag of Saint Mark and took away the flag of the most serene emperor, and then on the same tower they raised the flag of the sultan. When they had taken away these two flags, those of Saint Mark and of the emperor, and raised the flag of the Turkish dog, then all we Christians who were in the city were full of sorrow because it had been captured by the Turks. When their flag was raised and ours cut down, we saw that the whole city was taken, and that there was no further hope of recovering from this.

CHAPTER THREE

WARFARE IN SPAIN AND THE
WESTERN MEDITERRANEAN

Figure 3.1: Surrender of the Muslim town of Montefrio to the forces of Castile and
Aragon in 1486.

Source: Paul LaCroix, *Military and Religious Life in the Middle Ages and the Period of the Renaissance*
(London: Bickers and Son, n.d.), 193.

21. THE CONQUEST OF TOLEDO

In 1031, the caliphate of Cordoba collapsed after the death of the last caliph, Hisham III (r. 1027–31). Its downfall precipitated the fragmentation of Spanish Islam as the once powerful caliphate disintegrated into numerous small independent kingdoms known as taifas. These small states, ruled by groups from different ethnic and tribal backgrounds, constantly fought one another and, over time, the larger ones absorbed the smaller ones. As they fought and weakened each other, they opened themselves up to attack from the Christians from the north of the peninsula. These Christian kingdoms, led by Leon-Castile and Aragon-Navarre, took advantage of the weakness and fragmentation of the Muslims to advance their own territorial ambitions. They became a real threat to the taifas, which often survived by paying off the Christian kings with tribute. Throughout the eleventh century, Christian kings had some successes at the expense of the taifas, notably the conquest of Coimbra and the capture of Barbastro, which they subsequently lost. For the siege of Barbastro in 1064, Pope Alexander II (r. 1061–73) granted the Christian soldiers the plenary indulgence that would become the hallmark of the crusades. These minor triumphs, however, paled in comparison to the conquest of Toledo by Alfonso VI, king of Leon and Castile (r. 1065–1109) in 1085. The conquest of Toledo was of immense importance to the Christians. The city had been the capital of the Visigoths and the primatial seat of the Spanish church, thus giving it political and religious significance. Toledo also had a large Muslim population, many of whom now became Christian subjects known as mudejares. *The excerpt that follows, probably written by Abú Ja'far, narrates the story of the conquest of Toledo, placing particular blame on the internecine fighting among the taifas and the reliance of al-Qadir, the ruler of Toledo, on Alfonso VI for military and political support. The narrative highlights the complexities of peninsular politics, as Muslims and Christians often fought on the same side against their coreligionist and were often guided by pragmatic concerns more than by religious ones.*

Source: trans. Pascual de Gayangos, *The History of the Mohammedan Dynasties of Spain* (London: W.H. Allen and Co., 1843), vol. II: xxviii–xxxi; rev. Jarbel Rodriguez.

In the midst of these troubles, namely, in the year 477 [beginning 26 August 1074], died the king of Toledo, Ismael ibn Dhinun [better known as al-Mamun, r. 1043–75], the same who took Cordoba from Ibn 'Abbad [Muhammad Ibn Abbad al Mutamid, 1069–91], and defended it afterwards from his attacks. Ibn Dhinun surpassed many of the Muslim kings of his time in courage and military talents. When he died, his body was carried on the shoulders of his own men to Toledo, and there buried. He left no sons. That period of history in which the disastrous events above related took place has been called by the Arabian authors Ayyámu-l-firk [the days of division or confusion].

Ismail ibn Dhinun having left no male children, he was succeeded in the kingdom of Toledo by his grandson, Yahya, who assumed the title of al-Qadir [1075–85]. Yahya was imbecile in mind and weak in body. He had been brought up in his father's harem among women and eunuchs, dancers and singers; and he was as unfit for the command of the army as for the duties of the administration in those perilous times. He therefore abandoned himself completely into the hands of his slaves, and entrusted to his eunuchs the cares of the government. This made him the scorn of his subjects; hated and despised by them, he became at the same time a mark to the ambition of his equals among the rulers of Andalus.

The king of Seville, al-Mutamid, was the first to assail him in his own dominions. Being anxious to revenge upon him all the injuries he had received at his grandfather's hands, that monarch took the field at the head of considerable forces, and, after recovering Cordoba and the surrounding districts, reduced also Talavera, Gháfek, and all the territory lying between those two cities.

Nor was al-Mutamid the only one who attacked this imbecile prince; the king of Saragossa, Ibn Húd, made also an incursion into his territory, and, assisted by the tyrant Ibn Radmir [Sancho Ramirez, king of Aragon and Navarre, r. 1063–94], took from him the cities of Santa Maria and Molina. Unable to withstand alone the attacks of his two formidable adversaries, a task for which his cowardice and stupidity made him totally unfit, Yahya solicited the aid of the tyrant Alfonso [VI]. In the meantime the city of Valencia, which formed part of Yahya's dominions, as inherited from his grandfather, al-Mamum, threw off its allegiance; Ibn Húd having prevailed upon the governor, Abu Bekr Ibn 'Abdil-'azíz, to declare himself in open revolt, and to assume the command of the place. The king of Zaragoza then asked in marriage the daughter of Abu Bekr, expecting that the match would be the means of his getting possession of the kingdom of Valencia, which he ardently wished for.

At the same time the city of Cuenca, which belonged also to al-Qadir, was besieged by Ibn Radmir. That tyrant pressed the town until the inhabitants were on the point of starvation through hunger and thirst; when, unable to hold out any longer, they capitulated, and agreed to pay him a considerable sum of money if he would raise the siege, which he did. Al-Qadir then sent an army, under the command of Bashir the eunuch, to meet the combined forces of Ibn Húd and Ibn Radmir; but that general returned without encountering the enemy, who had already retired into their respective countries loaded with rich spoil.

When King al-Qadir saw himself thus surrounded by his enemies, he wrote to apprise Alfonso of his critical situation, and begged the Christian king to send an army to his assistance.

The tyrant's answer was thus conceived: "If you wish me to defend and protect you against your enemies, send me so much money; if not, I will deliver you into their hands." This king Alfonso was a very shrewd and perfidious man, and he saw with secret delight the disturbances raised in the very heart of the Muslim dominions by their ambitious rulers. He well knew that in proportion as they consumed their own resources and those of their subjects in useless and petty warfare, his own power would increase, and that the moment was fast approaching for conquering the whole of Andalus. He therefore took the first opportunity, which offered itself by the non-compliance of al-Qadir with the terms of the treaty, to invade the dominions of that monarch, as we shall presently relate. However, when Yahya received the above answer, he called together to a council the functionaries of the state, and the governors of his provinces, besides a considerable number of his subjects, and communicated to them Alfonso's proposal. "The Christian king," said Yahya to the assembly, "has pledged himself by a most solemn oath, that unless you bring me immediately the sums for which he asks, yourselves, wives, and children shall be made answerable for it." Not one of those present answered a word, with the exception of the Caid Abú Shajá' Ibn Lebun, who said to Yahya, "The words you have just uttered are the best proof of the instability of thy empire, but perhaps you trust and rely on him [Alfonso]." Abú Shajá' was right. So disgusted were the people of Toledo with Yahya's willingness to comply with the exorbitant demands made by the Christian king that they pronounced him to be utterly unfit to govern them, and decided to enter into a secret correspondence with al-Mutawakkil, king of Badajoz [r. 1067–94], and persuaded him to deprive al-Qadir of the empire.

No sooner was al-Qadir informed of the plot against him, that, not deeming himself secure in Toledo, he fled at night with his treasures and only a few of his adherents, and took the road to Huete; but the governor, named Ibn Wahb, shut the gates and refused him admission. During this interval, al-Mutawakkil arrived in sight of Toledo, and entered that city.

In this emergency al-Qadir again sought the aid of Alfonso. Surrounded on every side by enemies, his sole hope of salvation was in the Christian king. He wrote to him and implored his assistance, and the tyrant accordingly hastened to help him. Al-Qadir went out to meet the Christian, when it was mutually agreed that Alfonso should lay siege to Toledo, until he should expel al-Mutawakkil and restore the city to al-Qadir, who, on the restoration of his capital, was to hand over to Alfonso the whole of his treasures. As a security against any infraction of this treaty, Alfonso was to retain as pledges the fortresses of Soria and Conoria. These conditions being mutually agreed upon, the Christians were put in possession of the above fortresses, which they put in an excellent state of defense by considerably augmenting their fortifications, and garrisoning them with their best troops. Alfonso then laid siege to Toledo.

Al-Mutawakkil seeing himself closely besieged by the Christians, and not expecting assistance from any one, abandoned the city, and al-Qadir was again put in possession of it. Agreeably to his promise, al-Qadir collected all the money he could among the inhabitants of the place, and presented it to Alfonso; but this the tyrant would not receive. Al-Qadir then brought him the whole of the treasures and jewels which he had inherited from his father and grandfather, but still the amount not being equal to the promised sum, al-Qadir begged Alfonso to wait for the payment of the remainder. His request was granted by the Christian king on condition that the fortress of Canales should be given over to him as security. When Alfonso saw himself master of that important fortress, he immediately garrisoned it with his best troops, and filled it with provisions and military stores. After which he returned to Castile, rich, safe, and with his saddle-bags full of plunder.

Alfonso's interference on this occasion, far from being beneficial to al-Qadir, proved the cause of his ruin and of the loss of his kingdom. It alienated the hearts of his subjects entirely from him; many of whom left Toledo secretly, and repaired to the dominions of Ibn Húd, by whom they were kindly received and honorably entertained, this monarch bestowing on them all manner of favors and distinctions. The kingdom of Toledo, too, became a target for the ambition of neighboring princes, all of whom strove to gain possession of it. Thus, al-Mutamid attacked it from the west, while Ibn Húd made it feel on the east all the agonies of death.

When al-Qadir perceived that he was unable to resist the simultaneous attacks of his enemies, and that no way was left open to him to escape from their clutches, he again wrote to Alfonso, offering to cede to him Toledo and its environs, provided he would assist him in the conquest of Valencia and its dependencies. No sooner did Alfonso receive the letter containing this proposition, than he flew towards al-Qadir as if he had had wings, and, marching night and day, arrived in sight of Toledo, which city was immediately put at his disposal, and the inhabitants at his discretion. Before surrendering his capital to Alfonso, al-Qadir stipulated for the following conditions. Every Muslim was to enjoy security for himself, family, and children; he was, moreover, to retain possession of his property. Those who chose might quit the town with all their goods and chattels; those who preferred to remain were only to be subject to the payment of the customary tribute, in proportion to the number of individuals who composed their family. It was further stipulated that if any one of the inhabitants chose to return after an absence of some time, he should be allowed again to settle in Toledo with whatever goods or property he had, without being subjected to the payment of duties or other personal inconvenience owing to the amount of the same.

Alfonso gave his assent to this capitulation, which he confirmed by a touch of his right hand, swearing faithfully to observe every one of the conditions therein contained. The taking of Toledo by Alfonso happened in 478 (1085). Tariq ibn

Ziyad having taken it in the year 92, it had thus remained the abode of Islam for a period of 386 years. On the entrance of the Christians most of the inhabitants left the city, and retired to other provinces occupied by their brethren in religion. Toledo, in the mean time, remained in the hands of the infidels, who were left in undisturbed possession of it, as no attempt was made or wish manifested to snatch it from them, until the news came that the Almoravids, after defeating the tribe of Zeriatah, had conquered the whole of western Africa. These tidings filled with joy the Muslims of Andalus, whose hope was strengthened and whose spirit was revived in expectation of their powerful allies.

22. THE ARRIVAL OF THE ALMORAVIDS

The conquest of Toledo forced the remaining Muslim kingdoms to seek out allies from beyond the sea, lest they too be overthrown. In their desperation, they hesitantly turned to the Almoravids, who ruled northern Africa. This would significantly change the situation in the peninsula. The Almoravids crossed from northern Africa into Algeciras in June 1086. In late October, they clashed with the army of Alfonso VI of Castile, the king who had captured Toledo. The battle was a decisive Muslim victory that ultimately allowed Yūsuf Ibn Tashfin (r. 1061–1106), the ruler of the Almoravids, to bring most of Muslim Spain under his control and to put the Christians on the defensive.

Source: trans. Jarbel Rodriguez from Ambrocio Huici Miranda's Spanish translation of Ibn Abī Zar, *Rawd al-Qirtas* (Valencia: Graficas Bautista, 1964), 281–89.

The news of the arrival [of the Almoravids] reached Alfonso as he was laying siege to Zaragoza, crushing his hopes. He gave up on the siege and abandoned Zaragoza. He sent for Ibn Radmir and Alvar Fáñez; Ibn Radmir was laying siege to Tortosa and Alvar Fáñez to Valencia. The two of them quickly went with their troops to join Alfonso, who also sent word to Castile, Galicia, and Bayonne. From those regions, he received an incalculable number of Christians. When these infidel soldiers joined Alfonso and his regiments attained their full strength, he marched to meet the emir Yūsuf Ibn Tashfin and his Muslim troops. Yūsuf departed from Algeciras and headed to meet him. Before him, he sent his qadi Abū Sulaymān Dāwūd ibn 'A'ycha with ten thousand Almoravid horsemen. Following [Yūsuf] were Ibn 'A'ycha al-Mutamid ibn 'Abbād with the emirs from al-Andalus and their troops, among them Ibn Sumādih, Lord of Almeria; Ibn Habbūs, Lord of Granada; Ibn Maslima, Lord of the Upper Frontier; Ibn Dīl-nun, Ibn al-Aftas and Ibn Bādis. Yūsuf ordered all of them to join with al-Mutamid ibn 'Abbād and for the Andalusi forces to remain separate from the Almoravids.... Yūsuf then wrote a letter to Alfonso, giving him the option of paying tribute [*parias*], converting to Islam, or war. When the letter reached Alfonso, he was filled with pride and contempt and told the ambassador: "Tell the emir not to bother [coming to challenge us], we will come to you." Yūsuf and Alfonso both departed [from their respective mustering sites] and they made camp in the vicinity of Badajoz, with the emir Yūsuf making camp in a place known as al-Zallaqa in the region of Badajoz. Al-Mutamid and the nobles of al-Andalus also came forth and made camp in a nearby site, and between the two of them there was a hill, a barrier to protect them from the enemy. The Badajoz River separated these two armies and the Christian forces, and both sides drank from it. They remained there for three days, with messengers going back and forth between them, until they agreed to fight on Monday, the fourteenth of Rajab, 479 [AH/25 October 1086]. When the emir al-Mutamid agreed to this, he sent a message to Yūsuf ibn Tashfin to remind him to be ready and able for the battle as the enemy was very cagey and cunning in its responses. On the night of Thursday, tenth of Rajab, Ibn 'Abbad prepared his squadrons and made his soldiers ready for battle, sending light horsemen as scouts against the enemy to bring back any news of their movements.... Alfonso, the enemy of God, had divided his army into two corps and he himself led one against Yūsuf Ibn Tashfin, the emir of the Muslims. He clashed with Dāwūd ibn 'A'ycha and his soldiers and there was a great battle, in which the Almoravids offered a heroic resistance, but Alfonso thanks to his superior numbers, defeated and almost exterminated them. There was a fight between them in which the swords were broken and the lances shattered. The second corps of the damned [Alfonso] went with Alvar Fáñez and Ibn Radmir against the army led by Ibn 'Abbād and subdued it, crushing the armies of the nobles of al-Andalus. And none of them was able to withstand [the Christian army] except for Ibn 'Abbād, who kept his forces apart, and who fought without being defeated in a terrible battle and resisting as nobles in a wretched war. The news reached Yūsuf that the forces of al-Andalus had been defeated and that Ibn Abbād and Ibn 'A'ycha still fought on, unconquered. [He decided] to send his qadi Sīr Ibn Abī Bākr with the tribes from the Maghreb, and those of Zanata, Masmūda, Gomara, and other Berber tribes that were in his army to aid Ibn 'Abbād and Ibn 'A'ycha. He himself headed for Alfonso's camp with the army from Lamtūna and the Almoravid tribes from Sinhādja. While Alfonso was engaged with Ibn 'A'ycha, Yusuf set fire to his camp, burning it and killing the valiant defenders and other horsemen and soldiers that had been left behind to guard and defend it. The rest fled in defeat and headed for Alfonso, pursued by Yūsuf, the Muslim emir, with his rearguard, his drums, and his flags. The Almoravid soldiers went before him, striking their swords against the infidel and watering them in their blood. Alfonso said, "What is this?" It was then that he was told of the sacking and burning of his camp, the death of its defenders, and the capture of the women [camp followers]. Alfonso then turned to meet Yūsuf. The Muslim emir persevered against him and the battle became more heated. The Muslim emir, on a mule, rode among the Muslim ranks, exalting them and strengthening their morale so that they could prevail in the holy war. He told them, "Oh, gathered Muslims! Do not flinch in this battle with the infidel, enemies of God. Those among you who are martyred will be rewarded with paradise; and those among you who survive will win prizes and booty." The Muslims fought that day as if seeking martyrdom and wishing for death. Al-Mutamid and his companions who fought with him, had given up all hope of life, when, not knowing what was happening, they saw the Christian forces retreat and flee in defeat. When they saw the Christians turn their backs, they thought that it was due to their efforts. "Attack the enemies of God," shouted al-Mutamid to his men, and they attacked them. The qadi Sīr Ibn Abī Bākr also advanced with the tribesmen from the Maghreb that were with him. Those Muslims who had fled towards Badajoz, returned to the battle when they learned that the Muslim emir had triumphed. They joined up with each other, squadrons with squadrons, platoons with platoons, as the battle intensified around Alfonso forcing him to consider saving himself. He stayed on, however, continuing to fight until the sun set. When he noticed that night was fast approaching, that the bulk of his soldiers had perished, and the perseverance of the Almoravids and their intention to wage a holy war, he realized that he could not keep fighting, and he fled in defeat, lost, and with only 500 knights. The Muslims were on their heels, unleashing their swords upon them, slaughtering them over hills and valleys, and devouring them as a kit of pigeons devours a handful of grain, until darkness stopped their pursuit. The Muslims spent that night on horseback, killing, taking captives, claiming booty, and giving thanks to God for the victory that he had granted them. At dawn, they said their morning prayers in the midst of the battlefield. This was one of the worst defeats suffered by the enemies of God, losing their polytheistic kings and his auxiliaries, his defenders and his worthies, and the only one who survived was Alfonso, gravely wounded, with 500 wounded knights. Of these 400 died in the rout, and he entered Toledo with a mere one-hundred horsemen. This glorious victory occurred on Friday, the twelfth of Rajab, 479 [23 October 1086]. Over three-thousand Muslims were crowned in martyrdom, having already received many other gifts from God. Yūsuf, the Muslim emir, ordered his soldiers to cut off the heads of the dead Christians and arrange them in mounds before him. Ten thousand were sent to Seville and another ten thousand to Cordoba, Valencia, Zaragoza, and Murcia. Four thousand were sent to the Maghreb to be distributed among the cities, so that all could see them and give thanks to God for so great a blessing. The Christian army, it was said, numbered 80,000 horsemen and 200,000 infantry, and all died save for Alfonso and one hundred knights. The Christians were so humiliated that they were not able to do much for the next sixty years.

23. TWO VIEWS OF EL CID

The defeat suffered at the Battle of Zallaqa put the Christian forces on the defensive for much of the rest of the eleventh century. Alfonso, severely weakened, was barely able to defend his own territory, let alone come to the aid of the Muslim allies who sided with him and opposed the Almoravids. One region where the Christians forged some successes was in the east, where Rodrigo Diaz de Vivar (c. 1040–99), an exile from the court of Alfonso VI and better known as El Cid (from the Arabic sayyid *or lord), was able to capture Valencia in June 1094. Later that year, in October, he routed an Almoravid army that was coming to retake the city. Due to his near-legendary exploits, El Cid emerged as the iconic hero of the Reconquest, lionized in the Castilian sources for his exploits on the battlefield and for his chivalric and honorable conduct off it. The Muslim sources paint a different image, however, depicting a tyrannical ruler who was more than capable of torturing and executing his enemies. The two sources that follow are representative of these ambivalent feelings toward El Cid. The first source below, which narrates El Cid's activities around Zaragoza (starting around 1081), is drawn from the* Primera Cronica General, *a compilation of texts from the late thirteenth or early fourteenth century. In it, El Cid emerges as an honorable and duty-driven mercenary who fought on behalf of both Christian and Muslim rulers. The actions of El Cid are indicative of the fluid boundaries that separated Muslims from Christians in the Iberian Peninsula. Religious difference was not an impediment to alliances or truces, but an aspect of culture that could be negotiated and, at times, overshadowed by more pragmatic concerns. The second source, drawn from the* Al-Bayan al-Mughrib *and written by Ibn Idhari around 1312, takes a much harsher view of El Cid, notably in the polemical language that it uses to address him and in highlighting his ruthless tactics while dealing with Valencia.*

Sources: trans. Robert Southey, *Chronicle of the Cid* (London: George Routledge and Sons, 1885), 92–94, 102–9, rev. Jarbel Rodriguez; trans. Jarbel Rodriguez, from Ambrosio Huici Miranda, *Ibn 'Idari: Al-Bayan al-Mugrib—Nuevos fragmentos almorávides y almohades* (Valencia: Gráficas Bautista, 1963), 72–77, 87–89.

Chronicle of the Cid: El Cid and al-Mutamid

My Cid left the kingdom of King Don Alfonso, and [with his men] entered the country of the Moors. And at daybreak they were near the brow of the Sierra, and they halted there upon the top of the mountains, and gave barley to their horses, and remained there until evening. And they set forward when the evening had closed, that none might see them, and continued their way all night, and before dawn they came near to Castrejon, which is upon the Henares. And Alvar Fáñez said unto the Cid, that he would take with him two hundred horsemen, and scour the country as far as Fita and Guadalajara and

Alcala, and lay hands on whatever he could find, without fear either of King Alfonso or of the Moors. And he counseled him to remain in ambush where he was, and surprise the castle of Castrejon: and it seemed good unto my Cid. Away went Alvar Fáñez, and Alvar Alvarez with him, and Alvar Salvadores, and Galin Garcia, and the two hundred horsemen; and the Cid remained in ambush with the rest of his company. And as soon as it was morning, the Moors of Castrejon, knowing nothing of these who were so near them, opened the castle gates, and went out to their work as they were accustomed to do. And the Cid rose from ambush and fell upon them, and took all their flocks, and made straight for the gates, pursuing them. And there was a cry within the castle that the Christians were upon them, and they who were within ran to the gates to defend them, but my Cid came up sword in hand; eleven Moors he slaughtered with his own hand, and they abandoned the gate and fled before him to hide themselves within, so that he won the castle, and took gold and silver, and whatever else he would.

Alvar Fáñez meantime scoured the country along the Henares as far as Alcala, and he returned driving flocks and herds before him, with great stores of wearing apparel and of other plunder. He came with the banner of Minaya, and there were none who dared fall upon his rear. And when the Cid knew that he was close at hand he went out to meet him, and praised him greatly for what he had done, and gave thanks to God. And he gave order that all the spoils should be heaped together, both what Alvar Fáñez had brought, and what had been taken in the castle; and he said to him, "Brother, of all this which God has given us, take the fifth part, for you well deserve it," but Alvar Fañez would not, saying, "You have need of it for our support." And the Cid divided the spoil among the knights and foot-soldiers, to each his due portion; to every horseman a hundred marks of silver, and half as much to the foot-soldiers: and because he could find none to whom to sell his fifth, he spoke to the Moors of Castrejon, and sent to those of Fita and Guadalajara, telling them that they might come safely to purchase the spoil, and the prisoners also whom he had taken, both men and women, for he would take none with him. And they came, and valued the spoil and the prisoners, and gave for them three thousand marks of silver, which they paid within three days: they bought also much of the spoil which had been divided, making great gain, so that all who were in my Cid's company were full rich. And the heart of my Cid was joyous, and he sent to King Don Alfonso, telling him that he and his companions would yet do him service upon the Moors.

Then my Cid assembled together his good men and said unto them, "Friends, we cannot take up our abode in this castle, for there is no water in it, and moreover the king is at peace with these Moors, and I know that the treaty between them has been written; so that if we should abide here he would come against us with all his power, and with all the power of the Moors, and we could not stand against him. If therefore it seem good unto you, let us leave the rest of our prisoners here, for it does not befit us to take any with us, but to be as free from all encumbrance as may be, like men who are to live by war, and to help ourselves with our arms." And it pleased them well that it should be so. And he said to them, "You have all had your shares, neither is there anything owing to any one among you. Now then let us be ready to be on the move early in the morning, for I would not fight against my lord the king." So in the morning they went to their horses and departed, being rich with the spoils which they had won: and they left the castle to the Moors, who remained blessing them for this bounty which they had received at their bands. Then my Cid and his company went up the Henares as fast as they could go, and they passed by the Alcanas, and by the caves of Anquita, and through the waters, and they entered the plain of Torancio, and halted between Fariza and Cetina: great were the spoils which they collected as they went along. And the following day they passed Alfama, and leaving the Gorge below them they passed Bobierca, and Teca which is beyond it, and came against Alcocer. There my Cid pitched his tents upon a round hill, which was a great hill and strong; and the river Salon ran near them, so that the water could not be cut off. My Cid thought to take Alcocer, so he pitched his tents securely, having the Sierra on one side, and the river on the other, and he made all his people dig a trench, so that they would not be threatened, neither by day nor by night.…

… My Cid remained a while in Alcocer, and the Moors of the border waited to see what he would do. And in this time, King Fariz recovered from his wound, and my Cid sent to him and to the Moors, saying, that if they would give him three thousand marks of silver, he would leave Alcocer and go else-where. And King Fariz and the Moors of Techa, and of Teruel, and of Calatayud, were right glad of this, and the covenant was put in writing, and they sent him the three thousand marks. And my Cid divided it among his company, and he made them all rich, both knights and esquires and footmen, so that they said to one another, "He who serves a good lord, happiness is his dole." But the Moors of Alcocer were full sorry to see him depart, because he had been to them a kind master and a bountiful one, and they said to him, "Wherever you go, Cid, our prayers will go before you," and they wept both men and women when my Cid went his way. So the Campeador raised his banner and departed, and he went down the Salon, and crossed it; and as he crossed the river they saw good birds and [other] signs of good fortune. And the people of Za and of Calatayud were well pleased, because he went from them. My Cid rode on until he came to the knoll above Monte-Real; it is a high hill and strong, and there he pitched his tents, being safe on all sides. And from there he did much harm to the Moors of Medina and of the country round about. And he made Daroca pay tribute, and Molina also, which is on the other side, and Teruel also, and Celfa de Canal, and all the country along the river Martin. And the news went to the king of Zaragoza, and it neither pleased the king nor his people.

Ever after was that knoll called the Knoll of the Cid. And when the perfect one had waited a long time for Minaya and saw that he did not come, he removed by night, and passed by Teruel and pitched his camp in the pine-forest of Tebar. And from there he harassed the Moors of Zaragoza, insomuch that they held it best to give him gold and silver and pay him tribute. And when this covenant had been made, al-Muqtadir the king of Zaragoza [r. 1049–82], became greatly his friend, and received him full honorably into the town. Three weeks later, Alvar Fáñez came from Castile. Two hundred men of lineage came with him, every one of whom wore a sword girt to his side, and the foot-soldiers in their company were countless. When my Cid saw Minaya he rode up to him, and embraced him without speaking, and kissed his mouth and the eyes in his head. And Minaya told him all that he had done. And the face of the Campeador brightened, and he gave thanks to God and said, "It will go well with me, Minaya, as long as you live!" God, how joyful was that whole host because Alvar Fáñez was returned, for he brought them greetings from their kinswomen and their brethren, and the fair comrades whom they had left behind. God, how joyful was my Cid with the fleecy beard, that Minaya had purchased the thousand masses, and had brought him the biddings of his wife and daughters! God, what a joyful man was he!

Now it came to pass that while my Cid was in Zaragoza the days of King al-Muqtadir were fulfilled, and he left his two sons al-Mutamid and Abenalfange, and they divided his dominions between them. Al-Mutamid had the kingdom of Zaragoza [r. 1082–85], and Abenalfange the kingdom of Denia. And al-Mutamid put his kingdom under my Cid's protection, and bade all his people obey him even as they would himself. Now there began to be great enmity between the two brethren, and they made war upon each other. And King Don Pedro of Aragon [r. 1094–1104], and the count Don Ramon Berenguer III [r. 1082–1131] of Barcelona, helped Abenalfange, and they were enemies to the Cid because he defended al-Mutamid. And my Cid chose out two hundred horsemen and went out by night, and fell upon the lands of Alcañiz; and he remained out three days in this inroad, and brought away great booty. Great was the talk thereof among the Moors; and they of Monzon and of Huesca were troubled, but they of Zaragoza rejoiced, because they paid tribute to the Cid, and were safe. And when my Cid returned to Zaragoza he divided the spoil among his companions, and said to them, "You know, my friends, that for all who live by their arms, as we do, it is not good to remain long in one place. Let us be off again tomorrow." So in the morning they moved to the Puerto de Alucant, and from there they raided into Huesca and Montalban. Ten days were they out upon this inroad; and the news was sent everywhere how the exile from Castile was leading them, and tidings went to the king of Denia and to the count of Barcelona, how my Cid was overrunning the country.

When Don Ramon Berenguer, the count of Barcelona heard this, it troubled him to the heart, and he held it for a great dishonor, because that part of the land of the Moors was in his keeping. And he spoke boastfully saying, "Great wrong does the Cid of Vivar offer unto me; he smote my nephew in my own court and never would make amends for it, and now he ravages the lands which are in my keeping, and I have never defied him for this nor renounced his friendship; but since he goes on in this way I must take vengeance." So he and King Abenalfange gathered together a great power both of Moors and Christians, and went in pursuit of the Cid, and after three days and two nights they caught up with him in the pine-forest of Tebar, and they came on confidently, thinking to capture him. Now my Cid was returning with much spoil, and had descended from the Sierra into the valley when tidings were brought to him that count Don Ramon Berenguer and the king of Denia were at hand, with a great power, to take away his booty, and capture or slay him. And when the Cid heard this he sent to Don Ramon saying that the booty which he had won was none of his, and bidding him let him go on his way in peace. But the count answered that my Cid should now learn whom he had dishonored, and make amends once and for all. Then my Cid sent the booty forward, and bade his knights make ready. "They are coming upon us," he said, "with a great power both of Moors and Christians, to take from us the spoils which we have so valiantly won, and without doing battle we cannot be rid of them, for if we should proceed they would follow until they overtook us. Therefore let the battle be here, and I trust in God that we shall win more honor, and something to boot. They come down the hill, dressed in their hose, with their bright saddles, and their girths wet; we are with our hose covered and on our Galician saddles. A hundred men like us ought to beat their whole company. Before they get upon the plain, let us give them the points of our lances. For every that we run through, three will jump out of their saddles. And Ramon Berenguer will then see whom he has overtaken today in the pine-forest of Tebar, thinking to despoil me of the booty which I have won from the enemies of God and of the faith."

While my Cid was speaking, his knights had taken their arms, and were ready on horseback for the charge. Presently they saw the pendants of the Frenchmen [who fought in Ramon Berenguer's ranks] coming down the hill, and when they were near the bottom, and had not yet set foot upon the plain ground, my Cid bade his people charge, which they did with a right good will, thrusting their spears so stiffly, that by God's good pleasure not a man whom they encountered but lost his seat. So many were slain and so many wounded, that the Moors were dismayed forthwith, and began to fly. The count's people stood firm a little longer, gathering round their lord; but my Cid was in search of him, and when he saw where he was, he made up to him, clearing the way as he went, and gave him such a stroke with his lance that he felled him down to the ground. When the Frenchmen saw their lord in this plight they fled away and left him; and the pursuit lasted three leagues, and would have been continued farther if the conquerors had not had tired horses. So they turned back and collected the spoils, which were more than they could carry away. Thus was Count Ramon Berenguer made prisoner, and my Cid won from him that day the good sword Colada, which was worth more than a thousand marks of silver. That night did my Cid and his men make merry, rejoicing over their gains. And the count was taken to my Cid's tent, and a good supper was set before him. Nevertheless he would not eat, though my Cid besought him so to do. And on the morrow my Cid ordered a feast to be made, that he might do pleasure to the count, but the count said that for all Spain he would not eat one mouthful, but would rather die, since he had been beaten in battle by such a set of ragged fellows. And el Cid said to him, "Eat and drink, count, of this bread and of this wine, for this is the chance of war. If you do as I say you shall be free and if not you will never return again into your own lands." And Don Ramon answered, "You eat, Don Rodrigo, for your fortune is fair and you deserve it. Take you your pleasure, but leave me to die." And in this mood he continued for three days, refusing all food. But then my Cid said to him, "Take food, count, and be sure that I will set you free, you and any two of your knights, and give you wherewith to return into your own country." And when Don Ramon heard this, he took comfort and said, "If you will indeed do this thing I shall marvel at you as long as I live." "Eat then," said Rodrigo, "and I will do it, but mind you, of the spoil which we have taken from you I will give you nothing, for to that you have no claim neither by right nor custom, and besides we want it for ourselves, being banished men, who must live by taking from you and from others as long as it shall please God." Then was the count full of joy, being well pleased that what should be given him was not of the spoils which he had lost, and he called for water and washed his hands, and chose two of his kinsmen to be set free with him. The one was named Don Hugo, and the other Guillen Bernalto. And my Cid sat at the table with them, and said, "If you do not eat well count, you and I shall not part yet." Never since he was count did he eat with better will than that day! And when they had done he said, "Now, Cid, if it be your pleasure let us depart." And my Cid clothed him and his kinsmen well with comely skins and mantles, and gave them each an excellent palfrey, with rich caparisons [coverings], and he rode out with them on their way. And when he took leave of the count he said to him, "Now go freely, and I thank you for what you have left behind; if you wish to play for it again let me know, and you shall either have something back in its stead, or leave what you bring to be added to it."

The count answered, "Cid, you jest safely now, for I have paid you and all your company for this twelve months, and shall not be coming to see you again so soon." Then Count Ramon picked up his pace, and many times looked behind him, fearing that my Cid would repent what he had done, and send to take him back to prison, which the perfect one would not have done for the whole world, for never did he do a disloyal thing.

Then he of Vivar returned to Zaragoza, and divided the spoil, which was so great that none of his men knew how much they had. And the Moors of the town rejoiced in his good speed, liking him well, because he protected them so well that they were safe from all harm. And my Cid went out again from Zaragoza, and rode over the lands of Monzon and Huerta and Onda and Buenar. And King Pedro of Aragon came out against him, but my Cid took the Castle of Monzon in his sight; and then he went to Tamarit: and one day as he rode out hunting from there with twelve of his knights, he fell in with a hundred and fifty of the king of Aragon's people, and he fought with them and put them to flight, and took seven knights prisoners, whom he let go freely. Then he turned towards the sea-coast, and won Xerica and Onda and Almenar, and all the lands of Borriana and Murviedro; and they in Valencia were greatly dismayed because of the great feats which he did in the land. And when he had plundered all that country he returned to Tamarit, where al-Mutamid then was.

Now al-Mutamid had sent for my Cid, and the cause was this. His brother the king of Denia had taken counsel with Count Ramon Berenguer, and with the count of Cardona, and with the brother of the count of Urgel, and with the chiefs of Balsadron and Remolin and Cartaxes, that they should besiege the castle of Almenar, which my Cid had refortified by command of King al-Mutamid. And they came up against it while my Cid was away, besieging the castle of Estrada, which is in the rivers Tiegio and Sege, and which he had taken by force. And they fought against it and cut off the water. And when my Cid came to the king at Tamarit, the king asked him to go and fight with the host which besieged Almenar. But my Cid said it would be better to give something to King Abenalfange that he should break up the siege and depart, for they were too great a power to do battle with, being as many in number as the sands on the seashore. And the king did as he counseled him, and sent to his brother, King Abenalfange, and to the chiefs who were with him, to propose this accord, and they would not. Then my Cid, seeing that they would not depart for fair means, armed his people, and fell upon them. That was a hard battle and well fought on both sides, and much blood was shed, for many good knights on either party were in the field. Nevertheless, he of good fortune won the day at last, he who never was conquered. King Abenalfange and Count Ramon and most of the others fled, and my Cid followed, smiting and slaying for three leagues; and many good Christian knights were made prisoners. Rodrigo returned with great honor and much spoil, and gave all his prisoners to King al-Mutamid, who kept them eight days, and then my Cid begged their liberty and set them free. And he and the king returned to Zaragoza, and the people came out to meet them, with great joy, and shouts of welcome. And the king honored my Cid greatly, and gave him power in all his dominions.

Ibn Idhari: El Cid and the Conquest of Valencia

In the year 486 AH [February 1093–January 1094] the threat posed by the Christian leader [El Cid] against Valencia increased and the situation of its inhabitants worsened and became truly desperate. They then asked for help from the prince of the Muslims, Yūsuf Ibn Tashfīn, describing in extensive detail the sorrows they were enduring. The prince listened to their words and gave orders to his generals and his governors throughout Andalus to go to their aid. Muslim contingents gathered in Xativa [south of Valencia] and news of their marshaling reached the enemy, but he did not move nor cede his positions. The Muslim troops, accompanied by numerous volunteers, both infantry and cavalry, began to approach by forced marches, and it wasn't long before they were in sight of Valencia. Its inhabitants, anxiously awaiting them, rejoiced at their coming and the revenge they would now take against their enemy, and they felt reborn.

The enemy leader decided to move his forces to the far side of his encampment and divided his forces into two groups. Following their orders, the troops stayed in tight formations, and by divine will, this tactic forced the Muslims to retreat. The people of Valencia were dismayed with them and deeply troubled about their own survival. The enemy then increased his violent acts against them. He imposed extraordinary tributes on his Muslim subjects; launched foraging raids against them; blocked entrance to the city; and stopped all who tried to leave. Those who tried to leave their villages, or were suspected of doing so, saw their wives and children reduced to slavery. Nobody dared to move or even harbor the hope of emigrating. For its part, when the Muslim army of the Almoravids returned to Xativa, the emir Abū Bakr Ibn 'Ibrahīm hastened to inform the prince of the Muslims what had transpired.

In the year 487 AH [January 1094–January 1095], once fate had decreed the departure of the Muslim army led by the emir Abū Bakr Ibn 'Ibrahīm, the Muslims in the city became convinced that death awaited them. Desperation took hold of the inhabitants and they became incapable of further resistance, while their hatred for the enemy increased and their heart hardened against them. The majority of the people were dying of hunger, while they subsisted on, among other things, animal hides and the meat of beasts of burden. Those who fled to the Christian camp, had their eyes gouged, their hands cut off, their legs broken, or were killed, which is why most preferred to die inside the city. The situation became much worse than that endured by Toledo when that city was besieged [prior to its conquest in 1085] as the siege [of Valencia] was much tighter, and the hatred of the enemy more implacable as the siege dragged on and the people of Valencia continued to resist, asking for help.

When they had reached the height of adversity and the limit of their ability to resist and realizing that no help was coming, the people of Valencia had no choice but to begin negotiations with the enemy, by force and against their will. They gathered around their qadi [judge], Abu al-Mutarrif Ibn Chajjāf and they sent a delegation to El Cid—God damn him—to negotiate a truce. The Christian acceded favorably to their requests, but in his heart of hearts he treacherously planned to violate the pact and grant a truce such as other lords like him usually granted. The qadi of Valencia came out to meet El Cid under these conditions. El Cid made him sign the treaty and forced him to agree to specific clauses and conventions, which he vigorously demanded, while giving free reign to his own pretensions and leaving little room to discuss how these should be interpreted. With the truces signed, the gates to the city were opened to him and he entered with his soldiers. This occurred in the month of Jumada al-awwal [I] of said year [19 May to 17 June 1094]....

... When El Cid—God damn him—made himself lord of Valencia, his tyranny began to show and he jailed the qadi of the city, as well as members of his immediate family and other relatives. And all of them were tortured in his dungeons. What he wanted from them was that they hand him the treasures of al-Qādir Ibn Di'l'Nūn, and he did not stop taking all that they owned until they had nothing left of their riches or fortunes. Once they had nothing left, be it in the open or hidden, he ordered the construction of a huge bonfire. The qadi Ibn Chajjāf, who suffered in chains, was brought forth surrounded by his family and his children, and in the presence of many Muslims and Christians who had gathered. El Cid then asked a group of Muslims, "What is the punishment in your laws for someone who kills their prince?" As nobody answered, he added, "among our people, the law requires that he should be burnt alive." And he ordered Ibn Chajjāf and his family to be brought closer to the fire, where the flames, still distant, seared their faces. The gathered Christians and Muslims asked him to spare the qadi's wives and his children who were blameless and knew nothing of the matter. Upon considering it, El Cid agreed to their pleas and gave amnesty to the women and children. As for the qadi, they dug a hole where they buried him up to his waist, filling the ground around him with burning embers. When the fire reached his face, he called out, "In the name of the merciful and compassionate God." And then he proceeded to gather the burning faggots ever closer to him until his body was charred. God almighty have mercy upon him!

24. THE BATTLE OF LAS NAVAS DE TOLOSA

Over the course of the twelfth century, the Christian kingdoms, even as they battled one another, were able to stabilize their situation vis-à-vis the Almoravids. And by the 1130s, Leon-Castile and Aragon had enjoyed some major territorial successes. This Christian push coincided with an insurrection in northern Africa that threatened and ultimately overthrew the Almoravids. The rebels were religious and tribal rivals of the Almoravids, known as the Almohads. This insurrection, as well as revolts in Spain and coupled with Christian pressure, led to the collapse of the Almoravids. The revolt spread to the Iberian provinces of the Almoravid Empire, where new taifa kingdoms, weak and fragmented like their predecessors, emerged after throwing off Almoravid control, but they were so fragile that they were incapable of offering much resistance to the Christian advance. After the collapse of the Almoravids, the Almohads wasted little time in taking over northern Africa and began to extend their reach into Iberia. Over the following decades, al-Andalus was convulsed by warfare as the taifa kings fought one another, the Almohads, and the Christian kingdoms, which were having problems of their own. By 1175, however, the Almohads had emerged victorious from the Muslim civil wars, while powerful kings such as Alfonso VIII in Castile (r. 1158–1214) and Alfonso II of Aragon-Barcelona (r. 1162–96) had taken firm control over their realms, setting the stage for a protracted struggle between Christians and Muslims. In 1195, the Almohads won a stunning victory against Alfonso VIII at the Battle of Alarcos that threatened to roll back the Christian conquests made over the previous century, as even Toledo came under Muslim attack. But the Almohads had to divert their attention from Alfonso to deal with revolts and invasions in northern Africa, giving him a respite. In 1211, both sides found the strength for another major effort, and Alfonso's attacks on Muslim cities and strongholds were answered by a massive Almohad army crossing from Morocco, led by the caliph himself, Muhammad an-Nāsir (r. 1199–1213). Alarmed by the scale of the attack, Alfonso appealed to Pope Innocent III (r. 1198–1216) and other Christian kings for help. Innocent replied by granting full crusading privileges to all who went to help the Spanish Christians, and large numbers of French crusaders answered his call. In addition, the kings of Aragon and Navarre added their armies to Alfonso's. The two sides met at Las Navas de Tolosa on 16 July 1212. The battle, which turned into a rout, was a decisive Christian victory, shattering the power of the Almohads and opening up much of lower al-Andalus to conquest in the decades that followed. Al-Himyari, in his Kitab ar-Rawd al M'itar *(The Book of the Fragrant Garden), captures in a direct and simple style the loss felt by the Muslims.*

Source: trans. Jarbel Rodriguez, from Maria Pilar Maestro González's Spanish translation of Al Himyari, *Kitab ar-Rawd al-Mi'tar* (Valencia: Graficas Bautista, 1963), 276–80.

The sovereign Muhammad an-Nāsir, emir of the believers, had left Marrakech towards al-Andalus to undertake his enterprise. He spent a few days in Seville and from there marched to Cordoba. Later he advanced on the castles of Salvatierra and al-Lugg and laid siege to them. He first captured al-Lugg and then Salvatierra; the capture of the latter was possible due to powerful siege engines that launched massive stones against the walls. He took these positions to the detriment of Alfonso, king of Toledo and Castile, who was then left defenseless. This occurred in the year 608 AH [1211]. But, in the following year, the Christian king would take his revenge with his victory at al-'Ikāb [Las Navas de Tolosa]. The king an-Nāsir had been filled with pride over his capture of Salvatierra, and to announce the victory he sent messages throughout his domain, without realizing that there were dark forces at work plotting his next defeat.

He returned to Seville triumphant, but Alfonso did not hesitate to call on his coreligionists for help, urging them to defend the faith. They answered his call and from everywhere they came to his aid.

An-Nāsir departed Seville to meet him, leaving on Muharram 20 of the year 609 [22 June 1212] at the head of regiments that were in no condition to fight as he had stopped paying his soldiers, giving them the smallest of [salary] advances. He had also alienated his troops by having Ibn Kādis, the commander of the castle of Calatrava, put to death, after he had committed the grievous crime of handing the castle over to the Christians without attempting a defense. He had also banned the captains of his Andalusian troops from the salon where he greeted his family members, as a way of showing them his displeasure.

Additionally, the rest of the army fell victim to double-crossing by the Christians, who after announcing that they were stopping the fight, did just the opposite. The Christians mixed it up very quickly with the Muslims, without the latter noticing. The Muslims then fled very quickly after suffering an unparalleled defeat. This occurred in al-'Ikab, between Jaen and Cordoba, in mid Safar of the year 609 [17 July 1212], exactly as we have described. It was a horrific disaster. An-Nāsir was able to save himself, worrying little about the fate of his men, and he managed to escape to Seville. Those who fled with him, and had taken the royal tent, exhausted numerous horses and were pursued well into the night by the Christians, who chased after them on every possible road. A large number of Muslims was gravely wounded and among the dead in the battle were several important intellectual figures such as Ibn 'At and others.

An-Nāsir's horse was rather heavy and unable to go very fast. One of the Arabs dismounted and offered his own horse to the sovereign, telling him: "Ride my horse as it will be more useful to you than yours!" [Before the battle] an-Nāsir had ordered Abū Bakr, ibn 'Abd Allāh ibn Abī Hafs to stay with the royal standard. The Christians had charged toward the standard, thinking that an-Nāsir would be there. With their swords they wounded those soldiers who opposed and killed a good number of them, including Abū Bakr.

The Muslims were defeated, and the enemy captured the camp including most of the tents. Afterwards, the Christians took the cities of Baza and Priego and the surrounding fortresses, killing the men and taking the women and children captive.

This disaster was the first sign of weakness among the Almohads. After this, the people of the Maghreb were no longer willing to engage in these enterprises. When an-Nāsir returned to Seville, he tried to calm his people by issuing a proclamation in which he hid the truth, under flowery language. Later he crossed the sea toward Marrakech. He died in his palace in the capital in the year 610 [1213], as a result of a dog bite, according to some and due to other circumstances according to others.

25. CHRISTIAN CONQUESTS AND THE RISE OF THE NASRIDS

Las Navas de Tolosa was the decisive battle of the Christian conquest of Iberia. After 1212, the balance of power began to shift in favor of the Christian kingdoms. However, it was a gradual process, as Christian efforts to take advantage of their victory stalled after the battle. Peter II, who had led the armies of Aragon at Las Navas de Tolosa, died in 1213, leaving his son James I, only five years of age at the time, on the throne. A year later, Alfonso VIII died, and it would be a decade before a new Castilian king, Ferdinand III (r. 1217–54), felt strong enough to take an aggressive stance against the Muslim states in the peninsula. The defeat at Las Navas had left the Almohads in shambles, but it would take until 1224 for their empire to shatter into several pieces. The death of Muhammad an-Nāsir's successor, Yusuf II (r. 1213–24), provided the impetus for yet another period of fragmentation in Muslim al-Andalus. As in previous instances, the main benefactors of the disintegration of Muslim power were the Christian kings, notably Ferdinand III in Castile and James I in Aragon. Ferdinand took the lead and, by 1226, he had captured Baeza. He followed this conquest with a string of impressive additions that brought most of al-Andalus under his control. In 1236, he took Cordoba, the old capital of the caliphate in Spain; in 1246, it was the turn of the fortress city of Jaen; and in 1248, Ferdinand crowned his achievements by overpowering Seville. James I matched this remarkable series of Castilian victories with his own successes, taking Mallorca in 1229 and following that up with the conquest of Valencia in 1238. By mid-century, the only Muslim state left in Spain was the kingdom of Granada, led by the nascent Nasrid dynasty, in the southwest corner of the peninsula, and it was a tributary to Castile.

The Christian conquests of the thirteenth century are well attested in the surviving literature. The first excerpt below comes from the Muslim historian al-Makhzumi (c. 1189–1251) and recounts the Christian conquest of Mallorca. The second source is from the autobiography of James I and gives us a very personal account of his victory over

Valencia. The last source is from the north African polymath Ibn Khaldun (1332–1406). It relates the internecine warfare that plagued the Muslim polities after the downfall of the Almohads, the Christian conquests, and the rise of the Nasrids, the dynasty that would rule Granada until its collapse in 1492.

Sources: For al-Makhzumi and Ibn Khaldun, respectively, see trans. Pascual de Gayangos, *The History of the Mohammedan Dynasties of Spain* (London: W.H. Allen and Co., 1843), II: 329–32 and 339–41, both rev. Jarbel Rodriguez; for James I, see trans. John Forster, *The Chronicle of James I, King of Aragon, Surnamed the Conqueror (written by himself)* (London: Chapman and Hall, 1883), 369–98.

Al-Makhzumi: The Capture of Mallorca

Mallorca was governed at the time by an emir, named Mohammed Ibn 'Alí Ibn Músa, who, being a man of quality and influence among the people of the extinct dynasty of [the Almohads], had been entrusted with the government [of the Balearic Islands], which he held ever since 606 [beginning 5 July 1209]. Happening once to want some timber, which in the neighboring island of Ibiza is very abundant, Mohammed sent thither some light vessels under the convoy of a few of his war galleys. The Christian governor of Tortosa, having received intelligence of the departure of the expedition, sent out a fleet to capture the Muslim vessels, and succeeded; upon which Mohammed was so angry at the loss of his ships that he resolved upon declaring war against the Christians and making a descent upon their territory. In an evil hour did he form such a determination, for he lost his dominions in the contest. An occasion soon presented itself for carrying his project into execution. About the end of Dhū al-Hijja of the year 623 [December 1226], news came to him that a vessel from Barcelona had appeared in sight of Ibiza, and that another ship from Tortosa had also come up with it. Upon the receipt of this intelligence, Mohammed dispatched his son with some armed vessels in chase of the enemy. The son of Mohammed having entered the harbor of Ibiza, found lying there at anchor a large Genoese galley, which he attacked and took. This done, he sailed in chase of the Barcelonese ship, which he likewise boarded and took. This trifling success had the effect of completely turning the head of the governor of Mallorca, who from that moment fancied himself a conqueror, and thought that no king could resist his victorious arms, forgetting that he was as ill-fated as the camel cursed with sterility, and that the Christians would not fail to take ample vengeance for the injury they had received. And so it happened, for the people of Barcelona had no sooner heard of the capture of their vessel, than they said to their king, who was a successor to Alfonso [II], "How does the king like to see his subjects used in this manner? We are ready to assist thee with our persons and our money to avenge this insult." The king, taking them at their word, immediately raised an army of twenty thousand men in his dominions, and, having equipped a considerable fleet, set sail for Mallorca with upwards of sixteen thousand soldiers. This took place in 626 [1228], but as these immense preparations could not be made secretly, the news of the armament soon reached the governor of Mallorca, who began also to collect his forces, and prepared to repel the invasion. Having selected upwards of one thousand cavalry, he distributed them about the island, and he raised besides another body consisting of one thousand horse from among the country people and the inhabitants of the capital. His infantry amounted to eighteen thousand men. All these levies were ready by the month of Rabī, the first, of the said year [1228]. Unluckily, however, all these active preparations were counteracted by the following unfortunate event. One day Mohammed ordered the captain of his guards to bring into his presence four of the principal inhabitants of the town, and when, in pursuance of his order, they appeared before him, he caused them to be immediately beheaded. Among the number of these victims were two sons of his mother's brother, Abú Hafss Ibn Sheyrí, a man of rank and influence in the island. The people went to him and related what had occurred, warning him against the tyrant, and saying, "By Allah! This state of things can no longer be endured; the emir is not fit either to govern us or defend us, and as long as he rules, our lives will be entirely at his mercy." After this declaration, the citizens bound themselves to revenge the blood spilt by the tyrant, and Ibn Sheyrí having consented to become their chief, they determined upon ridding themselves of the emir at all costs. It was on a Friday, about the middle of the month of Shawwāl [1228] that with the fear of Mohammed's vengeance, should their plans be discovered, and the dread caused by the enemy, who was known to be at no great distance from the island, the citizens were actually trembling. Presently Mohammed summons to his presence the captain of his guards, and commands him to bring before him fifty of the principal citizens, the most distinguished by their birth, wealth, or talents. The tyrant's orders were immediately complied with, and the fifty individuals stood before him. They were all expecting to be marched to immediate execution, when, lo, a horseman appears, dressed as a courier, who, being introduced into the emir's presence, informs him that the Christian fleet, composed of upwards of forty sail, is in sight, and making for the shore. No sooner, however, had the horseman finished his recital, than a second messenger from a different quarter rushed breathless into the audience chamber, saying, "The Christian fleet is in sight, and I can count seventy sail." The fact it was soon ascertained, and the news found to be true. Mohammed then pardoned the fifty citizens who had been sentenced to death, and having apprised them of the arrival of the enemy, bade them go and prepare for the defense of the city. Accordingly they all went home, and were received by their families as if they had risen from the tomb. Soon after the news arrived that the Christians were just at hand, and that their fleet was composed of one hundred and fifty sail.

After crossing the bay, the Christians made for the harbor [intending to land], but the emir having sent against them some infantry and cavalry, with orders to station themselves on the shore and to remain there encamped both day and night, they were prevented from landing. At last, the Christians gained their object, and on the 18th of Shawwāl [1228], which was a Monday, an engagement took place in which the Muslims were completely defeated. After this, the enemy marched to the city and encamped on the deserted and uncultivated plain, close to the gate of Al-kahl, from where they made several assaults upon the city, and were on the point of taking it by storm. When Ibn Sheyrí saw that the Christians were masters of the neighboring country, and that the city could not hold out much longer, he left it secretly and made for the interior of the island, with such among the inhabitants as would follow him. On Friday, the eleventh of Safar, 628 AH [18 December 1230], the Christians made a general attack on the city, and on the following Sunday became masters of it. In the massacre that ensued no less than twenty-four thousand of the inhabitants were inhumanly sacrificed for the fault of a single individual. The emir was taken and subjected to all manner of torture, under which he expired forty-five days after his capture. As to Ibn Sheyrí, he betook himself to the mountainous part of the island, in which were many places strongly fortified by nature, and having collected around him a force of sixteen thousand men, he defended himself bravely for some time, until he was killed on Friday the tenth of Rabī the second, of the year 628 [14 February 1231].

James I: The Conquest of Valencia

255. When the Saracens of Valencia learned that I had got Paterna, the anger and grief they had were doubled, at seeing I was coming so close to them. I resolved, at the Puig of Santa Maria, to wait for nothing more, but to proceed at once to the siege of Valencia. I then had with me the master of the Hospital, En Hugh de Fullalquer; a commander of the Temple, who had about twenty knights with him; the commander of Alcaniz; Don Rodrigo Licana, who had some thirty knights under him; the commander of Calatrava; En Guillem de Aguilo, who had about fifteen; Don Exemen Perez de Taracona, and my own train of retainers, who might be from a hundred and thirty to a hundred and forty knights, all men of noble birth. There were also in the camp a hundred and fifty *almogavars* [elite light infantry] and well up to a thousand footmen.

256. I resolved that next day early, in the name of the Lord, I would begin to move, and would proceed to the siege of Valencia. I passed the marsh at a crossing I had made, and went along the sea shore to the Grau, and there forded the river. When I had got over it, we and the baggage-mules went to some houses half-way between Valencia and the Grau, but nearer the Grau than Valencia.

There I set up my banners and tents, and took my station; it might be a mile from that place to Valencia. My intention was to wait there for more troops to come from Aragon and Catalonia, with which to besiege Valencia. That day I saw Saracen horsemen from Valencia, who went about between us and the town, to see if they could steal anything from the army, but I kept my knights from foraging till they knew the country well.

257. Next day before dawn, without my knowledge, the *almogavars* and the camp-followers went to take the Rucafa [suburb of Valencia], close to the town, within two cross-bow shots. I had at the time a malady in the eyes, and could not open them till I had washed them with hot water. They came and told me that *almogavars* and footmen had gone to quarter themselves in the Rucafa, of which they had actually taken possession. En Hugh de Fullalquer, the master of the Hospital, came to me and said, "What do you order us to do? They have all gone to take quarters in the Rucafa." I said, "Let us put armor on the horses, and with banners spread let us go to succor them, or else all are dead men." And he said, "It shall be done as you command." Then we all armed and proceeded towards the suburb called Rucafa. Had I not made so much haste to come, all those in the place would have been killed or taken prisoners. When we entered it, the Saracens were at the other end of it. I made my people halt in an open space there was.

258. Then there came to me En Ramon Cavella, commander of Aliaga, and Lope Xemenez de Luzia, who said they could take full fifty Saracens if they made an assault towards Valencia. I said, I wished to see how that could be done. They took me to the gate looking towards Valencia, and there I saw Zaen [Zayyan ibn Mardanish, ruler of Valencia from 1229–38] posted with all the power of Valencia at a tower half-way between that city and the Rucafa, in a spot where there were some rocks, and where water had collected from the rains and the watercourses. The tower now belongs to En Ramon Riquer. I reckoned Zaen's force at four hundred horsemen, and of footmen, the greater part of those in Valencia; in my opinion, and in that of those who were round me, the Saracens might be about ten thousand, more or less. And within a stone's throw of us and of them, there were thirty or forty peasants gathering beans in a bean-field. These were the Saracens whom Cavella and Luzia said they could capture if they made an assault towards Valencia. I told them, "You are wrong. It is the nature of an attack, like the one you propose making, that if unsuccessful they who make it will have to come back as fugitives. I do not know whether those fields are cut and traversed by watercourses for the purpose of irrigation. If they are, the horses in coming back through them will get into the watercourses, some of them may fall inside, and we all may sustain great damage; peradventure also if the enemy drives us back in flight to the Rucafa, we might also lose that and the other places we have taken." Wherefore I would

not take their advice on that, but at night I would send trustworthy men to see if the fields were irrigated or not. If they were not, my men might return to me, and then I would allow a charge to be made. In this manner by the favor of God we did so much on that first day that we were actually quartered within two cross-bow shots of the city of Valencia.

259. We stayed under arms all that first day; so that no one of us even ate his food but sitting on his horse, and that was only bread, wine, and cheese. At vespers, the Saracens turned head and went back to the city; then I dismounted, put off my armor, as usual, and took food. After taking my repast, I made fifty knights arm themselves to watch the camp by night. When morning came, I heard mass. The Saracens did not come out against us, but let us rest, and so we stayed for five days.

260. Meantime there continued to come to me barons and knights from Aragon and Catalonia; among the first came the archbishop of Narbonne with forty knights and six hundred footmen; his name was Pedro Arnyell. So our army kept increasing, the Saracens being so confined that they did not dare come out against us, except to skirmish with some of our men, for which it would not do to put armor on our horses, as the Saracens did not close with us so as to do us harm, nor could we, as it was, get at them. So when the barons and the city bands came, they beset Valencia all around, and set themselves closer to the city than we had done when we first came to it. The city men who took post the nearest were those of Barcelona.

261. I had next to consider from what side I would push the siege, and a council was held for that purpose; some said that the attack should be against the Boatella, but I spoke against those who said so. Of that opinion were also the archbishop of Narbonne and the other barons who were with me; but I proved to them by reasoning, that we could not push the siege from any place so good as that where we were then for three reasons. One was that if we set our battering engines against the gate, it would only be where the Saracens could sally out and set fire to them, as it would be near their gate, which they could not do where we then were. The place is farther from their gate, and they will not dare to sally out as far. So I would set the engines there where we then were. If the Saracens attack the engines, the army can easily defend them and overtake the enemy before they got back to the city, for at that time there was no gate between the Boatella and the Xerea. Another reason was, that the city came to an angle there on that spot, and when the time came for our mining the barbican and the wall, the operation could not be hindered from the towers, for the wall came where the fight would be, and projected further than the rest of the city wall. The third reason was, that if the army shifted itself to the Boatella, they in the city could by their horse get command of the ways between the sea and the army, and we should be obliged to keep, in order to protect the camp, an

additional hundred horse in armor, who would considerably lessen the strength of the army, while it would harass those who had to do this guard. When the barons and knights heard my reasons, they all assented to what I said, and held my plan for the best.

262. Then the archbishop of Narbonne, who was a bold man, asked me why I was there and did nothing; I said I would act when the army came, I would then attack the Boatella. Meantime there came a trebuchet [a siege engine used for hurling projectiles against city walls] I had made at Tortosa, and two fonevols [similar to a trebuchet]. I set them up and battered the wall opposite to where the camp was. I had besides mantlets [large shield used to protect soldiers from enemy missiles] made, which extended beyond the engines, having underneath them men in armor. The mantlets were then pushed up to some cub-walls near the moat. Wood and faggots were next thrown into the moat, which was full of water; then three men in armor crossed over to the barbican. When they told me that three men had crossed to the barbican, I would not believe their word, and went to see what they were talking of. I saw that the men had actually lodged themselves and could well maintain their ground, and that they in the town could not reach them with missiles. I sent them two picks, and they worked with them and made three holes in the barbican, into each of which two men could very well go.

263. Meantime I sent one of the fonevols to Cilia under two barons, Don Pedro Fernandez de Acagra and Don Exemen de Urrea, who attacked it for eight days, at the end of which time the enemy surrendered. So was Cilia taken.

264. While we were mining into the barbican, and the Saracens were defending it as well as they could, there came against us, to the Grau of Valencia, twelve galleys and six atzaures [smaller vessels] of the king of Tunis, between first sleep and midnight. There came also during the night a message from those who were at the Grau, saying that many galleys had arrived, they thought from twelve to fifteen. Hearing that, I got ready fifty knights, with horses in armor, and about two hundred footmen, and I set them in ambush on a bank at some distance from the sea, between certain ditches and the bank, where they could lie well. I exhorted them not to sally out till the enemy were well advanced, and not to give up their ambush till half tierce. The Saracens, however, for fear of the ambush, did not land. When it was night, they put up full a hundred signal lights on the galleys, that they in the town might see, and they beat their drums. They in the town set full a thousand lights on the walls, and also beat their drums, to let them know that they held the king of Tunis for their lord. When they had done all that display and noise, I ordered the army also to prepare torches in every tent, and when it became dark to light them all, and throw them into the moat after setting up a great shout, and it was done as I had ordered, that the Saracens might understand that we cared little for their bravados. In this

manner did my men throw five hundred burning torches against the rampart. So the Valencians saw that we cared little for what they had done, and that the galleys could in no way help them.

265. Meantime I sent by the shore as far as Tortosa and Tarragona, bidding them be on their guard and to come in a body, which they did. I had three galleys at Tarragona and Tortosa, which were immediately armed. After stopping two days [at the Grau] the galleys of the Saracens went to Peñiscola, and landed to attack the place. Fernan Perez de Pina was inside with his men. He went out of the castle which he held for me; he had with him ten horsemen between himself, Don Fernan Ahones, and others who were there. With this small force and the Saracens of the town, who gave him very good aid, Don Fernan beat off the people of the galleys, of whom seventeen were slain. Meanwhile the convoy from Tortosa, which consisted of twenty-one sails, armed seven vessels [lenys] in such wise that any one of them could take a galley if it ran alongside of her. The three galleys [of Tarragona] and the seven vessels [of Tortosa] came all in a body, so that when the enemy's galleys came to know of this, they took flight and disappeared, not daring to wait for them. In this manner there came to me a great supply of bread, wine, barley, cheese, fruit, and other smaller articles. So large became the camp that there were at last in it no less than a thousand knights and sixty [thousand] footmen. One could find in it every article one wished to sell or buy, as in a city; nay, there were there apothecaries from Montpellier and Lerida, who sold drugs and spices, such as one could find in a great town, for the sick as well as the sound. Meanwhile I made my engines batter the walls every day, and my men had frequent skirmishes with those within, or made attacks. In one of these the Exerea was taken; more than a hundred horse in armor got into it, and full fifteen Saracens were killed in the defense.

266. At another time the men of the archbishop of Narbonne were skirmishing with those from inside, but the archbishop's men did not know the way of the Saracens, who on that occasion, as in others, fled from them to draw them nearer to the town. Perceiving that the enemy's footmen were only retreating with that end, I sent my people a message not to pursue, or else the Saracens would do them great hurt. They would not stay for my message; but I, fearing lest thirty or more of them should be killed by the Moors, went up to them on the same horse I was then riding, and made them draw back. As I was coming with the men, I happened to turn my head toward the town in order to look at the Saracens, who had come out in great force, when a cross-bowman shot at me, and hit me beside the sun-hood, and the shot struck me on the head, the bolt lighting near the forehead. It was God's will it did not pass through the head, but the point of the arrow went half through it. In anger I struck the arrow so with my hand that I broke it. The blood came out down my face. I wiped it off with a mantle of sandal [a light silk] I had, and went away laughing, that the

army might not take alarm. I then went and lay down in a tent, when all my face and eyes swelled, so that I could not see for the swelling of the eye on the wounded side. When the swelling in my face had gone down, I rode round the camp that the army might not be discouraged.

267. Meantime Don Pedro Cornell and Don Exemen de Urrea agreed that they would attack the tower which stands at the gate of the Boatella on the street of Saint Vincent. This they concealed from me and from everyone else in the camp. But though they made the attack and continued it for a good while, what with the forces that came out to it from the city, and the gallant defense of those within the tower, Don Pedro and Don Exemen could not take it, and had to retreat. I told them they had done ill to begin so great an undertaking without my counsel and that of the barons and knights of the army, and that it was right well that they had fared so ill.

268. Thereon I sent for the bishops and the barons of the army, and we agreed that since the thing had been begun, by all means the tower should be taken the next day, that we would arm two hundred horse and all the cross-bowmen of the army. At sunrise, we would go to the attack, resolved to take the tower, and no man should draw back until it was taken. At sunrise, I went there myself; there were about ten Saracens prepared to defend the tower. We attacked them, and they defended themselves well and gallantly; no men could defend themselves better than they did. But so great was the effect of the cross-bowmen on our side, and of the stones that were thrown against the tower, that no Moor could put his hand out of cover but it was immediately pierced by an arrow. With all that they would not surrender the tower when summoned. Then one of our men set fire to the tower. When they saw the fire they were cowed, and said they would surrender, but I said we would not give them quarter, as they had not surrendered at first. I burned them all there, took possession of the tower, and returned to the camp.

269. When that was done, great fear fell on those inside the city for the capture of that tower. We made our engines batter the city night and day. After a time, when a month was past, a Saracen trader came out of the city under safe conduct; the men of En Ramon Berenguer de Ager met with him and brought him in on the croup of a horse. He came before me and gave me news of Zaen, the king of Valencia, how he managed his affairs and what his plans were. He told me that three things had greatly discouraged the Valencians: first, that the galleys of the king of Tunis had done so little for them; the second, the tower that we had burnt; the third, the great army they saw, that had invested almost the whole of Valencia. He [the trader] thought they could not hold out long because they had not supplies for so many people as were in Valencia—men, women, and children—owing to our having surprised them and besieged the town before they got in their harvest. He believed it certain that it would not be long before we got it.

270. When I heard the words the Saracen said to me, they pleased me much, as well as those of the army who happened to know of them. And as this book is such that one should not put small matters into it, I leave telling many things there were, and will only tell the greatest, that the book may not be much lengthened, but the things that were great and good, of them will I speak and treat. As to our camp, I can say of it that I, who have made thirty of them at different times, have never seen one so well supplied as that was with the things that were necessary for man's help; so that sick people got the help of apothecaries as if they were at Barcelona or Lerida.

271. When it got to within fifteen days of Michaelmas [the Feast of Saint Michael, 29 September], Zaen sent me word that if I would give a safe conduct to a Saracen named Ali Albata, a native of Peñiscola, he would send him on to parley with me. I said I was well content that he should come, and that I would give him a safe conduct; when the messenger came, he told me what the king of Valencia had sent him for. I said I would consider it, and would give him an answer briefly. I reflected that it was not well to make those words of Ali known to anyone in the camp, whether baron, knight, or others, for there were many among them who would not be pleased that Valencia should be taken. They would rather it belonged to the Saracens than to me, as I afterwards had sufficient proof of it. I went to the queen [Violant of Hungary], and told her what Ali Albata had said, and what my intention was. If it seemed well to her, I prayed and commanded that no one in the camp but I and she, and the messenger who acted as interpreter, should know of it. She said that what I told her pleased her much. No one had so great an interest in my honor and welfare as herself; if God loved me and gave me honor, she thanked him for it, for her hopes were all centered in me. She thought it well that no one should know of these proposals, that I might not be hindered in my undertaking, for she had seen me take possession of other places and castles, which my barons would rather see as they were than in my power, and as to which they did many things they should not do; wherefore she well believed that since in small things they acted so, they would with regard to Valencia show their power in such wise that I should not take it. She thought secrecy good beyond everything, until I was sure of taking the city.

272. I then sent for Ali Albata to come again to me, and told him to state what he had come for. He said that the words Zaen had to say were great and of high import. "They are not for me to speak out, but Zaen, king of Valencia, sends me to say that if you will he will send to you the Rais Abulphamalet (or Abulamalet) his nephew, his sister's son, and after himself the most powerful man in Valencia and in the kingdom, and the one in whom he most trusts. If it pleases God, before you and he part, I trust that this business will come to a good conclusion." To that I replied that he might go back to the town, and that

the other one should come as soon as possible. I gave him a knight to escort him and take him back to Valencia. And he fixed a time, next morning at sunrise, when he would be with me, and that I should send then a knight to escort him to the camp. I agreed to do so. In the morning, I accordingly sent a knight, and he came. When he was before me, he said that Zaen, king of Valencia, saluted me. He told me besides, on that king's behalf, that next morning, between terce and sunrise, I was to send two nobles to escort Rais Abulphamalet, who would forthwith come to me. I ordered Don Nuño and En Berenguer Roger de Ager to get ready in the morning to meet Zaen's nephew, Rais Abulphamalet, and to escort him to me, and they said they would do so.

273. Meantime two Saracen knights challenged any two of our army to joust with them, and they made this known to me. Don Exemen Perez de Taracona, who, was afterwards lord of Arenos, came to me and asked me to give him that joust, together with Miguel Perez de Isor. I told him I marveled much at him, that a man, who was such a sinner as he was, and of so bad a life, could ask to joust. I had my fears that we all should be brought to shame through him. But he begged of me so hard that I assented. He jousted with the Saracen, and the Saracen overthrew him. Pere de Clariana then went against the other Saracen, and at coming together in the joust the Saracen turned and fled, and he pursued him, till he got across the Guadalaviar, and among his own people.

274. The next morning early, Rais Abulphamalet came out with the Saracen who had jousted, and with ten other knights, well equipped and dressed, with good horses and good new saddles, fit to go into any court as well-appointed men. I had my house well decked out to receive him. On entering, he would not kiss my hand, but prostrated himself and embraced me. Then he seated himself before me, and saluted me on behalf of Zaen, king of Valencia. He said that he had not before seen me, and was very glad to do so. I told him I prayed God to prosper him, that I was well pleased that he had come to see me, wherefore I would do him honor and good in such wise that he should have to thank me. He said that was what he expected of me, that I was such that those whom I loved had ever good and honor from me. I invited him to eat; he replied that he thanked me much for the invitation, but that he would not eat out of the city, that it was forbidden him by his lord, but he held himself as honored by an invitation from me. I told him that if he would not take dinner there, I would send it into the town to him. He said that he thanked me much more, that at another time he would come when he could take it better, but then he would not for he really could not. Then I said that if he wished I would send away every one, and he could speak in secret with me. He said that so he wished, that he would not speak to me, except before one or two only in whom I put much trust. I made every one go away, except myself, him, and the interpreter. Then I asked him what he wished to say.

275. He said that Zaen marveled much at me that I was so enraged against him that I had made my armies and my power come against his land and his power. He did not think he had done anything against me that he should receive so much harm from me. To that I answered and told him, that yes, he had, when I went to the conquest of Mallorca he came to make a raid in my land, going as far as Tortosa and Amposta. What harm he could do there against men and cattle he certainly did do. He also attacked Ulldecona, which is in my kingdom. And that yet in another thing he had wronged me, I sent him once a message that I wished to have peace and truce with him, and as during my childhood I was wont to have and take the fifths of Valencia and Murcia, he was told to make good what they of Valencia had failed to pay; I made demand on him of a hundred thousand besants, sending to him as messenger Don Pedro Sanz, my notary, and he, despising my message and my love, only offered me fifty thousand besants. Whereupon I discharged myself of his love, and decided to come against him, since he had preferred fifty thousand besants to my love.

276. Thereupon the Rais answered and said he did not think that I had been wronged in that, for at the time I was entitled to and received the fifths of Valencia and Murcia, Zait Abuzeit was the king. "Things, have since come to what God willed, but for, what there now is between us and you, let us take counsel, and let it be well settled for your honor, for such is the wish of Zaen." I answered that he spoke well, and that men had to consult what to do with things in actual sight, not with things past. He said that he wished to know from me what I intended doing in these affairs that God, had ordained should come upon them, wherefore he prayed me much that I should discover what my wish was. If I wished his lord to give me according to the means he had, he would give. But I ought to know well what loss in men the city of Valencia had suffered through our power ever since the building of the fortifications at the Puig and how I had laid waste the corn lands and the garden of Valencia, and done the same harm in other places of the kingdom, in the best of them. To that I replied that I thought it fit for the queen to be there, and no one else in the world to know but ourselves and she, and he who spoke those words as an interpreter. He said there were two things he gave me great thanks for; one was that I would bring no one but the queen into the conference, and that no one besides should be concerned in it; the other, because it pleased him well that I should keep the matter secret. It was better so for them and for me, for he knew well that I had to guard myself against many who did not wish my advantage or profit in that, nor in other things.

277. I accordingly sent for the queen, and when she came sent away all the women who came with her and all the rest. She alone remained with me, and I repeated to her the words that had passed between Rais Abulphamalet

and me, as above written. Then I told him that I would say more to him in the queen's presence than apart, and this was the answer: "I have reached this place where I now am encamped. God has conducted me in all undertakings up to this day, and I have succeeded in them all. Since I am here, it is my intent and my resolution, never to depart thence until I get Valencia. If the king wishes to avert the great mischief there will be at the capture of a city like Valencia—so many Saracens, men, women, and children, who may then die or lose all they have—it will please me well." I said, moreover, that for their good and profit I would take them under my protection, and would escort them, with all they could carry, for I should grieve at their death. If I could get the place by their willingness to surrender it, I would rather have it so than in the other wise, by force, "For the greater part of the army (said I) wishes for the sack of the town, and I will not have it so for the pity I have of you. This is my wish, and nothing else will I do, unless you positively force me to do you hurt." He, the Rais, then said, "Those words are very weighty. I cannot further confer with you without consulting my lord and uncle, Zaen." I saw that he spoke reason, and told him to do so in good speed. I invited him again to eat, but he declined.

278. On the third day, the Rais sent me word that if I would give him an escort he would come out to me. I sent one of my barons to him, and he came immediately. He told me that the king of Valencia, Zaen, had considered the thing, and that he knew that the town could not hold out in the end. Wherefore, that he might not cause the Valencians to bear more ill than they had already borne, he would surrender the city on this condition: that the Saracens, men and women, might take away all their effects; that they should not be searched, nor should any outrage be done to them; and they all, himself and they, should go under escort to Cullera. Since it was the will of God that I should have the city, he had to will it so. On that I said that I would consult the queen, who alone was in on the secret. He said that he thought that was good, and he went out of the house, where I and the queen remained. I then asked her what she thought of Zaen's proposal. She said, that if it seemed right to me to take those terms, she thought it right also, for Valencia was not a thing that a man who could have, should risk it from one day to another. I felt that she gave me good advice, and I told her that I agreed with what she said, but I would add what I thought a very good reason for accepting Zaen's terms, namely, that should the town be taken by force, it would go hard for me if a wrangling over it arose in the army. Not for base lucre nor for apparel of any sort ought I to put off what my ancestors and myself had so long desired to take and have, and even yet, if I were wounded or fell ill before the town could be taken by force, the whole thing might still be lost. Wherefore, so good a work as that should not be put to risk and one should follow it up well, and end it.

279. After saying that, I sent for Rais Abulphamalet, and answered him in this way: "Rais, you know well that I have made a great outlay in this business of mine, yet notwithstanding the outlay that I and my people have made and the ills we have suffered, for all that it shall not be but that I will agree to your terms, and have you escorted to Cullera, with all the goods that the Saracens, men and women, may be able to carry. For love of the king and of you, who have come here, will I do your people that grace, that they may go safely and securely with their apparel and with what they can carry, and wish to carry."

280. When the Rais heard that, he was content and he said he gave me great thanks, though their loss was to be great; nevertheless, he thanked me much for the grace I did them. After a time, I asked him on what day it should be. He said they needed ten days for clearing out. I told him that he asked too much, that the army was growing weary of the delay, for nothing was being done, and it was not for their good nor for mine. And so after long discourse we agreed that on the fifth day they would surrender the town, and would begin to depart.

When that was settled between me and him, I told the Rais to keep the thing secret until I had spoken with the archbishop of Narbonne, with the other bishops, and with my barons. He said he would do so, and I told him I would speak with them that very evening, and would give orders that from that time no harm should be done to them.

281. When that was done, and I had eaten, drunk, and taken sleep in a pavilion beside my quarters, I sent for the archbishop [of Tarragona], for the bishops and the barons, as well as for the archbishop of Narbonne, who was there in the camp. When all were present, I told them how Our Lord had done me many favors, and among others had now done me one for which I and they ought to give him great thanks. As they had a good share in that great gain of mine, I would make them know, that they all might rejoice in it, that Valencia was ours at last. When I had said that, Don Nuño, Don Exemen de Urrea, Don Pedro, Fernandez de Acagra, and Don Pedro Cornell lost color, as if someone had stabbed them to the heart. All murmured except the archbishop and some of the bishops, who said that they thanked Our Lord for giving me that gain, and that grace. Not one of the others thanked God for it, or took it well. Then Don Nuño and Don Pedro Fernandez de Acagra asked how it was done, and in what manner? I said that I had engaged for the safety of the king of Valencia and of the Saracens, all those living in the town, men and women, and for escorting them to Cullera and Denia, and that they were to surrender the town on the fifth day from that. All said that since I had done it, they approved of it. And the archbishop of Narbonne added, "This is the work of God, and I do not believe but that of three things one must be: either you have done service to God, or you are now serving him in this, or you will serve him hereafter." And En Ramon Berenguer said, "We ought to give God great thanks for the love he has shown

you, and since that which you and your ancestors had desired is now fulfilled through you, we ought to be very thankful to Our Lord."

282. Next day, at vespers, I sent to tell the king and the Rais Abulphamalet that in order that the Christians might know that Valencia was ours, and might do nothing against it, they should hoist my standard on the tower, which now is that called of the Temple. They said they were content, and I went on the Rambla, between the camp and the tower. When I saw my standard upon the tower, I dismounted, turned myself towards the east, and wept with my eyes, kissing the ground, for the great mercy that had been done to me.

283. Meantime the Saracens busied themselves about departing within the five days I had agreed on with them, so that on the third day they were all ready to leave, and I myself, with knights and armed men about me, brought them all out into the fields between Rucafa and the town. I had, however, to put some of my own men to death because of their attempting to take goods from the Saracens, and carry off some women and children. So it was, that though the people who came out of Valencia were so numerous—there being between men and women around fifty thousand—by the grace of God they did not lose between them one thousand sols, so well did I escort, and have them escorted, as far as Cullera.

Ibn Khaldun: The Rise of the Nasrids and the Christian Conquests

The Banu Nasr [Nasrids] were originally from Arjunah [Arjona], a castle in the jurisdiction of Cordoba. Their ancestors had been officers of rank [in the army], and were well known in that country as the Banu Nasr, or the sons of Nasr. They connected their genealogy with Sa'd Ibn 'Obádah, lord of the tribe of Khazrej. The head of the family, towards the close of the dynasty of the Almohads, was Muhammad ibn Yusuf Ibn Nasr Ibn al-Ahmar, better known as *Ash-sheikh* [the Sheikh]; his brother's name was Ismail. The former especially enjoyed considerable influence among his kindred. When the fortune of the Almohads began to decline, and rebels rose against them in al-Andalus—when the Seyds [lords] or members of the royal family began to give up their castles and fortresses to the Christian king—when, in short, Mohammed Ibn Yúsuf Ibn Húd rose at Murcia, and, having proclaimed the reigning caliph of the house of 'Abbas, took possession [in his name] of the eastern provinces of al-Andalus—the Sheikh [Ibn al-Ahmar] prepared also for rebellion, and in the year 629 AH [beginning 28 October 1231] caused himself to be proclaimed sultan of Andalus, although he ordered that the name of Abu Zakariyya [Hafsid sultan of North Africa, r. 1229–49], sultan of eastern Africa, should be mentioned in the public prayers, as commander of the Faithful. In the following year, 630 AH [beginning 17 October 1232], Jaen and Sherish [Xerez] submitted to him. All this Ibn al-Ahmar accomplished with the assistance of his relatives the Banu Nasr, and of the family of Ibn Ashqilūla, to whom he was related by marriage. Subsequently to this, in the year 631 AH [beginning 6 October 1233], hearing that Ibn Hūd had received from Baghdad a favorable answer to his petition, Ibn al-Ahmar sent in his allegiance to that sultan. Then happened the rebellion at Seville of Abu Marwan Al-baji, who, taking advantage of the departure of Ibn Hūd [from that city] to return to Murcia, rose and declared himself independent. With this chieftain Ibn al-Ahmar entered into a treaty of alliance, giving him one of his daughters in marriage, and promising to defend him against Ibn Hūd on condition that he would acknowledge himself his vassal. Al-baji accepted the proposition, and Ibn al-Ahmar accordingly entered Seville as its lord in 632 AH [beginning 25 September 1234]; but in the course of time he had Al-baji seized and put to death, through the means of Ibn Ashqilūla, whom he sent thither for that purpose.

One month after the above event, the people of Seville returned to the allegiance of Ibn Hūd, and expelled [the troops of] Ibn al-Ahmar; but in 635 AH [beginning 23 August 1237], the latter prince made himself master of Granada by means of his secret partisans there. An influential citizen of that place, named Ibn Abi Khaled, who was his friend, having risen against Ibn Hūd, prevailed upon the citizens to proclaim Ibn al-Ahmar, and, hastening to Jaen, where that sultan was at the time, tendered to him the allegiance of the inhabitants. Immediately upon the receipt of this news, Ibn al-Ahmar dispatched Ibn Ashqilūla to Granada with a portion of his forces. He himself followed with the rest of his army, and having taken up his abode in that city, built the fortress of the Alhambra, as a residence for himself. Soon after the acquisition of Granada, Ibn al-Ahmar obtained possession of Malaga, and in the year 643 AH [beginning 28 May 1245] received Almeria from the hands of Ibn al-Remimi, the vizier of Ibn Hūd, who had risen and taken the command of the place. Ibn al-Ahmar was next proclaimed by the people of Lorca, who, in 663 AH [beginning 23 October 1264], sent their allegiance to Granada.

During the events above related the Christians reduced several important cities of Andalus, chiefly through the division and perversity of their Islamic rulers. At the commencement of his reign, Ibn al-Ahmar had entered into an alliance with the Christian king [Ferdinand III of Castile], for the purpose of obtaining his aid [against Ibn Hūd]; and the infidel king had accordingly sent him occasional succors of troops. Ibn Hūd, on the other hand, wishing to detach the Christian from the cause of Ibn al-Ahmar, had offered him thirty castles on the western frontier of his dominions, if he would forsake that sultan and assist him to take possession of Cordoba. The offer was accepted, and the castles delivered to the Christians. At last, in the year 633 AH [beginning 15 September 1236], the enemy [Ferdinand of Castile] took possession of Cordoba (may God restore it to Islam!) and, in the year 646 AH [beginning 25 April 1248], laid siege to Seville, Ibn al-Ahmar himself co-operating with his forces [against the Muslims]. After a vigorous and long protracted defense, the city was taken by capitulation, and the Christians became masters of its districts. Murcia also fell into their hands in 665 AH [beginning 1 October 1266]; in short, the Christian king [Ferdinand III of Castile] ceased not to assail the dominions of Islam, and to take district after district and castle after castle until the whole of the Muslim population were driven to the coast between Ronda in the west and [Almeria in] the eastern parts of Andalus, about twenty marhala [about 30 miles] in length and one marhala or less in width from the sea to the furthermost point on the northern frontier.

Subsequently to this, Ibn al-Ahmar grew angry, and sought to obtain possession of the rest of the island; but he found the task too difficult, and was unable to accomplish his purpose. Troops, however, sent by the Banu Marin [the Merinids, rulers of Morocco and large parts of northern Africa] and other African dynasties, occasionally crossed over to his assistance, and with them Ibn al-Ahmar was enabled to keep the Christians at bay. For instance, in the year 660 AH [beginning 25 November 1261], according to previous stipulation, the sultan of Western Africa, Abu Yusuf Yaqub Ibn Abd al-Haqq [Merinid Sultan, r. 1258–86], sent him three thousand warriors, whose arrival Ibn al-Ahmar welcomed, and with whom he repelled the attacks of the enemy, and inflicted serious losses upon them. On the return of these auxiliary troops to Africa, others kept continually going over in their stead, until the death of the Sheikh Ibn al-Ahmar, which happened in 671 AH [1273].

26. WARFARE AT SEA

Although much of the warfare between Muslims and Christians occurred on land, naval encounters were also common, as the combatants sought to control the Mediterranean Sea. When Islamic forces began their expansion in the seventh century, the Byzantines were the dominant naval power in the Mediterranean. The Muslim conquest of the north African coast and numerous islands shattered this dominance, however, and by the early tenth century, control of the seas had clearly shifted to the Muslims. The beginning of the crusades in the late eleventh century seems to have led to another shift, as the Italian city-states, notably Venice and Genoa, joined somewhat later by the forces of Aragon-Catalonia, led an aggressive Latin Christian offensive for control of the seas, one that was largely successful. Adding to their troubles at sea, the Islamic states also seem to have had problems finding suitable supplies of wood and experienced manpower. Piracy added an additional layer of complexity to warfare at sea. Both Christians and Muslims engaged frequently in piracy during the Middle Ages and early modern period, making living in coastal regions and traveling by sea dangerous. Moreover, unlike regular warfare, which generally stopped during truces, piracy was a constant threat. The sources below capture much of the flavor of naval warfare in the medieval Mediterranean. The first source comes from the Cronica *of Ramon Muntaner (1265–1336), a Catalan soldier and historian, who chronicled his military exploits and those of his countrymen during the thirteenth and fourteenth centuries. The second entry is a letter from Yusuf I, Sultan of Granada (r. 1333–54) to Alfonso IV, king of Aragon (r. 1327–36), in which Yusuf responds to charges of piracy made by Alfonso.*

Sources: for Muntaner see trans. Lady Goodenough, *The Chronicle of Muntaner* (London: Hakluyt Society, 1920–21), 49–52; for the letter from Yusuf I to Alfonso IV see trans. Jarbel Rodriguez, from Maximiliano A. Alarcón y Santón and Ramón García de Linares, *Los Documentos Árabes Diplomáticos del Archivo de la Corona de Aragón* (Madrid: Imprenta de Estanislao Mastre, 1940), doc. 42.

Muntaner: *Cronica*, 1325–32

I will turn to speak a little of [Roger de Luria's] brother-in-law Conrado Lansa, and tell of a fine thing which, by the favor of God and of the lord king Peter of Aragon [surnamed the Great, r. 1275–85], happened to him. It is the truth that the lord, King Peter, should come first, but I wish to tell and recount it to you now, for it may as well be done at once than later, and I will do it now, while I remember the affairs concerning those two richs homens [rich men]; and it is better to speak now of that deed performed by the said noble Conrado Lansa than further on. For a man, when he speaks the truth, can relate any deed in any part of the book. And perhaps I should have to speak of it in a place where it would disturb my narrative; and, besides, it is not a long story. And so I pray all to forgive me if in this place or in another, they find I tell them things before their proper time. Nevertheless, if they ask me for reasons, I shall give them such as will make them excuse me; but, whatever the reasons I give you, be sure that everything you will find written is the truth, and of this have no doubt whatever. So then, I wish to tell you the favor God did to that rich hom [man] Conrado Lansa.

The lord king of Aragon has of old a right to a tribute from the king of Granada and from the king of Tlemcen and from the king of Tunis. And because, for a long time, this tribute had not been sent to the lord king of Aragon, he had four galleys equipped at Valencia and he made the said noble Conrado commander of them. He went to the port of Tunis and to Bougie and all along the coast, sacking and destroying all the ports. He came to the sea of the king of Tlemcen, to an island called Habibas and he went there to get water. And as he came to that place to get water, ten armed Saracen galleys of the king of Morocco also came to that place to get water. And these ten Saracen galleys were the best equipped, and manned by better Saracens of any that ever were equipped and they had already done much injury to lenys [small vessels] which they had captured from Christians and they had many captives in their galleys, which was a great sin.

And when the galleys of Conrado Lansa saw the ten galleys coming, they left the place. And the Saracens, who saw them and had had news of them already, shouted in their Saracen language, "Aur, Aur" and they came towards the galleys of Conrado Lansa with great vigor. And the galleys of Conrado Lansa formed in a circle, and all four collected together and held council. And Conrado Lansa said to them, "You, my lords, know that the favor of God is with the lord king of Aragon and with all his subjects; and you know how many victories he has had over Saracens. You may well consider that the lord king of Aragon is present with us in these galleys, for you see here his standard, which represents his person, and as he is with you, so is the favor of God and he will help us and give us victory. And it would be a great disgrace for the said lord and for the city of Valencia to which we all belong, if, because of those dogs, we faced about, a thing no man of the lord king of Aragon has ever done. Therefore I pray you all that you remember the power of God and of Our Lady Saint Mary, and the Holy Catholic Faith, and the honor of the lord king and of the city of Valencia and of all the kingdom; and that, roped together as we are, we attack resolutely, and that, on this day, we do so much that we be spoken of forever. And, assuredly, we shall defeat them and be prosperous forever. However, you can all see that we have so much the advantage of them that we can retire if we like, and that they cannot force us to fight, if we do not wish to. And so, let everyone say what seems best to him, but as for me I have told you my opinion already. Again, I tell you and pray you and require you, in the name of the lord king of Aragon and of the city of Valencia, to attack them."

And all began to shout, "Let us attack them! Let us attack them! They will all be ours!" And with that they armed themselves well and the Saracens did the same. And when both sides were armed, Conrado with great strokes of the rowers, advanced towards the Saracens. Some of these told their commander that the galleys were coming towards them in order to surrender, and a great many Saracens were of this opinion, because there was a very accomplished knight amongst them and they did not think the Christians would be so mad as to wish to fight with them. But the Saracen admiral was a wise seaman and had been in many feats of arms and had had proof of what the Catalans are, and he shook his head and said, "Barons, your opinion is foolish; you do not know the people of the king of Aragon as I know them. Now be sure that they are preparing well and wisely to fight with us; and they come so ready to die that woe is to the mother's son who is awaiting them. Wherefore as they come prepared to vanquish or die, so put the same resolution into your hearts; for this will be the day in which, if we make not great endeavors, you will all die or be taken captive. Would to God I were a hundred miles away from them; but as things are as they are, I commend myself to God and Muhammad."

And with that, he ordered trumpets and nakers [a small drum] to be sounded, and with great shouts they began a vehement attack. And the four galleys, most beautifully, and without shouts and words or any clamor, went to the attack in the midst of the ten galleys and there the battle was most grievous and hard, and it lasted from the morning until the hour of vespers [evening], and no one dared to eat or drink. But Our Lord the true God and his blessed mother, from whom come all favors, and the good luck of the lord king of Aragon, gave the victory to our men, in such manner that all the galleys were defeated and the men killed or taken. Blessed be the Lord who made it come to pass. And when they had won the battle and defeated and taken all the galleys, they delivered the Christian captives whom they found in them and gave to each of them as good a share of what God had enabled them to take as that of every man who had been in the battle. And so, with great honor and in great triumph, they returned to Valencia with the galleys which they brought there, and with many Saracen captives who had hidden below deck, of whom they had much profit.

Letter from Yusuf I to Alfonso IV, 1335

Your messenger Ramon Boil has informed us of the claim made by your people.

Among them is the incident of a galley captured by the people of Almeria [Yusuf's subjects] last year. This problem has already been resolved and all the munitions from the galley have been returned to you. The merchant goods which the galley carried were sold in Almeria and the proceeds from the sale turned over to its owner by the customs bureau of Almeria which settled the account.

We have made inquiries regarding Ibn al-'Ahsan, the captain of the saetia [a type of ship], which according to some accounts, was responsible for damages in your territories during times of peace. [Our investigation] discovered two lenys, one in Malaga, and the other in Vera, which he had captured. Both have been returned to their respective owners who came to claim them. Moreover, we have also sought all the Christians taken by him. We found seventeen, all of whom were returned to you with your ambassador. Previously, we had returned another eighteen Christians with Abū al-Hasan [ruler of Morocco, r. 1331–51], the son of Kumāsa. Whatever goods could be found [from what was taken] have been picked up by their owners.

In regards to Captain Ibn al-'Ahsan, whose origins you have denounced, you should know that the magnificent and peerless sovereign, Abū al-Hasan, prince of the believers, whom we regard as our father, had already asked us to send to him Ibn al-ʿAhsan and all he had captured. We have sent al-ʿAhsan, all his captives [alienígenas], and goods that he commandeered during his last raid. As such, if you have further claims against him, you should write to his excellent majesty [Abū al-Hasan] for his bounty knows no bounds.

The delay in returning all the captives and goods to you stemmed from us not knowing whether or not they came from a hostile country. But as soon as your letter arrived, we deemed it certain that they were yours and we have ordered that all be returned to you and to liberate all the captives, as we know that your words are true and wish to fulfill your wishes.

Written on the fourth day of Dhū al-Hijja, 735 AH [26 July 1335].

27. FRONTIER RAIDS

The people who settled and lived on the frontier regions between Christian and Muslim territory were constantly under the threat of attack by raiding parties. These attacks were sometimes part of sanctioned military campaigns, but more likely they were the result of frontier denizens acting on their own initiative, sometimes in open defiance of their own monarchs. Raids were a way of life on the frontier. Many of them were launched to obtain captives and booty, others orchestrated to recover stolen property, and yet others were punitive expeditions to discourage future attacks. Their net effect was to destabilize life on the frontiers, as a raid by one side prompted retaliatory strikes from the other, with many innocent non-combatants caught in the crossfire. The first source, from the observations of the great Muslim traveler Ibn Battuta (1304–68) and written by the Andalusi scholar Ibn Juzayy (1321–57), describes a raid on the town of Marbella in which a number of Christian pirates disembarked from their vessels and attacked the town, causing some damage. The second source is from the Anales de Orihuela, *by Pedro Bellot. Orihuela was a frontier town (the largest one in the municipality) in southern Valencia that experienced and participated in more than its share of raiding with neighboring Granada. In 1400, the Christians and Muslims living there came to an agreement that they hoped would limit the raids and the damage these caused. These* hermandades *imposed a collective civic responsibility on* aljamas, *self-governing Muslim towns in Christian territories, and Christian towns within the municipality. By belonging to an* hermandad, *the towns and* aljamas *were held accountable for the raiding activities of their coreligionists, even if a particular town or* aljama *was not directly responsible.*

Sources: for Ibn Battuta, trans. H.A.R. Gibb, Ibn Battuta, *The Travels of Ibn Battuta, AD 1325–1354*, 5 vols. (London: Hakluyt Society, 1956–94), 4:939–40; for Bellot, trans. Jarbel Rodriguez, from Mosén Pedro Bellot, *Anales de Orihuela*, 2 vols., ed. Juan Torres Fontes (Alicante: Real Academia Alfonso X El Sabio, 1954, repr. 2001), 184–86.

Ibn Battuta: The Raid of Marbella, 1352–55

I left the Mount of Victory for the city of Runda [Ronda], which is one of the strongest and best sited Muslim strongholds.... I stayed there for five days and then went to the city of Marbala [Marbella]. The road between these two cities is difficult and very rough. Marbella is a pretty, little town with abundant supplies of food. I found there a cavalry troop going to Malaqa [Malaga], and I wished to travel in their company. God Most High in his grace preserved me. They left before me and were taken prisoner on the road, as we shall relate. I left in their wake, and when I had gone beyond the limits of Marbella and entered those of Suhail I passed a dead horse in a ditch. Then I passed a basket of fish abandoned on the ground. This alarmed me. The guardian's watchtower was in front of me, and I said to myself: "If the enemy had appeared here the warden of the tower would have given warning." I went forward to a house and found in front of it a horse that had been killed. While I was there I heard cries from behind me. I had gone ahead of my companions, but I turned back towards them. I found the qadi [judge] of the Suhail fort with them. He informed me that four enemy war galleys had appeared there, some of those manning them had landed, the warden had not been in the tower, and horsemen coming from Marbella, twelve in number, had passed by them. The Christians had killed one of them, one had fled, and ten had been taken prisoner. A fisherman had been killed with them; it was he whose basket I had found lying on the ground.

The qadi advised me to stay the night in his station so that he could conduct me to Malaga. I spent the night with him in the fort of the frontier post named after Suhail, the aforesaid war galleys being moored nearby. Next day the qadi accompanied me on horseback and we reached the city of Malaga, one of the capitals of al-Andalus and one of its finest cities, combining as it does the amenities of land and sea; it has ample resources and fruits. I saw grapes sold in the bazaars at eight pounds for a small dirham; its Murcian ruby-red pomegranates have no equal in the world; its figs and almonds are exported from Malaga and its neighborhood to the east and the west.

Bellot: Anales de Orihuela

During that time [the year 1400], Alicante was under a state of alert fearful of a fleet of 22 vessels [*fustas*] which had formed in Africa and was suspected of headed towards Alicante. The town sent a message to the town council of Orihuela asking for help. The council gave their word to the messenger and made a promise in writing to Alicante that as soon as an attack was certain that all its forces, both horse and foot, would march to their aid. They also notified the town of Guardamar and ordered all the landowners to go to Alicante. And the governor Guillén Pérez Vaillo gave notice to other locales and the council sent a plea to the king to make Olfo de Próxita [a high-ranking Valencian official] their leader during the emergency. But the king replied that he [currently] had much need of him and as soon as he could return to Valencia, he would send him to Orihuela.

The Moorish armada did not attack Alicante, or any other place in this region, putting all of these fears to rest. The raids from Granada, however, did not stop. These were aided and guided by local Muslims, which was damaging and set a very bad example, and which obliged the local villages to seek a convenient solution. They put into action an agreement between Moors and Christians put forth by Carbonell, the royal commissioner, and it included many clauses.... The most important clause stipulated that if anyone from this municipality raided, captured or killed any Moors, the Christians were obligated to find them and ransom them at their own cost, and if they [the Muslims] were killed, the Christians had to pay 200 florins to their kin or to the *aljama* if they didn't have any relatives. If they killed or captured any Christians, the Muslims had the same obligation. The Christians benefited greatly from this agreement. Since the Muslims from the *aljamas* had to pay for any damages caused by raiders from Granada, not only did they not help them with intelligence or cover, but they would have done anything to avoid paying the damage caused by the brigands from Granada.

These safeguards did not stop the raiding from Granada, but oftentimes things turned out poorly for them thanks to the efforts of Lorca, Murcia, and Orihuela. On 4 May the town of Lorca warned that three companies of Moors had crossed their borders and the council ordered one company of horsemen and many on foot to sally forth, and the Moors retired in time. Another notice came from Murcia, announcing that war had been declared between Castile and Granada, and warning all to put their cattle in a safe place, as there were many companies of Moors in these parts.

This type of warfare was exhausting to the people of Orihuela as they had to be constantly on guard with their weapons at the ready and prepared to muster. What was worse, they seldom caught the enemy, as the territory was so large that by the time warning arrived, the Moors had already left. Because of this, they would be slow in marching out to their musters. To remedy this problem, the council ordered the horsemen to make multiple shows of force, and those whose turn it was to sortie when they heard the [warning] bell should do so through the portal where they had to muster. There, they should wait for the governor and the justiciar and a mule train loaded with bread, wine, sandals, horseshoes, and nails should follow them.

And since the Moors did not stop making raids into Murcia and this municipality [Orihuela], the people of Lorca wrote to Orihuela that the best solution was to place lookouts at all the passes through which the Moors could come. Moreover, since everyone would benefit from this, the cost should be distributed equally. Orihuela consulted with the other towns in the municipality and they all agreed to the plan. They then proposed it to Murcia, which quickly promised to pay half the costs and that the municipality [of Orihuela] should pay the other half.

On 15 August, Murcia sent notice to the council of Orihuela that Lope Barriga, one of its citizens, while traveling had come across the trail of two men on horse with grass horseshoes, even finding one of the horseshoes and that the trails came from the field of Matanza. Murcia urged the council to take every precaution so that the two would not escape, as it was certain that the two horsemen were the renegade Chinchilla and his brother-in-law. The council did everything it could to prevent the two renegades from escaping. The two had caused a lot of damage in the municipality and so much money had been spent on musters [to try to catch them] that the regular rents were not enough and taxes had multiplied. The council advised Murcia to take similar precautions. But this time they were unable to capture them.

28. THE CONQUEST OF GRANADA AND ITS AFTERMATH

In 1469, Isabel, sister of the king of Castile, and Ferdinand, son of the king of Aragon, married. In 1474, Isabel inherited the Castilian throne while Ferdinand came into his inheritance five years later. Their marriage, although it did not politically unite Castile and Aragon, created a unity of purpose in the two Christian kingdoms which spelled doom for the Nasrid kingdom of Granada. Ever since the mid-fourteenth century, Christian efforts to conquer Granada had amounted to little. There had been some minor successes, but the Muslim kingdom survived and even thrived as Castile and Aragon dealt with their own internal problems or were beckoned by the prospect of conquest and riches elsewhere. The marriage of Ferdinand and Isabel would change all that. In 1481, the Christian monarchs began a decade-long campaign to conquer the last remaining Muslim kingdom in Iberia. The city of Ronda fell in 1485, followed by Malaga in 1487. The Castilians spent most of 1490 raiding Granada's hinterland and by 1491 had surrounded and cut off the city itself, building a great encampment, known as Santa Fe, from which they coordinated the siege. Finally, on the night of 1–2 January 1492, the city capitulated, with the monarchs themselves entering the city on 6 January. With its fall, the last Muslim kingdom in Iberia had been conquered, and the entire peninsula was under Christian political control. The sources below approach the final conquest from very different points of view. The first is a description of the fall of Granada written by the Castilian priest Andrés Bernáldez. It is a triumphant retelling of the deeds of Ferdinand, Isabel, and their soldiers as they captured the city. The second source, extracted from the writings of the north African historian Ahmed Ibn Muhammad al-Maqqari (c. 1591–1632), recounts the fall of Granada from the Muslim perspective and gives a detailed list of the clauses that made up the surrender treaty. Lastly, al-Maqqari continues the story beyond the conquest itself with an overview of how the Muslims who stayed in Iberia fared under Christian rule until their eventual expulsion in 1610.

Sources: for Bernáldez, trans. Jarbel Rodriguez, from Andrés Bernáldez, *Historia de los Reyes Catolicos Dⁿ Fernando y Dᵃ Isabel*, 2 vols. (Seville: Imprenta que fue de D. José Maria Geofrin, 1870), I: 300–305; for al-Maqqari, trans. Pascual de Gayangos, *The History of the Mohammedan Dynasties of Spain* (London: W.H. Allen & Co., 1843), 2: 386–92, rev. Jarbel Rodriguez.

Bernáldez: The Siege and Conquest of Granada

July, August, September, October, and November all came and went and the Moors still refused to surrender. By December, however, as they ran out of supplies, they asked for [surrender] terms from the king and the queen, which were agreed to between the king and the Moors. They agreed to turn over all the fortresses that they and Boabdil [Muhammad XII, last ruler of Granada, r. 1482–83 and 1487–92] held in the Alhambra to King Ferdinand on 30 December in exchange for the right to keep using their own [Islamic] law and to keep their property. The king and the queen agreed to this along with some other conditions; that those who wanted to leave could go whenever they wanted and wherever they wanted; that all Christian captives would be returned. To confirm the agreement, the people and nobles of Granada, in conjunction with King Boabdil, sent four-hundred hostages, common and great men, but all valiant, until the time when the city was handed over.... And a certain Moor raised a revolt within the city, saying that the Moors could win, praising Muhammad and garnering support, he would walk throughout the city calling out and over 20,000 Moors rose up with him. When he saw the upheaval, King Boabdil refused to come out from the Alhambra to put it down, until the next day, which was a Saturday, when he came out to the Albaycin [a hill district facing the Alhambra] and called the council. They arrived very agitated and he asked them what was going on and they told him. He then explained his views and tried to calm them down as best he could, telling them that it was too late to do anything, first, because of the dire position they were in which limited their ability to resist, and second because of the hostages they had turned over. He warned them of the great danger and the many deaths that lay ahead without any hope of salvation [should they persist in their revolt], and having said his piece, he returned to the Alhambra. The agreement called for the forces inside the city to surrender on the Feast of the Three Kings [6 January]. But King Boabdil, seeing the deteriorating conditions and disorder, wrote to King Ferdinand about everything that had transpired, and how the Moors, like ignorant men, had renounced the treaty, but that he remained committed and true to it. He urged his majesty to come and receive the Alhambra immediately and not wait until the sixth of January as he had the hostages and in spite of the turmoil, Boabdil intended to follow through on the treaty. When the king and queen met the king's ambassadors and read his letter, they decided to go and take the Alhambra. They departed from their camp on Monday, 2 January with their army in battle formation. When they approached the Alhambra, the Moorish king Boabdil came out accompanied by many lords with the keys to the city in his hands, riding a horse which he wanted to dismount to kiss the king's hand. But the king did not let him get off the horse, nor did he offer him his hand, so the Moorish king kissed his arm, gave him the keys and told him, "Take them lord, the keys to your city. I and those inside are your subjects." And King Ferdinand took the keys and gave them to the queen, and the queen gave them to the prince [John, prince of Asturias and royal heir], and the prince gave them to the count of Tendilla, who with the duke of Escalona, the marquis of Villena, and with many other lords, three thousand horsemen and two thousand musket-men entered the Alhambra. They went inside and took over [the fortress] gaining control over its entirety and displaying on the tallest tower the standard of Jesus Christ which was the Holy Cross that the king always carried with him in this holy conquest. Then the king, the queen, the prince, and the entire army humbled themselves before the Holy Cross and gave many thanks and praise to Our Lord and the bishops and clergy all sang, "Te deum laudamus." And then those who were inside the city unfurled the banner of Saint James, which the master of [the military order of] Saint James had with him, together with the royal banner of King Ferdinand and then the royal heralds called out in loud voices: "Castile! Castile!" The royal heralds then discharged their duties and made their proclamations. Present to witness this [proclamation] and the felicitous victory with the king and the queen were their children, Prince John, and the princess Joanna [later better known by her unfortunate nickname Joanna the Mad], the cardinal of Spain, the archbishop of Seville, the master of Saint James, the duke of Cadiz, and many other knights, counts, prelates, bishops, and great lords, whose names are too numerous to list. When they had finished, the king and the queen, with all their troops, returned to the royal camp and left the count of Tendilla in the Alhmabra with all the soldiers that he needed to guard it. The Moors in Granada turned over to the king all the gates, towers, and fortresses of Granada and the king sent officials to each as he secured his control over the city. When this was accomplished, the king ordered that all weapons and strongholds, whether they were offensive or defensive, be seized and all were brought to the Alhambra except for some that the defenders had hidden. The Moorish king Boabdil, with the great lords of

Granada and with many others came out of the city and they departed according to the stipulations of the treaty. Many went across the sea [to the Muslim kingdoms of northern Africa], while others went to live with *mudejares* [Spanish Muslims who lived in Christian-controlled regions] in places that had already been conquered. King Boabdil left to live and rule in the Val de Porchena, which is in the lands which the king [Ferdinand] had conquered when he took Vera. It was filled with *mudejares* and King Ferdinand gave him a lordship there and rents that he could live on and many vassals. He also raised the pension that he was accustomed to giving him [Boabdil] and returned to him all the hostages that he was holding.

The king, the queen, and the court stayed in Santa Fe [the royal camp] which they had built for the siege, going sometimes to the Alhambra, until the end of May 1492 and even part of June, as they did not dare to depart until the city was secure. During that time, there were several riots by the Moors and our men found a large mine packed with weapons. The king filled the city with justices and royal officials [*alcaydes*] and such was the order he imposed that he subjugated the Moorish masses that lived there and numbered over forty-thousand. Moreover, due to the disturbances and upheavals which some Moors caused while the court was there, during which time they rioted on two or three different occasions, [the king's men] killed many in the name of justice, while others were quartered and dismembered. This put the Moors under the yoke of fear and obedience, which was convenient. And when Granada had been won, subjugated, and placed under the yoke of Castile, the king, the queen, and the court departed from the Alhambra in the first days of June. They celebrated the feast of the Holy Spirit, which that year fell on the tenth of June, in Cordoba, victorious and blessed with such triumphs of honor and fortune as was possible. And thus, they brought to a glorious end their holy and praiseworthy conquest. Their eyes saw what many kings and princes had desired to see, a kingdom of so many cities and towns, with such a multitude of places located in such defensible and difficult terrain, won in only ten years. And this was because God wanted to help them and put this land in their hands.

Al-Maqqari: The Conquest of Granada and Its Aftermath

On the 12th of Jumādā II, of the year 896 AH [22 March 1491], the king of Castile marched his army into the plain of Granada, and began destroying the crops, demolishing the towns and villages, and subduing the whole country. He also laid the foundations of a town [Santa Fe] with walls and a ditch, the building of which he superintended in person. It had been reported at Granada that the Christians intended to raise the siege of that capital and return to their country; but if they had any such intention they changed their determination, for, instead of raising their tents, they remained encamped, in the city which they had built, and pressed the siege with greater vigor than ever. The contest lasted for seven consecutive months, and the Muslims were reduced to great extremities; but still, as the Christians were encamped at some distance from Granada, and the communication between that city and the Alpujarras was not yet intercepted, the inhabitants received abundant supplies from the district of Jebal-Sholayr [Sierra Nevada]. But when the winter came on, and frost and snow covered the ground, the produce of the earth grew less, its conveyance to Granada became more difficult, and provisions became gradually so scarce, that famine began to be felt in that capital. The enemy, too, had purposely taken possession of almost every patch of ground out of the city, so that it became impossible to gather any crops from the surrounding fields, and the condition of the besieged became every day more distressing and hopeless. This was about the beginning of the year 897 AH [November 1491]. It was evident that the enemy's design was to reduce the city by famine, and not by force of arms. Things being brought to this plight, great numbers of the inhabitants quitted Granada and fled to the Alpujarras. Provisions grew every day more scarce, and in the month of Safar of the same year [December 1491] the privations of the people became almost intolerable. The inhabitants then began to deliberate among themselves as to the expediency of surrendering to the enemy. They therefore sought the advice of their *Ulemas* and other learned men, who recommended them to look to their own safety, and consult over the matter with the sultan.

Agreeable to this opinion, the sultan convened his officers of state and councilors, when this important affair was discussed in his presence. The people then said, "The Christians are daily receiving reinforcements, while we have none to expect; we all thought and expected that, at the approach of winter, the Christians would have raised the siege and retired to their country, whereas our hopes have completely failed; they have built a town in front of our city, and pressed the siege closer than ever. We ought, therefore, to provide for our safety and that of our children." It was then unanimously agreed to adopt this last determination, and it soon became public that the officers of the army, fearing for their lives and those of the inhabitants, had for some time been treating with the Christians about the surrender of the city. Negotiations then commenced, and a capitulation was drawn up on the same terms as that of Guadix [which had surrendered to the Christian forces in 1489], although with some additional articles, as, for instance, that the pope should be a guarantee for the faithful execution of the treaty, and the strict observance of every one of the articles therein contained, before the Christians should be put in possession of the Alhambra and the other forts; and that the king should bind himself by oath, after the Christian fashion, to observe the treaty. The deputies sent by the people of Granada insisted upon the insertion of this clause; but it was reported that when they came to discuss the article together, the Christians bribed the Muslim envoys, and gave them considerable sums of money, to have it omitted in the capitulation. The treaty was then read over to the inhabitants, who approved of it and gave it their sanction, some of the principal citizens signing it with their own hands, and pledging their allegiance to the Castilian king, who accepted it. This done, the sultan of Granada left the Alhambra on the second day of Rabī I, of the year 897 AH [3 January 1492], and the Christian sovereign immediately took possession of it, as well as of the other fortresses in Granada, not without having first received five hundred of the principal inhabitants of Granada as hostages, to guard against any treachery on the part of the inhabitants.

The capitulation contained sixty-seven articles, among which were the following:

- That both great and small should be perfectly secure in their persons, families, and properties.
- That they should be allowed to continue in their dwellings and residences, whether in the city, the suburbs, or any other part of the country.
- That their laws should be preserved as they were before, and that no one should judge them except by those same laws.
- That their mosques and the religious endowments appertaining to them should remain as they were in the times of Islam.
- That no Christian should enter the house of a Muslim or insult him in any way.
- That no Christian or Jew holding public offices by the appointment of the late sultan should be allowed to exercise his functions or rule over them.
- That all Muslim captives made during the siege of Granada from whatever part of the country they might have come, but especially the nobles and chiefs mentioned in the agreement, should be liberated.
- That such Muslim captives as might have escaped from their Christian masters, and taken refuge in Granada, should not be surrendered, but that the sultan should be bound to pay the price of such captives to their owners.
- That all those who might choose to cross over to Africa should be allowed to take their departure within a certain time, and be conveyed there in the king's ships, and without any pecuniary tax being imposed upon them, beyond the mere charge for passage, and that after the expiration of that time no Muslim should be hindered from departing, provided he paid, in addition to the price of his passage, the tithe of whatever property he might carry along with him.
- That no one should be prosecuted and punished for the crime of another man.

- That the Christians who had embraced the Islamic religion should not be compelled to relinquish it, and adopt their former creed.
- That any Muslim wishing to become Christian should be allowed some days to consider the step he is about to take; after which he is to be questioned both by a Muslim and a Christian judge concerning his intended change, and if, after this examination, he still refuse to return to Islam, he should be permitted to follow his own inclination.
- That no Muslim should be prosecuted for the death of a Christian slain during the siege and that no restitution of property taken during the war should be enforced.
- That no Muslim should be subject to have Christian soldiers billeted upon him, or be transported to provinces of this kingdom against his will.
- That no increase should be made to the usual imposts, but that, on the contrary, all the oppressive taxes lately imposed should be immediately suppressed.
- That no Christian should be allowed to peep over the wall, or into the house of a Muslim, or enter a mosque.
- That any Muslim choosing to travel or reside among the Christians should be perfectly secure in his person and property.
- That no badge or distinctive mark be put on them, as was done with the Jews and *mudejares*.
- That no muezzin should be interrupted in the act of calling the people to prayer, and no Muslim molested either in the performance of his daily devotions or in the observance of his fast, or in any other religious ceremony; but that if a Christian should be found laughing at them he should be punished for it.
- That the Muslims should be exempted from all taxation for a certain number of years.
- That the lord of Rome [the pope] should be requested to give his assent to the above conditions, and sign the treaty himself. These, and many others that we omit, were the articles of the treaty.

This matter being settled, and the Christians having taken possession of the Alhambra, and of the city, the king appointed a governor to that fortress, and civil officers and magistrates to govern the inhabitants. On learning the conditions granted to the people of Granada, the inhabitants of the Alpujarras agreed to the treaty, and made their submission upon the same terms. The king of Castile then ordered the necessary repairs to be made in the Alhambra, as well as in the other fortresses and towers, and applied himself to strengthen its fortifications. While these works were going on, he came daily to the Alhambra, but returned every night to his camp, fearing, no doubt, some treachery on the part of the inhabitants, and he continued to do so until his fears were entirely dissipated. He also entered the city and visited its different quarters, so as to gain exact information of the feeling of the inhabitants towards him, and learn other particulars which he wished to ascertain.

After this, the infidel king ordered the sultan of the Muslims to repair to the Alpujarras, which he said should be his, and to fix his residence at Andarax. In compliance with this order, the [deposed] sultan repaired to that town, and the Christian troops which occupied the Alpujarras were immediately withdrawn. However, some time after, the king made use of the following stratagem to induce the sultan to leave Andalus and cross over to Africa. He pretended that the latter had expressed to him the wish of leaving the country, and wrote to the governor of Almeria in the following terms: "On the receipt of this our letter, let no one hinder Muley Abú 'abd-Allah [Boabdil in the Christian sources] from going to whichever port of Africa he likes best. Let all those who read the present letter facilitate everything for his passage, and observe towards him the conditions stipulated in the treaty." Agreeable to the intimation contained in this letter, Abu 'abd-Allah set forth immediately for Almeria, and having embarked at that port, he sailed for the coast of Africa and landed at Melilla. From there he went to Fez, where he settled. His first intention, however, had been to fix his residence at Morocco, but hearing, on his landing, that the provinces of that empire were sadly afflicted by famine, pestilence, and other calamities, he desisted from his project.

After his landing at Melilla, the sultan directed his course towards the city of Fez, where, complaining of his unlucky fate, and regretting the kingdom he had lost, he settled with his family and his adherents, and built some palaces in imitation of those of Granada, which we ourselves saw and visited during our residence in that city. He died in Fez in the year 940 AH [1538], (may God forgive him!) and was buried in front of the chapel outside of Bábu-sh-shari'at [the gate of the law]. He left two male children, one named Yusuf and the other Ahmed, whose posterity may still be traced in Fez; for in our time, when we visited that city in 1037 AH [1635], we were acquainted with some of his posterity, who were reduced to the necessity of subsisting upon the charitable allowances made to the faquirs and poor people out of the funds of the mosques, and who in fact were nothing more than mere beggars.

Not many years elapsed before the Christians violated the treaty entered into with the Muslims, and began to infringe one by one the settled stipulations. Things even went so far that in the year 904 AH [beginning 18 August 1498], they set about forcing the Muslims to embrace the Christian religion under various pretences, the most specious of which was that their priests had written [books] on the convenience of compelling such Christians as had become Muslims to embrace their former religion. Notwithstanding the clamor excited among the Muslim community by so revolting an injustice, the people being helpless, the measure was carried into execution. Not satisfied with this breach of the treaty, the Christian tyrants went still further; they said to a Muslim, "Thy ancestor was a Christian, although he made himself a Muslim; thou must also become a Christian."

When these proceedings became public, the people of the Albayzin rose up in arms and slew their magistrates; but this was also made an excuse for more rigorous measures, for, soon after, the poor Muslims were told, "the king has promulgated a law by which anyone who revolts against his magistrates is condemned to death, unless he immediately becomes a Christian; so you must either die or be converted to Christianity."

In short, every Muslim, whether residing in Granada or in the neighborhood, was enjoined to embrace the religion of the idolaters within a certain time. A few, however, refused to comply with this order, but it was of no avail to them; seeing which, they had recourse to arms, and rose in several towns and villages, such as Belefique, Andarax, and others. Thither the enemy marched his forces, attacking and pursuing the inhabitants, until they almost exterminated them, killing a great number, and making the rest captives, except such as fortified themselves in Jebal-Balanca, and to whom God Almighty was pleased to grant victory over their enemies; for in a battle which took place there they killed a great number of the Christians, and amongst them the lord of Cordoba. After this the Muslims obtained terms of capitulation, and were allowed to cross over to Fez with their families and moveable property, although they were not permitted to take with them more money than that required for their journey.

Such of the Muslims as still remained in Andalus, although Christians in appearance, were not so in their hearts; for they worshipped Allah in secret, and performed their prayers and ablutions at the proper hours. The Christians watched over them with the greatest vigilance, and many were discovered and burnt. In the meantime, they were forbidden the use of arms, and even small knives, or any other sharp instrument made of iron. At last, these and other cruelties having driven the Muslims to despair, they again rose in arms in the mountainous districts, and on different occasions. But the Almighty not being pleased to grant victory to their cause, they were everywhere overpowered and slain, until they were ultimately expelled from the territory of Andalus—an event that took place in our times, in the year 1017 of the Hijra [1610]. Many thousands of the unfortunate emigrants went to Fez, thousands to Telemsan [Tlemcen] from Wahran [Oran]; the greater part took the road to Tunis. Few, however, reached the place of their destination; for they were assailed on the road by the Arabs and such as fear not God, and they were plundered and ill-treated, especially on the road to Fez and Telemsan. Those who directed their course to Tunis were more fortunate; they, for the most part, reached that place in safety, and peopled the desert towns and districts of the country, as also Tet-wan [Tetouan], Sale, and the plain of Metidja, near Algiers. Some entered the service of the Sultan of Maghreb al-Aqsa [Morocco], who formed them into a body, and allotted them for a residence the port of Sale, where they have since made themselves famous by their maritime expeditions against the enemy of God; they have also fortified the castle, and built themselves houses, palaces, and baths, and still continue to reside in that place. A few went to Constantinople, to Egypt, Syria, and to other countries where Islam is predominant and settled there, inhabiting now, as we have been told, the same places at which they first fixed their residence. God, indeed, is the master of all lands and dominions, and gives them to whomsoever he pleases.

CHAPTER FOUR

DIPLOMACY AND ALLIANCES

Figure 4.1: Messengers of the sultan.

Source: Paul LaCroix, *Military and Religious Life in the Middle Ages and the Period of the Renaissance* (London: Bickers and Son, n.d.), 129.

29. A COMPLEX ALLIANCE

The multitude of polities, ethnicities, religious proclivities, and personal relationships in Asia Minor and the Holy Land could make alliances quite complex. A region inhabited and contested by Byzantines, Turks, Arabs, Armenians, and Latin Europeans, among others, often witnessed the gathering of strange bedfellows when it came time to make treaties and to gather coalitions for wars. The source below by the Byzantine historian and soldier John Kinnamos describes the efforts of the emperor Manuel Comnenus (r. 1143–80) to put together an army with which to attack the Seljuk Turk sultan Kilij Arslan II (r. 1156–92). The emperor drew on his local Christians allies, as well Italian, Serbian, and Russian forces, while concurrently trying to undermine Kilij Arslan by making alliances with members of his own family.

Source: trans. Charles Brand, John Kinnamos, *Deeds of John and Manuel Comnenus* (New York: Columbia University Press, 1976), 150–53.

At what had befallen, the Turks were aggrieved and determined to injure the Romans [Byzantines] in turn; biding their time, they seized Phileta, an eastern city. Also, unexpectedly attacking Laodikeia in Lesser Phrygia, they seriously damaged it, carrying off at sword's point many of the inhabitants, from youth upwards, whom they had made captive, a great and innumerable multitude. When he heard this, the emperor was vexed and grieved; were it possible, he wished to cross to Asia forthwith and commence a campaign on Ikonion. But since he knew this required a time appropriate for such deeds and greater preparation for war than before, he deferred it.

Being minded to gather forces from every direction, he dispatched John Kontostephanos to Palestine [in early 1160] to meet King Baldwin [II, king of Jerusalem, r. 1143–62] and lead back from there the men whom he had agreed by their alliance to furnish on request to the emperor, as well as a mercenary corps. He ordered Reginald prince of Antioch to start out as swiftly as possible with the troops around him, as well as the then leaders of the Armenians, Toros and Tigranes, and the Cilician Chrysaphios and those whom people call Kogh Vasilii, who are commanders of martial forces, but who long since came over to the emperor as voluntary subjects. From the east he gathered thus great a band, and from the west he drew Ligurian [Lombard] knights and summoned the grand župan of Serbia with the troops under him, and he hired many Scyths from those tribes settled around Tauros [Tauroscyths or Russians]. Nor did he cease making preparation for war with these measures, but aware that the landfall for the Latin races bound for Palestine [the crusaders] was at the island of Rhodes, he recruited a mercenary band of knights from there. For provision-supply and other service, he ordered an unutterable quantity of oxen with their carts to be driven from the villages in Thrace.

So he had made these preparations, while, in order to render the sultan hostile to his compatriots and relatives, he wrote to his brother Shahan-Shah, who then governed Gangra and Galatian Ankyra [Ankara], and to his son-in-law Yaghi-Basan, who ruled both Kaisareia [Kayseri] and Amaseia [Amasya] and other outstanding cities which are situated in the Cappadocians' land. After he had rendered them suspect to the sultan, he was in a short time ready for war. The sultan learned of this, and since he was incapable of opposing either of those who had been roused against him by the emperor, he yielded his claim to many cities, especially ones recently acquired by him with great effort, in favor of those who lived near his own land. He wrote to the emperor and requested pardon. Should he succeed in this, he promised to restore the Roman captives, wherever they were concealed in his realm: the search would be his business.

While these things were under examination, something as follows befell. As he set out from Palestine [autumn 1161] with the knights, John [Kontostephanos] encountered a Turkish army which numbered upwards of twenty-two thousand fighting men. Stricken by surprise, he at first went with his followers quickly to a hill located nearby and took a stand; thereafter, cheered on by the whole army, he charged at them, and since the Romans engaged the foe with intense pressure, the Turks' retreat commenced. Many of them fell as they fled, many were taken by the Romans' soldiers, and the cavalry trampled many under foot. Then numerous other persons achieved deeds worthy of account and of their valor, but in that conflict the demonstration of excellence rested with the general, John. After this success, John returned to the emperor with tokens of victory.

When the sultan heard this, pricked by goads of regret, he cursed himself for their untimely rashness, not so much disturbed by what had befallen, but that he had still further invited the emperor's advance against himself and thereby had behaved so that they [the Byzantines] threatened those who were not yet ready. Therefore he quickly supplemented his previous offers with other, greater ones. He promised to give the Romans annually an allied force on request, and agreed that no Turk would set foot on their land with his permission; should anyone from another [Turkish] principality trouble the Romans' territory, he would straightway wage war upon him, and he would in every way hinder any treachery from whatsoever source it arose. He would without hesitation do everything commanded by the emperor, and should one of the cities subject to the emperor have previously fallen under Turkish sway, he agreed to restore it to the Romans. Persuaded by these things, the emperor bound him with mighty oaths; ending hostility, he returned home.

30. FREDERICK II AND AL-KAMIL

The relationship between Muslim and Christian rulers could at times be quite friendly, and perhaps none was reputed to be as friendly as the rapport enjoyed by the Holy Roman emperor and king of Sicily Frederick II (r. 1198–1250) and the sultan of Egypt al-Kamil (r. 1218–38). Frederick had launched the Sixth Crusade in 1228, as he sought to claim the crown of Jerusalem (which had come to him by marriage), but at the time he was also embroiled in an ongoing dispute with the papacy that culminated in his excommunication. Upon his arrival in the Holy Land as an excommunicate, Frederick managed to alienate most of the local nobility and ecclesiastical elites, but he also managed to secure a truce, the Treaty of Jaffa (1229), with al-Kamil, which included a ten-year cessation of hostilities and, most importantly, granted Frederick control over Jerusalem. His relations with al-Kamil and his successors appear to have been cordial, perhaps conditioned by his long experience dealing with his Muslim subjects in Sicily. This familiarity with Muslims did not endear Frederick to Christian chroniclers such as Matthew Paris (1200–59), the author of the first source below, who depicted this intimacy as part of a broader set of character flaws that also included heresy, immorality, and impiety. Matthew Paris's fears about the emperor are given some credence by Muslim sources. The last two sources in this section, by Qaratāy and Ibn Wasil, suggest that Frederick may have warned the Egyptians about the coming of Louis IX and his crusaders in 1248.

Sources: for Paris, trans. J.A. Giles, *Matthew Paris's English History: From the Year 1235–1273*, 3 vols. (London: Henry G. Bohn, 1852), I: 157–58; II: 83–84; rev. Jarbel Rodriguez; for Qaratāy and Ibn Wasil, trans. Peter Jackson, *The Seventh Crusade, 1244–1254: Sources and Documents* (Aldershot, UK: Ashgate, 2007), 46–47.

Matthew Paris: English History

In the course of the same year, the fame of the emperor Frederick was clouded and stained by his envious enemies and rivals; for it was imputed to him that he was wavering in Catholic faith, or wandering from the right way, and had given utterance to some speeches, from which it could be deduced and suspected that he was not only weak in the Catholic faith, but what was a much greater and more serious crime, that there was in him an enormity of heresy, and the most dreadful blasphemy, to be detested and execrated by all Christians. For it was reported that the emperor Frederick had said (although it may not be proper to mention it) that three conjurers had so craftily led away their contemporaries as to gain for themselves the mastery of the world. These were Moses, Jesus, and Muhammad; and that he had impiously put forward some wicked and incredible ravings and blasphemies respecting the most holy Eucharist. Far be it from any discreet man, much less a Christian, to unlock his mouth and tongue in such raving blasphemy. It was also said by his rivals that the emperor agreed and believed in the law of Muhammad more than that of Jesus Christ, and that he had made some Saracen harlots his concubines. A whisper also crept among the people (which God forbid to be true of such a great prince), that he had been for a long time past in confederacy with the Saracens, and was more a friend to them than to the Christians, and his rivals, who were endeavoring to blacken his name, attempted to establish this by many proofs. Whether they sinned or not, He alone knows who is ignorant of nothing....

... That he is guilty of sacrilege is certain for when the aforesaid bishops of Portua and Preneste, and several prelates and clerks of the churches, as well as religious men and seculars, were coming by water to the Apostolic See, for the purpose of attending the council (which he, the emperor, had asked to be convoked), all the roads of his territory were altogether stopped by his command; and having sent his son Henry with a number of galleys, and he lying in wait for them near the sea-coast, with some others which he had procured in Tuscany, in order to discharge upon them the full force of his heavy anger, dared to lay his sacrilegious hands upon them, some of the prelates and other persons being drowned at the time of capture, some slain, and others put to flight and pursued by their enemies. The rest were deprived of all their property, ignominiously carried about from place to place in the kingdom of Sicily, and were afterwards consigned to prison there, and some of them, worn away by sickness, and oppressed by want, have fallen away to a wretched condition. With good cause, moreover, a suspicion of heresy arisen against him, since, after he had incurred the sentence of excommunication issued against him by the aforesaid J., bishop of Sabina, and Cardinal Thomasius, and the aforesaid pope Gregory IX [r. 1227–41] had pronounced an anathema upon him, and after the capture of the Roman cardinals and the prelates and clerks of the churches while on their voyage from various quarters to the Apostolic See, he despised, and still despises the keys of the Church, causing, as far as he can effect it, divine service to be performed, or rather profaned, before him, and boldly asserting, as above stated, that he does not fear the sentences of excommunication pronounced against him by Pope Gregory. Besides, he is united by a detestable alliance with the Saracens, has often times sent messages and presents to them, and in turn received the same from them with respect and alacrity. He embraces their customs, notoriously keeping them with him in his daily service, and, after their fashion, he shamelessly appoints them as guards over his wives, whom he has received from the descendants of a royal race, certain eunuchs, especially those whom he has lately caused to be castrated. And what is a more execrable offense, he, when formerly in the country beyond sea, made a kind of arrangement, or rather collusion, with the sultan, and allowed the name of Muhammad to be publicly proclaimed in the temple of the Lord day and night. And lately, in the case of the sultan of Babylon [a reference to al-Kamil, sultan of Egypt], who, by his own hands, and through his agents, had done irreparable mischief and injury to the Holy Land and its Christian inhabitants, he caused that sultan's ambassadors, in compliment of their master, as is said, to be honorably received and nobly entertained in his kingdom of Sicily.

Qaratāy: On the Seventh Crusade

When the emperor, the leader of the Franks, had left the Holy Land and bade farewell to al-Malik al-Kamil at Ascalon, the two sovereigns had embraced and promised mutual friendship, assistance, and fraternity. Now the only route by which the Frenchman [Louis IX] could reach Egypt lay across the emperor's territory. The latter first went to him and offered him help in terms of horsemen, money, and livestock. But subsequently the two sovereigns had an interview [which is unlikely to have ever occurred], in which the emperor said to the Frenchman: "Where do you intend going?" "To Egypt and to Jerusalem," [was the reply]. To which the emperor responded, among other things: "That will do you no good. Do not go to Egypt, but reconsider, along with your barons.... I was there in the year [626/1229], in the reign of al-Kamil. I took from the Muslims Jerusalem and all the villages between it and Acre, and stipulated with al-Kamil that these localities should belong to the Franks, and that there should no longer be a Muslim force at Jerusalem. If I limited myself to that much, it is because I had realized the impossibility of fighting the princes, the emirs, and all the troops in the country, and my powerlessness before them. And so how do you hope to take Damietta, Jerusalem, and Egypt?" But on hearing this the Frenchman was scandalized and told the emperor: "Say no more. Nothing, by God and by the truth of my Faith—nothing shall prevent me from attacking Damietta, Jerusalem, and Egypt, and nothing shall deflect me from it except my death and that of my people."

So then, irritated by his obstinacy, the emperor wrote to King al-Salih [al-Kamil's son and successor, r. 1240–49] a letter in which he said, among other things: "In such-and-such a year the king of the French has arrived in my country accompanied by a vast host." And further on: "My lord Najm al-Din [al-Salih's honorific title], take good care. You must know that your attackers' intention is to take Jerusalem, and for that purpose to conquer Egypt first." And again: "The king of the French is convinced he will conquer Egypt in a few hours"; and "this prince is the most powerful of the princes of the West— animated by a jealous faith, the importance of his actions as a Christian and his attachment to his religion set him against everyone else." And he ended: "My nephew, in vain have I opposed his plans and sought to put him on his guard against the danger he runs in attacking you. To shake him I have insisted on the numbers and strength of the Muslims and on the impossibility of taking Jerusalem if one has not first reduced Egypt, which is [in any case] unfeasible. The Frenchman has not fallen in with my views. The number of those who follow him is constantly on the increase: they total more than 60,000, and in the course of this year they will land in Cyprus."

Ibn Wasil: On the Seventh Crusade

When the king of France, one of the greatest Frankish kings, attacked Egypt in the year 647 [1249–50], the emperor sent word to him in order to restrain him from doing so, to fill him with fear and to warn him what would come of it; but he did not accept [his advice]. Sir [name unintelligible] who was master of ceremonies to the emperor's son Manfred, told me: "The emperor sent me in secret to al-Malik al-Salih Najm al-Dīn to inform him of the king of France's determination to invade Egypt, to put him on his guard and to advise him to make preparations against it. Al-Malik al-Salih made ready, and I returned to the emperor. I had gone out to Egypt, and come back, in the guise of a merchant, and not one person learned that I had met with al-Malik al-Salih to alert him to the danger from the Franks or that the emperor had made common cause with the Muslims against them."

... When al-Malik al-Salih died and there befell the king of France what transpired—the destruction and annihilation of his army, his being taken prisoner by al-Malik al-Salih's son, al-Malik al-Mu'azzam Tūrān Shāh, then his release from captivity following al-Malik al-Mu'azzam's murder, and his return to his own country—the emperor sent to remind him of his [own] sound advice and the consequences of his obstinacy and recalcitrance, and to upbraid him for it.

31. CRUSADER/MAMLUK TREATIES

After the failure of Louis IX's crusades and the rise of the Mamluks, the situation for the Christian crusader states had grown desperate. The highly effective campaigns launched by the Mamluk sultan Baybars (r. 1260–77) had reduced the Christian holdings to a handful of coastal territories surrounded by a tight perimeter of Muslim fortresses. Baybars was also an adroit diplomat who used unequal and heavy-handed truces to formalize his conquests and keep the Christian polities from getting too strong during periods of peace. The sultan Qalāwun (r. 1279–90) continued many of these practices, including the renewal of truces with the Christians that strengthened his own position while limiting any advantages that Christians could hope to press after the cessation of hostilities—note the stipulations that Christians could not rebuild their defenses. The Christians, for their part, operating from a position of weakness, had little option but to accept. The treaty below between Qalāwun and Acre is illustrative of this practice. Ultimately, however, the truces would not save the Christian polities. Violation of any of the clauses was considered a casus belli, *prompting an immediate commencement of hostilities. In August 1290, Christian crusaders arriving from Europe attacked and killed dozens of Muslim merchants and peasants, bringing an end to the truce. By May 1291, Qalāwun's son and successor al-Ashraf Khalil (r. 1290–93) had assembled a mighty army at the gates of Acre, and, with its fall at the end of the month, the crusader states effectively came to an end.*

Source: trans. Francesco Gabrieli, *Arab Historians of the Crusades* (Berkeley: University of California Press, 1969), 326–31.

Treaty with Acre, 1283

In 682 (1283) our lord the sultan agreed to grant a request from the people of Acre, after their ambassadors had appeared before him time after time, in Syria and Egypt, asking for peace. He forbade them to travel overland, inviting them to come by sea only, whenever they should desire an audience of him. This they did. The agreement reached was that they should submit themselves to the will of the sultan, although before this, at the expiration of the truce [of al-Malik az-Zahir (Baybars)], they had put forward exorbitant claims. In Safar of this year [May 1283] delegates and notabilities came from Acre and signed the truce. The sultan took the oath in the presence of the Frankish ambassadors, who were: two Brethren of the Order of the Temple, two of the Order of the Hospital, two royal knights, the governor-general William and the vizier Fahd. The text was as follows:

A truce is declared between our lord the sultan al-Malik al-Mansūr [Qalāwun] and his son al-Malik as-Salih 'Alā' ad-Dunya wa'd-Din 'Ali—God make their power eternal—and the authorities of the Commune of Acre, Sidon, Athlith [Chastel Pèlerin] and the dependent territories, over which the truce extends. These are: the seneschal Odo, *bailli* of Acre, the grand master *frère* William of Beaujeu, grand master of the Order of the Temple, the grand master *frère* Nicholas Lorgne, grand master of the Order of the Hospital, and the marshal *frère* Conrad, representative of the grand master of the Teutonic Hospital. The truce is to last ten whole years, ten months, ten days, and ten hours, beginning on Friday 5 Rabī I 682 of the *hijra* of the Prophet, which corresponds to 3 hazirān 1594 of the era of Alexander, son of Philip the Greek [June 3, 1283]. The truce is to be effective throughout all the states of our lord al-Malik al-Mansūr and of his son al-Malik as-Salih 'Alā' ad-Dunya wa'd-Din 'Ali: forts, castles, territories, provinces, cities, villages, farmed and unfarmed land. This includes:

The kingdom of Egypt with all its regions and Muslim forts and castles, the district of Damietta, the district of Alexandria, Nastarawa, Santariyya, and every port and coast and town connected with them; the district of Fuwwa and of Rosetta: the country of the Hijāz; the well-guarded district of Gaza with all its harbors and territories; the province of Karak, Shaubak and its territory, as-Salt and its territory, Bustra and its territory; the province of the friend of God [Hebron]—on which be God's blessing!—the province of Jerusalem the noble and its territories, of the Jordan, of Bethlehem and its territory, with all the towns included in it and taken into account; Bait Gibrīl; the province of Nablus and its territory; the province of Alatrun and its territory; Ascalon and its territory, harbors and coasts; the province of Jaffa and Ramla, its port and territory; Arsūf, its port and territory; Caesarea, its port and coastline and territory; the fort of Qaqūn and its territory; Lydda and its territory; the al-'Aujā zone and the salt works therein; the zone of the blessed conquest with its territory and its farmland; Baisān and territory, at-Tur and territory, al-Lajūn and territory, Jubnīn and territory, 'Ain Jalūt and territory, al-Qaimūn and territory with all regions dependent on it; Tiberias with its lake and territory; the province of Safad and its dependencies; Tibnīn and Hunīn with all their towns and territories; ash-Shaqīf, known as Shaqīf Arnūn, with its territory and dependencies; the town of al-Qarn and its dependencies, apart from those specified in this treaty; half of the city of Alexandretta and of the suburb of Marūn with their villages and vineyards and gardens and fields—and the rest of the above-mentioned Alexandretta shall all, including all its confines and lands, be subject to our lord the sultan and to his son—while the other half shall go to the kingdom of Acre; al-Biqā' al-'Azizi and its territory, Mashghar and territory, Shaqīf Tirūn and its territory; all the caves, Zalaya and the rest; Baniyās and its territory; the fort of as-Subaiba with its lakes and territory; Kaukab and its territory; the fort of 'Ajlūn and its territory; Damascus and its province with its forts and towns and districts and territories; the fortress of Baalbek and its territory; the province of Hims with its territory and confines; the province of Hamāt with its city and fort and lands and confines; Balātunus and its territory; Sahyūn and its territory; Barzayya and its territory; the conquests of Hisn al-Akrād and its territory, Safithā and its territory; Mai'ār and its territory; al-'Uraima and territory; Maraqiyya and its territory; Halabā and its territory; the fort of 'Akkār and its territory and lands; al-Qulai'a and its territory; the fort of Shaizar and its territory, Apamea and its territory; Jábala and its territory, Abu Qubais and its territory; the province of Aleppo with all the forts, cities, towns, and castles connected with it; Antioch and its territory with everything that made up that blessed conquest; Baghrās and its territory, Darbsāk and its territory, Rawandān and its territory, Harīm and its territory, 'Aintāb and its territory, Tizīn and its territory, Saih al-Hadīd and its territory; the fort of Najm and its territory, Shaqīf Dair Kush and its territory; ash-Shughr and its territory, Bakās and its territory, as-Suwaida and its territory; al-Bab and Buza'a and their territories; al-Bira and its territory, ar-Rahba and its territory, Salamiyya and its territory,

Shumaimīs and its territory, Tadmur and its territory; and everything connected with these places, whether specified or not.

[The safety of all these places is guaranteed] by the authorities of the kingdom of Acre, i.e. the *bailli* of the kingdom, the grand master of the Templars *frère* William of Beaujeu, the grand master of the Hospitallers, *frère* Nicholas Lorgne and the marshal *frère* Conrad, representative of the grand master of the Teutonic Hospitallers; as well as all the Franks, Brethren and knights obedient to them and members of their state of Palestine; and by all the Franks without distinction who inhabit Acre and the coastal regions included in the treaty, and anyone of them to arrive there by land or sea, whatever his race or condition.

The territories of our lord the sultan al-Malik al-Mansūr and of his son the sultan al-Malik as-Salih, their castles, forts, towns, villages, and armies, Arab, Turcoman and Kurdish, and their subjects of every race, with all their possessions, flocks, goods, crops and everything else, shall have to fear no harm, injury or encroachment, attack, or assault. This shall apply to all conquests of our lord the sultan al-Malik al-Mansūr and of his son al-Malik as-Salih, by their own hand or by means of their armies and their commanders of castles and forts and provinces, by land and by sea, in the plains or in the mountains.

In the same way all the coastal lands of the Franks to which this treaty applies [shall be guaranteed their safety]; to wit: the city of Acre, with the gardens, terrain, mills, and vineyards dependent upon it, including the taxes received from its administrative area, and the regions agreed under this treaty, numbering seventy-three districts with their fields; all without dispute in possession of the Franks. In the same way Kaifa and its vineyards and gardens, with seven dependent districts. In the same way Marina and the region known by that name shall belong to the Franks, In the same way they shall hold the monastery of Sayāj and that of Mar Elias. Of the area of Carmel our lord the sultan shall take for himself 'Afā and al-Mansura, while the rest, consisting of thirteen districts, shall belong to the Franks. Of Athlith the fort and the city and the gardens that have been harvested, the vineyards and the cultivated land and terrains shall go to the Franks, with sixteen districts; our lord the sultan shall take the village of al-Haramīs herein mentioned, with its taxes and farmlands; the rest of the territory of Athlith shall be divided in half, apart from that which is in our lord the sultan's private possession: eight districts. The Hospitallers' estates in the province of Caesarea shall be Frankish property with everything that they contain. A half of the city of Alexandretta and the suburb of Marūn with all its contents shall belong to the Franks, and the rest to our lord the sultan; all the taxes and crops of Alexandretta and the suburb of Marūn shall be divided between them. In the case of Sidon, the fort and the city, the vineyards and the administrative area with all that it involves shall belong to the Franks; they shall take possession of fifteen districts with all their rivers, waters, springs, gardens, mills, canals, flowing streams and dikes, by which the land is watered according to ancient usage; the rest of the entire mountain region shall be in the sole possession of our lord the sultan and his son. All these territories belonging to Acre, and those specified in the treaty, shall be given guarantees of safety by our lord the sultan and his son on behalf of their armies and troops, whether the region is partly or wholly in Frankish hands; the guarantee shall apply to property and inhabitants.

Outside Acre, Athlith and Sidon and the walls of these three places the Franks may not rebuild walls, forts, fortifications or castles, whether old or new.

The galleys of our lord the sultan and his son that have been fitted out and sent to sea are forbidden to cause any harm to the coastal territories treaty. When the above-mentioned galleys are bound for a country other than those whose ruler is linked by treaty with the authorities of the commune of Acre the galleys may not drop anchor or take on provisions in countries affected by this treaty; if however the ruler of the country for which they are bound is not linked by treaty with the authorities of the commune of Acre the galleys may drop anchor and take on provisions in the aforementioned countries. If ever, which God forbid, one of these galleys should be wrecked on a harbor or on a coast affected by the treaty, if making for an ally of the commune of Acre and its ruler, the *bailli* of the kingdom of Acre and the grand masters of the Orders must take it into custody, enable the crew to take on provisions and to repair the damage to the ship and send it back to Muslim territory. The original objective of the ship that has been wrecked and cast up on the shore shall be cancelled. If, however, the country for which the ship was bound is not linked by treaty with the commune of Acre, the wrecked ship may take on provisions and crew in countries affected by the treaty and may proceed toward the original objective. This clause shall obtain equally in the case of Frankish ships cast up on Muslim territory.

Whenever one of the kings of the Franks or of Outremer shall leave his land and invade the territory of our lord the sultan or of his son, where that territory is under treaty, the *bailli* of the commune and the grand masters of Acre shall undertake to give notice of their movements to our lord the sultan two months before their arrival; in the event of their arrival after the two months have elapsed the *bailli* of the commune of Acre and the grand master shall be exempt from any obligations in the matter.

In the case of attack by the Mongols or other enemies whichever of the two signatories is the first to receive news of it shall inform the other. If an enemy force which God forbid, whether Mongol or from some other hostile power should attack Syria by the overland route and drive the [sultan's] armies before it as far as the coastal territories affected by this treaty and invade these lands, the *bailli* of the commune of Acre and the grand masters shall have the right to make provision by means of treaties for the defense of their persons, their subjects and their territories, to the best of their ability.

If God forbid sudden panic should cause Muslims to flee from their own lands into the coastal territories affected by the treaty, the *bailli* of the commune of Acre and the grand masters shall give protection and defense to these fugitives, and defend them from their pursuers, so that they and their possessions may be safe and secure. The *bailli* of the commune of Acre and the grand masters shall instruct all the other coastal territories under treaty not to permit pirates to take on food or water in their ports, to hold them if they capture them, and in the case of a pirate ship coming to sell its booty they shall detain the brigands until the rightful owner shall come to take back his property. The same conditions shall apply to the sultan.

The church at Nazareth and four houses close to it shall be reserved for the use of Christian pilgrims, great and small, of whatsoever race and station, coming from Acre and the coastal lands affected by the treaty. In the church priests and friars shall perform their offices, and the houses shall be reserved for the use of visitors to the church of Nazareth, who shall have complete freedom of movement within the area under treaty. Concerning the stones of the church, those that are picked up (having fallen from their place) shall be cast away, and stone shall not be set upon stone to rebuild the church; nor shall unlawful gifts be solicited by priests and friars for this purpose.

The treaty contained the usual stipulations. When our lord the sultan had taken the oath on it the amīr Fakhr ad-Din Ayāz, *amīr hajib* 'lord chamberlain,' and the Qadi Bahr ad-Din ibn Razīn took it to the Franks, who also swore to it, and so the truce was concluded.

32. OTTOMAN TREATY WITH THE VENETIANS

The conquest of the Byzantine Empire in 1453 left the Venetians in a precarious position. Bereft of whatever limited support the Byzantines could give them and forced out of their traditional position of power in Constantinople, the Venetian Empire found itself at the forefront of the war against the Ottoman Turks. The two sides were at war between 1463 and 1478, with the Venetians faring poorly and losing numerous territories and colonies in the Balkans and along the Adriatic to the Ottomans. In 1478, the two sides reached a truce agreement that, not surprisingly considering the military situation, favored the Ottomans and their sultan Mehmed the Conqueror.

Source: trans. Diana G. Wright in Barbara Rosenwein, ed., *Reading the Middle Ages: Sources from Europe, Byzantium, and the Islamic World* (Toronto: University of Toronto Press, 2006), 497–99.

I, the great lord and great emir, sultan Mehmed-Bey, son of the great and blessed lord Murad-Bey, do swear by the God of heaven and earth, and by our great prophet Muhammad, and by the seven *mushaf* which we Muslims possess and confess, and by the 124 thousand prophets of God (more or less), and by the faith which I believe and confess, and by my soul and by the soul of my father, and by the sword I wear:

Because my lordship formerly had peace and friendship with the most illustrious and exalted signoria of Venice, now again we desire to make a new peace and oath to confirm a true friendship and a new peace. For this purpose, the aforementioned illustrious signoria sent the learned and wise Sir Giovanni Dario, secretary, as emissary to my lordship so we might make the said peace with the following old and new provisions. For this my lordship swears by the above-written oaths that just as there was formerly peace and friendship between us, namely, with their lords and men and allies, I now profess good faith and an open peace by land and sea, within and without the straits [the Dardenelles], with the villages, fortresses, islands, and lands that raise the banner of San Marco [Saint Mark is Venice's patron saint], and those who wish to raise the flag in the future, and all those places that are in their obedience and supervision, and to the commerce which they have as of today and are going to have in the coming years.

[Confirmation of Previous Agreements.]

[1] First, no man of my lordship will dare to inflict injury on or opposition to the signoria of Venice or its men: if this happens, my lordship is obligated to punish them according to the cause: similarly, the most illustrious signoria is obligated toward us.

[2] Further, from this day forward, if either land or other goods of the most illustrious signoria and its men is taken by the men of my lordship, it will be returned: similarly, they are obligated to my lordship.

[3] Their men and their merchandise may come by land and by sea to every land of my lordship, and all the merchandise and the galleys and the ships will be secure and at ease: they are similarly obligated toward us in their lands.

[4] Similarly, the duke of Naxos and his brothers and their lords and men with their ships and other boats are in the peace. They will not owe my lordship any service, but the Venetians will hold them just as it all used to be.

[5] Further, all ships and galleys, that is merchantmen and the fleet of my lordship, wherever they may encounter the Venetians, will have good relations and peace with them. Corsairs and klefts, wherever they are taken, will be punished.

[6] If any Venetian incurs a debt or commits other wrong in the lands of my lordship, the other Venetians will bear no responsibility: similarly, the signoria of Venice [vows the same] to our men.

[7] If any Venetian slave flees and comes into Turkish hands and becomes a Muslim, they will give his master 1000 aspers: if he is a Christian he will be sent back.

[8] If any Venetian boat is wrecked on the land of my lordship, all the men will be freed and all the merchandise returned to their agent: they are similarly obligated to our men.

[9] If any Venetian man dies in the lands of my lordship, without a will or heir, his goods are to be given to the Venetian *bailo* [Venetian diplomatic representative to the Ottomans]; if no *bailo* is found, they will be given into Venetian hands. Venice will write what to do.

[10] Further, the most illustrious signoria will have the right and authority specifically to send a *bailo* to Constantinople, with his household, according to custom, who will be able to dispense justice and administer Venetian affairs, according to their custom. The [Ottoman] governor will be obligated to give him aid and cooperation.

[New Provisions and Conditions for Peace.]

[11] If the said *bailo* wants to secure his position during this time, he is obligated to give my lordship every year a gift of 10,000 Venetian florins from the commercial transactions.

[12] Further, the most illustrious signoria of Venice is obligated for every debt lying between us and for all debts whether common or private or of certain of their men, for all the past time before the war until today, to give to my lordship 100,000 Venetian ducats within two years. Further, my Lordship cannot look for past debts, either from the most illustrious signoria of Venice or from its men.

[13] Further, the most illustrious signoria of Venice is obligated to hand over to my lordship the fortress called Skodra in Albania, except that it may remove the lord who is *rettor* [governor], and the council, and all the other men who wish to depart, specifically, with their merchandise, if they have any. The signoria will take the equipment and all other military matériel or whatever is found in the fortress at present without any opposition.

[14] Further, the most illustrious signoria of Venice is specifically obligated to transfer to my lordship the island of Lemnos, except that they will take the *rettor* and the Venetian citizens. The other men who want to go will take whatever they have to go wherever they want. Those who want to remain on the island will be pardoned for what they did up to this point.

[15] Further, the most illustrious signoria of Venice will hand over to my lordship the present fortresses and lands which were taken in the war from my lordship, that is, the lands in the Morea [southern Greece], except that the men in their authority may go wherever they want with whatever they have. If any want to remain in the present territories and fortresses they will have complete pardons, specifically, for every act, if they did anything up to now.

[16] Further, my lordship is obligated to hand over to them the occupied lands, that is, to the former borders of their fortresses which abut the lands of my lordship on all sides.

The above-written provisions are confirmed and ratified and sworn.

The present writing was done in the year 6987 [25 January 1478], the 12th indiction, the twenty-fifth of the month of January, in Constantinople.

33. THE SULTAN BAYEZID SENDS A RELIC TO THE POPE

Upon the death of Mehmed the Conqueror in 1481, he was succeeded on the Ottoman throne by his son Bayezid II (r. 1481–1512), but not without controversy, as Bayezid was challenged by his younger brother Çem (1459–95). Ultimately unsuccessful in his challenge for the throne, Çem had to flee the Ottoman Empire and seek refuge in Christian Europe, first with the Knights of St. John in Rhodes (the Hospitallers) and finally with the pope. Upon learning this, Bayezid offered to pay the pope an annual sum in exchange for keeping his brother in a comfortable imprisonment. In the source below, the Spanish chronicler Andrés Bernáldez (c. 1450–1513) details the arrangement between the papacy and the sultan, as well as the successful efforts by Pope Innocent VIII (r. 1484–92) to convince Bayezid to turn over to him one of Christendom's most prized relics.

Source: trans. Jarbel Rodriguez, from Andrés Bernáldez, *Historia de los Reyes Católicos D⁻. Fernando y D⁻ Isabel*, 2 vols. (Seville: Imprenta que fue de D. José Maria Geofrin, 1870), I: 306–7.

In the year 1492, Bayezid the Turk, emperor of Constantinople and sultan of the Turks, sent to Pope Innocent VIII forty-thousand ducats as a pension or tribute, which he sent him every year in return for the safe-keeping of his brother Çem, who after being defeated on both land and sea sought refuge with the grand master of Rhodes [the Hospitallers]. He was first sent to King Louis [XI, r. 1461–83] of France who refused to receive him, nor did he want him in his kingdom or that he even see it. Then he was placed in the hands of Pope Innocent, and when his brother the sultan found out he was in Rome, he offered friendship to the pope and to give him every year a sum of ducats, in exchange for the pope keeping his brother in safe-keeping, as the sultan feared him very much. The pope kept him in Rome as long he [Çem] lived, allowing him to live and be treated as a great lord, but guarded zealously so that he could not escape. It is believed that in one of his embassies, the pope asked the sultan for the iron head of the lance which the centurion used to pierce the side of our Lord Jesus Christ when he was on the cross, and which was one of the relics housed in Constantinople. And the sultan sent it to him along with the payment of the ducats even though it was very dear to him as he knew how precious and valuable the Christians held the Holy Lance and the other relics that had been kept in Constantinople by the Byzantines. When the pope found out that the ambassadors were coming with the Holy Lance, he sent two bishops to Ancona [an Italian city on the Adriatic side of the Peninsula] to receive it, which they then escorted to Rome. The pope, dressed in his papal robes, with all the cardinals came out to receive it with a great procession on foot through the Porta del Popolo, although he felt ill and had to be carried in a chair lift. [Upon seeing the relic] the pope descended from his lift and threw himself on the ground with great reverence, and then took the gold box in which the lance was mounted in a glass monstrance of great craftsmanship that no matter how one looked at it, the lance always pointed up. The pope then showed it to the multitude that was there and they all venerated it as the sacred relic that had touched the side of Our Redeemer and which had witnessed his passion. The pope then carried it back on his chair lift to the church of St. Peter where it was given a place of honor.

34. A CHRISTIAN KING AND HIS MUSLIM VASSAL

The relationship between kings in medieval Iberia often transcended religious boundaries, as it was not unusual for Muslim and Christian kings to form friendships, political connections, and even military alliances, sometimes against their own coreligionists. The source below, from the Chronicle of Alfonso the Emperor, *a mid-twelfth-century Spanish source, highlights such a relationship. Alfonso VII (r. 1126–57), also known as the emperor (he claimed to be emperor over all of Spain), was the most powerful monarch in the Iberian Peninsula in the middle years of the twelfth century. Among his vassals was Zafadola, a minor Muslim king, whose family had ruled Zaragoza before its conquest by the Aragonese in 1118. In 1131, Zafadola became Alfonso's vassal by turning over the city of Roda to the Christian king, and he seems to have remained within Alfonso's circle of advisers until his death in 1146 at the hands of Christian knights.*

Source: trans. Glenn Lipskey, *The Chronicle of Alfonso the Emperor: A Translation of the Chronica Adefonsi Imperatoris, with Study and Notes* (Ph.D. dissertation, Northwestern University, 1972), 67–75.

The Vassalage of King Zafadola

At that time there was a certain Spanish Muslim king living in Rota. His name was Zafadola, and he was a descendant of one of the most noble families of the Spanish Muslim rulers. He had heard much about the exploits of Alfonso in his struggle against the king of Aragon. He had been informed of how our king had confronted him, how the Aragonese monarch had sworn to restore his kingdom to him, and how he had lied and become a perjurer. When King Zafadola had gathered all of this information, he called his entire family together. Included in this group were his children, his wives, his constables, his governors, and all his nobles. He said to them, "Do you know of the great deeds of Alfonso, the king of Leon, against the Aragonese ruler and against his rebels?" They replied that they had heard of them. Zafadola continued, "What course shall we take? How long shall we remain confined here?" They had, in fact, hidden themselves for fear of the Almoravids who had killed all of the descendants of the Spanish Muslims and had taken their kingdom from them. King Zafadola himself was in Rota confined there with some of his people who had fled to him. He told them, "Hear my plan. Let us go to the king of Leon, and let us make him our king and master and our friend. I know that he will be lord over all the Moors, because God is his deliverer and his helper. I know, indeed, that through him my sons and I will recover the honors which the Almoravids robbed from me, from my ancestors, and, from my people."

His nobles answered unanimously, "This is an excellent plan. Your idea seems sound to all of us." In the meantime, King Zafadola sent ambassadors to the king of Leon with this message: "Lend me some of your nobles with whom I may come to you in safety." Alfonso was very happy to hear this, and he quickly sent Count Rodrigo Martínez and Gutier Fernández to Zafadola. The latter noble was one of the king's counselors. When they arrived in Rota they were received honorably by King Zafadola. He presented them with magnificent gifts, and then he traveled to the king of Leon accompanied by them. Alfonso welcomed him, and honored him by making him sit at his side on the royal throne. He expressly ordered that Zafadola should not be allowed to give anything in return for his food. When the Moorish nobles witnessed all this, they were amazed and, said to each other, "Who among the kings is like the king of Leon?"

King Zafadola saw the wisdom and the wealth of Alfonso VII. He likewise saw the great peace that reigned in his palace and in all his kingdom. He then said to the Christian ruler, "What I have heard in Rota regarding your wisdom, your clemency, the peace in your kingdom and, your wealth is indeed true. Blessed are your men, blessed are your counselors who live here with you and who are in your kingdom." He gave the king a magnificent gift of very precious stones. He and his sons became Alfonso's knights and promised to serve him all the days of their lives. They gave him the city of Rota, which the king entrusted to his own son, Sancho the Castilian. Then Rota was populated with Christians, and they began to invoke the name of the Blessed Trinity in the city, and especially the Holy Spirit. No one living at that time ever conceived that the name of the Lord would be mentioned publicly in Rota. The king of Leon also gave Zafadola fortresses and cities. These were in the region of Toledo, in Extremadura and along the Duero River. Zafadola came and lived there, and served Alfonso all the days of his life....

The First Campaign to Andalusia; the Sackings of
Jerez and of Cádiz; Dealings with the Moors

... In the seventh year of his reign, 1171 of the Spanish Era [1133], Alfonso took counsel with King Zafadola. He gathered the nobles from his kingdom, and he revealed his secret plan to them. He disclosed that his highest ambition was to begin to make war throughout the land of the Moors. He wished to take revenge on King Texufin [Almoravid king, r. 1143–ca. 1145] and on the other rulers of the Almoravids. These were the infidel leaders who had come to the frontier region near Toledo and had killed many Christian captains. They had destroyed the castle at Aceca, and they had slain all the Christians they had found there. Tello Fernández had been carried across the sea along with other captives. He was the commander there. The king's proposal was subsequently approved by all.

The entire army from all the kingdom was mobilized in Toledo. They pitched their tents near the Tajo River. King Alfonso marched with his forces as did King Zafadola. The camp was divided into two divisions, because there was not enough drinking water for all the army, nor was there enough grass to feed the animals. Alfonso entered the territory of the Almoravids with his army through the Puertollano Pass. The other army, under the command of Rodrigo González, entered through Despeñaperro Pass. For fifteen days they marched through uninhabited lands. Both armies joined together near the Moorish castle of Galledo. From then on they were able to get fodder for the livestock and grain in abundance. The countless number of knights, infantrymen, and archers covered the face of the earth like locusts.

The king moved the camp from there and began marching through the fertile fields around Cordoba plundering on all sides. He occupied all that land, and pillaged it completely. He took a large quantity of booty and left behind nothing but fire and destruction. He then crossed the Guadalquivir River and continued the march. They left behind Cordoba and Carmona on the left and Seville (which the ancients called "Hispalis") on the right. It was the harvest season, so he set fire to all the fields and cut down the vineyards, olive groves, and fig trees. Consequently, fear of the Christian king weighed heavily on all those who lived in the lands of the Saracens. In a state of terror, the Moors abandoned their cities and smaller castles. They enclosed themselves in the most impregnable fortresses and in the fortified cities. They also hid in the mountains, in nearby caves, in the rocks and on the islands off the coast.

The entire Christian army camped in the territory around Seville. Large bands of armed men went out of the camp every day to carry out raids on the enemy. They would march throughout the region around Seville, Carmona, and Cordoba, plundering on all sides. They set fire to all the land, cities, and castles. They found many of these uninhabited, for the people had fled. They could not count the number of men and women who were captured, it was so great. They also seized a large number of horses, camels, asses, oxen, sheep, and goats. They carried off much grain, wine, and olive oil to the camp. They also destroyed all the mosques they came upon, and they killed all their priests and doctors of the Law. The sacred books which they found in the mosques were burned. These raids continued for eight days. Following that, they all returned to the camp with the booty.

When there were no more spoils to be had in the region, the king broke camp. He then arrived at a very rich city which the ancients called "Tuccis," but in our tongue it is known as Jerez de la Frontera. It was plundered and destroyed. Later the king moved camp and continued pillaging in the surrounding area. He went as far as Cádiz which is on the sea.

However, there were some senseless knights (the sons of certain nobles) who did not manifest sound judgment. In the eyes of the king, their actions were not at all sensible. They had heard that a nearby island was filled with horses and oxen, and that there were great riches there. They crossed the sea and eagerly went to the island. But the infidel forces were prepared for battle. They met them and joined in combat. The Christians were defeated because of their sins. Some of these nobles' sons returned to the camp. They informed the army of all that had happened to them. Then at last the Christian military forces began truly to respect the king's judgment. From that day on, not one of the soldiers dared leave the camp without his orders.

Alfonso remained there for many days until all of the plundering cohorts had returned. They came back with many victories to their credit and they captured many thousands of Moors. They also brought back a vast number of camels, stallions, mares, bulls, cows, sheep, goats, and many other riches belonging to the Moorish royalty.

The king again broke camp and departed for Seville. He arrived there and crossed the Guadalquivir River. A large army of Moors gathered around the walls of the city with their forces in battle array. Nonetheless, they were quickly blockaded by a few armed Christians. All of the land around Seville was plundered, and the crops and houses were burned down. They destroyed the vineyards, the fig trees, and the olive groves. They cut down many of the royal orchards located on both sides of the river. The Almoravids, however, did not capture one Christian. If any had been taken prisoner, the death penalty would have been certain.

The leaders of the Spanish Muslims observed all this in secret. They then sent envoys to King Zafadola with the following message: "Speak with the Christian king and, with his help, rescue us from the power of the Almoravids. We shall give even more tributes to the ruler of Leon than our forefathers gave to his ancestors. We shall serve him with you, and you and your sons shall rule over us." When Zafadola heard this, he took counsel with Alfonso and with his trusted advisors. He answered the envoys, "Go and tell my brothers, the leaders of the Spanish Muslims, to capture some of the very strong castles and some of the highly fortified towers within the cities. Provoke war in all parts, and the Leonese king and I will come swiftly to the rescue."

Alfonso moved his camp and crossed the Amarela Pass. From there he proceeded to Talavera. Since all of the objectives of the campaign had been accomplished, everyone returned home with great joy and triumph. They praised and blessed God who had granted vengeance and punishment for the death of Tello Fernández and his companions killed in Aceca. Vengeance had also been granted for the death of Gutier Armíldez, the governor of Toledo, and the other victims of the Almoravids.

35. ARRANGING THE SURRENDER OF A CASTLE

The conquest of the kingdom of Valencia by James I of Aragon continued long after the city of Valencia itself capitulated in 1238. The fall of the capital and its ruling dynasty left the rest of the kingdom of Valencia under a multitude of authorities, James and his nobles controlling much of the northern part of the kingdom and different Muslim leaders and warlords controlling numerous villages, cities, and castles in the south. James would have to invest these one at a time using diplomacy, threats, bribes, and, at times, war. Such was the case with the city of Jativa and its magnificent castle. After several aborted sieges, James led a large army to try to capture the castle and city in 1244. The siege, however, ended up being a protracted affair, and after five months, in May 1244, the two sides began negotiations to end it. Ultimately, James was not able to wrest the main castle from the qadi, instead having to settle for a smaller castle with the promise that the surrender of the larger castle would come two years later. James recorded the full details of the negotiations in his autobiography.

Source: trans. John Forster, *The Chronicle of James I, King of Aragon, Surnamed the Conqueror (written by himself)* (London: Chapman and Hall, 1883), 465–70; rev. Jarbel Rodriguez.

350. At the end of two months the qadi sent to me a Saracen named Albocacim; I made everyone leave my tent, and remained alone with him. When Albocacim saw there was no one there but us two, he said to me: "The qadi of Jativa salutes you, and commends himself to your favor, as to the man on earth he has most at heart to love, serve, and honor. He sends me to ask why you keep besieging him, for you must be aware that his father ordered him not to surrender the castle to any man in the world, whether Christian or Saracen, but to you, if he were to lose it. You ought not to keep it besieged or do him, the qadi, any harm, for he is in fact holding the place for you, and would do no one's will but yours." I replied that I knew by report the words which his father had delivered to him on his death-bed; but it had been God's will that I should become king of Valencia, and as Jativa was the noblest place in it except, perhaps, the capital itself, the qadi ought to make it up to me, for I then could do him such good that he and his could live in honor. There was besides, I said, another argument in my favor, for the castle of Jativa was the key of the kingdom, and I could not be king of Valencia if Jativa were not mine. Wherefore I prayed him to consent, as otherwise I would never leave the place till I had it in my possession. Besides which, the money I would have to spend in taking the castle would be out of proportion to what he would have to spend in defending it; there would be consequently two losses, one to him and one to me: all which expense and loss might be saved and compensated by the love and kindness I would show him hereafter; he would be better off for what I intended to give him instead, and Jativa would be mine.

351. "My lord," said Albocacim, "what do you wish of the qadi of Jativa?" I said, "Let him give me the castle, and I will endow him and his family." Albocacim replied, "How could he part with such a castle as that of Jativa, which is so good a place, without thinking first what he should ask you for, and what he should not ask?" I said, "He will part with it to one who will be his lord, and will henceforward protect him from evil, and will give him ten times as much as his family ever had." He said, "My lord, these words of yours are of great weight, and if it please you, I will return to the qadi and repeat them to him." I said, "It pleases me well that you should go and say those my words to the qadi; go, and work well for me; you are the chief scrivener of Jativa, and have great influence over the qadi. If you succeed, I will endow you well, and

give you more than ever you had in your life; you know well that you cannot avert the fall of your city."

352. Thereon Albocacim went into Jativa, and next day he returned to me and said that it was not the qadi's opinion that Jativa could be surrendered on any account. My answer was, "Since the qadi does not wish to give it to me, he must prepare for the defense, for certainly I must have it, and will stay here in this camp until I take it." Albocacim then prayed me to send Eximen de Toviá into the city, because the qadi wished to speak to him. "Eximen," he said, "should come with me into Jativa, that he may witness the love and affection the qadi entertains for you." This was on a Wednesday, and Albocacim prayed us not to do anything against the city until the following Sunday, for the sheikhs (he said) would meet in the Mosque on Friday, and deliberate until Saturday; for that reason he asked that the truce should last until Sunday. To this, I agreed, but I will not enter into many details as to the parley, for it lasted a long while, and it would lengthen this book of mine beyond measure.

353. Next day there came to me Albocacim, Sexí, Almofarix, and En Eximen de Toviá, to discuss with me the terms of the capitulation they had just made, and ask for my approval. Eximen de Toviá said, "My lord, the qadi of Jativa lays before you his whole mind, and opens his heart to you; what these his delegates may do, you may consider as secure as if he himself did it." The proposals were that the qadi should surrender immediately the lesser castle of Jativa, and keep the greater one for two years, to be counted from Pentecost next. I was to name what place of importance I would give him instead, for him to hold in fief of me. I then asked them what lordships suited the qadi best. They asked for Montesa and for Vallada, both good castles in the neighborhood of Jativa. I said I would consider of it. I left my tent and went to the queen's apartments. There I found some of my council, such as the master of the Hospital, En Hugh de Fullalquer, En Guillem de Moncada, Eximen Perez de Arenós, En Carrós, and others. I told them what capitulation the qadi proposed, and asked them to advise on it. They asked the queen to speak first, and the queen said, "My lord, what counsel can I give you in this matter? none at all, yet my advice is, that since you can have Jativa, you ought not to delay for the sake of a castle or two; for Jativa is the finest castle, and the richest that I or any man has ever seen." The master of the Hospital said, "I can add nothing to the queen's words: for her advice is good." All the rest assented; and I said they had given me good counsel, and as such I accepted it; for I bethought myself that when the lesser castle was surrendered, the larger one could no longer remain in the qadi's hands.

354. So I sent for Eximen de Toviá and for the Saracens, and made them this answer: that I so loved the father of the qadi and the son himself, whom the father had left in charge to me, that although I had not got the business ended as I wished, yet would I for his love grant the capitulation as proposed. They

then asked on behalf of the qadi, and of the sheikhs in the city, that I would consent to Eximen de Toviá holding the castle; for the qadi said they trusted in him, and I also. I consented to that, and took possession of the lesser castle. Thereupon I withdrew my army, furnished the castle with provisions and men, and returned to Valencia.

36. NEGOTIATING A TRUCE

The political situation in Iberia in the late thirteenth century was complex, with alliances constantly shifting as different monarchs tried to get the upper hand on their adversaries. The Almohad defeat at Las Navas de Tolosa (see Doc. 24) and their subsequent loss of much of al-Andalus to Christian expansion led to the downfall of their dynasty. In northern Africa they were supplanted by the Marinids, a Berber dynasty from Morocco led by the redoubtable emir Abu Yusuf Yaqub b. Abd al-Haqq (r. 1258–86). In Muslim Iberia, the power vacuum left behind by the Almohads was ultimately filled by the Nasrid Dynasty in Granada. On the Christian side, there was also much instability, particularly in Castile. Upon the death of Ferdinand III, the conqueror who had taken Cordoba, Jaen, and Seville from the crumbling Almohad Empire, Alfonso X (r. 1252–84), called "the Wise," came to the Castilian throne. But he was far from a gifted politician or military leader, and by 1284 his son, Sancho IV (r. 1284–95), had rebelled against him and Alfonso had to flee to Seville. There he called upon one of his enemies, Abu Yusuf and the Marinids, who promptly came to his aid and attacked Sancho, who now had to face this new threat. Alfonso died that same year, and Sancho sued for peace a year later. The source below from the Rawd al-Qirtas *takes us through the negotiations as seen from the Muslim side.*

Source: trans. Jarbel Rodriguez, from Ambrocio Huici Miranda, trans. and ed., Ibn Abī Zar, *Rawd al-Qirtas* (Valencia: Graficas Bautista, 1964), 671–81.

When the emir of the Muslims lifted the siege of Jerez [de la Frontera] and returned to his country due to the approaching winter, Sancho, king of the Christians, left Seville for Jerez and saw firsthand the effects of the raid by the warriors of the faith and the devastation they had left behind, burning, killing, looting, laying waste to his forests and valleys; he squeezed his chest, turned his dream [of conquest] to vigilance and sent his confidant Alzand Garcia with an embassy of bishops, monks, and nobles to the court of the emir of the Muslims. They arrived at court humbled and dejected, asking for peace, but the emir of the Muslims did not listen to one word, nor did he respond to them and they returned frustrated to their lord. But he sent them back saying, "Return to him and perhaps his demeanor will soften." They arrived [at the emir's court] a second time and said, "Oh conquering king! We come to you with contrite hearts and full of shame to ask your forgiveness and beg for peace, since peace is what we desire. Do not disappoint our expectations or reject our offer." The emir responded, "I will not make peace with your sultan [Sancho IV] unless he accepts my conditions. I will send him an ambassador [with my terms] and if he accepts, we shall have peace, otherwise war."

He then called Sheikh Abū Muhammad abd al-Haqq, a dragoman [translator], and told him, "Go to that accursed man and tell him that the emir of the Muslims says that he will not make peace with you, stop fighting you, or raiding your territories, except under these conditions: that you do not attack any Muslim territory, or any of their ships, or do any damage to them either on land or at sea, be they the emir's subjects or anyone else's. In your country, you will be servant, doing as I command or forbid. If Muslims go to your country for commerce or to make a living, by day or night, you will not interfere or charge them a dirhem or dinar [two units of currency]. You will not interfere in the affairs of Muslims kings, not even a word, and you will not make alliances for war with any of them." Abū Muhammad abd al-Haqq went to [Sancho] with the letter bearing the conditions that the emir of the Muslims had set forth. He found him at court in Seville, greeted him and presented him the letter of the emir of the Muslims, explained the conditions and he received and accepted them. Abū Muhammad abd al-Haqq then told him, "Oh sultan, since you have accepted the conditions, hear what I am about to say." "Say what you will," answered the king. "Oh sultan, it is well known among the followers of the two faiths and it is inscribed in the hearts of the two peoples that the emir of the Muslims, Abu Yusuf, is very pious and a faithful guardian of pacts. If he promises something, he carries it out. But little is known of your faith, since you have done what you have done to your father, rebelling against him unjustly; you have perjured yourself and your people have turned from you, having little faith in you." To this Sancho replied, "If I knew that the emir of the Muslims wanted me to be his servant, I would hasten to do so." Abū Muhammad abd al-Haqq replied, "God be praised! If you serve our lord, the emir of the Muslims, and demonstrate your sincerity in his service, you will be pleased with him." "And what do I need to do to please him," asked Sancho. "The first thing that you ought to do is stay out of Muslim affairs, do not be a tempter among them, or go into their country, and if you have any pact or treaty with Ibn al-Ahmar, end it now, put it aside, and return his ambassadors. Like that you will please the emir of the Muslims who will give you peace and respect your country."

Ibn al-Ahmar had sent him his envoys to arrange a peace between them and to unite to combat the Muslims. Sancho had ships armed and ready to go up the river when Abd al-Haqq finished talking and told him, "Tomorrow you will hear what I have to say and see what I will do." The next day Sancho went to the river bank and stopped there. Ibn al-Ahmar's envoys arrived and sat before him and after he began to negotiate with them, he summoned Abd al-Haqq, legate of the emir of the Muslims. When he arrived, Sancho sat him by his side and began to speak with him until the ships appeared with their sails open. The envoys of Ibn al-Ahmar told him, "What are these ships that come with their sails unfurled, oh king?" "They are the ships," Sancho told them, "that I have outfitted to serve the emir of the Muslims, Abu Yusuf; to obey his wishes and be at his call wherever he may need." When the envoys heard this, they lost all hope as they looked at each other. Afterwards, they said, "And what response should we take with us when we take our leave from you, oh king?" Sancho replied, "As concerns the peace treaty that you came to negotiate for Ibn al-Ahmar, I see no way of reaching it. How am I going to ally myself with him and what would I offer? Is he my equal or my kin, that I should be making a treaty with him? Wasn't it his custom to serve me and kiss the hand of my father, mine, and the hands of the great and small among us? The emir of the Muslims, on the other hand, is king of the Muslims on both sides of the Straits [of Gibraltar]. He is lord of Marrakesh and Fez and the kingdom of the Maghreb. He has subjugated all the kings, due to the purity of his intentions and his good fortune, and he has beaten them with his forceful decisions and the multitude of his soldiers. He has destroyed the kings descended from 'Abd al-Mu'min [first Almohad caliph, r. 1130–63], taken away their kingdom and put an end to their dynasty. There is no king on earth that I fear, except for him. You already know that he has defeated me and that he defeated my father, taking over our country. He killed our soldiers and our heroes, captured our women, took our goods; we have no strength left to fight him nor the power to make war that would make us his equal. Moreover, all Christian kings have written to him asking for peace and his friendship. How can I abandon a treaty with the emir of the Muslims, to negotiate with one who is his inferior in power and authority? Take my answer to Ibn al-Ahmar and tell him, "There will be never be a treaty between us because this is what is best for me, my country, and my subjects." Tell him that I cannot defend myself against the emir of the Muslims. How can I defend him [Ibn al-Ahmar] against others? Whatever money I have received from you, consider it lost, since to my anguish, the emir of the Muslims has taken it.

Ibn al-Ahmar's envoys departed, desperate to get Alfonso's help [Alfonso had died by this point]. Abū Muhammad abd al-Haqq then turned to Sancho, "Ibn al-Ahmar's envoys have left and I will return to my lord, the emir of the Muslims." And Sancho said, "I am one of his servants, ready to follow his orders and do what pleases him." Abd al-Haqq replied, "It would please him if you would go and meet with him." "It will be my honor," responded Sancho. When Sancho decided to go and meet with the emir of the Muslims, the Christians opposed this and closed the gates of Seville to prevent him from going, telling him, "We are worried about what might happen to you if you meet the emir of the Muslims." Sancho answered, "I have decided to go and meet him to bring peace between us. Let him do with me as he pleases." When the Christians heard his reasons, they let him go. He had been gone one day from Seville when fear overtook him and he spoke to Abū Muhammad abd al-Haqq, the dragoman, "I don't think that my countrymen would have opposed my leaving without cause. I want you to swear and promise to me that I will be safe with him [the emir] and that he will do nothing to me but what pleases me." Abd al-Haqq swore an oath on a tahali [small leather pouch containing a Quran] that he carried with him and Sancho felt at ease and he continued. Later, upon arriving at Jerez de la Frontera, his fear grew worse and he spoke to Abd al-Haqq again. "I will not appear before the emir of the Muslims, Abu Yusuf, until I meet his heir, Abu Yaqub. With him, I will go before his father, under his care and protection. With him, I will go." When Abd al-Haqq heard this, he became suspicious, fearing that Sancho was setting a trap for the Muslims. "Fine. He will come to you, but he is a great king and a powerful sultan. When he comes to see you with his army, if you are inside one of your cities and ask him to intercede on your behalf with his father, you will have to come out of your city. His royalty demands it and you'll have no alternative but to exit Jerez if he comes in. If you do not do this, it will be a sign of disrespect and show contempt for his power. Consider what will happen to you if you do that. As concerns him meeting with you, I can guarantee [that he will]." When Sancho heard these words from Abū Muhammad abd al-Haqq, wishing to keep the emir Abu Yaqub from entering Jerez he returned to his initial position and said, "I will meet him outside the city."

Abū Muhammad met with the emir Abu Yaqub and told him what Sancho had said. That he wanted his protection and his favor and to make a pact with him and put himself under his care, until such time as Sancho could present himself before the emir of the Muslims, accompanied by Abu Yaqub. Abu Yaqub accepted and offered to work on his behalf. He departed to meet with Sancho accompanied by Abū Muhammad abd al-Haqq and a great host of the most noble and courageous among the Benimerines [members of the Marinid dynasty]. Sancho met him some miles from Jerez, greeted him, and with great joy prepared a banquet for his whole entourage. The emir Abu Yaqub ordered camp to be made and the tents pitched outside the city. He then dismounted from his horse and Sancho did the same and they entered Abu Yaqub's tent together. Sancho said, "Know this fortunate emir and blessed sultan, I want to be your guest, come under your protection, and place myself in the shadow of your power, so that I can meet with your father, the emir of the Muslims." The emir Abu Yaqub gave him the amān [guarantee of safe passage], promised that he would be pleased with his father, and took care of all his wishes. Sancho told him, "I am now satisfied." That afternoon, the emir Abu Yaqub rode out from the camp and all of Jerez came out to see him. The knights of the Benimerines rode out as well and jousted before him. Sancho also trotted out and came to the side of the emir, watching the Benimerines at their games and said, "I am very happy that God has willed for you to come see me and charge you with negotiating a treaty that brings me peace and tranquility. I am truly the happiest one here today." He then grabbed his shield and lance and rode out to joust with his knights until nightfall as Abu Yaqub watched.

The next day the emir Abu Yaqub and Sancho went to meet the emir of the Muslims. They met him at the castle of Fuente de la Peña, close to the Guadalete [river]. The emir of the Muslims prepared to meet Sancho and ordered all his soldiers to dress in white and arm themselves fully. The land itself was whitened by the dress of the Muslim soldiers. Sancho advanced toward him with an escort of polytheists [Christians] dressed in black; that was a warning to the perceptive. "Oh emir of the Muslims! God has favored and honored me with your presence today. I hope to get some of the good fortune that has been given to you and with which you have defeated every Christian king. Don't think that I have come before you willingly. In fact, I come here against my will, as you have ruined our country, stolen our women and children, and killed our bravest men. We cannot wage war against you, nor resist you, so everything that you order, I will do. Every condition that you impose upon me, I will accept and suffer through. Your hand sits over my kingdom and you will judge it as you will." Sancho then gave him magnificent gifts and did the same to Abu Yaqub to earn their benevolence. The emir of the Muslims gave him even better ones, so as not to be outdone and they concluded a truce between them on the twentieth of Sha'bān [21 October 1285], a Sunday.

37. A TRUCE AGREEMENT

Truces in Iberia, much like those in the Holy Land, tended to favor one side to the detriment of the other, with the Christians clearly in a position to dictate terms in most truces sealed after the battle of Las Navas de Tolosa. The truce below was agreed to by Castile and Granada in 1439 and highlights some of the main themes of Iberian peace-making, including a conclusion of hostilities, a re-establishment of commercial transactions, an effort to bring some stability to the frontier regions, and the liberation of captives taken in raids and war. But as is made clear toward the end of the document, Granada also had to pay parias, or tributary payments, in gold and return captives to the more powerful Castilian kingdom. Moreover, these truces seldom brought the peace they promised. At best, they limited some of the endemic raiding that made frontier life so perilous for both Christians and Muslims. The Truce of 1439 was particularly damaging for Granada as it was followed by numerous civil wars in the Nasrid kingdom, which weakened it considerably and paved the way for the Castilian invasions that overwhelmed the kingdom in the last decades of the fifteenth century.

Source: trans. Jarbel Rodriguez, from José Amador de los Rios, *Memoria histórico-crítica sobre las treguas celebradas en 1439 entre los reyes de Castilla y de Granada* (Madrid: Real Academia de la Historia, 1879), 128–31.

First of all a firm peace is agreed to and ratified by land and by sea between the [kings of Leon-Castile and Granada], their kingdoms, lordships, and their people throughout Andalusia, for the villages, places, and castles that are newly won by the king of Castile and by his captains or were given to the king of Castile or to his captains or to anyone else in his name that once belonged to the king of Granada and for the cities, and villages which now belong to the king of Granada and to his kingdom. [The truce] will commence on 15 April of this year, 1439 and will last three years, expiring on 16 April 1442.

Item: the king of Castile will make available three ports, namely Alcala la Real in the bishopric of Cordoba; the village of Huelma in the bishopric of Jaen; and Antequera or Sahara, in the bishopric of Seville, whichever one of the two the lord king desires. And in these ports all Christians, Muslims, and Jews who wish it can come and go and buy and sell their goods and be safe with all the goods and wares that they bring and take, paying the customary tariffs. Moreover, the Christians and Jews who live in the lands of the king of Castile who want to take and sell their wares in the lands of the Moors in Granada, except those items that are forbidden, [that include] horses, weapons, bread, silver, cattle, and other prohibited goods, shall be able to do so by going through the aforementioned Alcala la Real and through the royal road down to the port of Lope, and there they shall be able to sell whichever goods they bring with them, but shall not travel farther.

Item: That all Moors who would like to bring and sell or buy goods in the lands of the king of Castile shall be able to do so in safety by coming through the royal road to Alcala la Real. They can come and go safely through the royal road up to the village of Alcaudete, but no farther.

Item: That the king of Castile grants license that in the aforementioned ports livestock can be sold to the Moors of Granada, for each of the three years that the truce is valid, to include seven thousand sheep or goats, which over the three years would total twenty-one thousand animals. Additionally, in each of the three years one-thousand head of cattle can be sold to the Moors, totaling three thousand head of cattle over three years. No more livestock can be sold or taken out through these ports, nor through any other place, except as stipulated above, without the license and consent of the king of Castile.

Item: The king of Granada will grant Alfonso de Estuñiga, who is a captive in the kingdom of Granada, his freedom freely, within ten days of the start of the truce.

Item: The king of Granada will receive the alcaide Abraham, son of Zeyde Alamin, within thirty days of the start of the truce.

Item: Abenasayde, who has been a captive of the wife of Alfonso de Estuñiga will be turned over to the king of Granada who will pay, either himself or someone on his behalf, one-thousand doblas de banda [a type of gold coin] of Castilian gold. This was the price paid by the wife of Alfonso de Estuñiga [for Abenasayde].

Item: The king of Granada will receive a black man they call Muhammad and a black woman named Axa who are being held hostage for the aforementioned Alfonso de Estuñiga. Likewise, the king of Granada will release from captivity a young and healthy Christian man and woman, of roughly the same age as Muhammad and Axa.

Item: Christian and Muslim *alfaqueques* [professional captive ransomers] who have the appropriate guarantees of safe passage from both sides, will be able to enter, leave, and move through all the kingdoms in safety without suspicion or delays as they search for and ransom captives. They shall be able to remove and take these captives with them, paying the accustomed fees and no other charges shall be levied against them.

Item: If any city, village, castle, fortress or any other place were to rebel in the kingdoms and lordships of the king of Castile or the king of Granada, they will be given no support with manpower, food, weapons, or anything else by either side until said city, village, castle fortress, or other place is returned to the king to whom it belongs.

Item: Both sides will guarantee the security of castles, fortresses, and other places, be it against attacks by either king or by others who cross the frontiers to cause damages or those who go into revolt with fortresses and other places. Likewise, they will provide guarantees for crops stolen from the fields and other places, as well as for raids and deaths according to the traditional custom with the accustomed punishments, resolve, and oaths.

Item: Concerning those who move from one kingdom to another with stolen or ill-gotten goods, the goods shall be returned and the ancient custom will apply to those who took them. Likewise, ancient custom will apply to those captives who flee.

Item: The two kings shall name and appoint judges with appropriate powers to determine damages, thefts, raids, deaths, and pledges and to hear plaintiffs and to settle the proper value of property that was taken, stolen, or killed and could not be returned.

Item: Moreover, it is agreed in this truce and peace that the king of Granada shall pay in *parias* to the king of Castile for the aforementioned three years 24,000 doblas valadies [another type of gold coin] and 550 Christian captives from among those who are held in the kingdom of Granada and captured in war and who originate from the kingdoms of the king of Castile; 30 of them shall be selected by the king of Castile [the others by officials from Granada]. It is not stipulated in this document how the aforementioned doblas and captives will be handed over. As such, the king of Granada has added an addendum on this matter. Letters will be drafted and executed in both Latin and Arabic which stipulate all of the above, etc. And I, Iñigo Lopes, by virtue of the power granted to me by the king of Castile vouch that this document is true and valid and I have signed the Latin version with my own name and it is sealed with my customary seal. Likewise, you, the aforementioned Alcayde Ally, signed with your name by virtue of the power you hold from the king of Granada the Arabic version and sealed it with your customary seal. The letters are prepared and executed by us, representatives of the two sides and by virtue of the powers granted to us in the very noble city of Jaen on 11 April in the year of our Lord 1439.

CHAPTER FIVE

ECONOMIC RELATIONS

Figure 5.1: Transport of merchandise on the backs of camels.

Source: Paul LaCroix, *Manners, Customs, and Dress during the Middle Ages and during the Renaissance Period* (London: Chapman and Hall, 1876), 250.

38. THE MARKETS OF SEVILLE

Muslim markets in medieval Spain were well regulated, having numerous officials to oversee their everyday operations. In the following selection by Ibn Abdun, an Islamic jurist residing in Seville in the twelfth century, we get an overview of the regulations that were in place to ensure an efficient, safe, and reputable market. The rules affected a whole range of merchants and craftsmen but went beyond the commercial aspects of the market, as they also placed numerous restrictions on women and included several regulations geared toward the Jewish and Christian minorities in the city.

Source: trans. Bernard Lewis, *Islam from the Prophet Muhammad to the Capture of Constantinople*, 2 vols. (New York: Harper Torchbooks, 1974), II: 157–65.

Shopkeepers must be forbidden to reserve regular places for themselves in the forecourt of the great mosque or elsewhere, for this amounts to a usurpation of property rights and always gives rise to quarrels and trouble among them. Instead, whoever comes first should take his place.

The *muhtasib* [market inspector] must arrange the crafts in order, putting like with like in fixed places. This is the best and most orderly way.

There must be no sellers of olive oil around the mosque, nor of dirty products, nor of anything from which an irremovable stain can be feared.

Rabbits and poultry should not be allowed around the mosque, but should have a fixed place.

Partridges and slaughtered barnyard birds should only be sold with the crop plucked, so that the bad and rotten can be distinguished from the good ones. Rabbits should only be sold skinned, so that the bad ones may be seen. If they are left lying in their skins, they go bad.

Egg sellers must have bowls of water in front of them, so that bad eggs may be recognized.

Truffles should not be sold around the mosque, for this is a delicacy of the dissolute.

Bread should only be sold by weight. Both the baking and the crumbs must be supervised, as it is often "dressed up." By this I mean that they take a small quantity of good dough and use it to "dress up" the front of the bread which is made with bad flour. A large loaf should not be made up out of the *poya* rolls.

These should be baked separately and as they are. The glaziers must be forbidden to make fine goblets for wine; likewise the potters.

The *ratl* weights for meat and fish and *harisa* and fritters and bread should be made of iron only, with a visible seal on them. The *ratl* weights of the shopkeepers should always be inspected, for they are bad people.

The cheese which comes from al-Madā'in [in lower Seville] should not be sold, for it is the foul residue of the curds, of no value. If people saw how it is made, no one would ever eat it. Cheese should only be sold in small leather bottles, which can be washed and cleaned every day. That which is in bowls cannot be secured from worms and mold.

Mixed meats should not be sold on one stall, nor should fat and lean meat be sold on one stall. Tripe should only be sold dry on boards, for water both spoils it and increases its weight. The entrails of sheep must be taken out, so that they should not be sold with the meat and at the same price, which would be a fraud. The heads of sheep should not be skinned, except for the young. The guts must always be removed from the bodies of animals, except lambs, and should not be left there, for this too would be an occasion for fraud.

No slaughtering should take place in the market, except in the closed slaughter-houses, and the blood and refuse should be taken outside the market. Animals should be slaughtered only with a long knife. All slaughtering knives should be of this kind. No animal which is good for field work may be slaughtered, and a trustworthy and incorruptible commissioner should go to the slaughterhouse every day to make sure of this; the only exception is an animal with a defect. Nor should a female still capable of producing young be slaughtered. No animal should be sold in the market which has been brought already slaughtered, until its owner establishes that it is not stolen. The entrails should not be sold together with the meat and at the same price. A lamb weighing six *ratls* with its offal shall not be sold at the same price as a lamb the meat of which alone is of that weight.

Fish, whether salt or fresh, shall not be washed in water for this makes it go bad. Nor should salted fish be soaked in water, for this also spoils and rots it.

[Word missing in text] should only be sold cut into small pieces and with the bones removed. Jerked meat should not be sold, for it is prepared with bad and rotten meat. There is no goodness in it, and it is a deadly poison.

Left-over and rotten fish should not be sold.

Sausages and grilled rissoles should only be made with fresh meat and not with meat coming from a sick animal and bought for its cheapness.

Flour should not be mixed with the cheese used for fritters. This is fraud, and the *muhtasib* must watch out for it.

The cream must always be pure and not mixed with cheese. The leftovers of the cooks and fryers should not be sold.

Vinegar should only be bought from a trustworthy merchant, for it can be mixed with much water, which is a fraud. The vinegar maker should be ordered not to use too much water when he makes vinegar for someone, for this spoils it.

The copper pots used by the *harisa* makers, as also the spans of the fritter makers and the fryers, should be lined with tin only, since copper with oil is poisonous.

Women should be forbidden to do their washing in the gardens, for these are dens for fornication.

Grapes in large quantities should not be sold to anyone of whom it is known that he would press them to make wine. This is a matter for supervision.

Fruit must not be sold before it is ripe for this is bad, except only for grapes, which are good for pregnant women and for the sick. Large cucumbers which can be counted should not be sold by weight.

Grocery products which have wastage in the form of liquid, powder, or a kernel should only be sold with an allowance for wastage determined by the merchants and generally agreed. Groceries which are purchased by the shopkeepers by measure of capacity should only be sold by measure of capacity.

Wild figs may only be sold in pairs.

The seller of grapes should have baskets and nets in which to arrange them, as this is the best protection for them.

Cakes should be properly baked and should only be made wide, as thin ones are good only for the sick.

If someone assays gold or silver coins for a person, and later it emerges that there is base metal in them, the assayer must make good, for he deceived and betrayed the owner of the coins, who placed his trust in him. Swindlers when detected must be denounced in all crafts, but above all in assaying coin, for in this case the swindler can only be a person who is expert in matters of coin.

Women should not sit by the river bank in the summer if men appear there.

No barber may remain alone with a woman in his booth. He should work in the open market in a place where he can be seen and observed.

The cupper. He should only let blood into a special jar with graduation marks, so that he can see how much blood he has let. He should not let blood at his discretion, for this can lead to sickness and death.

The water wheel. Most of the holes for the spindles should be wedged, as this is best for its working.

No one may be allowed to claim knowledge of a matter in which he is not competent, especially in the craft of medicine, for this can lead to loss of life. The error of a physician is hidden by the earth. Likewise a joiner. Each should keep to his own trade and not claim any skill of which he is not an acknowledged master—especially with women, since ignorance and error are greater among them.

Only a skilled physician should sell potions and electuaries and mix drugs. These things should not be bought from the grocer or the apothecary whose only concern is to take money without knowledge; they spoil the prescriptions and kill the sick, for they mix medicines which are unknown and of contrary effect.

The sale of tame pigeons must be prohibited, for they are used only by thieves and people of no religion. The sale of cats should also be banned. Any broker who is known to be treacherous and dishonest should be excluded from the market, for he is a thief. He must be watched and not employed.

The lime stores and [other] empty places must be forbidden, because men go there to be alone with women.

Only good and trustworthy men, known as such among people, may be allowed to have dealings with women in buying and in selling. The trades-people must watch over this carefully. The women who weave brocades must be banned from the market, for they are nothing but harlots.

On festival days, men and women shall not walk on the same path when they go to cross the river.

The tax farm on … must be suppressed [reading uncertain].

Cargo ships must be known, and their holds should not be overloaded, especially when there are storms, as we have said [elsewhere]. The owners and captains of ships carrying wheat, charcoal, and other goods must be instructed to lighten their loads and not endanger the Muslims.

The heads of sheep, the meat of which is brought to the market, must be washed clean of blood. Otherwise, in narrow or crowded places it would not be possible to secure passersby from pollution by the blood. The ends of the stalls which protrude from the shops must be sawn off, since the meat hanging there would soil the clothes of passersby and make the way narrow.

The bakers must be ordered to wash their pans every day and to scrape and polish their boards to prevent vermin from entering them. They must not make large loaves with the dough for *poya* rolls. These must be cooked separately and sold by weight.

Graves should be slightly lengthened and widened. I saw a corpse which was exhumed from the grave three times; graves should allow for this. I saw another which had to be forced into the grave. The first concern of the *muhtasib* should be to demolish buildings erected in the cemetery and to watch over this for reasons I have already explained [elsewhere].

Paper should be of somewhat larger format, with more glazing.

Raw bricks should be thicker and smoother.

The basins in the public baths should be covered. If they are left uncovered, they cannot be protected from pollution, yet this is a place of purity. The bath attendant, the masseur, and the barber should not walk about in the baths without a loincloth or drawers.

A Muslim must not massage a Jew or a Christian nor throw away his refuse nor clean his latrines. The Jew and the Christian are better fitted for such trades, since they are the trades of those who are vile. A Muslim should not attend to the animal of a Jew or of a Christian, nor serve him as a muleteer, nor hold his stirrup. If any Muslim is known to do this, he should be denounced.

Muslim women shall be prevented from entering their abominable churches, for the priests are evil-doers, fornicators, and sodomites. Frankish [that is, Christian] women must be forbidden to enter the church except on days of religious services or festivals, for it is their habit to eat and drink and fornicate with the priests, among whom there is not one who has not two or more women with whom he sleeps. This has become a custom among them, for they have permitted what is forbidden and forbidden what is permitted. The priests should be ordered to marry, as they do in the eastern lands. If they wanted to, they would.

No women may be allowed in the house of a priest, neither an old woman nor any other, if he refuses marriage. They should be compelled to submit to circumcision, as was done to them by al-Mu'tadid 'Abbād [ruler of Seville, 1040–69]. They claim to follow the rules of Jesus, may God bless and save him. Now Jesus was circumcised, and they celebrate the day of his circumcision as a festival, yet they themselves do not practice this.

The contractor of the bathhouse should not sit there with the women, for this is an occasion for license and fornication. The contractor of hostelries for traders and travelers should not be a woman, for this is indeed fornication. The broker of houses shall not be a young man, but a chaste old man of known good character.

Clothes must not be cleaned with beetles. Laundry men should be forbidden to do this, as it is harmful to the clothes.

A Jew must not slaughter meat for a Muslim. The Jews should be ordered to arrange their own butcher's stalls.

The qadi must order the people of the villages to appoint a keeper in every village to guard private property from encroachment, for the peasants regard the property of the people of the city as licit to them. No riding animal or cattle should be turned loose without a halter. In the words of the proverb, "In the keeper is the protection of the state."

The property of the people and of the Muslims must be protected at the time of the harvest and other times from any kind of injury whatsoever. When the ears of the grain begin to form, it must be forbidden to cut and sell them. This is done only to avoid paying the tithe.

The curriers and silk dyers must be ordered to ply their trades outside the city only.

The felt makers should be ordered to improve their work. They make the felts slack, with little wool, and useless. The wool must be shaken free of lime.

The furriers must be advised not to use pigeons' dung to disguise worn out furs. This is a deceit which they practice.

Dyers must be forbidden to dye green with passerine or to dye light blue with brazilwood. This is fraudulent, since these dyes lose their color quickly. Some grocers use lycium leaf to make the henna green. This gives the henna a bright and fine green color. This is fraud.

A garment belonging to a sick man [likely means lepers], a Jew, or a Christian must not be sold without indicating its origin; likewise, the garment of a debauchee. Dough must not be taken from a sick man for baking his bread [again, probably refers to lepers]. Neither eggs nor chickens nor milk nor any other foodstuff should be bought from him. They should only buy and sell among themselves.

The sewer men must be forbidden to dig holes in the streets, as this harms them and causes injury to people, except when they are cleaning the entire street.

Itinerant fortune-tellers must be forbidden to go from house to house, as they are thieves and fornicators.

A drunkard must not be flogged until he is sober again.

Prostitutes must be forbidden to stand bareheaded outside the houses. Decent women must not bedeck themselves to resemble them. They must be stopped from coquetry and party making among themselves, even if they have been permitted to do this [by their husbands]. Dancing girls must be forbidden to bare their heads.

No contractor, policeman, Jew, or Christian may be allowed to dress in the costume of people of position, of a jurist, or of a worthy man. They must on the contrary be abhorred and shunned and should not be greeted with the formula, "Peace be with you," for the devil has gained mastery over them and has made them forget the name of God. They are the devil's party, "and indeed the devil's party are the losers" [Quran 58:20]. They must have a distinguishing sign by which they are recognized to their shame.

Catamites must be driven out of the city and punished wherever any one of them is found. They should not be allowed to move around among the Muslims nor to participate in festivities, for they are debauchees accursed by God and man alike.

When fruit or other foodstuffs are found in the possession of thieves, they should be distributed in prisons and given to the poor. If the owner comes to claim his goods and is recognized, they should be returned to him.

39. MUSLIM MERCHANTS IN CHRISTIAN REGIONS

The Muslim scholar Ibn Jubayr was one of the great travelers of the medieval period. He embarked on a pilgrimage to Mecca from his native Iberia, and his peregrinations took him throughout the Mediterranean, western Asia, Arabia, and the Red Sea. His observations are filled with local color, and, like any good traveler, he was keenly aware of social and cultural differences when he encountered them. In the following selection, from his travels in the Holy Land in the late twelfth century, he describes the local mercantile activity between Christians and Muslims, as well as taxes and custom duties.

Source: trans. R.J.C. Broadhurst, Ibn Jubayr, *The Travels of Ibn Jubayr* (London: Jonathan Cape, 1952), 300–1, 315–18.

One of the astonishing things that is talked of is that though the fires of discord burn between the two parties, Muslim and Christian, two armies of them may meet and dispose themselves in battle array, and yet Muslim and Christian travelers will come and go between them without interference. In this connection saw at this time, that is the month of Jumada 'l-Ula [I], the departure of Saladin with all the Muslims troops to lay siege to the fortress of Kerak [Crac des Chevaliers], one of the greatest of the Christian strongholds lying astride the Hejaz road and hindering the overland passage of the Muslims. Between it and Jerusalem lies a day's journey or a little more. It occupies the choicest part of the land in Palestine, and has a very wide dominion with continuous settlements, it being said that the number of villages reaches four hundred. This Sultan invested it, and put it to sore straits, and long the siege lasted, but still the caravans passed successively from Egypt to Damascus, going through the lands of the Franks without impediment from them. In the same way the Muslims continuously journeyed from Damascus to Acre [through Frankish territory], and likewise not one of the Christian merchants was stopped or hindered [in Muslim territories].

The Christians impose a tax on the Muslims in their land which gives them full security; and likewise the Christian merchants pay a tax upon their goods in Muslim lands. Agreement exists between them, and there is equal treatment in all cases. The soldiers engage themselves in their war, while the people are at peace and the world goes to him who conquers. Such is the usage in war of the people of these lands; and in the dispute existing between the Muslim emirs and their kings it is the same, the subjects and the merchants interfering not. Security never leaves them in any circumstance, neither in peace nor in war. The state of these countries in this regard is truly more astonishing than our story can fully convey. May God by his favor exalt the word of Islam....

... This city [Banyas] is on the frontier of the Muslim territories. It is small, but has a fortress below the walls of which winds a river that flows out from one of the gates of the city. A canal leading from it turns the mills. The city had been in the hands of the Franks, but Nur al-Din—may God's mercy rest upon his soul—recovered it [in 1165]. It has a wide tillage in a contiguous vale. It is commanded by a fortress of the Franks called Hunin [Neuf] three parasangs distant from Banyas. The cultivation of the vale is divided between the Franks and the Muslims, and in it there is a boundary known as "The Boundary of Dividing." They apportion the crops equally, and their animals are mingled together, yet no wrong takes place between them because of it.

We departed from Banyas on the evening of the same Saturday for a village called al-Masiyah, near to the Frankish fort we have mentioned. We passed the night in it, and removed on Sunday at daybreak. Between Hunin and Tibnin we passed a valley thick with trees, most of which were bay. The valley was of great depth, like a deep ravine whose sides come together and whose heights reach to the skies. It is known as al-Astil. Should soldiers penetrate it, they would be lost, there being no refuge or escape for them from the hand of those that lay in wait for them. Its descent and ascent, on both sides, is toilsome. Marveling at the place, we passed it, traveling close beside, and came to one of the biggest fortresses of the Franks, called Tibnin. At this place customs dues are levied on the caravans. It belongs to the sow known as queen [Agnes of Courtenay] who is the mother of the pig who is the lord of Acre [Baldwin IV]—may God destroy it.

We camped at the foot of this fortress. The fullest tax was not exacted from us, the payment being a Tyrian dinar and a qirat [one-twentieth part] of a dinar [about eleven shillings] for each head. No toll was laid upon the merchants, since they were bound for the place of the accursed king [Acre], where the tithe is gathered. The tax there is a qirat in every dinar [worth of merchandise], the dinar having twenty-four qirat. The greater part of those taxed were Maghrebis, those from all other Muslim lands being unmolested. This was because some earlier Maghrebis had annoyed the Franks. A gallant company of them had attacked one of their strongholds with Nur al-Din—may God have mercy upon him—and by its taking they had become manifestly rich and famous. The Franks punished them by this tax, and their chiefs enforced it. Every Maghrebi therefore paid this dinar for his hostility to their country. The Franks declared, "These Maghrebis came and went in our country and we treated them well and took nothing from them. But when they interfered in the war, joining with their brother Muslims against us, we were compelled to place this tax upon them." In the payment of this tax, the Maghrebis are pleasingly reminded of their vexing of the enemy, and thus the payment of it is lightened and its harshness made tolerable.

We moved from Tibnīn—may God destroy it—at daybreak on Monday. Our way lay through continuous farms and ordered settlements, whose inhabitants were all Muslims, living comfortably with the Franks. God protect us from such temptation. They surrender half their crops to the Franks at harvest time, and pay as well a poll-tax of one dinar and five qirat for each person. Other than that, they are not interfered with, save for a light tax on the fruits of trees. Their houses and all their effects are left to their full possession. All the coastal cities occupied by the Franks are managed in this fashion, their rural districts, the villages and farms, belonging to the Muslims. But their hearts have been seduced, for they observe how unlike them in ease and comfort are their brethren in the Muslim regions under their [Muslim] governors. This is one of the misfortunes afflicting the Muslims. The Muslim community bewails the injustice of a landlord of its own faith, and applauds the conduct of its opponent and enemy, the Frankish landlord, and is accustomed to justice from him. He who laments this state must turn to God. There is comfort and consolation enough for us in the exalted Book. "It is nothing but a trial; Thou makest to err with it whom Thou pleasest, and guidest whom Thou pleases" [Quran 7:155].

On the same Monday, we alighted at a farmstead a parasang distant from Acre. Its headman is a Muslim, appointed by the Franks to oversee the Muslim workers in it. He gave generous hospitality to all members of the caravan, assembling them, great and small, in a large room in his house, and giving them a variety of foods and treating all with liberality. We were amongst those who attended this party, and passed the night there. On the morning of Tuesday the tenth of the month, which was the eighteenth of September, we came to the city of Acre—may God destroy it. We were taken to the custom-house, which is a khan prepared to accommodate the caravan. Before the door are stone benches, spread with carpets, where are the Christian clerks of the Customs with their ebony ink-stands ornamented with gold. They write Arabic, which they also speak. Their chief is the Sahib al-Diwan [chief of the Customs], who holds the contract to farm the customs. He is known as al-Sahib [the director or master], a title bestowed on him by reason of his office, and which they apply to all respected persons, save the soldiery, who hold office with them. All the dues collected go to the contractor for the customs, who pays a vast sum [to the government]. The merchants deposited their baggage there and lodged in the upper storey. The baggage of any who had no merchandise was also examined in case it contained concealed [and dutiable] merchandise, after which the owner was permitted to go his way and seek lodging where he would. All this was done with civility and respect, and without harshness and unfairness. We lodged beside the sea in a house which we rented from a Christian woman, and prayed God Most High to save us from all dangers and help us to security.

40. A VENETIAN TRADING LICENSE

The ongoing state of war between the Christian and Muslim worlds had commercial repercussions as well. While much trade between Christians and Muslims was allowed, Christian authorities banned the trade in items of a military nature, such as ships, horses, and weapons or raw materials that had military applications, such as iron and wood. These embargoes could often be quite effective, as was the case with timber. Large forests capable of producing enough wood to maintain a navy were largely confined to the northern (Christian) area of the Mediterranean, while the southern (Muslim) region was mostly deforested. Consequently, the inability of Muslim princes to get adequate supplies of timber may have helped to tip the balance of naval power in the Mediterranean in favor of the Christians. In the following source, Pope Innocent III (r. 1198–1216) responds to the Venetians, who were hoping to obtain an exemption to the ban as it was damaging their economy. The pope kept many of the restrictions against military items in place, while giving the Venetians license to trade other goods.

Source: trans. Oliver Thatcher and Edgar McNeal, *A Sourcebook for Medieval History* (New York: C. Scribner Sons, 1905), 536–37.

In support of the eastern province [that is, the crusading states], in addition to the forgiveness of sins which we promise those who, at their own expense, set out thither, and besides the papal protection which we give those who aid that land, we have renewed that decree of the Lateran council [held under Alexander III, 1179], which excommunicated those Christians who shall furnish the Saracens with weapons, iron, or timbers for their galleys, and those who serve the Saracens as helmsmen or in any other way on their galleys and other piratical craft. We also ordered that their property be confiscated by the secular princes and the consuls of the cities, and that, if any such persons should be taken prisoner, they should be the slaves of those who captured them. We furthermore excommunicated all those Christians who shall hereafter have anything to do with the Saracens either directly or indirectly, or shall attempt to give them aid in any way so long as the war between them and us shall last. But recently our beloved sons, Andreas Donatus and Benedict Grilion, your messengers, came and explained to us that your city was suffering great loss by this our decree, because Venice does not engage in agriculture, but in shipping and commerce. Nevertheless, we are led by the paternal love which we have for you to forbid you to aid the Saracens by selling them, giving them, or exchanging with them, iron, flax [oakum], pitch, sharp instruments, rope, weapons, galleys, ships, and timbers, whether hewn or in the rough. But for the present and until we order to the contrary, we permit those who are going to Egypt to carry other kinds of merchandise whenever it shall be necessary. In return for this favor, you should be willing to go to the aid of the province of Jerusalem and you should not attempt to evade our apostolic command. For there is no doubt that he who, against his own conscience, shall fraudulently try to evade this prohibition, shall be under divine condemnation.

41. MUSLIMS AND CHRISTIANS IN BUSINESS PARTNERSHIPS

In spite of the papal bans on the trade of certain goods, a vigorous trade existed between Christian and Muslim regions, with Christian merchants becoming a common sight in the cities of northern Africa, Egypt, and the Holy Land. Genoese, Pisans, Venetians, and Catalans, in particular, were easily found in the urban areas of the Islamic world, with many of these cities hosting funduks, or hostels, for foreign merchants, the local economies being deeply dependent on trade. The following two letters, dated from around 1201, from a Tunisian leather merchant to his partners in Pisa, suggest some of the complexities of having Christian merchants in Muslim cities. In this case, the Pisans had engaged in acts of piracy in Tunisian waters, which led to their goods being confiscated. This left their Muslim partners caught in the middle of the dispute, simultaneously trying to maintain their business ties with the Pisans while making sure they were paid.

Source: trans. Robert S. Lopez and Irving W. Raymond, *Medieval Trade in the Mediterranean World: Illustrative Documents Translated with Introductions and Notes* (New York: Columbia University Press, 1967), 384–87.

I

In the name of God, the Clement and Merciful!

To the most noble and distinguished sheikh, the virtuous and honored Pace, Pisan; may it please God to preserve his honor, to decree his salvation, and to help and to assist him in the performance of what is good! Hilal ibn Khalifat al-Jamunsi, your affectionate, well-wishing friend, to him who follows a good path [sends] greetings and the mercy and blessings of God.

After [wishing] that he may give you salvation, my dearest friend, [let me recall how] you departed on the day of the event which took place by decree and will of the Most High God, Whose orders cannot be resisted and against Whose judgment one strives in vain; and you left in Tunis both your goods and your debts.

Through 'Abd-Allah al-Zagag I had sold to the people of the tarida [a type of ship] Greco, Tegrimo, and Ildebrando—1,031 skins. Total price, at the rate of 16 dinars a hundred, 165 dinars. Then I sold to Tegrimo and Ildebrando 605 skins for the price of 90 dinars 7 dirhams in cash. And I had from Greco his third part of the price of the 1,000 skins, and from Ildebrando the third part of this price and his half of the 90 dinars 7 dirhams, so that I remain the creditor of Tegrimo for 100 dinars 3½ dirhams of the mint. Moreover, Greco had given security to me for Ibn Qasum, and when leaving he did not pay me anything.

Further I am letting you know, my dear friend Pace, that I had credits against the people who smuggled in the steel, among whom Sabi owed me 73 dinars. With this, since it was my own, I bought copper at the auction sale. But after his departure, when I demanded the said sum, I was told that I had no credits against him. Yet it appears from a record that 166 dinars 1½ dirhams in cash are owing to me under the name of Bukir al-Akrash by Sabi and his partners who smuggled in the steel. I have obtained from the sheikh 9 quintals of steel at the rate of 7 dinars the quintal, so that I still am creditor for 20 dinars. The truth is that Ibn Qasum does not pay what he owes us and demands what we owe him.

Therefore we beg you to get information about these men—who is dead and who is alive? For Sabi, to whom I am indebted for the copper, already was my debtor—so that the rest of my credit with him, I mean after [deducting] the copper, is 7 dinars. If he is no longer living, [before his death] he may have entrusted you by letter [to settle] his debt.

Because of the arrest of Greco after your departure from here, I have received nothing of what he guaranteed for Ibn Qasum.

All of your goods here are under seizure. Nobody has taken any of them, and the sultan has forbidden us to touch them until the owners come.

To him who follows a good path [I send] greetings and the mercy and the blessings of God.

[Address]

To the most illustrious, most honorable sheikh, the virtuous and dear friend … Pace, Pisan, may God decree his salvation and give him plenty of goods!

2

In the name of God, the Clement and Merciful!

To the illustrious sheikhs, my revered and dear friends Ser Forestano, Ser Viviano, Ser Benenato Cerchi, and Ser Albano; may God grant them salvation and keep them under His guard! Your friend who relies upon your affection, the pilgrim Sadaqa, dealer in leather in Tunis—may God protect that city—sends you the very fullest greetings.

And he reminds you that you bought from him 1,485 lambskins through 'Uthman ibn 'Ali, dragoman, for the sum of 251 dinars 6 dirhams in cash—

of which I did not receive a single dirham! Then, owing to the fact that the musattah [a type of ship] captured the ship at the mouth of the canal, you left without paying me at all; nor could I take anything of what you left at the customs house.

Therefore your kindness is requested to act as you should as gentlemen and prominent merchants, [that is], to come [back] to satisfy my credit against you. For we asked in the customs house, I and others like me, [that they pay us] from what assets of yours may be kept there; and they answered us that they would pay us nothing unless you first came to take all your goods and to honor our credits.

And if you do not come here now, we hope you will write us letters and send someone entrusted with getting your goods out of the customs house and paying what is owing to us. Let the one you send carry an order of the prince of Pisa, with letters of the latter [to our authorities] and with powers of attorney from you. It would be [still] better if you came in person. Commodities here are cheap. Moreover, [there is] security and prosperity as before you left, and [indeed] more of it. And you will be treated with every regard and honor as has been customary in the past.

Ser Forestano, whom may God honor, is requested to go to see Sigiero Barba, Pisan, and to give him special greetings from the sheikh Yusuf, dealer in leather—the man from whom he bought 500 lambskins for 80 dinars through the dragoman whose name, in Frankish language, is Azmat Dafraka—and to beg him to come with you in order to pay [the sheikh Yusuf] this sum, as is your practice and that of honorable merchants. We do not need to press you to do it, nor do we need to insist more urgently because your integrity is well known. [Indeed], we write down [in our records] that you arrive soon, if it please God; may He safely guide you. And we greet you.

[Address]

To the illustrious sheikhs, revered friends, Ser Forestano and partners, Pisans, their admirer, the pilgrim Sadaqa, dealer in leather in Tunis—may God protect it!

42. MUSLIMS AND ECONOMIC EXCHANGES IN *LAS SIETE PARTIDAS*

In the mid-thirteenth century, Castilian jurists working under the direction of the king, Alfonso X (r. 1252–84), compiled Las Siete Partidas *(The Seven Divisions) to provide uniformity to the complex legal system that existed in Castile in the thirteenth century. The* Partidas *is one of the most important European legal works of the medieval period, but there is conflicting evidence as to how widely the* Partidas *was promulgated during the reign of Alfonso X, as there was strong opposition from the nobility and the towns against the new legal codex and the implied abandonment of older traditions such as the fueros (town charters). By the mid-fourteenth century, the Partidas was declared the laws of the land in Castile by Alfonso XI (r. 1312–50). As Castile continued with the Reconquest and later began its overseas expansion, the influence of the Partidas grew, becoming an important element in the legal systems of Spanish colonies in Africa, Asia, the Americas, and the southwestern United States, where there have been legal battles involving the Partidas as recently as the 1990s. The Partidas addressed a multitude of moral, philosophical, and theological issues related to the law and covered everything from theft to apostasy, from contracts to inheritance, and from the rights of the clergy to rents. There are numerous laws addressing the relationship between Christians and the religious minorities of Jews and Muslims. The laws from the Partidas included here deal only with the economic and commercial aspects of this relationship.*

Source: trans. Samuel Scott Parsons, Robert I. Burns, ed., *Las Siete Partidas*, 5 vols. (Philadelphia: University of Pennsylvania Press, 2001), IV: 978–80, 1035, 1058.

Partida IV: XXI: IV—Christians Who Provide the Enemies of the Faith with Iron, Wood, Arms, or Ships, Become Slaves by Reason of Such Acts

There are some wicked Christians who give assistance or advice to the Moors, who are the enemies of the faith; as, for instance, when they give or sell them arms of wood and iron, or galleys or ships already built, or the materials with which to build them; and this also includes those who pilot or navigate their ships in order to inflict injury upon Christians; and those who give or sell them wood for the purpose of making battering-rams or other engines. And, for the reason that such persons are guilty of great wickedness, the Holy Church deemed it proper that whoever could seize individuals guilty of acts of this kind, might reduce them to slavery, and sell them if they desired to do so, or make use of them as they would of their own slaves. In addition to this, such persons are excommunicated solely on account of their deeds, as stated in the Title concerning Excommunications, and they should lose everything they have, and become the property of the king.

Partida IV: XXI: VIII—Neither a Jew nor a Moor Can Hold a Christian as a Slave

Neither a Jew, a Moor, a heretic, nor anyone else who does not acknowledge our religion, can hold a Christian as a slave. Anyone who violates this law, by knowingly holding a Christian in servitude, shall lose his life on that account, and forfeit all his property to the king. We also decree that if any of the persons aforesaid has a slave that does not acknowledge our religion, and said slave becomes a Christian, the latter will be free for that reason, as soon as he is baptized and accepts our faith; nor will he be required to pay anything for himself to the party to whom he belonged before he became a Christian; and even though the party who was his master may subsequently become a Christian, he will retain no rights in said person who was his slave and became a Christian before he did. This is understood to apply where a Jew or a Moor purchases a slave who becomes a Christian with the intention of making use of his services and not for the purpose of disposing of him in trade. If, however, he buys him with the intention of selling him, he should do so within three months; and if, before the said three months have expired, and while his master was making an attempt to sell him, he should become a Christian, the said Jew or Moor should not, for that reason, lose all the price he paid for him, but we decree that the slave shall be required to pay for himself, or the party who caused him to become a Christian should pay for him, twelve maravedis of the money current in that locality; and where he has not the means to pay them, he should give his services instead of them, not as a slave but as a freeman, until he is entitled to that amount. If he should not be sold within the three months aforesaid, the party who was his master will retain no rights in him, even though he may subsequently become a Christian.

Partida V: V: XXII—Neither Weapons of Wood or Iron Should Be Sold to the Enemies of the Faith

Christians should neither sell nor lend weapons made of wood or iron to the Moors or any other enemies of the faith. Moreover, we forbid any persons in our dominions to remove to the country of said enemies, so long as they are at war with us, either wheat, barley, rye, oil, or any other article of food, by means of which they can sustain themselves, or sell or give them to them in our dominions to be taken to their country. However, we deem it proper that those who come to our court upon a mission, or under any agreement, should be sold such provisions as they need to eat and drink, so long as they remain there. We order that anyone who violates this law shall for that reason forfeit all his property, and that his life shall be at the mercy of the king; for to furnish arms or other assistance to the enemies of the faith, by means of which they can maintain themselves, is a species of treason.

Partida V: VII: IV—How Merchants and Their Property Should Be Protected

Countries and districts frequented by merchants with their merchandise are, for this reason, more wealthy, better provided, and more populous, and for this reason all persons ought to be pleased with them. Wherefore, we decree that all persons who resort to the fairs in our kingdoms, not only Christians but also Jews and Moors, and also those who at any other time visit our dominions, although they may not come to the fairs, shall be safe and secure in body, property, merchandise, and all their effects both on sea and land, while they are on the way to our dominions, while they are present there, and while they are departing from our country. We also forbid anyone to dare to employ violence against them, or do them any wrong or injury whatever. And if anyone should violate this law, by robbing them of what they bring with them or by depriving them of it by force, and the robbery or force can be established by evidence, or by any certain indications, although the merchants may not prove what property he was deprived of, or what its value was; the judge of the district where said robbery takes place should take the oath of the party, making inquiry in the first place as to what kind of a man he is, and what species of merchandise he is accustomed to deal in. And having made this investigation and appraised the amount according to the property which was sworn to, he must cause an amount of the property of the robbers equal to that which the said merchant swore he was robbed of, to be delivered to him, together with all the damages and losses resulting from the violence with which he was treated, and prosecute the robbers as the law directs. When neither the robbers, nor any property belonging to them with which reparation can be made, can be found, either the council or the lord in whose jurisdiction the place where the robbery occurred is situated, must pay said amount out of their own property.

43. MARITIME COMMERCIAL LAW

Merchants in the medieval period had to deal with numerous laws and customs as they went from one principality to the next. This overlap of legal, religious, and cultural traditions often led to disputes between merchants and host cities or out in the open sea. Consequently, as early as the eleventh century, many cities in the Mediterranean began to appoint officials known as sea consuls who could arbitrate between the quarreling parties. The laws and customs that guided the work of these sea consuls were also codified over the course of the Middle Ages. Among the most important and influential of these codifications was the Consulate of the Sea, *the maritime law of Catalonia. The* Consulate of the Sea *consisted of a disparate series of articles, laws, and royal proclamations promulgated over the course of the thirteenth and fourteenth centuries, with the bulk of them codified in 1343. The* Consulate *regulated all aspects of maritime activity, including the rights and responsibilities of sailors, captains, and shareholders (of a ship's cargo), how to transport goods, and the negotiation of agreements, among others. Moreover, the influence of the* Consulate *extended all over the Mediterranean and not just to Catalonia. All of these regulations influenced the actions and behavior of individuals associated with maritime trade, irrespective of whether the parties were Muslim or Christian. There were, however, numerous articles that specifically referred to the relations between Muslims and Christians and others that, more generally, regulated interactions between enemies.*

Source: trans. Stanley Jados, *The Consulate of the Sea and Related Documents* (Tuscaloosa: University of Alabama Press, 1975), 126–30, 245, 254–55, 258–59.

228. A Vessel Lost in the Territory of the Saracens—If a patron sailed into the territory of the Saracens and due to misfortune, storm, or action of armed enemy ships the vessel perished, he will not be required to pay the crew any wages, unless the vessel was lost at the same location where he had been paid the lading fees. If he had received such fees, he shall pay the crew full wages due them. If he had reduced the lading fees for the merchants, the crew shall accept a reduction in wages in proportion to the reduction of the lading fees received. If the patron owed the crew wages for another voyage, he shall pay them, as had been stated in one of the previous articles.

The patron who lost his vessel under the circumstances mentioned above shall not be required to furnish either transportation or subsistence for the crew until such time as they reach a Christian territory, because he had lost everything he possessed, and often even more than he possessed.

This article was written because a patron who lost his vessel is not required to furnish transportation or subsistence until they reach a Christian nation, because he does not even have the means to provide these necessities for himself.

229. Circumstances under Which the Patron of the Vessel Shall Secure the Approval of the Shareholders of the Vessel before He Accepts Cargo for Shipment—A patron who contracts to carry cargo destined for the territory of the Saracens or other dangerous places, should, if there are any shareholders present at the site where the vessel is being cargoed, receive their approval before he takes such cargo aboard. If he received their approval, he may proceed to load such cargo aboard, and none of the shareholders shall voice any opposition. If he should cargo the vessel without their approval, the shareholders may protest and sell the vessel at auction because the patron did not ask their permission. If, however, he had asked their permission, the shareholders cannot sell the vessel before he returns from the journey.

If the shareholders force the auction of the vessel that the patron had cargoed without their permission, and due to the sale of the vessel or for any other reason the patron is relieved from the command of the vessel, and the shareholders regain control of the vessel, the vessel shall make the journey as had been agreed with the merchant who had leased the vessel or had arranged to ship cargo aboard it with the party who had been the master of the vessel when the agreement was made. Let all who buy shares in a vessel remember that all the agreements made by the patron of a vessel shall be carried out.

However, if a patron of a vessel finds himself in the territory where none of the shareholders are present, he may use his judgment in accepting any cargo for shipment to any destination. If the vessel was damaged, none of the shareholders shall make any claims. On the other hand, if the patron of the vessel gambled away, squandered, or lost the vessel in any other way due to his negligence, the shareholders will be able to press their claims against him.

Further, a patron who accepts cargo for shipment to a Christian territory shall not be required to ask the permission of the shareholders to undertake such a journey, if he does not wish to ask their permission, and no shareholder shall attempt to bring about the sale of the vessel that had been engaged to carry cargo, until after the completion of the journey and return of the vessel. If the patron, upon the demand of the shareholders, must provide them with a guarantor that he will not change the course of the vessel during the voyage until he returns the vessel for their disposition, the guarantor shall be liable only to the degree decreed by the customs and the laws of the sea.

If it should happen that the patron contracts to carry cargo to the location mentioned above, and the shareholders are conveniently at hand, and regardless of whether they know about this trip or are ignorant of it or whether the patron informed them about it, and they do not oppose such a voyage, they will not be able to lodge any demands for damages later. If the vessel should have been lost or damaged on such a voyage, the patron of the vessel shall not be held liable for any consequences that had occurred.

230. Ransom Paid or Other Arrangements Made with Armed Enemy Vessels—A patron who encounters armed enemy vessels in the port, the open sea, or any other place may negotiate and conclude an agreement with the officers and the admiral of such naval units as to the amount of ransom he shall be required to pay them, in order that they would not harm him or anything aboard the vessel, and the majority or all the merchants who are aboard his vessel should be informed of the agreement he was forced to make or will make with the officers of the above armed units. With the advice and approval of these merchants he shall pay the amount agreed as ransom. The merchants are required to repay him the sum paid out in proportion to the value of the cargo they have aboard the vessel.

The ransom shall be paid by an assessment levied on all the cargo aboard the vessel in proportion to the amount and the value of the cargo, and the patron of the vessel shall share in this payment to the extent of half the value of his vessel.

If there are no merchants aboard the vessel, the patron shall consult with the officers of the stern, the navigator, and officers of the prow. He shall pay the ransom with the approval of all those mentioned above. The merchants whose cargo is aboard the vessel shall not and cannot protest such payment of ransom, provided that the patron share in the payment of ransom in the amount equal to half the value of his vessel.

To continue: If the patron should come upon armed naval units in the places mentioned above, but these were units of a friendly power, and he would wish to present a gift to the commander of such units or entertain him aboard his vessel, and the merchants are aboard his vessel, he is required to get their approval to proceed in this manner, or to act in accordance with the expressed desire of the crew as stated before. If he proceeds in the manner outlined above, he shall be reimbursed for his expenditures.

Further, if, however, the patron did not conduct himself in accordance with the wishes of the merchants aboard his vessel, or in their absence with the wishes of the persons mentioned before, but acted in this matter arbitrarily and gave such gifts without the knowledge of the merchants or without the consultation of the individuals mentioned previously, he shall pay out these expenditures from his personal cash box, and the merchants will not be required to reimburse him for the expenditure of money used to buy such gifts that he presented to the officers of these armed vessels.

231. Payment of Ransom to or Concluding of Agreements with Armed Enemy Vessels—If at the moment the vessel is fully or partly cargoed, it is located in an enemy territory or other dangerous locality, and is threatened by the arrival in the vicinity of unfriendly armed vessels, and if the patron of the vessel in order to avoid damage to the cargo aboard the vessel attempted to approach the enemy craft with some proposition that would guarantee safety to his vessel and the cargo, and the majority or all of the merchants are aboard the vessel, he shall be obliged to inform them of the terms he offered or intends to offer to the enemy officers of these vessels. With the approval and consent of the merchants he shall pay the amount of ransom agreed upon, and the merchants shall share in the amount paid in proportion to the value of their cargo aboard the vessel.

If it should happen that there would not be a single merchant aboard the vessel, but the vessel is anchored in waters adjacent to where the merchants are domiciled and can be reached by the patron in order to apprise them of the situation and of the agreement he had concluded or will conclude with the armed vessels in order to save his life and all the cargo aboard, he is required to inform them of this turn of events. If there was not sufficient time to notify the merchants of this happening, he shall proceed in such manner after obtaining the support of all the members of the crew. If he had acted according to these instructions, the merchants shall be required to share in the damages, as if they had been present, and shall not and could not raise any objections to the action he had taken in this matter.

Further, if the patron of the vessel had concluded an agreement although the majority or all of them were aboard the vessel or within an easy reach, such an agreement, concluded or that will be concluded without the consultation and approval of the merchants who were aboard the vessel or nearby where they could have been notified of this matter, is not binding upon the merchants whether all or only part of their cargo was aboard the vessel, because the patron failed to consult them in this matter. If, however, the merchants were in a locality where communication with them was an impossibility, and the patron concluded an agreement after consultation of the other persons mentioned previously, the merchants shall be required to reimburse him for the expenditures described above.

If by chance he should have concluded such an agreement without the knowledge of the merchants and without a consultation with the parties mentioned before, solely upon his own responsibility, he shall pay for all the expenses from his own personal cash box, and no one else will be required to share in these expenditures, because the patron had acted without the knowledge of the parties mentioned.

Further, if the vessel is anchored in one of the locations enumerated above after unloading its cargo, and if the merchants had agreed with the patron that he shall wait for them and that they will provide him with a new shipment of cargo, and in the interim armed vessels approach his vessel, and the patron in order to avoid any damage concludes some agreement with the command of such vessels, or if some unfortunate accident occurs that will result in the loss of his vessel, the merchants shall not be required to share in the damage or in the expenditures he incurred while waiting for them, because they had unloaded their cargo. They may, however, if they wish, reimburse him for these losses of their own free will.

If it should happen that the merchants did not cargo and dispatch the vessel in the agreed period of time, and in the meantime armed vessels arrive in the vicinity and the patron shall be forced either to reach a protective covenant with them or to lose his vessel, the merchants shall be required to pay the amount of the ransom agreed upon between the patron and the armed vessels or to reimburse him for any expense that he had incurred due to their negligence, because they had failed to dispatch the vessel on the date agreed to mutually.

322. Servants—Servants shall receive two shares of the captured booty. They shall nurse the ill Saracens and others who are ill aboard the vessel, as well as clean the ship. If the servant is employed by the armed personnel, the captain shall properly adjudge him a reward in conformity with the oath he had taken.

331. Stewards—In there had been stewards hired aboard the vessel, they together with the clerk are required to guard faithfully the common property aboard the ship and to make inventory of it, and each of them shall have a copy of such inventory, and each of them should have his own lock, so that one cannot open the chest of another and cannot be able to put anything into it or take anything out; and the clerk shall be present each time any valuables are put in or taken out of these chests.

If it should happen that any of the stewards takes out or issues anything on the orders of the admiral or some other party in command of the ship without the knowledge of the other stewards aboard the ship or of the clerk, he shall lose his hand, and he shall be removed from his office and shall be given over to the mercy of the crew and lose his shares of the booty.

Stewards are paid a silver mark for every privateering expedition.

Stewards are given one chest from each captured vessel, the best that shall be found aboard, without any merchandise that it may have contained, just the wooden part of it.

Stewards receive all the locks that shall be taken off a captured vessel or ship.

Stewards shall receive all the ropes taken off the crates from the captured vessel.

Stewards shall receive all the nails found aboard the captured vessel that are not in chests, packs, or baskets.

Stewards receive two millares for every Saracen captured; but they shall be required to furnish the rivets needed to fasten the fetters of the prisoners.

Stewards receive all the chisels found aboard the captured vessel with the exception of those that belong to the carpenter, but they shall make them available for use aboard their ship.

They shall be required to furnish the ropes necessary to tie up the crates until these are sold at auction, and the chisels for putting on the fetters on the prisoners and for taking them off. They shall also furnish ropes to tie up the prisoners and fasten the sails, if there are no such ropes aboard the vessel.

333. Consuls—The consuls should take an oath in the presence of the crew of the vessel, the navigators, the outfitters, the sailors of the prow, the crossbowmen, and other armed personnel that they shall not be influenced by any means in dealing with anyone aboard the ship, that they shall not be partial to any relatives or anyone else, and that they shall act faithfully in accordance with their best knowledge and good will, and that they shall always act with the advice of all those who shall give their advice, and that they shall not be deterred from this course either by bonds of blood, offers of money, or any other reason.

They shall watch very carefully that everything sold aboard the vessel, whether wine or anything else, shall be honestly measured. They shall also have a clerk; and each of the consuls shall be paid fifteen bezants; and they shall give the captain from the share they received of all the fines imposed aboard the ship one third of the amount and to the clerk also a third of the amount.

In addition, they shall receive half of the imposed fines. They should also receive one rug from each captured vessel.

In addition, they shall receive two bezants for each of them for every person captured aboard the vessel taken, because they arbitrate disputes between the people.

In addition, every consul is to conduct his affairs faithfully and impartially, and should he tolerate any evil acts, he shall be deprived of his office, shall forfeit his shares in the booty, and shall be branded on his forehead.

The guards who are bailiffs or major-domos should take an oath that they shall honestly distribute the food rations among all aboard, with the exception of the admiral who shall receive three portions, and the captain and the chief navigator who shall receive one and one-quarter portions. They shall not be allowed to give a larger portion to either a large or small member of the crew without the consent of the admiral, the captain, and the clerk.

The guards shall receive the hides of the animals eaten aboard the ship. They shall also receive bags and bread baskets, if their ship takes booty.

In addition, for every Saracen captured they shall be paid four millares; they shall, however, be required to watch them, chain and unchain them, and if these Saracens should be able to give ransom, they shall be paid one bezant each.

In addition, the guards shall receive as large a share of the spoils as will be available. Should the Saracens escape, however, they shall be held answerable.

44. AN APPEAL FOR CHRISTIAN MERCHANTS

Although Christian and Muslim rulers were welcoming of foreign merchants in their lands, these merchants could sometimes run into overtly zealous local authorities or anti-foreigner sentiments, or simply overstay their welcome. Therefore, from time to time, rulers had to appeal to foreign merchants to come and trade. In the following letter, the Marinid ruler of Morocco Abd al-Rahman (better known as Abu Inan, r. 1348–58) responds to an embassy from the king of Aragon, Peter IV (r. 1336–87). The embassy was requesting better conditions for the Christian merchants in Morocco, to which Abd al-Rahman agreed while also promising to protect Christian merchants who came to his realm.

Source: trans. Jarbel Rodriguez, from M.A. Alarcón y Santón and R. Garcia de Linares, *Los documentos árabes diplomáticos del Archivo de la Corona de Aragón* (Madrid: Impresa de E. Maestre, 1940), 202–5.

From the servant of God, who puts his faith in him, Abd al-Rahman, prince of the Faithful, and warrior for the Lord of the Universe, son of our lord prince

Abū al-Hasan, son of our lord, prince of the Faithful, warrior for the Lord of the Universe, Abū 'Alī, son of our lord, prince of the Faithful, warrior for the Lord of the Universe, Abū Sa'īd, son of our lord, prince of the Faithful and defender of the faith, warrior for the Lord of the Universe, Abu Yusuf, son of 'Abd al-Haqq. May God enhance his [Abd al-Rahman's] power, lend him valuable aid, facilitate decisive victories, and give him his assistance so that his words and thoughts are a continuous stream of proof of his love for him and so that the best virtues become evident in him, being at the same time free of vices. To the chivalric, illustrious, indomitable, heroic, resolute in spirit, grand, regally born, most faithful, and preeminent lord of Aragon, Barcelona, Valencia, Zaragoza, Jativa, Mallorca, Minorca, Perpignan, Roussillon, Perelada, Tarragona, Tortosa, Morella, Geltru and Cervera and the fortresses and castles of their respective jurisdictions, the eminent king Pedro. May God preserve his life so that he can walk down the path of virtues which he has laid out and so that he may follow the road of loyalty under the guidance of his divine light....

... After giving thanks to God for the prodigious signs of his omnipotence, which undoubtedly occur, and for his mercies which reach us as so many pieces of intertwined lace....

My cousin, the magnificent and gallant sultan Abū al-'Abbās Ahmad and I, constitute a unique force whose thoughts are perfectly aligned and whose efforts against the enemy are ceaseless.

We have forced him [the enemy] to take refuge in his lair, having made him suffer a harsh punishment and God willing we will soon receive news of his capture and subjugation with the help and power of God.

The friendship that we profess for you and which you deserve, is bound to us by bows whose knots cannot be easily undone and by a love so faithful that after proven it should be praised for its selfless greatness. And we must pray that God strengthens our friendship and preserve your faithfulness. We have received your venerable letter and your interesting declarations by way of your envoy William Mariner—may God keep him on the straight path—and through him, we have come to learn of your faith and loyalty in all things.

Your envoy, who has been given every honor that befits his provenance, has conferred with us and explained the worthy goals that your majesty has planned and taken great interest to insure that they come to fruition. He has informed us of your desire to simplify the process and to facilitate the means to resolve the difficulties which Christian merchants encounter.

We had previously written to you on this issue and now wish to finalize the details....

Order, thus, the Christian merchants in your kingdoms and in all your dominions, to come and trade in our country where they will find the respect, attention, consideration, and protection to which they are accustomed. In this regard, we have made promises to your envoy which would reveal the most hidden folds of the spirit, intensify human eloquence, and anticipate the glory of Paradise.

People like you are the ones that draw out this kind of praise for those who are endowed with excellent qualities and noble gifts, worthy of all admiration.

We hope that you will inform us of any complications the moment they arise and that you keep us up to date on any problems that may occur so that we may offer you satisfaction on all accounts, based on your wishes and with the help of God.

May God—glory be to him—grant you unending fortune and watch over your illustrious house. I give unto you the peace, mercy and blessings of God. This letter has been written on the twenty-first day of the month of Dhū al-Hijja of 775 [18 December 1354].

45. REGULATING MUSLIMS IN LLEIDA

The Christian kingdoms of Spain all imposed numerous regulations on their minority communities throughout the medieval period. These regulations often controlled where members of minority communities could live and work and how they could interact with the Christian majority. As such, the regulations often played an important role in the commercial and economic life of any Muslim community or aljama. The regulations below were imposed by the queen of Aragon, Maria of Castile (1401–58), and include several economic restrictions. Maria was regent for her husband Alfonso V (r. 1416–58) while the latter spent much of his reign attempting to conquer and rule the kingdom of Naples. While Alfonso was away, Maria ruled in his place, and it was under her authority that the following ordinances were issued in 1436.

Source: trans. Jarbel Rodriguez, from Josefa Mutgé Vives, *L'aljama sarraïna de Lleida a l'edat mitjana* (Barcelona: CSIC, 1992), 380–82.

First, our lady orders and commands the Moors to have and hold their houses and domiciles, with their wives and families, within the limits of the old Moorish quarter of the aforementioned city [Lleida] and in no other place. And if it is necessary, they will be given sufficient space to build the houses for them to live in. The Moorish quarter will be closed in such a way that one can only enter or exit through a single gate. Thus, they will be separated and apart from the Christians. This they will do within three months of the publication of these ordinances or be fined ten pounds for each Moor who after three months is found living outside the Moorish quarter. And if they cannot pay, they will be given thirty lashes in the public and customary [for whipping] areas of the city.

Likewise, she orders and commands, that when the precious heart of Christ passes through any street in the city, even if it is during the feast of Corpus Christi, if any Moor, male or female, is on that street they will get on their knees and remain on their knees until it passes or they should hide inside a house and not be seen. And whoever does not do this will be punished for each transgression fifty solidi or twenty lashes.

Likewise, she orders and commands that all Moors wear a round haircut or have a beard so that Christians can tell who they are. And those who do not have beards shall wear their hair starting at the ears in the *lonchs* style so that it is halfway down the ear. And whoever does not do this will be fined fifty solidi or given twenty lashes.

Likewise, she orders and commands that in the aforementioned Moorish quarter there shall be a butcher's table, in which a Christian butcher will cut meat for the Moors as is necessary and will be paid for it by the *aljama* of said Moors.

Likewise, that the aforementioned butcher shall not sell the meat to any Christian under a penalty of a ten pound fine for each transgression. And if he is not able to pay, he shall spend twenty days in prison and be given only bread and water.

Likewise, she orders and commands that on fair and market days, the aforementioned Moors can bring to market their goods and things to sell and to make contracts on them.

Likewise, she orders and commands that those Moors who are blacksmiths shall move their smithies and shops to the Cap Pont [a suburb] so that they can do their work, as has been the customary practice. And they shall not have their homes or wives [there]. Moreover, they shall not dare to live or work [at their shops] except on work days, according to the observances and customs of the Christians; all under penalty of a ten pound fine or thirty lashes. This restriction does not apply, moreover, to the potters or those who work in earthenwares, who our lady orders can work in those places where they have customarily done so [within the Moorish quarter].

Likewise, she orders and commands that the Moors, as long as they are within the Moorish quarter and while its gate is closed, can work and labor at all times and any day that they please except on Christmas, New Year's Day, Epiphany, the Feast of the Virgin Mary, Easter, the Quinquagesima, the Feast of Corpus Christi, the feast of Saint John, and the Feast of Saint Lawrence. On these days they will not do any work, be it inside or outside the Moorish quarter, under penalty of a fine of fifty solidi or twenty lashes.

Likewise, any Moor who may have left the city for any reason shall be able to return to Lleida, without fear, to live and work, according to the guidelines laid out in these ordinances, as our lady has graciously forgiven any penalties or fines which may have been imposed [upon them].

Likewise, all fines shall be paid in three parts. The first shall go to the king, the second to the accuser, and the third to whichever official can claim it, according to their privileges.

Likewise, so that all of these ordinances shall be observed, our lady revokes from each and every official the faculty and power to remit, ease, arrange, or commute the aforementioned penalties. They shall all be rigorously enforced without grace or mercy.

46. LATIN CHRISTIAN TRAVELERS DESCRIBE FOREIGN MARKETS AND GOODS

Christian travelers and pilgrims typically commented on Islamic markets, giving descriptions that were filled with a sense of wonder, exoticism, and novelty. The heart of the Islamic world sat astride the major Eurasian and African trade routes. Consequently, cities such as Alexandria, Cairo, Damascus, and Baghdad were entrepôts for goods coming from India, China, eastern Africa, and the Mediterranean. Europeans who visited such places encountered goods, foods, clothes, and other items that ranged from the banal to the exotic, as well as customs and traditions that made them comment, sometimes in appreciation and other times with disdain and moral judgments. The two short excerpts below are taken from Christian travelers. The first is an account by the German traveler Ludolph von Suchem of Damascus. The second passage comes from the travels of Pedro Tafur, a Spanish writer and diplomat whose sojourns between 1436 and 1439 took him throughout the Mediterranean, including Cairo. In his writings, he included a description of its market.

Sources: trans. Aubrey Stewart, *Ludolph von Suchem's Description of the Holy Land and of the Way Thither*, Palestine Pilgrims' Text Society, Vol. XII (London: Palestine Pilgrims' Text Society, 1895), 129–30, rev. Jarbel Rodriguez; trans. Jarbel Rodriguez, from Marcos Jimenez de la Espada, *Andanças é viajes de Pero Tafur por diversas partes del mundo ávidos: 1435–1439* (Madrid: Imprenta de Miguel Ginesta, 1874), 116–18.

Ludolph von Suchem

Going on from this village, one comes to Damascus. Damascus is an exceedingly ancient city, founded by Damascus, Abraham's servant. It stands on the place where Cain killed his brother Abel, and is an exceedingly noble, glorious, and beautiful city, rich in all manner of merchandise, and everywhere delightful, but more by artificial than by natural loveliness, abounding in foods, spices, precious stones, silk, pearls, cloth-of-gold, perfumes from India, Tartary, Egypt, Syria, and places on our side of the Mediterranean, and in all precious things that the heart of man can conceive. It is filled with gardens and orchards, is watered both within and without by waters, rivers, brooks, and fountains, cunningly arranged, to minister to men's luxury, and is incredibly populous, being inhabited by diverse trades of most cunning and noble workmen, mechanics, and merchants, while within the walls it is adorned beyond belief by baths, by birds that sing all the year round, and by pleasures, refreshments, and amusements of all kinds. Each trade dwells by itself in a particular street, and each workman, according to his craft and his power, makes in front of his house a wondrous show of his work, as cunningly, nobly, and peculiarly wrought as he can, outdoing his neighbors if possible, so that he adorns and decorates his house more beautifully than I can tell you. The merchants do likewise with their merchandise, and all handicrafts are wrought there wondrously well and with exceeding great skill. But they sell everything very dear. Rich citizens have all kinds of singing-birds and birdlets hanging in front of their houses, such as nightingales, quails, larks, francolins, and the like, and they sing wondrously and equally well all the year round, but better in winter time than in the summer heat; and you may hear all other kinds of birds, such as crows, pies, hoopoes, blackbirds, and the like, who can be taught human speech, talking like men in diverse tongues. Though the city is so full of people, and though all the merchandise is left almost unguarded, yet there is no man so old that he can remember anyone ever to have been slain there, and it is very seldom that any of the goods for sale are stolen. Each sort of thing that is sold there has a special market to itself. In the market where victuals are sold there may be seen every day the greatest crowd of people ever seen together in one place, and every kind of food that you can think of may be found there most exquisitely cooked. They take the greatest care with these things, and sell them all by weight and scales; also sundry different sorts of bread are sold there.

Pedro Tafur

The best, richest, and most magnificent site to see in Babylonia [Cairo] is the Alcayceria [market] and all the things sold there which come from Greater India, especially pearls and precious stones, spices, perfumes and other aromatics, silk, and linens. And who can tell how many products come from India and are spread all over the world and are sold cheaply here. [In the market] there are some men who walk around with a mirror dangling on their chest and touting [their services]. These are the barbers who shave the heads and back of the necks of the Muslims. There are also little black boys, no more than ten or twelve years of age, who walk around calling out, "Who wants a shave?" And they are the ones who serve the women and clean those parts [of their bodies] which they secretly attend to in the baths. And there are representatives of every trade walking through the streets in case they are needed. Even the cooks walk around with a brazier and a fire and stew for sale. Others sell plates of fruit and untold vendors have water for sale, carrying it on camels, donkeys or even on their own backs, as there are many people and the river is the only source of water. The summer fruits are very succulent and as it is very hot there, God has provided what is necessary. Sometimes, a thin breeze breaks through the heat affecting the eyes, and many people walk around as if drunk finding sweet succor in the fruits. Otherwise, it is a very healthy land, with good air, good water, and good victuals. The camels in this country are exceedingly large and beautiful, but not very fast. The donkeys are the most gentle beasts, strong and restless and they come well-equipped with saddle and bridle.

47. TRUCE BETWEEN THE TURKS AND GENOESE SAFEGUARDING THE RIGHTS OF MERCHANTS

In the aftermath of the conquest of Constantinople by the Ottoman Turks, the Italian city-states that had developed critical trading networks through the city found themselves at a loss. Not surprisingly, soon after the city fell, the Genoese, who had held considerable stakes in Constantinople, set to work to try to maintain their presence in Ottoman Istanbul. The source below, a treaty between Genoa and Mehmed the Conqueror, details the rights and obligations that Genoese merchants would have in the city.

Source: trans. J.R. Melville Jones, *The Siege of Constantinople 1453: Seven Contemporary Accounts* (Amsterdam: Adolf M. Hakkert, 1972), 136–37.

We the great lord and emir, the sultan Mehmed-Bey, son of the great lord and emir, the sultan Murad-Bey.

Do swear by the God of Heaven and Earth, and by our great Prophet Muhammad, and by the Seven Names which we Muslims have and confess, and by the hundred and twenty-four thousand prophets of God, and by the spirit of Our Father's Father and of Our Father, and by the life of our children and by the sword which we wear.

That whereas the general magistrates of Galata have sent their worthy ambassadors to the Porte of Our Majesty, the noble Marchesis de Franchi and their dragoman [translator] Nicolo Pagliuzzi, and have done reverence to Our Majesty and humbled themselves before Our Majesty, and have placed themselves in the power of Our Majesty.

They are to obey the laws and customs in force throughout our dominions. We shall not destroy their fortifications. They are to keep their property and their houses, their shops and their vineyards, their mills and their ships, their boats and their merchandise entire, and their women and their children according to their wishes. They may sell their goods as freely as in any other part of our dominions. They may come and go freely by land and sea, without paying any taxes or tolls, except for the poll tax, as is the custom in every part of our dominions.

Let them observe their own laws and customs, and preserve them now and in the future; and we will keep them as earnestly and hold them as dear as those which are current in our own dominions. They may keep their churches and hold services in them, provided that they do not ring bells or sound semantra [pieces of wood beaten to attract attention]. We shall not try to turn their churches into mosques, but they are not to build any new churches.

The Genoese merchants are to come and go freely and transact their own business. We shall not take their children as janissaries, nor any other young person there. They are not to have Turks planted among them, unless they are of high rank, or in the event that Our Majesty should send one of our servants to oversee them. The people of Galata are also to have permission to appoint an official among themselves, to direct the administration which their trade demands. Janissaries and slaves are not to be lodged in their houses. Let them collect the taxes which they owe, and keep accounts of what they have spent in doing so; and let them recoup these expenses from their own people. Their merchants are not to be subject to requisition orders. The merchants of Genoa are to have freedom to come and to go, and are to pay taxes according to the laws in force and the prevailing custom.

This present treaty was written down, and the oath sworn by Our Majesty, in the year of the world 6961, and 857 since the Hejira [1453 CE].

CHAPTER SIX

RELIGIOUS INTERACTIONS

Figure 6.1: Bishop Adhemar blessing the crusaders.

Source: John Frost, *Pictorial History of the Middle Ages from the Death of Constantine the Great to the Discovery of America by Columbus* (Philadelphia: Charles J. Gillis, 1846), 237.

48. MUSLIM POLEMICS ON THE GOSPELS

Christians and Muslims both used polemical writings and arguments to undermine and belittle each other's beliefs and practices. These polemics often followed a predictable pattern. Christian polemical writings often accused Muslims of being pagans, heretics or followers of anti-Christ. Muslim polemics, for their part, typically sought to highlight what they perceived to be errors in Christian doctrine or accused them of being polytheists due to the Christian worship of the Trinity. The source that follows comes from the Andalusi poet, jurist, and theologian Ibn Hazm (994–1064). Ibn Hazm was one of the most prolific of all medieval Muslim scholars, producing, according to his son, 400 works. His early life was lived in the splendor of the caliphate of Cordoba, but starting in 1008 the caliphate fell into civil war, which ultimately led to its collapse in 1031. Thereafter, Ibn Hazm spent most of the rest of his life writing in his family estates outside of Seville. This short excerpt is from a much larger work on religion, in which he devotes considerable space to refuting Christianity and Judaism.

Source: trans. Thomas Burman, ed. Olivia Remie Constable, *Medieval Iberia: Readings from Christian, Muslim, and Jewish Sources* (Philadelphia: University of Pennsylvania Press, 1997), 81–83.

In this same chapter [of the Gospel of Matthew] the Messiah said to them, "Do not suppose that I have come in order to introduce peace among the people of the land, but rather the sword; and I have arrived only in order to make division between a man and his spouse and his son, and between a daughter and her mother, and between a daughter-in-law and her mother-in-law, and in order that a man will consider the people of his household enemies" [Matt. 10:34–36].

And in the twelfth chapter of the Gospel of Luke the Messiah said to them, "I have arrived only in order to cast fire upon the earth, and my desire is only the spreading of it, and verily we will plunge all of [the earth] into it. And I am appointed for the completion of this. Do you think that I have come to make peace among the people of the earth? Nay, rather to make division among them. For five men will be divided in a single house, three against two and two against three, the father against the son and the son against the father, the daughter against the mother and the mother against the daughter, the mother-in-law against the daughter-in-law and the daughter-in-law against the mother-in-law" [Luke 12:49–53].

These are the two passages just as you see them.

And in the ninth chapter of the Gospel of Luke the Messiah (upon him be peace!) said to them, "I was not sent for the destruction of souls but rather for the welfare of them."

And in the tenth chapter of the Gospel of John the Messiah said, "I will not judge him who hears my words but does not keep them, for I did not come in order to judge the world and punish it, but rather in order to preserve the people of the world."

[Ibn Hazm's commentary:] These [last] two passages contradict the two passages that preceded them, and each of the meanings [of the respective sets of passages] clearly refutes the other. For if it is said that [Jesus] meant only that he was not sent for the destruction of souls who believed in him, then we say, [that Jesus] was speaking in general and did not single out [any particular group]. The proof of the falseness of this explanation of yours—that is, that he only meant that he was not sent for the destruction of the souls who believed in him—is the text of this passage: In the ninth chapter of the Gospel of Luke ... he says about the Messiah that "He sent before him messengers and they made their way to Samaria in order to prepare for him there, but they did not receive him on account of his wending his way to Jerusalem; but when John and James saw this they said to him, 'O our Lord, does it suit you if we call out so that fire will descend upon them from heaven and burn all of them just as Elias did?' But he turned to them and scolded them and said, 'The One Who possesses [your] spirits did not send the [Son] of Man for the destruction of souls, but for the salvation of them.' And then they made their way to another city."

... Ambiguity disappears, therefore, since it is certain that he did not mean by the souls which he was sent to save some of the souls to the exclusion of others, but rather he meant all the souls, those disbelieving in him and those believing in him, for just as you heard, he said this only when his disciples wanted to destroy those who would not accept him. So the lies of the first statement are manifest. And God forbid that the Messiah (on him be peace!) should lie; rather the lying without doubt derives from the four iniquitous men who wrote these corrupted, altered gospels.

And in [chapter twelve of the Gospel of Matthew] the Messiah said to them: "John [the Baptist] came to you and he did not eat or drink and you said, 'He is possessed.' Then the Son of Man came—he means himself—and you said, 'This man is a glutton and imbiber of wine, a wanton friend of tax collectors and sinners'" [Matt. 11:18–19].

[Ibn Hazm's commentary:] In this [passage] there is lying and contradiction [to the teaching] of the Christians. As for the lying, it occurs when he says here that "John did not eat or drink" so that it is said about him that "he is possessed" for that reason. In the first chapter of the Gospel of Mark [it says] that the food of John son of Zachariah [John the Baptist] (May peace be upon both of them) was locusts and wild honey [Mark 1:6]. This is a contradiction; one of the two reports is a lie without doubt. As for the contradiction of the teaching of the Christians, [it occurs when this passage] relates that John did not eat and drink while the Messiah did eat and drink. Now without doubt whomever among mankind God (he is magnified and exalted!) makes able to do without food and drink he has distinguished, and he has raised his status above anyone who cannot do without food and drink. So John [the Baptist in that case] is more virtuous than the Messiah without doubt.... .

A third narrative [is relevant here] and it is the acknowledgment of Jesus about himself that he ate and drank, even though among [the Christians] he is considered a god. But how could this god eat and drink? What foolishness is greater than this? For if they say that "the human nature of him is that which ate and drank," then we say, "and this is a lie on your part in any case, for if the Messiah is considered by you as both a divine nature and a human nature together, then he is two things; now if the human nature alone ate then only one of the combination of the two things ate and not the other." So admit that in that case half the Messiah ate and half the Messiah drank. Otherwise you [Christians] have lied anyway and your forefathers have lied in their saying "the Messiah ate," and you have attributed to the Messiah falsehood [as well] in his report about himself that he ate, since only half of him ate.

[All this shows that] the [Christian] community is altogether vile.

49. THE KING OF ENGLAND CONTEMPLATES CONVERSION TO ISLAM

One of the most unusual and implausible stories to emerge from medieval England about Islam involved the king of England, John (r. 1199–1216), converting to Islam and turning England into a Muslim fief. John's historical legacy has often been a matter of debate among historians, as his reign was quite turbulent. In 1204, John lost a significant portion of his patrimony when the French wrested Normandy from his control. The efforts to recover Normandy forced John into high taxation and other tactics that led his barons to despise him. Ultimately, they revolted in 1215 and forced John to the negotiating table to seal the Magna Carta, *which limited royal power in England. The events described by the source below supposedly take place during these difficult times, in 1213, when John, beset by enemies, sought to find allies in the Islamic world. The story comes from the work of Matthew Paris, one of the most famous of all medieval English chroniclers, but one who despised John. The story of John's contemplated conversion depicted by Matthew Paris is meant to paint the king as a tyrant and a betrayer to his faith and is almost certainly false. It is best read as an indictment of John's character. Interestingly, Murmelius, the north African emir to whom John allegedly sent his ambassadors was Muhammad an-Nāsir (r. 1199–1213), the ruler of the Almohads. Even if the story about John's possible conversion and embassy were true, it is unlikely that an-Nāsir would have been able to provide him any assistance, as he had just suffered the disastrous defeat at Las Navas de Tolosa (see Doc. 24).*

Source: trans. J.A. Giles, *Roger of Wendover's Flowers of History*, 2 vols. (London: Henry G. Bohn, 1849; repr. 1968), II: 283–86.

He therefore immediately sent secret messengers, namely, the knights Thomas Hardington and Ralph Fitz-Nicholas, and Robert of London a clerk, to the emir Murmelius the great king of Africa, Morocco, and Spain, who was commonly called Miramumelinus, to tell him that he would voluntarily give up to him himself and his kingdom, and if he pleased would hold it as tributary from him; and that he would also abandon the Christian faith, which he considered false, and would faithfully adhere to the law of Muhammad. When the aforesaid messengers arrived at the court of the above-named prince, they found at the first gate some armed knights keeping close guard over it with drawn swords. At the second door, which was that of the palace, they found a larger number of knights, armed to the teeth, more handsomely dressed, and stronger and more noble than the others, and these closely guarded this entrance with swords drawn: and at the door of the inner room there was a still greater number, and, according to appearance, stronger and fiercer than the former ones. Having at length been led in peaceably by leave of the emir himself, whom they called the great king, these messengers on behalf of their lord the king of England saluted him with reverence, and fully explained the reason of their coming, at the same time handing him their king's letter, which an interpreter, who came at a summons from him, explained to him. When he understood its purport, the king, who was a man of middle age and height, of manly deportment, eloquent and circumspect in his conversation, then closed the book he had been looking at, for he was seated at his desk studying. At length after deliberating as it were for a time with himself he modestly replied, "I was just now looking at the book of a wise Greek and a Christian named Paul, which is written in Greek, and his deeds and words please me much; one thing however concerning him displeases me, and that is, that he did not stand firm to the faith in which he was born, but turned to another like a deserter and a waverer. And I say this with regard to your lord the king of the English, who abandons the most pious and pure law of the Christians, under which he was born, and desires, flexible and unstable that he is, to come over to our faith." And he added, "The omniscient and omnipotent God knows that, were I without a law, I would choose that law before all others, and having accepted it would strictly keep it."

He then inquired what was the condition of the king of England and his kingdom; to which Thomas, as the most eloquent of the messengers, replied: "The king is illustriously and nobly descended from great kings, and his territory is rich, and abounds with all kinds of wealth, in agriculture, pastures, and woods; and from it also every kind of metal may be obtained by smelting. Our people are handsome and ingenious, and are skilled in three languages, the Latin, French, and English, as well as in every liberal and mechanical pursuit.

Our country, however, does not of itself produce any quantity of vineyards or olive trees, nor fir trees, but of these it procures an abundance from adjoining countries by way of trade. The climate is salubrious and temperate; it is situated between the west and the north; and, receiving heat from the west, and cold from the north, it enjoys a most agreeable temperature. It is surrounded entirely by the sea, whence it is called the queen of islands. The kingdom has, from times of old, been governed by an anointed king, and our people are free and manly, and acknowledge the domination of no one except God. Our church and the services of our religion are more venerated there than in any part of the world, and it is peacefully governed by the laws of the pope and of the king."

The king at the conclusion of this speech drew a deep sigh and replied: "I never read or heard that any king possessing such a prosperous kingdom subject and obedient to him, would thus voluntarily ruin his sovereignty by making tributary a country that is free, by giving to a stranger that which is his own, by turning happiness to misery, and thus giving himself up to the will of another, conquered as it were without a wound. I have rather read and heard from many that many would procure liberty for themselves at the expense of streams of their blood, which is a praiseworthy action; but now I hear that your wretched lord, a sloth and a coward, who is even worse than nothing, wishes, from a free man to become a slave, who is the most wretched of all human beings." After this he asked, although contemptuously, what was his age, size, and strength; in reply he was told that he was fifty, entirely hoary, strong in body, not tall, but rather compact and of a form suited for strength. The king on hearing this, said: "His youthful and manly valor has fermented, and now begins to grow cool; within ten years, if he lives so long, his valor will fail him before he accomplishes any arduous enterprise; if he should begin now he would fall to decay, and would be good for nothing; for a man of fifty sinks imperceptibly, but one of sixty gives evident signs of decaying. Let him again obtain peace for himself and enjoy rest." The emir, then, after reading over all the questions and answers of the messengers, after a short silence burst into a laugh, as a sign of indignation, and refused King John's offer in these words: "That king is of no consideration, but is a petty king, senseless and growing old, and I care nothing about him; he is unworthy of any alliance with me;" and, regarding Thomas and Ralph with a grim look, he said: "Never come into my presence again, and may your eyes never again behold my face; the fame, or rather the infamy of that foolish apostate, your master, breathes forth a most foul stench to my nostrils."

The messengers were then going away with shame, when the emir beheld Robert the clerk, who was the third of the messengers, and who was a small dark man, with one arm longer than the other, and having fingers all misshapen, namely, two sticking together, and with a face like a Jew. Thinking, therefore, that such a contemptible looking person would not be sent to manage a difficult business unless he were wise and clever, and well understood it, and seeing his cowl and tonsure, and finding by it that he was a clerk, the king ordered him to be called; for when the others had been speaking he had till now stood silent at a distance from him. He therefore kept him and sent away the others, and then had a long secret interview with him, the particulars of which the said Robert afterwards disclosed to his friends.

The said king asked him if King John was a man of moral character, and if he had brave sons, and if he possessed great generative power; adding that, if Robert told him a lie in these matters, he would never believe a Christian again, especially a clerk. Robert then, on his word as a Christian, promised to give true answers to all the questions which he put to him. He therefore answered affirmatively that John was a tyrant rather than a king, a destroyer rather than a governor, an oppressor of his own people, and a friend to strangers, a lion to his own subjects, a lamb to foreigners and those who fought against him; for, owing to his slothfulness, he had lost the duchy of Normandy and many other of his territories, and moreover was eager to lose the kingdom of England or to destroy it; that he was an insatiable extorter of money, and an invader and destroyer of the possessions of his own natural subjects; he had begotten few strong children, or rather none at all, but only such as took after their father; he had a wife who was hateful to him and who hated him; an incestuous, evil disposed, adulterous woman, and of these crimes she had been often found guilty, on which the king ordered her paramours to be seized and strangled with a rope on her bed; yet nevertheless this same king was envious of many of his nobles and relations, and violated their marriageable daughters and sisters; and in his observance of the Christian religion he is wavering and distrustful, as you have heard.

When the king emir heard all this, he not only disdained John as he had before done, but detested him; and, according to his own law cursed him, adding, "Why do the wretched English permit such a man to reign, and lord it over them? They are indeed effeminate and servile." Robert replied: "The English are the most patient of men until they are offended and injured beyond endurance; but now, like a lion or an elephant, when he feels himself hurt or sees his blood, they are enraged, and are proposing and endeavoring, although late, to shake the yoke of the oppressor from their necks." When the king emir heard this, he blamed the too easy patience of the English, which the interpreter, who had been present all the time, rightly asserted to be fear. The said king conversed on many other subjects besides this with Robert, all which the latter afterwards told to his friends in England. He then made him several costly presents of gold and silver, various kinds of jewels and silks, and dismissed him on friendly terms; but the other messengers he neither saluted when they left him, nor did he honor them with any presents. They then returned home and told John all that they had seen and heard, on which he wept in bitterness of spirit at being despised by the king emir, and at being balked in his purpose. Robert however liberally regarded the king from the foreign gifts bestowed on him, so that it was evident he had been received more favorably than the others, though at first he had been repulsed and kept silence; on which account the king honored him more than the others, and by way of reward this wicked extortioner bestowed on him the charge of the abbacy of St-Alban's, although it was not vacant, so that this transgressor of the faith remunerated his own clerk with the property of another. This Robert then, without consulting, yea even against the will of the temporary abbot, John de Cell, a most religious and most learned man, seized on everything which was then in the church and the convent at pleasure, and appropriated it to his own use; and in each bailiwick, which we call obediences, he appointed a porter, as a careful and resolute searcher of everything, by which means the aforesaid clerk, Robert, cheated that house of more than a thousand marks.

50. SAINT FRANCIS PREACHES TO THE SULTAN OF EGYPT

Francis of Assisi (1181–1226), founder of the Franciscan Order, was born into a well-off family in Assisi, Italy. Francis lived a relatively carefree existence until his early twenties, when he began to grow disillusioned with his life and its surroundings. A series of spiritual crises led him to abandon his previous life and embrace the life of a mystic, ascetic, beggar, and preacher, and he soon began to attract like-minded young men, who had grown weary of materialism and sought to live a more spiritual life. In 1210, Pope Innocent III approved the fledgling group as an order of the Church. As the Franciscans took their place in the ranks of the Church, many of them, including Francis, were deeply influenced by those who sought martyrdom by preaching Christianity. Seeking to end the crusades by converting Muslims to Christianity, or perhaps to gain martyrdom spreading the word of Christ, Francis launched his first mission in the Islamic world in 1212, when he tried to reach Jerusalem. Cut short by shipwreck, he tried again the following year, this time with a mission to Morocco, but this expedition also failed. Finally, in 1219, in the midst of the Fifth Crusade, Francis made his way to the crusader camp outside the Egyptian city of Damietta. From there he made his way to the sultan of Egypt, who, according to most contemporary sources, welcomed him, listened to what he had to say, and then sent him on his way, without giving Francis his sought-after martyrdom.

Source: trans. Lawrence Cunningham, *Brother Francis: An Anthology of Writings by and about St. Francis of Assisi* (New York: Harper & Row, 1972), 43–45.

Saint Francis, fired by his zeal for Christ and a desire for martyrdom, once took twelve holy companions and journeyed across the ocean to go directly to the sultan of Egypt. When he arrived at the territory of the Saracens, the passes were guarded by ferociously cruel men who allowed no Christian to pass alive. However, it pleased God to save them all from death, but they were beaten, bound, and taken in chains to the sultan.

Before the sultan Saint Francis, filled with the Holy Spirit, preached the faith of Christ so fervently that he was even prepared to be tested by fire. The sultan was quite touched by this devotion, by his steadfast faith, and by the utter worldlessness that he saw in him. Saint Francis would not accept any gift, even though he was the poorest of men. He was concerned only to suffer willingly for his faith. The sultan, as a result of this, listened to him willingly, granted both he and his companions permission to preach where they wished, and invited him to come often to see him. He also gave them a safe-conduct so that they would not be harmed by his followers

Armed with this permission, Saint Francis sent his companions two by two to different parts of the country to preach the faith of Christ. He chose one area and with a brother went there. On arrival, they stopped at an inn to rest. At the inn, there was a woman, beautiful in body but tainted in soul, who tempted Saint Francis to sin. Saint Francis said, "I accept your proposition. Let us be off to bed." She led him to a room, and Saint Francis said to her, "I will show you a beautiful bed." There was a great fire there in the fireplace, and Saint Francis, rapt by the Spirit, stripped off his clothes and entered the fire and then invited the girl to likewise undress and come join him in that beautiful spot.

Saint Francis stood in that fire for a long time with a smiling face and was neither burned nor even scorched. The girl was so overcome by this miracle and so penitent in her heart for her sin that she not only repented her evil but converted perfectly to the faith of Christ, and through her many other souls were saved in that area.

After a bit Saint Francis realized that he could do no more in those parts and, through the intervention of divine guidance, decided to send all of his companions back to the Christian lands. All together they went back to the sultan to make their good-byes. The sultan said to him, "Francis, I would most happily embrace the faith of Christ, but I fear to do so now. For if those about me heard of it, they would kill not only me but you and all your companions. Since there is so much good that you can do and there are so many grave duties that I must discharge, I am unwilling to provoke either your death or mine. So tell me what I must do to be saved, and I will follow your advice as best I can."

Saint Francis responded, "My lord, I must go now and return to my country. After my return, when by the grace of God my death has come, and I have gone to heaven, I will send you two friars who will come to you to baptize you in the name of Christ, and so you will be saved. My Lord Jesus Christ has revealed this to me. In the interim, free yourself from all entanglements so that when the grace of God comes, he may find you devout and faithful." This the sultan promised, and this he did.

After this, Saint Francis and his companions returned to their land, and after a time Francis died and rendered his soul to God. The sultan, informed of the death, set guards at all the frontiers with instructions that if two men should come with clothing similar to that of Saint Francis, they should be brought to the sultan without the least delay to bring him the promised salvation. In the meantime, Saint Francis appeared to two friars and told them to go across the ocean to the sultan and bring him the long-sought-after salvation. They immediately complied, and the guards on seeing them brought them to the sultan. The sultan received them with great joy and said, "Now I know that the good God has sent his servants for my salvation, just as Saint Francis promised me after his divine revelation." Receiving the instruction of the Faith of Christ, he was baptized by the brothers and regenerated in Christ. He later died of his illness, and his soul was saved by the merits and intervention of Saint Francis. In the praise of Christ. Amen.

51. MUSLIMS AND CHRISTIANS DEFEND MONOTHEISM

One of the most remarkable religious exchanges involving Christians and Muslims in the Middle Ages took place far away from the Mediterranean and was recorded by a Christian friar named William of Rubruck. In 1253, in the aftermath of the failed Seventh Crusade, Louis IX, king of France (r. 1226–70), sent William and a handful of companions as ambassadors to the Mongols. Their mission was of a religious nature, seeking to convert the Mongols to Christianity. Upon departing from Constantinople, they made their way from one Mongol khanate to another, starting with that of Sartach Khan (great-grandson of Genghis Khan) and then proceeding to the court of Batu Khan (ruler of the Golden Horde), until finally they reached Karakorum, the court of Mongke, the great khan (r. 1251–59). The European missionaries were surprised to find numerous Nestorian Christians in the great khan's court. During their stay, Mongke invited William to participate in a religious debate with the local Tuins (either Taoists or Buddhists) and Muslims. As the Tuins were polytheists, William, the Nestorians, and the Muslims banded together to defend the God of Abraham.

Source: trans. William Woodville Rockhill, *The Journey of William of Rubruck to the Eastern Parts of the World, 1253–1255* (London: Hakluyt Society, 1900), 226–35; rev. Jarbel Rodriguez.

The next day, which was Sunday before Pentecost [24 May], they took me to court and the grand secretaries of the court came to me, and one was the Moal who handed the khan his cup, and the others were Saracens, and they inquired on the part of the khan why I had come. Then I repeated what has previously been said; how I had come to Sartach, and from Sartach to Batu, and how Batu had sent me thither. Then I said to him, "I have nothing to say from the part of any man. [This he must have known from what Batu had written to him.] I have only to speak the words of God, if he wishes to hear them." They interrupted me, asking what words of God I wished to speak, thinking that I wanted to foretell some piece of good fortune to him, as many others do. I replied to them, "If you want me to speak the words of God to him, procure for me the interpreter." They said, "We have sent for him, but speak [now] through this one as well as you can. We understand you very well." And they urged me greatly that I should speak. So I said, "Of him unto whom much has been given much shall be required. And furthermore, of him to whom much has been given much love is required. By these words of God I teach Mongke, for God hath given him great power, and the riches which he has were not given him by the idols of the Tuins, but by Almighty God, who made heaven and earth, in whose hand are all kingdoms, and who removes it [power] from one nation to another on account of the sins of men. So if he shall love him, it shall be well with him, if otherwise, he must know that God will require all things of him to the last farthing." Then one of the Saracens said, "Is there anyone who does not love God?" I replied, "God says, 'If one loves me, he keeps my commandments, and he who loves me not keeps not my commandments.' So he who keeps not the commandments of God loves not God." Then he said, "Have you been to heaven, that you know the commandments of God?" "No," I replied, "but he has given them from heaven to holy men, and finally he descended from heaven to teach us, and we have them in the Scriptures and we see by men's works when they keep them or not." Then he said, "Do you wish, then, to say that Mongke Khan does not keep the commandments of God?" I said to him, "Let the dragoman [translator] come, as you have said, and I will, in the presence of Mongke, if it pleases him, recite the commandments of God, and he shall judge for himself whether he keeps them or not." Then they went away, and told him that I had said that he was an idolater, or Tuin, and that he did not keep God's commandments.

The next day [25 May] [the Khan] sent his secretaries to me, who said, "Our lord sends us to you to say that you are here Christians, Saracens, and Tuins. And each of you says that his doctrine is the best, and his writings—that is, books—the truest. So he wishes that you shall all meet together, and make a comparison, each one writing down his precepts, so that he himself may be able to know the truth." Then I said, "Blessed be God, who put this in the khan's heart. But our Scriptures tell us, the servant of God should not dispute, but should show mildness to all, so I am ready, without disputation or contention, to give reason for the faith and hope of the Christians, to the best of my ability." They wrote down my words, and carried them back to him. Then it was told the Nestorians that they should look to themselves, and write down what they wished to say, and likewise to the Saracens, and in the same way to the Tuins.

The next day [26 May] he again sent secretaries, who said, "Mongke Khan wishes to know why you have come to these parts." I replied to them, "He must know it by Batu's letters." Then they said, "The letters of Batu have been lost, and he has forgotten what Batu wrote to him; so he would know from you." Then feeling safer I said, "It is the duty of our faith to preach the Gospel to all men, so when I heard of the fame of the Moal people, I was desirous of coming to them, and while this desire was on me, we heard that Sartach was a Christian. So I turned my footsteps toward him. And the lord king of the French sent him letters containing kindly words, and among other things he bore witness to what kind of men we were, and requested that he would allow us to remain among the men of Moal. Then he [Sartach] sent us to Batu, and Batu sent us to Mongke Khan, so we have begged him, and do again beg him, to permit us to remain."

They wrote all these things down, and carried it back to him on the morrow.

Then he again sent them to me, saying, "The khan knows well that you have no mission to him, but that you have come to pray for him, like other righteous priests, but he would know if ever any ambassadors from you have come to us, or any of ours gone to you." Then I told them all about David and Friar Andrew, and they, putting it all down in writing, reported it back to him.

Then he again sent them to me, saying, "You have stayed here a long while, [the khan] wishes you to go back to your own country, and he has inquired whether you will take an ambassador of his with you." I replied to them, "I would not dare take his envoys outside his own dominions, for there is a hostile country between us and you, and seas and mountains, and I am but a poor monk, so I would not venture to take them under my leadership." And they, having written it all down, went back.

Pentecost eve came [30 May]. The Nestorians had written a whole chronicle from the creation of the world to the Passion of Christ, and passing over the Passion, they had touched on the Ascension and the resurrection of the dead and on the coming to judgment, and in it there were some censurable statements, which I pointed out to them. As for us, we simply wrote out the symbol of the mass, "Credo in unum Deum [I believe in one God]." Then I asked them how they wished to proceed. They said they would discuss in the first place with the Saracens. I showed them that that was not a good plan, for the Saracens agreed with us in saying that there is one God, "So you have [in them] a help against the Tuins." They agreed with this. Then I asked them if they knew how idolatry had arisen in the world, and they were in ignorance of it. Then I told them, and they said, "Tell them these things, then let us speak, for it is a difficult matter to talk through an interpreter." I said to them, "Try how you will manage against them; I will take the part of the Tuins, and you will maintain that of the Christians. We will suppose I belong to that sect, because they say that God is not; now prove that God is." For there is a sect there which says that whatever spirit [*anima*] and whatever virtue is in anything, is the God of that thing, and that God exists not otherwise. Then the Nestorians were unable to prove anything, but only to tell what the Scriptures tell. I said, "They do not believe in the Scriptures. You tell me one thing, and they tell another." Then I advised them to let me in the first place meet them, so that, if I should be confounded, they would still have a chance to speak. If they should be confounded, I should not be able to get a hearing after that. They agreed to this.

We were assembled then on Pentecost eve at our oratory, and Mongke Khan sent three secretaries who were to be umpires, one a Christian, one a Saracen, and one a Tuin. And it was published aloud, "This is the order of Mongke, and let no one dare say that the commandment of God differs from it. And he orders that no one shall dare wrangle or insult any other, or make any noise by which this business shall be interfered with, on penalty of his head." Then all were silent. And there was a great concourse of people there, for each side had called thither the most learned of its people, and many others had also assembled.

Then the Christians put me in the middle, telling the Tuins to speak with me. Then they—and there was a great congregation of them—began to murmur against Mongke Khan, for no other khan had ever attempted to pry into their secrets. Then they opposed to me one who had come from Cathay, and who had his interpreter; and I had the son of Master William, who began by saying to me, "Friend, if you think you are going to be hushed up, look for a more learned one than yourself." I remained silent. Then [the Tuin] inquired by what I wished to begin the discussion, by the subject how the world was made, or what becomes of the soul after death. I replied to him, "Friend, this should not be the beginning of our talk. All things proceed from God. He is the fountain-head of all things, so we must first speak of God, of whom you think differently from us, and Mongke Khan wishes to know who holds the better belief." The umpires decided that this was right.

He wished to begin with these questions, as they consider them to be the weightiest; for they all hold this heresy of the Manicheans, that one half of things is evil, and the other half good, and that there are two [elemental] principles, and, as to souls, they believe that all pass from one body into another. Thus, a most learned priest among the Nestorians questioned me [once] concerning the souls of animals, whether they could escape to any place where, after death, they would not be forced to labor. In confirmation furthermore of this error, as I was told by Master William, there had been brought from Cathay a boy who, from the size of his body, was not more than twelve years old, but who was capable of all forms of reasoning, and who said of himself that he had been incarnated three times; he knew how to read and write.

So I said to the Tuin, "We believe firmly in our hearts and we confess with our mouths that God is, and that there is only one God, one in perfect unity. What do you believe?" He said, "Fools say that there is only one God, but the wise say that there are many. Are there not great lords in your country, and is not this Mongke Khan a greater lord? So it is of them, for they are different in different regions."

I said to him, "You choose a poor example, in which there is no comparison between man and God. According to that every mighty man can call himself god in his own country." And as I was about to destroy the comparison, he interrupted me, asking, "Of what nature is your God, of whom you say that there is none other?" I replied, "Our God, besides whom there is none other, is omnipotent, and therefore requires the aid of none other, while all of us require his aid. It is not thus with man. No man can do everything, and so there must be several lords in the world, for no one can do all things. So likewise, he knows all things, and therefore requires no councilor, for all wisdom comes of him. Likewise, he is the supreme good, and wants not of our goods. But we live, move, and are in him. Such is our God, and one must not consider him otherwise."

"It is not so," he replied. "Though there is one [God] in the sky who is above all others, and of whose origin we are still ignorant, there are ten others under him, and under these latter is another lower one. On the earth they are in infinite number." And as he wanted to spin some other yarns, I asked him of this highest god, whether he believed he was omnipotent, or whether [he believed this] of some other god. Fearing to answer, he asked, "If your God is as you say, why does he make the half of things evil?" "That is not true," I said. "He who makes evil is not God. All things that are, are good." At this all, the Tuins were astonished, and they wrote it down as false or impossible. Then he asked, "Whence then comes evil?" "You put your question badly," I said. "You should in the first place inquire what is evil, before you ask whence it comes. But let us go back to the first question, whether you believe that any god is omnipotent; after that I will answer all you may wish to ask me."

He sat for a long time without replying, so that it became necessary for the secretaries who were listening on the part of the Khan to tell him to reply. Finally, he answered that no god was omnipotent. With that, the Saracens burst out into a loud laugh. When silence was restored, I said, "Then no one of your gods can save you from every peril, for occasions may arise in which he has no power. Furthermore, no one can serve two masters. How can you serve so many gods in heaven and earth?" The audience told him to answer, but he remained speechless. And as I wanted to explain the unity of the divine essence and the Trinity to the whole audience, the Nestorians of the country said to me that it sufficed, for they wanted to talk. I gave in to them, but when they wanted to argue with the Saracens, the [Tuins] answered them, "We concede your religion is true, and that everything is true that is in the Gospel: so we do not want to argue any point with you." And they confessed that in all their prayers they besought God to grant them to die as Christians die.

There was present there an old priest of the Iugurs, who say there is one god, though they make idols, they [the Nestorians] spoke at great length with him, telling him of all things down to the coming of the Antichrist into the world, and by comparisons demonstrating the Trinity to him and the Saracens. They all listened without making any contradiction, but no one said, "I believe; I want to become a Christian." When this was over, the Nestorians as well as the Saracens sang with a loud voice, while the Tuins kept silence, and after that they all drank deeply.

52. PLANS TO RECOVER THE HOLY LAND

The fall of Acre, the last Christian outpost in the Holy Land, in 1291 led to numerous suggestions for a new crusade to the East. It was also clear to many of the crusading proponents that new ideas were needed, as a direct attack on Jerusalem was likely to meet with failure. One of the most unusual and original proposals was put forth by Pierre Dubois, a French pamphleteer and political activist who directed much of his propaganda at the French king, Philip IV, the Fair (r. 1285–1314). Dubois put forth his ideas for a new crusade in a pamphlet entitled The Recovery of the Holy Land. *Central to any new crusading enterprise, Dubois argued, was the establishment of a new school system run by a foundation that trained boys and girls for future service in the East. These future crusaders were to be trained in foreign languages, notably Greek and Arabic, administration, preaching, medicine, and science. Among the possibilities Dubois imagined for the female graduates was for them to be given in marriage to Muslim rulers and nobles. The girls would then use their training and education to try to convince their Muslim husbands to convert to Christianity.*

Source: trans. Walter I. Brandt, Pierre Dubois, *The Recovery of the Holy Land* (New York: Columbia University Press, 1956), 124, 138–39.

69. While others are pursuing a policy of inflicting injury on the Saracens, making war upon them, seizing their lands, and plundering their other property, perhaps girls trained in the proposed schools may be given as wives to the Saracen chiefs, although preserving their faith lest they participate in their husbands' idolatry. By their efforts, with the help of God and the preaching disciples so they may have assistance from Catholics—for they cannot rely on the Saracens— their husbands might be persuaded and led to the Catholic faith. Little by little our faith might be made known among them. Their wives would strive the more zealously for this because each of them has many wives. All the wealthy

and powerful among them lead a voluptuous life to the disadvantage of their wives, anyone of whom would rather have a man to herself (nor is it to be wondered at) than that seven or more wives should share one husband. It is on that account, as I have generally heard from merchants who frequent their lands, that the women of that sect would easily be strongly influenced toward our manner of life, so that each man would have only one wife....

... 85. All the girls of the foundation, like the males, should be instructed in Latin grammar and afterwards in logic and in one foreign language; then in the fundamentals of the natural sciences, and finally in surgery and medicine. Such instruction beyond grammar and surgery is, I judge, for those who will be found more teachable and apt for it than others; too, they will be instructed only in those parts of each science which have a bearing on medicine and surgery, and in a manner as far as possible more understandable, plainer, and easier, owing to the weakness of their sex. Because they mature more rapidly than males, they more quickly attain such perfection as is possible for them, which is a mark of the frailty of their natural powers. We see the same thing in trees and other plants; as the Philosopher [Aristotle] says, speaking of this matter in his book On Animals, "The short-lived mature more rapidly."

Some of the more skillful of these girls who seem too delicate for crossing the sea might remain with us permanently to have charge of others. With their help the others will be cared for more faithfully and will be instructed more fully in both the theoretical and the practical knowledge of surgery and medicine, and in those matters known to be related to the art and handicraft of apothecaries.

[86.] The girls who are destined to marry those who do not adhere to the articles of our faith, as the Roman Church holds, teaches, and observes them, ought to be instructed in the articles as held by the Roman Church so that they may carry with them all the articles briefly and plainly written in a manner they can comprehend adequately. The same knowledge would not harm, it might even benefit, the several disciples of the aforesaid foundation who have not been more fully instructed in theology. Moreover, in the several schools of medicine and surgery to be established for girls, it would be well that two girls, more learned in medicine and surgery than the others, and more experienced in those arts, remain to be of service. They will instruct the others in both theory and practice so that when the girls leave school they may have had some practical experience as well as theoretical knowledge. In school, rather than afterwards, they can learn more easily and get much experience, without which such theoretical knowledge would be of little use, as witness the Philosopher, who says, "We have seen that in human affairs those who have experience without theoretical knowledge progress much further than those who have theoretical knowledge of their subject without practical experience."

53. A RESPONSE TO CHRISTIANITY

Among the most important Muslim polemics against Christianity is the Al-Jawab al-Sahih li-man Bad-dal Din al-Masih *(The Correct Answer to Those Who Changed the Religion of Christ) by Taqi al-Din Ahmad ibn Taymiyya (1263–1328), a legal scholar, theologian, and resident of Damascus, written around 1317. The work was a response to a Christian apology written by Paul of Antioch in 1150 and is deeply concerned not just with what ibn Taymiyya saw as the errors of the Christians, but with how similar errors could also endanger Muslim communities. As such, it stands as a cautionary tale for Muslims, who were ultimately his primary concern. By pointing out how Christians had taken the message of Christ and corrupted or misunderstood it, he was warning Muslims of pitfalls in their own spiritual development.*

Source: trans. Thomas F. Michel, *A Muslim Theologian's Response to Christianity: Ibn Taymiyya's Al-Jawab al-Sahih* (Delmar, NY: Caravan Books, 1984), 198–209.

It should be known that the cause of error among Christians and similar extremists—like the extremism of pious Muslims and Shi'a—are basically three:

1. Complex, general, ambiguous expressions handed down from the prophets. They hold fast to these and forego straightforward univocal expressions. Whatever passage they hear which has in it some obscure meaning for them they hold firmly to it and bring it to bear upon their belief, even if there is no indication for that. The clear-cut expressions opposed to that they either ignore or they interpret as do those in error. They follow ambiguity in rational and revealed proofs and stray from what is straightforward and unambiguous in both.

2. Extraordinary wonders. They suppose them to be signs when they are demonic affairs. It is through these things that many wayward idolaters and others have gone astray. For example, the demons enter into the idols and speak to people; demons also disclose to sorcerers unseen matters, and there is no doubt that they report falsehood to them as well. Like that also are various kinds of behavior which occur from the demons.

3. Information handed down to them which they suppose to be truthful, but which is false. Aside from these things, Christians and other people in error have no sound rational argumentation or correct revealed information for their false beliefs or any sign from the prophets. If they speak from rational argument, they use general ambiguous passages. Were they to seek an explanation of the meanings of those passages and the distinction between what is true and false in them, the deception and ambiguity which is in them would become clear. If they speak

from what is handed down as revealed, either their information would be correct but not a proof for their erroneous beliefs, or else it would not be established [as sound] but rather forged.

Similarly, the supernatural wonders which they mention either are correct and were manifested at the hand of a prophet, like the miracles of Christ and other prophets before him like Elijah and Elisha and the miracles of Moses—all these are true—or they would have been manifested at the hand of upright persons like the apostles. This would not make it necessary that these latter be inerrant like the prophets. The prophets are inerrant in what they communicate, and it cannot be imagined that they speak about God anything but the truth, or that there resides in their teaching anything but the truth, either intentionally or accidentally. But with upright persons, some one of them may err and make a mistake despite the manifestation of wonders at his hands. He would not thereby cease to be an upright individual. It would not be necessary that he be inerrant if he had not claimed inerrancy or brought the signs which indicate that. If he claimed inerrancy and was not a prophet, then he would be lying and would undoubtedly manifest his falseness. The demons would associate themselves with him and lead him astray so that God's statement would apply to him:

Shall I inform you upon whom the devils descend? They descend upon every sinful, false one. [Quran 26:221–22]

Among the Christians it is handed down in the Gospels that the one who was crucified and buried in the grave was seen by some of the apostles and others after he was buried. He rose from his grave two or three times. He showed them the place of the nails and said, "Do not suppose that I am a demon." If this [report] is sound, then that was a demon who claimed he was Christ and thereby deceived them. Things like that have happened to many people in our time and in earlier times. For example, there were people in Palmyra who saw a huge person flying in the air who appeared to them several times in various kinds of dress. He said to them "I am Christ the son of Mary" and gave them commands which it would have been impossible for Christ to have commanded for them. He arrived among the people and they saw clearly that he was a demon intending to lead them astray.

Among other people also, someone comes to the grave of someone he extols and considers to be among the upright or others, and sometimes he sees the grave open and a person in the likeness of that individual emerge from it, and at other times he sees that individual enter the grave. Sometimes he sees him either riding or walking, entering the place of that dead person, like the dome built over the grave. Sometimes he sees him emerging from that place and supposes that that is the upright man or he may suppose that this is a person to whom he can appeal for help, and so he goes to him. But that is a demon imitating his likeness.

This has occurred to more than one person I know. Sometimes people seek help from a person either dead or absent whom they suppose to be good. When he comes, they see him with their own eyes. He may speak to them and he may fulfill some of their needs. They suppose him to be the dead person, but it is only a demon who claimed that he was that person. However, it is not the person.

There are many stories of people to whom someone comes after death in the likeness of the dead person, who speaks to them, fulfills their debts, and returns back those things entrusted to his custody and informs them about the dead. They suppose that he is the dead person himself who has come to them, but it is only a demon impersonating his likeness.

This is extremely common, especially in idolatrous countries like India. Among these people you may see someone [who has died] under his bed taking the hand of his son at the funeral. One of them might say, "When I die do not summon anyone to wash me, for I am coming from this direction to wash myself." After his death someone comes in the air in his likeness. The one to whom he entrusted his final command thinks that he has come, but it is only a demon impersonating his likeness.

Sometimes one of them sees a person flying in the air or of great size or someone who discloses to affairs of the unseen and things like that. He may say to him "I am al-Khidr" but that is a demon lying to that person. The one who sees him may be a person of religion, asceticism, and worship. This has happened to more than one.

Sometimes it is seen at the grave of a prophet or others that the dead person comes forth either from his chamber or from his grave and embraces the visitor and greets him. That is a demon impersonating his likeness.

Sometimes someone will come to the grave of some person and ask his permission about things. He asks him about [various] matters, and a person responds to him. He may see him or hear a voice or see a person, but that would be a demon to lead him astray.

While he is awake, someone may see persons either riding or on foot who say this is such-and-such a prophet—whether Abraham, Christ, or Muhammad— or this is such-and-such a righteous person—whether Abu Bakr or one of the apostles. This may be some individual who is believed to be upright—either Saint George or others whom the Christians extol. It may be one of the Muslim sheikhs. In reality that is a demon claiming that he is a prophet, that sheikh, that righteous individual, or that saint.

Things like this occur very often to many idolaters and Christians and to many Muslims. One of them sees a sheikh whom he supposes to be good who says to him "I am Sheikh So-and-so." It is only a demon. I know a great many things of this kind. I know more than one person who sought help from one of the dead or absent sheikhs, who saw someone who came to him while waking and helped him.

Something like this has happened to me and to someone I know. More than one person has mentioned that he sought my help from a distant country and that he saw me when I came to him. Some of them say, "I saw you riding in your own clothes and in your likeness." Some say, "I saw you on a mountain." Some say other things than that. I told them that I did not help them, and that that was only a demon impersonating my likeness to lead them astray since they were making a partner to God and praying to other than God.

Similarly, more than one person I know among our friends was appealed to for help from someone who supposed him to be good. Then that person saw him come to him and he fulfilled his request. My friend said, "And I don't know anything about that."

One of these sheikhs relates that he heard the voice of the person who was appealing to him for help and he answered him. Actually, the demons were making him hear a voice resembling that of the person who was calling upon him for assistance. The sheikh answered him back in his normal voice, and the demons made the one seeking help hear a voice which resembled that of the sheikh, so that the other thought that it was actually the voice of the sheikh.

This has occurred to someone I know who told me about it himself. He said, "The *jinni* who was addressing me went on addressing me with the voice of those who were imploring me for help, and he was addressing them in a voice like mine. He was appearing to me in something white the likes of what I would be asking about. He informed people that I had seen him and that he would come. But I did not see him [at all]; I only saw his likeness." The *jinn* do many things like this to those who invite them and swear by them.

Similarly the cross which Constantine saw among the stars and the cross which he saw another time are what the demons fashion and show to lead people astray. Demons have done what is even greater than that for the worshippers of idols.

In the same way whoever has stated that Christ came to him while he was awake and said that he was Christ [actually saw] one of the demons. Similar things have happened to more than one person. Satan only leads people astray and causes them to err by that in which he supposes they obey him. He speaks to Christians in what agrees with their religion. He addresses whatever wayward Muslim he confronts by that which agrees with his belief, and he hands on to him whatever he deems necessary for them in accordance with their belief.

For this reason he represents himself in the likeness of Saint George to whomever among the Christians seeks help from Saint George or in the likeness of whichever of the great men of their religion Christians seek for assistance—one of their patriarchs, bishops, or monks. To wayward Muslims seeking help from one of the sheikhs he represents himself in the likeness of that sheikh, as he showed himself to a group of people I know in my likeness and in the likeness of a group of sheikhs who mentioned it. He appears often in the guise of one of the dead. Sometimes he says "I am Sheikh 'Abd al-Qadir [al-Jiliani]," sometimes "I am Sheikh Abu al-Hajjaj al-Uqsuri," sometimes "I am Sheikh Adi," sometimes "I am Sheikh Ahmad al-Rifa'i," sometimes "I am Abu Maydan al-Maghribi." If he used to say "I am Christ" or Abraham or Muhammad, he could do so about others *a fortiori*.

The prophet said:

Whoever has seen me in sleep has truly seen me; for Satan cannot imitate my likeness.

In another account he said "in the likeness of the prophets." Thus the vision of the prophets in sleep is true, but the vision of the dead while awake is a *jinni* impersonating his likeness.

Some people call this the "spiritual nature" of the sheikh, while others call it his comrade. There are many demons who take someone's place or they may leave that person's likeness in some other place. Often the person [himself] and the demon appearing in his image are seen in two places [at once], or they may be seen standing on Mount Arafat while they are in their own land and have never left it.

People who do not know become confused, but sound reason knows that one body cannot be at one time in two places. Trustworthy people have seen that with their own eyes and do not doubt it. Thus a dispute may often arise between one group of people and the next, as has occurred more than once. One person believes what he has seen and witnessed, the next person believes in what sound [reason] shows him.

What is seen is a *jinni* impersonating the likeness of a human. Sense perception, if it is not accompanied by rational proofs which uncover the real natures of things, will only fall into much error. This kind of thing which is witnessed in external reality is different from what a person imagines within himself. This is something everyone knows, and all intelligent people know that they imagine things within themselves just as a sleeper fantasizes in his dream but knows that the picture existing in his imagination is not found in external reality.

The philosophers and many intelligent people know this, but many philosophers suppose the angels which the prophets saw and the speech which they heard to be of this kind. They suppose that the *jinn* which are seen are of this nature. They are ignorant and erring in this matter, just as those people were ignorant and erring who supposed that the cause of supernatural wonders was natural, psychological, or astrological powers, and that the difference between the prophet and the magician is only the good intention of the former and the presumed false intention of the latter. Except in that, the cause of the wonders of both of them are psychological or astrological powers. This rejection [of true prophethood] is false, as we have discussed at length elsewhere and have pointed out the ignorance and error of these people in other matters.

The existence of [true revelations] in external reality is established among those who have witnessed that outside the mind by trustworthy reports successively handed down. They know that these others are ignorant, erring people. They know that angels have appeared in the form of men, as they appeared to Abraham, Lot, and Mary in human form. Jibril used to appear to the prophet, sometimes in the form of Dahya al-Kalbi and at other times in the form of a bedouin. Many people saw him with their own eyes, whereas whatever is in the imagination of someone is not seen by others than him. Similarly Satan appeared to the idolaters in the form of Al-Sheikh al-Najdi and others, and he appeared to them on the day of Badr in the likeness of Suraqa ibn Malik ibn Ja'tham. When he saw the angels, he fled [Quran 8:48]. It is related from Ibn 'Abbas and others that he said:

> Iblis appeared among the army of demons. He had with him a banner in the likeness of that of the men from Mudallaj. Satan was in the likeness of Suraqa ibn Malik ibn Ju'shum. He said: There will be no victor from among mankind over you today, for I am a neighbor to you. Jibril drew near to Iblis, and when he saw him, his hand was in the hand of one of the idolaters' men, and Iblis withdrew his hand and headed for the rear—he and his people. The man said, "Hey Suraqa! Didn't you say you were a neighbor to us?" He said, "I see what you do not see; I fear God, for God is severe in punishment."

Ibn 'Abbas said, "That was when he saw the angels." Al-Dahhak said:

> Satan traveled with them with his banner and his army. He cast into the hearts of the idolaters that "No one will overcome you while you are fighting for your religion and the religion of your fathers."

Many people have been carried off by the *jinn* to a distant place. They have borne away many people to Arafat and to other places than Arafat. Should someone see one of these people in a land other than their own that would be someone [who was] carried off; sometimes it was a case of the *jinn* having carried him off and at other times of their having impersonated his likeness. This person would not be one of the God-fearing friends of God to whom were granted special favors [*karamat*], but he could be even an unbeliever or a dissolute person. I know many stories about that, but I will not go into the details here.

Among the idolaters and the Christians there are many things like that which they suppose to be in the nature of signs which belong to the prophets, but they are rather of the nature of what pertains to magicians and sorcerers. Whoever does not distinguish between the friends of the Merciful One and the friends of Satan and distinguish between the miracles of the prophets and the special favors of the upright on one hand, and the wonders of magicians and sorcerers on the other, whoever lumps them all together is in likelihood that the demons will make him confuse truth and falsehood. He will either reject the truth brought by the trustworthy prophets or will believe the falsehood spoken by unbelievers and mistaken individuals.

These matters are elaborated elsewhere. The point here is to elucidate this principle. Christian scholars accept this, and on this matter they have many reports of stories of the friends of Satan who opposed the friends of the Merciful One. These latter have proven false the affairs of the former. Moses proved false the magicians who opposed him with wonders, as is stated in the Torah. They [Christians] relate it about one individual or another, like the story of Simon Magus and the apostles.

If they accept this, they should admit that what they mention is of this kind. If it is opposed to what is established from the prophets, it is from Satan. It is not permissible to argue from anything which opposes the Laws of the prophets which have been established on them; rather, such people are of the same nature as the great Dajjal, against whom all the prophets warned. Even Noah warned his people [against him]. The Seal of the prophets [Muhammad] said;

There has never been a prophet but he has warned his community, so that even Noah warned his community. But I will tell you a statement about him which no prophet said to his community. He is one-eyed, but your Lord is not one-eyed. There is written between his eyes "unbeliever" [k-f-r] which every believer, literate or not, can read. He said: know that no one of you will see his Lord until he die.

All of this is established in the sound hadiths from the prophet. He has commanded his community to seek refuge in God from his [al-Dajjal's] machinations. He said:

If one of you is seated speaking the shahada [Muslim creed] during prayer, let him take refuge in God from four things: from the punishment of hell, from the punishment of the grave, from the machinations of life and death, and from the machination of the Anti-Christ al-Dajjal.

All the prophets warned against the liars who imitate the prophets. There are people who intend falsehood. Many people, however, do not intend it, but are deceived and err, reporting what they suppose to be the truth when it is not. They may see in a waking state what they suppose to be such-and-such a friend of God or a prophet, or Al-Khidr, when it is not.

Error is possible for everyone except the prophets, for they are inerrant. Therefore if anyone does not weigh his learning, his acts, his views, and his deeds by what is known from the prophets, he will go astray. We ask the great God that He guide us along the straight Path, the path of those on whom His blessing rests—prophets, the righteous, martyrs, doers of good works. May their goodness be a companion.

The supernatural occurrences by which the demons have led the sons of Adam astray, such as Satan appearing in the form of some dead or absent person, through which occurrences many people adhering to Islam as well as the People of the Book and others have fallen into error—these events are all based on two premises.

1. Those at whose hands such events occur are friends of God, or as Christians would say, "a great saint."

2. Those who perform such actions are inerrant, and everything they teach is true and everything they command is just.

It may be that what occur are not supernatural events at all, neither divine nor satanic, but it is possible that their perpetrator has performed some trick of the kind done by liars and charlatans. These liars and charlatans have deceived a great number of people who think that their tricks are a type of supernatural miracle. But they are not like that, just as the tricks related about the monks are not.

Someone has written a book about the tricks of the monks. There is the trick related about one of them who made water into oil. The oil was in a hidden cavity of a tower, so that if it ran low, he would pour water on it, and the oil would float to the top of the water, and those present would think that the water itself had changed into oil.

Similarly there is the trick told about them of the rising of the palm tree. Someone passed by a monk's hermitage, and below him there was a palm tree. Then the monk showed him the palm tree rise up until it towered over the monastery. He took the dates from it and then it descended until it was back in its customary position. Finally the man discovered the trick. He found the palm tree was on a boat in a low-lying place. If the monk released water on it, it would fill and the boat would rise; if he diverted the water to another place, the boat would go down.

Another trick related about them is that of putting *kohl* [a cosmetic] on the Virgin's eyes for tears. They put *kohl* in water moving with a very slight movement, which then flowed slowly so that it ran down the picture of the Virgin and came out her eyes. People thought that it was tears.

There is also the trick which they have performed with the picture which they call the icon in Saydnaya. It is their greatest place of pilgrimage after Calvary, where Christ's tomb is found, and Bethlehem, where he was born. The basis of the trick is palm branches dipped in fats so that they become greasy and fat begins to exude from the picture. It is produced naturally, but people think that it is a *baraka* [miraculous property] of the picture.

Another of their many tricks is the fire which crowds believe to be descending from heaven during their feast at Calvary. It is a ruse which more than one Muslim and Christian have witnessed, and have seen with their own eyes that the fire is naturally produced while the praying crowds believe that it has descended from heaven and blessed them. Actually it is merely an invention and deception performed by those in charge of the place.

There are many other tricks of the Christians like these; in all the extraordinary events which the Christians follow they are changing the religion of Christ. These things are either demonic wonders or clever absurdities in which there is nothing of the *karamat*—the miraculous favors granted to upright persons.

Similarly the heretics who are changing the religion of the messengers—the religion of Christ and the religion of Muhammad—adopt a religion not legislated by God and His messenger; they designate a path to God and may choose it in preference to the path which God and his Messenger have ordained. For example, they may prefer hearing tambourines and flutes to hearing the Book of God. There may occur to one of these people a satanic emotion and passion by which the demon deceives them until he speaks by the tongue of one of them a message which that person on regaining consciousness is unaware that he uttered. It is just like one of the *jinn* might speak through the voice of a madman. He may inform one of those present of something that person knows, but this is actually from Satan. When the demon departs from that person, he will not be aware of what he said.

There are those whom the devil will carry in the air and raise up before people. There are those who point at someone present and that person dies, becomes sick or stiff like a board. Others point at one of those present so that the demon deceives him and his mind ceases operation and becomes absent for a long time against his will. Still others either enter a fire or eat it and their bodies and hair are engulfed in flames. Some people are presented with food, drugs, liquor, saffron, or rosewater by the demons, while others are brought money which the devils have stolen elsewhere. Then if the money is parceled out by these people among those present, the money disappears, so that it is not possible to spend it.

There are other matters which would take too long to describe, as well as other people who have no one among the demons helping them with these things, and so they perform extraordinary ruses. Thus act the heretics who are changing the religion of the prophets—the religion of Christ or that of Muhammad—and those like them among the renegades, the wayward, the idolatrous apostates, and others like Musaylima the Liar, Al-Aswad al-ʿAnsi, Al-Harith al-Dimashqi, the pope of Rome, and others who perform satanic preternatural deeds.

Charlatans—and there are many of them—are not friends of God. Even if their wonders are of the demonic order like those of the sorcerers and magicians, they possess no satanic state [*hal*] but [perform] pointless deceptions. They depend on falsehood and deception, in contrast to those who associate with demons. There are those among them who can deceive one so that he thinks these wonders are of the type of supernatural gifts granted to the holy men, just as others among them know such things to be from the demons and yet perform them to accomplish their own goals. The point is that many wonders, whether those which are from demons or those which are clever tricks and ingenious feats, are often thought to be extraordinary gifts [*karamat*] of upright persons.

Those feats whose purpose is *shirk* [idolatry] and rebelliousness come only from the demons. For example, when someone engages in idolatrous worship of God, claiming a share in divine worship for the stars or some created person, dead or absent, or making decisions and swearing by unknown names whose meaning he does not know or which he knows to be names of demons, or having recourse to things of darkness and obscenity, whatever miraculous events occur from these practices are from Satan. This we have elaborated at length more than once.

The holy men, such as the holy men of this community and the apostles and others who followed the religion of Christ, have wondrous gifts, but the existence of wonders performed at the hands of holy men does not necessitate that these men be inerrant like the prophets. Rather, he is simply a holy man, a friend of God who has these wondrous gifts. Nevertheless, he may err or make an error in what he thinks, or in what he hears, relates, and sees, or in what he understands of the Books. This is the case for everyone except the prophets. There must be extracted from their opinion what is contrary to the prophets, and it must be renounced. It is necessary for people to put faith in everything the prophets disclosed concerning the unknown and to obey them in all they have commanded. God has obligated men to faith in everything which they brought, but did not obligate them to faith in all that others than they have brought [Quran 2:136; 2:177].

Therefore, Muslims are in agreement that whoever rejects a prophet whose prophethood is known is an apostate unbeliever. It is necessary that anyone who curses a prophet be killed. It is even necessary to put faith in everything all the prophets have brought, and not to distinguish between them by believing in some and rejecting others [Quran 4:150–51]. However, this is not the case with anyone other than the prophets, even though these others be messengers of the prophets and among the early great friends of God.

The error of the wayward among these people is based on two premises.

1. This person does wondrous deeds, therefore he is a friend of God.

2. It is not possible that a friend of God err, but it is necessary to put faith in all that he teaches and to obey all he commands.

Actually there is no human who should be believed in all that he teaches or obeyed in all that he commands, unless that person be a prophet. Of these two premises which we have mentioned, it may be that one of them is false, and it may be that both of them are false. A certain man may not be one of the friends of God, but his miraculous deeds might be from the demons. Conversely, he may be one of the friends of God, but as he is not inerrant, it would be possible that he make a mistake. Again he may not be one of the friends of God, or even be performing miraculous acts, but might be a master of tricks and deception.

Muslims and People of the Book agree on confessing two Christs—the Messiah of True Guidance of the line of David, and the False Messiah whom the People of the Book say to be of the line of Joseph. Muslims and Christians say that the Messiah of True Guidance is Jesus the son of Mary, whom God has already sent and will send again. Muslims say he will descend before the Resurrection Day and kill the False Messiah, break the cross, and kill the pig. Then there will not remain any religion but that of Islam, in which the People of the Book, Jews and Christians, will believe [Quran 4:159]. The correct opinion on which the majority agree is [that this will occur] before the death of Christ [Quran 43:61].

Christians, however, think that Christ is God and that he will come on the Resurrection Day to reckon up the good deeds and the bad. This is one of the cases in which they are in error. The Jews also confess the coming of the Messiah of True Guidance. He is coming, they say. But they claim that Jesus was not this Messiah because of their claim that he brought the corrupted religion of the Christians, and whoever brought that is false. Thus they await the two Messiahs.

54. RAMON LLULL AND BOCCACCIO

Christian/Muslim polemics did not always need to be antagonistic, as the two sources below illustrate. The first comes from the Book of the Gentile *by Ramon Llull, one of the critical figures of his age. Llull was born in Palma, Mallorca, part of the Crown of Aragon in 1232 (d. 1315). Over the course of his life, he was a troubadour, a government official, a member of the Franciscan Order, a linguist, a scholar, and a philosopher. He was an avowed believer in amicable dialogue between members of the different faiths, being fully convinced that when presented with a clear and logical argument, non-Christians would quickly convert to Christianity. It is in this spirit that he wrote the* Book of the Gentile, *in which three wise men, representing Judaism, Islam, and Christianity, each make a strong and convincing argument as to why the gentile should convert to his particular faith. The section below comes from the dramatic conclusion, as the gentile gets ready to announce his decision after hearing each of the wise men. Surprisingly, Llull never tells the reader the gentile's decision, leaving the whole question in ambiguity. A similar situation occurs in the third story of the first day of the* Decameron *by Giovanni Boccaccio (1313–75). As with the* Book of the Gentile, *Boccaccio leaves the question of which is the true faith uncertain and leaves it up to the reader to decide.*

Sources: trans. Anthony Bonner, *Selected Works of Ramon Llull (1232–1316)*, 2 vols. (Princeton, NJ: Princeton University Press, 1985), I: 300–3; trans. J.M. Rigg, *The Decameron of Giovanni Boccaccio* (London: George Routledge and Sons, 1920), 38–40, rev. Jarbel Rodriguez.

Llull: Book of the Gentile

How the Three Wise Men Took Leave of the Gentile

When the Gentile had finished his prayer, he went to the lovely spring and washed his hands and face, because of the tears he had shed, and dried himself with a white cloth he carried, the one he had formerly used to wipe away his continual tears of sorrow. He then sat down next to the three wise men and said: "Through God's grace and blessing, I happened to meet you gentlemen here where God saw fit to remember me and take me as his servant. Blessed be the Lord, therefore, and blessed be this place, and may God bless you, and blessed be God for making you want to come here! And in this place, where I have received such good fortune, in the presence of you gentlemen, I want to select and choose that religion which, by the grace of God and by your words, seems to me to be true. And in that religion I want to be, and I want to work for the rest of my life to honor and proclaim it."

When the Gentile had spoken thus and stood up in order to kneel, and kneeling, proclaim the religion he preferred, he saw far away, coming through the forest, two gentiles who were from his land, whom he knew, and who were in the same error in which he had once been. And the Gentile therefore said to the three wise men that he wanted to await the arrival of these two Gentiles, so that he could proclaim the true religion in their presence. The three wise men then stood up and most agreeably and devoutly took leave of the Gentile. Many were the blessings the three wise men wished on the Gentile, and the Gentile on the three wise men; and their leave-taking and the end of their conversation was full of embraces, kisses, tears, and sighs. But before the three wise men left, the Gentile asked them in astonishment why they did not wait to hear which religion he would choose in preference to the others. The three wise men answered, saying that, in order for each to be free to choose his own religion, they preferred not knowing which religion he would choose. "And all the more so since this is a question we could discuss among ourselves to see, by force of reason and by means of our intellects, which religion it must be that you will choose. And if, in front of us, you state which religion it is that you prefer, then we would not have such a good subject of discussion nor such satisfaction in discovering the truth." With these words, the three wise men returned to the city from which they had come. But the Gentile, looking at the flowers of the five trees and recalling what he had decided, waited for the two gentiles who were coming.

What the Three Wise Men Said as They Returned

One of the three wise men said: "If the Gentile, who was so long in error, has conceived such great devotion and such great fervor in praising God, that he now states that in order to do so he would not hesitate to suffer any hardship or death, no matter how harsh it were, then how much greater should be our devotion and fervor in praising the name of God, considering how long we have known about him, and all the more so since he has placed us under such obligation by the many blessings and honors he has given us and gives us every day. We should debate and see which of us is in truth and which in error. For just as we have one God, one Creator, one Lord, we should also have one faith, one religion, one sect, one manner of loving and honoring God, and we should love and help one another, and make it so that between us there be no difference or contrariety of faith or customs, which difference and contrariety cause us to be enemies with one another and to be at war, killing one another and falling captive to one another. And this war, death, and servitude prevent us from giving the praise, reverence, and honor we owe God every day of our life."

When this wise man had finished, another began to speak, saying that people were so rooted in the faith in which they found themselves and in which they were raised by their parents and ancestors, that it was impossible to make them break away by preaching, by disputation, or by any other means man could devise. And this is why, as soon as one starts discussing with them, showing them the error of their ways, they immediately scorn everything one tells them, saying they want to live and die in the faith their parents and ancestors gave them.

The other wise man replied, saying: "It is in the nature of truth to be more strongly rooted in the mind than falsehood, since truth and being are in accord, as are falsehood and nonbeing. And therefore, if falsehood were strongly opposed by truth, continually and by many people, then truth would necessarily have to vanquish falsehood; and all the more so since falsehood never receives any help, great or small, from God, and truth is always helped by that divine virtue which is uncreated truth, which has created truth for the purpose of destroying falsehood. But since men are lovers of temporal posses-sions, and lukewarm and of little devotion in loving God and their neighbor, they therefore care little about destroying falsehood and error; and they live in fear of dying and of suffering illness, hardship, and poverty, yet they do not want to give up their wealth, their possessions, their lands, or their rela-tives to save those who are in error, so they may go to everlasting glory and not undergo infinite suffering. And they should do this mainly in order to be counted among those who praise the name of God and proclaim his virtue, for God wants it to be proclaimed among all nations, and every day he waits to see how we will honor him among those who dishonor, despise, and are ignorant of him; and God wants us to do what we can to exalt his glorious name among us. For if we do what we can to praise God, how much more would God do as a result of having his name praised! For if he did not, it would be contrary to himself and to his honor, which is impossible and against the conditions of the trees. But because we do not prepare ourselves to receive God's virtue and blessing, nor to be his valiant servants, who praise him, strengthened by stout hearts to face any hardship to exalt his honor, God therefore does not bestow on us that virtue which must be present in those who, through God's virtue, would destroy the error of people on the road to damnation who think they are on the road to salvation."

While the wise man was speaking these words and many others, the three of them arrived at the place where they had first met by the city gates; and there they took leave of one another most amiably and politely, and each asked for-giveness of the other for any disrespectful word he might have spoken against his religion. Each forgave the other, and when they were about to part, one wise man said: "Do you think we have nothing to gain from what happened to us in the forest? Would you like to meet once a day, and, by the five trees and the ten conditions signified by their flowers, discuss according to the manner the Lady of Intelligence showed us, and have our discussions last until all three of us have only one faith, one religion, and until we can find some way to honor and serve one another, so that we can be in agreement? For war, turmoil, ill will, injury, and shame prevent man from agreeing on one belief."

Each of the three [some original sources read two] wise men approved of what the wise man had said, and they decided on a time and place for their discussions, as well as how they should honor and serve one another, and how they should dispute; and that when they had agreed on and chosen one faith, they would go forth into the world giving glory and praise to the name of our Lord God. Each of the three wise men went home and remained faithful to his promise.

Boccaccio: The Story of the Three Rings

Saladin, who by his great valor had from small beginnings made himself sultan of Egypt, and gained many victories over kings both Christian and Saracen, having in diverse wars and by diverse lavish displays of magnificence spent all his treasure, and in order to meet a certain emergency being in need of a large sum of money, and being at a loss to raise it with a celerity adequate to his necessity remembered a wealthy Jew, Melchisedech by name, who lent at usance [interest] in Alexandria, and who, were he but willing, was, as he believed, able to accommodate him, but was so miserly that he would never do so of his own accord, nor was Saladin disposed to constrain him to do so. So great, however, was his necessity that, after pondering every method whereby the Jew might be induced to be compliant, at last he determined to devise a seemingly reasonable pretext for extorting the money from him. So he sent for him, received him affably, seated him by his side, and presently said to him, "My good man, I have heard from many people that you are very wise, and of great knowledge in divine things. Thus, I would gladly have you tell me, which of the three laws you believe to be the true law, the law of the Jews, the law of the Saracens, or the law of the Christians?" The Jew, who was indeed a wise man, saw plainly enough that Saladin meant to entangle him in his speech, that he might have occasion to harass him and he realized that he could not praise any of the three laws above another without furnishing Saladin with the pretext which he sought. So, concentrating all the force of his mind to shape such an answer as might avoid the snare, he presently lit on what he sought, saying, "My lord, a pretty question indeed is this which you propose and it pleases me to answer it. To which end it is appropriate that I tell you a story, which, if you will listen, goes as follows:

If I am not mistaken, I remember to have often heard tell of a great and rich man of long ago, who among other most precious jewels had in his treasury a ring of extraordinary beauty and value, which by reason of its value and beauty he was minded to leave to his heirs forever. As such, he decided that whichever of his sons was found in possession of the ring as by his bequest, should thereby be designated his heir and be entitled to receive from the other sons the honor and homage due to a superior. The son to whom he bequeathed the ring left it in like manner to his descendants, following in the footsteps of his father. In short, the ring passed from hand to hand for many generations and in the end came to the hands of one who had three sons, goodly and virtuous all, and very obedient to their father, so that he loved them all the same. The rule as to how the ring was passed on was known to the young men, and each aspiring to hold the place of honor among them did all he could to persuade his father, who was now old, to leave the ring to him at his death. The worthy man, who loved them all equally, knew not how to choose from among them a sole heir, promised the ring to each in turn, and in order to satisfy all three, had a cunning crafts-man secretly to make another two rings, so like the first that the maker himself could hardly tell which was the true ring. So, before he died, he disposed of the rings, giving one in secret to each of his sons. Then it came to pass, that after his death each of the sons claimed the inheritance and the place of honor, and, his claim being disputed by his brothers, produced his ring to prove his case. And the rings being found to be so alike that it was impossible to distinguish the true one, the suit to determine true heir remained pending to this day." And so, my lord to your question, touching the three laws given to the three people by God the Father, I answer, "Each of these peoples deems itself have the true inheritance, the true law, the true commandments of God; but which of them is justified in so believing, is a question which, like that of the rings, remains pending." The excellent adroitness with which the Jew had contrived to evade the snare which he had laid for his feet was not lost upon Saladin. He therefore determined to let the Jew know his need, and did so, telling him at the same time what he had intended to do, in the event of his answering less circumspectly than he had done.

Thereupon the Jew gave the sultan all the money that he required, which the sultan afterwards repaid him in full. He also gave him most munificent gifts with his lifelong friendship and a great and honorable position near his person.

55. THE CONVERSION OF ANSELM DE TURMEDA

Christian conversions to Islam in the medieval period do not appear to have been uncom-mon. Numerous stories about renegades, as these converts were called by their former core-ligionists, making new lives for themselves in Granada, northern Africa, and the Middle East attest to the relative frequency with which this occurred. However, we know very little about most of the converts. When they enter the historical record, it is often briefly and just as often anonymously. One of the rare exceptions is the conversion of Anselm de Turmeda (1355–1423). Anselm was born in Mallorca and became a well-known and respected Fran-ciscan friar. As Anselm himself tells us in the Tuhfa, *a post-conversion polemical work that also included autobiographical sections, at the age of 35 he decided to convert to Islam. He went on to have a very successful career under the Hafsid dynasty in Tunis, eventually becoming vizier as well as a diplomat to his former country. He may be the only medieval writer who enjoyed literary success in both a European language (Catalan) and Arabic. In the selection below, Anselm describes the immediate events surrounding his conversion.*

Source: trans. Jarbel Rodriguez, from Míkel de Epalza, *Fray Anselm de Turmeda y su polémica islamo-cristiana: Edición, traducción y estudio de la Tuhfa* (Madrid: Libros Hiperión, 1994), 222, 224, 226, 228.

I promised him [his former mentor] what he wanted to leave him satisfied. Later I gathered the provisions for my voyage and went to say to good bye. He gave his blessings when I left and gave me 50 gold dinars to help with the trip. I took ship and headed for my homeland, the city of Mallorca, where I remained for six months. Then I left for Sicily and stayed there for another five months. I was in search of a ship that was headed to an Islamic country and finally such a ship arrived, headed for Tunis. In it I made the trip from Sicily. We set sail as the sun was setting and arrived in the Marsa [port] of Tunis near midday.

When I got off the ship, some of the Christian troops [mercenaries] stationed there who had heard about me came with mounts and took me with them to their homes. They were accompanied by some [Christian] merchants who also lived in Tunis. I was their guest, and treated very well, for four months.

After this, I asked them if there was anyone in the sultan's household who spoke the language of the Christians. During that time, the sultan was our sovereign Abū al-'Abbās Ahmad [r. 1370–94]—God have mercy on him. The Christians told me that there was a man in the sultan's palace, who was one of highest ranked officials in his service, by the name of Yūsuf the Physician [possibly a renegade]. He was the sultan's doctor and one of his closest confidants. I was very pleased when I learned this.

I asked around as to where this doctor lived and had someone take me to him. I introduced myself, and told him my situation and the reason for my visit; that it was my wish to convert to Islam. The doctor became very happy and took much joy in participating in this process.

He then got on his horse and took me with him to the sultan's palace. He went to the sultan and told him my story and asked him for an audience for me, an audience which the sultan granted. I presented myself to the sultan and the first thing he asked was my age. I told him I was 35 years old. He then asked me several questions on the sciences which I had studied, which I described to him. He then told me, "you have come at a good time (and gave me 50 gold dinars) as you have abandoned your land for ours. Now become a Muslim with God's blessing."

I then told the translator, Yūsuf Al-Tabīb [the doctor], "Tell our sovereign, the sultan, that no one leaves one's religion without his fellows raising their voices against him and maligning him. I beg him, thus, out of his benevolence, that he summon the most worthy [Christian] soldiers and merchants who live here, ask them about me, and hear what they have to say. After this, I will make myself a Muslim, God willing."

The sultan replied, using the translator, "You have asked of me the same thing that 'Abdullah b. Salām asked of the Prophet—may the blessings and peace of God be abundantly upon him—when he wanted to become a Muslim."

He then sent for the Christian soldiers and some of the merchants, and he asked me to wait in an alcove near his audience hall. When the Christians entered, he asked them, "What would you tell me of this priest who arrived on the ship?" [They replied,] "My lord, he is very learned in our faith. Our scholars have even said that they have not seen a greater authority on science of religion in all of Christendom."

"And what would you say if he were to become a Muslim?"

"May God save us from this! He would never do that."

When the sultan heard the opinion of the Christians, he called for me. I presented myself before him and made a profession of the true faith in front of the Christians. They made the sign of the cross and said, "He has only done this because he wishes to marry, as our priests are not allowed to marry." They then left, dejected and saddened.

The sultan—may God have mercy upon him—assigned to me [a stipend of] four dinars a day and gave me in marriage to the daughter of Hajji Muhammad al-Saffâr. When I took her to my house on our wedding day, she gave me 100 dinars and a magnificent new outfit. We joined each other and I had a son by her. I named him Muhammad, after the blessing that the name of our prophet Muhammad—blessings and peace be upon him—carries with it.

56. JOHANN SCHILTBERGER'S VIEWS ON ISLAM

Johann Schiltberger (1380–ca. 1440) was a German traveler and slave whom fate took from one momentous event to the next, making him an eyewitness to many of the most important occurrences of the late fourteenth and early fifteenth centuries. At the age of 16 he was a participant at the Battle of Nicopolis (1396), which he survived, likely because of his young age. Falling into Turkish captivity, he became a slave, serving as a page to the Turkish Sultan Bayezid for six years, until Bayezid himself was overwhelmed and captured by the Mongol forces of Timur the Lame (Tamerlane). Schiltberger then went to serve this new master, with whom he traveled through Armenia and Georgia until Timur's death in 1405. Remaining in servitude with Timur's descendants, he traveled widely through Russia, going as far as Siberia, central Asia, Persia, and the Middle East. After decades of peregrinations in the service of his Mongol masters, he was finally able to escape to Constantinople and return to Germany in 1427, 33 years after he had left. His wide travels gave him an unusual and far-ranging perspective on Islam, upon which he focused much of his narrative. In this brief selection from his Travels, *Schiltberger offers his description of Islam, its customs, and rituals—as he understood them, but with many inaccuracies—along with what Muslims thought of Christians and Christianity.*

Source: trans. J. Buchan Telfer, *The Bondage and Travels of Johann Schiltberger: A Native of Bavaria in Europe, Asia, and Africa, 1396–1427* (London: Hakluyt Society, 1879), 65–79.

Of the Many Religions the Infidels Have

It is to be noted, that the Infidels have five religions. First, some believe in a giant called Aly, who was a great persecutor of Christians. Others believe in one who was called Molwa who was an infidel priest. The third believe, as the three kings believed, before they were baptized. The fourth believe in fire, because they say that Abel, the son of Adam, brought his offering to Almighty God, and the flames of the fire were the offering; therefore they believe in this offering. Among the fifth, some believe, and the largest number among the infidels believe, in one who is called Muhammad.

How Muhammad and His Religion Appeared

It is here to be noted of Muhammad, how he came and how he brought his religion. Item, his father and mother were poor people, and he was a native of Arabia. When he was thirteen years old he went away from home, went to [some] merchants who wanted to go to Egypt, and asked them to take him with them. They took him, agreeing that he must look after the camels and horses, and wherever Muhammad went, or stood, there stood always a cloud over him, which was black; and when they came to Egypt, they encamped near a village. Now at that time there were Christians in Egypt; the pastor of the village came to the merchants, and invited them to dine with him. They did so and told Muhammad that he must look after the horses and camels. This he did. And now when they came into the pastor's house, the pastor asked them if they were all there? The merchants said, "We are all here, except a boy who is guarding our camels and horses." Now this priest had read in a prophecy, how one, born of two persons, would spread a doctrine against that of Christianity, and that as a sign of who the man was to be, a black cloud would stand over him. The pastor went out, and saw a black cloud over the little boy, who was Muhammad. When he had now seen him, he asked the merchants that they should bring the boy and they brought him. The pastor asked him his name. He said, "Muhammad." This, the priest also found in prophecy and more [than this], that he would be a mighty lord and man, and that he would greatly trouble Christianity; but that his doctrine would not last one thousand years, and then it would decrease. When the pastor knew that he was named Muhammad, and saw the black cloud stand over him, he understood that he was the man who would introduce this doctrine, and he placed him at his table above the merchants, and showed him great honor. After the meal, the pastor asked the merchants if they knew the boy. They said, "No, but he came to us, and asked us to take him with us into Egypt." Then the pastor told them how he had read in a prophecy, how this boy would introduce a doctrine against Christians, through which they would suffer much, and for a sign [of this], a black cloud would be always over him; and showed them the cloud and said, that when he was in the galley, the cloud was there also. He said to the boy, "Thou shall be a great teacher, and shall introduce a particular doctrine amongst the infidels, and thou shall overpower the Christians by your might, and your descendants will also acquire great power. Now I pray to you that you will leave my race, the Armeny [Armenians], in peace." This he promised him, and then went with the merchants to Babiloni, and became a great scholar in infidel writings, and preached to the infidels that they should believe in God who had created heaven and earth, and not in the idols that were the creatures of men; they have ears and hear not; they have eyes and see not; they have a mouth and speak not; they have feet and walk not; nor can they save either the body or soul; and he converted the king of Babylonia and many people with him. Then the king took him, and gave him power over the land. This he exercised and when the king died, he took the king's wife, and became a mighty calpha [caliph], which is as much as to say, a pope. He had four men with him who were well learned in infidel writings, and to each he gave an office. To the first, he gave charge of ecclesiastical jurisdiction; to the other, lay jurisdiction; the first was named Omar, the other, Otman; the third was named Abubach, to whom he gave charge of weights and manufactures, so that he was over them, and each one should be faithful in his work. The fourth was named Aly; he made him chief over all his people, and sent him into Arabia that he should convert Christians, because Christians were there at the time; but if any would not be converted, then he should compel them by the sword. We read in the Infidel book, Alkoran [the Quran], that in one day ninety thousand men were killed for [the sake of] Muhammad's doctrine, and the whole of Arabia was converted.

Muhammad gave them a law, how they were to conduct themselves before God, who had created heaven and earth. And the law of the infidels begins in this way. First, when a boy was born, when he comes to be thirteen years old, he must be circumcised, and he has instituted five daily prayers, which must be daily repeated. The first prayer is when the day breaks; another, in the middle of the day; the third, at the time of vespers; the fourth, before the sun goes down; the fifth, when day and night part. With the first four, they praise God, who has made heaven and earth; with the fifth, they pray to Muhammad, that he will intercede for them with God. And they must go into the temple at certain times of the day; and when they want to go into the temple, they must wash the mouth, then the hands, feet, ears, and eyes. And when any one has sinned with his wife, he cannot go into the temple, until he has washed his whole body; this they do in the same belief as we Christians who confess; and the infidels believe that, after they have washed, they are as pure as Christians, who, with full penitence, have confessed to the priest. And when they want to enter the temple, they take off their shoes and go in bare footed. They cannot take in any arms, or weapons that cut, and they do not allow any woman in the temple, so long as they are inside. And when they go into the temple, they stand near each other, with their hands close to each other, and they bend and kiss the ground, and their priest sits on a seat before them, and begins a prayer which they repeat after him. It is also to be noted, that in the temple no one speaks to another, nor looks at another, until the prayer is ended. In the temple they do not put one foot far from the other, but keep them close together; they do not go to and fro, nor look here and there, but they stand still in one place, and keep their hands together until they have quite finished their prayer; and when they have quite finished, they bow to each other, and only then go out of the temple. It is also to be noted, that no door of the temple is left open. They have no painting and no picture inside, only their writings, plants, roses, and flowers. They do not willingly allow Christians to enter, and more than this, it is to be noted, that infidels must not spit, cough, or do anything of the sort in their temple; but if someone does so inside, he must go out and wash himself, and, added to this, must suffer much reproach from the infidels; and when one coughs, sneezes, or [unclear text], he must go out of the temple and wash himself after it. It is also to be noted, that they keep Friday as we keep Sunday, and whoever does not go to the temple on their holy-day, is taken and tied to a ladder, and carried about the town from one street to the other, and tied in front of the temple until their prayer is finished; and then they beat him twenty-five times with a rod on the naked body, whether he is rich or poor.

Item, all the young dropped by their cattle on the Friday, are given to the hospital. Their priests also say, that when prayer is finished on a holy day, people may work, because work is holy, and that man commits more sin by being idle than with work, and therefore they allow their people to work on holy days after they have finished their prayer. And when they finish their prayers on holy days, they raise their hands towards God, and all pray with common voice for vengeance on Christendom, and say, "Almighty God, we pray thee not to suffer Christians to be united," and say, that if Christians are united and have peace amongst themselves, they must succumb. It is also to be noted, that they have three kinds of temples; one, to which they all go, is Sam, a parish church; the other, into which priests go, is a monastery, and in which they also go through their probation; the third, is where their kings and mighty vassals have their burial, and in it poor people are received for the love of God, whether they be Christians, infidels, or Jews, and the temple is like a hospital. The first temple is also called Mesgit, the other Medrassa, the third, Amarat. It is also to be noted, that they do not bury their dead either in the temples, or around them; they bury in the fields and on the high roads; this they do that those who pass by, may pray to God for them. And when one is about to die, they stand around him, and tell him that he must think of God, and call to God to have mercy upon him; and when he dies, they wash him, and then their priests carry him, singing, to the grave, and bury him. It is also to be noted, that the infidels fast one month in the year, and this fast changes every year to another month, and they fast one whole day without eating or drinking, until they see the stars in the sky. Then the priest goes up the tower, and calls the people to prayer, and they go into the temple and say their prayers, and only when they have finished their prayer, they go home and eat all night until the morning, meat, or whatever they may have. Also, they do not lay with their wives during their fast; and when a woman is pregnant or in childbed, she may eat during the day, and the sick may do the same. They do not take payment during fast, either for houses or for any thing that pays interest.

Of the Infidels' Easter-day

It is also to be noted of the infidels' Easter day, that, after they have fasted four weeks, they have Easter for three days following, and on the morning of Easter day they go to the temple, and finish their prayer as is their custom; and when they have done, the common people put on their arms, and then come to the high priest's house, with the chiefs of the town and the soldiers, and then take out of the priest's house, the tabernacle, and ornament it with cloth of gold and velvet, and the chiefs and the principal [people] carry it in front of their temple, and in front of the tabernacle they carry their banners, and all the musicians they can find also go before it; and when they bring it to the temple, they put it down, and the chief priest goes into the tabernacle and preaches inside it. "When he has preached, they put a sword in his hand; he draws it and speaks to the people, and calls upon God that he should give us might and strength against all the enemies of Muhammad's faith, so that we may overcome them with the sword. Then they all put out their hands, and pray to our Lord that it may so happen, and after this, the mighty lords go into the temple and pray, and during that time, the people must guard the tabernacle and the lords. When their prayer is finished, they take the tabernacle with the priest inside, and carry him back to his house, with the musicians and banners. Afterwards, they go to their houses and have great rejoicings for three days.

Of the Other Easter-day

And then, after a month, they have another Easter day in honor of Abraham. On this [day] they kill lambs and oxen, and give to the poor, by the will of God, [and] to the honor of Abraham, because he was obedient, and wanted to sacrifice his son to God. At this time, the infidels go to the grave of Muhammad, and to the temple which Abraham built and which lies in front of the city, and Muhammad has his grave in it, and it is called Medina. On Easter day, the king-sultan covers the temple of Abraham with velvet, which is black, and then their priest cuts off a small piece for each infidel pilgrim that comes, that he may take it away as a sign that he has been there.

Of the Law of the Infidels

It is also here to be noted, what Muhammad has forbidden in the laws he has given to the infidels. First, he has forbidden the infidels that they should dare to cut the beard, because it would be against the will of God when he created Adam, the first man, in his divine image; and the infidels also say, that he who would have a face different to that he received from God, does it against God's command, whether he be young or old. They also say that whoever cuts his beard, he does it from vanity and pride, and to please the world, and scorns the creation of God; it is particularly the Christians who do this to please their women, and this is a great misfortune for them, because, for the sake of vanity, they disfigure the image in which God created them. Then Muhammad forbade that any one should lift his hat or uncover his head to another, whether he be king, emperor, noble, or plebeian, which they also observe; but when they go before a mighty man, they bow and kneel before him. They say, when one's father, and mother, or another friend dies, they should uncover the head before him. This they also do. When they lament for one, they take off their hat, and lift it high and throw it on the ground, and then they lament. This also has Muhammad allowed, that a man may take as many wives as he can support. It is also their law, that when a woman is pregnant, they do not go near her until the child is born, nor for fourteen days after; but they may have a concubine. The Infidels also say that after the last day they will have wives, with whom they will lie; but they will always remain virgins. They also say that God has established marriage only for those who die in the faith of Muhammad. He has also ordered that they must not eat any animal, or bird, unless they cut its throat and let the blood flow, which they observe. They do not eat pig's flesh, because Muhammad has also forbidden it.

Why Muhammad Has Forbidden Wine to Infidels

It is also to be noted, that Muhammad has forbidden wine to infidels, because as the infidels say: One day he was passing, with his servants, a public-house, in which were many people making merry. He asked why those people were so merry; one of his servants told him it was caused by wine. Muhammad said: "Is it such a drink that people become so merry from it!" Now in the evening Muhammad went out again, and there was a great noise because a man and his wife were fighting, and two persons were killed. He spoke and asked what was the matter? One of his servants said that the people who were merry have now lost their senses, because they have taken too much wine, and they knew not what they did. Then Muhammad forbade wine to all, under a heavy penalty, whether ecclesiastic or lay, emperor, king, dukes, barons, counts, knight and varlet, servants, and all those who were of his faith, and that they should no longer drink wine, whether they be well or ill, and this is why he has forbidden wine to them, as the infidels have told me. He has also ordered that the Christians and all those who are against his faith, should be persecuted day and night, except the Armeny who are to be free amongst them; and where there are Armeny amongst them, then they should not take from them a monthly tax greater than two pfennings, because Muhammad had promised the Armenian priest, as has been stated. He has also ordered, that when they overcome Christians, they should not kill them, but they should pervert them, and should thus spread and strengthen their own faith.

Of a Fellowship the Infidels Have among Themselves

It is also to be noted, that during the time he was on earth, Muhammad had forty disciples. They have a special fellowship and have made an alliance against Christendom, and this is their law. Whoever wants to be of their fellowship, must swear that if he meets a Christian, he will not let him live nor take him a prisoner, whether from favor or for the sake of profit; and if it should happen that in a battle which infidels [might] have with Christians, he cannot succeed to take one, he must buy a Christian and kill him. Those who are in this fellowship are called They; there are many of them in Turkey, and they always go against the Christians because it is their law.

How a Christian Becomes an Infidel

It is also to be noted how a Christian, from the beginning, becomes an infidel. When a Christian wants to become an Infidel, he must before all men raise a finger, and say the words, "La il lach illallach," Muhammad is his true messenger.

And when he says this, they take him to the high priest; then he must repeat the above written words before the priest, and must deny the Christian faith, and when he has done that, they put on him a new dress, and the priest binds a new kerchief on his head; and this they do that it may be seen he is an infidel, because Christians wear blue kerchiefs, and the Jews, yellow kerchiefs, on the head. Then the priest asks all the people to put on their armor, and who has to ride rides; also all the priests who are in the neighborhood. And when the people come, they put him on a horse, and then the common people must ride before him, and the priests go behind him, with trumpets, cymbals, and fifes, and two priests ride near him; and so they lead him about in the town; and the Infidels cry with a loud voice and praise Muhammad, and the two priests say to him these words, "Thary wirdur, Messe chulidur, Maria cara baschidur, Muhammad kassuldur," which is as much as to say, There is one God, and the Messiah his servant, Mary his maid, and Muhammad his chief messenger. After they have led him everywhere in the city, from one street to another, then they lead him into the temple and circumcise him. If he is poor, they make a large collection and give it to him, and the great lords show particular honor to him, and make him rich. This they do, that Christians may be more willing to be converted to their faith. If it is a woman who wants to change her religion she is also taken to the high priest, and must say the above words. The priest then takes the woman's girdle, cuts it in two, and makes of it a cross; on this, the woman must stamp three times, deny the Christian faith, and must say the other words above written. The infidels have a good custom among their merchants, when one wants to buy from another, whatever be the merchandise. The buyer says to the seller, that he should make a just profit on what he buys, so that he also might live; so that he takes no more profit than one pfenning in forty pfennings, which is equal to one gulden in forty guldens, and no more. This they call a right purchase and profit, and this Muhammad has also commanded them, so that the poor, like the rich, might live. The priests also always say in their sermons, that they should help each other and be subject to their superiors, and the rich are to be humble before the poor, and when they do this, God Almighty gives them strength and might against their enemies; and whatever their priest says to them about spiritual things, they are obedient and submissive to it. This is the faith of Muhammad which he has given to the infidels as his law, such as it is, as I then heard it from them.

What the Infidels Believe of Christ

It is also to be noted, that the Infidels believe that Jesus was born of a virgin, and that after the birth, she remained a virgin. They also believe that when Jesus was born, he spoke to his mother and comforted her, and they believe that Jesus is the highest prophet of God amongst all prophets, and that he has never committed sin; and they do not believe that Jesus was crucified, but that it was another who was like him; therefore Christians have a wicked faith, because they say that Jesus was crucified, who was the highest friend of God, and has never committed any sin, therefore God would not have been a just judge if Jesus was crucified and innocent. And when one converses with them of the Father, and Son, and Holy Ghost, they say that they are three persons, and not one God, because their book Alkoran [Quran] says nothing of the Trinity. When anybody says that Jesus is the word of God, they say, this we do know, that the word of God has spoken, otherwise he would not be God; and when one says that wisdom is the Son of God who was born of the Virgin Mary, from a word which the angels announced to her, and on account of which word we must all rise and come to judgment—they say it is true that no one can go against the word of God. They also say that the strength of the word of God cannot be conceived by any one, and therefore their book Alkoran says, and gives them a sign, by the word which the angel spoke to Mary, that Jesus was born of the word of God. They say that Abraham was the friend of God, Moses the prophet of God, Jesus the word of God, so was Muhammad the true messenger of God. They also say, that Jesus, of the four, was the most worthy, and was the highest with God, and it will be he also who will judge the last judgment of God over all men.

What the Infidels Say of the Christians

The infidels also say that whatever territory they possess of the Christians, they do not owe it to their power, nor to their wisdom, nor to their holiness, but they have it because of the injustice, perversity, and arrogance which Christians have against them. Therefore Almighty God has decreed, that they should take the land from Christians, because they do not conduct their affairs, whether spiritual or temporal, with justice, because they look to wealth and favor, and the rich treat the poor with haughtiness, and do not help them either with gifts or with justice, and do not hold to the doctrine which the Messiah has given them. They also say, that they find it and read it in their prophecies, that the Christians will yet expel them out of the country, and will again possess the country; but so long as Christians are such, and are perverse, and their spiritual and temporal lords live such a disordered life, we are not afraid that they will expel us out of our country; because we fear God, and do always what is right and just, and worthy, according to our faith, for the love of God and in honor of our prophet Muhammad, who is the highest messenger of God, who has given us the right doctrine by his teaching; to him we are obedient, and always willingly follow his commandments which are in the book called the Alkoran, which has been touched upon often before.

How Christians Are Said Not to Hold to Their Religion

The infidels also say that Christians do not hold to the commandment, nor to the doctrine of the Messiah, which the Messiah has commanded them, and they also do not observe the law of the book Inzil, which is called Ewangely, nor the rules which stand in that book. They hold to particular laws, spiritual and temporal, which are against the laws of the book Inzil, and the commandments and laws contained therein are all holy and just; but the law and belief which they have set up and invented, are all false and unjust, because the laws which they have made are for profit and favor, which is all against God and his dear prophets; and whatever misfortunes and troubles they have, are all decreed to them by God for their unrighteousness.

CHAPTER SEVEN

VIEWS OF THE OTHER

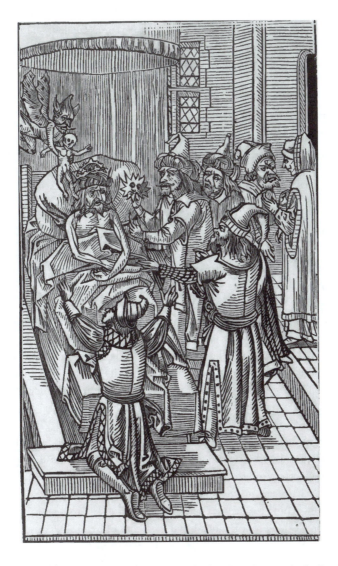

Figure 7.1: Christian representation of the death of Mehmed II, as a devil takes his soul.

Source: Paul LaCroix, *Military and Religious Life in the Middle Ages and the Period of the Renaissance* (London: Bickers and Son, n.d.), 178.

57. A TALE OF TWO CITIES

Medieval travelers often commented on the strangeness and peculiarities of foreign cities, selecting details and characteristics that they found exotic, troubling, or unusual. The source below is no exception. It is the work of the Spanish Jewish traveler Benjamin Tudela (1130–73) and describes Constantinople, the Byzantine capital, and Baghdad, the capital of the Abbasid caliphate. Tudela traveled extensively throughout the Mediterranean basin and western Asia between 1165 and 1173, visiting hundreds of locations and providing vivid descriptions of many of them. As he was neither a Muslim nor a Christian, Tudela's narrative gives us the opportunity to see the two faiths through the eyes of an external observer while avoiding the polemical discourse typically used by Muslims and Christians to describe each other. One of Tudela's main interests in his narrative is describing the conditions of the local Jewish communities. As such, his views on Christianity or Islam are sometimes colored by the treatment that his fellow Jews received.

Source: trans. Marcus Nathan Adler, *The Itinerary of Benjamin of Tudela: Critical Text, Translation and Commentary* (New York: Philipp Feldheim, 1907, repr. 1965), 11–14, 35–42; rev. Jarbel Rodriguez.

A three days' voyage brings one to Abydos, which is upon an arm of the sea which flows between the mountains, and after a five days' journey the great town of Constantinople is reached. It is the capital of the whole land of Javan, which is called Greece. Here is the residence of the king Emanuel the emperor [Manuel Comnenus, Byzantine emperor, r. 1143–80]. Twelve ministers are under him, each of whom has a palace in Constantinople and possesses castles and cities; they rule all the land. At their head is the king Hipparchus, the second in command is the *megas domesticus*, the third *dominus*, and the fourth is *megas ducas*, and the fifth is *oeconomus megalus*; the others bear titles like these. The circumference of the city of Constantinople is eighteen miles; half of it is surrounded by the sea, and half by land, and it is situated upon two arms of the sea, one coming from the sea of Russia, and one from the sea of Sepharad.

All sorts of merchants come here from the land of Babylon, from the land of Shinar, from Persia, Media, and all the sovereignty of the land of Egypt, from the land of Canaan, and the empire of Russia [duchy of Kiev], from Hungary, Patzinakia, Khazaria, and the land of Lombardy and Sepharad. It is a busy city, and merchants come to it from every country by sea or land, and there is none like it in the world except Baghdad, the great city of Islam. In Constantinople is the church of Santa Sophia, and the seat of the pope of the Greeks [the patriarch of Constantinople], since the Greeks do not obey the pope of Rome. There are also churches according to the number of the days of the year. A quantity of wealth beyond telling is brought hither year by year as tribute from the two islands and the castles and villages which are there. And the like of this wealth is not to be found in any other church in the world. And in this church there are pillars of gold and silver, and lamps of silver and gold more than a man can count. Close to the walls of the palace is also a place of amusement belonging to the king, which is called the Hippodrome, and every year on the anniversary of the birth of Jesus the king gives a great entertainment there. And in that place men from all the races of the world come before the king and queen with juggling and without juggling, and they introduce lions, leopards, bears, and wild asses, and they engage them in combat with one another; and the same thing is done with birds. No entertainment like this is to be found in any other land.

This king Emanuel built a great palace for the seat of his government upon the sea-coast, in addition to the palaces which his fathers built, and he called its name Blachernae. He overlaid its columns and walls with gold and silver, and engraved thereon representations of the battles before his day and of his own combats. He also set up a throne of gold and of precious stones, and a golden crown was suspended by a gold chain over the throne, so arranged that he might sit thereunder. It was inlaid with jewels of priceless value, and at night time no lights were required, for every one could see by the light which the stones gave forth. Countless other buildings are to be seen within the city. From every part of the empire of Greece, tribute is brought here every year, and they fill strongholds with garments of silk, purple, and gold. Like unto these storehouses and this wealth, there is nothing in the whole world to be found. It is said that the tribute of the city amounts every year to 20,000 gold pieces, derived both from the rents of shops and markets, and from the tribute of merchants who enter by sea or land.

The Greek inhabitants are very rich in gold and precious stones, and they go clothed in garments of silk with gold embroidery, and they ride horses, and look like princes. Indeed, the land is very rich in all cloth stuffs, and in bread, meat, and wine.

Wealth like that of Constantinople is not to be found in the whole world. Here also are men learned in all the books of the Greeks, and they eat and drink every man under his vine and his fig-tree.

They hire from amongst all nations warriors called Loazim [barbarians] to fight with the Sultan Masud, king of the Togarmim [Seljuks], who are called Turks; for the natives are not warlike, but are as women who have no strength to fight.

No Jews live in the city, for they have been placed behind an inlet of the sea. An arm of the sea of Marmora shuts them in on the one side, and they are unable to go out except by way of the sea, when they want to do business with the inhabitants. In the Jewish quarter are about 2,000 Rabbanite Jews and about 500 Karaites, and a fence divides them. Among the scholars are several wise men, at their head being the chief rabbi R. Abtalion, R. Obadiah, R. Aaron Bechor

Shoro, R. Joseph Shir-Guru, and R. Eliakim, the warden. And among them there are artificers in silk and many rich merchants. No Jew there is allowed to ride on horseback. The one exception is R. Solomon Hamitsri, who is the king's physician, and through whom the Jews enjoy considerable alleviation of their oppression. For their condition is very low, and there is much hatred against them, which is fostered by the tanners, who throw out their dirty water in the streets before the doors of the Jewish houses and defile the Jews' quarter [the Ghetto]. So the Greeks hate the Jews, good and bad alike, and subject them to great oppression, and beat them in the streets, and in every way treat them with rigor. Yet the Jews are rich and good, kindly and charitable, and bear their lot with cheerfulness. The district inhabited by the Jews is called Pera....

... Thence it is two days to Baghdad, the great city and the royal residence of the caliph Emir al Muminin al Abbasi [al-Mustanjid, r. 1160–70] of the family of Muhammad. He is at the head of the Muslim religion, and all the kings of Islam obey him; he occupies a similar position to that held by the pope over the Christians. He has a palace in Baghdad three miles in extent, wherein is a great park with all varieties of trees, fruit-bearing and otherwise, and all manner of animals. The whole is surrounded by a wall, and in the park there is a lake whose waters are fed by the river Hiddekel. Whenever the king desires to indulge in recreation and to rejoice and feast, his servants catch all manner of birds, game and fish, and he goes to his palace with his counselors and princes. There the great king, Al Abbasi the caliph [Hafiz] holds his court, and he is kind unto Israel, and many belonging to the people of Israel are his attendants; he knows all languages, and is well versed in the law of Israel. He reads and writes the holy language [Hebrew]. He will not partake of anything unless he has earned it by the work of his own hands. He makes coverlets to which he attaches his seal; his courtiers sell them in the market, and the great ones of the land purchase them, and the proceeds thereof provide his sustenance. He is truthful and trusty, speaking peace to all men. The men of Islam see him but once in the year. The pilgrims that come from distant lands to go unto Mecca, which is in the land El-Yemen, are anxious to see his face, and they assemble before the palace exclaiming "Our Lord, light of Islam and glory of our Law, show us the effulgence of thy countenance," but he pays no regard to their words. Then the princes who minister unto him say to him, "Our Lord, spread forth thy peace unto the men that have come from distant lands, who crave to abide under the shadow of thy graciousness," and thereupon he arises and lets down the hem of his robe from the window, and the pilgrims come and kiss it, and a prince says unto them "Go forth in peace, for our master the lord of Islam grants peace to you." He is regarded by them as Muhammad and they go to their houses rejoicing at the salutation which the prince has vouchsafed unto them, and glad at heart that they have kissed his robe.

Each of his brothers and the members of his family has an abode in his palace, but they are all fettered in chains of iron, and guards are placed over each of their houses so that they may not rise against the great caliph. For once it happened to a predecessor that his brothers rose up against him and proclaimed one of themselves as caliph; then it was decreed that all the members of his family should be bound, that they might not rise up against the ruling caliph. Each one of them resides in his palace in great splendor, and they own villages and towns, and their stewards bring them the tribute thereof, and they eat and drink and rejoice all the days of their life. Within the domains of the palace of the caliph there are great buildings of marble and columns of silver and gold, and carvings upon rare stones are fixed in the walls. In the caliph's palace are great riches and towers filled with gold, silken garments, and all precious stones. He does not issue forth from his palace save once in the year, at the feast which the Muslims call El-id-bed Eamazan, and they come from distant lands that day to see him. He rides on a mule and is attired in the royal robes of gold and silver and fine linen; on his head is a turban adorned with precious stones of priceless value, and over the turban is a black shawl as a sign of his modesty, implying that all this glory will be covered by darkness on the day of death. He is accompanied by all the nobles of Islam dressed in fine garments and riding on horses, the princes of Arabia, the princes of Togarma and Daylam [Gilan] and the princes of Persia, Media, and Ghuzz, and the princes of the land of Tibet, which is three months' journey distant, and westward of which lies the land of Samarkand. He proceeds from his palace to the great mosque of Islam which is by the Basrah Gate. Along the road the walls are adorned with silk and purple, and the inhabitants receive him with all kinds of song and exultation, and they dance before the great king who is styled the caliph. They salute him with a loud voice and say, "Peace unto thee, our lord the king and Light of Islam!" He kisses his robe, and stretching forth the hem thereof he salutes them. Then he proceeds to the court of the mosque, mounts a wooden pulpit and expounds to them their Law. Then the learned ones of Islam arise and pray for him and extol his greatness and his graciousness, to which they all respond. Afterwards he gives them his blessing, and they bring before him a camel which he slays, and this is their Passover sacrifice. He gives thereof unto the princes and they distribute it to all, so that they may taste of the sacrifice brought by their sacred king; and they all rejoice. Afterwards he leaves the mosque and returns alone to his palace by way of the river Hiddekel, and the grandees of Islam accompany him in ships on the river until he enters his palace. He does not return the way he came; and the road which he takes along the riverside is watched all the year through, so that no man shall tread in his footsteps. He does not leave the palace again for a whole year. He is a benevolent man.

He built, on the other side of the river, on the banks of an arm of the Euphrates which there borders the city, a hospital consisting of blocks of houses and hospices for the sick poor who come to be healed. Here there are about sixty physicians' stores which are provided from the caliph's house with drags and whatever else may be required. Every sick man who comes is maintained at the caliph's expense and is medically treated. Here is a building which is called Dar-al-Maristan, where they keep charge of the demented people who have become insane in the towns through the great heat in the summer, and they chain each of them in iron chains until their reason becomes restored to them in the winter-time. While they abide there, they are provided with food from the house of the caliph, and when their reason is restored they are dismissed and each one of them goes to his house and his home. Money is given to those that have stayed in the hospices on their return to their homes. Every month the officers of the caliph inquire and investigate whether they have regained their reason, in which case they are discharged. All this the caliph does out of charity to those that come to the city of Baghdad, whether they be sick or insane. The caliph is a righteous man, and all his actions are for good.

In Baghdad there are about 40,000 Jews, and they dwell in security, prosperity and honor under the great caliph, and among them are great sages, the heads of academies engaged in the study of the law. In this city, there are ten academies ... [A list follows which names the rabbis who head each academy] ... These are the ten Batlanim, and they do not engage in any other work than communal administration; and all the days of the week they judge the Jews their countrymen, except on the second day of the week, when they all appear before the chief rabbi Samuel, the head of the Yeshiba Gaon [Jacob], who in conjunction with the other Batlanim judges all those that appear before him. And at the head of them all is Daniel the son of Hisdai, who is styled "Our lord the head of the Captivity of all Israel." He possesses a book of pedigrees going back as far as David, king of Israel. The Jews call him "Our lord, head of the Captivity," and the Muslims call him "Saidna ben Daoud," and he has been invested with authority over all the congregations of Israel at the hands of the emir al Muminin, the lord of Islam. For thus Muhammad commanded concerning him and his descendants; and he granted him a seal of office over all the congregations that dwell under his rule, and ordered that every one, whether Muslim or Jew, or belonging to any other nation in his dominion, should rise up before him [the exilarch] and salute him, and that any one who should refuse to rise up should receive one hundred stripes [lashes].

And every fifth day when he goes to pay a visit to the great caliph, horsemen, Gentiles as well as Jews, escort him, and heralds proclaim in advance, "Make way before our lord, the son of David, as is due unto him," the Arabic words being "Amilu tarik la Saidna ben Daud." He is mounted on a horse, and is attired in robes of silk and embroidery with a large turban on his head, and from the turban is suspended a long white cloth adorned with a chain upon which the cipher of Muhammad is engraved. Then he appears before the caliph and kisses his hand, and the caliph rises and places him on a throne that Muhammad had ordered to be made for him, and all the Muslim princes who attend the court of the caliph rise up before him. And the head of the Captivity is seated on his throne opposite to the caliph, in compliance with the command of Mohammad to give effect to what is written in the law: "The scepter shall not depart from Judah nor a lawgiver from between his feet, until he come to Shiloh: and to him shall the gathering of the people be." The authority of the head of the Captivity extends over all the communities of Shinar, Persia, Khurasan, and Sheba, which is El-Yemen, and Diyar Kalach [Bekr] and the land of Aram Naharaim [Mesopotamia], and over the dwellers in the mountains of Ararat and the land of the Alans [the Caucasus], which is a land surrounded by mountains and has no outlet except by the iron gates that Alexander made, but which were afterwards broken. Here are the people called Alani. His authority extends also over the land of Siberia, and the communities in the land of the Togarmim unto the mountains of Asveh and the land of Gurgan, the inhabitants of which are called Gurganim who dwell by the river Gihon and these are the Girgashites who follow the Christian religion. Further, it extends to the gates of Samarkand, the land of Tibet, and the land of India. In respect of all these countries, the head of the Captivity gives the communities power to appoint rabbis and ministers who come unto him to be consecrated and to receive his authority. They bring him offerings and gifts from the ends of the earth. He owns hospices, gardens and plantations in Babylon, and much land inherited from his fathers, and no one can take his possessions from him by force. He has a fixed weekly revenue arising from the hospices of the Jews, the markets and the merchants, apart from that which is brought to him from far-off lands. The man is very rich, and wise in the Scriptures as well as in the Talmud, and many Israelites dine at his table every day.

At his installation, the head of the Captivity gives much money to the caliph, to the princes and the ministers. On the day that the caliph performs the ceremony of investing him with authority, he rides in the second of the royal equipages, and is escorted from the palace of the caliph to his own house with timbrels and fifes [instruments resembling tambourines and flutes]. The exilarch appoints the chiefs of the academies by placing his hand upon their heads, thus installing them in their office. The Jews of the city are learned men and very rich.

In Baghdad, there are twenty-eight Jewish synagogues, situated either in the city itself or in Al-Karkh on the other side of the Tigris; for the river divides the metropolis into two parts. The great synagogue of the head of the Captivity has columns of marble of various colors overlaid with silver and gold, and on these columns are sentences of the Psalms in golden letters. And in front of the ark are about ten steps of marble; on the topmost step are the seats of the head of the Captivity and of the princes of the House of David. The city of Baghdad is twenty miles in circumference, situated in a land of palms, gardens and plantations, the like of which is not to be found in the whole land of Shinar. People come thither with merchandise from all lands. Wise men live there, philosophers who know all manner of wisdom, and magicians expert in all manner of witchcraft.

58. THE ECCENTRICITIES OF THE FRANKS

Usamah Ibn-Munqidh was a Muslim nobleman, warrior, diplomat, poet, and scholar. He was born in Syria in 1095 (d. 1188) and lived an eventful life in the shadows of the crusades, being an eyewitness to many of the critical events that transpired in the region over the course of the twelfth century. He served in an official and unofficial capacity many contemporary Muslim leaders including Zengi, Nur al-Din, and Saladin. He was also a prolific writer, penning numerous books of poetry. At the age of 90, he wrote the Kitab al-I'tibar, *a memoir that has made him widely known to modern readers. The* Kitab al-I'tibar *is a collection of anecdotes from his life, ranging from stories about hunting to tales of war and court life. The stories are often amusing, insightful, and humane, and they remain thoroughly appealing due to their accessibility and Usamah's ability to construct an engaging narrative. Included in his memoirs are numerous stories about his interactions with the crusaders (Franks), many of whom he considered his friends. Yet, he was often astounded by what he saw as the uncivilized and, at times, barbaric behavior of many of the crusaders. The selections below capture the complex relationship between Usamah and the Latin Christians with whom he interacted, lived with, and later wrote about.*

Source: trans. Philip K. Hitti, *An Arab-Syrian Gentleman and Warrior in the Period of the Crusades: Memoirs of Usamah Ibn Munqidh* (New York: Columbia University Press, 2000), 163–70.

Newly arrived Franks are especially rough: One insists that Usamah should pray eastward.—Everyone who is a fresh emigrant from the Frankish lands is ruder in character than those who have become acclimatized and have held long association with the Muslims. Here is an illustration of their rude character.

Whenever I visited Jerusalem I always entered the Aqsa Mosque, beside which stood a small mosque which the Franks had converted into a church. When I used to enter the Aqsa Mosque, which was occupied by the Templars who were my friends, the Templars would evacuate the little adjoining mosque so that I might pray in it. One day I entered this mosque, repeated the first formula, "Allah is great," and stood up in the act of praying, upon which one of the Franks rushed on me, got hold of me and turned my face eastward saying, "This is the way thou shouldst pray!" A group of Templars hastened to him, seized him and repelled him from me. I resumed my prayer. The same man, while the others were otherwise busy, rushed once more on me and turned my face eastward, saying, "This is the way thou shouldst pray!" The Templars again came in to him and expelled him. They apologized to me, saying, "This is a stranger who has only recently arrived from the land of the Franks and he has never before seen anyone praying except eastward." Thereupon I said to myself, "I have had enough prayer." So I went out and have ever been surprised at the conduct of this devil of a man, at the change in the color of his face, his trembling and his sentiment at the sight of one praying towards the *qiblah* [towards Mecca].

Another wants to show to a Muslim God as a child.—I saw one of the Franks come to al-Amir Mu'in-al-Din [emir of Damascus, r. 1140–49] (may Allah's mercy rest upon his soul!) when he was in the Dome of the Rock and say to him, "Dost thou want to see God as a child?" Mu'in-al-Din said, "Yes." The Frank walked ahead of us until he showed us the picture of Mary with Christ (may peace be upon him!) as an infant in her lap. He then said, "This is God as a child." But Allah is exalted far above what the infidels say about him!

Franks lack jealousy in sex affairs.—The Franks are void of all zeal and jealousy. One of them may be walking along with his wife. He meets another man who takes the wife by the hand and steps aside to converse with her while the husband is standing on one side waiting for his wife to conclude the conversation. If she lingers too long for him, he leaves her alone with the conversant and goes away.

Here is an illustration which I myself witnessed:

When I used to visit Nablus, I always took lodging with a man named Mu'izz, whose home was a lodging house for the Muslims. The house had windows which opened to the road, and there stood opposite to it on the other side of the road a house belonging to a Frank who sold wine for the merchants. He would take some wine in a bottle and go around announcing it by shouting, "So and so, the merchant, has just opened a cask full of this wine. He who wants to buy some of it will find it in such and such a place." The Frank's pay for the announcement made would be the wine in that bottle. One day this Frank went home and found a man with his wife in the same bed. He asked him, "What could have made thee enter into my wife's room?" The man replied, "I was tired, so I went in to rest." "But how," asked he, "didst thou get into my bed?" The other replied, "I found a bed that was spread, so I slept in it." "But," said he, "my wife was sleeping together with thee!" The other replied, "Well, the bed is hers. How could

I therefore have prevented her from using her own bed?" "By the truth of my religion," said the husband, "if thou shouldst do it again, you and I would have a quarrel." Such was for the Frank the entire expression of his disapproval and the limit of his jealousy.

Another illustration:

We had with us a bath-keeper named Salim, originally an inhabitant of al-Ma'arrah, who had charge of the bath of my father (may Allah's mercy rest upon his soul!). This man related the following story:

> I once opened a bath in al-Ma'arrah in order to earn my living. To this bath there came a Frankish knight. The Franks disapprove of girding a cover around one's waist while in the bath. So this Frank stretched out his arm and pulled off my cover from my waist and threw it away. He looked and saw that I had recently shaved off my pubes. So he shouted, "Salim!" As I drew near him he stretched his hand over my pubes and said, "Salim, good! By the truth of my religion, do the same for me." Saying this, he lay on his back and I found that in that place the hair was like his beard. So I shaved it off. Then he passed his hand over the place and, finding it smooth, he said, "Salim, by the truth of my religion, do the same to madam [al-dama]" (al-dama in their language means the lady), referring to his wife. He then said to a servant of his, "Tell madam to come here." Accordingly, the servant went and brought her and made her enter the bath. She also lay on her back. The knight repeated, "Do what thou hast done to me." So I shaved all that hair while her husband was sitting looking at me. At last he thanked me and handed me the pay for my service.

Consider now this great contradiction! They have neither jealousy nor zeal but they have great courage, although courage is nothing but the product of zeal and of ambition to be above ill repute.

Here is a story analogous to the one related above: I entered the public bath in Sur [Tyre] and took my place in a secluded part. One of my servants thereupon said to me, "There is with us in the bath a woman." When I went out, I sat on one of the stone benches and behold! the woman who was in the bath had come out all dressed and was standing with her father just opposite me. But I could not be sure that she was a woman. So I said to one of my companions, "By Allah, see if this is a woman," by which I meant that he should ask about her. But he went, as I was looking at him, lifted the end of her robe and looked carefully at her. Thereupon her father turned toward me and said, "This is my daughter. Her mother is dead and she has nobody to wash her hair. So I took her in with me to the bath and washed her head." I replied, "Thou hast well done! This is something for which thou shalt be rewarded [by Allah]!"

Another curious case of medication.—A curious case relating to their medicine is the following, which was related to me by William of Bures, the lord of Tabarayyah [Tiberias], who was one of the principal chiefs among the Franks. It happened that William had accompanied al-Amir Mu'in-al-Din (may Allah's mercy rest upon his soul!) from 'Akka to Tabarayyah when I was in his company too. On the way, William related to us the following story in these words:

We had in our country a highly esteemed knight who was taken ill and was on the point of death. We thereupon came to one of our great priests and said to him, "Come with us and examine so and so, the knight." "I will," he replied, and walked along with us while we were assured in ourselves that if he would only lay his hand on him the patient would recover. When the priest saw the patient, he said, "Bring me some wax." We fetched him a little wax, which he softened and shaped like the knuckles of fingers, and he stuck one in each nostril. The knight died on the spot. We said to him, "He is dead." "Yes," he replied, "he was suffering great pain, so I closed up his nose that he might die and get relief."

Let this go and let us resume the discussion regarding Harim.

A funny race between two aged women.—We shall now leave the discussion of their treatment of the orifices of the body to something else.

I found myself in Tabarayyah at the time the Franks were celebrating one of their feasts. The cavaliers went out to exercise with lances. With them went out two decrepit, aged women whom they stationed at one end of the race course. At the other end of the field they left a pig which they had scalded and laid on a rock. They then made the two aged women run a race while each one of them was accompanied by a detachment of horsemen urging her on. At every step they took, the women would fall down and rise again, while the spectators would laugh. Finally, one of them got ahead of the other and won that pig for a prize.

Their judicial trials: A duel.—I attended one day a duel in Nablus between two Franks. The reason for this was that certain Muslim thieves took by surprise one of the villages of Nablus. One of the peasants of that village was charged with having acted as guide for the thieves when they fell upon the village. So he fled away. The king [Fulk of Anjou, r. 1131–42] sent and arrested his children. The peasant thereupon came back to the king and said, "Let justice be done in my case. I challenge to a duel the man who claimed that I guided the thieves to the village." The king then said to the tenant who held the village in fief, "Bring forth someone to fight the duel with him." The tenant went to his village, where a blacksmith lived, took hold of him and ordered him to fight the duel. The tenant became thus sure of the safety of his own peasants, none of whom would be killed and his estate ruined.

I saw this blacksmith. He was a physically strong young man, but his heart failed him. He would walk a few steps and then sit down and ask for a drink. The one who had made the challenge was an old man, but he was strong in spirit and he would rub the nail of his thumb against that of the forefinger in defiance, as if he was not worrying over the duel. Then came the viscount, that is, the seignior of the town, and gave each one of the two contestants a cudgel and a shield and arranged the people in a circle around them.

The two met. The old man would press the blacksmith backward until he would get him as far as the circle, then he would come back to the middle of the arena. They went on exchanging blows until they looked like pillars smeared with blood. The contest was prolonged and the viscount began to urge them to hurry, saying, "Hurry on." The fact that the smith was given to the use of the hammer proved now of great advantage to him. The old man was worn out and the smith gave him a blow which made him fall. His cudgel fell under his back. The smith knelt down over him and tried to stick his fingers into the eyes of his adversary, but could not do it because of the great quantity of blood flowing out. Then he rose up and hit his head with the cudgel until he killed him. They then fastened a rope around the neck of the dead person, dragged him away and hanged him. The lord who brought the smith now came, gave the smith his own mantle, made him mount the horse behind him and rode off with him. This case illustrates the kind of jurisprudence and legal decisions the Franks have—may Allah's curse be upon them!

Ordeal by water.—I once went in the company of al-Emir Mu'in-al-Din (may Allah's mercy rest upon his soul!) to Jerusalem. We stopped at Nablus. There a blind man, a Muslim, who was still young and was well dressed, presented himself before al-emir carrying fruits for him and asked permission to be admitted into his service in Damascus. The emir consented. I inquired about this man and was informed that his mother had been married to a Frank whom she had killed. Her son used to practice ruses against the Frankish pilgrims and cooperate with his mother in assassinating them. They finally brought charges against him and tried his case according to the Frankish way of procedure.

They installed a huge cask and filled it with water. Across it, they set a board of wood. They then bound the arms of the man charged with the act, tied a rope around his shoulders and dropped him into the cask, their idea being that in case he was innocent, he would sink in the water and they would then lift him up with the rope so that he might not die in the water; and in case he was guilty, he would not sink in the water. This man did his best to sink when they dropped him into the water, but he could not do it. So he had to submit to their sentence against him—may Allah's curse be upon them! They pierced his eyeballs with red-hot awls.

Later this same man arrived in Damascus. Al-Emir Mu'in-al-Din (may Allah's mercy rest upon his soul!) assigned him a stipend large enough to meet all his needs and said to a slave of his, "Conduct him to Burhan-al-Din al-Balkhi (may Allah's mercy rest upon his soul!) and ask him on my behalf to order somebody to teach this man the Quran and something of Muslim jurisprudence." Hearing that, the blind man remarked, "May triumph and victory be thine! But this was never my thought." "What didst thou think I was going to do for thee?" asked Mu'in-al-Din. The blind man replied, "I thought you wouldst give me a horse, a mule, and a suit of armor and make me a knight." Mu'in-al-Din then said, "I never thought that a blind man could become a knight."

A Frank domesticated in Syria abstains from eating pork.—Among the Franks are those who have become acclimatized and have associated long with the Muslims. These are much better than the recent comers from the Frankish lands. But they constitute the exception and cannot be treated as a rule.

Here is an illustration. I dispatched one of my men to Antioch on business. There was in Antioch at that time al-Ra'is Theodoros Sophianos, to whom I was bound by mutual ties of amity. His influence in Antioch was supreme. One day he said to my man, "I am invited by a friend of mine who is a Frank. You should come with me so that you may see their fashions." My man related the story in the following words:

I went along with him and we came to the home of a knight who belonged to the old category of knights who came with the early expeditions of the Franks. He had been by that time stricken off the register and exempted from service, and possessed in Antioch an estate on the income of which he lived. The knight presented an excellent table, with food extraordinarily clean and delicious. Seeing me abstaining from food, he said, "Eat, be of good cheer! I never eat Frankish dishes, but I have Egyptian women cooks and never eat except their cooking. Besides, pork never enters my home." I ate, but guardedly, and after that we departed.

As I was passing in the market place, a Frankish woman all of a sudden hung to my clothes and began to mutter words in their language, and I could not understand what she was saying. This made me immediately the center of a big crowd of Franks. I was convinced that death was at hand. But all of a sudden, that same knight approached. On seeing me, he came and said to that woman, "What is the matter between you and this Muslim?" She replied, "This is he who has killed my brother Hurso." This Hurso was a knight in Afamiyah who was killed by someone of the army of Hamah. The Christian knight shouted at her, saying, "This is a bourgeois [a merchant] who neither fights nor attends a fight." He also yelled at the people who had assembled, and they all dispersed. Then he took me by the hand and went away. Thus, the effect of that meal was my deliverance from certain death.

59. A VICTORY SERMON

The conquest of Jerusalem by Saladin in 1187 brought much rejoicing to the Islamic world. On the first Friday after Saladin and his army entered the city, the Muslim preacher Muhammad Ibn Zeky delivered the sermon below in exultation of the Muslim victory. The sermon is one of thanksgiving and praise for the Islamic warriors who had taken the city. Ibn Zeky also uses the sermon to warn his listeners of vices that could nullify their victory. But in the sermon, praise for Muslims and Islam is often contrasted with insults and mockery of Christians and Christianity. The sermon draws a stark difference between the two faiths and their followers and casts the Islamic victory and Christian defeat as the will of God, who, in the discourse of the sermon, had clearly made a choice as to who were his chosen people and who were not.

Source: trans. W. Robson in Joseph Francois Michaud, *The History of the Crusades*, 3 vols. (London: George Routledge and Sons, 1881), III: 376–79; rev. Jarbel Rodriguez.

Praise to God, who has raised Islam into glory by his aid; who has abased polytheism by his power; who rules worldly things by his will; who prolongs his blessings according to the measure of our gratitude; who defeats infidels by his stratagems; who gives power to dynasties, according to his justice; who has reserved future life for those who fear him, by an effort of his goodness; who extends his shadow over his servants; who has caused his religion to triumph over all others; who gains the victory over his servants without any one being able to oppose him; who triumphs in his caliph, without any one being able to resist him; who orders what he wills, without any being able to make objections to it; who judges according to his will, without any one being able to avert the execution of his decrees. I praise this God for having by his assistance rendered his elect victorious; for the glory he has given them; for the aid he has granted to his defenders; I praise him for having purified the house filled with pollution, from the impieties of polytheism. I praise him inwardly and outwardly. I give testimony that there is no other God but this God; that he is the only one, and has no associate; the only one, the eternal one, who begets not, neither is he begotten, and has no equal. I give testimony that Muhammad is his servant and his messenger, this prophet who has removed doubts, confounded polytheism, extinguished falsehood; who traveled by night from Medina to Jerusalem; who ascended into the heavens, and reached even the cedar Almontehy. May the eternal felicity of God be with him, with his successor Abou Bakr Alsadic, etc.

O men! Publish the extraordinary blessing by which God has made easy to you the recapture and deliverance of this city which we had lost, and has made it again the center of Islam, after having been during nearly a hundred years in the hands of the infidels. This house was built and its foundations laid for the glory of God and in the fear of Heaven. For this house is the dwelling of Abraham; the ladder of your prophet (peace be with him!); the kiblah towards which you prayed at the commencement of Islam, the abode of prophets, the aim of saints, the place of revelation, the habitation of order and defense; it is situated in the land of the gathering, the arena of the meeting; it is of this blessed land of which God speaks in his sacred book. It was in this mosque that Muhammad prayed with the angels who approach God. It was this city to which God sent his servant, his messenger, the word which he sent to Mary. The prophet he honored with a mission did not stray from the rank of his servant. For God said, "the Messiah will not deny that he is the servant of God; God has no son, and has no other God with him." Truly, they have been in impiety, they who have said that the Messiah, the son of Mary, was God.

This house is the first of the two kiblah, the second of the mosques, the third of the héramëin; it is not toward it that the people come in crowds after the two mesdjed; it is toward it that the fingers are pointed after the two places [Mecca and Medina?]. If you were not of the number of the servants whom God has chosen, truly he would not have favored you particularly by this advantage which has been granted to no other brave men, the honor of which no one can dispute with you; how fortunate you are in being the soldiers of an army which has made manifest the miracles of the prophet, which has made the expeditions of Abu Bakr, the conquests of Omar, etc. God has rewarded you by the best of rewards in that which you have done for his prophet. He has been grateful for the courage you have shown in punishing rebels; the blood which you have shed for him has been acceptable to him; it has introduced you into the Paradise which is the abode of the blessed. Acknowledge, then, the value of this blessing, offer up to him necessary thanksgivings; for God has shown for you a marked beneficence in granting you this blessing, in selecting you for this expedition. For the gates of Heaven have been opened for this conquest; its splendor has cast a light which has penetrated even to the deepest darkness; the angels who approach the Divine Majesty have rejoiced at it; the eye of the prophets and the messengers has beheld it with joy. Since, by the favor of God, you are the army which will conquer Jerusalem at the end of time, the troop which will raise the standards of the faith after the destruction of the prophecy.

This house, is it not that of which God spoke in his book? For he says, "Be he praised who made his servant travel by night." Is this not the house which the nations have revered; towards which the prophets came, in which the four books sent from God have been read? Is this not the house for which God stopped the sun, under Joshua, and retarded the march of day, in order that his conquest should be easy, and should be accelerated? Is this not the house which God committed to Moses, and which he commanded his people to save; but, with the exception of two men, these people would not; God was angry against these people, and cast them into the desert, to punish them for their rebellion.

I praise the God who has conducted you to the place from which he banished the children of Israel; and yet these were distinguished above other nations. God has seconded you in an enterprise in which he had abandoned other nations that had preceded you; which has caused there to be but one opinion among you, while formerly opinions differed; rejoice that God has named you among those who are near him, and has made of you his own army, after you became his soldiers by your own free will. The angels [who were sent toward this house] have thanked you for having brought here the doctrine of the unity.

Now the powers of the heavens pray for you, and pour benedictions upon you. Preserve this gift in you, by the fear of God. Whoever possesses it is saved. Beware of the passions, of disobedience, of falling back, of flying from an enemy. Are you eager to take advantage of the opportunity to destroy what anguish remains? Fight for God as you ought; sacrifice yourselves to please him, you his servants, since you are of the number of the elect. Beware that the devil do not come down among you again, and that irreligion introduce not itself into your hearts. Did you figure to yourselves that your swords of steel, your chosen horses, your untiring perseverance, have gained you this victory? No, it was God; it was from him alone that your success came. Beware, servants of God after having obtained this victory, of becoming disobedient and rebellious; for then you will be like her who cut to pieces that which she had spun, or like him to whom we have sent our verses, and who has rejected them; the devil has laid hold of him, and he has wandered from the faith. The holy war! The holy war! That is the best of your worships, the most noble of your customs; help God, and he will help you; hold to God, and he will hold to you; remember him, and be will remember you; do good towards him, and he will do good towards you; endeavor to cut off every diseased member, to destroy even to the last enemy; purify the rest of the earth of those nations with whom God and his messenger are angry. Lop off the branches of impiety, and fear, for already the days have grown. Vengeance of Muslim attacks, of the Islamic nation. God is great: he gives conquests, he degrades impiety; learn that this is a great opportunity—seize it; it is a prey, cast yourselves upon it; it is a booty, get possession of it. It is an important business, apply your whole means to it, give yourselves up to it entirely; put the battalions of your tribes on the march for it. For this business draws towards its end, and the treasuries are filled with wealth. God has already given you the victory over these vile enemies. These enemies were equal to you, or perhaps more numerous than you; but however that might be, he has manifested that one of you is worth twenty other men. God will aid you as you cause his orders to be obeyed, and abstain from that which he has prohibited. He will strengthen all us Muslims by a victory; if God helps you, you have no other conqueror to fear; but if he withdraws his help from you, who will be he that shall help you after him?

60. A CHRISTIAN VIEW OF ISLAM

Much of the Christian polemical language on Islam focused on the figure of the prophet Muhammad and his teachings. The earliest Latin biographies of Muhammad date from the early twelfth century and depict the prophet as a trickster, magician, and heresiarch. Much of this was the result of a dearth of real information in Europe about Islam or Muhammad. In the absence of reliable sources, Christian writers often turned to established archetypes or their own imaginations to construct an image of Islam and Muslims that made them acceptable enemies to a Latin Europe in the midst of crusading fever. Moreover, Christian concerns about the wealth, power, and influence of the Islamic world on Christian Europe meant that Islam and its prophet had to be discredited by attacking Muhammad's character and mission and claiming that Islam was little more than a heresy. The source below, from the English historian Matthew Paris, is part of this tradition, albeit from the mid-thirteenth century. In it, Matthew Paris follows in the footsteps of twelfth-century forebears such as Guibert of Nogent, Petrus Alfonsi, and Peter the Venerable, abbot of Cluny, and writes a narrative that is a mixture of fantastic, xenophobic, and pejorative claims mixed with misinterpretations and misunderstandings—as well as some accurate facts.

Source: trans. J.A. Giles, *Matthew Paris's English History from the Year 1235 to 1273*, 2 vols. (London: Henry G. Bohn, 1852), I: 21–23.

The Belief of the Saracens According to the Commands of Muhammad

Many of the Saracens believe that there is one God, the creator of all men: they have, however, no belief in the Trinity, which they reject entirely. According to the writings of Muhammad, they abominate idolatry, for he mixed some good doctrines with his evil ones, in order the more warily to make persons drink his poison seasoned with honey. They state that our Lord Jesus Christ was born of the Virgin Mary, by the Holy Ghost, and they say that he was a creator by the virtue of God, as also, they say was Adam, for they place him on a level with

Adam, or Moses, or one of the prophets. They also believe that he was taken to Heaven and still is alive there, for, as he came from God, so he has returned to, and remains with God, and they expect that he will still reign for forty years on earth. His crucifixion, suffering, and death, they altogether deny, and say that some other man was substituted to suffer in his stead, and, that when he was about to suffer, it became so dark in order that this might not be found out. They also declare that, from the days of Noah, all the patriarchs and prophets, and Jesus Christ himself, have observed the same law as they, and by it have been saved. They say that we have perverted the law of the Gospel, and have erased the name of Muhammad from it. For the scripture of the Saracens has it that, before the heavens and the earth were made, the name of Muhammad existed with God, and if there had been no Muhammad, there would have been no heaven, earth, paradise, or hell; wherefore, from this sole sentence, so pregnant with folly, all wise Saracens may see the vanity of his other doctrines. They expect and believe in the resurrection, but they say that, at the Day of Judgment, no one of their adherents will perish or be doomed to punishment, but that they will all be saved. For they say that all who keep their law will obtain salvation of God by the intercession of Muhammad, and will never be punished. They believe that, after this temporal life, they will live eternally, and dwell forever in paradise, whence there flow forth rivers of honey, wine, and milk, for the enjoyment of every one living there; and that whatever any of them may ask to eat and drink, will at once be sent to them from heaven. Also, that however many male or female children any one of them may desire to be born, they shall at once be born to him; they declare that there no one will mourn or be sorrowful, but that they shall be refreshed with various and universal delights and enjoy endless felicity, and they believe that the advantages, riches, and pleasures of the present life will not prevent their future happiness.

Of Marriage among the Saracens

According to their law, a man may take three or four wives, if he has sufficient means to support them; their wives ought to be free women; but of female slaves and concubines, they keep as many as they can manage or feed; contrary to what is said in Genesis, "There shall be two in one flesh." It does not say, "three or four." Again, Lamech, who first introduced polygamy, was rebuked by God, and punished worse than the first murderer. If anyone among them is displeased with his wife, or if any contention, dispute, or hatred arises between them, a divorce is at once effected both on the part of the husband and of the wife, and each releases the other. If, however, a man, after putting away his wife, repents of so doing, and wishes her to be restored to him, unless she has previously formed a connection with another man, and she herself consents to return to him, he is in no wise allowed to take her to wife. This is so, because among them there is no legitimate marriage. They pay their dowries, not according to the law, but after the manner of the heathens, for they have no doctrinal guidance in these things, and no blessing is bestowed upon their nuptials.

Their Superstition

They chiefly have connection with their wives during their time of fasting, thinking that they the better please God by this. They fast only one month in the year, and then from the morning till night; from the beginning of the night till the morning they eat continually; on their days of fasting it is not proper for them to pray with an empty belly, but then they mostly have intercourse with their wives, as if they will obtain a greater recompense. If at the time of fasting anyone is sick, or troubled in any way, or is on a pilgrimage, he is allowed to eat, and to renew his fasting when he is restored to health. At their time of fasting they eat flesh and all richer sorts of food, except wine. They hold no intercourse with their wives when pregnant, but only before conception, alleging as an honorable motive, that they ought not to do it unless to obtain offspring. They always perform their devotions looking towards the south; and they reverence Friday above all other days. In their judgments, whoever is accused of murder, if he is proved guilty, by any witnesses, is at once condemned to death as an atonement for his crime; and in their law it is written, "If any one does not observe the law, and denies Muhammad, let him be kept till the third day; and if he does not then repent, let him be put to death."

61. BURCHARD OF MOUNT SION ON THE PEOPLE OF THE EAST

The German friar Burchard of Mount Sion spent many years in the Holy Land, Egypt, and Syria, including ten years at the Monastery of Mount Sion in Jerusalem. Based on his experiences he wrote a long treatise around 1280, describing the lands of the East, which focuses on the many different faiths and sects that he encountered in his travels. Modern editors of his work have found him to be a very observant, accurate, and tolerant writer. Some of this comes through in the selection below, but so do some of the prejudices of the age.

Source: trans. Aubrey Stewart, *Burchard of Mount Sion, A.D. 1280* (London: Palestine Pilgrim's Text Society Vol. XII (1896; repr. New York: AMS Press, 1971), 102–11; rev. Jarbel Rodriguez.

There are dwelling therein men of every nation under heaven, and each man follows his own rite, and, to tell the truth, our own people, the Latins, are worse than all the other people of the land. The reason of this, I think, is that when any man has been a malefactor, as, for example, a homicide, a robber, a thief, or an adulterer, he crosses the sea as a penitent, or else because he fears for his skin, and therefore dares not stay at home. Wherefore men come thither from all parts—from Germany, Italy, France, England, Spain, Hungary, and all other parts of the world; yet they do but change their climate, not their mind: for when they are there, after they have spent what they brought with them, they have to earn some more, and therefore return again to their vomit, and do worse than they did before. They lodge pilgrims of their own nation in their houses, and these men, if they know not how to take care of themselves, trust them, and lose both their property and their honor. They also breed children, who imitate the crimes of their fathers, and thus bad fathers beget sons worse than themselves, from whom descend most vile grandchildren, who tread upon the holy places with polluted feet. Hence, it comes to pass that, because of the sins of the dwellers in the land against God, the land itself, and the place of our redemption, is brought into contempt.

Besides the Latins there are many other races there; for example, the Saracens, who preach Muhammad and keep his law. They call our Lord Jesus Christ the greatest of the prophets, and confess that he was conceived of the Holy Ghost and born of the Virgin Mary. But they deny that he suffered and was buried, but choose to say that he ascended into heaven, and sits upon the right hand of the Father, because they admit him to be the son of God. But they declare that Muhammad sits on his left hand. They are very unclean, and have as many wives as they can feed; yet, nevertheless, they practice unnatural sins, and have ephebiae [boys] in every city. Yet they are very hospitable, courteous, and kindly.

Besides these there are the Syrians. The whole land is full of these. They are Christians, but keep no faith with the Latins. They are clothed most wretchedly, and are stingy, giving no alms. They dwell among the Saracens, and for the most part are their servants. In dress they are like the Saracens, except that they are distinguished from them by a woolen girdle.

The Greeks in like manner are Christians, but schismatics, save that a great part of them returned to obedience to the Church at a General Council held by our Lord Gregory X [in 1274 at Lyons]. In the Greek Church all the prelates are monks, and are men of exceeding austerity of life and wondrous virtue.

The Greeks are exceedingly devout, and for the most part greatly honor and revere their prelates. I have heard one of their patriarchs say in my presence: "We would willingly live in obedience to the Church of Rome, and venerate it; but I am much surprised at my being ranked below the inferior clergy, such as archbishops and bishops. Some archbishops and bishops wish to make me a patriarch, kiss their feet, and do them personal service, which I do not hold myself bound to do, albeit I would willingly do so for the pope, but for no one else."

There are also Armenians, Georgians, Nestorians, Nubians, Jacobites, Chaldeans, Medes, Persians, Ethiopians, Egyptians, and many other peoples who are Christians. Of those there is an infinite number. Each of them have their own patriarch and obey him. Their prelates declare that they would most willingly belong to the Church of Rome. Of these the Nestorians, Jacobites, and the like are so named after certain heretics who once were their chiefs.

Moreover, there are in the Holy Land Midianites, who now are called Bedouins and Turcomans, who apply themselves solely to feeding flocks and camels, of which they have exceeding great numbers. These people have no fixed dwellings, but wherever they learn that there is pasture, thither they go and pitch their tents. They are exceedingly warlike, yet only use swords and lances in battle. They do not use arrows, saying that it is base beyond measure to steal away a man's life with an arrow. They are brave in war, but wear only a red shirt, and over it a large flowing mantle, covering their heads only with a cloth. All Syria is full of them, but for the most part, they dwell round about the river Jordan, from Lebanon even to the wilderness of Paran, because there are mountains for sheep and goats, and plains for cattle and camels. The sheep in those parts, and especially the rams, are very big, and have tails of such a size that one tail is as much as three or four men can eat.

Round about the castle of Arachas, beyond Tripoli, up to the castle of Krach [Crac des Chevaliers], dwell the Saracens called Vannini. Adjoining them are the Saracens called Assassins, who dwell in the mountains beyond Antaradus near the castle of Margat. They have many castles and cities and a fertile land, and are said to have forty thousand fighting men. They have one chief, not by hereditary succession, but by personal merit, who is called the Old Man of the Mountains—not because of his age, but of his wisdom. These people are said to be of Persian origin. I have passed through a part of this country. They are obedient even to death, and at their superior's bidding slay anyone so ever, and say that thereby they gain paradise, even if they be slain before they have fulfilled their orders. A few years ago they wished to become obedient to the Church of Rome, and to this end sent an ambassador to Acre, who transacted the negotiation to his complete satisfaction, but on his homeward journey he was murdered by his escort just before entering his own land, to the loss of the Church as a body, because the others, when they saw that Christians were not to be trusted, straightway drew back. The boundary between these people's land and that of the Christians is marked by some stones, on which on the side of the Christians are carved crosses, and on that of the Assassins knives. None of the sultans have hitherto been able to subdue them, but they make their own laws and customs and follow them as they choose. They are a terror to all the nations round about because of their exceeding great fierceness.

Now, it must be noted as a matter of fact, albeit some, who like to talk about what they have never seen, declare the contrary, that the whole East beyond the Mediterranean Sea, even unto India and Ethiopia, acknowledges and preaches the name of Christ, save only the Saracens and some Turcomans who dwell in Cappadocia, so that I declare for certain, as I have myself seen and have heard from others who knew, that always in every place and kingdom, besides Egypt and Arabia, where Saracens and other followers of Muhammad chiefly dwell, you will find thirty Christians and more for one Saracen. But the truth is that all the Christians beyond the sea are easterners by nation, and albeit they are Christians, yet, as they are not much practiced in the use of arms, when they are assailed by the Saracens, Turks, or any other people so ever, yield to them and buy peace and quiet by paying tribute, and the Saracens, or other lords of the land, place their bailiffs and tax-gatherers therein. Hence, it arises that their kingdom is said to belong to the Saracens, whereas, as a matter of fact, all the people are Christians save those bailiffs and tax-gatherers and their families, as I have seen with my own eyes in Cilicia and Lesser Armenia, which is subject to the rule of the Tartars. I lived for three weeks in the palace of the king of Armenia and Cilicia, and there were a few Tartars at his court; but all the rest of his household were Christians, to the number of about two hundred. I used to see them frequent the church, hear masses, kneel, and pray devoutly. Moreover, whenever any of them met me and my companion, they did us great honor by taking off their hats and respectfully bowing to us, greeting us, and rising up at our approach. Many, too, are frightened when they are told that in parts beyond seas there dwell Nestorians, Jacobites, Maronites, Georgians, and other sects named after heretics whom the Church has condemned, wherefore these men are thought to be heretics, and to follow the errors of those after whom they are called. This is by no means true. God forbid! But they are men of simple and devout life; yet I do not deny that there may be fools among them, seeing that even the Church of Rome itself is not free from fools. Now, all these aforesaid nations, and many others whom it would take long to write down, have archbishops, bishops, abbots, and other prelates, even as we ourselves, and call them by the same names, all save the Nestorians, whose chief prelate is called Iaselich. He is their pope, and I have learned for certain that his jurisdiction reaches much farther in the East than that of the entire western church. The other prelates of that sect, however, are called archbishops and bishops like our own.

The chief prelate of the Armenians and Georgians is called the catholicus. I stayed with him for fourteen days, and he had with him many archbishops and bishops, abbots, and other prelates. In his diet, his clothes, and his way of life, he was so exemplary, that I have never seen anyone, religious or secular, like him; and I declare of a truth that in my opinion all the clothes that he wore were not worth five shillings sterling, and yet he had exceedingly strong castles and great revenues, and was rich beyond any man's counting. He wore a coarse red sheepskin pelisse, very shabby and dirty, with wide sleeves, and under it a gray tunic, very old, and almost worn out. Above this, he wore a black scapular, and a cheap rough black mantle. I have seen the king of Armenia and Cilicia with all his nobles sitting humbly and with the greatest reverence at his feet, the king often having with him his eldest son, and most devoutly hearing from him the word of God. He and all his prelates used to fast all Lent on bread and water, and so did the king and all his nobles, save on the Feast of the Annunciation, when in my presence the catholicus allowed himself to eat some fish and drink wine. On that day I heard a mass in the presence of the same catholicus, and of the king and queen. Their ritual is an exceedingly devout one: their priests and bishops are robed like ours. They use unleavened bread in their mass, and chant the Epistles, Gospels, and prefaces, the Sanctus, Pater Noster, and Agnus Dei in the Mass, in the same words that we do; but in their own language and letters, for they have a language and alphabet of their own. The catholicus and all the other prelates are monks, and throughout all the East no one of any nation can be a prelate unless he be a monk. All monks are greatly revered and honored. Clerks and priests have no authority, neither do the laity pay any regard to them, and they have no duties save celebrating divine service. They mark all the canonical hours by beating a plank or other piece of wood, because they have no bells. When notice is given at night, they go to matins calling out to the people as they go through the streets to come to matins. After matins they do not go to sleep again, but sit in church and teach the people until dawn, when they say the first mass, or till about the hour of tierce, if it be a feast-day. They have no authority besides this, save what is granted them by their vartabeds [theological scholars]. All priests are married, and no one is suffered to conduct service unless he has a wife. They never celebrate masses on Monday, nor yet thenceforth till Friday, inclusively, however great a feast may fall on those days, but are at liberty to converse with their wives; but on Saturday and Sunday they celebrate masses with great solemnity. After his wife's death a priest must be continent, and not marry a second wife. If he be guilty of fornication or adultery, he must lose his church and his office; nor can any dispensation be made in his favor. If a priest's wife be guilty of adultery, he must either be continent, or he must lose his office and his church, and his wife must lose her nose, and her paramour be castrated, even though he be a married man. This was done in my presence. When a priest dies, his wife must be continent. If she marries again, she shall be burned alive; but if she becomes a courtesan, no harm is done to her. And they have a new commandment among them, that a priest, like the apostle, should have a virgin to wife. The Armenian and Georgian priests are distinguished from the laity by a white linen cloth, which they wrap round their neck and shoulders.

Thieves who are guilty of petty thefts, or other evildoers who commit the lesser sorts of crime, are castrated, that they may not beget children to imitate their fathers' misdeeds. This seems to me to be one reason why there are so many courtesans there, for there are many eunuchs there, and all of them are in the service of noble ladies. I believe that the queen of Armenia had more than forty eunuchs when I was at her palace. No man visits her save by the king's special leave, and the king assigns to him some eunuch by name to show him in. So likewise is the custom with all noble ladies, both widows and married.

All the kings, princes, and nobles are most willing to hear the word of God; wherefore every day at the hour of tierce [around 3:00 A.M.] some doctors or monks go to the court of every king or prince. The princes or lords straight-way come themselves together with their children and their great men. Some book of Scripture is brought, and is read in their presence in the vulgar tongue, for they know no other. The monk expounds the text to them, and whenever the laymen feel doubts and raise questions, the monks instruct them according to the words of the saints. I have questioned these monks as to which doctors they chiefly follow, and they replied that their chief authorities were John Chrysostom, Gregory Nazianzen, and Cyril of Alexandria. Both clergy and laity are very devout in church, and never do anything there but pray or sing or do whatever else ought to be done there. I never saw anyone laugh or behave himself unseemly in church.

The Office of the Mass is devoutly performed in their church. The cup is placed on the left hand of the altar in a place made for the purpose in the wall. At the offertory prayer the deacon, wearing a precious silk cloth, reverently raises it above his head. With a subdeacon carrying the thurible [a metal censer], and two acolytes carrying candles walking before him, they circle round behind the altar to the right-hand side thereof, and then the bishop reverently takes it and offers it, even as our priests do. Two stand with lighted candles behind the priest while the canon of the Mass is being read, and near them two with thuribles, wearing albs. Two deacons stand on the right and left hand sides of the altar, praying devoutly with joined hands, their faces turned to the body of Christ, singing a sweet and pious melody and answering one another. Indeed, it is a most holy thing to see and hear.

I have seen many other very commendable practices in that land, both among laymen, clerks, and monks, which in our land would scarce be believed to be done.

I have traveled over the whole of this land, even to Cappadocia and Seleucia by the sea, and have sailed thence to Cyprus, and wandered over the greater part thereof. Thence I sailed to Syria and came to Tyre, and some days afterwards, sailing along the coast of Palestine or Philistia, I passed by Haifa, Mount Carmel, Dora, Caesarea of Palestine, Antipatris, Joppa, Iamnia, Ekron, Ashdod, Ascalon,

Gaza, and the whole sandy desert even to the mouths of the river Nile. Thence I came to Damietta, which of old was called Memphis. This is the land of Goshen, wherein the children of Israel sojourned of old, serving pharaoh in mortar and in brick. In this land also Jeremiah was afterwards stoned.

Blessed be God and Saint Matthew. Amen.

62. THE POPE, THE PATRIARCH, AND THE KOHEN

Ibn Khaldun's Muqaddimah *delved into many areas of human knowledge. Among them was the following discussion on Christianity (both Latin and Greek) and Judaism in which Ibn Khaldun addresses the leadership of each group and uses the offices of kohen, patriarch, and pope to organize his information. He displays not only his religious interest in the other two monotheistic faiths but his historical knowledge of their development as well. As with many of his contemporaries, Muslim and Christian, Ibn Khaldun used his writings to compare and contrast his own faith to that of others.*

Source: trans. Franz Rosenthal, Ibn Khaldun, *The Muqaddimah: An Introduction to History*, ed. N.J. Dawood (Princeton, NJ: Princeton University Press, 1967, repr. 1989), 183–88.

Remarks on the Words "Pope" and "Patriarch" in the Christian Religion and on the Word "Kohen" Used by the Jews

It should be known that after the removal of its prophet, a religious group must have someone to take care of it. Such a person must cause the people to act according to the religious laws. In a way, he stands to them in the place of their prophet, inasmuch as he enjoins the obligations which the prophet had imposed upon them. Furthermore, in accordance with the aforementioned need for political leadership in social organization, the human species must have a person who will cause them to act in accordance with what is good for them and who will prevent them by force from doing things harmful to them. Such a person is the one who is called ruler.

In the Muslim community, the holy war is a religious duty, because of the universalism of the Muslim mission and [the obligation to] convert everybody to Islam either by persuasion or by force. Therefore, caliphate and royal authority are united in Islam, so that the person in charge can devote the available strength to both of them at the same time.

The other religious groups did not have a universal mission, and the holy war was not a religious duty to them, save only for purposes of defense. It has thus come about that the person in charge of religious affairs in [other religious groups] is not concerned with power politics at all. [Among them] royal authority comes to those who have it—by accident and in some way that has nothing to do with religion. It comes to them as the necessary result of group feeling, which by its very nature seeks to obtain royal authority, as we have mentioned before, and not because they are under obligation to gain power over other nations, as is the case with Islam. They are merely required to establish their religion among their own people.

This is why the Israelites after Moses and Joshua remained unconcerned with royal authority for about four hundred years. Their only concern was to establish their religion. The person from among them who was in charge of their religion was called the kohen. He was in a way the representative [caliph] of Moses. He regulated the prayers and sacrifices of the Israelites. They made it a condition for him to be a descendant of Aaron, as it had been destined for him and his children by divine revelation. For [supervision of the] political matters which naturally arise among human beings, the Israelites selected seventy elders who were entrusted with a general legal authority. The kohen was higher in religious rank than they and more remote from the turbulent legal authority. This continued to obtain [among the Israelites] until the nature of group feeling made itself fully felt and all power became political. The Israelites dispossessed the Canaanites of the land that God had given them as their heritage in Jerusalem and the surrounding region, as it had been explained to them through Moses. The nations of the Philistines, the Canaanites, the Armenians, the Edomites, the Ammonites, and the Moabites fought against them. During that time political leadership was entrusted to the elders among them. The Israelites remained in that condition for about four hundred years. They did not have any royal power and were harassed by attacks from foreign nations. Therefore, they asked God through Samuel, one of their prophets, that he permit them to make someone king over them. Thus, Saul became their king. He defeated the foreign nations and killed Goliath, the ruler of the Philistines. After Saul, David became king, and then Solomon. His kingdom flourished and extended to the borders of the Hijaz and further to the borders of the Yemen and to the borders of [what became] the land of the Byzantines. After Solomon, the tribes split into two dynasties. This was in accordance with the necessary consequence of group feeling in dynasties, as we have mentioned before. One of the dynasties was that of the ten tribes in the region of Nablus, the capital of which is Samaria [Sabas-tiyah], and the other that of the children of Judah and Benjamin in Jerusalem. Nebuchadnezzar, the king of Babylon, then deprived them of their royal author-ity. He first [dealt with] the ten tribes in Samaria, and then with the children of Judah in Jerusalem. Their royal authority had had an uninterrupted duration of a thousand years. Now he destroyed their temple, burnt their Torah, and killed their religion. He deported the people to Isfahan and the Iraq. Eventually, one of the Persian Kayyanid [Achaemenid] rulers [Cyrus the Great] brought them back to Jerusalem, seventy years after they had left it. They rebuilt the temple and re-established their religion in its original form with priests only. The royal authority belonged to the Persians.

Alexander and the Greeks then defeated the Persians, and the Jews came under Greek domination. The Greek rule then weakened, and, with the help of their natural group feeling, the Jews rose against the Greeks and made an end to their domination over them. Jewish royal authority was in charge of their Hasmonean priests. The Hasmoneans fought the Greeks. Eventually, their power was destroyed. The Romans defeated them, and the Jews came under Roman domination. The Romans advanced toward Jerusalem, the seat of the children of Herod, relatives by marriage of the Hasmoneans and the last remnant of the Hasmonean dynasty. They laid siege to them for a time, finally conquering Jerusalem by force in an orgy of murder, destruction, and arson. They laid Jerusalem in ruins and exiled the Jews to Rome and the regions beyond. This was the second destruction of the temple. The Jews call it "the Great Exile." After that, they had no royal authority, because they had lost their group feeling. They remained afterwards under the domination of the Romans and their successors. Their religious affairs were taken care of by their head, called the kohen.

The Messiah [Jesus] brought the Jews his religion, as is known. He abolished some of the laws of the Torah. He performed marvelous wonders, such as healing the insane and reviving the dead. Many people joined him and believed in him. The largest group among his following were his companions, the apostles. There were twelve of them. He sent some of them as messengers to all parts of the world. They made propaganda for his religious group. That was in the days of Augustus, the first of the Roman emperors, and during the time of Herod, the king of the Jews, who had taken away royal authority from the Hasmoneans, his relatives by marriage. The Jews envied Jesus and declared him a liar. Their king, Herod, wrote to the Roman emperor, Augustus, and incited him against Jesus. The Roman emperor gave the Jews permission to kill him, and the story of Jesus as recited in the Quran occurred.

The apostles divided into different groups. Most of them went to the country of the Romans and made propaganda for the Christian religion. Peter was the greatest of them. He settled in Rome, the seat of the Roman emperors. They then wrote down the Gospel that had been revealed to Jesus, in four recensions according to their different traditions. Matthew wrote his Gospel in Jerusalem in Hebrew. It was translated into Latin by John, the son of Zebedee, one of the apostles. Luke wrote his Gospel in Latin for a Roman dignitary. John, the son of Zebedee, wrote his Gospel in Rome. Peter wrote his Gospel in Latin and ascribed it to his pupil Mark. These four recensions of the Gospel differ from each other. Not all of it is pure revelation, but the Gospels have an admixture of the words of Jesus and of the Apostles. They consist chiefly of sermons and stories. There are very few laws in them.

The apostles came together at that time in Rome and laid down the rules of the Christian community. They entrusted them to Clement, a pupil of Peter, noting in them the list of books that are to be accepted and in accordance with which one must act.

The books which belong to the old religious law of the Jews are the following:

> The Torah, which consists of five volumes.
> The Book of Joshua.
> The Book of Judges.
> The Book of Ruth.
> The Book of Judith.
> The four Books of Kings.
> The Book of Chronicles.
> The three Books of Maccabees, by Ibn Gorion.
> The Book of Ezra, the religious leader.
> The Book of Esther and the story of Haman.
> The Book of Job the Righteous.
> The Psalms of David.
> The five Books of David's son, Solomon.
> The sixteen Prophecies of the major and minor prophets.
> The Book of Jesus, the son of Sira, the minister of Solomon.

The books of the religious law of Jesus that was received by the apostles are the following:

> The four recensions of the Gospel.
> The Book of Paul which consists of fourteen epistles.
> The Katholika [General Epistles] which consist of seven epistles, the
> eighth being the Praxeis [Acts], stories of the Apostles.
> The Book of Clement which contains the laws.
> The Book of the Apocalypse [Revelation] which contains the vision
> of John, the son of Zebedee.

The attitude of the Roman emperors toward Christianity varied. At times, they adopted it and honored its adherents. At other times, they did not recognize it and persecuted its adherents and killed and exiled them. Finally, Constantine appeared and adopted Christianity. From then on, all [the Roman emperors] were Christians.

The head of the Christian [community] and the person in charge of [Christian religious] institutions is called patriarch. He is their religious head and the representative [caliph] of the Messiah among them. He sends his delegates and representatives to the remote Christian nations. They are called "bishop," that is, delegate of the patriarch. The man who leads the prayers and makes decisions in religious matters is called "priest." The person who withdraws from society and retires into solitude for worship is called "monk." The latter usually seeks solitude in monastic cells.

The apostle Peter, the chief apostle and oldest of the disciples, was in Rome and established the Christian religion there. Nero, the fifth Roman emperor, killed him. Successor to Peter at the Roman see was Arius.

Mark the Evangelist spent seven years in Alexandria and Egypt and the Maghreb making propaganda. After him came Ananias, who was called patriarch. He was the first patriarch there. He appointed twelve priests to be with him, and it was arranged that when the patriarch died, one of the twelve should take his place, and one of the faithful be elected to take his place as the twelfth priest. Thus, the patriarchate fell to the priests.

Later on, dissension broke out among the Christians with regard to the basic principles and articles of their religion. They assembled in Nicaea in the days of Constantine, in order to lay down [the doctrine of] true Christianity. Three hundred and eighteen bishops agreed upon one and the same doctrine of Christianity. They wrote it down and called it "the Creed." They made it the fundamental principle to which they would all have reference. Among the things they set down in writing was that with respect to the appointment of the patriarch as the head of Christianity, no reference should be made to the independent judgment of the priests, as Ananias, the disciple of Mark, had prescribed. That point of view was abolished. The patriarch was to come from a large group and to be elected by the leaders and chiefs of the believers. It has been so ever since. Later on, other dissensions arose concerning the basic principles of Christianity. Synods concerned with regulating [the religion] were assembled, but there was no dissension with regard to the basic principles of the method of selecting the patriarch. It has remained the same ever since.

The patriarchs always appointed bishops as their delegates. The bishops used to call the patriarch "Father," as a sign of respect. The priests similarly came to call the bishop "Father," when he was not together with the patriarch, as a sign of respect. This caused confusion in the use of the title over a long period, ending, it is said, with the patriarchate of Heraclius in Alexandria. It was considered desirable to distinguish the patriarch from the bishop in the matter of respect [shown to him by style of address]. Therefore, the patriarch was called "pope," that is, "Father of fathers." The name first appeared in Egypt, according to the theory expressed by Jirjis b. al-'Amid in his History. It was then transferred to the occupant of the most important see, the see of Rome, which was the see of the apostle Peter, as we have mentioned before. The title of pope has remained characteristic of the see of Rome down to this day.

Thereafter, there were dissensions among the Christians with regard to their religion and to Christology. They split into groups and sects, which secured the support of the various Christian rulers against each other. At different times there appeared different sects. Finally, these sects crystallized into three groups, which constitute the Christian sects. Others have no significance. These are the Melchites, the Jacobites, and the Nestorians. We do not think that we should blacken the pages of this book with discussion of their dogmas of unbelief. In general, they are well known. All of them are unbelief. This is clearly stated in the noble Quran. To discuss or argue those things with them is not for us. It is [for them to choose between] conversion to Islam, payment of the poll tax, or death.

Later on, each sect had its own patriarch. The patriarch of Rome is today called "pope." He is of the Melchite persuasion, Rome belongs to the European Christians. Their royal authority is established in that region.

The patriarch of the Christian subjects in Egypt is of the Jacobite persuasion. He resides among them. The Abyssinians follow the religion of [the Egyptian Christians]. The patriarch of Egypt delegates bishops to the Abyssinians, and these bishops arrange religious affairs in Abyssinia. The name of "pope" is specially reserved for the patriarch of Rome at this time. The Jacobites do not call their patriarch "pope." The word is pronounced pappa.

It is the custom of the pope with respect to the European Christians to urge them to submit to one ruler and have recourse to him in their disagreements and agreements, in order to avoid the dissolution of the whole thing. His purpose is to have the group feeling that is the strongest among them [concentrated upon one ruler], so that he has power over all of them. The ruler is called "emperor." [The pope] personally places the crown upon the head of [the emperor], in order to let him have the blessing implied [in that ceremony]. The emperor, therefore, is called "the crowned one." Perhaps that is the meaning of the word "emperor."

This, briefly, is our comment on the two words pope and kohen.

63. THE EMPEROR AND THE GRAND TURK

Pedro Tafur was born in Cordoba, Spain, around 1410. In 1435, he set out on a grand journey that took him to northern Africa, Egypt, the Holy Land, Constantinople, and Cyprus, as well as numerous stops on the European mainland. He returned to Spain in 1439, and sometime in the mid-1450s he recorded the memoirs of his far-reaching travels. Tafur was a daring and charismatic traveler, meeting some of the most important figures of his day and visiting a long list of renowned cultural sites. During his stay in Jerusalem, for example, he convinced a Christian convert to Islam to sneak him into the Mosque of Oman, which was partly built on the ruins of the Temple of Solomon. His description of the Mosque and Jerusalem itself lacks the verbal jabs that other pilgrims leveled against

Muslims and Islam in their writings. Instead, Tafur writes his narrative like a travelogue, noting things that his readers would find interesting or useful. The same holds true for his description of his trip to Constantinople. Tafur believed that his descendants had emigrated from the Byzantine Empire. Thus, the trip to the Byzantine capital was akin to a home-coming. He only had kind words about the Greeks, while still being a realist and noting the decay that had overwhelmed the once-mighty empire. In fact, when Tafur arrived in Constantinople, the emperor John Paleologus VIII (r. 1425–48) was preparing a last ditch effort to secure western help against the Turks. In the resulting Council of Ferrara-Florence (1438–39), the emperor agreed to bring the Byzantine church under western Catholic dominion. This agreement was utterly rejected by the Greek population, which ultimately meant little help came from the West when the Turks invaded and conquered Constantinople in 1453. After the emperor left on his desperate mission to Italy, Tafur remained in Constantinople and took this opportunity to visit the court of the grand Turk, Murad II (r. 1421–44) at Adrianople. Tafur found the grand Turk and his court impressive, and he made numerous notes on Murad's personality, wealth, and lifestyle. As with other parts of his narrative, his description of Murad and his court is generally devoid of polemics and filled with the knowledgeable observations of a man who had seen much.

Source: trans. Malcolm Letts, *Pero Tafur: Travels and Adventures, 1435–1439* (London: George Routledge and Sons, 1926), 59–62, 117–18, 124–29.

The pilgrims had to return that night to sleep at Jericho and to go the next day to Quarantana, where our Lord fasted. But I arranged with a Moor to take me to the desert of Arabia, three leagues farther on, where Saint John preached, and where the first hermit, Saint Anthony, as well as other holy fathers, retired to live, and from there I returned by the Dead Sea, where were Sodom and Gomorrah and three other cities, five cities in all, which were overthrown for the sin of sodomy. The water is so foul that it cannot be described, and they say that no fish can breed there and that no birds frequent the place. The Moor who traveled with me told me a great marvel: that the river Jordan enters the lake and emerges at the other side without mixing with the fetid waters, and that in the midst of the lake one can drink of the sweet water of the river. All about this valley there are certain tall and very straight trees, much burdened with a fruit like citrons, and if one touches them with the fingers, however lightly, they break and a smoke comes out, and the evil smell remains on the hand all that day.

The following day I returned and dined at Jericho, which is a village with about a hundred inhabitants, and there I gathered some of those roses which are beneficial to women in labor, and saw many holy places associated with our Lord. At the head of that river is the province called Bethany-trans-Jordan. That night I slept at the mountain where our Lord fasted where I again joined the pilgrims. This is a very high mountain range in the center of which are some small chapels, and there is a road for the ascent, made by Saint Helena to do honor to the place. But as we were ascending, a squire of France, going to the assistance of a lady, fell headlong from the mountain and was dashed to pieces on the rocks below, for the place is very perilous to climb. We then descended, and by another and easier route we reached the very summit where our Lord was tempted by the devil. We then returned and came to a fountain where the people from Jericho had brought food to sell to us. We remained there that night, and the next morning we took up the corpse of that squire and carried it to the before-mentioned house on the mountain, and there we buried it, after which we remained there that day.

The next morning we returned to the castle of Madalon, but the governor [of Jerusalem] remained behind as he was going hunting. He commended us, however, to one of his knights, who accompanied us to the church where Lazarus was raised from the dead. The officer there demanded tribute, but the Moor who was with us refused to pay, saying that it was not customary, and the quarrel grew so heated that the officer and his men took up arms against the knight who had charge of us and wounded him. But we went to his assistance and attacked and wounded many of the Moors, and finally we captured the officer and his fellows and carried them before the governor, who meanwhile had drawn near. The governor at once held his enquiry and pronounced sentence of death on the officer, whose head was cut off without more ado, while the other prisoners were ordered to be flogged. We remained there until evening, and then returned to sleep at Jerusalem. The next day we departed with the same knight and came to Bethany, where they showed us many holy places, including Mount Tabor, where our Lord was transfigured, and it is said that here also is the Vale of Hebron, where are the graves of Adam and Eve. We returned that night to Jerusalem, passing several holy places, among them the garden where our Lord prayed and was taken, and we reached the city early.

That night I bargained with a renegade, a native of Portugal, and offered him two ducats if he would get me into the Temple of Solomon [Mosque of Omar], and he consented. At one o'clock in the night I entered, dressed in his clothes, and saw the Temple which is a single nave, the whole ornamented with gold mosaic work. The floor and walls are of the most beautiful white stones, and the place is hung with so many lamps that they all seemed to be joined together. The roof above is quite flat and is covered with lead. They say, in truth, that when Solomon built it, it was the most magnificent building in the whole world. Afterwards it was destroyed and rebuilt, but today, without doubt, it is still unmatched. If I had been recognized there as a Christian I should have been killed immediately. Not long ago this Temple was a consecrated church, but a favorite of the sultan prevailed on him to take it and turn it into a mosque. The renegade who had escorted me now returned with me to Mount Sion where the friars mourned for me as one already dead, since I had not come at the appointed time, and they rejoiced greatly to see me again, as did also the gentlemen of my company....

After two days, during which time I rested myself, I went to make my reverence to the emperor of Constantinople, and all the Castilians accompanied me. I arrayed myself as best I could, putting on the Order of the Escama, which is the device of King Juan, and I sent for one of the emperor's interpreters, called Juan of Seville, a Castilian by birth, and they say that the emperor chose him to be interpreter because he sang him Castilian romances to the lute. He came with me to the palace, and went in to advise the emperor that I was there to make my reverence, and they made me wait an hour while the emperor sent for certain knights and prepared himself. I then entered the palace, and came to a hall where I found him seated on a tribune, with a lion's skin spread under his feet. I made my reverence there, and told the emperor that I had come to see his person and estate, and to take knowledge of his lands and lordships, but principally to learn the truth concerning my lineage, which I had been told had sprung from that place, and from his imperial blood, and I commenced to tell him the manner in which this was said to have come about. He replied at once that I was very welcome, and that he was greatly pleased to see me, and as to that which I spoke of he would order the ancient records to be searched, so that the truth of everything might be ascertained. He asked me for news of the Christian lands and princes, especially concerning the king of Spain, my master, and of his estate and his war with the Moors, and I replied to everything to the best of my knowledge, and so took leave of him and went to my lodging. The next day he sent for me to ask me to go hunting, and he sent horses for me and mine, and I went with him, and with the empress, his consort, who was there, and that day he told me that he was now acquainted with the matters about which I enquired, and that on his return he would order me to be exactly informed concerning them, and I thanked him. When we returned, about Vesper time, after we had dismounted, he sent to summon before him those whom he had instructed to make search concerning my enquiries, and it was on this wise....

[A long discussion follows on the history of Pedro's Byzantine ancestors.]

... This day the emperor sent for me to go hunting, and we killed many hares, and partridges, and francolins, and pheasants, which are very plentiful there, and when we returned to the palace I took my leave and went to my lodging, where he had ordered that I should be provided with whatever I had need of. Without doubt, it was the emperor's wish to show me much honor and favor, and from that day onwards, when he or the empress, his consort, desired to hunt, he sent horses for me, and I went with them, and they said that they had great pleasure in my company. After fifteen days of my visit had passed, the emperor had to depart in the Venetian galleys to meet the pope, and he begged me repeatedly to accompany him, which I should have done had I not been forced to excuse myself on the plea that I was obliged first to see Greece, Turkey, and also Tartary. When the emperor saw that he could not persuade me, he commended me to the empress, his wife, and to Dragas, his brother, who was heir to the imperial throne—that one whom the Turks have since killed—and he departed in great splendor. There went with him two of his brothers, and 800 men, all noblemen of high rank. On the day of his going there was a great celebration, and everyone went in procession with the members of the religious orders to the place of embarkation, and a great company went one day's journey out to sea with the fleet, and I went also. I then took my leave and returned to Constantinople, but the emperor gave me license very unwillingly, saying that if I had had my people with me he would not have let me go. So I left him, he commanding me to visit him before returning to my country, which I promised and later performed.

Having returned to Constantinople, I asked leave of the despot Dragas, who now represented the emperor, to go to Adrianople, the greatest city in Greece except Constantinople, where the Turks had their armies. The despot sent for certain Genoese merchants who were there, and directed that they should arrange for me to see the grand Turk, his state and person, and return without danger. It happened that a brother of one of those merchants had arrived, who was very acceptable to the despot and was much trusted by him, and this merchant agreed, in order to serve the despot, to carry me with him and show me everything. We departed in three days, taking the road to Greece, and passing certain small places which need not be described here, until we arrived at Adrianople, a nine days' journey. Here I lodged with the Genoese who had his house in the city. The grand Turk sent for me to enquire when and how the emperor had departed, and in what state, and in whose ships, and accordingly, while telling him these things, I saw his person and household and people. He must be about 45 years of age, of good stature, and handsome of feature. He seemed from his bearing to be a discreet person, grave in his looks, and he was so handsomely attended that I never saw the like, for he had with him all his forces, which amount to 600,000 horsemen, and, lest it should appear that I am exaggerating, I refer to those who gave me the information. In good faith, I am afraid to repeat all that was told me. There is not a pedestrian in the whole country, but all go on horseback, on very small and lank horses. The grand Turk and his people are always in the field in tents, both in winter and summer, and although the city is close at hand, he never enters it unless it is to go with his women to the bath, which thing, with the help of the Genoese, I was enabled to see. He went thither with drums and music and buffoons singing, and a great crowd of women, who, they said, were his body-women, to the number of 300 and more. Thus, with great noise and shouting they entered the city and remained there until midnight, when the grand Turk returned to his tents. The next day he went hunting, and the Genoese arranged for me to go as well. There were many people on horseback with falcons, goshawks, and leopards, and all the hunting accoutrements. The Turks have the custom to carry in the saddle an iron staff, and a tambourine with their bows and quivers. This is the whole of their fighting outfit, and since the country is cold and often frozen, and the horses fall easily, the men wear boots of Damascine leather up to the knees, which are very hard, and to which the spurs are fixed. These they wear always, and if the horse falls they can free their legs without receiving any injury, and the boot remains in the stirrup. There are many pheasants and francolins, and every kind of bird which is in Spain. The men are clad in the manner of the country, with long cloaks and mantles of the same material, which are open in front. These are made of fine woolen cloth, and of silk and brocades from Italy. But what surprised me more than anything else was the display of furs: martins, sable, and less valuable skins, ermine, with the teeth, and fox, which latter they value very highly, as well for its quality as also for its softness, and because it is very warm and suitable for such a cold country. Many wear linen on their heads, others hats made like those worn at rustic merry-makings in Burgos. Their saddles are like asses' saddles, but very rich and covered with fine cloths, and their stirrups are rather short than long.

That day we returned to the city, and my companion took me about the camp, looking at the quarters of the knights and the other people. There, as in their own houses, they keep all that is necessary for their comfort, their women, and everything besides. The tents are excellent with good personal accommodation, but nevertheless the people endure much hardship, and long usage has so accustomed them to it that they do not show any aversion. The horses are always kept in the open without any shelter, and I believe that, although they are lank and small by nature, the way in which they are neglected makes them work still less, and, indeed, it seems at times as if they could scarcely carry their masters. Although the number of their horses is difficult to count, yet considering how many beasts there are in Castile, hacks in Galicia and in the mountains, he-mules, she-mules and asses, I think our country could show as many. I would as lief [gladly] ride to war or to tourney on one of our asses as on any of their horses.

The Turks have a vast dominion, but the country is very sterile and sparsely populated and mountainous. Greece, which they occupy, is a flat and fruitful land, although now it is depopulated by war, for the Greeks bear the whole burden of the struggle, and the Turks are ruthless and treat them with great cruelty. Indeed, it is difficult to believe how so great an army can be provisioned. The Turks are a noble people, much given to truth. They live in their country like nobles, as well in their expenditure as in their actions and food and sports, in which latter there is much gambling. They are very merry and benevolent, and of good conversation, so much so that in those parts, when one speaks of virtue, it is sufficient to say that anyone is like a Turk. Having seen the person, household and estate of the grand Turk, I told my companion that it would be well to return to Constantinople, but we were forced to remain for two days more on account of some business which he had to complete with certain merchants of the grand Turk's household. On one of those days the grand Turk went out to hunt, and I went with him to see the assembly, which was the greatest I had ever beheld, in point of numbers and horses, and general display. The men were very well and richly clad, according to their fashion, but such linings I never saw in my life, neither so many nor so rich.

CHAPTER EIGHT

LIVES OF MINORITY COMMUNITIES

Figure 8.1: View of the cathedral, one-time mosque, of Cordoba.

Source: Albert F. Calvert, *Moorish Remains in Spain* (London: John Lane, 1906), 203.

64. THE REGULATION OF *DHIMMIS*

According to the Quran, Christians, Jews, and other people of the Book such as Zoroastrians enjoyed protected status under Islamic law. They were called dhimmis. Their protected status allowed them certain liberties, including the right to practice their religious traditions. These protections came at a price, however, as Muslim authorities enforced numerous discriminatory practices to differentiate between Muslims and non-Muslims. As the following source makes clear, most of these regulations forced the dhimmis to wear distinctive items of clothing to mark their religious status and made them show deferential treatment to any Muslims whom they might meet. One of the Muslim officials charged with ensuring that the dhimmis followed these laws was the muhtasib, a judge-like figure who was responsible for regulating the marketplace and all related activities. The original source from which the following section is drawn, the Nihāyat al-Rutba fiTalab al-Hisba, was most likely written in Syria sometime in the twelfth century. It would become a deeply influential manual to guide the activities of the muhtasib and his assistants.

Source: trans. R.P. Buckley, *The Book of the Islamic Market Inspector* (Oxford: Oxford University Press, 1999), 121–23.

The covenant of protection is only valid from the imam, or from someone whom the imam authorizes. No one shall be given a covenant of protection unless he has a holy book or similar belonging to the unbelievers, such as the Jews, the Christians, and the Magians [Zoroastrians]. As for anyone else who does not have a holy book or similar, like the polytheists, idol worshippers, apostates from Islam or atheists and heretics, they are not permitted to have the covenant of protection nor to be confirmed in their beliefs. Nothing should be accepted from them apart from submission [conversion to Islam].

The *dhimmis* must be made to observe the conditions laid down for them in the treatise on *jizya* [poll tax] written for them by Umar b. al-Khattāb, and must be made to wear the *ghiyār* [compulsory mark on their clothing]. If he is a Jew, he should put a red or a yellow cord on his shoulder; if a Christian he should tie a *zunnār* [girdle] around his waist and hang a cross around his neck; if a woman she should wear two slippers, one of which is white and another black. When a protected person goes to the baths, he must wear a steel, copper or lead neckband to distinguish him from other people.

The *muhtasib* should stop them from riding horses and carrying weapons and swords. When they ride mules, they should do so with side saddles. Their buildings should not be higher than those of the Muslims nor should they preside over meetings. They should not jostle Muslims on the main roads, but should rather use the side streets. They should not be the first to give a greeting, nor be welcomed in meetings. The *muhtasib* must stipulate that they offer hospitality to any Muslim who passes by and give him lodging in their houses and places of worship.

They must not be allowed to display any alcoholic drinks or pigs, to recite the Torah and the Bible openly, to ring the church bells, to celebrate their festivals, or to hold funeral services in public. All this was stipulated by Umar b. al-Khattāb in his treatise, so the *muhtasib* must keep an eye on their affairs regarding these things and force them to comply.

The *muhtasib* must take the *jizya* from them according to their social status. Thus, at the beginning of the year a poor man with a family pays one dinar, while someone of middling wealth pays two dinars and a rich man pays four dinars. When the *muhtasib* or his agent comes to collect the *jizya*, he should stand the *dhimmi* in front of him, slap him on the side of the neck and say: "Pay the *jizya*, unbeliever." The *dhimmi* will take his hand out of his pocket holding the *jizya* and present it to him with humility and submission.

Along with the *jizya*, the *muhtasib* should stipulate that they abide by the laws of Islam, for if the *dhimmi* does not do this, wages war against Muslims, fornicates with a Muslim woman or acquires her in the name of marriage, entices a Muslim away from his religion, robs a Muslim on the highway, shelters polytheists or shows them the vulnerable points of any Muslim or kills a Muslim, then his status as a protected person is annulled, he is immediately executed and his wealth is confiscated. This is because it is stipulated that the *dhimmi*s do none of this. The *muhtasib* must be acquainted with these things and compel the *dhimmi*s to abide by all of them. But God knows best.

65. IBN JUBAYR IN SICILY

One of the most memorable stops in the long travels of Ibn Jubayr occurred when he stopped on the island of Sicily in 1185. Sicily had once been in Muslim hands, but shortly before the beginning of the crusades, Norman mercenaries under Roger Guiscard began to conquer the island, a process that they completed by 1091. Thereafter, a Norman dynasty held control of the island through the twelfth century. Although the Normans were Latin Christian kings, Sicily emerged as one of the most cosmopolitan polities in Latin Christendom, with a significant Muslim, Jewish, and Byzantine population, all of whom found a measure of toleration and success on the island. By the time Ibn Jubayr arrived in 1185, William II, also known as the Good (r. 1166–89), ruled Sicily. His acceptance of, and dependence on, Muslims seems to have led to a further integration of the Muslim and Christian inhabitants, as well as their customs, languages, and traditions. Ibn Jubayr's description highlights the stable and prosperous situation of Sicily's Muslims, while still expressing distaste that they had to live under a Christian king.

Source: trans. R.J.C. Broadhurst, *The Travels of Ibn Jubayr* (London: Jonathan Cape, 1952), 338–50.

Recollections of the City of Messina in the Island of Sicily

May God Restore It [to the Muslims]

This city is the mart of the merchant infidels, the focus of ships from the world over, and thronging always with companies of travelers by reason of the lowness of prices. But it is cheerless because of the unbelief, no Muslim being settled there. Teeming with worshippers of the Cross, it chokes its inhabitants, and constricts them almost to strangling. It is full of smells and filth; and churlish too, for the stranger will find there no courtesy. Its markets are animated and teeming, and it has ample commodities to ensure a luxurious life. Your days and nights in this town you will pass in full security, even though your countenance, your manners and your tongue are strange.

Messina leans against the mountains, the lower slopes of which adjoin the entrenchments of the town. To its south is the sea, and its harbor is the most remarkable of maritime ports, since large ships can come into it from the seas until they almost touch it. Between them and the shore is thrown a plank over which men come and go and porters take up the baggage; thus no boats are needed for loading and unloading save for ships anchored far out.

You will observe ships ranged along the quay like horses lined at their pickets or in their stables. This is all because of the great depth here of the sea which forms the strait, some three miles wide, that separates the island from the continent. On the coast opposite to Messina, is the town known as Rayah [Reggio], the capital of a large province.

This town of Messina is at the extremity of Sicily, an island having many towns, cultivated places, and hamlets that it would take long to name. Its length is seven days' journey, and its width five. On it is the aforementioned volcano [Mt. Etna], draped in clouds so high it is, and forever, summer and winter, covered by snow.

The prosperity of the island surpasses description. It is enough to say that it is a daughter of Spain in the extent of its cultivation, in the luxuriance of its harvests, and in its well-being, having an abundance of varied produce, and fruits of every kind and species.

But it is filled with the worshippers of the Cross, who promenade in its upper districts and live at ease in its sheltered parts. The Muslims live beside them with their property and farms. The Christians treat these Muslims well and "have taken them to themselves as friends" [Quran 20:41], but impose on them a tax to be paid twice yearly, thus taking from them the amplitude of living they had been wont to earn from that land. May Almighty and Glorious God mend their lot, and in his goodness, make a happy recompense their heritage.

The mountains are covered with plantations bearing apples, chestnuts and hazel-nuts, pears, and other kinds of fruits. There are, in Messina, no Muslims save a small number of craftsmen, so the Muslim stranger there will feel lonely.

The finest town in Sicily and the seat of its sovereign, is known to the Muslims as al-Madinah, and to the Christians as Palermo. It has Muslim citizens who possess mosques, and their own markets, in the many suburbs. The rest of the Muslims live in the farms [of the island] and in all its villages and towns, such as Syracuse and others. Al-Madinah al-Kabirah ["the great city"—Palermo], the residence of their king, William [II, also known as "the Good"], is however the biggest and most populous, and Messina is next. In al-Madinah, God willing, we shall make our stay; and thence we hope to go to whichever of the western countries that Great and Glorious God shall at his will determine.

Their king, William, is admirable for his just conduct, and the use he makes of the industry of the Muslims, and for choosing eunuch pages who all, or nearly all concealing their faith, yet hold firm to the Muslim divine law. He has much confidence in Muslims, relying on them for his affairs, and the most important matters, even the supervisor of his kitchen being a Muslim; and he keeps a band of black Muslim slaves commanded by a leader chosen from among them. His ministers and chamberlains he appoints from his pages, of whom he has a great number and who are his public officials and are described as his courtiers. In them shines the splendor of his realm for the magnificent clothing and fiery horses they display; and there is none of them but has his retinue, his servants, and his followers.

This king possesses splendid palaces and elegant gardens, particularly in the capital of his kingdom, al-Madinah. In Messina he has a palace, white like a dove, which overlooks the shore. He has about him a great number of youths and handmaidens, and no Christian king is more given up to the delights of the realm, or more comfort and luxury-loving. William is engrossed in the pleasures of his land, the arrangement of its laws, the laying down of procedure, the allocation of the functions of his chief officials, the enlargement of the splendor of the realm, and the display of his pomp, in a manner that resembles the Muslim kings. His kingdom is very large. He pays much attention to his [Muslim] physicians and astrologers, and also takes great care of them. He will even, when told that a physician or astrologer is passing through his land, order his detainment, and then provide him with means of living so that he will forget his native land. May God in his favor preserve the Muslims from this seduction. The king's age is about thirty years. May God protect the Muslims from his hostility and the extension of his power. One of the remarkable things told of him is that he reads and writes Arabic. We also learnt from one of his personal servants that his 'alamah [motto] is: "Praise be to God. It is proper to praise him." His father's [William I, r. 1131–66] 'alamah was "Praise be to God in thanks for his beneficence." The handmaidens and concubines in his palace are all Muslims. One of the strangest things told us by this servant, Yahya ibn Fityan, the embroiderer, who embroidered in gold the king's clothes, was that the Frankish Christian women who came to his palace became Muslims, converted by these handmaidens. All this they kept secret from their king. Of the good works of these handmaidens there are astonishing stories.

It was told to us that when a terrifying earthquake [1163] shook the island this polytheist [a Muslim would deem William to be so, since he accepted the dogma of the Trinity] in alarm ranged round his palace, and heard nothing but cries to God and his Prophet from his women and pages. At sight of him, they were overcome with confusion, but he said to them, "Let each invoke the God he worships, and those that have faith shall be comforted."

The pages, who are the leaders of his state and the managers of his affairs, are Muslims, there being none who do not, voluntarily and for a heavenly reward, fast in the holy month [of Ramadān], and give alms that they might be nearer to God. They redeem prisoners and bring up their young ones, arranging for their marriage and giving them assistance, and doing all the good they can. All this is done by Great and Almighty God for the Muslims of this island and is one of the mysteries of his care for them.

In Messina we met one of their leading and most distinguished pages called 'Abd al-Massih, whose wish [to see us] had been conveyed to us. He entertained us with regard and generosity, and then spoke openly to us, revealing his close-guarded secrets. He had first looked about his audience-room, and then, in self-protection, dismissed those servants about him whom he suspected. He then questioned us about Mecca—may God hallow it—and about its venerable shrines, and those of Holy Medina and of Syria. As we told him, he melted with longing and fervor, and asked if we would give him some blessed token we had brought from Mecca and Medina—may God hallow them—and begged us not to be sparing of what we could give him. "You can boldly display your faith in Islam," he said, "and are successful in your enterprises and thrive, by God's will, in your commerce. But we must conceal our faith, and, fearful of our lives, must adhere to the worship of God and the discharge of our religious duties in secret. We are bound in the possession of an infidel who has placed on our necks the noose of bondage. Our whole purpose therefore is to be blessed by meeting pilgrims such as you, to ask for their prayers and be happy in what precious objects from the holy shrines they can give us to serve us as instruments of faith, and as treasures on our bier [in token of the life to come]." Our hearts melted in compassion for him, and we prayed that his end might be happy, and gave him some of our treasures as he wished. Profusely he expressed his thanks and gratitude, and told us in confidence of his colleagues the other pages, who have a notable repute for good works. In the release of prisoners, they most acquire merit in God's eyes, and all their servants are of a like temper.

Another singular circumstance concerning these pages is that when in the presence of their lord and the hour for prayer is at hand they will leave the chamber one by one that they might make their prayers. They sometimes do so in a place where the eye of their king might follow them, but Almighty and Glorious God conceals them. They thus continue to labor in their purpose, covertly advising the Muslims in their unending struggle for the faith. May God, in his grace, advantage them and bring them to a happy end.

In Messina, the king has a shipyard containing fleets of uncountable numbers of ships. He has a similar yard at al-Madinah [Palermo].

We lodged [in Messina] at an inn, and stayed there nine days. Then, on the night of Tuesday the twelfth of the holy month [Ramadān] and 18 December, we embarked on a small ship sailing to al-Madinah. We steered close to the shore, so that we might keep it within sight. God sent us a light breeze from the east that most pleasantly urged us on our way. So we sailed along, bending our gaze on the continuous cultivations and villages, and on the fortresses and strongholds at the tops of the lofty mountains. To our right we saw nine islands [Aeolian or Lipari], rising up like lofty mountains in the sea, close to the shores of Sicily. From two of them [Vulcano and Stromboli] fire issues unendingly, and we could see the smoke ascending from them. At the close of night a red flame appeared, throwing up tongues into the air. It was the celebrated volcano. We were told that a fiery blast of great violence bursts out from air-holes in the two mountains and makes the fire. Often a great stone is cast up and thrown into the air by the force of the blast and prevented thereby from falling and settling at the bottom. This is one of the most remarkable of stories, and it is true.

As for the great mountain in the island, known as the Jabal al-Nar [Mountain of Fire, Etna], it also presents a singular feature in that some years a fire pours from it in the manner of the "bursting of the dam." It passes nothing, it does not burn until, coming to the sea, it rides out on its surface and then subsides beneath it. Let us praise the author of all things for his marvelous creations. There is no God but he.

On the evening of Wednesday following the Tuesday we have chronicled, we came to the port of Shafludi [Cefalu], between which and Messina lies a day and a half's sailing.

Recollections of the Town of Cefalu in the Island of Sicily

May God Restore It [to the Muslims]

Cefalu is a coastal town, with an ample produce from its soil and with many commodities, beset with vine and other trees, and having well-ordered markets. A community of Muslims lives there. Set over the town is a mountain, on whose-large circular summit is a fortress, than which I have never seen any more formidable. They hold it in readiness for any sea attack that a fleet from the lands of the Muslims—may God render them victorious—might make upon them unawares.

We sailed from Cefalu at midnight, and came to the town of Thirmah [Termini] in the early forenoon of Thursday, after an easy voyage. The two towns are five and twenty miles from each other. At Termini, we changed from that ship to another which we chartered, that the sailors accompanying us might be of the country [through which we should travel].

Recollections of the Town of Termini in the Island of Sicily

May God Deliver It [to the Muslims]

Better situated than the place we have just described, this town is strongly fortified, and surmounts and towers above the sea. The Muslims have a large suburb, in which are their mosques. The town has a high and impregnable fort, and in its lower part is a thermal spring which serves the citizens as baths. It enjoys an extreme fertility and abundance of victuals; indeed, the whole island in this regard is one of the most remarkable in God's creation. We passed Thursday the fourteenth anchored in a river below the town into which the tide from the sea flowed and ebbed, and there we stayed the night of Friday. The wind then changed to the west, and we had no way to sail.

Between us and our destination, al-Madinah, the town known to the Christians as Palermo, lay five and twenty miles, and we feared that we would be held long at Termini. But we thanked God Most High for his gracious favor in having [already] brought us in two days across a passage that stayed other ships, as we were told, twenty or thirty days and more; and on the morning of Friday in the middle of the holy month, we rose determined to journey overland by foot. We discharged our design, and, carrying some of our effects, and having left some of our companions to guard the chattels remaining in the ship, we set forth.

We traveled along a road like a market so populous it was, with men coming and going. Groups of Christians that met us themselves uttered the first greetings, and treated us with courtesy. We observed in their attitude and insinuating address towards the Muslims that which would offer temptation to ignorant souls. May God, in his power and bounty, preserve from seducement the people of Muhammad—God's blessings upon him.

We came at last to Qasr Sa'd [Solanto Castle], which lies a parasang [about 4 miles or 6 kilometers] from Palermo, and being seized with fatigue, turned aside and passed the night in it. The castle is on the seashore, and is lofty and ancient, for it was built in the time of the Muslim occupation of the island. It always was, and still is, by the grace of God, inhabited by pious [Muslims]. Around it are numerous tombs of ascetic and pious Muslims, and it is known for its grace and blessedness, being visited by men from all countries. Opposite it is a spring known as 'Ayn al-Majnunah [the Spring of the Mad Woman]. The castle has a strong iron door. Inside are the living quarters, and commanding belvederes, and well-planned suites; the place indeed has all the conveniences of living. At its summit, is one of the finest mosques in the world. It is an oblong building with long arcades spread with spotless mats of a workmanship such as I have never seen better; and within it are hung forty lamps of brass and crystal. In front of the mosque is the broad road which girdles the upper part of the castle. In the lower part is a well containing sweet water.

We passed the most pleasing and agreeable night in that mosque, and listened to the call to prayer, which long we had not heard. We were shown high regard by the residents of the mosque, among whom was an imam who led them in the obligatory prayers and, in this holy month, the tarawih [special and additional prayers of twenty prostrations, performed in the month of Ramadān].

Near this castle, about a mile away in the direction of Palermo, is a similar castle known as Qasr Ja'far, which contains a spring of sweet water.

We noticed on this road churches prepared for the Christian sick. In their cities they have them after the model of the Muslim hospitals, and we have seen their like at Acre and Tyre. We marveled at such solicitude.

After the morning prayers, we bent our way to al-Madinah. On arrival we made to enter, but were stopped and directed to a gate near the palace of the Frankish king—may God relieve the Muslims of his dominance. We were then conducted to his commissioner that he might question us as to our intentions, as they do in the case of all strangers. Over esplanades, through doors, and across royal courts they led us, gazing at the towering palaces, well-set piazzas and gardens, and the ante-chambers given to the officials. All this amazed our eyes and dazzled our minds, and we remembered the words of Almighty and Glorious God, "But that all mankind would become one people [infidels], we would have given those who denied merciful God silver roofs for their houses, and stairways to mount to them" [Quran 43:33; gold and silver having no value in the sight of God].

Among the things we observed was a hall set in a large court enclosed by a garden and flanked by colonnades. The hall occupied the whole length of that court, and we marveled at its length and the height of its belvederes. We understood that it was the dining-hall of the king and his companions, and that the colonnades and the ante-chambers are where his magistrates, his officials, and his stewards sit in presence.

The commissioner came out to us, walking majestically between the servants who surrounded him and carried the train of his robes. We looked upon a stately old man with long white mustaches, who questioned us in supple Arabic as to our design and our country. We told him, and he showed pity for us, and, with repeated salutations and invocations, ordered that we be allowed to depart. He gave us much cause to wonder. His first question to us had been for news of Constantinople and what we knew of it, but alas we had nothing we could tell him. We shall give news of it later.

One of the strangest examples of seducement into waywardness that we witnessed happened as we left the castle, when one of the Christians seated at the gate said to us, "Look to what you have with you, pilgrims, lest the officials of the customs descend on you." He thought, of course, that we carried merchandise liable to customs duty. But another Christian replied to him saying, "How strange you are. Can they enter into the king's protection and yet fear? I should hope for them [to receive] nothing but thousands of rubayyat. Go in peace, you have nothing to fear." Overwhelmed with surprise at what we had seen and heard, we departed to an inn where we took lodgings on Saturday the sixteenth of the holy month and 22 December. On leaving the castle, we had gone through a long and covered portico down which we walked a long way until we came to a great church. We learn that this portico was the king's way to the church.

Recollections of al-Madinah [Palermo], the Capital of Sicily

May God Restore It [to the Muslims]

It is the metropolis of these islands, combining the benefits of wealth and splendor, and having all that you could wish of beauty, real or apparent, and all the needs of subsistence, mature and fresh. It is an ancient and elegant city, magnificent and gracious, and seductive to look upon. Proudly set between its open spaces and plains filled with gardens, with broad roads and avenues, it dazzles the eyes with its perfection. It is a wonderful place, built in the Cordoba style, entirely from cut stone known as *kadhan* [a soft limestone]. A river splits the town, and four springs gush in its suburbs. The king, to whom it is his world, has embellished it to perfection and taken it as the capital of his Frankish kingdom—may God destroy it.

The king's palaces are disposed around the higher parts, like pearls encircling a woman's full throat. The king roams through the gardens and courts for amusement and pleasure. How many—may they not long be his—palaces, constructions, watch-towers, and belvederes he has, how many fine monasteries whose monks he has put in comfort by grants of large fiefs, and how many churches with crosses of gold and silver! May it be that God will soon repair the times for this island, making it again a home of the faith, and by his power delivering it from fear to security. For he can perform what he desires.

The Muslims of this city preserve the remaining evidence of the faith. They keep in repair the greater number of their mosques, and come to prayers at the call of the muezzin. In their own suburbs they live apart from the Christians. The markets are full of them, and they are the merchants of the place. They do not congregate for the Friday service, since the khutbah is forbidden. On feast-days [only may] they recite it with intercessions for the Abbasid caliphs. They have a qadi to whom they refer their lawsuits, and a cathedral mosque where, in this holy month, they assemble under its lamps. The ordinary mosques are countless, and most of them are used as schools for Quran teachers. But in general, these Muslims do not mix with their brethren under infidel patronage, and enjoy no security for their goods, their women, or their children. May God, by his favor, amend their lot with his beneficence.

One point of resemblance between this town and Cordoba—for one thing always resembles another in some direction—is its having in the middle of the new city an old one known as the Qasr al-Qadim [the old castle], just as there is in Cordoba—God protect it. In this old castle are mansions like lofty castles with towers hidden in the skies, bewildering the sight with their splendor.

One of the most remarkable works of the infidels that we saw was the church known as the church of the Antiochian. We examined it on the Day of the Nativity [Christmas Day], which with them is a great festival; and a multitude of men and women had come to it. Of the buildings we saw, the spectacle of one must fail of description, for it is beyond dispute the most wonderful edifice in the world. The inner walls are all embellished with gold. There are slabs of colored marble, the like of which we had never seen, inlaid throughout with gold mosaic and surrounded by branches [formed from] green mosaic. In its upper parts are well-placed windows of gilded glass which steal all looks by the brilliance of their rays, and bewitch the soul. God protect us [from their allurement]. We learnt that its founder, after whom it was named, spent hundredweights of gold on it. He had been vizier to the grandfather of this poly-theist king. This church has a belfry supported by columns of colored marble. It was raised cupola over cupola, each with its separate columns, and is therefore known as the columned belfry, and is one of the most wonderful constructions to be seen. May God, in his kindness and benevolence, soon exalt it with the *adhan* ["call to prayers," and so make it a Muslim mosque].

The Christian women of this city follow the fashion of Muslim women, are fluent of speech, wrap their cloaks about them, and are veiled. They go forth on this Feast Day dressed in robes of gold-embroidered silk, wrapped in elegant cloaks, concealed by colored veils, and shod with gilt slippers. Thus they parade to their churches, or [rather] their dens [a play on the words *kana'is*, "churches," and *kunus*, "dens"], bearing all the adornments of Muslim women, including jewelry, henna on the fingers, and perfumes. We called to mind—in the way of a literary witticism—the words of the poet, "Going into the church one day, he came upon antelope and gazelle."

We invoke God's protection for this description which enters the gates of absurdity and leads to the vanities of indulgence, and seek protection also from the bewitchment that leads to dotage. In truth, he is the Lord of power and forgiveness.

Seven days we spent in this city, living in a hostel used by Muslims. We left it on the morning of Friday, the twenty-second of this holy month and 28 December, bound for Trapani, where there are two ships, one waiting to sail to Andalusia and the other to Ceuta. We had sailed to Alexandria in this, and both were carrying pilgrims and Muslim merchants.

66. MUSLIMS UNDER CASTILIAN LAW

Muslims were not the only ones who had what a modern reader might consider to be prejudiced laws, nor were they the only ones to enforce them. Christian authorities also relegated their religious minorities to second-class status with numerous discriminatory statutes. Between the eleventh and fifteenth centuries, the Spanish Christian kingdoms conquered all the territory previously held by Muslim polities in Iberia. As part of these conquests, many Muslim communities came under Christian control while still maintaining their own internal institutions and legal systems. These Muslims were known as mudejares, *and they were also subject to Christian law that regulated different aspects of their daily activities, notably how they interacted with the surrounding Christian communities. This interaction was extensive and intimate. In the kingdom of Castile these laws were codified in a thirteenth-century legal compendium called the* Siete Partidas *(The Seven Divisions; see Doc. 42) from which the following source is drawn. While the text here has a patronizing tone similar to that found in Doc. 64, the concerns are somewhat different from those expressed in Islamic legal codes, with a significant emphasis on conversion by Christians to Islam and the harsh penalties imposed on those who went this route.*

Source: trans. Samuel Parsons Scott, *Las Siete Partidas*, 5 vols., ed. Robert I. Burns (Philadelphia: University of Pennsylvania Press, 2001), 1438–42.

Title 25—Concerning the Moors

The Moors are a people who believe that Muhammad was the Prophet and Messenger of God, and for the reason that the works which he performed do not indicate the extraordinary sanctity which belongs to such a sacred calling, his religion is, as it were, an insult to God. Wherefore, since in the preceding Title we treated of the Jews and of the obstinacy which they display toward the true faith, we intend to speak here of the Moors, and of their foolish belief by which they think they will be saved. We shall show why they have this name; how many kinds of them there are; how they should live among Christians, and what things they are forbidden to do while they live there; how Christians should convert them to the Faith by kind words, and not by violence or compulsion; and what punishment those deserve who prevent them from becoming Christians, or dishonor them by word or deed after they have been converted, and also to what penalty a Christian who becomes a Moor, is liable.

Law 1

WHENCE THE NAME OF MOOR IS DERIVED, HOW MANY KINDS OF THE LATTER THERE ARE, AND IN WHAT WAY THEY SHOULD LIVE AMONG CHRISTIANS.

Sarracenus, in Latin, means Moor, in Castilian, and this name is derived from Sarah, the free wife of Abraham, although the lineage of the Moors is not traced to her, but to Hagar, who was Abraham's servant. There are two kinds of Moors; some do not believe in either the New or the Old Testament; the others accept the five books of Moses, but reject the prophets and do not believe them. The latter are called Samaritans because they first appeared in the city called Samaria, and these are mentioned in the Gospel where it is stated that the Jews and the Samaritans should not associate with one another or live together.

We decree that Moors shall live among Christians in the same way that we mentioned in the preceding Title that Jews shall do, by observing their own law and not insulting ours. Moors, however, shall not have mosques in Christian towns, or make their sacrifices publicly in the presence of men. The mosques which they formerly possessed shall belong to the king; and he can give them to whomsoever he wishes. Although the Moors do not acknowledge a good religion, so long as they live among Christians with their assurance of security, their property shall not be stolen from them or taken by force; and we order that whoever violates this law shall pay a sum equal to double the value of what he took.

Law 2

CHRISTIANS SHOULD CONVERT THE MOORS BY KIND WORDS, AND NOT BY COMPULSION

Christians should endeavor to convert the Moors by causing them to believe in our religion, and bring them into it by kind words and suitable discourses, and not by violence or compulsion; for if it should be the will of our Lord to bring them into it and to make them believe by force, he can use compulsion against them if he so desires, since he has full power to do so; but he is not pleased with the service which men perform through fear, but with that which they do voluntarily and without coercion, and as he does not wish to restrain them or employ violence, we forbid anyone to do so for this purpose; and if the wish to become Christians should arise among them, we forbid anyone to refuse assent to it, or oppose it in any way whatsoever. Whoever violates this law shall receive the penalty we mentioned in the preceding Title, which treats of how Jews who interfere with, or kill those belonging to their religion who afterwards become Christians, shall be punished.

Law 3

WHAT PUNISHMENT THOSE DESERVE WHO INSULT CONVERTS

Many men live and die in strange beliefs, who would love to be Christians if it were not for the vilification and dishonor which they see others who become converted endure by being called turncoats, and calumniated and insulted in many evil ways; and we hold that those who do this wickedly offend, and that they should honor persons of this kind for many reasons, and not show them disrespect. One of these is because they renounce the religion in which they and their families were born; and another is because, after they have understanding, they acknowledge the superiority of our religion and accept it, separating from their parents and their relatives, and abandoning the life which they have been accustomed to live, and all other things from which they derive pleasure. There are some of them who, on account of the dishonor inflicted upon them after they have adopted our Faith, and become Christians, repent and desert it, closing their hearts against it on account of the insults and reproaches to which they are subjected; and for this reason we order all Christians, of both sexes, in our dominions to show honor and kindness, in every way they can, to persons of other or strange beliefs who embrace our religion; just as they would do to any of their own parents or grandparents, who had embraced the faith or become Christians; and we forbid anyone to dishonor them by word or deed, or do them any wrong, injury, or harm in any way whatever. If anyone violates this law we order that he be punished for it, as seems best to the judges of the district; and that the punishment be more severe than if the injury had been committed against another man or woman whose entire line of ancestors had been Christians.

Law 4

WHAT PUNISHMENT A CHRISTIAN DESERVES WHO BECOMES A MOOR

Men sometimes become insane and lose their prudence and understanding, as, for instance, where unfortunate persons, and those who despair of everything, renounce the faith of our Lord Jesus Christ, and become Moors; and there are some of them who are induced to do this through the desire to live according to their customs, or on account of the loss of relatives who have been killed or died; or because they have lost their property and become poor; or because of unlawful acts which they commit, dreading the punishment which we deserve on account of them; and when they are induced to do a thing of this kind for any of the reasons aforesaid, or others similar to them, they are guilty of very great wickedness and treason, for on account of no loss or affliction which may come upon them, nor for any profit, riches, good fortune, or pleasure which they may expect to obtain in this world, should they renounce the faith of our Lord Jesus Christ by which they will be saved and have everlasting life.

Wherefore we order that all those who are guilty of this wickedness shall lose all their possessions, and have no right to any portion of them, but that all shall belong to their children (if they have any) who remain steadfast in our faith and do not renounce it; and if they have no children, their property shall belong to their nearest relatives within the tenth degree, who remain steadfast in the belief of the Christians; and if they have neither children nor relatives, all their possessions shall be forfeited to the royal treasury; and, in addition to this, we order that if any person who has committed such an offense shall be found in any part of our dominions he shall be put to death.

Law 5

WHAT PENALTY A CHRISTIAN DESERVES WHO BECOMES A MOOR, EVEN IF HE
SUBSEQUENTLY REPENTS AND RETURNS TO OUR FAITH

Apostata, in Latin, means, in Castilian, a Christian who becomes a Jew or a Moor, and afterwards repents and returns to the Christian religion; because a man of this kind is false, and manifests contempt for our faith, he should not remain unpunished, even though he repents; for which reason the learned men of the ancients declare that such a person must remain forever infamous, so that his testimony could never be taken, nor he hold office or any honorable position, nor make a will, nor be appointed an heir of others in any way whatsoever. And, in addition to this, we do not permit that any sale or donation which may be made to him or which he may make to another party shall be valid, after the day on which it entered into his heart to do this; and we hold that a penalty of this kind inflicted upon such a person is more severe than if he were put to death; for a dishonorable life will be worse to him than death itself, since he will not be able to make use of the honors and advantages which he sees others enjoy.

Law 6

WHAT PENALTY A CHRISTIAN OF EITHER SEX WHO BECOMES A JEW, A MOOR, OR A
HERETIC, DESERVES

Our Lord God desired that kings and princes should have dominion over the people, in order that through them justice might be maintained, and also because as often as disputes and controversies arise among men which cannot be decided by the ancient law, through their means new advice might be obtained by means of which said controversy could be equitably decided; and therefore we order that if, from this time forward, as it has formerly occurred, any married woman acknowledging our faith becomes a Jewess, a Moor, or a heretic, and marries again in accordance with the rites of her new religion, or commits adultery; her dowry, her marriage gifts, and all property which she held in common with her husband at the time when she committed this offence, shall belong to him; and we decree that her husband if he becomes a Jew, a Moor, or a heretic, shall undergo the same penalty which we stated should be inflicted upon his wife. Where, however, the said woman has children, they, after the death of their father, shall inherit the property which the husband obtains on account of the offense committed by his wife, and although he may have children by another wife, the latter shall not be entitled to any of said property. We decree that the same disposition shall be made of his property if he committed an offense of this kind.

Law 7

WHERE ANYONE RENOUNCES THE FAITH OF OUR LORD JESUS CHRIST HIS REPUTATION
CAN BE ATTACKED FIVE YEARS AFTER HIS DEATH

Where anyone renounces the religion of our Lord Jesus Christ and subsequently returns to it, as stated above, and he should not happen to be accused of said offense in his lifetime; we consider it proper, and we order, that any man can attack his reputation within five years after his death. If during said time anyone should accuse him and he should be convicted, his property shall be disposed of as we stated in the preceding law; but if he should not be accused while alive, or within five years after his death, then no one can accuse him afterwards.

Law 8

FOR WHAT REASON A CHRISTIAN WHO BECOMES A JEW OR A MOOR AND AFTERWARDS REPENTS, RETURNING TO THE FAITH OF THE CHRISTIANS, CAN ESCAPE THE PENALTY AFORESAID

It may happen that some of those who renounce the Catholic Faith and become Moors will attempt to render some great service to the Christians resulting in the substantial benefit of the country; and for the reason that they who endeavor to perform such a service may not remain unrewarded, we consider it proper and we order that they be pardoned, and released from the penalty of death which we stated in the fourth law preceding this one shall be inflicted upon them on account of the offense of which they are guilty. For a party who commits an act of this kind makes it sufficiently understood that he is attached to the Christians, and would return to the Catholic faith if he had not left it through shame, or on account of some reproach by his relatives or friends; and therefore we order, and we desire that his life be granted him, even though he may remain a Moor. And if after he has rendered the service to the Christians, as aforesaid, he repents of his sin and returns to the Catholic Faith, we order, and we consider it proper that he also be released from the penalty of being considered infamous, that he shall not lose his property; and that no one thereafter shall dare to reproach him or his conduct, or interfere with him in any way; and that he shall enjoy all the honors, and make use of all the things which Christians have and ordinarily use, just as if he had never renounced the Catholic faith.

Law 9

MOORS WHO COME ON A MISSION FROM OTHER KINGDOMS TO THE COURT OF THE KING SHOULD, WITH THEIR PROPERTY, BE SAFE AND SECURE

Envoys frequently come from the land of the Moors and other countries to the court of the king, and although they may come from the enemy's country and by his order, we consider it proper and we direct that every envoy who comes to our country, whether he be Christian, Moor, or Jew, shall come and go in safety and security through all our dominions, and we forbid anyone to do him violence, wrong, or harm, or to injure his property.

Moreover, we decree that although an envoy who visits our country may owe a debt to some man in our dominions, which was contracted before he came on the mission, he shall not be arrested or brought into court for it; but if he should not be willing to pay any debts which he contracted in our country after he came on the mission, suit can be brought against him for them, and he can be compelled to pay them by a judgment of court.

Law 10

WHAT PENALTY A MOOR AND A CHRISTIAN WOMAN DESERVE
WHO HAVE INTERCOURSE WITH ONE ANOTHER

If a Moor has sexual intercourse with a Christian virgin, we order that he shall be stoned, and that she, for the first offense, shall lose half of her property, and that her father, mother, or grandfather, shall have it, and if she has no such relatives, that it shall belong to the king. For the second offense, she shall lose all her property, and the heirs aforesaid, if she has any, shall obtain it, and if she has none, the king shall be entitled to it, and she shall be put to death. We decree and order that the same rule shall apply to a widow who commits this crime. If a Moor has sexual intercourse with a Christian married woman, he shall be stoned to death, and she shall be placed in the power of her husband who may burn her to death, or release her, or do what he pleases with her. If a Moor has intercourse with a common woman who abandons herself to everyone, for the first offense, they shall be scourged together through the town, and for the second, they shall be put to death.

67. AN INCIDENT IN CAIRO

The guidelines laid down for the muhtasib *(see Doc. 64 above) were more than mere rhetoric, but they also seem to have often been ignored by Muslim authorities, allowing the* dhimmis *much more freedom than the law permitted them. The following source, a description of an incident that took place in Cairo in the early fourteenth century, highlights some of the ambiguities of the* dhimmi *status. On the one hand, depending on how zealous local authorities were in enforcing the laws that regulated their activities,* dhimmis *could get away with a lot and ignore many of the regulations that guided their everyday lives. On the other hand, this type of insubordination and going above their social position could have painful repercussions for the protected minorities. Dhimmi transgressions often angered Muslims, who then forced the local authorities to crack down on the Christians and Jews with harsher terms.*

Source: trans. Bernard Lewis, *Islam from the Prophet Muhammad to the Capture of Constantinople*, 2 vols. (New York: Harper Torchbooks, 1974), II: 229–32.

In the month of Rajab [700/March–April 1301] a misfortune befell the people of the protected religions [*ahl al-dhimma*]. This happened because they lived a life of increasing luxury in Cairo and Fustat and indulged in such things as riding on fine horses and splendid mules with magnificent trappings and wore sumptuous clothes and received high positions. It happened that the vizier of the king of the Maghreb came on his way to the pilgrimage and foregathered with the sultan and the emirs at a time when he was under the citadel, and suddenly a man passed by on horseback, surrounded by a number of people walking on foot by his stirrup and begging him and beseeching him and kissing his feet, while he turned his back on them and took no notice of them—or rather, rebuffed them and called on his henchmen to drive them away. The Maghrebi was told that this rider was a Christian. This disturbed him greatly. He met two of the emirs, Baybars and Salar, and told them what he had seen and condemned this and wept greatly and denounced the business of the Christian and said, "How can you hope for victory when the Christians ride among you on horseback, wear white turbans, humiliate the Muslims, and have them run in their service?" So he went on in his denunciation and spoke of the duty of rulers to humble the *dhimmi*s and to moderate their dress. His words influenced the emirs, and a decree was issued convening a meeting in the presence of the judges. Qadis and jurists were invited and the patriarch of the Christians was summoned, and a decree of the sultan was issued, requiring the *dhimmi*s to conform to the prescriptions of the law of Muhammad. The qadis assembled in the Sālihī *madrasa* situated in the Bayn al-Qasrayn quarter, and the chief qadi Shams al-Dīn Ahmad al-Surūjī al-Hanafi was appointed to act for them in this matter. The patriarch of the Christians was summoned with a group of their bishops, the leading priests among them, and the notables of their community, and likewise the *dayyan* [judge] of the Jews and the chiefs of their community. They were asked about the pact which was fixed with them in the caliphate of the commander of the Faithful Umar ibn al-Khattāb, may God be pleased with him, and they gave no answer to this. The discussion with them went on a long time until it was settled that the Christians should be distinguished by wearing blue turbans and the Jews by wearing yellow turbans; that they be forbidden to ride horses or mules or to do any of the things which they were forbidden to do by the Lawgiver, may God bless and save him; and that they be bound to fulfill the conditions which the Commander of the Faithful Umar ibn al-Khattāb, may God be pleased with him, had imposed on them. They pledged themselves to this, and the patriarch testified that he forbade all Christians to break these rules or to disregard them. The chief of the Jews and their *dayyan*, said, "I have made this known to all the Jews that they may not break these rules or disregard them." The meeting was dissolved, and the sultan and the emirs were informed of what had happened, and letters were sent to the provinces of Egypt and Syria concerning this.

On Maundy Thursday, which fell on 20 Rajab [30 March 1301], the Christians and the Jews were called together in Cairo, Fustat, and their surroundings, and it was decreed that no one of them should be employed in the office of the sultan or in the offices of the emirs, that they should not ride horses or mules, and that they should observe all the conditions imposed upon them. Proclamation to this effect was made by criers in Cairo and Fustat, and warning given that if anyone disobeyed this, his blood would be shed. The Christians felt constrained by this and tried with money to procure its abrogation, but the emir Baybars, the Taster, who had taken a praiseworthy stance in the execution of the decree, pursued it with increased persistence, and the Christians were compelled to conform. The *amīn al-mulk* 'Abdallāh ibn al-Ghannām, the chief accountant attached to the sultan's person, and many others became Muslims because they desired to remain in their positions of authority and disdained to wear blue turbans and ride on donkeys. Couriers were sent by the postal service to impose on the Christians and the Jews from Dongola in Nubia to the Euphrates that which has already been mentioned.

The common people laid their hands on the synagogues of the Jews and the churches of the Christians and destroyed them in accordance with a *fatwā* of the jurist Sheikh Najm al-Din Ahmad ibn Muhammad ibn al-Rif'a. The emirs convened the qadis and jurists to examine the case of the synagogues and churches. Ibn al-Rif'a declared that it was a duty to destroy them, but the chief qadi Taqī al-Dīn Muhammad ibn Daqīq al-'Id disagreed and argued that if there was proof that they had been built after the advent of Islam they should be destroyed, but if not, they should not be touched. The others concurred and they dispersed. When the decree of the sultan concerning the *dhimmi*s became known to the people of Alexandria, they turned on the Christians and destroyed two of their churches. They also destroyed Jewish and Christian houses that overtopped the houses of their Muslim neighbors. They lowered the benches of their shops until they were lower than the benches of the Muslim shops. Two churches were also destroyed in Fayyūm.

The decree concerning the *dhimmi*s reached Damascus by courier on Monday, 7 Sha'bān [17 April 1301]. The qadis and notables met at the house of the emir Aqqush al-Afram, and the Sultan's decree to this effect was read to them. On the fifteenth of the month [25 April] criers proclaimed that the Christians were to wear blue turbans, the Jews yellow turbans, and the Samaritans red turbans, with threats of punishment for disobedience. The Christians and Jews in all the realm of Egypt and Syria had to do as they were ordered and dyed their turbans, except for the people of Kerak, for the emir Jamal al-Dīn Aqqush al-Afram al-Ashrafī who was governor saw fit to leave them as they were, with the excuse that most of the people of Kerak were Christians. The Christians in Kerak and Shawbak did not therefore change their white turbans.

The churches in the land of Egypt remained closed for a year until the envoys of al-Ashkarī, the king of the Franks, came and interceded for their reopening, whereupon the Mu'allaqa church in Fustat and the Melchite church of

Michael were opened. Then envoys came from other kings, and the church in the Zuwayla quarter and the Church of Nicholas were opened.

68. MINORITY COMMUNITIES AND INTERNATIONAL RELATIONS

The minority communities on both sides of the Muslim/Christian divide were not without their protectors. Muslim and Christian rulers often intervened on behalf of their coreligionists who lived in foreign lands. To what extent this intervention protected minority communities varied from situation to situation, but rulers could often exert pressure on their counterparts by explicitly or implicitly threatening their own minorities if the rights of their coreligionists were not protected. The case of the Spanish Christian kingdom of Aragon is instructive in illuminating some of these issues, as the two sources below make clear. Aragon had a large minority Muslim population as well as extensive mercantile and diplomatic relations with Muslim rulers throughout the Mediterranean. Maintaining good relations between Aragon and these Muslim polities often depended on how well each side treated the other's minority communities. The first letter, dated from 1306, is from Al-Nasir Muhammad, sultan of Egypt, to James II, king of Aragon, promising the protection of all Christians living in his realm as well as guaranteeing the right of Christian pilgrims to visit Jerusalem. In return, he asks for the same from the king of Aragon. The second letter, dating from 1314, has a similar message. In it the ruler of Granada thanks James II for the protection he has given Muslim subjects in his realm and offers to do the same for those Christians who lived in Granada.

Source: trans. Jarbel Rodriguez, from Maximiliano Alarcón y Santón and Ramón García de Linares, *Los Documentos Árabes Diplomáticos del Archivo de la Corona de Aragón* (Madrid: Impresa de Estanislao Maestre, 1940), 357–60, 24–25.

Letter from Egypt to Aragon, 1306

From the sultan, the triumphant king, the illustrious, just and wise lord, defender of the material and spiritual interests of the people, sultan of Islam and of the Muslims, defender of the Mohammedan faith, life giver of the Abbasid Dynasty, sultan of the Egyptian nation, of the coastal regions, of the countries of Syria, Aleppo, and the Euphrates, sultan of kings, king of the Orient to its far reaches, sultan of Nubia and Jerusalem, servant of the two most noble sacred places [Mecca and Medina]—may God glorify them— sultan of Yemen and Hichaz, sultan of all Arabs and all of Islam, conqueror of all the districts and regions of Egypt, destroyer of the Tartars [Mongols], king of the Seas, lord of Mecca and Jerusalem, lord of kings and sultans, Abū al-Fatah Muhammad—may God protect his empire eternally—the sultan, son of al-Mansūr Qalāwun, warrior for the faith, may God bless his soul.

In the name of the benevolent and compassionate God.

May God grant a long life to your majesty, the illustrious, honorable, heroic, spirited, and courageous lion, the wisest among the people of his faith, the most just in his states, the monarch, King James, king of Aragon, Valencia, Sardinia and Corsica, count of Barcelona, standard-bearer of the Church of Rome, and prince and representative of said church, sustenance of the people of the cross, defender of the Christian religion, friend of kings and sultans.

This letter is sent to your majesty, the illustrious monarch—may God grant you a long life—to inform you ... of the arrival of your message by the hand of your envoy, the venerable Aul Aymeric. We have received it [the letter] as one would a valued and respected object. We have read it carefully and have richly informed ourselves of [the topic] about which you write. Your emissary, Aul Aymeric, has appeared before us and we have received him with every honor and have provided him with excellent lodging. We have been verbally informed of his declarations and manifestations that show the love that your majesty professes for us and the firmness of your friendship with us.

By his [the emissary's] declarations we have come to know the love that the king has for us as well as the sincerity of his friendship and the loyalty that he holds for us, and, thank God, all that Prince Fajr al-Dīn has told us about the gratitude of the king, we have come to recognize as truthful by our own faculties, and from the bottom of our heart we know that this is certain.

We are also fully aware of what he [the king of Aragon] proposes concerning the Christians who find themselves in our kingdoms and in our domains and his desire that they enjoy our protection, that they be authorized to celebrate their rituals in their churches, that we give orders prohibiting anyone from causing them harm of any kind, and that the treatment of Christians in our kingdoms and our domains be identical to the treatment of Muslims that he has adopted in his countries and domains, and what he presently has done so that they are treated with respect.

Let the king know that all Christians who find themselves in our domains and in our kingdoms are given maximum and explicit attention to avoid any harm coming to them, and currently they are in control of their churches and celebrate their rituals as they have customarily done without anyone daring to prevent them from conducting their prayers at the appropriate times, and there is no one who causes them any problems in the churches that belong to them.

The king should know that all Christians who find themselves anywhere in the extent of our kingdoms and our domains, are our vassals and whose defense and protection weighs upon us in a special fashion. And if anyone were to carry out any abuse against any of them, we would impose the harshest sanction and would order that the authorities proceed against [the transgressors] as the situation demanded.

Now, we must insist with his majesty, the king, regarding royal protection for the Muslims that find themselves in his kingdom, [and that he assure their protection] much as we protect them in our [kingdom], as they are our subjects and natives of this country, and in this present occasion, we are insisting in our sovereign instructions to renew the protection for every Christian who resides in our kingdoms, in consideration of the request made by the king. Likewise, we are aware of his thoughts concerning those people who come from his kingdom to visit the Holy House and his desire that they be safe and sound of any abuse against themselves or their goods. We have already forwarded to our representatives in the Holy House—may God increase its glory—our orders to protect everyone who comes from the king's domains or resides in his kingdoms and to allow them to visit, watching after them from the moment they enter our kingdom until the moment they leave, and that they and their goods will be protected as well as anyone who is traveling with them.

We have also sent royal orders to our representative in the city of Alexandria so that he might take under his protection all pilgrims who come by sea from the king's kingdoms and domains and who are going to the Holy House that they be allowed to visit. Moreover, we have insisted that every means necessary be used to assure their safety.

Let the king inform the people of his country and his kingdom that all those who come to visit the Holy House can do so in peace and safety concerning themselves, their associates and their goods.

Moreover, the custom and norms followed in our kingdoms and territories with Christians who come here for the pilgrimage to the Holy House has been to allow them to proceed and not impede them in any way. Thus, everyone who comes here from the king's country and the inhabitants of his domains will be subject to every consideration and respect until they finish their pilgrimage and return safely to their own country.

We have also been informed of his views regarding the captives native to his kingdom that he says we are holding and whose names his emissary, Aul Aymeric, will specify, as well as the king's desires that they should be freed in consideration of his intercession.

Keeping in mind that the king deserves our highest consideration and that, in our estimation, he holds an esteemed place that he shares with no one, there is no doubt that his demand will not be in vain and his intercession will not be unheeded. Thus, we are sending [him] the captives, whose freedom we have presently ordered, in the company of our ambassador Prince Fajr al-Dīn. The captives number twelve: Friar Lope, Friar William of Failats, Friar Delmas, as well as nine other captives. The rest of those claimed, if God—may He be praised—wishes it, when our ambassador, the prince Fajr al-Dīn, returns from the king's domain, they will be released in accordance with the king's demand, [and in consideration] of his love, his loyal friendship and his affection. As such we have hurried the return of these [captives] who go with Prince Fajr al-Dīn, our emissary.

We have also been informed concerning King Alfonso and his wish that the king [of Aragon] intercede with us on the matter of freeing three people whose names he specifies. On this issue we have sent word with our emissary Prince Fajr al-Dīn, whom we have entrusted with expressing our greetings, testimonies of friendship, and other news that he will convey verbally to the king—may God grant him a long life. Listen closely to his words and phrases, and proceed accordingly so that our foregoing friendship and ancient promises can be maintained. ...

... Let the king know all this. May God—let him be praised—grant him a long life if that is what he wants.

This letter has been written on the first day of the moon of the venerable [month of] Sha'bān of the year 705 [16 February 1306 CE] ... according to the instructions of the sovereign. God be praised, only him, and let there be blessings and salvation for our Prophet Muhammad, his family, and his companions. In God we have all we need. Excellent healer, he is.

Letter from Granada to Aragon, 1314

To the illustrious, glorious, magnificent, etc. King James [II], king of Aragon, lord of Valencia, and Xativa and their respective territories, count of Barcelona and admiral to the pope. ...

He, who cares very much for his majesty, who loyally carries his obligation to esteem him and respect out of true friendship, the prince, servant of God, Ismail, son of Faraj and of Nasr. We write to you from the Alhambra of Granada. May God watch over it. ...

... Your royal highness is truly exalted and highly esteemed. We are very grateful for your proposals, inspired in friendship and the most excellent loyalty, and the way you have proceeded, firmly bound by faithful promises, is worthy of imitation. We might also add, that your valued letter where you confirm the sincerity of your affection [for us] and your plausible proposals, has arrived. We welcome [its contents] with gratitude, inextinguishable esteem, and profound respect.

You write that all of our subjects and natives of our territories, who reside through the breadth of your domains, are guaranteed their safety and their persons and property will be respected, under all circumstances. In this, we recognize the faithfulness of your promises and the sincerity of your friendship.

In a like manner, for our part, and in reciprocity, we lavish our gratitude in such a way that it will merit your praise. Any merchant or other subject of yours found in our domains will be given every respect, consideration, and solicitude, and they will enjoy complete security, both in their persons and their goods. Ask any who comes here or who has returned from here and they will tell you just how true these words are, since when it comes to you we are guided by high esteem, which manifests itself in our desire to please you and to treat you as befits one, such as yourself, who is among the greatest of kings. On this you can you be very sure....

... In response to your greetings, you have my abundant and indelible salutations. Written on the twenty-third day of the month of Safar of the year 714 [29 May 1314]. May God in his grace and generosity make evident his blessings. End.

69. A *FATWĀ* AGAINST CHRISTIAN MERCHANTS

Not all Christians in Islamic lands enjoyed dhimmi *status. That was reserved for Christians who lived in these regions on a permanent basis. Those who traveled temporarily to Islamic territory, such as merchants or pilgrims, did not have the protections of the* dhimmis. *Instead, they were granted guarantees of safe conduct by a local ruler, guarantees that offered limited protection and could be rescinded if they broke Islamic law. The following* fatwā *(legal decision) concerns the status of these foreigners and the rights they enjoyed under Islamic law. The source dates from 1370 and includes the original* fatwā *(sections 3–4) as well as notes and commentary by a copyist (sections 1–2 and 5–6). The case concerns some Frankish merchants who held a public Christian prayer, an act banned by Islamic law, but for which the local Muslim authorities had granted permission. The jurist in this case had to decide whether the Franks had broken the guarantee of safe conduct and what penalties should be imposed if they had. The legal rigor that the Muslim authorities applied to this case ensured that everything was done by the letter of the law. The jurist determined that the Franks had violated the law and could be treated as captives and used in exchange for Muslim captives held by the Christians. The case reveals the precarious position under which minority groups operated and in which something as simple as ignorance or misunderstanding (on either their part or that of the local authorities) could ultimately have dramatic implications.*

Source: trans. A.S. Atiya, "An Unpublished XIVth Century Fatwā on the Status of Foreigners in Mamlūk Egypt and Syria," in *Studien Zur Geschichte and Kultar Des Nahen Und Fernen Ostens* (Leiden: Brill, 1935), 58–63.

1. Title

An event in 'Akkā, a town of [the province of] Safad in the time of Shaikh al-Islām, the *mujtahid* of the time, Qāḍi 'l-Quḍāt, Taqī al-Dīn al-Subkī.

2. Copyist's Introduction

In the name of Allah etc.... A juridical consultation from Safad sent to Malik al-Umarā' in Damascus, al-maqarr al-'Alā'ī, may God fortify his followers. There came a letter from the Nā'ib of Safad, al-Maqarr al-Karīm al-Shihābī ibn Subh to Shaikh al-Islām, the *mujtahid* of the time, Qāḍi 'l-Quḍāt, Taqī al-Dīn al-Subkī.

The summary of the received letter is that the town of 'Akkā on the coast of the province of Safad has a harbor to which the merchants of the Franks resort by sea to sell what they bring with them and buy other goods instead and return to their homeland. And it was not their custom to celebrate their festivities publicly in 'Akkā nor did they practice the usages of their native countries. Then one day the Franks gathered together and engaged persons who cut down olive branches for them, and they laid these on the shoulders of Muslim carriers with beams of wood. Then the Franks mounted on the beams a number of their boys with drums and flutes. And the said boys, while in the harbor, publicly prayed for the sultan al-Malik al-Sāliḥ. Then all went to the ruins of 'Akkā, and at the head of the procession were the Muqaddim of the province and the harbor and a number of Muslims with drawn swords. When they reached the church, the boys riding [on the shoulders of Muslims] prayed to the Christ to succor the religion of the Cross; and one of them raised a lance with a banner attached to it. Meanwhile, the Mamluk mustered forces which [seized and] brought the aforesaid Franks together with the governor of 'Akkā, the judge of the city, *Muqaddim* of the harbor and the province, and the carriers. When they came in the presence of the mamluk, he asked the carriers about that [event]. They stated that it happened and the *Muqaddim* of the province had ordered them to carry the olive-tree with the Franks. They added that the Franks stated that they had consulted the governor, and he dispatched them to the qadi, who ordained that if the governor had enjoined them to act in this wise they were authorized to do so. He [the mamluk] made a procès-verbal of the case with [a statement of] what all the aforementioned persons had deliberately done. He wished to enforce the law against them, but for fear of complaint and of contention that he had unnecessarily and wrongfully ill-treated them, he had searched for a *mufti* [legal scholar] whom he might consult as to his action, and failed to find such a juris-consult at Safad, whose *ḥākim* asserted that there were three views on this matter; and a good deal of discussion took place among the *Faqīhs* [jurists] of Safad [in regard to this]. The mamluk therefore chose to put on record what

344

was necessary against all the aforesaid in order that he might deal with them according to the requirements of the religious law; and he would thus leave no room for argument or complaint on the part of the Franks. He thus prepared [a request for] a *futyā* [*fatwā*] and, after a reading thereof, submitted it to our lord, the *Malik al-Umarā*,' for consideration and endorsement in conformity with the religious law. It was on this account that the shaikh al-Islām wrote the *futyā* in question.

3. Text of the *Fatwā*

Praise be to God! [This is] the reply.

Those who come to the land of Islam for trade under safe-conduct are not subject to the same law as *ahl al-dhimma*. Unlike them, their status is that of persons enjoying the pledge of safe-conduct or treaty. And the pledge of safe-conduct is a weaker obligation than the covenant of *al-dhimma*; and it is liable to revocation in circumstances wherein the latter cannot be revoked. Now this action which has been committed by those under safe-conduct, in publicly professing [the aforenamed] things and proclaiming the religion of the Cross together with the sum total of such [offenses] as are cited, is one whereby their safe-conduct is broken and they become equivalent to outlaws. The verdict of the *faqihs* in the matter of *ahl al-dhimma* whose covenant is violated, is that the imam has the right to choose in dealing with them between execution, grace, slavery, and ransom, but cannot drive them out, according to the correct [view], but they [the *faqihs*, further] say that he who has a safe-conduct, is to be sent back to a place of safety [abroad]; and it is possible that their view should be brought into accord with what is decided for *ahl al-dhimma*. And my view is that both are alike in this situation. Hence, the imam can deal with them [the Franks] too as he may with *ahl al-dhimma* whose covenant is violated, that is, choose between the aforesaid four ways of execution, slavery, grace, and ransom. Yet his selection is not dependent on his pleasure, but on what seems to be for the good of the Muslims; and the final verdict lies with the sultan himself and not with the sultan's *naib* [second in command], for execution in this case is a serious matter, and the *naib* is not at liberty to enforce it without consulting our lord the sultan. And this applies to the rest of the four measures. Nevertheless, the infliction of a minor punishment is necessary in any case, and the sultan's *naib* is free to impose it without consultation as it is compulsory. And the [choice] of minor punishment on such people depends on the judgment of the *naib* of the sultanate—may God the High confirm him!—for this varies with what is apparent of their circumstances. As for this act [of the Franks], it is an act of violence against Muslims, and hushing it would be an injury towards them. Their responsible authority [the mamluk] should be rewarded for his rejection [of their action]. And no one would say that they [the Franks] might be ransomed without [minor] punishment. And he who ordered and allowed them to do so, if he be a *wali*, he should be dismissed and corrected by beating which must not reach the minimum limits; and if he be a qadi, he should be discharged from office. And the carriers should be corrected gently together with the Muslims who were in their company and did not disapprove of their action. And God knows best! Written by 'Ali al-Subki al-Shafi'i.

4. Postscript

And my opinion in the aforesaid case is that, together with punishment or other-wise, we should detain those Franks here until they set free the Muslim captives in their countries for they have the means of doing so by influence or money. The *naib* of the sultanate—may God the High confirm him!—is thus bound to hold them in custody till they find a way to deliver the Muslim prisoners. And this is to be considered among the four measures which we have enumerated, that is, ransom, which the *naib* of the sultanate may impose without consultation providing no harm accrues therefrom, namely, their imprisonment until they find a way thereto. For such measure at this time is preferable to execution, or to showing mercy to them or to enslaving them. And God the Exalted knows best!

5. Copyist's Commentary

This is what he [al-Subki] wrote in the *futya* without enlargement; and I may add to that for the benefit of a *faqih* without his book [?], and thus I say: Be it known that their mere advent for trade does not imply safe-conduct until the imam, his *naib*, or any of the Muslims has granted it to them by a clear word of mouth or writing or an intelligible sign. And the safe-conduct given by sign is as binding as that given by writing, whether this emanates from one capable of speech or incapable thereof on our side and by a word of mouth or an act on their side. Without this, no obligation is established, unless they are [diplomatic] envoys or [otherwise] have come with the intention of hearing the word of God. If they do not fall under any of these three categories, there will be no safe-conduct for them. And safe-conduct is not of necessity a result of their mere coming for trade, for he who comes without permission is without security. And the *faqihs* have declared that if a person from enemy country comes into the lands of Islam and says: "I have come for trade and I have assumed that the visiting of merchants is similar to that of ambassadors and convoys," his assumption is to be disregarded and it will be lawful to slay him, since his contention is an assump-tion, not a validated statement. For such merchants are without a warrant for safe-conduct and are therefore liable to the treatment of enemies of war, so that we may take their lives and confiscate their goods and chattels. For the condition of their safe-conduct is that the *wali* should say: "Anyone who comes for trade is safe," or, if one of the Muslims says [so] to a specific person, and thus that person earns his safety. General safe-conduct cannot be binding as a result of a word from one of the community of Muslims, but only by the word of the imam or his *naib*. Special safe-conduct may be established by one of the community of Muslims. And if a written document [to this effect] is found without intention, it is null and void but involves no slaying and [the person concerned] is conveyed abroad. Moreover, if safe-conduct is granted, but the infidel has not recognized it, the grant will not come into effect and the grantee may be slain even by him who has given the safe-conduct, for this has not been established owing to the infidel's misunderstanding thereof. And if persons have had permission to come for trade without anything to testify to their safe-conduct, will safe-conduct be binding for them or not, while there is no proof to it either by an outspoken promise or by writing or sign? I have seen no tradition concerning this matter. And this is the case of these Franks, and it is evident that they have no safe-conduct for that reason. For they are neither persons under safe-conduct, nor are they under treaty before or after their action, how much less indeed thereafter! This, however, we have said by way of further interpretation of that case and by way of amplification, which we do not need, for we are definitely convinced that as a result of their guilt they have no safe-conduct. We have, nevertheless, wished to draw attention to this special case and also to those who come on pilgrimage to the Church of the Resurrection. Although they may have permission without safe-conduct for that [purpose], their status will be as follows. They have no safe-conduct, but they are not to be slain. The advantage of leaving them without safe-conduct is that if one of them is killed, there has been no guarantee for his life, although it is illegal for anyone to kill him, but he can be sent back abroad for he has not trespassed in coming by permission. On the contrary, the person who has committed that shameful act has thereby violated [his own safe-conduct], and we are thus under no obligation for [returning him to] security. And it is admitted in the argument of the *faqihs* that safe-conduct is for the purpose of trade; of this there can be no doubt if it is issued by the imam or his *naib* generally or specifically, or by any specific member of the Muslim community to a specific person or small number of merchants. But in the case where a subject declared it and the infidel says its legality is validated, there are two views as to the lawfulness of slaying him, the more correct of which is that he should not be slain. But if his safe-conduct proves to be harmful to Muslims, it is abrogated. He will have no right of conveyance to refuge, and it will be lawful to slay him in the circumstances, even if safe-conduct has been granted, for such is null and void. In contrast, there is a safe-conduct, vicious in nature, yet inviolable, such as the safe-conduct of a child. The revocable safe-conduct may be illustrated by that of a spy and likewise. And no safe-conduct for property binds until it is openly stated according to the most correct view. And my opinion is that a safe-conduct granted to a person for trade also binds for property imported for this purpose which is the original object thereof. And if safe-conduct is violated by his committing a crime, it is retracted from person and property which becomes booty for Muslims, unless the culprit takes to refuge and leaves his property behind. In this case, safe-conduct remains inviolate for his property according to the more correct view, and indeed it has to be ceded to his lawful heirs, because the safe-conduct in that case is without crime against us—[the breach] being confined to the person and not the property. And here [in the case of the Franks] the crime originated from the person and the property suffers the consequences. And God knows best.

6. Explicit

Shaikh al-Islām—may the mercy of God be upon him!—said that he wrote this on the eve of 25 Safar 754 [1 April 1353]. And it was copied from his own autograph—may the mercy of God be upon him!—by Abu 'l-Barakāt on 4 Shawwāl 771 [1 May 1370].

70. ORDINANCES OF VALLADOLID

The situation for minority religious communities was also difficult in the Christian world, and one could argue that their status declined over the course of the Middle Ages. This was particularly true for Muslims and Jews living in Iberia, where the fourteenth century had witnessed a decline in their rights and living conditions, culminating in massive pogroms against the Jews in 1391 throughout the peninsula. A series of wars and weak kings, particularly in Castile, created tremendous instability that undermined the position of minorities. Under these circumstances, Muslims and Jews often became scapegoats for broader social problems, and the weakness of the monarchs upon whose protection they depended put them at further risk. The source below, the Ordinances of Valladolid, captures the extreme legal restrictions under which minorities were living by the early fifteenth century. The Ordinances were promulgated by John II of Castile (r. 1406–54), seven years of age at the time, and under the guidance of his regents, his mother Catherine of Lancaster and his uncle Ferdinand of Antequera. The legislation placed extensive limits on where Jews and Muslims could live, what trades they could engage in, their personal appearance, and their interactions with Christians. In spite of the harshness of the Ordinances, it does not appear that they were widely enforced, and some of the laws do not seem to have been applied outside of Valladolid. Nevertheless, the laws do capture the discriminatory environment in which Jews and Muslims toiled, and the uncertainty of their social position as their lives were often at the whim of the king and his advisors.

Source: trans. Jarbel Rodriguez, from Francisco Fernandez y Gonzalez, *Estado social y politico de los Mudejares de Castilla* (Madrid: Imprenta a cargo de Joaquin Muñoz, 1866), 400–5.

1. First of all, from this moment forth all Jews and Muslims in every one of my kingdoms and lordships shall live apart from Christians, in a separate locale in the city, village or place where they live, and they shall be enclosed with a surrounding wall that shall only have one gate on the perimeter. And within said enclosure, shall live all the Jews and Muslims that have so been assigned, and not in any other place, nor shall they have a domicile outside of said enclosure. And this process [of separation] shall begin on the day on which they are assigned their living quarters and for eight days thereafter. And any Jew or Muslim who resides outside of said enclosure shall lose all their goods and their bodies shall be at my mercy, to be physically punished, as I deem fit.

2. Moreover, no Jew or Muslim shall be a spicer, pharmacist, surgeon, or physician. They shall not sell bread, lard, or any other foodstuff to Christians. They shall not have stores, pharmacies or [food] tables either in public or in hiding to sell any food items. And any Jew or Muslim who goes against this law, shall be fined 2,000 maravedis for each transgression and their bodies shall be at my mercy, to be physically punished, as shall be deemed appropriate and I see fit.

3. Moreover, if any Jew or Muslim is inspired by the Holy Spirit and wants to be baptized or convert to the holy Catholic faith, they shall not be held or bound from the Holy Catholic Faith. They shall not be turned away by Jew, Muslim, or Christian, be they man or woman, father, mother, brother, or any other person. And any who goes against this law shall face the stiffest civil and criminal penalties that apply.

4. Moreover, no Jew or Muslim shall, inside or outside their homes, eat or drink among Christians, nor shall Christians [eat or drink] among Jews or Muslims. [Jews and Muslims] shall not have Christian squires, servants, pages, or maids who serve them and obey their commands or do any domestic work in their homes, not even helping with food or doing any errands on Saturday such as lighting their lamps, going for wine, or similar things. They shall not have Christian nannies that help with the raising of their children or plowmen, gardeners, or shepherds. They shall not attend the funerals, weddings, or burials of Christians, nor shall they be godfathers or godmothers of Christians, nor shall Christians be godfathers or godmothers to them, go to their weddings or burials, nor have any conversations at any of the aforementioned [gatherings], all under penalty of 2,000 maravedis for each time that the Jews or Muslims break these laws.

5. Moreover, no Jew or Muslim shall own property to rent, or be a lawyer, tax collector, [land] steward, or lessor for any of my properties or that of any Christian lord or lady. They shall not be brokers or money changers or carry weapons in the cities, villages, or places. And any Jew or Muslim who breaks this law shall pay a fine of 2,000 maravedis. And that any Christian, of any rank, who uses a Jew or a Muslim in any of these offices, shall pay the same penalty.

6. Moreover, no Jew or Muslim shall have in their neighborhoods or quarters either squares or marketplaces in which they can buy or sell anything to eat or drink to Christians, under penalty of 500 maravedis for each transgression. [This is] so that they buy and sell only among themselves.

7. Moreover, the *aljamas* [communities] of Jews and Muslims in my realms and lordships shall not have, now or in the future, judges, be they Jewish or Muslim, to adjudicate civil or criminal disputes which might occur among them. And I hereby revoke any power that they may have on this matter, which they may have obtained by privilege or in any other form from me or from my ancestors. And I command that henceforth all such disputes, civil or criminal, among Jews or Muslims shall be adjudicated by the [Christian] magistrate of the city, village or place where they dwell. But it is my will that the magistrates in their judgments of civil cases shall protect the customs and statutes which had been hitherto preserved by Jews and Muslims, as long as these [the customs and statutes] are authentic and have been approved by them since long ago.

8. Moreover, no *aljama* or community of Jews or Muslims shall dare to levy a tax or tribute among themselves nor place any tariffs on any item without my license or that of my wife, the queen, my mother, or the prince, my uncle, [the latter two] who are my tutors and regents. And if any right has been given to the aforementioned Jews and Muslims, or if any rights of taxation have been granted to them, either in common or in any other form, be it on individuals, foodstuffs, merchants, or for anything else, [and these rights have been granted] either to their judges or anyone else so that they have certain privileges or writs from past kings (my ancestors) or from me to do so, henceforth they shall no longer have the right to tax or have to pay any such taxes, as I, in my royal power, revoke any and all privileges that have previously been granted on this question. And I command the aforementioned Jews and Muslims to stop using these [past] privileges under penalty of bodily punishment. Likewise, I order the aforementioned Jews and Muslims to neither impose nor pay any such assessment that may be imposed on them without my order and license expressly given to this purpose.

9. Moreover, no *aljama* or community of Jews or Muslims from this moment forth shall dare to assess or allocate taxes without my license and consent, and whenever they impose any taxes in my service, they shall divide out among themselves only what I order and no more. And if they charge or impose any more [taxes than what I have approved], those who do so, even if by mistake, or who advised to do so, shall lose all their good and be put to death in the name of justice.

10. Moreover, no Jew or Muslim shall dare to visit any sick Christians or bring them medicines or curative concoctions. The Jews and Muslims shall not bathe in baths with Christians [this applies to both men and women]. They shall not send them gifts of pastries, spices, baked bread, wine, fowls, or any other dead animals or fish, nor any fruit or any other dead foodstuffs. And any who breaks this law, Jew or Muslim, shall pay a 300-maravedi fine for each offense.

11. Moreover, no Christian woman, married, single, loose or public woman [prostitute] shall dare to enter by day or by night the enclosure where Muslims live. And any Christian woman who so enters, if married, she shall pay 100 maravedis each time she enters the enclosure; if single or a loose woman, she shall lose the clothes she is wearing; and if a prostitute, she shall be flogged 100 times in the name of justice and expelled from the city, town or place where she resides.

12. Moreover, no Jew or Muslim, shall call themselves from this day forth "sir" either orally or in writing. And any who does so shall be flogged 100 times for each transgression.

13. Moreover, from this day forth no Jewish man from my realms and lordships shall wear hoods with cowls, unless the cowls are short—up to a hand span—made in the shape of a funnel and sewn all around, up to the tips. Moreover, they shall wear coats with tails, not cloaks, and continue wearing the red badges which they now carry; all under penalty of losing all the clothes they are wearing [if they break these regulations].

14. Moreover, starting ten days hence, the Jewish and Muslim women from my realms and lordships shall wear long veils without trimmings that reach to their feet, and headdresses without gold, and they shall cover their heads with the aforementioned veils folded over. And any who goes against this [law], shall lose all the clothes they are wearing down to their undershirt for each transgression.

15. Moreover, starting ten days hence the Jews and Muslims from my realms and lordships shall not wear any clothes made from cloth that is worth more than 30 maravedis a yard; and any who goes against this [law] shall lose all the clothes they are wearing down to their undershirt for the first offense; shall lose all their clothes

and be flogged 100 times for the second offense; and shall lose all their clothes, be flogged fifty times, and lose all their property for the third offense. It is my will that they be allowed to make coats and veils with the clothes they have now.

16. Moreover, no Jew or Muslim shall leave Valladolid or the place where they now reside. Any who do so shall lose all their property and their body will be at my mercy.

17. Moreover, no lord, knight, or squire shall dare to welcome in their villages or other holdings any Jew or Muslim who has abandoned the place where they currently live. And if any of them has taken in any Jew or Muslim from Valladolid or any other city, village or place, they shall return them and all their belongings to the place where they lived previously. Moreover, if they have taken them in and fail to send them back as stipulated above, they shall be fined 50,000 maravedis for the first offense and lose the lordship where a Jew or Muslim has taken residence for the second offense.

18. Moreover, from this moment forth the Jews and Muslims of my realms and lordships shall not shave their beards, with either scissor or razor, but wear them long nor will they cut their hair, but keep it as they used to in antiquity. And any who goes against this [law] shall be flogged 100 times and pay a fine of 100 maravedis for each offense.

19. Moreover, no Jew or Muslim from my realms or lordships shall employ any Christian woman for pay, or any Christian man to work on their land, vineyards, houses or any other building. And any who goes against this [law] shall be flogged 100 times for the first offense; be fined up to 1,000 maravedis and again flogged 100 times for the second offense; and lose all his or her goods and flogged 100 more times for the third offense.

20. Moreover, no Jew or Muslim from my realms or lordships shall be a veterinarian, farrier, carpenter, maker of jackets, tailor, shearer, hosier, butcher, furrier, or one who sells rags to Christians, nor shall they sell to Christians shoes, jackets, stockings, nor sew their clothes or jackets or any other articles. And any who goes against this [law] shall suffer the penalties prescribed in the previous law.

21. Moreover, no Jew or Muslim from my realms and lordships shall work on a [commercial] mule-train or bring any merchandise such as oil, honey, rice or other edible goods to sell to Christians. And any who goes against this [law] shall suffer the penalties prescribed in the previous law.

22. Moreover, for any of the aforementioned transgressions any resident of the city, village, or place where the offense occurred can act as an accuser. And said

accuser is entitled to one third of the fine prescribed for the offense; the remaining two-thirds belong to my treasury. It is my will that said accusers shall not take into custody any Jew or Muslim who, instead, shall be brought to trial.

23. Moreover, any Jew or Muslim from my realms and lordships who leaves my kingdom and is captured on the road or any other place, shall [because of their leaving] lose all their goods and become my captive in perpetuity.

24. Moreover, that no mayor, judge, royal official, magistrate, or any other person from any city, village or place, even if they are lords and have judicial rights, shall lift, dispense with, add to or lessen any of the aforementioned civil and criminal penalties under penalty of losing their lordship or office.

25. Since I have made these ordinances, they shall be kept and maintained as stipulated and I order all councils, mayors, justices, judges, magistrates, constables, and any other officials in my realms and lordships to publicize and proclaim them in each city, etc.

Given in Valladolid, on the second of January, in the year of the birth of our lord Jesus Christ, 1412.

71. MUSLIM MINORITIES AND THE COMPLEXITIES OF THE LAW

Those Muslims who lived under Christian law had to negotiate a host of competing interests that sought to influence and dictate how they lived their lives. Not only were there Christian laws and officials to deal with, but there were also their own internal legal traditions and officials that ran the day-to-day affairs of Muslim communities (known as aljamas *in Spain), as well as legal decisions from the broader Muslim world that also had an impact upon them. The source that follows reflects some of the difficulties minority Muslim communities faced. It is the* Breviary *written in 1462 by Ice de Gebir, a mudejar jurist from Segovia. It is a source full of contradictions reflecting the conflicting legal traditions that* mudejares *had to negotiate. For example, it reminds its readers to flee the lands of the unbelievers, yet it is written in Castilian and aimed at a community that had been living in the lands of the unbelievers for generations. And while it exhorts all Muslims to teach the law (of Islam) to everyone, this would have been fatal for* mudejares, *as the preaching of Islam to Christians in Castile was punishable by death.*

Source: trans. Jarbel Rodriguez, from *Memorial Historico Español—Vol. V* (Madrid: La Real Academia de Historia, 1853), 250–53.

Ice de Gebir—Breviary

The sovereign Creator who revealed his honored Quran to his honored prophet Muhammad the Blessed and who speaks in seven different ways and as such has included in the Law and Sunnah [practices instituted by Muhammad that all Muslims are expected to follow] commandments, histories and revelations, punishments, and threats. [What follows is an] abridged Breviary of all the commandments and obligations found in the Law and the Sunnah. The most important among them are the following:

1. You will only worship the Creator, but never attribute any images or likenesses to him, and honor his chosen and blessed Muhammad.
2. You will desire for your neighbor the same good that you desire for yourself.
3. Keep yourself continuously clean by means of ablutions and purification and the five prayers.
4. Obey your father and mother even if they are infidels.
5. Do not take your Creator's name in vain.
6. Do not murder, steal, or fornicate with any creature.
7. Pay your tithes [*zakat*].
8. Keep the fast in the holy month of Ramadān.
9. Perform the *hajj* [pilgrimage to Mecca].
10. Do not lie with your wife unless you are both [ritually] clean.
11. Honor the day of prayer [Friday], especially the holy days, in cleanliness and devout prayers and by visiting the poor and those who are learned in the Law.
12. Honor those who are learned in the Law.
13. Defend the Law with your goods and with your person.
14. Honor your neighbor, be he a stranger, a relative, or an infidel.
15. Give lodging willingly to the traveler and to the poor.
16. Do not break your oath, word, surety or pledge except in cases that violate the Law; if you do you must make amends [to those you wrong].
17. Be faithful. Do not traffic in goods that you know to be stolen.
18. Do not be the cause of sin or allow it or you will be associated with it.
19. Do not falsify weights and measures to their owners; do not lie or betray; do not engage in usury.
20. Do not drink wine or anything that can inebriate you.
21. Do not eat pork, dead animals, blood, things of questionable provenance, or animals that have been improperly slaughtered, offered to a creature [as food] or on an altar [as a sacrifice].

22. Whenever you encounter a Muslim, offer him your greetings [*salaam*] and help him in the service of the Creator; visit him if he is sick and bury him if he dies.

23. Oppose any Muslim that goes against the Law or the Sunnah.

24. He who speaks should speak well or remain silent; do not speak ill [of others] even if it is true.

25. When you judge, be a fair judge; do not profit and guard against greed; be faithful to your lord even if he is not a Muslim as he will be your heir if you lack one and pay him his dues; honor the rich; do not scorn the poor; guard yourself against envy and malice; be patient; do not fall in with sorcerers, diviners, augurs, astrologers, or casters of lots, remaining true only to your Lord.

26. Do not live in the land of the infidels, in a land without justice, or with bad neighbors; do not befriend bad Muslims.

27. Live among the worthy and devote one-third of your goods, more if you can afford it and do not have to regret it.

28. Do not play dice or other banal games.

29. Do not take pleasure from that which is sinful [haram]; do not desire with your heart or covet with your eyes that which does not belong to you; guard yourself against your enemies; forgive those who wrong you and ask for forgiveness of those you have wronged; guard against pride; obey your elders, have pity on the young, and be a brother to those who are your own age.

30. Do not be two-faced; be a peacemaker; put the sinful on the right path, calm those who are angry, and ensure that Allah gets his due.

31. Use your wealth to redeem captives; lend succor to the orphan and the widow and be a neighbor to your lord.

32. Learn the Law and teach it to all, as on this action you will be judged and be found worthy or wanting.

33. Hinder those who transgress the Law or Sunnah as those who sin or consent to sin are equally guilty; turn your efforts to them and Allah will reward you.

34. If you are truly repentant you will be worthy of eternal praise.

35. Be in contempt of the world and in good hope you will have eternal life and blessings.

36. Do not adopt the manners, uses, and customs of the Christians nor their dress or affectations, or that of the sinful, and you will be free of infernal sin.

37. Keep and guard the words, doctrines, uses, customs, habits, and dress of the excellent and blessed Muhammad, God bless and save him, and of his Companions upon whom the Almighty bestowed so much grace, and on the day of judgment, you will be among those without temptation who enter paradise.

72. PIETRO CASOLA IN JERUSALEM

Religious minorities not only included those who permanently lived in a given place, but also transient populations such as merchants, travelers, foreign mercenaries, and pilgrims. These groups often lacked the protections of their more permanent coreligionists, but that certainly did not stop the adventurous, the enterprising, and the pious from traveling to foreign regions. One of these devout travelers was the Milanese priest Pietro de Casola (1427–1507) who made a pilgrimage to the Holy Land in 1494 at the age of 67. In an account that mirrors many of the same observations and complaints made by Ibn Jubayr (see Doc. 65), but from a Christian perspective, Casola made numerous comments both on the interaction between local Christian communities with the ruling Muslims and on his own experiences as a pilgrim. The section below is taken from Casola's description of his stay in Jerusalem and is brimming with details that describe the wonders and difficulties encountered by pilgrims; it also provides an outsider's viewpoint on daily life for the local Christian community.

Source: Margaret Newett, *Canon Pietro Casola's Pilgrimage to Jerusalem in the Year 1494* (Manchester: Manchester University Press, 1907), 246–65.

On Wednesday, the 6th of August, Mass having been said in the midst of the hospital, all the pilgrims set out early, guided by certain friars of Mount Sion, who were familiar with all the places to be visited by the pilgrims.

Leaving Jerusalem and passing that torrent called in the Holy Scriptures the torrent Cedron, we came to a monument built in the ancient fashion which was said to be that of Absalom, the son of David, who was killed by Joab, David's captain, when he was hung up by his hair while he was pursuing his father. On seeing it, I thought it was more probably the monument of Helena, queen of the Adiabene, because so I had read in Josephus's wars of the Jews.

Then, going further, we visited all those sacred places on the Mount of Olives where the mysteries which preceded the passion of our Lord Jesus Christ were shown to us: where he remained to pray, where the three disciples were when he prayed "Pater si possible est transeat a me calyx iste," ["Oh my father, if it be possible, let this cup pass from me," Matt. 26:39] and where he was apprehended. Then we mounted higher to where there was a small church, or part of one, and over the altar there was a stone still bearing the mark of the foot of our Lord Jesus Christ when he ascended into heaven, and this was touched with the rosaries and other objects of devotion. In these places—because they are so despised by those Moorish dogs and are not otherwise venerated—it is necessary to open the third sack, called the sack of faith, otherwise the voyage would be made in vain [earlier in his narrative Casola describes three "sacks" that every pilgrim needed: a sack of patience, a sack of faith, and a sack of money]. I do not mention that any antiphons or prayers were said there, because those Fathers did not say any; they only explained in Latin and in the vulgar tongue what those places were and nothing else. Many itineraries, however, both Italian and Ultramontane, written in the vulgar tongue and in Latin, mention that formerly antiphons and prayers appropriate to the places visited used to be said. I can only say that in fact this was not done. I can well believe that as the friars were in such a hurry to show us those places, they omitted some of the usual ceremonies.

Afterwards we descended the Mount of Olives and, turning to the right hand, we went into the valley of Jehoshaphat, who was king of Jerusalem. It is a small valley, nevertheless, it is said that it will be the place of the Last Judgment of Our Lord Jesus Christ. In this valley there is a beautiful church containing the Sepulcher in which the body of Our Lady was placed by the eleven Apostles. The place of the Sepulcher proper is governed by the Latin friars—that is, by those of Mount Sion. In the same church there are several other altars served by Greek priests. The said church, from what I could hear, is held in great veneration also by the Moorish women. At the entrance to that church the Moors made a charge for each person. I do not know how much it was because the captain [of the pilgrim's ship] paid.

After the prescribed prayers had been offered in the said church, which descends many steps, we returned to Jerusalem by the gate called the gate of Saint Stephen, where he was stoned. Above the torrent Cedron, outside the gate on the left-hand side of the entrance, there is what looks like a little church. When I asked a Christian of the Girdle [local Christian] what it was, he said that the lord of Damascus had built it in memory of one of his sons who was buried there, and that he had placed there a reservoir of water for wayfarers, which is never empty; and this is the will of the said lord, even though the water should have to be brought from Damascus. And all this he has done for the repose of the soul of his said son.

Within the said gate, a house was pointed out which they said was the house of Pilate, and another which they said was Herod's. We went to a certain place said to be the pool of Siloam, where the blind man was sent to bathe his eyes. There is no water now, and the place is full of ruins.

We went to see the Probatic pool [Pool of Bethesda]. This has running water, and there are even a few vestiges of the five porches which the Holy Scripture says were there at the time of Christ. This was a pool which had the virtue that an angel descended from heaven into the said pool and moved the water, and the first sick person who entered the pool after the moving of the water was cured of all his infirmities. Therefore, under those porches, there used to lie a great multitude of sick persons in order to be ready to enter the water quickly; and Christ with a word only healed one who had been there eighteen years. Now, as could be seen, the Moors washed there the hides which had been in lime. Many of the pilgrims drank the water. When I saw that filth I left it alone, it was enough for me to wash my hands there.

As it was on our way, we afterwards saw the Mosque—which they say stands on the site of the temple of Solomon. It is a beautiful building to look at from the outside, and strong compared with the greater part of the habitations in Jerusalem. It is wonderful to see the courts—so well paved with the whitest marble—which are built around at the base of the Mosque.

When we had seen what the friars wanted us to see—opening the first and third sacks where it was necessary and where I judged it advisable to do so—we arrived at the hospital all hot and covered with dust, and took a little repose and also some refreshment, and whoever had a lodging went there. The Prior of Mount Sion now sent to tell the pilgrims that every man must be ready to enter the Holy Sepulcher that evening. But when he wanted to arrange for the entrance with Abrayno, who was the person in authority, he demanded first a thousand ducats. An altercation followed, and in consequence, the project of entering the Sepulcher was given up.

As the captain's house was frequented by a very agreeable Moor who had formerly been forced into slavery at Rhodes, and who knew a little Latin, to while away the time, I got him for a few *marchetti* [small Italian coin] to take me and certain other pilgrims to see as much as possible of the city; and I studied it as carefully as I could.

The city of Jerusalem is very ancient. Its first founder was Canaan, the grandson of Ham, son of Noah—that son as I said who was cursed by his father Noah because seeing him uncovered he mocked him. When the three sons of Noah—that is, Shem, Ham, and Japhet—divided the world among them after the deluge, that part called Judea fell to the progeny of Ham, and in Judea Jerusalem has always been the chief city.

At first it was called Solyma, and was an insignificant place, but afterwards from time to time it was enlarged, as Rome was. Although it lies between various mountains or rather hills, it seems that there are many flat parts, nevertheless it is in the mountains. As is generally known, Titus Caesar in the second year of the reign of Vespasian destroyed it so completely that no one who looked on the ruins could have imagined that it had ever been inhabited. He did not leave there one stone upon another except in three towers preserved as a record that the Romans had subdued such a great city. I saw the foundations of the said towers; they are very wonderful. They are on the way down from Mount Sion before crossing the torrent Cedron.

After a long time Hadrian caused the city to be rebuilt and wished it to be called Helias. To judge by the ruins it was not re-built as it had been at first, and he gave it for a habitation to the Christians. Since that time, it has been attacked very often—now by the Saracens, now by the Christians. As all the histories relate, Saint Helena, mother of the emperor Constantine, caused all the mysteries of the humanity of our Lord Jesus Christ to be adorned, but afterwards many of them were destroyed and few remain to us because those Moorish dogs will not permit any restorations to be made.

As I went about the city I did not see beautiful dwelling-houses. There are a great number, and they are close together, but they are ugly. All the houses appear to be vaulted and have vaults above vaults. The roofs are flat, and there is little woodwork inside. The more a man wishes to say about this city the less he has to say, except that such a famous city, called by Christians the Holy Place, is a great *cavagniaza* [market basket made of rushes; meaning unclear here]. There are some very honorable dwellings, though not many. Among the number is the house of the governor, who, as I said, is like a commissioner. There is also the habitation of the Grand Cathibissa, or as they call him the Old Man of the Faith, to whom honor and reverence is paid as if he were a saint.

What pleased me most was the sight of the bazaars—long, vaulted streets extending as far as the eye can reach. In one of them all the provisions are sold—I mean also the cooked provisions, as they sell the chestnuts at home. When I marveled at this I was told that not a single person in Jerusalem does the cooking in the house; and whoever wishes to eat goes to buy in the bazaar. However, they make bread at home—that is, flat cakes made without leaven; they are good when there is no other bread to be got. Leavened bread can only be had in the monastery at Mount Sion. Cooked fowls, cooked meat, eggs and all other eatables are very cheap. I saw another long bazaar like the other, with both sides full of merchandise, and of the things the people know how to make, and this was a beautiful sight.

The city has one beautiful building; that is its mosque. Neither Christian nor Jew can enter there. Outside one can see what a beautiful place it is with those courts round it as I mentioned above. I heard from the Moors that there are neither paintings nor images inside. They say that there are a thousand lamps within, which on certain occasions are all lighted at the same moment.

Many people say that this mosque is the temple built by Solomon. But I cannot believe it, because I have not found any writing which would give me a reason for believing this, or that it is on the site of the Temple of Solomon; because the Holy Scripture relates that Nebuchadnezzar, king of Babylon, caused the Temple of Solomon to be thrown to the ground. We know also that Ezra, with the permission of Cyrus, king of the Medes and Persians, caused it to be re-built from the foundations. Then in true histories we find that Herod the Great—the one who was king of Judea at the time of the birth of Christ—caused it to be rebuilt. And besides all that, the Temple of Solomon was built on a mountain, and on that mountain called Mount Moriah, which was pointed out by God to Abraham when he told him he must sacrifice his son Isaac. This was also the place where the sleeping Jacob saw in a dream the ladder which reached from earth to heaven, and the angels ascending and descending, and said, "This is the house of God and the gate of Heaven." And it was also the place where David saw the angel, sword in hand, striking the people with the plague, and prayed God to pardon the people and strike him instead. And God commanded him to build an altar there and offer sacrifices, and David did at once as God commanded him. He bought the site from Hornan, who was a Jebusite—that is a Gentile; and he commanded Solomon, his son, to build a temple there after his death, and this was done. Therefore, this mosque cannot be on the site of the Temple of Solomon because it is in the valley, and that was on a mountain. Further, there is authentic record that after Titus caused the temple to be leveled to the ground because it was the greatest fortress the Jews then possessed, it has never been rebuilt.

It appears to me that there are no vestiges remaining of the said temple, and that this mosque was built according to the will of the Moors after the Christians had lost Jerusalem, which was in the reign of Saladin, lord of Babylon, and they have never been able to recover it since. However that may be, like the other smaller one which the Usbech—the present governor of Jerusalem—caused to be built ten years ago, it is a stupendous thing; and it appears to me that the Moors do not lack good master workmen for their buildings. I heard from certain of the friars at Mount Sion that he used many of the marbles which were round at Joppa—that is, Jaffa—buried under the ruins; and some were also raised out of the water. Our magnificent captain assured me that this was true, because a few years ago he was obliged with his boats to help to raise certain columns which were in the water there at Jaffa, and which were afterwards dried and taken to Jerusalem to be used in the building of the new mosque about which we have been talking. So that, in my judgment, there is not a vestige left of the said Temple of Solomon. At the side of this mosque there is a beautiful dwelling, almost the most beautiful in Jerusalem, where lives one who is called the Old Man of his Faith. He is a handsome man, and besides the faith he is worth looking at. He has the care of these mosques, and especially of this new one. It is not an article of belief or unbelief—what was said while our magnificent captain was with the said old man—that is, that in the said new mosque there were a thousand lamps constantly burning. I wanted to find out for certain, but it was impossible. I saw nothing else beautiful in the said city.

I saw indeed a thing worth recording; that is, a miracle. There is a palace ruined on one side. It is built in the modern style, rooms above rooms; in short, there is not its equal in Jerusalem. It belonged to a rich Moor. When the friars of Mount Sion were building at the side of their monastery a certain chapel of Our Lady, which was greatly venerated, the said Moor stirred up all the people on account of the said building to such an extent that all the Moors in a state of fury rushed there and destroyed the said chapel. And immediately the said palace was ruined, and no one has been able to rebuild it since. I recount this because I saw both places, and heard the story from the fathers of Mount Sion.

The Mount of Sion is the highest in Jerusalem, and in ancient times it was called the rock or city of David. The said rock was so strong that the children of Israel—that is, the Jews or Hebrews—even when they had entered the Promised Land and divided it by lot could never conquer it until David became king, and even he was king several years before he could take it. At last, he took it and made it his dwelling. Now the observant friars of Saint Francis live there, and they have a very well kept convent, and as the friars say, if it were not for the prohibition of the Moors who will not let them build, they would make it much more beautiful.

The friars' church is very beautiful, but it is not very large. They say that at the time of our Lord Jesus Christ this church was the large room in which he ate the last supper with his disciples before his passion. Where the high altar stands was the place where, after supper, he first ordained the Sacrament of his Body and Blood and gave it to his disciples. At the right of the said altar there is another altar said to be the place where our Lord Jesus Christ washed the feet of his disciples. In these two places, in spite of my unworthiness, I said Mass and prayed to God for all my friends.

Outside the said church, on the right-hand side going in towards the habitation of the friars, there is the place where the apostles were gathered together when the Holy Spirit descended upon them. Under the said church there is a certain little chapel, where it is said that Saint Thomas put his hand into the side of our Lord Jesus Christ, when he said to him, "Be not faithless but believing."

The convent is in good order considering that there are so few friars; they say there are always twenty friars who administer their part of the Sepulcher and also the place at Bethlehem. As I said above, if it were not for the prohibition of the Moors, the friars would do great things. As to building, they can do nothing, and if they do any repairs in the house they do them very secretly.

At the side of the church there is a chapel of our Lady which was destroyed by the fury of the Moors, as I mentioned before, and immediately the house of him who caused the evil fell down.

The said friars have certain gardens round the monastery, but when we were there everything was dried up. When I went into the said gardens I saw many ruins all round, which showed that the city of Sion had been an important place in the time of the kings. Near the said monastery there is what looks like a grand palace, and within the gate there is a little church belonging to certain Christians of the Girdle. They say that Saint James, who was said to be the brother of our

Lord, was beheaded in that place by order of Herod, the son of that Herod who killed the Innocents.

A little further on, going towards the gate of Jerusalem—because the Mount called Sion is a good way outside Jerusalem—there is the castle of the Pisans. Seen from outside it appears to be strong. In my opinion no care is taken of it. I never saw a guard there, although I often passed that way, going from the lodging of the captain where I also lodged, to the monastery of the friars at Mount Sion.

The said city, as I said above, has not strong walls nor any moat. I have not said anything yet about the place of the Holy Sepulcher because up to this day I had not seen it.

Among the inhabitants of Jerusalem, there are many of good condition and handsome men. They all go about dressed in the same way, with those clothes that look like quilts. Many are white, others are made of camlet, and of other silks of the Moorish kind. According to their means they display great care and magnificence in the white cloths they wear on their heads. This cloth is called a *sexula* if it is all white, and *moro naturale* if there are some black stripes woven in the said *sexula*.

Whether they are renegade Christians or true Christians of the Girdle, they all live in the same way, and eat on the ground on carpets; they have a few white cloths, but they are rare. They do not drink wine—I mean in public—but if they get the chance they take a good long drink of it. They like cheese very much. They would not eat a fowl which had had its neck drawn, as is the custom with us. They always cut the fowls' throats; otherwise they are clean in their cooking. For sleeping they have no place but the ground. They lie upon carpets, of which they have a great many. In their manner of eating, they are very dirty; even persons of importance thrust their hands into the dishes. They do not use knives or forks or spoons but they thrust their hands into everything.

With regard to their prayers, I observed—from a window which overlooked certain Moors who slept in the open air because of the extreme heat—that in the morning when they rose they went through so many genuflexions—throwing themselves all their length stretched out on the ground—that it was a marvel to see them. When I inquired further I learned that when they go to pray in the Mosque they go barefooted, and first they wash themselves in certain places set apart for that purpose, but only from the waist downwards, and then they uncover their heads, which they never uncover even in the presence of the greatest lord in the world. It is great madness to talk to them about our faith, because they have no rational sentiment in them. They are very impetuous and easily excited to anger, and they have no gracious or courteous impulses or actions. And I declare that they may be as great and as learned as you like, but in their ways they are like dogs.

In Jerusalem I was never able to see a beautiful woman; it is true that they go about with their faces covered by a black veil. They wear on their heads a thing which resembles a box, a *braccio* [unit of length ranging between 15 and 39 inches] long, and from that, on both sides, a long cloth, like the white towels in Italy, hangs down.

I know nothing more about these Moorish people, except that they are very disagreeable to us Italians and to other kinds of Christians in asking for money, which is an extreme annoyance. On this account, I was obliged to use a great deal of two of the three sacks. On Thursday, 7 August, all the pilgrims went to Mount Sion, and there many confessed and also communicated in that most holy place where this most holy Sacrament was instituted; and many said Mass there. We had amongst us sixty-three priests of different Orders. I said Mass and communicated one of our Milanese—Bernardino Scotto by name—and two Ragusans. Then the friars chanted very solemnly a Mass of the Holy Spirit, and a beautiful sermon was preached in Latin by one of the friars of Mount Sion, in which he expounded all the mysteries contained in the said church of Mount Sion. When Mass was ended a procession was formed to the places of the said mysteries; and when the said procession was finished the said friars of Mount Sion refreshed all the pilgrims with a good dinner.

After dinner, all the pilgrims were advised to go and take a rest in order to be ready that evening either to enter the Holy Sepulcher or to go to Bethlehem. At a very late hour the order was given to enter the Sepulcher. And this was because of a new extortion which was invented out of the ordinary way. Thus in the evening, at the twenty-third hour, all the pilgrims congregated before the door of the church of the Holy Sepulcher in a little court very beautifully paved with slabs of marble. In the middle of the court there is a stone which is honored because it is said that Christ rested there on the way to the place of his passion.

The deputies who had been appointed to count the pilgrims were now ready. They were ten Moors—men of imposing appearance and not priests—who wore dresses as white as snow and had those large *sexule* on their heads. It made me feel very hot only to look at them. These men were seated on a certain small platform raised about two *braccia* from the ground and arranged with mats over the boards, because the said platform was made of wood; and there they were all seated on their legs, like the tailors sit at home. They made, however, a fine picture.

We waited until sunset expecting the Moor who keeps the keys and who could not be found. You must know that although the Sepulcher is governed by the friars of Mount Sion and by other sects of Christians, as you will hear, nevertheless they cannot go in or out at pleasure, but must do so at the pleasure of that dog who always keeps the keys. He is the Moor who auctions the tolls on the pilgrims and on those who wish to visit the Sepulcher even at other times.

It is indeed true that in the door of the church there are certain cracks through which victuals and other things can be passed to those within.

The pilgrims were finally dismissed, as it was said that for that evening they could not enter, and the company therefore began to depart. The captain had already gone some distance when he encountered the man who had the keys. After much altercation and many words which I did not understand because they were in Moorish—although the prior of Mount Sion understood them—we returned to the church of the Sepulcher and the door was opened to the praise of God. The deputies mentioned above began to count the pilgrims like sheep in Moorish, and the interpreter in Italian; and by the grace of God we entered that Holy Church.

Because it was already night every pilgrim immediately lighted his candle, and the friars of Mount Sion who had come for that purpose began to form the procession, beginning at a Chapel of Our Lady where the offices are said continually by the friars who are shut up there all the year. In that place Christ appeared to his blessed Mother after the Resurrection. When an anthem had been chanted there and the appointed prayer said, one of the friars declared in Latin all the mysteries and relics contained in the said chapel; in which, besides the apparition I mentioned, a large piece of the cross of Christ is honored. It is placed in a window in the said chapel on the gospel side of the altar, and can be seen but not touched. On the other side of the said altar a large piece of the column at which our Lord Jesus Christ was scourged is honored. It is a wonderful relic, because the marks of the blows can be seen sculptured upon it; but they cannot be touched too much or they would disappear. This column may be touched with one hand, and also with a few rosaries. In all the places there are large indulgences.

On leaving the said chapel the procession entered the body of the church and visited all the other places usually visited, and first the place where Christ appeared to Mary Magdalen in the form of a gardener. All the time the appointed anthems were being sung, and the Litanies chanted by the way. We then visited the place where Christ remained in prison whilst the hole was being made in which the cross was erected. Then we visited the place where the garments of Christ were divided, and where the lots were cast for them. Then we went into the Chapel of Saint Helena, which goes down several steps, and after descending several other steps we saw the place where the cross of Christ was found, which is below the place of the Calvary. Then returning above, we visited a chapel where there is the column to which Christ was bound when the crown of thorns was placed on his head. Then we mounted to the place of the Calvary, by a wooden staircase, with the greatest reverence.

There a beautiful sermon was preached on the passion of Christ by one of the friars of Mount Sion, in such a way that I believe that if those Moorish dogs had been present, together with all the pilgrims, they would have wept. We stayed there for over an hour, and when the sermon was finished and the usual prayer had been chanted we descended to the Holy Sepulcher and entered one by one.

When the offices commenced by the said friars finished, the company set about refreshing themselves as well as they could—that is, those of the pilgrims who had laid in a store of provisions. I went with the magnificent captain to a small place belonging to the friars of Mount Sion, and had supper, although it was late, because he had made good provision. The other pilgrims stayed in the church on the floor, some in one place, some in another. When the refection was over some lay down on the ground to sleep, others did not.

As soon as I saw that the crowd of Ultramontanes had diminished, I went again with my lighted candle to make all the visitations, and I touched the places and relics with my rosaries without any impediment. Then after the scrutiny had been made, and the number of the pilgrims taken by the friars—I mean of those who wanted to say Mass—they made out the clear lists, and we were divided between three places—that is, the Sepulcher, the place of the Calvary, and the Chapel of Our Lady. Mass could also be said in the place where the body of Christ was laid when he was taken down from the Cross, while he was being anointed with the mixture brought by Nicodemus and by Joseph of Rama [Aramathea], before he was laid in the Sepulcher. In that place anyone who wished could say Mass without any other order. According to this first arrangement, I said Mass above the Sepulcher.

On Friday, 8 August, at the third hour of the day, we were let out of the church of the Sepulcher, and each of the pilgrims went to his lodging to rest as well as he could.

On Saturday, 9 August, early in the morning, all the pilgrims were gathered together in Mount Sion, and we were led by two friars of the monastery on a pilgrimage—that is, to seek certain places usually visited by pilgrims, and which we had not yet visited. Meanwhile the venerable father Don Fra Francesco was ill with the fever and suffering pain; he was doubtful, but full of courage.

After the said visitation we all returned to Mount Sion, and that day a Frenchman, also a pilgrim, who had been ill from the time we went on board the galley, was buried.

Immediately after Mass had been heard, every man went to prepare to go to Bethlehem according to the order given by the friars, and thus at the nineteenth hour we set out in extreme heat, riding the usual animals; and we went along a very gay and beautiful road with beautiful gardens on both sides. In my opinion, the road from Jerusalem to Bethlehem is the most beautiful we saw in those parts, there are so many beautiful things there—grapes, figs and olives. By the way, we came to three springs. The prior said that those springs began to flow when the star appeared to the wise men as they went from Jerusalem to Bethlehem to seek our Lord Jesus Christ to adore him. Further on, near to Bethlehem, I saw the sepulcher of Rachel, the wife of the patriarch Jacob, who died in childbed. It is beautiful and much honored by the Moors.

At the twenty-third hour we reached Bethlehem. It was the vigil of Saint Lawrence, and we went to the convent of the friars, which is a very comfortable place. Immediately the procession was set in order by the friars and we went into the grotto where Christ was born, and there a sermon was preached. Then we sought out the other places usually visited.

After the devotions were performed, the pilgrims were lodged as well as possible. As I have said several times, thanks to the captain, I fared extremely well compared with the others.

At midnight, the pilgrims began to say Masses in the place where Christ was born, and where he was laid in the manger. The places are near together. In the same grotto, down several steps, there was the place where Saint Jerome made his dwelling for many years. Mass was also said there. I said my Mass where Christ was laid in the manger.

On Sunday, 10 August, the prior, having made instance, whoever wished to visit those holy places again could do so—that is, where Saint Jerome translated the Bible from Hebrew into Latin, where his body was laid, and where the innocents were killed by order of King Herod, who sought thus to slay Christ, when he was deceived by the three wise men.

The church at Bethlehem seems to me the most beautiful between Venice and Bethlehem. It is not only fine but extremely beautiful. Besides the body of the church in the center, it has two shoulders, or as we say, two naves, each supported by eleven columns, so thick that one man alone cannot put his arms round them. They are very tall and all of one piece. The church is all adorned with most beautiful mosaics that look quite new. I was never tired of looking at the many beautiful pillars. I counted up to forty-four of them.

The said church is inhabited by a sect called Armenian Christians, although it is administered by the friars of Mount Sion. The Armenians, both big and little, male and female, live there on the ground, like pigs. They did nothing but cry out all night without intermission. At the entrance to the church it is necessary to pay money to the Moors.

From the ruins which are to be seen, the city of Bethlehem must have been a beautiful place. The country is fine and fruitful. There are few inhabitants now. A few families live there in certain ruins arranged for keeping cattle, which they keep even up to the door of the said church, to our great shame.

When day broke and the pilgrims had finished saying their Masses, the order was given that every man must mount the animal assigned to him, and we went to the hills of Judea. There we visited a ruined church said to be the place where Saint Elizabeth greeted Our Lady, and where she made that canticle, "Magnificat anima mea Dominum," and then another church. Although this last was not in ruins and was a fine body of a church, yet those Moorish dogs keep their animals inside, and make all kinds of filth.

We visited the place where Saint John the Baptist was born, and the place where Saint Zachariah, his father, made the canticle, "Benedictus Dominus Deus Israel quia visitavit, etc." Then we departed from there and returning to Jerusalem by another way, we visited the Church of the Holy Cross, which is in very good order and served by certain Greek monks. They say that the wood was cut down there of which the cross of our Lord Jesus Christ was made.

After this visitation we returned to Jerusalem to rest a little, because in truth the heat exhausted us greatly. The venerable don Era Francesco Trivulzio, who, as I said, was more ill than well, and who yet wanted to visit every place, remained behind in Bethlehem, saying that he did not want to ride in so much dust, and that he wanted to make that visitation with certain friars of Mount Sion.

The rest of us went again that evening into the church of the Holy Sepulcher, but without the captain, because between age—for he is old—the great heat and the great trouble given him by those Moorish dogs, he was very sick. We made the visitations as we did the first time we entered, but without either procession or friars, and each one performed his devotions as his feeling dictated. A new list was made, arranging how Masses were to be said by the pilgrims, in order that there should be no confusion. I said Mass in the place of the Calvary because this was the order.

That night ten knights were created in the Sepulcher, and they belonged to every nation of Italy. One was Don Giovanni Simone Fornaro of Pavia, who, as I said, had come with Fra Francesco from Ferrara; another was Don Giovanni de Burgho of Antwerp, in Burgundy; others were Germans and also Spaniards. As there was a dearth of scribes, I wrote several letters testifying that they had been created knights at the Sepulcher, according to the form given me by the superior, and he sealed the letters.

CHAPTER NINE

INTELLECTUAL CONTACTS

Figure 9.1: A lesson in astronomy.

Source: Paul LaCroix, *Science and Literature in the Middle Ages and at the Period of the Renaissance* (London: Bickers and Son, 1877), 87.

73. A STOREHOUSE OF KNOWLEDGE

The Islamic world had a highly developed scientific, medical, and philosophical tradition. This tradition was nurtured by Muslim rulers who considered it a sign of status and prestige to have numerous scholars in their courts. Moreover, sitting on the crossroads between Africa, Asia, and Europe, the Islamic world had inherited many of the great works of antiquity from Greek, Roman, and Persian sources. These texts were carefully preserved and translated into Arabic in places such as Alexandria, Damascus, and Baghdad and included some of the great works of Aristotle, Plato, Euclid, Ptolemy, and Galen, works that had largely been lost to Europe since the collapse of the western Roman Empire in the fifth century. But the Muslims had done more than simply translate and preserve the ancient texts. They had also interpreted and absorbed them into their own scholarly and scientific traditions, in the process writing extensive commentaries such as Ibn Sina's (ca. 980–1037; known in Europe as Avicenna) glosses on the works of Aristotle, and Ibn Rushd's (1126–98; known in Europe as Averroes) compilations of the medical texts of the Roman physician Galen. Muslim Spain, particularly under the leadership of Abd al-Rahman III (r. 912–961) and his son al-Hakam II (r. 961–976), was an active participant and leader in the wider world of Islamic scholarship—indeed Ibn Rushd was born in Cordoba and spent most his life in Iberia and Morocco. The Library of Cordoba, for example, was reputed to have a catalog consisting of 44 volumes. The library may have had close to 400,000 books and rolls, a truly astonishing amount. In the selection below from his Tabaqat al-'Umam *(written in 1068), the Iberian historian and judge Said al-Andalusi (1029–70) provides an accounting of the impressive state of learning in Muslim Spain.*

Source: trans. and ed. Semaan I. Salem and Alok Kumar, *Science in the Medieval World: "Book of the Categories of Nations" by Said al-Andalusi* (Austin, TX: University of Texas Press, 1991), 69–78.

During our present time, there are many young scholars who have distinguished themselves in the study of philosophy and demonstrated great energy and ability to acquire a knowledge of most of its branches. Those of them who live in Toledo or around it include Abu al-Hasan Ali ibn Khalaf ibn Ahmar al-Saydalani [the pharmacist], Abu Ishaq Ibrahim ibn Yahya al-Naqqash, known by the name Walad al-Zarqali, Abu Marwan Abd Allah ibn Khalaf al-Istiji, Abu Jafar Ahmad ibn Yusuf ibn Ghalib al-Tamlaki, Isa ibn Ahmad al-Alim [the scholar], and Ibrahim ibn Said al-Sahli, the constructor of astrolabes.

Among those who live in Zaragoza, we have al-Hajib Abu Amir, son of al-Amir al-Muqtadir bi-Allah Ahmad ibn Sulayman ibn Hud al-Jadhami, and Abu Jafar Ahmad ibn Jawshan ibn Abd al-Aziz ibn Jawshan.

Among those who live in Valencia, we have two outstanding geometers; they are Ali ibn Khalaf ibn Ahmar al-Saydalani [the pharmacist] and Abu Jafar Ahmad ibn Jawshan [he could have lived in both Zaragoza and Valencia]. Also in Valencia, Abu Zayd Abd al-Rahman ibn Sayyid is the most knowledgeable among its scientists in astronomy and the movements of the stars.

Abu Ishaq Ibrahim ibn Yahya al-Naqqash, known by the name Walad al-Zarqali, is the best in our time when it comes to astronomical observations, the study of celestial shapes, and the calculation of the movements of the stars. He is the most knowledgeable in astronomical tables and in the invention and construction of astronomical equipment.

Abu Amir ibn al-Amir ibn Hud, although equal to his contemporaries in the study of mathematics, surpassed them all in the study of logic, natural philosophy, and theology.

Among those who specialized in the study of logic to the neglect of the other branches of philosophy, we have Abu Muhammad Ali ibn Ahmad ibn Said ibn Hazm ibn Ghalib ibn Salih ibn Khalaf ibn Madan ibn Sufyan ibn Yazid al-Farisi, *mawla* [master] of Yazid ibn Abu Sufyan ibn Harb ibn Umayyah ibn Abd Shams al-Qarshi, whose ancestors came originally from the village of Mont Lisham in the district of al-Zawiyah of the county of Unabat of the province of Lablat [Niebla] of the western parts of al-Andalus. He and his parents settled in Cordoba, where they gained wide respect and influence. His father, Abu Amru Ahmad ibn Said ibn Hazm, was one of the great viziers of al-Munsur Muhammad ibn Abd Allah ibn Abu Amir [*hajib* or grand vizier of al-Andalus until 1002] and also of his son al-Muzaffar [*hajib* from 1002–08], and the chief administrator of their two governments. His son al-Faqih Abu Muhammad was the vizier of Abd al-Rahman al-Mustazhir hi-Allah ibn Hisham ibn Abd al-Jabbar ibn cAbd al-Rahman al-Nasir li-Din Allah. Later, he abandoned this profession and began his study of the sciences, history, and tradition. He paid special attention to the study of logic and wrote a book that he called *Kitab al-Taqryb li-Hudud al-Mantiq* [*A Book on Approaching the Limits of Logic*], in which he simplified the methods of scientific acquisitions and utilized examples of legal arguments and Islamic laws. In this book he contradicted Aristotle, the founder of this science [logic], on some basic points, but his contradictions demonstrate that he did not fully understand the object of Aristotle's work. For this reason, his book is weak and contains many obvious errors. Following his work on logic, he became deeply involved in the study of Islamic law until he knew it better than anyone who lived before him in al-Andalus. He wrote on this subject a large number of treatises of high quality and noble aim. Most of these treatises dealt with the foundations and the branches of jurisprudence and were written to conform with the doctrine that he had adopted from Dawud ibn Ali ibn Khalaf al-Asbahani and his followers of the Zahir school, although he neglected analogy and interpretation.

I have been informed by his son al-Fadl, nicknamed Abu Rafi, that the total number of books that he wrote on jurisprudence, traditions, religious foundations, rites, and sects and his books on history, genealogy, literature, and his replies to his critics amount to about four hundred volumes, containing some 80,000 pages. In all of Islam, we do not know of a more productive author except Abu Jafar Muhammad ibn Jarir ibn Yazid al-Tabari, who was the most prolific of them all. Abu Muhammad Abd Allah ibn Muhammad ibn Jafar al-Farghani stated in his book on history entitled *Al-Silah* [*Connection*], which contains detailed information about Abu Jafar al-Tabari al-Kabir, that a group of his students counted the days of his life, from the time he reached maturity until his death in AH 310 [922 CE] at age eighty-six, and divided into it the total number of pages that he had written and showed that he had written fourteen pages per day. Such a feat cannot be accomplished by a person without the generous care and gracious support of his creator. In addition to all that, Abu Muhammad ibn Hazm wrote large volumes on the Arabic language and its grammar, and a good section on prosody and the art of oratory. I received a letter from him, written in his own handwriting, in which he informed me that he was born after the morning prayer and before sunrise on Wednesday, the last day of Ramadān in AH 384 [994 CE]. He died, may Allah have mercy upon him, toward the end of Sha'bān in the year AH 456 [1064 CE].

We also have Abu al-Hasan Ali ibn Muhammad ibn Sydih, al-Ama [the blind]. His father was also blind. He studied the science of logic for a long time and wrote many simplified works on this subject in which he followed the method of Matta ibn Yunus. Among all the people of al-Andalus, he was the most knowledgeable in the Arabic language, grammar, and poetry. He was a man of superb memory who knew by heart several scientific works such as *al-Gharyb al-Musannaf* [*Strange But Correct*] and *Islah al-Mantiq* [*Correction of Enunciation*]. He wrote great works, among them *Kitab al-Muhakkam* [*The Precise*] and *al-Muhyt al-Azam* [*The Great Encyclopedia*], arranged in alphabetic order, and his book *al-Mukhassas* [*Specialized*], arranged in sections similar to *al-Gharyb al-Musannaf*. He also wrote a commentary on *Islah al-Mantiq* and an explanation of *Kitab al-Hamasah* as well as others. He died, may Allah have mercy upon him, around AH 458 [1066 CE], when he was about sixty years old. Among the scientists of al-Andalus, these are the most famous logicians.

None of the scientists of al-Andalus paid much attention to the study of natural sciences or theology, and I do not know of anyone who cultivated these sciences except Abu Abd Allah Muhammad ibn Abd Allah ibn Hamid, better known as ibn al-Nabbash al-Bajjani, who will be mentioned with the physicians Abu Amir ibn al-Amir ibn Hud and Abu al-Fadl ibn Hasday al-Israeli.

Similarly, medical science was not well understood by the people of al-Andalus and none of its scientists progressed to lead in this field. Their interest was reduced to reading some of the books that treat branches of this subject and not its foundations, such as the books of Hippocrates and Galen. They were satisfied with such superficial knowledge to cut short their study time and make their fortunes serving the kings as physicians. There were a few exceptions; they were those who disdained these aims and who chose medicine for its own sake and studied, in proper order, most of the appropriate books.

The first to become known as a physician in al-Andalus was Ahmad ibn Iyas of Cordoba, a very rich and a very influential person who lived at the time of al-Amir Muhammad ibn Abd al-Rahman al-Awsat [r. 852–886]. Before him, the people were medically treated by a group of Christians who were not qualified either in medicine or in any of the other sciences. They followed in their treatment one of the Christian books that was in their possession, which they called al-Ibryshim or al-Ihryshim. The word means the universal and the united.

Also during the period of al-Amir Muhammad ibn Abd al-Rahman al-Awsat, there came into al-Andalus a man from Harran who became known in al-Andalus by the name al-Harrani. I was never told his real name. He performed some good medical experimentation and attained great fame and a good reputation in Cordoba.

Those who came after these two physicians or were contemporary to them, but did not become as famous, include Yahya ibn Ishaq, one of the viziers of Abd al-Rahman al-Nasir li-Din Allah [r. 912–961] during the beginning of his reign. His father Ishaq was an able Christian physician who became famous for his medical experimentation during the reign of al-Amir Abd Allah [r. 888–912]. Yahya was very intelligent and very knowledgeable about medical procedures. He was a Muslim and was highly rewarded by Abd al-Rahman al-Nasir, who appointed him governor of prestigious states. He composed a medical pandect containing five volumes, in which he followed the methods used by the Romans [Christians].

There was also Said ibn Abd al-Rahman ibn Muhammad ibn Abd Rabbih ibn Habib ibn Muhammad ibn Salim, a confidant of al-Amir Hisham al-Radi ibn Abd al-Rahman al-Dakhil. He was the nephew of Ahmad ibn Muhammad ibn Abd Rabbih [d. 940], the poet and the author of *Kitab al Iqd [Necklace]*. He was a noble physician and a good poet. He wrote a good medical treatise, of excellent style, in which he demonstrated his grasp of this science and of the methods used by early scientists. He was also familiar with the movements of the planets, the directions of the winds, and climatic changes. It was reported that after a surgical operation he sent after his uncle, Ahmad ibn Muhammad ibn Abd Rabbih, the poet, asking him to come and keep him company. His uncle did not accept his invitation, so Said wrote him the following two verses:

> When I have no guests or companions,
> I entertain Hippocrates and Galen.

> I take their books as a remedy for my loneliness.
> They are the cure for every wound they treat.

When these two verses reached his uncle, he replied with verses, of which we choose the following:

> You have accepted the company of Hippocrates and Galen,
> Because they do not eat and cost their host nothing.
> At the exclusion of your relatives,
> You accepted them as friends and companions.
> I believe your greed will leave you with no body,
> And after them you will accept the company of the Devil.

Said ibn Muhammad was a man of beautiful doctrines who avoided the company of kings. Toward the end of his life, he wrote:

> After I plunged into the study of the truth,
> And enjoyed, for a long time, the gifts of my Creator.
> And when I came close to getting into his kingdom,
> I saw those demanding wealth, but no giver.
> The age of a man is but an hour of pleasure
> That passes fast as if it were a flash of lightning.
> My soul is coming close to its departure,
> And he who drives me toward death is pressing hard.
> If I remain here or run away from death,
> To faraway places; death will catch up with me.

There were also Umar ibn Baryq, Asbagh ibn Yahya, and others. These were the physicians of al-Andalus during the period that we have mentioned, from before the time of al-Amir Muhammad until the time when al-Hakam al-Mustansir bi-Allah expressed interest in *Al-Ilm* [knowledge or science] and in those interested in it.

Of the known physicians who lived in the period between the time of al-Hakam al-Mustansir bi-Allah and the present time, we have Ahmad ibn Hakam ibn Hafsun, who was a noble physician of intelligence and talent. He was very perceptive. He knew logic well and was versed in all the branches of philosophy. He had connections with al-Hajib Jafar al-Saqlabi or al-Saqli [from Sicily] and was in charge of his entourage. Al-Hajib put him in touch with al-Hakam al-Mustansir bi-Allah and he remained in the service of that prince until the death of al-Hajib Jafar. After that time, he was dropped from the medical *diwan* [guild] and was neglected until his death.

There was also Muhammad ibn Tamlyh, a scholar of dignity and respect having a deep knowledge of medicine, grammar, language, poetry, and history. He served al-Nasir and al-Mustansir bi-Allah [r. 961–976] as their physician. He was also the orator of al-Hakam [al-Mustansir bi-Allah], who charged him with the supervision of the addition to the south side of the mosque of Cordoba. The work was completed under his direction and responsibility. I have seen his name written in gold and pieces of mosaic on the wall of *al-mihrab* [the part of the mosque reserved for the prayer leader] of that section. This structure was completed under his direction by the order of Caliph al-Hakam in AH 358 [969 CE].

There was also Abu al-Walid Muhammad ibn Husayn, known as ibn al-Kinani. He was a very knowledgeable physician, an able and kind practitioner who was loved and respected by his patients. He also served al-Nasir and al-Mustansir bi-Allah.

There was also Abu Abd al-Malik al-Thaqfi, an expert in medicine, mathematics, and geometry, but he spent most of his time practicing medicine and served as the physician of al-Nasir and al-Mustansir.

There were also Umar and Ahmad, the two sons of Yunus ibn Ahmad al-Harrani. They both traveled to the East during the reign of al-Nasir and stayed there for ten years. They entered into Baghdad and studied the work of Galen under the tutelage of Thabit ibn Sinan ibn Thabit ibn Qurrah al-Sabi [of the Sabians]. They also entered into the service of ibn Wasyf, where they learned how to treat the eye. Then they returned to al-Andalus during the reign of al-Mustansir bi-Allah and this was in AH 351 [962 CE]. He invited them into his service and chose them as his own personal physicians from among all the other physicians of his time. Umar died while serving al-Mustansir, but his brother Ahmad continued in the service of al-Hakam until the end of his [al-Hakam's] days. His successor, Hisham al-Muayyad bi-Allah [r. 976–1009 and 1010–13] put Ahmad in charge of police and commerce. But he continued his medical practice, providing remarkable eye treatment. His marvelous cures are well documented in the city of Cordoba.

There was also Muhammad ibn Abdun al-Jabali. He traveled to the East in AH 347 [958 CE] and lived in Basra [Iraq] and in Egypt, where he worked as the director of the hospital. He became a very able physician and searched great many of the fundamental roots of medicine. He was also well versed in the study of logic, which he learned from Abu Sulayman Muhammad ibn Tahir ibn Bahrain al-Sajistani al-Baghdadi [from Baghdad]. Then he returned to al-Andalus in the year AH 360 [971 CE] and entered the service of al-Mustansir bi-Allah and al-Muayyad bi-Allah as their physician. Prior to entering the field of medicine, he was a teacher of mathematics and geometry and authored a good book on *al-taksyr* [fractions]. I was informed by Abu Uthman Said ibn Muhammad ibn al-Baghunish of Toledo that, when he was studying in Cordoba, there was no physician there who could be considered the equal of Muhammad ibn Abdun al-Jabali in the practice of medicine or in the understanding of all its branches, especially in its obscure cases.

During the time of ibn Abdun and afterward, until the end of the Amiriyah [al-Amirid dynasty], lived some scientists who experimented in medicine and practiced it as a profession, but they were all at a level considerably below that of ibn Abdun. Among them there were Sulayman ibn Hassan, also known as ibn Jaljal, Abd Allah ibn Ishaq, known as ibn al-Shana'ah al-Muslamani al-Israeli. There were also others, of whom the youngest was Muhammad ibn al-Husayn, known as ibn al-Kinani. He studied medicine under the direction of his uncle, Muhammad ibn al-Husayn, and his colleagues. He worked in the service of al-Munsur Muhammad ibn Abu Amir and his son al-Muzaffar. At the beginning of Ahd al-Fitnah, he moved into the city of Zaragoza and settled there. He was a distinguished and able physician. He also had knowledge of logic, astronomy, and many of the branches of philosophy. The vizier Abu al-Mutarraf Abd al-Rahman ibn Muhammad ibn Abd al-Kabir ibn Wafid al-Lakhmi informed me about him, saying that he was very intelligent, a deep thinker, and endowed with the power of original productivity and induction. He was also a man of great wealth. Ibn al-Kinani died about AH 420 [1029 CE]. He was about eighty years old. I have read some of his books, in which he says, "I learned logic from Muhammad ibn Abdun al-Jabali, Umar ibn Yunus ibn Ahmad al-Harrani, Ahmad ibn Hafsun, the philosopher, Abu Abd Allah Muhammad ibn Masud al-Bajjani, Muhammad ibn Maymun, known by the name Markus, Abu al-Qasim Fyd ibn Najm, Said ibn Fathun of Zaragoza, known as al-Hammar [the muleteer], Abu al-Haryth al-Usquf [the priest], a student of Raby ibn Zayd, priest and philosopher, ibn Maryn al-Bajjani, and Muslamah ibn Ahmad al-Majrit."

Belonging in the same *tabaqat* [class] with ibn al-Kinani, there was Abu al-Arab Yusuf ibn Muhammad, one of the researchers in medical science with profound knowledge of the medical field. I have been informed by the vizier Abu al-Mutarraf ibn Wafid and Abu Uthman Said ibn Muhammad ibn al-Baghunish that Abu al-Arab was an authority on the fundamentals of medicine, with a knowledge of all its branches, and a very skillful practicing physician. I also heard from other authorities that there was no one, after ibn Abdun, equal to Abu al-Arab in the practice of medicine or in his knowledge of the medical field. Toward the end of his life, he was overcome by his desire for *al-khamr* [wine]. He was hardly ever sober or free from the influence of alcohol. By so doing, he prevented many people from profiting from his knowledge and ability. He died at the age of about ninety, in AH 430 [1039 CE].

From the period of these physicians until the present time there have lived several medical scientists, of whom the most famous are Abu Uthman Said ibn

Muhammad ibn al-Baghunish, who was originally from Toledo, but moved to Cordoba in his quest for scientific knowledge. He studied mathematics and geometry under the tutelage of Muslamah ibn Ahmad and medical science under the tutelage of Muhammad ibn Abdun al-Jabali, Sulayman ibn Juljul, Muhammad ibn al-Shanaah, and others; then he returned to Toledo and got in touch with its prince, al-Zafir Ismail ibn Abd al-Rahman ibn Ismail ibn Abd al-Rahman ibn Ismail ibn Amir ibn Mutarraf ibn Dhi al-Nun. He progressed well in the prince's court and became one of his state administrators. I met him there during the early years of the reign of al-Ma'mun, the man of glory, ibn Yahya ibn al-Zafir Ismail ibn Dhi al-Nun; by then he had abandoned the study of sciences and adhered to the study of the Quran. He kept to himself at home and away from people. I found him to be a very sage man of great reputation and high moral principles, a cleanly dressed and a pious man, who had in his possession great books on the various branches of philosophy and other fields of knowledge. I came to realize by talking with him that he had studied geometry and logic and that he had precise knowledge of both fields, but he neglected this area to give special attention to the books of Galen, of which he had a private collection that he had critically corrected, thus becoming an authority on the works of Galen. He never did practice medicine and he did not have a complete understanding of diseases. He died during the morning prayer on Tuesday, the first day of Rajab, AH 444 [27 October 1053 CE]. He told me, may Allah have mercy upon him, that he was born in AH 369 [980 CE]. Thus, he lived to be seventy-five years old.

Among the physicians of this period, we have the vizier Abu al-Mutarraf Abd al-Rahman ibn Muhammad ibn Abd al-Kabir ibn Yahya ibn Wafid ibn Muhammad al-Lakhmi [active ca. 1010 CE], one of the nobility of al-Andalus and a descendant of a good family. He studied with great care the books of Galen and Aristotle as well as those of other philosophers. He distinguished himself in his study of *al-mufradah* [single ingredient] medication and knew it better than anyone else of his generation. He wrote on this subject a great book of no equal, in which he presented the content of the book of Dioscorides and the book of Galen, which were written on this same subject. He presented the material in an excellent arrangement in a single volume of some five hundred pages. He informed me that it took him some twenty years to collect, organize, state the properties and relative strengths of all the medications, and present this in his book in the fashion he deemed appropriate. As a physician, he adopted an honest approach and simple methods; he preferred not to treat his patients with medications if they could be cured with proper nutrients or something equivalent. If medication became necessary, he did not prescribe the complex if simple cures could be effective, and if compound remedies became indispensable, he preferred the use of the least complex. There are many documented cases where he cured his patients from difficult and frightful diseases with the simplest and most common medications. At the present time, al-Lakhmi is living in Toledo, and he informed me that he was born in Dhi al-Hijjah in AH 398 [August 1008 CE].

There was also Abu Marwan Abd al-Malik, son of the jurist Muhammad ibn Marwan ibn Zuhr al-Ishbili [of Seville]. He traveled to the Middle East and lived in al-Qayrawan and in Egypt, where he studied medicine for a long time before he returned to al-Andalus and lived in the city of Denia, where his fame as a physician reached most of the provinces of al-Andalus. He had medical recommendations, one of which was the forbiddance of bathing, in the belief that it encourages the growth of fungus on the body and disturbs personal behavior. This is an opinion contradicted by ancient and modern physicians and the public knows that it is erroneous. If baths are taken gradually and in proper order, they serve as a good form of exercise and a good method to open the pores and assist in getting rid of extractions and in soothing the heavy parts of chymes [a stomach fluid].

There was also Abu Muhammad Abd Allah ibn Muhammad, known as ibn al-Dhahabi, one of those who practiced in the medical profession and read many of the books of philosophy without getting deeply into them. He was very interested in the science of chemistry, a subject that he studied intensely. He died in the city of Valencia in Jumada II, in the year AH 456 [May 1064 CE]. I was present at his funeral. May Allah have mercy upon him.

There was also Abu Abd Allah Muhammad ibn Abd Allah ibn Hamid al-Bajjani, known as ibn al-Nabbash. He practiced the medical profession and helped cure many patients. He had a good knowledge of natural sciences and participated to some extent in the study of theology. He performed some research in the science of morals and politics and had some understanding of logic, but his knowledge of mathematics was limited. At the present time, he lives in the Murciyah [Murcia] region.

There was also Abu Jafar ibn Khamis al-Tulaytili [of Toledo], who was mentioned earlier with the mathematicians. He studied the books of Galen in their proper order and adopted their content in his practice of medicine.

Among the young physicians of our time who also cultivated the study of philosophy, we have Abu al-Hasan Abd al-Rahman ibn Khalaf ibn Asakir, who studied well the books of Galen, mostly under the direction of Uthman Said ibn Muhammad ibn Baghunish. He is a young scientist of great character and good methods of practicing medicine. He is also very good with his hands, especially at manufacturing minute equipment. At the present time, he is working hard at understanding the science of geometry and logic. He enjoys a powerful memory and great intelligence and this, with good work and favorable conditions, may lead him to the summit in his understanding of philosophy.

In al-Andalus, the practice of astrology has met some acceptance, both in the past and at the present; there were some well-known astrologers in every period, including our own. Of the most famous astrologers during the reign of the Banu Umayyah [Umayyads], we have Abu Bakr ibn Yahya ibn Ahmad, known as ibn al-Khayyat [the tailor]. He was one of the students of Abu al-Qasim Muslamah ibn Ahmad al-Majriti, who taught him the science of number and geometry. Later, he showed interest in astrology and became a well-known astrologer. In this capacity, he served Sulayman ibn al-Hakam al-Nasir li-Din Allah, al-Amir al-Muminin [prince of the believers], during Ahd al-Fitnah as well as other princes, of whom the last one was al-Amir al-Mamun Yahya ibn Ismail ibn Dhi al-Nun. In addition to that, he practiced medicine with great care. He was kind in his judgment, a man of noble character and good reputation. He died in Toledo in AH 474 [1082 CE]. He was about eighty years old.

Among the young astrologers of our time, we have Abu Marwan Abd Allah ibn Khalaf al-Istiji, one of those who studied astrology well and understood the old and the new books that treat the subject. I do not know anyone in al-Andalus, past or present, who has known all the secrets and marvels of this science as well as he does. He has written an excellent treatise on *Tasyrat wa Matarih al-Shu'a'at* [*The Directions and Projections of Light Rays*] and some explanations of the foundation of this science. No one wrote anything like it before him. He mailed it to me from the city of Cuenca [or Fuenca].

Those are the famous Muslim scholars knowledgeable in the ancient sciences in both the East and the West. I do not pretend that I know them all; it is possible that, among those who are not known to me, there are some who are better than the ones I have mentioned. Allah—the Highest—has the distinction of being all-knowing. There is no God but him.

74. ADELARD OF BATH AND ARABIC SCIENCES

The twelfth century witnessed the great flowering of the western European medieval intellectual tradition in the so-called Renaissance of the Twelfth Century. This renaissance, however, would have been stunted had it not been for the copious knowledge that Europe was importing from the Islamic world. The crusades and the Christian expansion in Spain and Sicily, which had brought cities such as Palermo and Toledo under Christian control, brought European scholars into broader contact with Muslim scholars and exposed them to the vast reserves of learning housed in Arabic texts. Over the course of the twelfth century, many of these classical and Arabic texts were translated into Latin, mostly in Iberia and Sicily, and became the soil upon which much of the Renaissance of the Twelfth Century bore fruit. One of the most important figures in this process of adoption and translation was the Englishman Adelard of Bath (ca. 1080–ca. 1153). Sometime in the 1110s, Adelard traveled to Sicily and then to the Muslim East, where he spent seven years, learning from his "Arab friends." Upon his return to England, he wrote numerous books, including a translation of Euclid's Elements, *a critical text for the understanding of geometry. He also penned numerous original works, including the* Quaestiones Naturales (Natural Questions), *written sometime between 1107 and 1133, most likely toward the latter part of that period. The* Quaestiones *takes the form of a dialogue between Adelard and his nephew on 76 questions about the natural world. The Arab influence on Adelard, as the selection below illustrates, was ever-present. Adelard may have been hiding behind his "Arab friends" as a way of presenting concepts that were not popular and perhaps even heretical. If they proved too controversial, he could always claim that he was simply presenting Arab learning and not his own ideas.*

Source: trans. Hermann Gollancz, *Dodi-Venechdi (Uncle and Nephew)* (London: Oxford University Press, 1920), 91–92, 97–99; rev. Jarbel Rodriguez.

Preface

On my return the other day to England, in the reign of Henry [I, r. 1100–35], son of William—it was he who had long maintained me abroad for the purpose of study—the renewal of intercourse with my friends gave me both pleasure and benefit.

After the first natural enquiries about my own health and that of my friends, my particular desire was to learn all I could about the manners and customs of my own country. Making this then the object of my enquiry, I learnt that its chief men were violent, its magistrates wine-lovers, its judges mercenary; that patrons were fickle, private men sycophants, those who made promises deceitful, friends full of jealousy, and almost all men self-seekers: this realized, the only resource, I said to myself, is to withdraw my thoughts from all misery.

Thereupon my friends said to me, "What do you think of doing, since you neither wish to adopt this moral depravity yourself, nor can you prevent it?" My reply was to "to give myself up to oblivion, since oblivion is the only cure for evils that cannot be remedied; for he who gives heed to that which he hates in some sort endures that which he does not love." Thus we argued that matter together, and then as we still had time left for talking, a certain nephew of mine, who had come along with the others, rather adding to the tangle than unraveling it, urged me to publish something fresh in the way of Arabian learning. As the rest agreed with him, I took in hand the treatise that follows. Of its profitableness to its readers I am assured, but am doubtful whether it will give them pleasure. The present generation has this ingrained weakness, that it thinks that nothing discovered by the moderns is worthy to be received—the result of this is that if I wanted to publish anything of my own invention I should attribute it to someone else, and say, "Someone else said this, not I." Therefore, (that I may not wholly be robbed of a hearing) it was a certain great man that discovered all my ideas, not I. But of this enough.

Since I have yielded to the request of my friends so far as to write something, it remains for you to give your judgment as to its correctness. About this point I would that I felt less anxiety, for there is no essay in the liberal arts, no matter how well handled, to which you could not give a wider range. Grant me, therefore, your sympathy. I shall now proceed to give short answers to questions put by my nephew.

Here Begins Adelard's Treatise to His Nephew

You will remember, Nephew, how seven years ago when you were almost a child in the learning of the French, and I sent you along with the rest of my hearers to study with a man of high reputation, it was agreed between us that I should devote myself to the best of my ability to the study of Arabic, while you on your part were to acquire the inconsistencies of French ideas.

NEPHEW: I remember, and all the more because, when departing, you bound me under a solemn promise to be a diligent student of philosophy.

The result was that I applied myself with great diligence to this study. Whether what I have said is correct, the present occasion will give you an opportunity of discovering; since when you have often set them forth, I, as hearer only, have marked the opinions of the Saracens, and many of them seem to me quite absurd; I shall, therefore, for a time cease to exercise this patience, and when you utter these views, shall attack them where it seems good to me to do so.

To me it seems that you go too far in your praise of the Arabs, and show prejudice in your disparagement of the learning of our philosophers. Our reward will be that you will have gained some fruit of your toil; if you give good answers, and I make a good showing as your opponent, you will see that my promise has been well kept.

ADELARD: You perhaps take a little more on you than you ought; but as this arrangement will be profitable not only to you but to many others, I will pardon your forwardness, making however this one stipulation, that when I adduce something unfamiliar, people are to think not that I am putting forward an idea of my own, but am giving the views of the Arabs. If anything I say displeases the less educated, I do not want them to be displeased with me also. I know too well what is the fate which attends upon the teachers of the truth with the common herd, and consequently shall plead the case of the Arabs, not my own.

NEPHEW: Let it be as you will, provided nothing causes you to hold your peace.

ADELARD: I think then that we should begin with lighter matters, and if here I fail to give you a reasonable account, you will know what to expect in more important subjects. Let us begin then at the bottom, and so proceed upwards.

Chapter V: Do Creatures of Airy Nature Live in Air, and of Fiery Nature in Fire, Just as Creatures of Earthy Nature Do in Earth

NEPHEW: In very truth, it is obvious to the purblind or the sightless. How grievously did the Saracens befool you with their subtle trifling. But not today shall you trick me out of laying bare your deceitful and obscure arguments, covered up though they be with subtle falsity. I can see clearly what you are aiming at.

ADELARD: You are putting a question which is unintelligible to both of us, to the end that I may out of disgust grant you what is false.

NEPHEW: You do not know to whom you are talking, but this will teach you. By your own proposition you are forced to admit, that in water certain objects exist which are of a nature more watery than earthy or airy or fiery, and in air certain others which are more airy than earthy or watery or fiery, and others in fire more fiery than earthy or watery or airy; for this is the natural consequence of what you said before. But it will not do, and so you ought to go no further.

ADELARD: Of a truth your *reductio ad absurdum* breaks down altogether. What you have stated is exactly true; in water there are things of watery nature, that is fishes, which are mere compacted water; and in air, airy powers. In fire also, that is in the upper ether, there live fiery animals which we can see. Therefore, my argument will do, and we are agreed.

NEPHEW: Well, for my part let the argument rest a while. So as not to excite your anger, I will say no more on this.

ADELARD: It is then established how roots grow, and why they are called warm and live, and why they last longer in earth than elsewhere, and why they die.

Chapter VI: Why the Fruit Follows Not the Natural Graft

NEPHEW: Let us now pass on to the natures of trees. I ask you then why it is that when a cutting is engrafted on a stock, the fruit follows entirely the nature of the thing grafted. It is agreed that the graft and the stock are of different nature, and, as I have said, these things when growing get their nourishment from the ground. Consequently, they will draw from it either the same nourishment or else unlike and opposite nourishments. But to live on the same food is impossible for them, since they are of different and opposed natures; so that the graft requires food from the stock. Now this it draws either through the stock or otherwise, but the latter course is impossible. Consequently then it draws it through the stock. Again, the stock either draws the same food or does not. If it does not do so, then there is a break in the drawing, and the graft cannot receive the food it wants; while if the stock draws the same food as the graft, then it is drawing what is its opposite. If this is so, it is drawing and seeking for the means of its own destruction—a thing which is neither possible, nor in keeping with the arguments already adduced.

ADELARD: You are handling the matter like a sophist, and I must put an end to your quibbling. I grant you that the graft draws its food from the earth and through the stock. You go on "just as the stock also does." Granted. You then go down a step and say, "consequently, it is drawing in its own opposite." This too I willingly accept. Lastly, you make the inference that therefore it is of its own accord drawing in its own destruction. This, indeed, is not a descending, but tumbling down a whole flight; and I will clear up the matter in a word or two. The stock is drawing for itself and for a second thing: that which it draws for itself it keeps, that which it draws for the benefit of the graft, it passes on to it. In like manner, the stomach draws and seeks after whatever is necessary to the parts of the body, keeps what it wants for itself, and gives to those others what belongs to them. Similarly, both the stock and the graft abide by their own nature; and if after three days or a longer time you were to cut off the graft, you would find the stock of the same nature as it had been before.

NEPHEW: What you have said on this point is childish—mere probable conjectures rather than necessary truths. Let us then proceed to the nature of living beasts for there I cannot help thinking I shall put a spoke in your wheel.

ADELARD: It is a little difficult for you and me to argue about animals. I, with reason for my guide, have learned one thing from my Arab teachers, you, something different; dazzled by the outward show of authority you wear a head-stall. For what else should we call authority but a head-stall? Just as brute animals are led by the head-stall where one pleases, without seeing why or where they are being led, and only follow the halter by which they are held, so many of you, bound and fettered as you are by a low credulity, are led into danger by the authority of writers. Hence, certain people arrogating to themselves the title of authorities have employed an unbounded license in writing, and this to such an extent that they have not hesitated to insinuate into men of low intellect the false instead of the true. Why should you not fill sheets of paper, aye, fill them on both sides, when today you can get readers who require no proof of sound judgment from you, and are satisfied merely with the name of a time-worn title? They do not understand that reason has been given to individuals that, with it as chief judge, distinction may be drawn between the true and the false. Unless reason were appointed to be the chief judge, to no purpose would she have been given to us individually: it would have been enough for the writing of laws to have been entrusted to one, or at most to a few, and the rest would have been satisfied with their ordinances and authority. Further, the very people who are called authorities first gained the confidence of their inferiors only because they followed reason; and those who are igno-rant of reason, or neglect it, justly desire to be called blind. However, I will not pursue this subject any further, though I regard authority as matter for contempt. This one thing, however, I will say. We must first search after reason, and when it has been found, and not until then, authority if added to it, may be received. Authority by itself can inspire no confidence in the philosopher, nor ought it to be used for such a purpose. Hence, logicians have agreed in treating the argument from authority not as necessary, but probable only. If, therefore, you want to hear anything from me, you must both give and take reason. I am not the man whom the semblance of an object can possibly satisfy; and the fact is, that the mere word is a loose wanton abandoning herself now to this man, now to that.

75. A MUSLIM GEOGRAPHER IN KING ROGER'S COURT

Along with Toledo in Spain, Palermo in Sicily was one of the great centers of transmission and translation of Arabic learning in Christian Europe. Sicily had seen its share of foreign powers come and go during its history. Greeks, Carthaginians, Romans, Byzantines, Muslims, and finally Normans had all laid claim to the island and enriched it with their cultures, traditions, and people. The Muslims had conquered the island and much of southern Italy from the Byzantines in the early tenth century. Their almost two-century rule left a deep impression, particularly on the architecture, ethnic makeup, and admin-istrative practices of the island. The Normans, led by the Guiscard family, arrived in the late 1040s and slowly began to take over. In 1072, they captured Palermo, the adminis-trative center, and by 1091, the conquest was largely completed. Roger Guiscard would become the first count of Sicily. Upon his death he was succeeded by his son, Roger II (r. 1105–54), who would become the first king of Sicily in 1130. His reign may have been the highpoint of Sicilian history in the Middle Ages, as the island underwent a period of unmatched cultural, economic, and administrative growth. This Sicilian golden age was one to which the island's different cultures, faiths, and ethnicities all contributed.

Roger and his Normans were quick to adopt many practices from the Arabs, Jews, and Byzantines and Arabic, Greek, and Latin all became courtly languages. Roger was also eager to welcome Muslim scholars, poets, and philosophers to Palermo, where they often worked side by side with Latin Christians, Jews, and Byzantines. One of the central figures in Roger's court was Muhammad al-Idrisi (1099–1165), a Moroccan-born poet and geographer. His seminal work was the Nuzhat al-Mushtaq fi ikhtirak al-afaq (Amusements for those who long to traverse the horizon). *It is also known by its Latin title, the* Tabula Rogeriana (The Book of Roger) *or more simply as the* Geography. *Roger commissioned the* Tabula *in 1138 and al-Idrisi finished it in 1154, having spent the intervening 16 years patiently collecting the accounts of travelers who came to Sicily and writing the manuscript. In its finished form, the* Tabula *included a thorough description of the known world and an extensive and detailed map. It would remain authoritative for centuries. The passage below is from the introduction, in which al-Idrisi explains his purpose and methods.*

Source: trans. Karla Mallette, *The Kingdom of Sicily, 1100–1250: A Literary History* (Philadelphia: University of Pennsylvania Press, 2005), 146–48.

As evidence of Roger's splendid learning and his illustrious and lofty inclinations, once he ruled an ample kingdom, once the aspirations of the people of his realm had been advanced, once the lands of the Rumi [Christians] acceded to him and their peoples accepted obedience to him, it pleased him to know the nature of his land and to know it with certainty and with precision. So he acquired knowledge about its boundaries, its roads and sea routes, into how many regions it was divided, and the nature of its seas and bays. He also wished to know about other lands, their division into the seven climate zones upon which the scholars agree and which the translators and authors confirm in their registers, and what parts of them belonged to which of the climate zones. He researched and calculated the matter by studying what was contained in books written in this branch of knowledge, such as *On Marvels* by al-Masudi, and the books of Abu Nasr Said al-Jihani, Abu al-Qasim Muhammad Abdullah ibn Khurdadhba, Ahmad ibn Umr al-Udhri, Abu al-Qasim Muhammad al-Hawqali al-Baghdadi, Khanaj ibn Khaqan al-Kaymaki, Musa ibn Qasim al-Qaradi, Ahmad ibn Yaqub (known as al-Yaqubi), Ishaq ibn al-Hasan the astronomer, Qudama al-Basri, Ptolemy al-Aqludi [that is, Claudius], and Orosio the Antiochene.

But he did not find the information he sought thoroughly explained and set forth in these books; in fact, he found them to be rather simple-minded. So he summoned to his presence experts in these things, discussed the matter with them, and sought their knowledge on the subject. But he did not find among them any more knowledge than he had found in the books mentioned above.

When he saw how things stood, he dispatched an order throughout his lands and summoned those who had knowledge in these matters and had traveled in these lands, and he had them questioned by an intermediary, in groups and one by one. When their accounts agreed with each other and corroborated each other, he recorded what was most reliable and most trustworthy. When they varied among each other, he put their information aside and disregarded it. He worked in this manner for about fifteen years. Not for a single moment during this time did he neglect his research and his search to uncover the truth, until his work became complete as he wished it. Then he asked the aforementioned people for certain, sound, and corroborated information concerning the distance in length and breadth of the lands.

Then he ordered that a drawing tablet be brought, and he began to test their information with a measuring device made of iron, point by point, keeping in mind the books previously mentioned and giving precedence among them to those that seemed most authoritative. He applied himself assiduously to this project until he hit upon the truth. Then he ordered that a great sphere be made for him of pure silver, large in volume and great in mass, which weighed 400 Rumi pounds, each pound being worth 112 dirhams. When this had been completed, he ordered that the outline of the seven climate zones be engraved on it with their nations and regions, their coastlines and seashores, their bays, seas, rivers, and the mouths of rivers, the populated regions and the unpopulated, and the well-traveled internal roads of each nation and those between nations with the distance figured and recorded in miles, as well as the best-known anchorages: all this information was transcribed from the drawing tablet and inscribed on the silver sphere, with nothing left out, its likeness set down and its form etched on it with precision.

Next the king commanded that a book be written corresponding to the details included in the sphere, matching its description of the nature of the countries and the lands, their nature and nations and places and the situation of the lands, their seas and mountains, their crops, the sorts of buildings and the other peculiarities found there, the employments of men in each, the industries that were marketed in each, the merchandise that was imported to and exported from each, the marvels that were reported and related about each, and where it was in the seven climate zones, along with reports about the condition of its people: their appearance, their nature, their faith, their clothing and ornaments, their languages. And he ordered that the book be called *Nuzhat al-mushtaq fi ikhtirak al-afaq*. This was during the first ten days of the Christian month that corresponded to the month of Shawwāl during the year 548 AH [January 1154 CE]. And I have obeyed the king's command and interpreted the inscriptions on the sphere.

76. STRANGE MEDICINES

Usamah Ibn-Munqidh (see Doc. 58) was fascinated by many aspects of Latin Christian culture. In the brief selection below, he describes several instances in which he saw Latin medical practices in action. Usamah was often shocked at some of the barbaric practices used by the Europeans, but he was also more than willing to give them credit when their practices proved efficacious.

Source: trans. Philip K. Hitti, *An Arab-Syrian Gentleman & Warrior in the Period of the Crusades: Memoirs of Usamah Ibn Munqidh* (New York: Columbia University Press, 2000), 162–63.

Their Curious Medication

A case illustrating their curious medicine is the following: The lord of al-Munaytirah wrote to my uncle asking him to dispatch a physician to treat certain sick persons among his people. My uncle sent him a Christian physician named Thabit. Thabit was absent but ten days when he returned. So we said to him, "How quickly hast thou healed thy patients!" He said:

They brought before me a knight in whose leg an abscess had grown; and a woman afflicted with imbecility. To the knight I applied a small poultice until the abscess opened and became well; and the woman I put on diet and made her humor wet [Galenic medicine taught that health was dependent on four humors that had to be in balance]. Then a Frankish physician came to them and said, "This man knows nothing about treating them." He then said to the knight, "Which wouldst thou prefer, living with one leg or dying with two?" The latter replied, "Living with one leg." The physician said, "Bring me a strong knight and a sharp ax." A knight came with the ax. And I was standing by. Then the physician laid the leg of the patient on a block of wood and bade the knight strike his leg with the ax and chop it off at one blow. Accordingly he struck it— while I was looking on—one blow, but the leg was not severed. He dealt another blow, upon which the marrow of the leg flowed out and the patient died on the spot. He then examined the woman and said, "This is a woman in whose head there is a devil which has possessed her. Shave off her hair." Accordingly they shaved it off and the woman began once more to eat their ordinary diet—garlic and mustard. Her imbecility took a turn for the worse. The physician then said, "The devil has penetrated through her head." He therefore took a razor, made a deep cruciform incision on it, peeled off the skin at the middle of the incision until the bone of the skull was exposed and rubbed it with salt. The woman also expired instantly. Thereupon I asked them whether my services were needed any longer, and when they replied in the negative I returned home, having learned of their medicine what I knew not before.

I have, however, witnessed a case of their medicine which was quite different from that. The king of the Franks [Fulk of Anjou, king of Jerusalem, r. 1131–43] had for treasurer a knight named Bernard, who (may Allah's curse be upon him!) was one of the most accursed and wicked among the Franks. A horse kicked him in the leg, which was subsequently infected and which opened in fourteen different places. Every time one of these cuts would close in one place, another would open in another place. All this happened while I was praying for his perdition. Then came to him a Frankish physician and removed from the leg all the ointments which were on it and began to wash it with very strong vinegar. By this treatment all the cuts were healed and the man became well again. He was up again like a devil.

Another case illustrating their curious medicine is the following: In Shayzar we had an artisan named abu-al-Fath, who had a boy whose neck was afflicted with scrofula [a type of tuberculosis that manifests itself most prominently with large masses around the neck]. Every time a part of it would close, another part would open. This man happened to go to Antioch on business of his, accompanied by his son. A Frank noticed the boy and asked his father about him. Abu-al-Fath replied, "This is my son." The Frank said to him, "Will thou swear by thy religion that if I prescribe to thee a medicine which will cure thy boy, thou wilt charge nobody fees for prescribing it thyself? In that case, I shall prescribe to thee a medicine which will cure the boy." The man took the oath and the Frank said:

Take uncrushed leaves of glasswort, burn them, then soak the ashes in olive oil and sharp vinegar. Treat the scrofula with them until the spot on which it is growing is eaten up. Then take burnt lead, soak it in ghee butter [*samn*] and treat him with it. That will cure him.

The father treated the boy accordingly, and the boy was cured. The sores closed and the boy returned to his normal condition of health.

I have myself treated with this medicine many who were afflicted with such disease, and the treatment was successful in removing the cause of the complaint.

77. TRANSLATIONS OF GERARD OF CREMONA

The work of translation begun by Adelard of Bath and his contemporaries gained momentum over the course of the twelfth and thirteenth centuries. Primarily dependent on Muslim, Jewish, and Mozarab (Iberian Christians who had lived under and adopted Arabic culture) translators at first, Latin Christians increasingly began to learn Arabic and then to translate works themselves. Working largely in Toledo, which became a major translation center soon after its capture by the Castilians in 1085, Jewish, Muslim, and Christian scholars worked in teams, bringing works of Greek and Arabic learning to a

Latin Christian audience. Among those who came to Toledo hoping to learn from the wisdom stored there was the Italian Gerard of Cremona (ca. 1114–87). Gerard first came to Toledo no later than 1144, in search of a copy of Ptolemy's Almagest, *a codex of mathematical and astronomical learning. Once there, he learned Arabic and then began his remarkable career as a translator. The source below was created by his students, who compiled a brief biography of his life and bibliography of his translated works, which they appended to Gerard's translation of Galen's* Ars Parva. *The translations, which number over 70, include some of the seminal works produced by classical and Arabic scholars, including Aristotle, Ptolemy, Archimedes, Galen, Alkindi, and al-Khwarizmi.*

Source: trans. Michael McVaugh, "The Translation of Greek and Arabic Science into Latin," in Edward Grant, ed., *A Source Book in Medieval Science* (Cambridge, MA: Harvard University Press, 1974), 35–38.

As a light shining in darkness must not be set under a bushel, but rather upon a candlestick, so too the splendid deeds of the great must not be held back, buried in timid silence, but must be made known to listeners today, since they open virtue's door to those who follow, and in worthy memorial offer to modern eyes the example of the ancients as a model for life. Thus, lest master Gerard of Cremona be lost in the shadows of silence, lest he lose the credit that he deserved, lest in brazen theft another name be affixed to the books translated by him (especially since he set his name to none of them), all the works he translated—of dialectic as of geometry, of astronomy as of philosophy, of medicine as of the other sciences— have been diligently enumerated by his associates at the end of this Tegni [the *Ars Parva*] just translated by him, in imitation of Galen's enumeration of his own writings at the end of the same book; so that if an admirer of their works should desire one of them, he might find it the quicker by this list, and be surer of it.

Although he scorned fame, although he fled from praise and the vain pomp of this world; although he refused to spread his name in a quest for empty, insubstantial things, the fruit of his works diffused through the world makes plain his worth. For while he enjoyed good fortune, possessions or their lack neither delighted nor depressed him; manfully sustaining whatever chance brought him, he always remained in the same state of constancy. Hostile to fleshly desires, he clove to spiritual ones alone. He worked for the advantage of all, present and future, mindful of Ptolemy's words: when approaching your end, do good increasingly. He was trained from childhood at centers of philosophical study and had come to a knowledge of all of this that was known to the Latins; but for love of the Almagest, which he could not find at all among the Latins, he went to Toledo; there, seeing the abundance of books in Arabic on every subject, and regretting the poverty of the Latins in these things, he learned the Arabic language, in order to be able to translate. In this way, combining both language and science (for as Hamet says in his letter *De proportione et proportionalitate*, a translator should have a knowledge of the subject he is dealing with as well as an excellent command of the languages from which and into which he is translating), he passed on the Arabic literature in the manner of the wise man who, wandering through a green field, links up a crown of flowers, made from not just any, but from the prettiest; to the end of his life, he continued to transmit to the Latin world (as if to his own beloved heir) whatever books he thought finest, in many subjects, as accurately and as plainly as he could. He went the way of all flesh in the seventy-third year of his life, in the year of our Lord Jesus Christ 1187.

These are the titles of the books translated by master Gerard of Cremona, at Toledo:

On Dialectic
  [1] Aristotle, *Posterior Analytics*
  [2] Themistius, *Commentary on the Posterior Analytics*
  [3] Alfarabi, *On the Syllogism (Liber Alfarabii de syllogismo)*

On Geometry
  [4] Euclid, The Fifteen Books [of the *Elements*] (*Liber Euclidis tractatus XV*)
  [5] Theodosius, Three Books *On the Sphere*
  [6] Archimedes, [*On the Measurement of the Circle*]
  [7] [Ahmad ibn Yusuf], *On Similar Arcs (De similibus arcibus)*
  [8] Mileus [Menelaus], Three Books [on Spherical Figures]
  [9] Thabit [ibn Qurra], *On the Divided Figure (De figura alchata)*
  [10] Banu Musa [the Three Sons of Moses or the Three Brothers], [*On Geometry*]
  [11] Ahmad ibn Yusuf, [Letter] *on Ratio and Proportion (Liber Hameti de proportione et proportionalitate)*
  [12] [Abu 'Uthman or Muhammad ibn 'Abdal-Baqi], *The Book of the Jew on the Tenth Book of Euclid*
  [13] Al-Khwarizmi, *On Algebra and Almucabala*
  [14] Book of Applied [or Practical] *Geometry*
  [15] Anaritius [al-Nairizi], [*Commentary*] on [*the Elements of*] *Euclid*
  [16] Euclid, *Data*
  [17] Tideus [Diocles], *On [Burning] Mirrors*
  [18] Alkindi, *On Optics (De aspectibus)*
  [19] *Book of Divisions (Liber divisionum)*
  [20] [Thabit ibn Qurra], *Book of the Roman Balance (Liber Karastonis)*

On Astronomy
  [21] Alfraganus [al-Farghani], *The Book Containing XXX Chapters*
  [22] [Ptolemy], The Thirteen Books of the *Almagest*

[23] [Geminus of Rhodes], *Introduction to the Spherical Method of Ptolemy (Liber introductorius Ptolomei ad artem spericam)*

[24] Geber [Jabir ibn Afiah], *Nine Books [on the Flowers from the Almagest]*

[25] Messehala, *On the Orb (De orbe)*

[26] Theodosius, *On Habitable Places (De locis habitabilibus)*

[27] Hypsicles, [*On the Rising of the Signs (De ascensionibus signorum)*]

[28] Thabit [ibn Qurra], *On the Exposition of Terms in the Almagest (Liber Thebit de expositione nominum Almagesti)*

[29] Thabit [ibn Qurra], *On the Forward and Backward Motion (De motu accessionis et recessionis)*

[30] Autolycus, *On the Moving Sphere (De spera mota)*

[31] Book of the Tables of Jaen with Its Rules *(Liber tabularum iahen cum regulis suis)*

[32] [Abu Abdallah Muhammad ibn Mu 'adh], *On the Dawn (De crepusculis)*

On Philosophy

[33] Aristotle, *On the Exposition of Pure Goodness (De expositione bonitatis pure)*

[34] Aristotle, *Physics (De naturali auditu)*

[35] Aristotle, Four Books *On the Heavens and World (Celi et mundi tr. IV)*

[36] Aristotle, *On the Causes of Properties and the Four Elements*, Book I *(Liber Aristotelis de causis proprietatum et elementorum primus)*; he did not translate the second treatise of this work, because he could find only a little bit of its ending in Arabic

[37] Aristotle, *On Generation and Corruption*

[38] Aristotle, *Meteorology*, Books I-III; the fourth he did not translate, since it was already translated

[39] Alexander of Aphrodisias, *On Time (De tempore), On the Senses (De sensu)*, and another *That Augment and Increase Occur in Form, Not in Matter (Quod augmentum et incrementum fuit in forma et non in yle)*

[40] Alfarabi, *Commentary on Aristotle's Physics (Distinctio Alfarabii super librum Aristotelis de naturali auditu)*

[41] Alkindi, *On the Five Essences (De quinque essentiis)*

[42] Al Farabi, *On the Sciences*

[43] Alkindi, *On Sleep and Vision*

On Medicine *(De fisica)*

[44] Galen, *On the Elements*

[45] Galen, *Commentary on Hippocrates' Treatment of Acute Diseases*

[46] [pseudo-]Galen, *Secrets [of Medicine] (De secretis)*

[47] Galen, *On the Temperaments (De complexionibus)*

[48] Galen, *On the Evils of an Unbalanced Temperament (De malicia complexionis diverse)*

[49] Galen, *On Simple Medicines, Books I-V (Liber Gal. de simplici medicina tr. V)*

[50] Galen, *On Critical Days*

[51] Galen, *On Crises*

[52] Galen, *Commentary on Hippocrates' Prognostics*

[53] [pseudo-]Hippocrates, *Book of the Truth (Liber veritatis)*

[54] Isaac [Ishaq al-Isra'ili], *On the Elements*

[55] Isaac [Ishaq al-Isra'ili], *On the Description of Things and Their Definitions (De descriptione rerum et diffinitionibus earum)*

[56] Rhazes [Abu Bakr Muhammad ibn Zakariya al-Razi], *The Book of Almansor (Liber Albubatri rasis qui dicitur Almansorius tr. X)*

[57] [Rhazes], *The Book of Divisions*, containing CLIIII chapters

[58] [Rhazes], *Short Introduction to Medicine (Liber ... introductorius in medicina parvus)*

[59] Abenguefit [Abu al-Mutarrif 'Abd al-Rahman ibn al-Wafid], *Book of Simple Medicines and Foods*, in part *(Pars libri Abenguefiti medicinarum simplicium et ciborum)*

[60] John Serapion [Yahya ibn Sarafyun], *Breviary (Breviarium)*

[61] Azaragui [Abu-al-Qasim al-Zahrawi], *Surgery*

[62] Jacob Alkindi, *On Degrees [of Compound Medicines]*

[63] Avicenna, *Canon*

[64] Galen, *Tegni*, with the commentary by Ali ab Rodohan ['Ali ibn Ridwan]

On Alchemy

[65] [Jabir ibn Hayyan, attrib.], *Book of Divinity of LXX (Liber divinitatis de LXX)*

[66] [pseudo-Rhazes], *On Alumens and Salts*

[67] [pseudo-Rhazes], *The Light of Lights (Liber luminis luminum)*

On Geomancy

[68] A book on geomancy concerning the divining arts, beginning "Estimaverunt indi"

[69] Alfadhol [de Merengi], *[Book of Judgments and Advice]* (*Liber Alfadhol id est arab de bachi*)

[70] *Book on Accidents (Liber de accidentibus alfel)*

[71] [Harib ibn Zeid, Calendar] *(Liber anoe)*

78. ISLAMIC LEARNING AND ROGER BACON

The service rendered by Gerard of Cremona and other translators became readily apparent in the thirteenth century, as a host of scientific and philosophical disciplines in Europe bore a strong Muslim influence, perhaps none more so than philosophy. The rediscovery of much of the Aristotelian corpus, as well as the growing appreciation for the work of

Averroes and Avicenna, pushed European philosophers in new directions and resulted in the full development and maturation of the scholastic method. Scholasticism sought to reconcile Christian theology with Aristotelian philosophy and became the dominant methodology taught in medieval universities. Among those who practiced the scholastic method was the Englishman Roger Bacon (ca. 1210–94), a university lecturer at Oxford and Paris and later a member of the Franciscan order. Bacon was the author of numerous works, but his most wide-ranging and important one was the Opus Majus (The Greater Work), *a compilation of his learning in mathematics, astronomy, grammar, optics, the natural sciences, and philosophy, which he dedicated and sent to Pope Clement IV (r. 1265–68). When he finished it in 1267, Bacon intended the* Opus *to be used by the Church to aid in the saving of souls, but perhaps more importantly as part of its proselytizing mission to convert non-Christians. The selection from the* Opus *below is instructive in highlighting the importance of Aristotle and Muslim philosophers and then provides an exhortation for the use of philosophy by Christians.*

Source: trans. Robert Belle Burke, *The Opus Majus of Roger Bacon*, 2 vols. (Philadelphia: University of Pennsylvania Press, 1928), I: 62–64, 65–67.

On Philosophy

Before the death of Socrates, Aristotle [384—322 BCE] was born, since he was his auditor for three years, as we read in the life of Aristotle. According to Bede he was born under Artaxerxes [II, king of Persia, r. 404–358 BCE] surnamed Memnon, the successor of Darius Nothus. In his seventeenth year, he was an auditor of Socrates and listened to him for three years. After the death of Socrates [in 399 BCE] he became an auditor of Plato [*ca.* 424–*ca.* 348], according to [the Anglo-Saxon monk and historian] Bede [*ca.* 672–735], and remained so for twenty years, as we read in his life. After Plato's death he lived twenty-three years. As is clear from the statements made, the extent of his life was sixty-three years. This statement is likewise made in [the Roman writer] Censorinus's book on the natal day. Censorinus's book states that Aristotle maintained a struggle against a mortal disease for three years by the greatness of his soul rather than by the virtue of medicine. Aristotle became the teacher of Alexander the Great [r. 336–323 BCE] and on the authority of his pupil sent two thousand men throughout the world to inquire into the secrets of nature, as Pliny [Roman historian, first century CE] tells us in the eighth book of his *Natural History*, and Aristotle composed a thousand books, as we read in his life. He purged away the errors of preceding philosophers, and enlarged philosophy, aspiring to that full measure of this subject possessed by the ancient patriarchs, although he was not able to perfect each of its parts. For his successors have corrected him in some particulars, and have added many things to his works, and additions will continue to be made until the end of the world, because there is no perfection in human discoveries, as has been shown in what precedes. Nature made this man strong, as Averroes says in the third book on the Soul, that she might discover the ultimate perfection of man. Aristotle, on the testimony of all great philosophers, is the greatest of them all, and that alone must be ascribed to philosophy which he himself has affirmed; whence at the present time he is called by the title Philosopher in the realm of philosophy, just as Paul is understood by the title of Apostle in the doctrine of the sacred wisdom. But the larger portion of the philosophy of Aristotle received little attention either on account of the concealment of the copies of his work and their rarity, or on account of their difficulty, or unpopularity, or on account of the wars in the East, till after the time of Muhammad, when Avicenna and Averroes and others recalled to the light of full exposition the philosophy of Aristotle. Although only some of his works on logic and certain others have been translated from Greek by Boethius, yet from the time of Michael Scotus [1175–ca. 1232], whose translations with authentic expositions of certain parts of Aristotle's works on nature and metaphysics appeared in the year of our Lord 1230, the philosophy of Aristotle has grown in importance among the Latins. But in comparison with the vastness of his wisdom contained in a thousand books, only a very small portion up to the present time has been translated into Latin, and still less is in common use among students. Avicenna in particular, the imitator and expositor of Aristotle, and the man who completed philosophy as far as it was possible for him to do so, composed a threefold volume of philosophy, as he states in the prologue of his book *Sufficiency*: one part popular in character like the philosophical dicta of the Peripatetics who are of the school of Aristotle; the second part in conformity with the pure truth of philosophy, which does not fear the thrusts of the spears of contradicters, as he himself asserts; and the third part conterminous with his own life, in which he gave an exposition of the earlier parts and collected together the more hidden facts of nature and art. But of these volumes two have not been translated; the Latins have the first in certain parts; which is called the book of *Assipha*, that is the book of *Sufficiency*. After him came Averroes, a man of sound wisdom, correcting many statements of his predecessors and adding much to them, although he must be corrected in some particulars and completed in many others. For of making many books there is no end, as Solomon writes in Ecclesiastes....

... Hence, it follows of necessity that we Christians ought to employ philosophy in divine things, and in matters pertaining to philosophy to assume many things belonging to theology, so that it is apparent that there is one wisdom shining in both. The necessity of this I wish to establish not only on account of the unity of wisdom, but because of the fact that we must revert below to the lofty expressions relating to faith and theology, which we find in the books of the philosophers and in the parts of philosophy: so that it is not strange that in philosophy I should touch upon the most sacred truths, since God has given to the philosophers many truths of his wisdom. The power of philosophy must be applied to sacred truth as far as we are able, for the excellence of philosophy does not otherwise shine forth, since philosophy considered by itself is of no utility. The unbelieving philosophers have been condemned, and "they knew God, and did not glorify him as God, and therefore became fools and perished in their own thoughts," and therefore philosophy can have no worth except in so far as the wisdom of God required it. For all that is left is in error and worthless; and for this reason Alpharabius [al-Farabi, *ca.* 872–*ca.* 950] says in his book on *Sciences* that an untaught child holds the same position with respect to a very wise man in philosophy as such a man does toward the revelation of God's wisdom. Wherefore philosophy by itself is nothing, but it then receives vigor and dignity when it is worthy to assume the sacred wisdom. Moreover, the study of wisdom can always continue in this life to increase, because nothing is perfect in human discoveries. Therefore we of a later age should supply what the ancients lacked, because we have entered into their labors, by which, unless we are dolts, we can be aroused to better things, since it is most wretched to be always using old discoveries and never be on the track of new ones, as Boethius [Christian philosopher, born in Rome, *ca.* 480–*ca.* 524] says, and as we proved clearly above in the proper place. Christians likewise ought to handle all matters with a view to their own profession, which is the wisdom of God, and to complete the paths of the unbelieving philosophers, not only because we are of a later age and ought to add to their works, but that we may compel the wisdom of the philosophers to serve zealously our own. For this the unbelieving philosophers do, compelled by truth itself as far as it was granted them: for they refer all philosophy to the divine wisdom, as is clear from the books of Avicenna on Metaphysics and Morals, and from Alpharabius, Seneca, and Tullius, and Aristotle in the Metaphysics and Morals. For they refer all things to God, as an army to its chief, and draw conclusions regarding angels and many other things; since the principal articles of the faith are found in them; for as will be set forth in the morals, they teach that there is a God and that he is one in essence, of infinite power and goodness, triune in persons, Father, Son, and Holy Spirit, who created all things out of nothing; and they touch on many things concerning Jesus Christ and the Blessed Virgin. Likewise also, they teach us of Antichrist and the angels and of their protection of men, and of the resurrection of the dead and of future judgment and of the life of future happiness promised by God to those obedient to him, and of the future misery which he purposes to inflict on those who do not keep his commandments. They write also innumerable statements in regard to the dignity of morals, the glory of laws, and concerning a legislator who must receive the law from God by revelation, who is to be a mediator of God and men and a vicar of God on earth, the Lord of the earthly world. When it shall be proved that he has received the law from God, he must be believed in all things to the exclusion of all doubt and hesitation; who must direct the whole race in the worship of God and in the laws of justice and peace, and in the practice of virtues because of the reverence of God and because of future felicity. [We must avail ourselves of their teachings] because they wrote that the worship of idols should be destroyed, and because they prophesied of the time of Christ. From whatever source the philosophers got these statements and similar ones, we find them in their books, as a clear proof will show in what follows, and anyone can discover the fact who cares to read through the books of the philosophers. For we cannot doubt that these things were written by them, from whatever source they received them. Nor should we be surprised that philosophers write such statements; for all the philosophers were subsequent to the patriarchs and prophets, as we brought out above in its proper place, and therefore they read the books of the prophets and patriarchs which are in the sacred text.

79. LEARNING ARABIC IN THE CHRISTIAN WORLD

Roger Bacon's Opus Majus *was partly meant to help Christian missionaries convert non-Christians to Christianity. As part of this effort, he made an impassioned plea in the* Opus *to encourage Latin Christians to learn foreign languages, including Arabic. In this effort he was not alone, as numerous churchmen, scholars, and rulers actively supported the teaching of Arabic to Christians as a means not only to help the proselytizing efforts of the Church, but also to help translate foreign-language works into Latin and for other practical applications. The two sources below share this vision of language education and speak to an increasingly multilingual Christian elite over the course of the Middle Ages. The first source is part of Pierre Dubois's visionary plan to help recover the Holy Land (see Doc. 48). The second source is a proclamation made by the papal council held in the French city of Vienne in 1312.*

Sources: trans. Walter I. Brandt, Pierre Dubois, *The Recovery of the Holy Land* (New York: Columbia University Press, 1956), 128–29, 136; trans. Lynn Thorndike, "Statute of the Council of Vienne," in *University Records and Life in the Middle Ages* (New York: Columbia University Press, 1944), 149–50.

Pierre Dubois: Training Future Crusaders

72. On the completion of these studies let the boys transfer to another school and begin their instruction in logic. At the same time they should begin their instruction in Greek, Arabic, or such other language as the founders [of the new schools] shall direct them to choose. In the study of this new language they should first be taught its word forms and their grammatical construction. In

logic let them hear the [standard] treatises and the compendia written to explain them. Care should be taken to have someone skilled in this art summarize for them briefly and clearly the matter obscurely handed down by the Philosopher in each of his books on logic; and succinctly, so that after the treatises they may hear that brief art—which would not need an explanation of the writings—twice or thrice in cursory lectures. Afterwards let them hear the books once in formal lectures. This ought to be accomplished by their fourteenth year.

Then let them begin to hear natural science. Because of its prolixity and profundity it is desirable that the *Naturalia* of friar Albertus [Magnus, scholastic philosopher, d. 1280] containing verbosely the whole thought of the Philosopher [Aristotle] with many additions and digressions, be abridged as much as possible, but so clearly that intelligent persons could comprehend this extract without [consulting] the complete writings. The youths would hear this entire extract during the first year in four lectures a day, without questions; they would then hear it for a second time with questions. Afterwards they would hear the books as they are [customarily] read in the schools.

It would also be well for them to have natural questions selected from the writings of friar Thomas [of Cantimpré, theologian and natural philosopher, d. 1272], Siger [of Brabant, Averroist philosopher, d. 1280s], and other doctors, all arranged in a single compilation, as on primary matter, its form, composition, generation, and corruption; on all the senses and their functions; on all the faculties of the soul, their workings and nature; on the elements of nature and their workings; on the heavenly bodies, their nature, influence, and motion. By presenting the material in such a systematic order, it can readily be found and can the more readily be grasped because of its arrangement. It would be very difficult to arrange [the material] in such a manner, although it would be of great advantage on the road to learning, which would by this means be acquired easily in a short time; once acquired, it would be retained, and readily called to mind....

83. In every school of this foundation it would be well to retain some who might be too weak to cross the sea. When they had been educated beyond the prescribed course of study as far as circumstances permitted, they might teach others and ultimately be made chancellors of the schools. Many Greek, Arab, and Chaldean [Aramaic] teachers should be sought, as well as teachers of other idioms considered useful. They would give instruction in their lettered languages to our more brilliant students, and to others for whom less study of the lettered and mother tongues would be sufficient to enable them to act as speech interpreters for the unlearned. I think that, just as among us Latins we see that diverse mother tongues are included under each lettered idiom, it would be well for those who are believed inept for the study of foreign languages to learn the more common of these, which among us Latins is French.

The Council of Vienne, 1312

Clement, bishop, servant of the servants of God. In perpetual memory of the matter.

Among our cares ... and so, imitating the example of him whose place on earth we unworthily fill who wished the apostles to go throughout the world preaching the Gospel trained in every language, we desire the holy church to abound in Catholics acquainted with the languages which the infidels chiefly use, who may come to know the infidels themselves, and be able to instruct them in sacred institutions, and add them to the company of worshippers of Christ by knowledge of the Christian faith and reception of baptism. Therefore, that linguistic ability of this sort may be obtained by efficacy of instruction, with the approval of this holy council we have provided for establishing courses in the languages to be mentioned, wherever the Roman curia happens to reside, also in the universities of Paris, Oxford, Bologna, and Salamanca, decreeing that in each of these places Catholics having sufficient knowledge of the Hebrew, Greek, Arabic, and Aramaic languages, namely two trained in each tongue, shall offer courses there and, translating books faithfully from those languages into Latin, teach others those languages carefully and transfer their ability to these by painstaking instruction, so that, sufficiently instructed and trained in these languages, they may produce the hoped for fruit with God's aid and spread the faith salubriously to infidel nations. For whom we wish provision made: for those lecturing at the Roman curia by the apostolic see, in the university of Paris by the king of France, at Oxford by that of England, Scotland, Ireland, and Wales, in Bologna by Italy's and in Salamanca by Spain's prelates, monasteries, chapters, convents, colleges, exempt or not, and rectors of churches in competent stipends and expenses, imposing the burden of contribution according to the ability of each to pay regardless of any privileges and exemptions to the contrary, by which however we do not wish prejudice to be generated so far as other matters are concerned.

80. MUSLIM INFLUENCE ON LATIN MEDICINE

The increased access to Arabic and other languages had a tremendous impact on the teaching of medicine in Latin Europe. Islamic (and to a lesser extent Byzantine) influence on Christian European medicine had begun with the crusades, as western pilgrims, travelers, and doctors were exposed to eastern practices and began to adopt them. The increased translation efforts of the twelfth century accelerated this process, and the writings and concepts of Hippocrates, Galen, Rhazes, and Avicenna became widely accepted and diffused in western Europe. By the fourteenth century, the work of these writers, among others, dominated the medical curriculum at the universities of Montpellier and Bologna, widely considered to be among the most prestigious medical schools in Europe at the time. Moreover, Latin writers were beginning to take some of these eastern sources and build upon them. Among the most important and famous Latin medical practitioners was the Frenchman Guy of Chauliac (ca. 1300–68), who served as papal physician from 1342 until his death. While at the papal court, he wrote his great work on medicine entitled the Chirurgia Magna *(Great Surgery). In it, he gives us a short but useful history of the many doctors that had influenced medicine in his time and describes some of the different types of medical practitioners, which included not only trained physicians but also those without traditional medical training.*

Source: trans. James Bruce Ross, "The History of Surgery—Gui de Chauliac" in James Bruce Ross and Mary Martin McLaughlin, eds., *The Portable Medieval Reader* (New York: Viking Press, 1949, repr. 1968), 640–44.

Guy of Chauliac: History of Surgery

The workers in this art, from whom I have had knowledge and theory, and from whom you will find observations and maxims in this work, in order that you may know which has spoken better than the other, should be arranged in a certain order.

The first of all was Hippocrates [fifth century BCE] who (as one reads in the *Introduction to Medicine*) surpassed all the others, and first among the Greeks led medicine to perfect enlightenment. For according to Macrobius and Isidore, in the fourth book of the *Etymologies* ... medicine had been silent for the space of five hundred years before Hippocrates, since the time of Apollo and Aesculapius, who were its first discoverers. He lived ninety-five years, and wrote many books on surgery, as it appears from the fourth of the *Therapeutics* and many other passages of Galen [129–ca. 217 CE]. But I believe that on account of the good arrangement of the books of Galen the books of Hippocrates and of many others have been neglected.

Galen followed him, and what Hippocrates sowed, as a good laborer he cultivated and increased. He wrote many books, indeed, in which he included much about surgery, and especially the *Book on Tumors Contrary to Nature*, written in summary, and the six first *Books on Therapeutics*, containing wounds and ulcers, and the last two concerning boils and many other maladies which require manual operation. In addition, seven books which he arranged, *Catageni* (that is, about the composition of medicaments according to kinds), of which we have only a summary. Now he was a master in demonstrative science in the time of the emperor Antoninus [Marcus Aurelius], after Jesus Christ about one hundred and fifty years. He lived eighty years, as is told in *The Book of the Life and Customs of the Philosophers*. Between Hippocrates and Galen there was a very long time, as

Avicenna says in the fourth of the *Fractures*, three hundred and twenty-five years, as they gloss it there, but in truth there were five hundred and eighty-six years.

After Galen we find Paul [of Aegina, *ca.* 625–*ca.* 690] who … did many things in surgery; however, I have found only the sixth book of his *Surgery*.

Going on we find Rhazes [Persian physician, d. *ca.* 923], Albucasis [Andalusi physician. d. *ca.* 1013], and Alcaran, who (whether they were all one and the same, or several) did very well, especially in the *Books for Almansor* [by Rhazes] and in the *Divisions*, and in the *Surgery* by Albucasis. In these as Haly Abbas [Persian physician, d. late tenth century] says, he put all his particulars, and in all the *Continens* (which is called *Helham* in Arabic) he repeated the same things, and he collected all the sayings of the ancients, his predecessors; but because he did not select and is long and without conclusion, he has been less prized.

Haly Abbas was a great master, and besides what he sowed in the books on *The Royal Disposition*, he arranged on surgery the ninth part of his *Second Sermon*.

Avicenna [980–1037], illustrious prince, followed him, and in very good order (as in other things) treated surgery in his fourth book.

And we find that up to him all were both physicians and surgeons, but since then, either through refinement or because of too great occupation with cures, surgery was separated and left in the hands of mechanics. Of these the first were Roger [of Salerno, flourished *ca.* 1170], Roland [of Parma, flourished *ca.* 1200], and the Four Masters [anonymous], who wrote separate books on surgery, and put in them much that was empirical. Then we find Jamerius [fl. *ca.* 1230–52] who did some rude surgery in which he included a lot of nonsense; however, in many things he followed Roger. Later, we find Bruno [of Longo-burgo, fl. *ca.* 1252], who, prudently enough, made a summary of the findings of Galen and Avicenna, and of the operations of Albucasis; however, he did not have all the translation of the books of Galen and entirely omitted anatomy. Immediately after him came Theodoric [Borgognoni, 1205–98], who gathering up all that Bruno said, with some fables of Hugh of Lucca [d. *ca.* 1252–58], his master, made a book out of them.

William of Saliceto [*ca.* 1210–*ca.* 1280] was a man of worth who composed two compendia, one on medicine and the other on surgery; and in my opinion, what he treated he did very well. Lanfranc [*ca.* 1250–*ca.* 1306] also wrote a book in which he put scarcely anything but what he took from William; however, he changed the arrangement.

At that time, Master Arnauld of Villanova [*ca.* 1235–1311] was flourishing in both skills, and wrote many fine works. Henry of Mondeville [*ca.* 1260–*ca.* 1325] began in Paris a very notable treatise in which he tried to make a marriage between Theodoric and Lanfranc, but being prevented by death he did not finish the treatise.

In this present time, in Calabria, Master Nicholas of Reggio [d. 1350], very expert in Greek and Latin, has translated at the order of King Robert many books of Galen and has sent them to us at court; they seem to be of finer and more perfect style than those which have been translated from the Arabic. Finally, there appeared a faded English rose [*Rosa Anglica* of John of Gaddesden, *ca.* 1280–1361] which was sent to me, and I have seen it. I had thought to find in it sweetness of odor, but I have found only the fables of the Spaniard, of Gilbert, and of Theodoric.

In my time there have been operating surgeons, at Toulouse, Master Nicholas Catalan; at Montpellier, Master Bonet, son of Lanfranc; at Bologna, Masters Peregrin and Mercadant; at Paris, Master Peter of Argentiere; at Lyons (where I have practiced for a long time), Peter of Bonant; at Avignon, Master Peter of Aries and my companion, Jean of Parma.

And I, Guy of Chauliac, surgeon and master in medicine, from the borders of Auvergne, diocese of Mende, doctor and personal chaplain to our lord the pope, I have seen many operations and many of the writings of the masters mentioned, principally of Galen; for as many books of his as are found in the two translations, I have seen and studied with as much diligence as possible, and for a long time I have operated in many places. And at present, I am in Avignon, in the year of our Lord 1363, the first year of the pontificate of Urban V. In which year, from the teachings of the above named, and from my experiences, with the aid of my companions, I have compiled this work, as God has willed.

CHAPTER TEN

OF LOVE AND BONDAGE

Figure 10.1: Garden of the Generalife, Granada.

Source: Stanley Lane-Poole, *The Moors in Spain* (London: T. Fisher Unwin, 1888), 227.

81. THE WEDDING OF LADY THERESA

Interfaith marriages and liaisons appear to have been common at the time of the caliphate in Spain, as Muslim rulers, nobles, and officials often took Christian concubines and engaged in sexual relations with Christian slaves. Some modern scholars have seen this exchange as complementing Muslim domination of the Iberian Peninsula and as serving to symbolize Muslim power as well as emasculating and humiliating Christian men. Among the many stories that emerged to support this tradition, the wedding of the lady Theresa is one of the most famous. The story tells how Theresa, sister to Alfonso V of Leon (r. 999–1028), was betrothed by her brother to a Muslim prince (whose identity is far from clear). The story of Theresa was first recorded by the bishop Pelayo of Oviedo sometime between 1121 and 1132. Afterwards, numerous other chronicles incorporated the story into their narratives. The story also became the basis for a ballad, which was first published in a cancionero *(song-book) in the sixteenth century and is our source below.*

Source: trans. J.G. Lockhart, *The Spanish Ballads and the Chronicle of the Cid* (New York: The Century Co., 1907), 54–55; rev. Jarbel Rodriguez.

1. It was when the fifth Alfonso in Leon held his sway,
King Abdalla of Toledo an embassy did send;
He asked his sister for a wife, and in an evil day
Alfonso sent her, for he feared Abdalla to offend;
He feared to move his anger, for many times before
He had received in danger much succor from that Moor.

2. Sad heart had fair Theresa when she their bargain knew,
With streaming tears, she heard them tell she among the
    Moors must go,
That she, a Christian damsel, a Christian firm and true,
Must wed a Moorish husband, it well might cause her woe;
But all her tears and all her prayers they are of small avail;
At length she for her fate prepares, a victim sad and pale.

3. The king has sent his sister to fair Toledo town,
Where then the Moor Abdalla his royal state did keep;
When she drew near, the Muslim, from his golden throne,
    came down
And courteously received her, and bade her cease to weep;
With loving words he pressed her, to come his bower within,
With kisses he caressed her, but still she feared the sin.

4. "Sir king, Sir king, I pray thee," thus Theresa spake,
"I pray thee have compassion, and do to me no wrong;
For sleep with thee I may not, unless the vows I break
Whereby I to the holy Church of Christ my Lord belong;
But thou has sworn to serve Muhammad, and if this thing
   should be,
The curse of God it must bring down upon thy realm and thee.

5. "The angel of Christ Jesus, to whom my heavenly Lord
Has given my soul in keeping, is ever by my side;
If thou does me dishonor, he will unsheathe his sword,
And smite thy body fiercely, at the crying of thy bride.
Invisible he stands; his sword, like fiery flame,
Will penetrate thy bosom, the hour that sees my shame."

6. The Muslim heard her with a smile; the earnest words she said,
He took for bashful maiden's wile, and drew her to his bower.
In vain Theresa prayed and strove—she pressed Abdalla's bed,
By force received his kiss of love, and lost her maiden flower.
A woeful maiden there she lay, a loving lord beside,
And earnestly to God did pray her succor to provide.

7. The angel of Christ Jesus her sore complaint did hear,
And plucked his heavenly weapon from out its sheath unseen,
He waved the brand in his right hand, and to the king came
   near,
And drew the point over limb and joint, beside the weeping
   queen.
A mortal weakness from the stroke upon the king did fall,
He could not stand when daylight broke, but on his knees
   must crawl.

8. Abdalla shuddered inwards, when he this sickness felt,
And called upon his barons, his pillow to come nigh;
"Rise up," he said, "my liegemen," as round his bed they knelt,
"And take this Christian lady, else certainly I die;
Let gold be in your girdles, and precious stones beside,
And swiftly ride to Leon, and render up my bride."

9. When they were come to Leon, Theresa would not go
Into her brother's dwelling, where her maiden years were spent;

But over her downcast visage a white veil she did throw,
And to the ancient nunnery of Saint Pelagius went.
There long, from worldly eyes retired, a holy life she led;
There she, an aged saint, expired—there sleeps she with
    the dead.

82. FORBIDDEN LOVE

One of the arts that flourished in Islamic Spain was poetry. Andalusi poets became renowned throughout the Muslim world, and their influence extended north of the Pyrenees with the birth of the troubadour movement in Aquitaine, in what is now southern France. One of the themes that delighted audiences was the eternal one of love, especially illicit or forbidden love. In the source below from ca. 1075, the poet Abu 'Abd-Allad ibn Haddad (1051–91) writes of his love for a Christian girl from Guadix whom he calls Nuwaira. Love between Christians and Muslims was forbidden, but it also seems to have been fairly common, as this source and some of the upcoming ones in this chapter attest.

Source: trans. Charles Melville and Ahmad Ubaydli, "Forbidden Love (about 1075)" in *Christians and Moors in Spain: Volume 3, Arabic Sources (711–1501)* (Warminster, UK: Aris and Phillips, 1992), 75, 77.

My heart is at the place of the tamarisk trees, a hostage to desires
    and alarms,
So turn towards them, they are the *qibla* [object] of my desires,
    even though they treat me badly.
Take a rest from the winding sands in the folds of the
    mountains covered in blooms,
Stop, you two young men of Amir, at the place where the
    Christian girls are.
I have a girl among the Christians, who bolts like a shy gazelle
    round the churches.
I am in raptures over her; but passion among the cloisters and
    the churches is a sin.
In relation to the gazelles of the desert, who would not prefer
    the gazelles who live in towns?
I alone celebrate on their Easter Day, among the lofty trees and
    the *artas*;
They had come from there to a rendezvous, and congregated
    there at the appointed time,
To stand before a bishop holding a lantern and a staff,

And many priests displaying piety, with signs of ostentatious
  quietness and humility before God,
His eyes wandering over theirs like a wolf who longs to devour
  the ewes.
What man could be safe from passion when he had seen these
  gazelles?
And from moon-like cheeks set above willowy figures?
They recited the scriptures of their Gospels, with beautiful
  voices and intonations,
Increasing their gazelles' shunning of me, and [raising] the
  pressure of my passions.
The [only] sun is the sun of beauty, [shining] among them
  beneath the clouds of [her] veils;
My gaze snatches hers, and her glance kindles my torments.
My insides blaze with the fire of Nuwaira, by whom I have
  been captivated since my youngest years,
[The fire] has not gone out for a moment, though how often
  have I wished it; rather, it blazes ever more fiercely.
Wish the gazelle at the bend in the valley a long life, from me,
  even if it refuses to return my greetings.

83. ALFONSO VI AND SA'IDA

*After the conquest of Toledo in 1085, the Christian forces of Alfonso VI of Leon-Castile
found themselves on the defensive. The invasion by the Almoravids from northern Africa
in 1086 had arrested any momentum gained from the conquests, and the intricate web
of alliances and tributaries that had supported Alfonso began to fray. Checked militarily
by his enemies, Alfonso turned his efforts to diplomacy. It is likely that early in 1091,
he began negotiations with al-Mutamid, the ruler of Seville (r. 1069–91) to enter into
a relationship with Sa'ida, the latter's daughter-in-law (not daughter, as our source
claims), whose husband had only recently died. This relationship (it is unclear if it was a
marriage) helped bind Seville to Alfonso. Moreover, as Bernard Reilly, who has written
extensively on Alfonso (*The Kingdom of León-Castilla under King Alfonso VI,
1065–1109 [Princeton: Princeton University Press, 1988]), argues, it bolstered Alfonso's
claim that he was the defender of Spanish Islam in the face of Almoravid aggression. An
alternative interpretation of events makes Sa'ida a refugee fleeing from the Almoravid
invasion of al-Andalus, an invasion that resulted in the death of her husband and the
exile of her father-in-law. In any case, the relationship lasted only a few years, as Sa'ida
died in childbirth. By the time she died, however, she had given Alfonso the male heir,
Sancho, that he so desperately needed and that his two previous wives (not five as the
source claims; Alfonso likely married his last three wives after Sa'ida's death) had failed*

to provide. Sancho, although illegitimate, became his father's heir but died in 1108, forcing the old king to marry for one last time in a desperate attempt to secure a male heir. This marriage proved childless and Alfonso was dead by 1109, leaving his kingdom to his eldest legitimate daughter Urraca (r. 1109–26).

Source: trans. Colin Smith, *Christians and Moors in Spain: Volume I, 711–1150* (Warminster, UK: Aris and Phillips, 1988), 105, 107.

The reason for the crossing of the Almoravids from Africa to Spain was as follows. We have earlier told you that this king Alfonso [VI] was married to five women in succession: Ines, Constanza, Berta, Elizabeth, and the fifth Beatrice, who was French. Since all five died, King Alfonso was free to marry again. At this time there reigned in Seville al-Mutamid, a Moor of goodly habits in himself, and very powerful, since he possessed here in what we now call Castile the cities and places and castles we mentioned earlier: Cuenca, Ocaña, Ucles, Consuegra, and all the other places listed. This king al-Mutamid had a daughter, fully grown and very beautiful, unmarried and of a goodly style of life. The king loved her dearly, and in order to improve her lot and improve her chances of marriage, he gave her Cuenca and all the other places and castles we have mentioned, granting them to her under firm agreements. King Alfonso, ever energetic and successful and known for great deeds, even though he had won Toledo, did not for all that cease in military endeavors, to the extent that both Moors and Christians had to take account of him. With King Alfonso's great fame so widely known, this lady, Princess Sa'ida, came to hear of it; and so much did she hear about King Alfonso being a great knight and very handsome and strong in arms and in all else that he did, that she fell in love with him; not by seeing him (for she never did), but on account of his good reputation and his high honor which grew day by day and was more talked of, this kind of love being stronger than the other. She being so deeply in love, and since women are clever and wise when they put their minds to a matter that closely concerns them, she sent her messengers to speak to the king and ask that she should meet him, for she was mightily impressed by the reputation and handsomeness in him that all spoke of, adding that she loved him and wanted to see him; this being easy for the messengers, since King Alfonso was at the time in the area of Toledo and was then capturing places around the city and also adjacent to the lands of Princess Sa'ida. Also, in order to bring the matter more quickly to the conclusion she desired, she sent him in writing a list of the places her father had given her, saying that if Alfonso would marry her, she would hand over to him Cuenca together with all those castles and fortresses she had received from her father. When King Alfonso received this message he was very pleased with the news, and sent to ask her to come to him at whatever place she might choose, and that he promised to be there. Some say that she came to Consuegra, which was hers and which was not far from Toledo, others say that it was Ocaña which was also hers, others again say that the meeting was in Cuenca. Wherever the meeting took place, the fact is that what Princess Sa'ida wished was achieved.

Let us continue with the narration of the text we are following: King Alfonso called out the flower of his cavalry, and, taking care in case any deceit or treachery should be planned in this matter, went to meet Princess Sa'ida. Once they were together, if she was already much in love and delighted with King Alfonso, he was no less delighted with her, for he found her full-grown and very beautiful and well-educated and very attractive, just as people had said she was. Then the king asked her formally whether, since she was asking for an agreement [to marry] from him, she would be willing to become a Christian. She replied that she would, and that she would give him Cuenca and all the other places that her father had given her, and that she would do anything else in the world that he might order, provided only that he would marry her. King Alfonso, aware that his capture of Toledo was recent, and that the lands in the possession of Sa'ida would be of the greatest help in making Toledo more secure, took counsel with his counts and nobles. Then he had Sa'ida baptized, as we mentioned earlier, and married her; and a son was born to them. She handed over Cuenca and all the other places to the king. The king ordered that his son should be called Sancho Alfonso, and he handed him over to be brought up by Count Garcia of Cabra. After this King Alfonso of Castile and Leon, realizing how much he owed to al-Mutamid King of Seville, the father of Princess Maria, "la Zaida," his wife, was thenceforth on terms of close friendship with him.

84. BOHEMOND AND THE TURKISH PRINCESS

The English historian Orderic Vitalis (1075–ca. 1141) wrote one of the great Latin Christian Chronicles of the Middle Ages, the Historia Ecclesiastica (Ecclesiastical History). *In the* Historia, *Orderic includes a story about the relationship between Bohemond, prince of Antioch, and Melaz, a Turkish princess. The narrative, which is rich in detail and involves love affairs, battles, religious conversion, betrayal, and interfaith alliances, is a mix of history and fictional accounts. Bohemond was a leader of the First Crusade. During the crusade, Bohemond became prince of Antioch, a city the Byzantines claimed, and in 1100 he was captured by the Turks while trying to defend the city. His refusal to return the city to the Byzantines after its conquest only added to the distrust and antagonism that existed between him and the emperor Alexius and serves to explain the delight with which the latter received the news of Bohemond's capture. He spent several years in captivity until he was ransomed in 1103. Beyond the historical framework provided mostly by Bohemond's capture, there are numerous details that are uncorroborated by other historical accounts and are likely fictional. Included among these is the participation of Bohemond and his French knights in the battle between Danishmend (r. 1071–1104) and Kilij Arslan (sultan of Rum, r. 1092–1107) and, most importantly, Melaz herself. It is very likely that she is a literary construction drawing on a tradition that extended back to the Roman writer Seneca (d. 65 CE) and that may have come to Orderic influenced by the* Thousand and One Nights *and French Romances. The story includes many of the biases and misunderstandings of Christian writers of the early twelfth century. Note, for example, how Orderic misidentifies Muhammad as the God of the Muslims and has Muslim soldiers denigrate Islam. These examples, and others, remind us to read the source carefully and to consider what it says about Christian expectations and beliefs as much as any factual historical evidence it may provide.*

Source: trans. Marjorie Chibnall, *The Ecclesiastical History of Orderic Vitalis*, 6 vols. (Oxford: Clarendon Press, 1975), V: 355, 359–79 (odd-numbered pages only).

About this time another event with serious consequences for the Christians took place in Syria. The famous duke, Mark Bohemond, led an expedition against the Turks; but the Danishmend emir unexpectedly fell on him with a great army, killed many men, captured Bohemond with Richard of the principality and several valiant men of rank, and kept them in chains in his dungeon for a long time. When Tancred [Bohemond's nephew], the commander of the army, heard of the misfortune of his lord and kinsman, he was greatly distressed, but he did not give way like a woman to vain tears and laments. He mustered the whole army of the faithful from all the province round about, strengthened Antioch and all the villages and towns around with vigilant garrisons, and defended the principality admirably against all assaults of his enemies as long as the duke was in captivity; indeed he even enlarged its boundaries....

... Melaz, the daughter of the Danishmend, was beautiful and very wise; she had much authority in her father's house and owned great riches and many slaves to wait on her bidding. This lady loved the Franks passionately when she heard of their great feats, and was so eager to enjoy their company that often, after distributing liberal bribes to the guards, she would go down into the dungeon and engage in subtle discourse with the captives about the Christian faith and true religion, learning about it by constant discussion interspersed with deep sighs. Their gentle kindness meant more to her than the love of her parents, and she procured for them an abundance of all the food and clothing they needed. Her father, who was occupied with many other affairs, either knew nothing of this or perhaps, relying implicitly on the virtue of his beloved daughter, was not disturbed by it.

Two years later a worse than civil war broke out between the Danishmend and his brother [in the Islamic faith]. Kilij Arslan, bursting with aggression, turned against the Danishmend; gathering a huge army, he invaded his brother's territory and rashly provoked him to battle. The Danishmend, roused by this attack, procured support from all sides, while he himself, intoxicated with many past victories, thirsted for the bloody conflict, and as the hour of battle drew near took the field with his battalions. Meanwhile Melaz had spoken privately with the Christians, addressing them with these words, "I have heard the chivalry of the Franks praised by many for a long time; now in my father's pressing need I would like to test it, so that what my ears have heard may be confirmed by my eyes." Bohemond replied, "Most fortunate and honorable lady, if it would please your highness in your kindness that we should be allowed to go out into the field of battle armed for the fray, be assured that we will demonstrate how mightily Franks strike with sword and lance, and make a good showing of our blows on your enemies' bodies before your people's eyes." The maiden said, "Promise me on your faith as Christians that, in the matter we are discussing, you will act entirely in accordance with my advice, and will not presume to do anything contrary to my bidding. Assure me of this by pledging your faith, and I will no longer hesitate to reveal the secrets of my heart to you."

Bohemond was the first to swear on oath what she had asked, and all the others after him pledged their word as the maiden required. Then she said with joy, "Now I know that I can trust you, for in my opinion you are men of your word and will never compromise your honor. Give help to my father, who is just about to engage in battle, and prove your valor nobly by going immediately to his aid. If victory falls to you—as I trust it will—refrain from pursuit of the fleeing enemy, come back here quickly, fully armed, and do not lay aside your arms until I give the word. In the meanwhile, I will make all the guards come down from the upper room in the highest tower to the lower gates, and stand with me in the courtyard as if they were waiting for you. But when you return and I command the guards to fasten your fetters as before, you must boldly lay hands upon them, seize all resolutely, and thrust them into the dungeon in your place. At sight of this, I will run away from you as if you were ravening wolves, and you must occupy the strongest tower and guard it resolutely until you have made a satisfactory truce with my father. There are doors at the top of the tower through which you may descend by a stone staircase into the hall and take possession of all the treasures and apartments of my father. But if my father is angry and wishes to punish me for these offences then, I beseech you, my friends, whom I love as I do my life, come immediately to my rescue."

When she had spoken these words she armed the knights and sent them out at once. She had already deceived and corrupted the guards of the tower and, after informing them of the matter, had said among other things, "I am disturbed by great fear on my father's account, for a multitude from many nations is gathered to fight him. But because he is a courageous warrior, he will not stoop to ask for help from captives. However, I may tell you that he has authorized me to see to this, namely to provide the Christians with arms and send them into battle to assist our forces. If they defeat the enemy troops, the honor and profit will be ours. If however they fall and are slain by the swords of our enemies, we shall not weep for the loss of foreigners, whose customs and religion are detestable to the whole Saracen people." They listened and gratefully agreed, warmly praising the maiden's wise foresight. At once she released the captives, led them out of the house of bondage and sent them, fully armed, into battle. They found the armies locked in fierce conflict and confidently uttered the battle cry of the Normans, "Dieux aide"; at their shouts and ferocious attack the squadrons of Kilij Arslan wavered. There were a certain number of Christians in his army; when they recognized the famous Duke Bohemond they were jubilant and, deserting Kilij Arslan, threw in their lot with the Catholics.

When Marciban, the proud young son of Kilij Arslan, heard that Bohemond was there he charged into the battle, calling him by name and eager to fight him in single combat. At last they met under the eyes of the Danishmend, and dealt each other doughty blows. But the warlike Norman struck down the Turk and, drawing his sword, cut off his head. As the Danishmend cried out, "Spare him, spare him: he is my nephew," the Christian champion realized what he had done and, hiding a joyful heart under a sorrowful countenance, replied ironically, "Pardon, my lord, what I have done in ignorance. I took him for an enemy, not your nephew, and slew him to please you."

After much slaughter on both sides the army of Kilij Arslan was shattered, and the enemy force pursued the remnants all day. The Christians, however, according to their agreement, returned immediately and found their lady waiting with the custodians before the tower. She said at once to the guards, "The Franks are undoubtedly men of their word, and will keep the promise they have made. Go to meet them. Take back their arms and escort them back to their former prison, until my father returns and gives them worthy rewards for their prowess." The Turks moved to obey the maid's commands, but the Franks surrounded them and thrust them as prisoners into the dungeon, carefully secured the doors with bolts, and occupied all the inner rooms of the tower without causing a disturbance, successfully achieving their aims without bloodshed. The whole town was emptied of soldiers, who had all gone to the battle, and only their trembling wives and children occupied the houses. The dungeon was in a very strong tower, and great stores of rich treasure and various furnishings and great wealth were kept there; the main royal palace communicated with the tower.

The following night Melaz brought the Christians from the tower into the hall, showed them all the chambers and hidden recesses, and instructed them in what they should do when the Danishmend arrived. Next day the victor returned home with his governors and officers and nobles, and his daughter ran joyfully to greet him with other maidens. "Welcome," she said, "glorious conqueror." He, however, answered in terrible anger, "Hold your peace, shameless harlot. I do not want your feigned greetings; I hold your false praises not worth a straw. By the divine stock of Muhammad, who gave me the victory, I will make you die tomorrow with your lovers. You gave arms to my adversaries to my utter confusion, and with them you shall be burnt in fierce flames as an abominable traitress." As yet he did not know that his guards were imprisoned in the dark dungeon, while the noble Franks were enjoying freedom in the solar above, and were plotting to attack him with Christ's help. Pale and trembling, the girl fled from the sight of her angry father and took refuge in her chamber, wretched and afraid.

When some hours later the angry prince was sitting in judgment, having only his chief nobles with him, since the rest of his people and the squires and other attendants were dispersed in their own quarters, and were attending to their horses and arms and their other duties, he ordered some men to go to his daughter's chamber and bring the rash traitress to him. When, summoned, she stood before the raging tyrant and all alone, without help, heard his terrible threats and abuse, Bohemond looked from the tower through a window into the palace and, seeing his liberator standing deserted before the judgment seat, said in sorrow, "See, our protectress is in sore distress. Now we must go out from here and help her with all our might." At once they crept cautiously from the tower, down the steps into the hall. Armed, they surrounded the Danishmend and all his officers and companions, barred the doors of the house, and occupied all the defenses round it. All were equally filled with trepidation, and doubtful what they ought to do. The Turks were unable to escape because the doors were barred; they were unable to slip away because they were surrounded by armed men and, being few and unarmed, they could not resist by putting up a fight against men more numerous and better armed than they. The Christians for their part could have cut down all the Turks there and then, but because of the oath they had sworn to the maiden they dared not strike or in any way harm anyone without her sanction. So all looked towards her, waiting for what she might command, because they were resolved not to break faith.

At length Melaz, feeling safer, began to smile and, holding command over the Franks like their lady, said, "Dear father, you are angry with me without cause; you frighten me with terrible threats and heap reproaches on me because of the timely help which, out of concern for you, I have carefully provided with great kindness. The Franks helped your men in the conflict by their deeds and broke the enemy ranks more quickly. Note well how honorable the Christians are. They have loyally helped you in battle; as they fought, the enemy turned and fled. Even the half-blind could see that they had every opportunity of escaping but, because they did not wish to depart without taking leave of you, they returned voluntarily and confidently ask for rewards for their chivalry from your generosity. At this moment they have their hands on their sword-hilts, they have the power to cut all our throats if they choose; they hold the citadel and the palace with all the wealth that is in them, and your guards, being captives, cannot breathe a word against them. In these circumstances, father, think carefully before you act, and consult wisely with your counselors who are with you."

Having said this, the lady placed herself at the head of the Christians, while the Danishmend drew apart with his men to seek their advice. Then he resumed his seat, saying, "First, my daughter, we wish to hear what you recommend." To this she replied, "I will not hesitate to state what I think expedient. Make peace with the Christians and let an inviolable treaty bind you together as long as you live. Free all the captive Christians who are anywhere in your dominions, and let them in return release all those of your race who are in their power. Offer a suitable reward for admirable service to Bohemond and his fellow knights, with whose timely aid you won the victory. Besides this, let me tell you that I am a Christian; I wish to be reborn through the sacrament of the Christian faith and will no longer remain here with you. For the religion of the Christians is holy and honorable, and your religion is full of vanities and polluted with all filth."

On hearing this the Turks were greatly offended; they showed their ferocity with their burning eyes and stern gestures, but God restrained them so that they could not express in action the hatred in their evil hearts. As they were debating what should be done, Melaz called the Christians apart and said, "Now, brave knights, who have been proved in many hardships and dangers, who have come here from distant lands of your own free will and have survived after gallantly completing many labors and battles, act boldly in the name of your God whom you declare to be omnipotent. Now you need both courage and skill in arms, so that you may bring to a glorious conclusion the enterprise so bravely begun. My father is very angry, and is plotting with his men to destroy us by every means in his power. Up to now you have loyally observed the terms I proposed to you. From now on I absolve you from the undertaking you made on oath. Now fortify the citadel and palace and the wall around and the chambers, both large and small; keep a close watch and guard the approaches, so that no one may go in or out without your knowledge. For if my father leaves this place, he will call together all the neighboring peoples and blockade you cruelly until he has brought you to death or shameful surrender. So keep him a prisoner with all his friends in one room, and compel them to make peace using all the force that is necessary, but as far as possible restrain your hands from bloodshed. I entrust the design and control of this course which I recommend to you, Lord Bohemond, because you are a man of wide experience and your sound judgment and good sense are praised all over the world. From now onwards I shall be joined to you as a sister, and will share joys and sorrows with you in the faith of our Lord Jesus Christ."

So Bohemond, greatly pleased, violently thrust the Danishmend with all his men into a chamber and set armed guards over the cell. Then he placed the other knights in different stations, and instructed each one in what he was to do. In this way, he governed the royal palace and all who were in it for about fifteen days. He allowed the wives of the men and their female attendants and unarmed eunuchs to enter and bring them adequate supplies of food and whatever else they needed. The Danishmend complained bitterly that his home had become a prison and his daughter the gaoler who confined him strictly. So he cursed his God, Muhammad, loudly and poured abuse on all his friends and subjects and neighbors, because they allowed him to be wretchedly treated in the heart of his own kingdom by a few foreign captives. The lords who were imprisoned persuaded him to make peace with the Christians, so that they might at least escape with their lives. At length his hardness gave way to fear. He spoke with Bohemond and asked to make peace, promised to allow him and his men to depart freely, liberated all the captives who were suffering under his rule, and offered him his daughter in marriage.

When Melaz heard these proposals from Bohemond, she replied in her shrewdness, "Words are easily spoken, but not all of them are invariably to be believed. Listen courteously to the smooth but devious promises of my father; at the same time continue to keep close watch on all the places that are in your power until you are assured of safety through certain victory. Have envoys acceptable to both sides sent to Antioch to bring back an armed force of your knights, with whose support you may be honorably escorted without fear of deceit to your own land; in this way you will escape from the treacherous snares of all your ill-wishers." This advice pleased all. So Richard of the principality and Sarcis of Mesopotamia were sent to Antioch, and informed the men of Antioch to their great delight of the course of events. Tancred, the commander of the army, immediately sent out officials to fetch the knights and the captive gentiles, and when they were assembled delivered them to the lords Richard and Sarcis to escort back. At that time the daughter of Yaghi-Siyan, the emir of Antioch, was released, weeping bitterly as she was brought out of the Christian prison. When she was asked why she wept so, she replied that it was because in future she would not be able to eat the excellent pork that Christians eat. The Turks and many other Saracen peoples detest the flesh of pigs, although they eat with enjoyment the flesh of dogs and wolves, demonstrating in this way that they hold to the law neither of Moses nor of Christ, and are neither Jews nor Christians.

During this time Bohemond had frequent conversations with the Danishmend and, being a prudent and forbearing man, treated him courteously and flattered him to some extent to obtain better terms for the many whom the tyrant was in a position to oppress. By his complaisant and kind words he soothed both the Danishmend and all who were with him, and won his affection by the attentiveness of his courteous companionship. Little by little the provincial officials and nobles learnt of the new governor, and made every effort to find out about the foreign prince who was the lord of their true prince; when they talked with their lord with Bohemond's permission they praised him greatly. They urged their natural lord to act for the advantage of the state, advised him to try to win the friendship of the great duke by any means, and often recalled the saying of the comedian,

Since you cannot do what you wish, wish for what you can do.

They added further, "We were badly misled in the victory we have lately won, because we made use of able allies who are enemies of our faith to slaughter our compatriots, and we wickedly and stupidly found cause to rejoice in our common loss. Our own God, the abominable Muhammad, utterly deserted us and fell helpless before the God of the Christians. See how wonderfully the crucified Christ, whom they call omnipotent—and rightly, as all their enemies learn and feel to their cost—unexpectedly, through your daughter, freed the men whom you believed to be closely fettered in prison, where you intended to guard them closely for ever. He armed them and caused them to triumph gloriously in battle, stained their swords with the blood of our brothers and kinsmen, and besides this delivered to them the royal stronghold where all your treasures are, gave into their hands both you and the chief nobles of your kingdom so that you are guarded, groaning, in the prison of your own hall like helpless slave-girls, without a fight. We from outside cannot visit you without the permission of the foreigners, and are powerless to give you any help. We dare not rise up and attack them all together, because they would immediately vent their fury on you. Even if the great king, the sultan of Persia, came here with all his might and attempted to storm this fortress, so great is the valor of the Franks and so great the strength of the fortress that they would dare to resist him there, and would inflict great losses on our men before they were taken. Therefore it is better to placate the enemy with friendship than by rash acts to incite him to a fury that would cause your death."

The Danishmend acquiesced in such advice. Accepting the friendship of the gallant duke, he freely issued orders in his house for the good of both, and dispensed generous gifts from his treasures to the Christians voluntarily; he also ordered that all the captives throughout his kingdom should be set free. They were carefully sought out and when found were brought to the Danishmend, who clothed them liberally and handed them over to Bohemond. He immediately added them to his company and assigned various duties to them, to swell the ranks and ensure the safety of his companions, so that they should not be tricked by any evil subterfuge of the pagans.

Richard and Sarcis returned after fifteen days, their mission accomplished, and brought a large force of Christian knights. The Danishmend ordered them to be received with great honor; he had sumptuous viands prepared for them according to the custom of his country, and provided in plenty for all their needs. Then Bohemond and the Danishmend made a treaty of perpetual peace between themselves, and for three days prepared suitable equipment of all kinds for them. At length Bohemond, Richard, and their fellow captives went forth joyfully from captivity and, like Zerubbabel and Nehemiah, blessed the Lord God of Israel. The Danishmend and his nobles, rejoicing because they too had been freed from prison, escorted them for some way. They traveled with deceit in their hearts, for they were plotting to harm the Christians in some way or other on the journey, but failed to do so because God protected his own. For the faithful feared some trick, and so traveled fully armed as if ready for battle; they also carefully retained hostages for their security until they had reached the safe place which had been appointed. At length the Danishmend asked his allies as a friend for license to depart and, receiving it, returned regretfully because he had not been able to harm them on the way by any trick.

The prudent Melaz departed from her father's house with her servants and eunuchs and noble household, and, voluntarily leaving all her own people, was devoutly associated with the Christians, as Bithiah, Pharaoh's daughter, accompanied Moses and the Hebrews in safety when the Egyptians perished. The men of Antioch, rejoicing, went out to meet the men they had long wished to see, and the clergy and all the people fervently blessed the Lord King who saves all who put their trust in him. Then Bohemond sent Richard, the companion of his captivity, to Gaul, and dispatched silver fetters by his hand to the holy confessor, Saint Leonard, giving devout thanks for his delivery.

After the highly born Melaz had been regenerated by holy baptism in the catholic Church, Bohemond, choosing a convenient moment, addressed her thus in an assembly of the magnates, "Noble maiden, who so unexpectedly came to our rescue when you were yet a pagan, who have wisely preferred the Lord Jesus to all your kindred, and have cherished him in us who are his members and servants, and in so doing have incurred the wrath of your father almost to the point of death, choose from us the spouse whom you desire to have in the name of Christ. For it is not right that we should in any way refuse your just requests, since we are all deeply in your debt for the virtues you have already shown. First of all, hear my advice, which I hope, sweet lady, may be profitable to you. I acknowledge certainly that you have been given to me by your father, but I wish to make better provision for you, so listen attentively to the reason for this. From my youth I have been a restless man and, living in strife, have endured many trials, yet I fear still graver lie ahead of me. For I am at war with the emperor and with the pagans on all sides.

Besides this, I made a vow to the Lord when I was in prison, that if I were liberated from the bondage of the infidel I would go to the shrine of Saint Leonard, which is in Aquitaine. I offer these excuses to you out of sincere devotion, for I do not wish to see you who are more than daughter or sister to me forsaken in any way, or to enter into the bonds of a marriage that you will soon have cause to regret. What joy or delight could there be for you in our union, if immediately after the marriage I am obliged to set out on a long journey over sea and land, and depart as a pilgrim to a distant country near the ends of the earth? Reflecting on these things, my lady, choose for yourself from many, and choose a better fate. See now, Roger [of Salerno, regent of Antioch, 1112–19], the son of Prince Richard, is my kinsman and younger than I, more handsome than I am, equal to me in birth, wealth, and power. I advise you to take him as your husband, and hope that you will live with him for many years."

All who were present approved the advice of the prudent duke. The wise maiden readily fell in with the counsel accepted by so many lords. So Roger married the maiden honorably, with great joy, and the whole of Antioch celebrated the wedding with loud cheers and rejoicing, while Bohemond served as steward at the wedding banquet, with the chief lords of the country. Some six years later, after Bohemond and Tancred were dead, Roger became ruler of the principality of Antioch. Two years later he was killed on the field of Sarmada [1119] with seven thousand Christians, by the Persian Il-Ghazi.

85. THE EGYPTIAN AND HIS FRANKISH WIFE

The Thousand and One Nights *is one of the masterpieces of Arabic literature. The history of its composition is a complex one, but most historians and literary critics now agree that although some of the stories may date from at least the tenth century, the first fully extant manuscript dates from the fourteenth century from Syria. The* Thousand and One Nights *is a collection of tales framed together by the story of the fictional Persian king Shahryar and the young virgin Scheherazade. According to the story, Shahryar would request a new virgin every day to marry while beheading his wife from the previous day. After going through one thousand virgins, he met Scheherazade who was determined to avoid the fate of her predecessors. The first night they were together, she began a tale, which she failed to finish by the coming morning. The intrigued Shahryar decided to spare her life and keep her as his wife for a second night so that she could finish her account. However, as soon as she finished this story, she began a second one, which again she was unable to finish before dawn, prompting the king to grant her another reprieve. This went on for a thousand and one nights, until finally Scheherazade ran out of stories. By this point, however, the king had fallen in love with her and fathered her three children. He married her and made her his queen. Among the stories that Scheherazade told*

Shahryar are some that remain popular to this day, including those of Aladdin and the Magic Lamp, Ali Baba and the Forty Thieves, and Sinbad the Sailor. The tale below concerns an Egyptian man who fell in love with a Frankish woman, and the twists and turns that ultimately would lead them to marriage.

Source: trans. Richard F. Burton, *The Book of the Thousand Nights and a Night*, 10 vols. (London: Burton Club, 1885), IX: 19–24; rev. Jarbel Rodriguez.

We lay one night in the house of a man of the Sa'id or Upper Egypt, and he entertained us and entreated us hospitably. Now he was a very old man with exceedingly dark skin, and he had little children, who were white, of a white dashed with red. So we said to him, "Tell us, how is it that these children of yours are white, while you yourself are dark?" And he said, "Their mother was a Frankish woman, whom I took prisoner in the days of Al-Malik al-Nasir Salah al-Din [Saladin], after the battle of Hattin, when I was a young man." We asked, "And how did you get her?" And he answered, "I had a rare adventure with her." We said, "Favor us with it;" and he responded, "With all my heart! You must know that I once sowed a crop of flax in these parts and pulled it and scutched it and spent on it five hundred gold pieces; after which I would have sold it, but could get no more than this therefore, and the folk said to me, 'Carry it to Acre: for there you will happily make a good profit.' Now Acre was then in the hands of the Franks, so I carried my flax there and sold part of it at six months' credit. One day, as I was selling, behold, there came up a Frankish woman, (now it is the custom of the women of the Franks to go about the market streets with unveiled faces), to buy flax from me, and her beauty dazed my wits. So I sold her some of the flax and was easy with her concerning the price and she took it and went away. Some days after, she returned and bought some more flax from me and I was yet easier with her about the price; and she repeated her visits to me, seeing that I was in love with her. Now she was used to walking in company of an old woman to whom I said, 'I am very enamored of your mistress. Can you arrange for me to enjoy her?' She said, 'I will arrange this for you; but the secret must not go beyond us three, me, you, and her, and there is no help but that you be lavish with money, to boot.' And I answered, saying, 'Though my life were the price of her favors, I would pay it.' So it was agreed (continued the man of Upper Egypt), that I should pay her fifty dinars and that she should come to me; whereupon I procured the money and gave it to the old woman. She took it and said, 'Make ready a place for her in your house, and she will come to you this night.' Accordingly, I went home and made ready what I could of meat and drink and wax candles and sweetmeats. Now my house overlooked the sea and it was the season of summer; so I spread the bed on the terrace roof. Soon, the Frankish woman came and we ate and drank, and the night fell dark. We lay down under the sky, with the moon shining on us, and fell to watching the shimmering of the stars in the sea, and I said to myself, 'Are you not ashamed before Allah (to whom belong Might and Majesty!) and you a stranger, under the heavens and in presence of the deep waters, to disobey Him with a Nazarene woman and merit the torment of Fire?' Then said I, 'O my God, I call you to witness that I abstain from this Christian woman this night, out of shame before you and fear of your vengeance!' So I slept until the morning, and she arose at the break of day full of anger and went away. I walked to my shop and sat there; and behold, presently she passed, as if she were the moon, accompanied by the old woman who was also angry. Thereupon my heart sank within me and I said to myself, 'Who are you that you should refrain from such a woman? Are you Sari al-Sakati or Bishr Barefoot or Junayd of Baghdad or Fuzayl bin 'Iyaz [famous ascetics]?' Then I ran after the old woman and coming up with her said to her, 'Bring her to me again,' and said she, 'By the virtue of the Messiah, she will not return to you but for one hundred gold pieces!' I said, 'I will give you a hundred gold pieces.' So I paid her the money and the damsel came to me a second time; but no sooner was she with me than I returned to my former way of thinking and abstained from her and resisted her for the sake of Allah Almighty. She soon went away and I walked to my shop, and shortly after the old woman came up, in a rage. I said to her, 'Bring her to me again,' and she said, 'By the virtue of the Messiah, you shall never again enjoy her presence, except for five hundred gold pieces, and you shall perish in your pain!' At this, I trembled and resolved to spend the whole price of my flax and with it ransom my life. But, before I could think, I heard the crier proclaiming and saying, 'Listen, all Muslims, the truce which was between us and you is expired, and we give all of you Muslims who are here a week from this time to have done with your business and depart to your own country.' Thus, her visits were cut off from me and I applied myself to collecting the money for my flax which men had bought upon credit, and to bartering what remained in my hands for other goods. Then I took with me fair merchandise and departed Acre with a soul full of affection and longing for the Frankish woman, who had taken my heart and my coin. So I journeyed to Damascus, where I sold what I had brought from Acre, at the highest price, because of the cutting off of communication due to the term of truce having expired, and Allah (extolled and exalted be He!) vouchsafed me good gain. Then I fell to trading in captive slave-girls, thinking thus to ease my heart of its pining for the Frankish woman, and in this traffic I engaged for three years, until there Saladin met the Franks at Hattin and other places and Allah gave him the victory over them, so that he took all their kings prisoners and he captured the coast cities by his leave.

"As luck would have it, one day after this, a man came to me and sought to buy a slave-girl from me for Saladin. Having a beautiful handmaid, I showed her to him and he bought her from me for one hundred dinars and gave me ninety on the spot, leaving ten still due to me, for that was all that was left in the royal treasury that day, because he had spent all his monies in waging war against the Franks. Accordingly, they took counsel with him and he said, 'Take him to the treasury where the captives are held and give him his choice among the damsels of the Franks, so he may take one of them for the ten dinars that are due to him.' They brought me to the captives' lodging and showed me all who were there, and I saw among them the Frankish damsel with whom I had fallen in love at Acre and knew her right away. Now she was the wife of one of the cavaliers of the Franks. So I said, 'Give me this one,' and carrying her to my tent, asked her, 'Do you know me?' She answered, 'No,' and I rejoined, 'I am your friend, the sometime flax-merchant with whom you had to do at Acre and what happened between us happened. You took money from me and said, "You shall never again see me but for five hundred dinars." And now you have become my property for ten gold pieces.' She said, 'This is a mystery. Your faith is the True Faith and I testify that there is no god but the God and that Muhammad is the Messenger of God!' And she made perfect profession of Al-Islam. Then said I to myself, 'By Allah, I will not have relations with her until I have set her free and acquainted the Kazi.' So I went to Ibn Shaddad [judge under Saladin] and told him what had transpired and he married me to her. Then I lay with her that night and she conceived, after which the troops departed and we returned to Damascus. But within a few days there came an envoy from the king of the Franks, to seek the captives and the prisoners, according to the treaty between the kings. So Saladin restored all the men and women captive, until there remained but the woman who was with me and the Franks said, 'The wife of such and such a knight is not here.' Then they asked after her and making strict search for her, found that she was with me; whereupon they demanded her of me and I went to her very concerned and with color changed, and she said to me, 'What troubles you and what evil bedevils you?' I said, 'A messenger has come from the king to take all the captives, and they demand that I return you.' She said, 'Have no fear, bring me to the king and I know what to say to him.' I took her into the presence of the sultan Saladin, who was seated, with the envoy of the king of the Franks on his right hand, and I said to him, 'This is the woman that is with me.' Then said the king and the envoy to her, 'Will you go to your country or stay with your current husband? For Allah has loosed your bonds and those of your fellow captives.' She said to the sultan, 'I have become a Muslim and am pregnant, as you can see by my figure, and the Franks shall have no more profit of me.' The envoy asked, 'What is dearer to you, this Muslim or your first husband, the knight? She answered him even as she had answered the sultan. Then said the envoy to the Franks with him, 'You heard her words?' They replied, 'Yes.' And he said to me, 'Take your wife and depart with her.' So I took her and went away, but the envoy sent after me in haste and cried, 'Her mother gave me a charge for her, saying, "My daughter is a captive and naked, and I would have you carry this chest to her. Take it and deliver it to her."' Accordingly, I carried the chest home and gave it to her. She opened it and found in it all her garments as she had left them and inside I saw the two purses of fifty and one hundred dinars which I had given her, untouched and tied up with my own knot, wherefore I praised Almighty Allah. These are my children by her and she is alive to this day and it was her that prepared this food for you." We marveled at his story and at that which had befallen him of good fortune, and Allah is All-knowing.

86. HOW TO PURCHASE A SLAVE

Love and marriage between Christians and Muslims was closely linked to slavery and captivity, as some of the sources above have already shown. Slavery and the taking of captives was widely practiced by both Christians and Muslims and considered legal as long as slaves were of the other faith. The urban and rural areas of the Mediterranean, including those of Iberia, Italy, northern Africa, Egypt, and western Asia had significant slave populations. These slaves worked in all types of jobs, including agricultural labors, domestic work, professional crafts, construction, and the transport of goods, among others. The work was often exhaustive and humiliating and, at times, dangerous. In addition to these occupations, many Islamic regions had castes of slave soldiers, typically children recruited from Christian regions and converted to Islam. Among these, we find the Mamluks and the elite troops of the Ottoman Empire, the Janissaries (see Doc. 88). For women, captivity and enslavement often meant a loss of control over their own sexuality, as their bodies were at the whim of their masters. The harem, a common institution in Muslim countries, was typically populated by slave women, some of whom rose to prominence and power when they became the mothers of future sultans. The ubiquity of slavery, moreover, ensured that there would be plenty of advice available to those who wanted to purchase slaves. Numerous variables had to be considered when purchasing a slave, including age, gender, physical strength, beauty or comeliness, provenance, and any special skills. These characteristics also helped to determine the market price of the slave. In the following source, the eleventh-century Arab Christian physician and philosopher Ibn Butlan provides information on how best to select slaves based on their personal characteristics, as well as their region of origin. His writing highlights some of the qualities that a prospective buyer should look for when selecting slaves, along with some of his own preconceptions, strongly mediated by a sense of geographic determinism, which assigned virtues and faults based on where a slave came from.

Source: trans. Bernard Lewis, *Islam from the Prophet Muhammad to the Capture of Constantinople*, 2 vols. (New York: Harper Torchbooks, 1974), II: 243–51.

Useful advice when buying slaves, according to the sayings of the wise men and philosophers; ten pieces of advice, of which four apply equally to male and female slaves, viz:

1. Their injunction that the shopper should make a careful examination before buying and should not decide at first glance. They said: one who shops for a thing should not be in dire need of it, for the hungry man approves any food that appeases his hunger, and the naked man finds suitable any rag that warms and covers him. Accordingly, they said: a lecher should not shop for slave-girls, for the tumescent has no judgment since he decides at first glance, and there is magic in the first glance and charm in the new and strange. If he feels an urgent need, he will make a choice at first glance which his senses will later belie when the need is no more. Therefore, it is said: Repeated looking wears out novelty, and constant examination reveals artifice and exposes deceit.

2. The warning of the ancients before purchase. They said: beware of buying slaves at fairs and festivals, for it is at such markets that the slave-dealers perfect their cunning tricks. How often has a scraggy girl been sold as plump, a dirty brown as a golden blond, an aging man as a full-bottomed boy, a bulging paunch as a trim, flat waist, a stinking mouth as perfumed breath. How often do they dye blemishes in the eyes and leprous sores on the body, and make light blue eyes dark blue. How often do they dye yellow cheeks red, make thin cheeks fat, enlarge small orifices, remove hair from cheeks, stain fair hair jet black, curl lanky hair, whiten brown faces, make spindly legs rounded, thicken falling hair, and gild pockmarks, tattoo marks, freckles, and scabies.... How often has a sick slave been sold as healthy, and a boy as a girl. All this in addition to the slave-merchants' practice of encouraging the slave-girls in shameless flirtation with passing young men who regard carrion as lawful meat, as well as their bedecking themselves with rouge and henna and soft, dyed garments. We have heard a slave-dealer say, "A quarter of a dirham's worth of henna raises the price of a slave-girl by 100 silver dirhams."

3. Their injunction not to decide at the first hearing of male and female slaves. They said: Do not decide at the first sight of a slave or slave-girl ... but be more inclined to doubt than to trust. It is safer to be suspicious.

4. A special warning for the great. They said: Let the great—anyone with an enemy who he fears may seek to murder him or to penetrate his secrets—beware of buying a eunuch or a slave-girl, especially if she can write and has come out of a ruler's household, without thoroughly investigating her; also beware

of buying a mulatto slave-girl from a merchant or broker, for this is a trick by which many kings and great ones have perished.

Three pieces of advice relating especially to the purchase of male slaves, viz:

1. Their warning to the purchaser against buying a slave accustomed to beating and argument. They said: do not buy a slave whose master used to beat him very much, and do not omit to inquire about the previous owner and his reason for selling the slave, and find out about this before you buy him from the slave himself and from others, for there is great benefit in such an inquiry, either in binding him to you or in leaving him.

2. [Is the cause] the boldness of the slave in blaming his master and belittling him or the master's resentment at his slave's complaints and disrespect for him? Is the cause of the selling in the master or in the slave?

3. Their advice on what to do before employing him. They said: The slave's character will be determined by your treatment of him from the moment when he first enters your house. If you embolden him, he will be bold; if you train him, he will be obedient; if he associates with bad slaves or other bad people, he will be bad.

Two pieces of advice relating to female slaves, viz:

1. How to make sure that slave-girls are free from pregnancy before purchase. They said: Be careful to ascertain that female slaves are free from pregnancy before taking possession of them, and beware of their spurious discharge and lying claims. Many of them insert other girls' blood in their private parts. The one to ascertain this is a woman who would not wish you to have another man's child foisted on you. Order her to examine her breasts and feel her stomach. You can also know this from the pallor of her complexion and her desire for salty food, for this is a craving due to pregnancy.

2. On taking care after purchase of tricks to become pregnant against the owner's will. They said: Be careful on two points. If you buy a slave-girl who has not yet reached puberty, it often happens that she reaches puberty while in your possession without your knowledge, concealing this from you because she desires motherhood.

Beware of lesbian [?] slave-girls who fancy that they are barren and that they dislike pregnancy, for often they will deceive you in this.
One piece of advice which concerns the seller, not the buyer.

They said: never send a slave-girl from your house to the slave-dealer, except during the menstrual flow. Otherwise she is likely to become pregnant in the slave-quarters and claim that it is yours.

We have indeed seen one in our time who bled during pregnancy, but this is rare.

On the Different Kinds of Slaves, According to Their Countries and Origins

We shall report what we have found out, what is well-known, what we have gathered from books, and what we have learned by inquiry from travelers, concerning the various races of slaves and the differences between them in body and in character, so that we may satisfy the inquirer in this matter with the fruit of experience and trial. Twenty-five sections, as follows:

The first section contains the explanation of terms, the meanings of which the reader needs to know.

If you hear me say "Farisiyya," know that I mean a woman who is born in Fars. Both parents may be Farisi, but the father alone suffices. If the offspring of a negress mate with whites for three successive generations, thereafter black gives way to white, a flat nose gives way to a long nose, the limbs become dainty, and the character changes accordingly. The same usage is to be understood with reference to all races.

If you hear me speak of a slave-girl as a "fiver," by this I mean that her height is five spans.

If I say shahtvdriyya, this is not the name of a race but is a Persian word derived from [the Arabic] shahwa [passion] and means "perfect passion."

If I say Mansuriyya, I am referring to al-Mansura which is beyond the river [Indus], that is, to Multan, and not to al-Mansura of the Arabs.

Then come four sections, relating to the four points of the compass.

The first concerns the eastern lands. The color of the people of these lands is white tinged with red. Their bodies are fertile, their voice clear, their sicknesses few, their faces handsome, their characters noble, their sheep plentiful, their trees tall. There is no anger in them and no courage because of their equitable dispositions; they are a people of calm and of meek temper. All this is because of the temperate sun in that region, their temperate food, and their clear water.

The second concerns the western lands. These are almost the exact opposite of what we have described in the eastern lands, since the sun does not rise over them in the mornings.

The third concerns the northern lands. These are the ones whose inhabitants live under the signs of the Bear and the Goat, such as the Slavs. These are broad-chested and brave, of portly build to conserve heat, but with thin legs because the heat escapes from the extremities. They live long because of their excellent digestion, but their women are barren because they are never clean from menstrual blood.

The fourth concerns the southern lands. These are the ones whose people live under the southern Pole [sic], such as the Ethiopians, and their condition is the opposite of that of the people of the northern lands. Their color is black, their waters are brackish and turbid, their stomachs cold, and their digestion bad. Their natures are calm, their lives short, and their bellies soft because of bad digestion.

Then follow twenty sections dealing with the countries, one by one.

The Indian women are in the southeast. They have good stature, brown color, and a plentiful share of beauty, with pallor, a clear skin, fragrant breath, softness, and grace, but old age comes quickly upon them. They are faithful and affectionate, very reliable, deep, sharp-tongued, and of fine character. They cannot support humiliation but endure pain without complaint until they are killed. They can master great things when compelled or provoked. Their women are good for childbirth, their men, for the protection of persons and property and for delicate handicrafts. They catch cold easily.

The women of Sind are between the east and the south. They closely resemble the Indians whose country adjoins theirs, except that their women are distinguished by their slender waists and long hair.

The women of Medina are brown in color, and of upright stature. They combine sweetness of speech and grace of body with charm, roguishness, and beauty of form and flesh. These women are not jealous of men, are content with little, do not grow angry, and do not scold. There are negresses among them, and they are suitable for training as singing girls.

The women of Ta'if are golden brown and shapely. They are the most cheerful of all God's creatures, the funniest, and the merriest. They are not good as mothers of children, for they are slow to pregnancy and die at childbirth. Their men are the most active of mankind in courtship, the most assiduous in company, and the most excellent in song.

The Berber women are from the island of Barbara [sic], which is between the west and the south. Their color is mostly black, though some pale ones can be found among them. If you can find one whose mother is of Kutama, whose father is of Sanhaja, and whose origin is Masmuda, then you will find her naturally inclined to obedience and loyalty in all matters, active in service, suited both to motherhood and to pleasure, for they are the most solicitous in caring for their children. Abu 'Uthman the slave-dealer says, "If it happens that a Berber girl with her racial excellence is imported at the age of nine, spends three years in Medina and three years in Mecca, comes to Iraq at the age of fifteen and is educated in Iraq, and is bought at the age of twenty-five, then she adds to the excellence of her race the roguishness of the Medinans, the languor of the Meccans, and the culture of the women of Iraq. Then she is worthy to be hidden in the eyelid and placed in the eye."

The Yemeni women are of the same race as the Egyptians, with the body of the Berbers, the roguishness of the Medinans, and the languor of the Meccans. They are the mothers of handsome children somewhat resembling the Bedouin Arabs.

The Zaranji women are from a country called Zaranj. Ibn Khurradadhbeh says that from this place to the city of Multan is a journey of two months, and Multan is in the middle of India. A peculiarity of this race is that during sexual intercourse they sweat a liquid like musk, but they are not good for motherhood.

The Zanj women have many bad qualities. The blacker they are, the uglier their faces, the more pointed their teeth, the less use they are and the more likely to do some harm. For the most part, they are of bad character, and they frequently run away. It is not in their nature to worry. Dancing and rhythm are innate and ingrained in them. Since their utterance is obscure, they have been compensated with music and dance. It is said that if a Zanji were to fall from heaven to earth, he would beat time as he fell. They have the cleanest teeth of mankind because they have much saliva, and they have much saliva because they have bad digestion. They can endure hard work. If the Zanji has had enough to eat, you can chastise him heavily and he will not complain. There is no pleasure to be got from their women because of their stench and the coarseness of their bodies.

The Ethiopian women. Most of them have gracious, soft, and weak bodies. They are subject to phthisis and hectic fever and are no good for singing or dancing. They are delicate and do not thrive in any country other than that in which they were born. They are good, obliging, tractable, and trustworthy, and are distinguished by strength of character and weakness of body, just as the Nubians are distinguished by strength of body despite their slenderness and also by weakness of character and shortness of life because of their bad digestion.

The women of Mecca are languorous, feminine, with supple wrists and of a white color tinged with brown. Their figures are beautiful, their bodies lissom, their mouths clean and cool, their hair curly, their eyes sickly and languid.

The women of Zaghawa are of vicious character and full of grumbles. Their ill nature and evil disposition lead them to do terrible things. They are worse than the Zanj and than all the black races. Their women are useless for pleasure, and their men are useless for service.

The Bujja women are between the south and the west in the country which lies between Ethiopia and Nubia. They are golden in color, with beautiful faces, smooth bodies, and tender flesh. If, as slave-girls for pleasure, they are imported while they are still young, they are saved from mutilation, for they are circumcised and all the flesh from the upper part of their pudenda is incised with a razor until the bone appears; they have become a byword. Similarly the nipples of men are cut off and a bone removed from the knee.... Bravery and thievery are innate and ingrained in them; they cannot therefore be trusted with money and are unsuitable for use as treasurer or custodian.

The Nubian women, of all the black races, have ease and grace and delicacy. Their bodies are dry, while their flesh is tender; they are strong and at the same time slender and firm. The climate of Egypt suits them, since they drink the water of the Nile, but if they are removed to some place other than Egypt, diseases of the blood and acute sicknesses overcome them and pain racks their bodies. Their characters are pure, their appearance attractive, and there is in them religion and goodness, virtue, chastity, and submissiveness to the master, as if they had a natural bent for slavery.

The women of Qandahar are like the Indian women. They have one merit above all other women, that the widow or divorcee again becomes like a virgin....

The Turkish women combine beauty and whiteness and grace. Their faces tend to look sullen, but their eyes, though small, are sweet. They have a smooth brownness and their stature is between medium and short. There are very few tall ones among them. The beautiful ones are extremely beautiful and the ugly ones exceptional. They are treasure houses for children, gold mines for generation. It very rarely happens that their children are ugly or badly formed. They are clean and refined. Their pots are their stomachs on which they rely for preparing, cooking, and digesting food [?]. Bad breath is hardly ever found among them, nor any with large buttocks, but they have some nasty characteristics and are of little loyalty.

The Daylami women are both outwardly and inherently beautiful, but they have the worst characters of all and the coarsest natures. They can endure hardship like the women of Tabaristan in every respect.

The women of Allan are reddish-white and well-fleshed. The cold humor predominates in their temperaments. They are better suited for service than for pleasure since they have good characters in that they are trustworthy and honest and are both reliant and compliant. Also, they are far from licentious.

The Greek women are blond, with straight hair and blue eyes. As slaves they are obedient, adaptable, serviceable, well-meaning, loyal, trustworthy, and reliable. They are good as treasurers because they are meticulous and not very generous. Sometimes they are skilled in some fine handicraft.

The Armenians would be beautiful were it not for their peculiarly ugly feet, though they are well-built, energetic, and strong. Chastity is rare or absent among them, and thievery widespread. Avarice is very rare among them, but they are coarse in nature and speech. Cleanliness is not in their language. They are slaves for hard work and service. If you leave a slave for an hour without work, his nature leads him to no good. Only fear and the stick make them behave properly, and their only merit is endurance of toil and heavy labor. If you see one of them idle, it is because of his bad character and not because of any lack of strength; therefore, use the stick. Be watchful in striking him and making him do what you want because this race is untrustworthy even when they are contented, not to speak of when they are angry. Their women are useless for pleasure. In fine, the Armenians are the worst of the whites as the Zanj are the worst of the blacks. And how much do they resemble one another in the strength of their bodies, their great wickedness, and their coarse natures!

87. CAPTIVE TALES

Among Usamah Ibn-Munqidh's many anecdotes, we find numerous stories about captivity. The two stories below highlight the important role played by other Muslims in the liberation of Muslim captives—this was true for Christian captives as well, who were heavily dependent on help from their coreligionists back home to gain their freedom. In the first story, a Bedouin helps a captive escape. In the second, Usamah himself plays the role expected of pious Muslims and ransoms captives out of his own pocket.

Source: trans. Philip Hitti, *An Arab-Syrian Gentleman & Warrior in the Period of the Crusades: Memoirs of Usamah ibn-Munqidh* (New York: Columbia University Press, 2000), 109–12.

The fidelity of a Bedouin.—This same servant of mine, who in the year 538 [ended 3 July 1144 CE] had accompanied me to Egypt, told me a story about the son of the lord of al-Tur [Mt. Sinai] who told it to him in the following words (al-Tur being a distant province belonging to Egypt and close to the land of the Franks and over which al-Hafiz li-Din-Allah—may Allah's mercy rest upon his soul!—would appoint as governor any one of his emirs whom he desired to banish):

My father was appointed governor of al-Tur, and I went out with him to the province. I was fond of hunting. So I went out one day to hunt and a group of Franks fell upon me, captured me and took me to Bayt-Jibril. There they shut me up all alone in a dungeon. The master of Bayt-Jibril fixed my ransom at two thousand dinars. I remained in the dungeon a year without anybody inquiring about me.

But one day as I was in my dungeon, behold! the trapdoor was uplifted and a Bedouin was lowered towards me. I said, "Where did they take you from?" "From the road," he replied. After staying with me a few days, his ransom was fixed at fifty dinars. One day he said to me, "Do you want to know that none can deliver you from this dungeon but me? Deliver me, therefore, so that I may deliver you." I said to myself, "Here is a man who, finding himself in distress, seeks for himself a way of deliverance." So I answered him not. A few days later he repeated the same request to me. So I said to myself, "By Allah, I will surely make an effort to deliver him, for maybe Allah will deliver me in recompense." So I shouted to the jailer and said, "Tell the lord I wish to confer with him." The jailer went away and returned. Then he made me mount out of the dungeon and presented me before the lord. I said to the lord, "I have been in thy prison for one year without anybody inquiring about me, and nobody knows whether I am alive or dead. Then you imprisoned with me this Bedouin and fixed his ransom at fifty dinars. Now, add his ransom to mine and let me send him to my father so that he may buy me off." "Do so," replied the lord. Accordingly, I returned and notified the Bedouin, who went out, bade me farewell and departed.

I awaited results from him for two months, but I saw no trace of him nor heard any news about him. So I despaired of him. But one night, to my great surprise, he appeared before me from a tunnel in the side of the dungeon and said, "Arise. By Allah, I have been five months digging this subterranean passage from a village in ruins until I got to you." I arose with him and we went out through that subterranean passage. He broke my chain, and accompanied me to my own home. And now I know not what to admire more—his fidelity in carrying out his promise or his precision in digging a tunnel that hit the side of the dungeon.

When Allah (worthy of admiration is he!) decrees that relief should come, then how easy become the causes which bring it about!

Usamah ransoms captives.—I used to visit frequently the king of the Franks [Fulk of Anjou and king of Jerusalem, r. 1131–43] during the truce between him and Jamal-al-Din Muhammad ibn-Taj-al-Muluk [lord of Damascus, r. 1139–40] (may Allah's mercy rest upon his soul!), on account of the fact that King Baldwin [II, r. 1118–31] , father of the queen [Mélisende], who was the wife of King Fulk, son of Fulk, was under obligation to my father (may Allah's mercy rest upon his soul!). During these visits the Franks used to bring before me their captives so that I might buy them off, and I would buy off those of them whose deliverance Allah (exalted is he!) would facilitate.

Once a devil of a Frank named William Jiba set out in his vessel for a piratical raid, and captured a vessel in which were Maghribi pilgrims numbering about four hundred souls, men and women. Now some of these Maghribis would be brought to me by their owners, and I would buy from among them those whom I could buy. One of the captives was a young man who would salute and sit without uttering a word. I inquired about him and was told that he was an ascetic owned by a tanner. So I said to the tanner, "For how much will you sell me this one?" The tanner replied, "By the truth of my religion, I will not sell him except in conjunction with this sheikh, and that for the same price that I paid for them, namely forty-three dinars." I bought them both, and

I bought for my own use a few others. I also bought for the Amir Mu'in-al-Din [Usamah's patron] (may Allah's mercy rest upon his soul!) a few others costing one hundred twenty dinars. I paid the money that I had with me and offered a bond for the balance.

Later I came to Damascus and said to the Amir Mu'in-al-Din (may Allah's mercy rest upon his soul!), "I have purchased some captives especially for you, but I did not have their full price. And now that I have arrived in my home, if you want them you shall pay their price; otherwise I shall pay it myself." "Oh no," said he, "I would, by Allah, rather pay their price myself. And of all men, I desire most the reward that comes thereby." In truth, Mu'in-al-Din (may Allah's mercy rest upon his soul!) was the quickest of men in doing good and in gaining the reward thereof. He paid their price. A few days afterwards I returned to 'Akka [Acre].

There remained with William Jiba thirty-eight of the captives, among whom was the wife of one of those whom Allah had delivered through my hand. So I bought her off without paying her price on the spot. Soon after, I rode to Jiba's home (may Allah's curse be upon him!) and said, "Will you sell me ten of the captives?" "By my religion," he replied, "I won't sell them but all together." "I haven't got on my person the price of them all," I replied. "So I will now buy some, and then another time I will buy the rest." "I will not sell them to you but all together," he repeated. So I departed. But Allah (worthy of admiration is he!) decreed and they fled away that very night, all of them. The inhabitants of the villages of 'Akka being all Muslims, whenever a captive came to them they would hide him and see that he got into Muslim territory. That accursed one sought his runaways, but succeeded in capturing none, for Allah (worthy of admiration is he!) made their deliverance good.

The second morning he began to demand from me the price of the woman whom I had purchased but whose price I had not paid and who was one of those who had fled away. I said to him, "Deliver her to me and then take her price." He replied, "Her price is mine by right since yesterday before she fled away." And he forced me to pay her price. So I paid it and considered it an easy thing since I was so happy at the deliverance of those miserable ones.

88. ON THE JANISSARIES

The Ottoman Turks relied on an excellent military to wage their campaigns of conquest. One of the most celebrated units was the elite Janissary Corps. The Janissaries likely originated during the reign of Orhan I (r. 1324–61) or, at the latest, that of his son Murad I (r. 1362–89). Their ranks were largely filled either by the purchase of foreign slave boys or through the devshirme system of tribute, whereby Christian boys from areas under Ottoman control were taken from their families, converted to Islam, and trained in a life of military servitude. However, to see the Janissaries as simple slaves misses much

of the context, as there was an element of pride, respect, professionalization, and esprit
de corps *among the Janissaries that placed them among the elites of Ottoman society.
The author of the source below, Konstantin Mihailovic, knew the Janissaries well. He
was born in Serbia and found himself at the siege of Constantinople as part of a Serbian
contingent sent to help defend the city. When the city fell, he was captured and pressed
into Turkish service, participating in many of Mehmet II's campaigns. It is unclear if
he was actually a Janissary, although that seems unlikely. Nevertheless, he was closely
associated with the corps and knew its workings well.*

Source: trans. Benjamin Stolz, *Konstantin Mihailovic: Memoirs of a Janissary* (Ann Arbor: University of
Michigan Press, 1975), 157, 159.

Whenever the Turks invade foreign lands and capture their people an imperial
scribe follows immediately behind them, and whatever boys there are, he takes
them all into the Janissaries and gives five gold pieces for each one and sends them
across the sea. There are about two thousand of these boys. If, however, the number
of them from enemy peoples does not suffice, then he takes from the Christians in
every village in his land who have boys, having established what is the most every
village can give so that the quota will always be full. And the boys whom he takes
in his own land are called *cilik*. Each one of them can leave his property to whomever he wants after his death. And those whom he takes among the enemies are
called *pendik*. These latter after their deaths can leave nothing; rather, it goes to the
emperor, except that if someone comports himself well and is so deserving that he
be freed, he may leave it to whomever he wants. And on the boys who are across
the sea the emperor spends nothing; rather, those to whom they are entrusted must
maintain them and send them where he orders. Then they take those who are
suited for it on ships and there they study and train to skirmish in battle. There the
emperor already provides for them and gives them a wage. From there he chooses
for his own court those who are trained and then raises their wages. The younger
must serve the older, and those who come of age and attain manhood he assigns to
the fortress so that they will look after them, as mentioned earlier.

And at the court there are about four thousand Janissaries, and among them
there is the following organization. They have over them a senior hetman called
an aga, a great lord. He receives ten gold pieces a day, and his steward, one gold
piece a day. To each centurion they give a gold piece every two days, and to
their stewards, a gold piece every four days. And all their sons who grow out of
boyhood have a wage from the emperor. And no courtier who permits himself
something will be punished by the honest ones by fine, but rather by death; they
dare not, however, punish any courtier publicly, but secretly, because of the
other courtiers, for they would revolt. And no Janissary nor any decurion of
theirs dare ride a horse, save the hetman himself and the steward. And among

them it is so arranged that some are archers who shoot bows, some are gunners who shoot mortars, others muskets, and still others, crossbows. And every day they must appear with their weapons before their hetmans. And he gives each one a gold piece per year for a bow, and in addition a tunic, a shirt, and large trousers made, as is their fashion, of three ells of cloth, and a shirt of eight ells. And this I myself distributed to them for two years from the imperial court.

89. THE TAKING AND FREEING OF CAPTIVES IN IBERIA

The last stages of the Christian conquest of al-Andalus changed the lives of many residents of the Iberian Peninsula. Hundreds and thousands went into and came out of captivity as the fate of captives and masters came to rest on the whim of advancing armies and falling cities. As Isabel and Ferdinand's victorious armies swept through one Muslim stronghold after another, they liberated multitudes that were in captivity. Emotional scenes on the part of captives and liberators, as well as religious processions to offer thanksgiving, often accompanied these manumissions. A quite different fate awaited the Muslims who had the misfortune to be in the path of the advancing Christian forces. While many were allowed to stay in their homes, but now under Christian rule, others chose exile, and others still became captives themselves. The source below, by the Castilian chronicler Andrés Bernáldez, captures both of these extremes in its description of the fall of Malaga and the surrounding fortresses. The conquest of Malaga meant a joyful liberation for the hundreds of Christian captives held in the city, but it also meant captivity for many of its defenders, and in the case of some of those described here, a humiliating parade through Rome as they became the human trophies of a victorious enemy. Of course, the same had happened when Constantinople fell in 1453, only in reverse. Thousands of Christians were captured, paraded through the city, and shipped off to slave markets, some to be ransomed, but most to live and die in slavery.

Source: trans. Jarbel Rodriguez, Andrés Bernáldez, *Historia de los Reyes Católicos D. Fernando y Doña Isabel*, 2 vols. (Seville: Imprenta que fue de D. José María Geofrin, 1870), I: 249–52.

On Saturday, 18 August, in the year of our Lord 1487, the city [of Malaga] surrendered. It had been besieged since 7 May, thus the king had it surrounded for three months and eleven days, until it capitulated. The king then sent a crier through the city to tell the Muslims that they and their property would be safe in their homes, and he placed many guards among them so that none would leave, and no one would bother them, annoy them, or take what they had. And then he demanded that the Christian captives held in Malaga be turned over to him and he ordered a large pavilion set up near the Granada gate. There, the king, the queen, and their daughter, the princess, received them all, almost six-hundred men and women in total. Through the gate where the captives emerged there were many people with crosses and royal pennons and they marched in procession together to where the king and queen awaited. And arriving before their majesties they prostrated themselves and fell to their knees wanting to kiss the royal feet, but the king and queen would not allow it, instead taking them by the hand, giving praise to God, and weeping from joy. The captives were all emaciated, their skin yellowish from hunger, on the verge of death, with shackles on their feet and necks, and long beards. And when they kissed the feet of the king and queen, they fervently praised God, praying for the well-being and success of their majesties. Then the king ordered that they be fed and given drink, their shackles removed, and that they be given fresh clothes and alms so that each could return to their homes, and so it was done. And among the captives there were some who had been asked for large ransoms and now they were rescued. And there were some who had been in captivity for ten, fifteen, even twenty years, and some who had been captive for less....

... Two strong and powerful fortresses, one named Mijas, the other Osuna, situated between Malaga and Fonjirola, had refused to surrender while Malaga was besieged. The king had always kept a garrison [to watch them] and when Malaga fell, the king demanded their surrender. Believing that the people of Malaga had made a good treaty [with the king], they sided with them and handed over the fortresses. The king sent the galleys from his armada to fetch all eight-hundred of them along with their movable property. But when they got to Malaga, they realized that they were now captives and lost. The king took these Muslims, as well as those who had gone to Malaga to help defend it, but were not citizens of the city [and thus not bound by the terms of the surrender treaty], and divided them among his knights [as slaves], allocating shares to each based on their rank. To each duke, he gave one-hundred Muslims; the same to the master of Santiago; fifty to each count and other lord; less to some and more to others among the rest. He made gifts [of the slaves] to the king of Naples and the king of Portugal. He also sent to Pope Innocent VIII, who then ruled in Rome, one-hundred Muslims as a gift. The pope received them and had them paraded throughout Rome, as a heroic deed, and in celebration of the Christian victory. He then forced them to convert and become Christian. And thus were remembered the victories which illustrious Romans had won, notably those of the Scipios, Lucius Metellus, Fabius, Quintus, Publius, Lucius, Marius, Gaius, Pompey, Marcelus, Julius Caesar, and many others who conquered large parts of the world for Rome. And when they returned with their victories or sent the captured booty that they had, the whole city would be moved upon receiving them and witnessing [the spectacle]. And thus the whole city of Rome was moved upon seeing the captives that the king sent to the holy father, from the victory which God had granted to him in Malaga and its hinterland. And the holy father was very grateful and he had prayers sung and thanks offered to God, our Lord.

SOURCES

Saìd al-Andalusi. *Science in the Medieval World: "Book of the Categories of Nations."* Trans. and ed. Semàan I. Salem and Alok Kumar, 69–78. Austin, TX: University of Texas Press, 1991. Copyright © 1991. Reprinted by permission of the University of Texas Press.

A.S. Atiya, trans. "An Unpublished XIVth Century Fatwā on the Status of Foreigners in Mamlūk Egypt and Syria," from *Studien Zur Geschichte Kultar Des Nahen Und Fernen Ostens*, 58–63. Leiden: Brill, 1935. Reprinted by permission of Koninklijke BRILL NV.

Ibn Battuta. *The Travels of Ibn Battuta, AD 1325–1354.* 5 Vols. Translated by H.A.R. Gibb. London: Hakluyt Society, 1956–94. Vol. 4: 939–40. Reprinted by permission of the publisher.

Anthony Bonner, trans. *Selected Works of Ramon Llull 1232–1316.* Volume 1, 300–3. Princeton, NJ: Princeton University Press, 1985. Copyright © 1985 Princeton University Press. Reprinted by permission of Princeton University Press.

R.J.C. Broadhurst, trans. *The Travels of Ibn Jubayr*, 300–1, 315–18, 338–50. London: Jonathan Cape, 1952. Reprinted by permission of The Random House Group Limited.

R.P. Buckley, trans. *The Book of the Islamic Market Inspector*, 121–23. Oxford: Oxford University Press, 1999. Copyright © Oxford University Press. By permission of Oxford University Press.

Robert Belle Burke, trans. *The Opus Majus of Roger Bacon.* 2 Vols. Philadelphia: University of Pennsylvania Press, 1928. 1: 62–64, 65–67. Reprinted with permission of the University of Pennsylvania Press.

Thomas Burman, trans., Olivia Remie Constable, ed. *Medieval Iberia: Readings from Christian, Muslim, and Jewish Sources*, 81–83. Philadelphia: Pennsylvania University Press, 1997. Reprinted with permission of the University of Pennsylvania Press.

Gui de Chauliac. "The History of Surgery." Trans. James Bruce Ross. From *The Portable Medieval Reader*, ed. James Bruce Ross and Mary Martin McLaughlin. Copyright © 1949 by Viking Penguin, Inc.; copyright renewed © 1976 by James Bruce Ross and Mary Martin McLaughlin. Used by permission of Viking Penguin, a division of Penguin Group (USA) LLC.

Marjorie Chibnall, trans. *The Ecclesiastical History of Orderic Vitalis, Volume 5*, 355, 359–79. Oxford: Clarendon Press, 1975. By permission of Oxford University Press.

Jim Colville, trans. *Contra Christianorum*, from *Sobriety and Mirth: A Selection of the Shorter Writings of al-Jāhiz*, 73–80. London: Kegan Paul, 2002. Reprinted by permission of Jim Colville.

E. J. Costello, trans., Francesco Gabrieli, ed. *Arab Historians of the Crusades*, 10–11, 28–29, 50–53, 225–34, 326–31. Berkeley, CA: University of California Press, 1969. Copyright © 1969 Routledge & Kegan Paul. Reproduced by permission of Taylor & Francis Books, UK; reprinted by permission of The University of California Press.

Lawrence Cunningham, trans. *Brother Francis: An Anthology of Writings by and about St. Francis of Assisi*, 43–45. New York: Harper & Row Publishers, 1972. Reprinted by permission of Dr. Lawrence Cunningham.

Paul Edward Dutton, trans. and ed. *Charlemagne's Courtier: The Complete Einhard*, 148–49. Toronto: University of Toronto Press, 1998. Reprinted with permission of the publisher.

Philip K. Hitti, trans. *An Arab-Syrian Gentleman and Warrior in the Period of the Crusades: Memoirs of Usamah Ibn Munqidh*, 109–12, 162–63, 163–70. New York: Columbia University Press, 2000. Copyright © 2000 Columbia University Press. Reprinted with permission of the publisher.

P.M. Holt. *The Memoirs of a Syrian Prince: Abu'l-Fidā, Sultan of Hamāh (672–732/1273–1331)*, 16–17. Weisbaden: Franz Steiner Verlag GMBH, 1983. Reprinted by permission of the publisher.

Peter Jackson, trans. *The Seventh Crusade, 1244–1254: Sources and Documents*, 46–47. Aldershot, UK: Ashgate, 2007. Copyright © Ashgate. Reprinted by permission of the publisher.

J.R. Melville Jones, trans. *The Siege of Constantinople 1453: Seven Contemporary Accounts*, 136–37. Amsterdam: Adolf M. Hakkert, 1972. Reprinted by permission of the publisher.

Walter Emil Kaegi, trans. "Initial Byzantine Reactions to the Arab Conquest." *Church History* 38:2 (1969): 144–46. Reprinted with the permission of Cambridge University Press.

Ibn Khaldun. *The Muqaddimah: An Introduction to History*. Trans. Franz Rosenthal, ed. N. J. Dawood, 183–88. Princeton, NJ: Princeton University Press, 1967. Copyright © 1967 Princeton University Press. Reprinted by permission of Princeton University Press.

John Kinnamos. *Deeds of John and Manuel Comnenus*. Trans. Charles Brand. New York: Columbia University Press, 1976. Copyright © 1976 Columbia University Press. Reprinted with permission of the publisher.

Malcolm Letts, trans. *Pero Tafur: Travels and Adventures, 1435–1439*, 59–62, 117–18, 124–29. London: George Routledge and Sons, 1926. Reprinted by permission of Gorgias Press.

Bernard Lewis, trans. *Islam: From the Prophet Muhammad to the Capture of Constantinople*, 157–65, 229–32, 243–51. New York: Harper Torchbooks, 1974. Copyright © 1974 by Bernard Lewis. By permission of Oxford University Press, USA.

Robert S. Lopez and Irving W. Raymond, trans. *Medieval Trade in the Mediterranean World: Illustrative Documents Translated with Introductions and Notes*, 384–87. New York: Columbia University Press, 1967. Copyright © 1967 Columbia University Press. Reprinted with permission of the publisher.

Karla Mallette, trans. *The Kingdom of Sicily, 1100–1250: A Literary History*. Philadelphia: University of Pennsylvania Press, 2005. 146–48. Reprinted with permission of the University of Pennsylvania Press.

Michael McVaugh, trans. "The Translation of Greek and Arabic Science into Latin," from *A Sourcebook in Medieval Science*, 35–38. Ed. Edward Grant. Cambridge, MA: Harvard University Press, 1974. Reprinted by permission of the publisher. Copyright © 1974 by the President and Fellows of Harvard College.

Charles Melville and Ahmad Ubaydli, trans. "Forbidden Love (about 1075)," from *Christians and Moors in Spain: Volume 3, Arabic Sources (711–1501)*, 75, 77. Warminster, UK: Aris and Phillips, 1992. Reprinted by permission of Oxbow Books.

Thomas F. Michel, trans., *A Muslim Theologian's Response to Christianity: Ibn Taymitta's Al-Jawab al-Sahih*, 198–209. Delmar, NY: Caravan Books, 1984. Reprinted by permission of the publisher.

Samuel Scott Parsons, trans., Robert I. Burns, ed. *Las Siete Partidas*. 5 Vols. IV: 978–80, 1035, 1058, 1438–42. Philadelphia: University of Pennsylvania Press, 2001. Reprinted with permission from the University of Pennsylvania Press.

Bernhard Walter Scholz, trans., with Barbara Rogers. "Royal Frankish Annals," from *Carolingian Chronicles*, 56, 77–78, 86–87, 91, 96, 101–2, 120–22. Ann Arbor: University of Michigan Press, 1970. Reprinted by permission of The University of Michigan Press.

Colin Smith, trans. *Christians and Moors in Spain: Volume I, 711–1150*, 105, 107. Warminster, UK: Aris and Phillips, 1988. Reprinted by permission of Oxbow Books.

Lynn Thorndike, trans. "Statute of the Council of Vienne," from *University Records and Life in the Middle Ages*. New York: Columbia University Press, 1944. Copyright © 1944 Columbia University Press. Reprinted with permission of the publisher.

A.S. Tritton, trans. *The Caliphs and Their Non-Muslim Subjects: A Critical Study of the Covenant of Umar*, 12–16. London: F. Cass, [1930] 1970. Reprinted by permission of Oxford University Press.

Kenneth B. Wolf, trans. *The Chronicle of 754 in Conquerors and Chroniclers of Early Medieval Spain*, 130–35. Liverpool: Liverpool University Press, 1990. Reprinted by permission of Liverpool University Press.

Diana G. Wright, trans., Barbara Rosenwein, ed. *Reading the Middle Ages: Sources from Europe, Byzantium, and the Islamic World*, 497–99. Toronto: University of Toronto Press, 2006. Reprinted by permission of Diana Wright.

Figures

Figure 2.1: Façade of the Holy Sepulcher. From Paul LaCroix, *Military and Religious Life in the Middle Ages and the Period of the Renaissance* (London: Bickers and Son, n.d.), 106. Image copyright © duncan1890/iStock-photo.com.

Figure 2.2: Urban II at Clermont. From Paul LaCroix, *Military and Religious Life in the Middle Ages and the Period of the Renaissance* (London: Bickers and Son, n.d.), facing 262, Private Collection Ken Welsh/Bridgeman Images.

Figure 2.3: Claude Sauvageot, Crac des Chevaliers, reconstruction (engraving), Private Collection Giraudon/Bridgeman Images.

Figure 3.1: Surrender of the Muslim town of Montefrio to the forces of Castile and Aragon in 1486. From Paul LaCroix, *Military and Religious Life in the Middle Ages and the Period of the Renaissance* (London: Bickers and Son, n.d.), 193, Private Collection Ken Welsh/Bridgeman Images.

Figure 4.1: Messengers of the sultan. From Paul LaCroix, *Military and Religious Life in the Middle Ages and the Period of the Renaissance* (London: Bickers and Son, n.d.), 129. Image copyright © Ann Ronan Picture Library/Heritage Images/Imagestate.

Figure 5.1: Transport of merchandise on the backs of camels. From Paul LaCroix, *Manners, Customs, and Dress during the Middle Ages and during the Renaissance Period* (London: Chapman and Hall, 1876), 250. Image copyright © Universal Images Group/Getty Images.

Figure 9.1: A lesson in astronomy. From the Breviary of St. Louis, illustration from *Science and Literature in the Middle Ages and the Renaissance*, written and engraved by Paul LaCroix, 1878 (engraving), French School (13th century), Private Collection/Bridgeman Images.

INDEX OF TOPICS

Topics are listed by document number, not page number.

READINGS IN MEDIEVAL CIVILIZATIONS AND CULTURES
Series Editor: Paul Edward Dutton

"Readings in Medieval Civilizations and Cultures is in my opinion the most useful series being published today."
—William C. Jordan, Princeton University